Politics and Health Care Organization

LAWRENCE D. BROWN

Politics and Health Care Organization

HMOs as Federal Policy

THE BROOKINGS INSTITUTION
Washington, D.C.

Library of Congress Cataloging in Publication data:

Brown, Lawrence D. (Lawrence David), 1947–
  Politics and health care organization.
  Includes bibliographical references and index.
    1. Health maintenance organizations—United States.
  2. Medical policy—United States.   I. Title.
  RA413.5.U5B76   1982   362.1'0425   81-70466
  ISBN 0-8157-1158-1
  ISBN 0-8157-1157-3 (pbk.)

1   2   3   4   5   6   7   8   9

THE BROOKINGS INSTITUTION is an independent organization devoted to nonpartisan research, education, and publication in economics, government, foreign policy, and the social sciences generally. Its principal purposes are to aid in· the development of sound public policies and to promote public understanding of issues of national importance.

The Institution was founded on December 8, 1927, to merge the activities of the Institute for Government Research, founded in 1916, the Institute of Economics, founded in 1922, and the Robert Brookings Graduate School of Economics and Government, founded in 1924.

The Board of Trustees is responsible for the general administration of the Institution, while the immediate direction of the policies, program, and staff is vested in the President, assisted by an advisory committee of the officers and staff. The by-laws of the Institution state: "It is the function of the Trustees to make possible the conduct of scientific research, and publication, under the most favorable conditions, and to safeguard the independence of the research staff in the pursuit of their studies and in the publication of the results of such studies. It is not a part of their function to determine, control, or influence the conduct of particular investigations or the conclusions reached."

The President bears final responsibility for the decision to publish a manuscript as a Brookings book. In reaching his judgment on the competence, accuracy, and objectivity of each study, the President is advised by the director of the appropriate research program and weighs the views of a panel of expert outside readers who report to him in confidence on the quality of the work. Publication of a work signifies that it is deemed a competent treatment worthy of public consideration but does not imply endorsement of conclusions or recommendations.

The Institution maintains its position of neutrality on issues of public policy in order to safeguard the intellectual freedom of the staff. Hence interpretations or conclusions in Brookings publications should be understood to be solely those of the authors and should not be attributed to the Institution, to its trustees, officers, or other staff members, or to the organizations that support its research.

Foreword

WITH THE enactment of Medicare and Medicaid in 1965, the federal government became the nation's largest single purchaser of health care, and the rising costs of that care soon became a central concern of national policy. Told that the choice of cost containment techniques lay between competitive and regulatory strategies, the federal government has hesitated, cautiously committing itself to small measures of both. The hope has remained lively, however, that analytic acumen and political ingenuity might devise a general cost containment strategy that will forgo regulation in favor of the discipline of a medical marketplace working by means of improved incentives and enhanced competition.

One prominent example of such a proposal is the health maintenance organization (HMO). Throughout the 1970s, policymakers were impressed with the prospect that prepaid group practice arrangements (as HMOs were once called) might bring about great improvements in efficiency. An HMO delivers comprehensive medical services to voluntarily enrolled subscribers in exchange for premiums fixed, known, and paid in advance. It does so through physicians employed by or under contract to it, whose remuneration depends on their success in living within the plan's annual budget. Therefore, it was argued, the HMO is uniquely able to overcome the seemingly illogical incentives at work in the larger medical system, which is based on fees for services and reimbursement on the basis of third parties' retrospective computations of the costs of care. HMOs might not only realize economies of their own, but, if widely diffused, might also put competitive pressure on traditional sources of financing, thus generating system-wide savings.

Impressed by these possibilities, President Richard M. Nixon proposed in 1971 that the federal government make available small sums of grants and loan funds to aid the formation and growth of HMOs. After two and a half years of battling with the administration and within its own ranks, Congress finally created an HMO development program at the end of

1973. The program immediately met criticism from various sources—
criticism that the federal bureaucracy's troubled efforts to administer the
program in the mid-1970s did little to alleviate. In 1976, Congress tried to
improve the law with amendments. In 1977, the Carter administration
made several efforts to breathe new life into it. By 1980, however, after
roughly a decade of federal encouragement, the HMO presence remained
modest. About 235 HMOs enrolled about 4 percent of the population. In
1981, the Reagan administration proposed, and Congress agreed, that
federal financial aid for HMOs should be phased out. Even as the program
wound down, however, HMOs were widely cited as the conceptual
prototypes of the competitive health care system the Reagan administration
had promised to promote.

In this study, Lawrence D. Brown, a Brookings senior fellow, examines
the promise and performance of HMOs as exemplars of federal policy.
Beginning by asking what it is reasonable to expect of HMOs, Brown
explores central problems of organizational formation, management, and
performance. With this organizational perspective as background, he asks
what the political process has in fact done for (or to) the HMO strategy.
He derives answers from analysis of the legislative-executive struggle over
what became the HMO law of 1973, its administration in the federal
bureaucracy, and the varied efforts to revive the program in the late 1970s.
He then explores the interplay between policy prospects and political
outcomes, assessing some familiar accounts of the program's problems,
offering alternative explanations, and discussing the future of HMOs—
and of competitive strategies more generally—in the political arena and
the health care system.

The conclusions are the author's alone and should not be ascribed to
the trustees, officers, or other staff members of the Brookings Institution.

BRUCE K. MACLAURY
President

August 1982
Washington, D.C.

Author's Acknowledgments

I AM deeply grateful to the many persons in HMOs, government and elsewhere who kindly and generously granted interviews and supplied documents. My Brookings colleague, Martha Derthick, offered valuable insights and suggestions from the conception of the project through its several drafts, strengthening it in countless ways. Three HMO practitioners, James A. Lane, John Smillie, M.D., and Michael J. Taylor, offered detailed and insightful advice on a draft. Though they may disagree with much of it, they improved the book significantly. David Nexon, Bruce C. Vladeck, and Steven Rhoads made many useful suggestions on the whole manuscript. Individual chapters were improved by the advice of David Alexander (who also generously made available his own extensive research materials and notes), David Benor, Sidney Edelman, George Greenberg, Margaret Henrickson, Bonnie Lefkowitz, William J. McLeod, Steve Morris, and Louise B. Russell. Nina M. Lane and Anna T. Stocker, librarians at the Group Health Association of America, patiently helped for over five years in the search for documents and literature on HMOs.

David Morse was the principal typist; Joan Milan, Radmila Nikolič, and Celia Rich also typed portions of the manuscript. Donna Daniels Verdier, Colleen Copley, and Diane Hodges provided administrative support. Alice Carroll edited the manuscript; Florence Robinson prepared the index. Needless to say, I alone am responsible for any errors of fact or interpretation.

Most important throughout were the love, encouragement, and counsel of my wife, Adela J. Gondek.

L.D.B.

For my parents

Contents

Politics and Health Care Organization

I have served in the Cabinet or sub-Cabinet of four Presidents. I do not believe I have ever heard at a Cabinet meeting a serious discussion of political ideas—one concerned with how men rather than markets behave. These are the necessary first questions of government.

Daniel P. Moynihan, "Floccinaucinihilipilificationism," *The New Yorker*, August 10, 1981.

CHAPTER ONE

Politics, Organization,
and Health Care Policy

If enough people don't like something, it becomes a problem; if the intellectuals agree with them, it becomes a crisis; any crisis must be solved; if it must be solved, then it can be solved— and creating a new organization is the way to do it.

James Q. Wilson, "The Bureaucracy Problem," *The Public Interest* (Winter 1967)

To THE SURPRISE of many onlookers, in the 1970s the benefit-and government-expanding public philosophy of the 1960s was sharply challenged and in some respects routed by a cost- and government-containing spirit. This challenge, which began in earnest in the late 1960s and had gained wide legitimacy by about 1975, is perhaps the single most important development in the recent politics of social welfare policy in the United States.

Changing Public Philosophies

The 1960s began with widespread acceptance of a public philosophy vividly embodied in John Kenneth Galbraith's famous critique of the incongruous coincidence of "private opulence and public squalor."[1] In the view of many social critics, a long list of urgent social needs was addressed— to the degree it was addressed at all—in piecemeal and largely futile fashion by an underdeveloped, lethargic public sector. The politics of American democracy was said to suffer from a lingering, perhaps chronic, case of deadlock,[2] resulting from the overwhelming power of various veto groups in the private sector to block the progressive intentions that elected officials in the federal government might adopt. By default of federal capacity,

1. *The Affluent Society* (Mentor Books, 1958), p. 203.
2. James MacGregor Burns, *The Deadlock of Democracy: Four-Party Politics in America* (Prentice-Hall, 1963), especially pp. 1–7, 323–25.

therefore, social policy lay largely in the hands of state and local governments, thought to be "unresponsive" and "backward," or was entrusted to the private sector in the faith that major social problems would yield to the all-purpose solution of strong, rapid economic growth. These evils of privatization and decentralization were viewed as both cause and symptom of a failure of central government activism that set the United States off by unfortunate contrast from other major Western industrial democracies.

In the early and middle 1960s, and especially between 1964 and 1968, the federal government moved quickly and forcefully to end these long-deplored deadlocks by means of a series of programmatic "break-throughs." In these years the Kennedy and Johnson administrations proposed and the Democratic Congress quickly enacted (under Johnson) new federal efforts to wage a "war on poverty" and to build a "Great Society." There followed close upon one another programs to encourage community action in localities across the nation, to bring new job opportunities to youth, to help pay the medical bills of the elderly and of the poor, to build neighborhood health centers, to support coordinated efforts at urban problem-solving in various "model" cities, to subsidize the renting and purchasing of decent housing by poor and moderate income families, to give disadvantaged youngsters a head start in school and to give them the advantages of compensatory education, and much more.[3] Although most of these programs were implemented by and generally deferred very substantially to the private sector and state and local governments, they amounted to a massive new set of federal commitments undertaken within a very short period of time. The number of categorical federal grant-in-aid programs increased into the hundreds.[4] In an extraordinary burst of creative energy and effort the federal government had answered the indictments of the public philosophy of the 1950s and early 1960s.

No sooner had these programs begun to take root than disillusionment began setting in, and it grew steadily throughout the 1970s. By mid-decade a very different public philosophy had taken hold. In this view, the problem is not that the public sector, and especially the federal government, is underdeveloped, but rather that the United States suffers from an excess of governmental, especially federal governmental, intrusion, interference, and intervention, often subsumed by the general term "overregulation."

---

3. For the politics of enactment of many of these programs see James L. Sundquist, *Politics and Policy: The Eisenhower, Kennedy, and Johnson Years* (Brookings Institution, 1968).

4. The Advisory Commission on Intergovernmental Relations (ACIR) counted 442 categorical grants by the mid-1970s; *Categorical Grants: Their Role and Design*, A-52 (Washington: ACIR, 1978), p. 92.

Attempting to do too much and crudely insisting on "throwing money at problems" the federal government is said to suffer from "overload," both of its own institutions and of subnational governments and the private sector laboring under the burdens imposed by federal institutions. Exorbitant federal taxing, spending, and regulation, it is said, are depleting private capital, depressing investment and saving, and hampering the productivity and efficiency of the private sector. These allegations, compounded by a widespread impression that the federal government's own efforts at public sector planning have miscarried, have generated a passion for "reprivatization," "deregulation," and "market alternatives." Federal "dictation," especially federal bureaucratic dictation, it is said, has robbed state and local governments of their natural vitality; has confounded their executives, overwhelmed by federal burdens and demands; and has flouted traditional American values of states' rights and local control. The urgent need for "devolution" and "decentralization" is pressed by those determined to make the federal government stop trying "to run the cities and states from Washington."

The Galbraithian thesis of an underdeveloped public sector has, within little more than a decade, been replaced by an antithetical image of gross public overdevelopment. Today little is said about the needs of the poor and disadvantaged, in part because many of these needs have been met, but in part too because the mood of austerity and of public resentment over rising taxes no longer supports "bold, new" programs on behalf of the less well-off. The older abhorrence of the power of a few well-placed, well-heeled pressure groups to veto public progress has given way to a concern with the "democratic distempers" attending excessive community action, citizen participation, citizen group politics, single-issue interest groups, public interest lobbies, and—in consequence of all this mobilization—a sense that democracies are no longer governable. The preoccupation with assembling bits and scraps of fragmented power in the private sector and at the state and local levels into a mandate for federal leadership has been driven out by derision of the federal government's "social pork barrel,"[5] and by intense nervousness over the approximately 75 percent of the federal budget deemed "relatively uncontrollable."[6] A political scientist Rip Van Winkle who fell asleep in 1965 or 1968 to reawaken in 1975, would have been astonished—especially if he was an incrementalist—at

5. The term is taken from David A. Stockman, "The Social Pork Barrel," *The Public Interest*, no. 39 (Spring 1975), pp. 3–30.
6. *The Budget of the United States Government, Fiscal Year 1980*, p. 561.

so remarkable and extensive a change in political climate and context in so short a time. After the sudden offensives of the 1960s, the American welfare state abruptly went on the defensive. Efforts to add new victories to the accumulating stock of policy breakthroughs have yielded to efforts to rationalize the breakthroughs of the past.[7] National health insurance and comprehensive welfare reform, annually proclaimed to be imminent in the late 1960s and early 1970s, are now widely viewed as ideas whose time has passed. The rhetoric of overcoming cycles of poverty and addressing unmet needs has been driven back by the esoteric lexicon of cost-containment, cost-effectiveness thinking, cost-benefit analysis, zero-based budgeting, and evaluation.[8]

A cynical but perfectly reasonable explanation of this transformation points to the world of ideas, to the mind-set of those intellectual elites who work to transform their personal philosophies into public philosophies. For this group, government (or at any rate the U.S. federal government) can do no right. When the federal government did little, much of the intellectual community complained bitterly of government's incapacity to take timely and decisive action. Now that the federal government does more, a sizable portion of the intellectual community complains bitterly of government's incapacity to learn not to take on too much. This is known as the "critical spirit." Because of it, public philosophies may be the poorest of guides to understanding public events.

On the other hand, these changes in public philosophy may be rooted in reality, in new and unexpected developments in the political and policymaking systems. The argument to be developed briefly here as a

7. The term "rationalizing" politics, as used here, means an attempt to improve the workings (management, efficiency, effectiveness, and so on) of existing programs while holding constant their size and scope. This mode of politics may be contrasted with efforts to expand the size and scope of programs without making major internal improvements in them ("incremental expansion" politics) and with efforts to add major new commitments to the governmental agenda ("breakthrough" politics). For a longer discussion see Lawrence D. Brown, New Policies, New Politics: Government's Response to Government's Growth (Brookings Institution, 1983).

8. To say that the welfare state has been put on the defensive is not to say that it has been forced to retreat or that it has been routed. The "uncontrollable" entitlement programs have of course continued to grow rapidly—a major source of the rationalizing challenges discussed here. Moreover, especially in the early 1970s, some very costly new commitments—most notably a large benefit increase and the introduction of indexing in the social security program in 1972, and the adoption of the supplemental security income program—were undertaken. New commitments grew fewer as the 1970s progressed, however, and after 1975 the percentage of gross national product devoted to federal domestic spending began to decline, ending two decades of uninterrupted growth. ACIR, Significant Features of Fiscal Federalism, 1979–80, M-123 (ACIR,1980), table 1. For evidence that "in constant dollars, Federal spending per capita has been leveling off over the past five years, and state and local spending is actually declining," see Rudolph G. Penner, New York Times, December 7, 1980.

preface to the particular concerns of this book is that one may discern a broad sequence of changes mediating the transition between the government- and benefit-expanding and government- and cost-containing philosophies. These changes appear to be inherent in (or at any rate copresent in) the interplay between policy and politics in the American welfare state and perhaps in other mature Western industrial democracies too.

Equalization. Since World War II (and in a few cases before it) the United States has launched by means of public policy sizable and often successful assaults on serious sources of inequality. The cataloguers of unmet needs in the 1950s could point accurately to a significant portion of the population suffering from poverty, lack of education, poor housing, malnutrition, poor health and limited access to medical care, unemployment, and discrimination. In each case, prevailing notions of justice encouraged a policy definition, or more accurately, estimation, of the standard or quality of life enjoyed by the majority, that is, by the modal member of the middle class, and then defined those enjoying less as afflicted by an inequality or inequity.[9] Public programs were then enacted to bring the incomes, educational opportunities, housing, nutrition, health care, job opportunities, and legal status of the disadvantaged closer to (though seldom actually to) the levels enjoyed by the majority.

Welfare state programs here and abroad have by and large been equalizing programs, and they have achieved some impressive results. The percentage of the American population living in poverty declined dramatically in the 1960s and 1970s and would be even smaller today if the benefits of government transfer programs were counted as income. The proportion of the population living in substandard housing has declined steadily. The food stamp program has done much to improve nutrition among the poor. Medicare and Medicaid have significantly enhanced the access of the elderly and of the poor to medical care. Civic equality between the races has increased remarkably. These are formidable moral accomplishments, in which the federal government has played a central role. However, these equalizing programs also have carried with them institutional consequences received far less enthusiastically than this social progress.

Politicization. Equalizing programs have produced many new occasions for public (especially federal) involvement in the private sector. As the 1950s notion that a strong and growing economy would inevitably

9. See Lawrence D. Brown, "The Scope and Limits of Equality as a Normative Guide to Federal Health Care Policy," *Public Policy*, vol. 26 (Fall 1978), pp. 481–532.

trickle down to solve the problems of the poor lost favor, governments initiated or expanded their role in policy areas previously viewed as the nearly exclusive preserve of the private sector. For example, housing markets felt the impact of new federal rent and home-purchase subsidy programs on behalf of low- and moderate-income persons, medical markets were influenced by the federal government's new role as a purchaser of care for the elderly and for the poor, and employment markets (including of course individual firms) across the country found a new and often unwelcome partner in hiring and promotion decisions as the federal government moved to prevent discrimination and to enforce "affirmative action" on behalf of disadvantaged groups.

It is a mistake, albeit a common one, to view politicization as a "shift" in a zero-sum game in which each increment of public power diminishes private power proportionately. In reality, new public undertakings define new areas of private as well as of public action. In the United States, private actors may have reasons of their own for clamoring for new public programs (the housing industry, for example, hoped to "stay alive with 235"), and they tend to have an important say in both design and administration of programs.[10] Nonetheless, so rapid an increase in the public presence in so wide a range of policy areas in recent years must be counted as a social fact of first importance.

Centralization. Equalizing programs have greatly expanded the scope and scale of federal involvement in the affairs of state and local governments. Regional or interstate disparities or inequities in welfare, housing, food, medical, or other benefits, or in the legal treatment of minorities, are plain targets for programs that aim to bring all disadvantaged citizens, regardless of location, closer to majority standards, and the major equalizing programs have—with varying success—tried to define reasonably clear national entitlements. Again, it is easy to exaggerate the extent to which federal decisionmaking has supplanted state and local discretion in these programs, and critics more impressed with Washington's assertiveness than with the realities of intergovernmental relations have persistently exaggerated it. In practice, the pervasive localism of the U.S. political system, strongly expressed in pressures on both the executive and Congress, tends to generate laws containing large scope for local discretion, and tends to lead mid-level federal bureaucrats, fearful of exceeding their ambiguous statutory mandates and of antagonizing state and local elected

10. See Morton Grodzins, *The American System* (Rand McNally, 1966).

officials with powerful federal allies, to forgo substantive in favor of procedural restraints.[11] Nonetheless the new, extensive federal presence, embodied in a sizable number of programs enacted and implemented in a very short span of time, has disturbed the standard procedures of state and local political, administrative, and "delivery" systems and has made the central government much more a force to be reckoned with (if only subverted) in state and local affairs than it was in, say, 1960.

Participation. It was not to be expected that the United States, with its decentralized political structures, pluralistic political culture, and egalitarian ethos, could sustain an increase in politicization and centralization without a corresponding increase in political participation. This increased participation has taken three main forms. The first is a great acceleration of the normal pulling and hauling among groups in a system of "interest group liberalism."[12] Debates over new programs, and the working out of the programs themselves, have engaged the interested energies of lobbies of state and local officials, physicians, hospitals, the housing industry, teachers, the elderly, organized labor, organized business, and more, all holding opinions about, and many having a tangible stake in, the design and implementation of new federal efforts.

Second, some new federal programs have built in their own participatory mechanisms. The provisions for "maximum feasible" participation of the poor in the community action program and for "widespread" citizen participation in model cities are best remembered, but other programs too instituted advisory boards, locally elected governing bodies, consumer representatives, and public hearing procedures to assure that unrepresented or underrepresented interests would have a voice in them. These participatory mechanisms seldom ran deep (that is, they mobilized relatively few people), but they were broad (that is, they extended to many new programs and communities). The result was to create and nourish new elites, often consisting of the most mobile and articulate beneficiaries of a program, and to encourage their involvement in shaping public policy. And some of these participants have in turn formed or joined new groups of their own—welfare rights and tenant counseling groups, for example.

Third, although the precise cause-and-effect pattern is not entirely clear, new federal programs have stimulated the formation and growth of new

11. For a case in point see Lawrence D. Brown and Bernard J. Frieden, "Rulemaking by Improvisation: Guidelines and Goals in the Model Cities Program," *Policy Sciences,* vol. 7 (December 1976), pp. 455–88.

12. The term is taken from Theodore J. Lowi, *The End of Liberalism* (Norton, 1969), p. 71.

groups. For example, federal consumer and environmental legislation seems to have stimulated as much as reflected the activism of consumer and environmental organizations. The net result of these three patterns is a much enlarged scale and intensity of political participation by organized groups, new and old, generalist and program-specific.

Pluralistic stagnation. The cumulative effects of these equalizing programs and the increased politicization, centralization, and participation that accompanied them, taking place both widely and suddenly, soon raised questions whether the political structures that had generated these programs and concomitants could safely sustain their consequences. Even in Great Britain, a unitary nation with a strong party system and a civil service that has long evoked admiration, the concerted demands of program beneficiaries, professional elites, governmental administrators, local authorities, and other increasingly mobilized interests seem increasingly to defy discipline and direction.[13] In the United States, extremely decentralized by Constitution and custom, with a federal system, extensive sharing of power between the public and private sectors, and formal separation of powers among governmental institutions at all three levels of government, the capacity of the federal government to discipline and direct newly mobilized interests is still more in doubt. The leadership capacity of the system has been questioned all the more sharply because the informal mechanism usually said to be the major tool of overcoming the high degree of formal decentralization in the American system—the political party— appears to be losing popular support and integrative capacity even as the need for a systemwide integrative mechanism grows.

As observers contemplated the difficulties of managing the demand for expansion of existing programs, and for addition of new ones, and as they witnessed the rapidly rising costs of "uncontrollable" programs like social security and Medicare, they coined a new vocabulary of political despair. "Interest group liberalism," "overinstitutionalization," the "immobility-emergency cycle," the "democratic distemper," the "crisis of democracy," the "ungovernability" of democracy,[14] and other such utterances gave

---

13. Samuel H. Beer, "British Pressure Groups Revisited: Pluralistic Stagnation from the Fifties to the Seventies" (Harvard University, July 1979).

14. See Lowi, *The End of Liberalism,* p. 71 ("interest group liberalism"); Mark Kesselman, "Overinstitutionalization and Political Constraint: The Case of France," *Comparative Politics,* vol. 3 (October 1970), pp. 21–44 ("overinstitutionalization"); Karl W. Deutsch, *Politics and Government: How People Decide Their Fate,* 2d ed. (Houghton Mifflin, 1974), pp. 61–63("immobility-emergency cycle"); Samuel P. Huntington, "The United States," in Michel J. Crozier and others, *The Crisis of Democracy: Report on the Governability of Democracies to the Trilateral Commission* (New York University Press, 1975), pp. 102–13 ("democratic distemper"); and Crozier and others, *Crisis of Democracy* (abundant use of the title phrase and the "ungovernability" theme).

expression to the view that welfare state politics had unleashed forces government could no longer direct, and that rationality, deliberation, and purposiveness had all somehow been thwarted by democratic excesses. In short, the United States (along with other Western welfare states) appeared to be suffering from "pluralistic stagnation."[15]

Rationalizing politics. From these interconnected developments and from the discontents and fears they generated grew a new political style of increasing importance as the 1970s progressed. This style looked skeptically on demands for new programs and on the steady expansion of existing ones and emphasized instead the importance of rationalizing what existed, of making programs work better. Under various guises and dressed in diverse rhetorical cloaks, the rationalizing theme came to dominate political discourse in the United States in the 1970s and gave practical content to the new government- and cost-containing public philosophy. The keynotes were management, coordination, reorganization, efficiency, cost-effectiveness, and planning, terms that described the search for a rearrangement of governmental elements in a new and more rational pattern. Other key words—reprivatization, incentives, market approaches, devolution, and deregulation—captured the growing demand for alternatives to federal, or indeed governmental, action and the call for renewed vigor in the private sector or at the state and local levels.

The objective of this rationalizing process was not to abolish or even greatly to cut back the programmatic breakthroughs of the 1960s. Rather, it was to trim their rough edges, improve their effectiveness and efficiency, and contain their costs. Thus, recognizing both the virtues and the vices of recent public commitments, the former ideological partisans of action or inaction were seized by a new ambivalence. Programs designed to improve, contain, or challenge—but not to undo or fundamentally obstruct—the expansionist breakthrough programs entered the statute books, thus institutionalizing this ambivalence.

The Political Evolution of Federal Health Care Policy

Although the political consequences of the rapidly growing federal presence may be seen in many areas of social policy, none exhibits them more clearly than does health care. Until the end of World War II, health care was considered an almost exclusive prerogative of the private sector.

15. Samuel H. Beer, *British Politics in the Collectivist Age* (Vintage Books, 1969), p. 408; and "British Pressure Groups Revisited."

When government "interfered," it did so gingerly, supporting activities that private practitioners agreed to cede to state and local public health departments. The federal government's inactivism was reinforced by the firm opposition of the American Medical Association (AMA) to initiatives such as national health insurance—regularly proposed over the years and regularly beaten back with little effort by organized medicine—that would expand the federal role. As critics often remarked, health care was a classic case of the "deadlock" of American politics.

After the end of World War II, conditions began gradually to change. The first breakthrough was an expansion in the late 1940s of federal financial support for biomedical research in the ever larger and more numerous National Institutes of Health (NIH). These programs concentrated funds and research energy on the needs of persons suffering from such dread diseases as cancer and heart ailments. In Cochrane's phrase, they attacked "inequalities between diseases."[16] A second breakthrough (1946) committed federal funds to the planning, construction, and renovation of hospital facilities, especially in rural areas. This program, termed Hill-Burton after its two principal legislative sponsors, redressed inequalities of resources among regions. Although these programs enlarged the federal presence in the health care system, they posed little threat to its privatism and decentralization. They were essentially subsidy programs, extending federal aid to support activities the private sector already performed and wished to perform on a larger scale. The importance of AMA support for, or at any rate nonopposition to, these programs is evident from the fate of a third subsidy program, federal funding for the training of physicians, which was continually discussed after the early 1950s, and strongly opposed by the AMA, and passed only in 1963, more than fifteen years after the NIH expansion and the Hill-Burton enactment.

In 1965, with enactment of the Medicare and Medicaid programs, the federal government added a new strategy—financing[17]—to the policy mix and launched an assault on the major remaining inequality in the health care field—inequality between classes. The federal government became for the first time a major purchaser of medical care—indeed the single largest

16. The conception of the three major forms of inequality in the health field is taken from A. L. Cochrane, *Effectiveness and Efficiency: Random Reflections on Health Services* (London: Nuffield Provincials Hospital Trust, 1972), chap. 8. The application to U.S. health care programs follows Brown, "Scope and Limits of Equality," pp. 496–501.

17. As used here, "subsidy" programs are federal aid to providers of health care services (broadly defined) that enable them to pursue accustomed or new activities on a larger scale. "Financing" programs are federal aid to consumers that help them pay their medical bills.

purchaser—and did so on behalf of the elderly and the poor. By the late 1960s, therefore, the policy deadlock had been decisively broken. Through a series of breakthroughs achieved over twenty years, the federal government had become deeply involved on both sides of the medical economics equation, at once building up the supply of medical care providers and services (the production of biomedical research and technology, the construction of hospitals, and the training of physicians) and generating new demand for care among previously deprived parts of the population (the elderly and the poor). Major steps toward equality had been taken: sufferers from dread and chronic diseases benefited from federally supported biomedical research, regions lacking medical facilities now had better access to care because of federally supported construction activities, and social groups that had faced financial barriers to access were no longer shut out of the system. The political concomitants of these equalizing programs brought along new and difficult problems of their own, however.

First, the subsidy and financing policies entailed a new and extensive politicization of health care. The traditional view that health care was properly left to the private sector, aided only by such marginal public health activities as private institutions could not or did not choose to adopt, had been violated. Government now strongly influenced the flow of funds to biomedical researchers and medical schools, to hospital planners and builders, and to physicians and hospitals caring for Medicare and Medicaid beneficiaries. Moreover, politicization brought centralization; although the roles of the states and localities increased (Hill-Burton and Medicaid funds, for example, went to state agencies and were spent largely according to state plans), most of the new action was initiated and much of it conducted at the *federal* level. The years 1945–65 had witnessed a major change not only in the distribution of health functions between the private and public sectors but also among levels of the federal system.

As might be expected, politicization and centralization affected in turn the cast of characters seeking to participate in health care policy. One major change was the self-sustaining participation of the federal government itself. Now a major subsidizer and purchaser of care, the federal government stood on the sidelines of policy no longer, and it began to discern and articulate interests and agendas of its own. Thus in the decentralized American system Congress, White House, multiple elements of the federal bureaucracy, and more, began wrangling with one another for control of the newly expanded federal health agenda.

At the same time, new programs generated and responded to new constituencies: the biomedical research community, medical schools, and the research lobby in the case of NIH and manpower training programs; . the American Hospital Association, state health planners, and individual localities in Hill-Burton; the AFL-CIO, the elderly, the poor, and others in the financing programs. The growth of "public sector politics"[18] at the federal level and the diffusion of participation throughout the system in turn demoted the AMA from its privileged status as veto group to the position of one pressure group among others in a newly politicized, pluralized, and democratized policy field.

In the wake of these developments, when the Nixon administration took office in 1969, severe doubts were being entertained and expressed about the direction of federal health care policy. More than twenty years of freely flowing federal funds had failed to produce the long-awaited cure for cancer and other dread diseases, and the managerial competence and cost-effectiveness of NIH were questioned. Years of federal hospital construction funds had endowed the nation with many overbedded, underoccupied hospitals which fueled the fires of medical cost inflation. Federal efforts to overcome the doctor shortage had made little change in the maldistribution of physicians by area and specialty and seemed merely to subsidize the training of doctors who followed one another to attractive and remunerative metropolitan locations and pursued their "target incomes" there. During their short lives, Medicare and Medicaid had proved to be much more costly than legislators and planners had expected (or at any rate acknowledged), and they threatened to inflict grave damage on the integrity of federal (and state) budgets.

No less clear than these problems were the enormous political obstacles to addressing them. Efforts to shake up the status quo at NIH would be (and were) opposed by the biomedical research community, the medical schools, the research lobby, and others. Efforts to end the construction of hospitals in areas with little need for new beds were opposed by acquisitive localities and medical communities and, most important, by congressmen eager to bring home more bacon. Medical schools and the AMA would fight energetically against any federal effort to alter the nature of the manpower training quid pro quo—for example, proposals making aid contingent on service in rural areas or on an increase in the number of family practitioners the schools trained. Medicare and Medicaid were uncontrollable by their very design—they committed the federal govern-

18. The term is taken from Samuel H. Beer, "The Adoption of General Revenue Sharing: A Case Study in Public Sector Politics," *Public Policy*, vol. 24 (Spring 1976), pp. 127–95.

ment to pay the bills run up by those statutorily entitled to aid, regardless of the total annual sum and independent of the annual budget and appropriations processes. Efforts to introduce control would meet objections from the poor, the elderly, and organized labor (if controls fell on the recipients) or from organized providers (should they fall on hospitals and doctors). By 1970 the United States was said to be suffering from a health care crisis, as annual costs shot up. The federal government, it was widely agreed, should do something.

Thus by painful steps did the federal government begin under the Nixon administration in 1970 the search for "rationalizing" programs in the health field, programs that would reorganize and make more manageable, cost-effective, and controllable the accumulated, expanding commitments the federal government had undertaken. The quest was largely an exercise in "public sector politics," launched and sustained mainly by federal officials worried about the fiscal consequences to the federal government of the uncontrollability (in all its various senses) of the federal health care agenda. In search of rationalizing policies and distrustful of those bastions of presumed self-interest, the bureaucracy and the universe of affected interest groups, the federal policymakers turned to policy analysts, a swelling legion of academics, quasi- and pseudo-academics, consultants, and others trained in esoteric disciplines, especially economics.[19] Hearing the call of duty, the analytic community did not shrink. Even as the new governmental willingness to act and the demand for the conceptual stuff of which breakthroughs were made stimulated an intellectual effervescence of ideas for action in the 1960s, so now the demand for managerial,

19. The terms "policy analysis" and "policy analyst" have several possible meanings. Throughout this book, policy analysis will generally mean recommendations about what government ought to do or how it should approach its problems based on esoteric (often meaning academic) theoretical or empirical propositions. (By this is meant propositions unlikely to occur to policymakers relying solely on their intuitions, experiences, or political maintenance concerns.) By making "recommendations" part of the definition, this usage includes an element of policy "advocacy." Advocacy ranges from simple publication of policy views to aggressive "selling" of them (in which case the advocate is a policy "entrepreneur"). Policy analysts need not make recommendations, that is, also be advocates. The Congressional Budget Office, for example, notes in the preface to its background papers that its mandate is "to provide objective and impartial analysis," and so it "offers no recommendations of policy options." This study, however, is heavily concerned with analysts who are also advocates and in some cases entrepreneurs. Policy analysis may also mean efforts to explain rigorously the workings and results (especially the "outcomes" or "outputs") of the policy process. The best-known examples of this type are the implemenation studies. Except where explicitly noted, this is not the type of policy analysis discussed in this book. Implementation studies are usually the preserve of political scientists, whereas policy analysis in the earlier sense is mainly based on economics (a more "esoteric" discipline) though it need not be. However, policy analysts need not be card-carrying (that is, Ph.D.) social scientists. Indeed, most of the policy analysts, advocates, and entrepreneurs discussed in this book were not. Analysts may—and often do—apply propositions from academic disciplines they have not necessarily mastered.

reorganizational, and cost-effective strategies of control in the 1970s stimulated new minds to supply new ideas, which were often in tension with those of the best (or at any rate most influential) minds of the previous decade.

By 1970 the federal government constituted a fertile market for health care cost-control strategies. This rapid change of perspective was extraordinary; few observers of the political developments of the 1960s had doubted that the federal government would go on steadily expanding benefits over time, letting the chips fall where they may, and even fewer believed that the government would itself take the lead in the quest to impose controls—that is, limits and constraints—on the medical care system a mere five years after enactment of Medicare and Medicaid. Yet even as the struggle for national health insurance grew increasingly lethargic as the 1970s progressed, the struggle to define and implement effective health care controls grew increasingly urgent.

The Federal Government and HMOs

This book examines one of the federal government's first sustained, programmatic efforts at health care controls, the health maintenance organization (HMO) program. (Readers unfamiliar with this term may wish to consult the opening pages of chapter 2.) Judged by the size of its budget and by the scope of its accomplishments, the HMO program is not very significant. It has (as federal programs go) spent little money and has accomplished little. Nonetheless the program is singularly revealing about the emergence of rationalizing politics in the 1970s and has much to teach about the interplay between politics and policy in government's quest for control over programs it had earlier and hopefully brought into being, a quest earnestly pursued today in health care and in other policy fields.

Specifically, the HMO program offers instruction in three features of rationalizing politics. First, these politics give rise to new professional-intellectual elites, policy analysts, who wield the weapons of cost-benefit and cost-effectiveness analysis, incentives, reorganization, evaluation, and more in battle against "professional-bureaucratic complexes"[20] that defend and seek to extend the benefit-expanding breakthroughs of the past. Public sector politics is not simply a stage on which professionals and

20. Beer, "Adoption of General Revenue Sharing," p. 157.

bureaucrats conspire to produce incremental program expansion. Increasingly it is a scene of conflict between program-oriented elites and analytic-oriented elites, the latter gaining influence as disappointment grows with the former and seeking to persuade policymakers of the results of new approaches couched in the distinctive propositions, largely economic, of policy analysis. Rationalizing politics issue a challenge to benefit-expanding cadres and offer an opportunity to the "partisan efficiency advocates"[21] in the policy analysis community. The HMO program, a quintessential embodiment of many tenets of policy analysis, is of special interest as a case of how analysis gets on the public agenda and of what happens to it once it gets there. Proponents of HMOs posed the policy issue in stark terms: the choice for health care policy lay between increasing public regulation on the one side and innovative efforts at reorganization and market-building on the other. A federal HMO program was to be an effort at what Charles L. Schultze called institution-building[22] for competition, an attempt to revitalize the health care market, to reorganize institutional arrangements predicated on faulty incentives, and to put to work the internal (organizational) and external (systemwide) discipline of competition on tasks that might otherwise be entrusted to regulatory bureaucracies.

This line of policy reasoning, which encapsulated and put to work virtually every major concept and theme in the lore of contemporary policy analysis—reorganization, markets, competition, incentives, efficiency, cost-effectiveness, and more—rested on a number of assumptions about health care, its costs, and how to control them. The major assumptions were that the root of the cost crisis was faulty incentives embodied in faulty institutional structures in need of reorganization; that markets could be made strong and responsible, and therefore into adequate agents of this reorganization, in the health field; that the market discipline following from the union of prepayment and group practice in one organization (the HMO) would produce greater efficiency; that the presence of such efficient organizations in the larger health care system would generate vigorous price competition and therewith new systemwide efficiencies and cost-containment; that HMOs were self-regulating entities, whose competitive and market-based discipline would keep them free of undesirable side effects; that such self-regulation led the HMO to combine within itself

---

21. The term is taken from Charles L. Schultze, *The Politics and Economics of Public Spending* (Brookings Institution, 1968), p. 96.

22. *The Public Use of Private Interest* (Brookings Institution, 1977), p. 13.

improved quality, increased access, and lower costs, without the trade-offs among these goals said to be enforced in the fee-for-service, third-party-payment world; that such an approach was an obviously preferable alternative to public regulation; and that HMO-building was something that the federal government might easily "catalyze."

All of these propositions are of obvious interest to a citizenry tired of regulation, bureaucracy, and big government and bent on discovering ways to realize the "public use of private interest."[23] The notion that the proper manipulation of incentives, markets, competition, reorganization, and the like can improve on present arrangements is ardently advanced not only in health but also in the fields of pollution control, energy development, and others. Although these theories are often asserted, they are seldom tried. In the HMO case they were tried; the results may be instructive.

To understand and evaluate the trial this incentive-based approach received, it is necessary to begin by analyzing the major arguments behind the HMO development effort. It is necessary, that is, to set forth the policy analysis on which the HMO approach rested and to subject it to some further policy analysis in turn. Because HMOs are, after all, health maintenance *organizations,* it is important that their organizational prop-erties—especially the fundamental processes of organizational formation, maintenance, and performance—be considered in some detail. For reasons that will be illustrated throughout part 1, these processes should be considered not only in detail but also in sequence. Formative experiences by definition determine whether development of an HMO in a given area is feasible at all. In HMOs that survive the early years, such experiences tend to influence growth and management. Approaches to growth and management, in turn, influence not only the organization's financial stability and internal tranquillity, but also its organizational "outputs," or performance. These projects occupy part 1 of this book. Chapter 2 examines the opportunities and difficulties that attend the formation of HMOs. Chapter 3 explores the problems of managing and maintaining HMOs over time. Chapter 4 discusses the complexities of passing judgment on the performance of HMOs, that is, on the quality, access, and cost of care they provide. Answers to these three questions—how are HMOs formed? how are they run? and how do they perform?—taken together, offer a basis for answering the question, what is it reasonable to expect from the HMO approach in public policy?

23. Ibid. Interestingly, Schultze does not discuss HMOs as an application of this strategy.

A second central feature of rationalizing politics is a preoccupation, indeed an obsession, with governmental failure. Political failures (deadlock, inaction, and failure of will) haunted the 1950s and early 1960s; governmental failures (deficiencies of intelligence, foresight, and competence) torment the 1970s.[24] Of the two, governmental failure is probably the more serious and more difficult to overcome. Political failures may be overcome by acting; governmental failures may be dispelled only by acting well and rightly.

This preoccupation with governmental failure largely explains the growing appeal of policy analysts with new perspectives on problems that the entrenched professional-bureaucratic complexes have helped to bungle. (The preoccupation is also to some degree a result of the growing number and assertiveness of these analysts.) It largely explains the rapid growth of policy analytic, economic-based alternatives and of political science implementation studies devoted to cataloguing and ridiculing governmental errors. It also largely explains the major "solutions" of these analytic schools: make government action more closely resemble that of the theoretical private economy (the first school) or insist that government take on less (the second).

The severity and scope of the indictment and the assurance of the purveyors of the alternatives invite attention to the relation between politics and policy that defines governmental failure. Broadly speaking, there have been two general accounts of failure. One view, generally that of the economics-influenced analysts, is that the analytic universe is abundantly populated with good ideas (policies), but that the political system (government) somehow manages persistently to overlook them or, if it tries them, constantly botches their translation from the analytical to the political realm. The second view, generally that of political scientists sobered by their studies of implementation, is that many seemingly good and simple ideas turn out to be poor ones on closer inspection, but that the political system, through an excess of naïve good will or a shortage of foresight and common sense (or both), often embraces these ideas and tries to put them into practice. The respective remedies, as noted above, are "do differently" and "do less."

It may be, however, that the sources of governmental failure are more complex and less amenable to solution than these views imply. It is worth

24. Of course in a democracy governmental failures are a species of political failure. In the special sense used here, "political" failure means the inability of elective officials (and of their local or interest group constituents) to adopt desired programs. "Governmental" failure means the inability of elective and appointed officials to make programs on the statute books work as critics think they should.

pressing a bit on the permutations contained in the policy-politics combinations noted here, and worth raising the possibility that the roots of failure may lie neither in government ineptness nor in deceptive ideas. What if the "normal" failure finds government taking up reasonably good ideas and then doing a reasonably good job with them, but with unimpressive or dismal results?

This possibility suggests a need to look more deeply into the interplay between policy and politics, and to introduce some conceptual distinctions on each side. First, one should distinguish between policies as "ideas" and as "strategies." Not everything that makes sense in theory or on paper works well in the real world; recognizing the difference in concrete cases is what distinguishes policy analysis from analysis simply. Second, one should distinguish between political "processes" (that is, the behavior of flesh-and-blood politicians in and over time) and political "structures" (those enduring constitutional and other formal relations among institutions that constrain political behavior). What politicians try to do and what political structures permit, encourage, or constrain are two different matters; recognizing the difference in concrete cases is what distinguishes the political scientist from the political reporter. The usual views, which call attention to miscarried interplays between ideas and processes, may operate at the wrong level of analysis; a richer level and source of explanation may be the fit between strategies and structures.

Too little attention has been given to these issues. First (the policy side of the coin), it is too often assumed that any good idea is ipso facto a good strategy, that anything that makes sound intellectual sense should work smoothly when put into practice by men intelligent enough to understand *that* it makes good intellectual sense. This must be proved, however, not assumed. If there is a difference between idea and strategy, and the difference goes unrecognized, the result is likely to be diminished legitimacy as government fails to fulfill the misconceived demands of the policy analysts.

Second (the political side), the distinction between processes and structures has some suggestive implications for prevailing images of the American political system. The dominant emphases in political science in the United States have gradually shifted from (1) a structural view, emphasizing formal-legal-constitutional arrangements among institutions, to (2) an institutionalist focus, concentrating on the more particular roles, powers, and functions of particular institutions, to (3) a behavioral persuasion examining the micro-level bargaining, decisionmaking, or whatever of actors within institutions. The third, reigning, view pictures policymaking as a mode of political behavior, which is to say a function of the decisions or choices of actors or of their accumulated choices reconciled in "bargains" that produce "outcomes." This view, like that of the policy analysts, implies that good ideas may be adopted as policy strategies, and poor ideas avoided, if only policymakers are properly enlightened and thereby protected against "the unanticipated consequences of purposive social action"[25] that will be revealed in the implementation process.

This is an attractive rationalist image and there is no doubt some truth to it. But the view that policymaking is mainly a function of behavior, and therefore of individual choice, and therefore of the insightfulness, information, and public-spiritedness of the choosers may obscure crucial elements of the *context* of choice. Choice takes place within institutional settings—White House, federal department, legislative committee, and so forth—which are themselves set within enduring political structures. Of central importance are those structures that define the degree of separation or integration among major organs of government (executive, legislative, judiciary), the mutual powers of levels of government in a federal system, and the degree of sharing of power and responsibilities for collective affairs between the public and private sectors of society.

These three structural variables—which might be called parliamentarism, federalism, and privatism—may be assigned "values" for any society.[26] In the United States these values are extensive separation of powers, extensive dispersion of powers among three levels of a federal system, and extensive sharing of responsibilities between a robust private sector and the public sector. In a word, these values define an extreme decentralization of political structures in the United States. Unless the discrete choices of the policymaking process are traced back to and contemplated in their structural context, an important source of explanation for the interplay between politics and policy may be missed. Not all policy strategies fit equally well with all political structures; strategies and structures cannot be mixed and matched indiscriminately. This, at any rate, is a central theme of this study.

25. This is the title of Robert Merton's essay, *American Sociological Review*, vol. 1 (December 1936), pp. 894–904.

26. A fourth structural variable, of great importance in comparative studies but of less significance in this single-nation study of one program, might be termed "collectivism," meaning the role assumed by large formal organizations in the politics of policymaking. The degree to which the major formal organizations—public bureaucracies and interest groups—are many and fragmented ("decentralized") or few and unified ("centralized") is a key element of the structural context of policy.

The HMO program offers excellent opportunities to test this hypothesis that a deeper problem of fit between strategy and structure underlies the apparent problem of matching idea to process. The HMO development effort is a federal exercise in taking up a bright idea advanced by policy analysts and trying to make it work on a large scale in practice.[27] Born of perceived governmental failure—to control the rising costs of medical care—the HMO program was in its turn branded a governmental failure, an allegedly unworkable program embodied in a badly drafted law poorly administered by the federal bureaucracy.

To understand the debate surrounding the enactment and progress of the program, the asserted unworkability of the law, and the changes later introduced into it, it is necessary to look closely at the political history of the HMO effort. This is the focus of part 2 of this work. The proposition that the federal government should take the lead in promoting and developing health maintenance organizations (a newly minted term for prepaid medical group practices) found a prominent place on the federal agenda for the first time in 1970. President Richard M. Nixon proposed HMO legislation in 1971, Congress debated the proposal between 1971 and 1973, leading finally to the Health Maintenance Organization Act of 1973 (Public Law 93-222). The legislative-executive struggles over the law's enactment are the subject of chapter 5. The Department of Health, Education, and Welfare (HEW) wrestled with the administration of the law—a law roundly deplored by much of the HMO industry itself—between 1974 and 1976. The bureaucratic politics of the administrative process are treated in chapter 6. In 1976 Congress made the law more acceptable to its many critics by amending it. Then HEW wrestled with it anew, and Congress amended it again in 1978, but serious problems continued to afflict the program. Chapter 7 examines these changes and recurrent difficulties from 1976 to 1980. Examination of these three phases—legislative-executive formulation of the HMO law, HEW administration, and political change in both Congress and executive—answers the central question of part 2 of this study: what have the federal

27. A word about terminology is in order here. The HMO program authorized by Public Law 93-222 dates from December 1973. However, in 1970 the Department of Health, Education, and Welfare established an "HMO program" using discretionary provisions of categorical grants to launch HMOs. The first formal effort of the federal government to encourage citizens to join HMOs was the Nixon administration's proposal in March 1970 to add a "part C" HMO option to the Medicare law (see chapter 5, below). For the most part the term "HMO program" will be used in this book to refer to HMO development activities authorized by P.L. 93-222. The terms "federal HMO effort" or "development effort" will refer to all the diverse forms of encouragement undertaken since early 1970.

government and the political process done for (or to) the HMO strategy? To what degree has the political process realized or failed to realize the policy potential of HMOs discussed in part 1?

A third element basic to rationalizing politics is a preoccupation with the *organization* of public policy and of social institutions and arrangements more generally. In the breakthrough period of the 1960s (as in a similar period in the New Deal) organizational questions were often neglected. In the rush to launch new organizations entrusted with urgent social purposes and to create new egalitarian entitlements to confer benefits on needy and worthy groups, mundane questions of organizational design and of the administrative and implementation capacities of those complex organizational networks that constitute "delivery systems" tended to be overlooked. In the reappraisals of the 1970s, questions of organization and management came to center stage as attention turned to means of rationalizing both delivery systems and government's own efforts. There appears to be a cyclical pattern here. Breakthrough periods accompanied by inattention to the niceties of organizational design and administrative detail tend to be followed by "rationalizing" periods in which organizational questions become paramount.

As government expands the scope and scale of its activities, government organizations (bureaucracies) increasingly clash with and bang into private sector (and subnational governmental) organizations implicated in government's new doings. As these frictions develop, government faces four basic choices. First, it may attempt to displace or eliminate recalcitrant organizations. (For example, it could in theory put an end to the private practice of medicine and install a national health service.) Second, it may attempt to regulate existing organizations. Third, it may enter into bargaining relationships with these organizations in hope of winning, by means of persuasion and concession, some of its objectives. Fourth, it may attempt to induce change in these organizations by indirection—for example, by sponsoring the creation of new organizations to compete with or otherwise influence the behavior of existing ones.

The strategies actually chosen reflect the will and power of policymakers. For example, the idea of eliminating or greatly displacing established organizations is virtually unthinkable in the United States; here, whatever is, is deemed functional and legitimate. Regulation presupposes both the conviction that it is workable and necessary and the political support (notably votes in the legislature) to impose it on hostile and politically active organizations. Bargaining implies that the government has the leverage to oblige private organizations to come to and remain at the bargaining table, an assumption met only slightly in the largely private U.S. health care system. In short, when the search for means of controlling the health care system got under way at the end of the 1960s, a thorough-going assault on the prerogatives of private medical practice was unthink-able, regulation was highly unattractive, and bargaining relations were very weak between a federal government that had enacted financing programs for only a part of the population but five years before and a private medical community that had resisted those programs bitterly. Of political necessity, therefore, the search for controls began with a strategy of indirection, an attempt to induce change in the larger system by building new, exemplary organizational forms that would stand apart from the larger system but would at the same time act in and on it and would pressure it, by means of economic processes elaborated in detail by the partisans of medical efficiency, toward change.

The HMO effort, then, is of interest not only as a policy approach and as a political undertaking but also as a social beginning, an early step down a still dimly discerned road to stronger measures of federal influence on the U.S. health care system. The HMO effort mediated politically and captures analytically the transition between the benefit- and government-expanding public philosophy of the 1960s and the cost- and government-containing philosophy of the 1970s.[28] Health maintenance organizations, a federally encouraged means of controlling costs by means of decentralized market-building, have been supplemented by calls for and experiments with more centralized and regulatory approaches. But although HMOs may be viewed as a beginning, as a means of mediating a major social transition,[29] they are also a recurring encounter along the road. A decade after HMO development first gained prominence on the federal agenda, despite the modest accomplishments of the effort, federal interest in HMO-building remained high. Indeed in the 1980s the HMO banner is being unfurled anew and held high as a leading "market alternative" to regulatory controls. A grasp of the interplay between policy and politics in the HMO

28. Some may think it contradictory to assert that "an early step . . . to stronger measures of federal influence" mediated a transition to a "cost- and government-containing philosophy." But in the HMO effort, the federal government attempted to exert influence over health care costs by stimulating the development of new organizations that would introduce market competition in private, local settings. The proponents of HMOs have all along emphasized that this private, market-oriented effort is a distinct alternative to public regulation. Thus it is fair to say that the federal government has taken the lead in promoting an approach designed to contain both costs and government.

29. On the mediation of social transitions, see John Dewey, *Liberalism and Social Action* (Capricorn, 1963), p. 48.

program can shed valuable light on the nature of the "mediation of social transitions" now in progress in the health care field (and in other fields) in the United States.

Put simply, there are two central questions about the HMO program. First, why did the federal government undertake, with such high hopes, an HMO development effort in the first place? Second, having undertaken it with such hope, why did it manage to accomplish so little? The answer offered in this study focuses on the paradox that the source of the program's appeals was also the source of its difficulties. The key attraction—and key difficulty—of the HMO approach is that it is a reorganization strategy. The strategy has both "macro" and "micro" components. The macro objective is a systemwide reorganization of health care as HMOs go to work on the faulty incentives of a system thought to be illogically organized in fragmented, irresponsible clusters of fee-for-service providers and third-party-payment insurers. The micro means to this end is an ambitious exercise in organization-building, the launching—with federal dollars, encouragement, and guidance—of hundreds, perhaps indeed thousands, of HMOs across the United States. In the arguments of the policy analysts who sold the HMO proposal and of the governmental generalists who bought it, these organization-building and -changing processes were nonproblematic, indeed semiautomatic. In practice, however, these processes proved to be very complex and problematic.

In the organization-building process, policy and politics interacted in ways no one had fully foreseen or intended. Legislators rapidly discovered that, far from following logically from the self-regulating, seemingly self-evident idea of HMO, writing a law that would encourage desirable HMOs required esoteric and controversial judgments of value and fact. As they went about their work, the legislators collided rudely with an HMO industry consisting both of long-established prepaid group practices intensely concerned with how federal requirements might affect their complex organizational patterns and of new and newly planned HMOs whose executives often entertained notions about HMO-building sharply at odds with those of important federal policymakers. After the law finally emerged in 1973, legislative-industry conflict and negotiation became administrative-industry conflict and negotiation as HEW attempted to devise administrative rules that were faithful both to the legislative instructions of its political superiors and to the practical needs of its constituency, the HMO industry. In short, the HMO program has been the scene of a protracted, angry government-industry clash, and although the conflict grew more muted over time, the program is not yet free from it or from its lingering effects. Such clashes do not of course assume the same form or involve the same issues in other areas of government-industry relations. Yet they grow increasingly common and increasingly important as the federal government impinges increasingly on organized interests in the private sector. Thus, the HMO case may offer lessons about the conditions and conduct of "corporatism" in the United States today.

Working from the hypothesis that the source of both the policy attractions and the political vicissitudes of the HMO program lies in its character as an organization-building strategy, part 3 of this book attempts to explain the poor fit between the HMO policy strategy and the structural characteristics of American government discussed in parts 1 and 2. Chapter 8 evaluates the decade of experience with the HMO strategy and explores the reasons for the clash between the federal government and the HMO industry. Chapter 9 elaborates on the distinction between HMOs as idea and as strategy and attempts to show why the strategic properties of the HMO proposal fit poorly with the structural properties of the U.S. political process. Chapter 10 sets HMOs in the context of the continuing and developing interplay between policy and politics in the health care field and attempts to draw some conclusions about the future of politics, organization, and health care policy.

Despite the size of this manuscript, the study it contains is a limited and highly selective treatment of the policy and politics of the federal HMO development effort.[30] The policy issues discussed in part 1 have been chosen with an eye to the politics treated in part 2, and vice versa. No attempt has been made to exhaust the many issues germane to assessing the policy potential of HMOs; nor is the account of HMO politics complete and comprehensive. Of necessity, therefore, the synthetic conclusions about the interplay between policy and politics in part 3 are also limited in scope.

The research presented here draws mainly on that subset of the vast HMO literature deemed relevant to the selective concerns of this study and on unstructured interviews conducted by this writer with about one hundred persons, most of them executives in HMOs or participants in one or another phase of the federal HMO program. (These interviews are the

30. Among many important additions to the literature, two, which appeared after this study was substantially completed, and which deal deeply with matters reviewed more lightly here, may be of special interest—Joseph L. Falkson, *HMOs and the Politics of Health System Reform* (Chicago: American Hospital Association, and Bowie, Md.: Robert J. Brady Co., 1980), and Harold S. Luft, *Health Maintenance Organizations: Dimensions of Performance* (Wiley, 1981).

source of unattributed quotations in the chapters to follow.) As HMO executives often insist, each of the roughly 235 HMOs in the United States today is unique; no generalizations hold with equal validity for all of them. Limits of time, budget, and energy made it impossible to survey every HMO to learn the details of its practices on each of the various points discussed here. Nor did it seem sensible to construct a list of standard indicators or measures and then apply them to a representative sample of HMOs. Such a quantitative approach presupposes that one can set up a clear list of indicators that mean very much the same thing in all (sampled) plans and that one can also decide what any given subset of the HMO universe is representative *of*. These presuppositions depend in turn on a stock of qualitative information about HMOs adequate to support these feats of categorization. Developing this qualitative knowledge seemed to this writer to be both more worthy and more pressing a task than pursuing the quantitative regimen, which so often entails establishing "testable" hypotheses that do not speak clearly to the theories with which one began; testing those hypotheses against indicators that fail to capture the heart of the hypotheses; applying to the indicators data that are available but, alas, suspect or largely beside the analytic point; and finally, applying to these data statistical methods based on unrealistic or ludicrous premises (for instance, that variables that common sense and observation show to be highly interrelated may be usefully treated as independent). The price of avoiding these pitfalls—the inevitable cries of HMO executives that one or another generalization offered herein fails exactly to fit one or another HMO—is well worth paying. In any case these objections are largely beside the point. As Henry Sumner Maine put it almost one hundred years ago:

> All generalization is the product of abstraction; all abstraction consists in dropping out of sight a certain number of particular facts, and constructing a formula which will embrace the remainder; and the comparative value of general propositions turns entirely on the relative importance of the particular facts selected and of the particular facts rejected.[31]

Of the relative importance of the facts emphasized and the comparative value of the general propositions offered here the reader may now judge for himself.

31. Henry Sumner Maine, *Popular Government* (Indianapolis: Liberty Classics, 1976), p. 120.

Part One

CHAPTER TWO

Organization Building: The HMO as a System of Contributions

Men always dislike enterprises where the snags are evident.   Niccolò Machiavelli

THE MOST conspicuous fact about prepaid group practices, now often called health maintenance organizations (HMOs), in the United States is their small numbers (about 235 in 1980) and the small percentage of the population they enroll (about 4 percent).[1] Curiously, little attention has been given to explaining the slow progress of this form of medical organization. Some economists offer the simple explanation that HMOs have been suppressed by fee-for-service practitioners who prefer not to compete and who have employed political power and public authority to enforce their preference. If the anticompetitive uses of public power were ended, so this argument runs, the economic appeals of the HMO would produce substantial consumer demand for them, which in turn would soon generate a correspondingly abundant supply. Critics of HMOs reply that the small supply accurately reflects consumer demand, which is small. But, because political and other obstacles have undeniably been put in the way of these groups, true consumer demand is difficult to gauge. The chicken-and-egg problem that arises from the economic logic of supply and demand cannot be easily resolved. There is another explanation for the slow progress of HMOs, however: they are complex organizations that are hard to build and maintain. Even if obstacles were removed from their path, and even if consumer demand were strong and clearly expressed, developing and sustaining a sizable HMO presence in the medical system might

1. U.S. Department of Health and Human Services, Office of Health Maintenance Organizations, *National HMO Census of Prepaid Plans, June 30, 1980,* DHHS Publication no. (PHS) 80-50159 (HHS, 1980), p. 1.

remain difficult. To assess this possibility, and its explanatory power relative to the anticompetitive argument, it is necessary to understand the elements of which HMOs consist and how these organizational elements come together. It is necessary, in short, to explore the organization-building process.

No two HMOs are entirely alike. Nevertheless most of them face a common set of problems of organizational formation (the subject of this chapter) and of organizational maintenance and growth (the subject of the next chapter). Their leaders also face a delimited range of "strategic choices"[2] as they address these common problems. Although it is seldom possible to generalize about the actual detailed choices that are made—these depend on a host of contingencies and peculiarities—it is both possible and useful to generalize about the problems and options that these groups face.

The argument of this chapter is that in order to succeed, an HMO must find effective means of creating a balance of positive over negative inducements for a range of contributors essential to the formation of the organization—sponsors, physicians, subscribers, and hospitals. The prospect of involvement with an HMO carries benefits and risks for each of these potential contributors. If the benefits can be made to outweigh the risks for all four, an HMO can be founded with reasonable hope of success. If not, it either cannot be established or is unlikely to succeed over time.

Organizational Types

The ancestors of HMOs go back many years. In Europe, from medieval times until the advent of national health insurance, health care was often provided under the auspices of benevolent societies, guilds, unions, churches, and other associations that collected small "premiums" from their members and paid physicians who agreed to care for those members for fixed sums, usually a capitation payment of so much per member per unit of time.[3] In nineteenth-century America, similar arrangements were included in company medical or "contract medicine" plans developed by firms concerned about the health of work forces in areas where physicians and

2. The term is borrowed from John Child, "Organizational Structure, Environment, and Performance: The Role of Strategic Choice," *Sociology*, vol. 6 (January 1972), pp. 1–22.
3. William A. Glaser, *Paying the Doctor* (Johns Hopkins Press, 1970), pp. 9–11.

facilities were few.⁴ Labor unions too have developed prepaid plans for their members.

This form of medical care system is usually termed "prepaid group practice" (PGP). The essential elements are these: a health "plan" (the administrative and marketing arm) employs physicians (a "staff" model plan) or contracts with a physicians' group (a "group" model plan), who agree to provide, in exchange for fixed remuneration (often a salary, sometimes a bonus in addition to a salary, occasionally a capitation sum) a wide and contractually specified range of medical services to an enrolled population. Unlike a conventional insurance plan, a PGP does not indemnify subscribers against risk; rather, a single organization both markets its coverage and delivers care with a closed panel of its own physicians. Two basic differences between PGPs and conventional plans should be underscored: first, conventional insurers usually reimburse physicians on a fee-for-service basis; prepaid groups, which employ or contract with their own physicians, do not. Second, conventional insurers are third parties, reimbursing one or both of the first two parties to a medical transaction—the insured and the provider—for services rendered or received. By combining the financing and delivery of care in one organization, PGPs eliminate third-party payment. The specific advantages said to follow from the elimination in the PGP of conventional fee-for-service, third-party-payment arrangements will be discussed in due course.

In addition to these basic elements, two other features have often been considered important, if not essential, to the "pure" PGP. First, physicians work full-time for the plan (that is, do not engage in outside fee-for-service practices) and serve an overwhelmingly prepaid membership. Second, the plan owns its major facilities—its central clinic, offices, and other outpatient facilities certainly, and its own hospital if possible. The best example of "pure" PGPs are the Kaiser-Permanente Medical Program plans about which more will be said in the next chapter.⁵

The major alternative to the PGP is the independent practice association (IPA). Like the PGP, the IPA is a health plan enrolling subscribers entitled to health services in exchange for prepaid premiums. It differs from the

4. For background, see the 1978 annual report of the Kaiser Foundation Medical Care Program, *Organized Health Care Delivery Systems: A Historical Perspective*, pp. 4–9.

5. See National Advisory Commission on Health Manpower, *Report* (U.S. Government Printing Office, 1967), vol. 2, app. 4: *The Kaiser Foundation Medical Care Program;* Anne R. Somers, ed., *The Kaiser-Permanente Medical Care Program: A Symposium* (New York: Commonwealth Fund, 1971).

PGP in several ways, however. First, the IPA preserves fee-for-service reimbursement. The plan usually pays doctors according to a fee schedule, in which fees are set at about 10 percent (and perhaps more) below prevailing charges. Second, the doctors under contract with an IPA usually devote only a small fraction of their practices to prepaid patients; most of their time is spent with conventionally insured patients. Third, IPAs seldom own their facilities; usually the doctors see prepaid patients, like other patients, in their private offices and send them to private clinics or hospitals (that is, ones not owned or controlled by the plan) for more specialized services. In an IPA, in short, the group may be little more than an administrative convenience.

Plans may combine elements of both the PGP and the IPA. For example, some fee-for-service multispecialty group practices have set up prepaid plans and then devoted some fraction of their time—in some cases a sizable fraction—to the prepaid members.[6]

The term "health maintenance organization," coined in the late 1960s by Dr. Paul Ellwood, embraces all of these variations.[7] The combination of prepayment and group practice in a single organization, and the consequent elimination of conventional fee-for-service, third-party-payment arrangements were supposed to yield a distinctive, desirable set of incentives and practice patterns, independently of the elements of purity about which proponents of group and staff PGPs, IPAs, and mixed types often hotly dispute. Advocates of HMOs argued that the synthesis of prepayment and group practice gives physicians an incentive to treat members early, before symptoms become illnesses, and to practice prevention to keep members well. (The HMO must live within a fixed annual budget, and a condition prevented or kept from getting worse is less expensive to treat than a condition neglected.) Hence the term "health maintenance organization." The federal government took up the term in its development effort in the early 1970s and incorporated it in public law in the Health Maintenance Organization Act of 1973 (Public Law 93-222).

The accuracy of the term is open to question. Some studies suggest that HMOs do provide more preventive services to their members than control

6. There are further terminological variations reflecting different combinations of these elements. For instance, the federal employees health benefits plan calls its PGPs and IPAs "comprehensive medical plans," Medicare uses the term "group practice prepayment plans," and California created "prepaid health plans" for Medicaid recipients in the 1970s.
7. Paul M. Ellwood and others, "Health Maintenance Strategy," *Medical Care,* vol. 9 (May–June 1971), pp. 291–98.

populations receive, but whether this finding points to an inherent virtue of HMOs, to a deficiency in the health coverage of the control groups, to a different incidence of prevention mindedness among self-selected HMO enrollees, or to still other factors is not clear. Moreover, offering preventive services and "maintaining health" are not the same thing; many doubt that doctors, however they may be organized, have the ability to maintain the health of consumers constrained by heredity and exercising free choice over their smoking, diet, driving patterns, and so forth. Finally, in the HMO, as in other medical modes, physicians spend the great majority of their time treating people who are or claim to be sick, not in "maintaining health."

Repelled by the hyperbole of the term "HMO," some have preferred to use the older and more precise terms "PGP," "IPA," and so on. Although there is no intention here to condone the hyperbole, this study will use the term "HMO," except when greater specification is required, for two reasons. First, the arguments to follow often discuss the generic features of prepaid medical groups and an inclusive shorthand term, albeit an extravagant term, is useful. Second, the term has become so widely used since 1970, for better or worse, that avoiding it in a discussion of the events since 1970 that brought it such familiarity would be precious.

The Roots of HMOs

The inspirations for prepaid group practices are diverse, but most derive from the presence in local communities of individuals involved in, but dissatisfied with, the purchase or delivery of fee-for-service medical care. Labor leaders may become displeased with the benefits that conventional insurance plans offer to unionists and may seek to sponsor an alternative. A local physician may feel morally uncomfortable with fee-for-service medicine and envision another mode of practice. The dean of a medical school may look for means of involving students directly in primary care, thus answering charges that the teaching system is too oriented toward hospitalized patients and too little concerned with prevention and ambulatory services. The head of a business firm may seek ways to economize on health care benefits for its employees. An insurance company, weary of battling providers over costs, may decide to experiment with new combinations of financing and delivery of health care. Consumer groups may seek a delivery system in the running of which they have a voice. A state (or the federal) government, nervous over uncontrollable spending for health care, may experiment with cost-conscious delivery mechanisms. Fee-for-service physicians may organize to meet competition from other HMOs.

Would-be organization-builders, pondering the wisdom of establishing an HMO, must answer four fundamental questions. Is sufficient money available to get the organization launched and working? Can doctors be recruited to provide medical services? Are there consumers in the projected service area in sufficient number and with requisite enthusiasm and purchasing power to enroll? Is a hospital of adequate quality and proximity willing to cooperate? Unless each question can be answered affirmatively, the organization-building process will probably grind to a halt.

Sponsors

Perhaps the basic constraint on the formation of HMOs is the large sums of capital they require. By one account, the process of building an HMO involves eight separate stages, with a total of twenty-six distinct steps.[8] Before an HMO can open its doors, its founders must hire lawyers to explore the complexities of state law and regulation; hire an architect; build, acquire, or renovate office facilities; buy furniture and medical equipment; hire planning staff; do a marketing survey; purchase insurance; begin assembling a permanent staff; and more. Each step requires money, and construction expenses in particular are likely to be high. Moreover, HMOs have little hope of recouping their investment quickly. Most, in their early years, must support a very wide range of medical services on the premiums of a limited number of subscribers. As a result, an HMO must expect a flood of red ink—perhaps two million dollars or more—in its early years, partly a consequence of large start-up costs and partly a result of operating deficits from year to year. Unforeseen complications— a local recession, a shift in top management, uncertainty over federal requirements, and so on—may push achievement of the enrollment necessary to reach the break-even point (usually estimated at somewhere between 20,000 and 50,000 members for a metropolitan HMO) beyond the date originally anticipated. Surmounting all of this takes money.

It is seldom hard for an HMO entrepreneur to secure small grants for

8. Committee for Economic Development, *Building a National Health-Care System* (New York: CED, 1973), pp. 54–55.

early planning purposes. (The federal government calls them "feasibility" grants.) Philanthropic foundations, universities, labor unions, the federal government, established prepaid groups, Blue Cross and Blue Shield, commercial insurance companies, and others, all make small sums available for research and early planning. Finding the millions of dollars needed to cover start-up costs and operating deficits is a much more difficult task.

The economic realities of sponsorship heavily influence the organizational type an HMO becomes. If large sums cannot be found, the entrepreneur must settle for creating an IPA or a small prepaid plan within a new or existing fee-for-service group practice. The prepaid plan then becomes an island of prepayment in a fee-for-service sea. In a multispecialty group of, say, 20 physicians, 20 percent of patients (2,000, say, of a total of 10,000) may be prepaid. Although HMO advocates sometimes sniff at this model because it does not correspond to their image of a true PGP, most of the roughly 235 HMOs in the United States are of this "impure" form. Purity is a luxury these groups cannot afford.

When, however, the founder has secured a generous sponsor, he may attempt to set up a pure—almost 100 percent prepaid—plan, with its own facilities; full-time bookkeeping, paramedical, and administrative staffs; and a full-time, salaried, core medical staff of a dozen or more physicians. Both the limited number of HMOs and the preponderance of the impure type are in part a result of the scarcity of generous sponsors.

Six types of sponsors are of central importance: industry, labor, insurance companies, government, medical schools, and fee-for-service group practices. Each may hope to realize two types of benefit from involvement with HMOs. First, they may value the progressive image accompanying association with a mode of medical delivery often said to be the medicine of the future. Second, and more important, each sponsor may seek a measure of control over processes in which it is implicated but which it cannot readily influence by other means. Conversely, each sponsor confronts two risks or costs attending its involvement. One is that sponsorship of an HMO will involve the patron directly in the delivery of medical services, an enterprise that all sponsors but fee-for-service physicians tend to avoid or to enter fearfully. A second, more specific disadvantage is that, apart from the money involved, building a workable HMO entails so many complications of recruiting and monitoring medical staff, marketing, negotiating with hospitals, fighting with local doctors, and more, that many sponsors decide that the aggravation, controversy, and publicity are not worth the trouble. The precise nature of the benefit-cost balance varies with time, circumstances, and personalities in ways that are impossible to define in detail but quite possible to portray in outline.

Industry

At various times and places, business firms have established prepaid groups. The most famous, of course, are those that constitute the Kaiser-Permanente Medical Care Program, an outgrowth of industrialist Henry Kaiser's personal commitment to improve the delivery of medical care. In theory, major corporations should be eager to sponsor HMOs. Employers pay about 75 percent of health insurance premiums in the United States[9] and costs keep rising.[10] An HMO may possibly improve workers' health, increase productivity, and reduce absenteeism; it may also hold the line on insurance costs, especially those resulting from hospitalization.

In fact, however, corporations rarely sponsor HMOs—indeed, one survey of national corporations discovered that fully 93.4 percent of its sample had no interest in developing one.[11] For one thing, their economic stake in cost-containment is often indirect and minor;[12] they can pass the costs of health plans along to consumers as part of the costs they incur in the production process and can deduct them from their taxes as a business expense at that. Moreover, even if the direct economic stake were greater, many would still refrain from direct involvement and responsibility in an alien and forbidding field. "The health-care system is difficult to understand and businessmen feel uncomfortable dealing with it," a Marriot executive explained. Moreover, corporate efforts to control health costs "are hard to quantify, complicating the task for managers who must deal with the typical profit-and-loss orientation of companies."[13] The logistical difficulties of setting up an organization to deliver comprehensive medical care are disturbing and the political complexities intimidating. Particularly

9. Robert M. Gibson and Charles R. Fisher, "National Health Expenditures, Fiscal Year 1977," *Social Security Bulletin,* vol. 41 (July 1978), p. 5.

10. In 1976, Victor M. Zink, General Motors' director of employee benefits, told the Council on Wage and Price Stability that health insurance coverage cost GM $825 million annually and was rising each year. He observed that "Blue Cross–Blue Shield plans are our number one supplier, if you take them all together. Metropolitan Life Insurance Company is our number two supplier and United States Steel is a rather distant third." Council on Wage and Price Stability, *The Complex Puzzle of Rising Health Care Costs: Can the Private Sector Fit It Together?* (Executive Office of the President, Council on Wage and Price Stability, 1976), p. 23.

11. John K. Iglehart, "The Federal Government as Venture Capitalist: How Does It Fare?" *Milbank Memorial Fund Quarterly/Health and Society,* vol. 58 (Fall 1980), p. 664.

12. For a different view, see J. Warren Salmon, "The Health Maintenance Organization Strategy: A Corporate Takeover of Health Services Delivery," *International Journal of Health Services,* vol. 5, no. 4 (1975), pp. 609–24.

13. *Baltimore Sun,* November 18, 1979.

worrisome are the prospects of angry exchanges with local medical societies, fear that capricious legislation or regulation in Washington may make a plan obsolete or unworkable, and the risk that the learning process will end unexpectedly in scandal, lawsuits, or financial failure, giving the company in general and its health staff in particular a reputation for bad management. There are exceptions, a notable one being the Winston-Salem Health Care Plan founded by R. J. Reynolds Company in North Carolina, but these (like Reynolds) may limit enrollment to the company's employees.

As the health-care cost crisis deepens, businessmen are likely to participate more fully in the rhetoric of solving it. Just as businessmen were urged to bring a new sense of corporate responsibility to bear on the late urban crisis, so now they are being asked to assume a major role in containing medical care costs. In these circumstances, a business leader who fails to rise to the occasion with a concrete plan to do something may be thought unprogressive or backward. For this reason alone HMOs are likely to grow more prominent in the conceptual armamentarium of business leaders. Moreover, business leaders, like other men of affairs, often respond to an artful mixture of flattery and appeals to the public interest. At a conference of business leaders convened in Washington by Secretary Joseph A. Califano, Jr., of the Department of Health, Education, and Welfare, in March 1978 an abundance of both was in evidence, the themes being that HMOs ought to proliferate and that "whatever government can do, business can do better."[14] Although some top corporate statesmen may heed the call and begin building HMOs, it is not likely that many of their less prominent colleagues will follow their lead. Business is likely to become a major sponsor of HMOs only if the widespread success of other sponsors shows that the risks are easily avoided or if increases in medical costs are somehow brought directly to bear on the industry instead of being passed along to consumers and taxpayers.

Labor

Before the surge of interest in HMOs in the 1970s, the labor and cooperative movements gave such plans their greatest impetus. Dr. Michael Shadid's medical cooperative at Elk City, Oklahoma, generally considered to be the first PGP in the United States, was founded in the late 1920s with the support of the Farmers' Union, and labor-sponsored plans are promi-

14. *Group Health News*, vol. 19 (April 1978), pp. 4–5.

nent in St. Louis, Detroit, Providence, and elsewhere.[15] The possible advantages of HMOs to the labor movement are more medical benefits for the member's money and more political muscle for the leader's effort. An HMO usually offers a wider range of benefits to members than conventional alternatives and although premiums tend to be higher (often requiring a sizable payroll deduction), out-of-pocket costs may be lower, leaving total costs below those of the competition. Moreover, when labor sponsors (or retains strong influence on) an HMO, it gains a say not only about the financing of care but also about its organization. Staffing, waiting times, hours of service, referral patterns, and the like become benefits on which union officials can deliver. Thus, labor leaders ideologically or otherwise concerned with delivery and financing of health care find that an HMO concentrates previously individual and fragmented transactions into an organized system that labor can call its own and on which it can exert influence.

Despite these benefits, labor unions are no longer major sponsors of HMOs. The major reason is the growth of work-related conventional health benefits since the 1950s. Many union benefit officials have become integral and stable parts of three-way agreements among employers, unions, and health insurers. Union leaders who have found satisfactory ways to deliver, have no incentive to create and subsidize competition by creating an HMO and may sense that their constituents will be reluctant to commit millions of dollars of their funds to sponsor an HMO—especially when most of them visit personal physicians they do not wish to abandon. Other obstacles too deter union sponsorship of HMOs. One is that unions share with industry the reluctance to enter the unfamiliar terrain of direct service delivery. Another is that a union leader who perceives that the employer is loath to accept the administrative and other inconveniences of adding an HMO option to the health insurance he offers may prefer to devote his energies to a push for higher benefits under existing plans rather than to a fight to add the HMO option. Yet another deterrent is that unions are far less likely than corporations to contain the managerial expertise and resources to launch a plan and to see it through the rough early days. Finally, ideological commitment to HMOs, always uneven, appears to be waning in the labor movement as "impure" plans launched by such alien

15. See Dr. Michael A. Shadid, *Crusading Doctor: My Fight for Cöoperative Medicine* (Boston: Meador Publishing, 1956), pt. 3; William A. MacColl, *Group Practice and Prepayment of Medical Care* (Washington: Public Affairs Press, 1966); Raymond Munts, *Bargaining for Health: Labor Unions, Health Insurance, and Medical Care* (University of Wisconsin Press, 1967), chap. 12.

elements as local medical societies, profitmaking insurance companies, and other capitalistic entrepreneurs increasingly turn the PGP movement into an HMO industry. As one observer put it, "labor's not that hot for HMOs now. A few of the big shots are, but the locals don't understand HMOs, could care less about them, and distrust anything that smacks of the corporate practice of medicine." Some union leaders are pleased to have an HMO option made available, for they gain bargaining leverage with local insurers and providers by holding out the plausible threat that they may take their business elsewhere.[16] Few unions, however, will devote much of their own energy and money to build such an option from the ground up.

Medical Schools

Universities with medical schools have recently become important sources of money for HMOs. Deans and faculties of medical schools have come to see HMO sponsorship as a defense against criticism that they train students to care for the sick while neglecting maintenance of the healthy, concentrate on inpatient care with little attention to ambulatory care, teach the cure of limited disease episodes rather than concern for the "whole person" or the whole family, and continue to prepare students for solo practice while technology and medical economics make group settings increasingly rational and efficient. Moreover, since 1976, federal legislation has required that the schools increase the training of general and family practitioners as a condition of receiving federal aid.[17] A university-sponsored HMO sometimes appears to be a natural setting in which to teach the "medicine of the future."

A university-affiliated HMO also gives a medical school a chance to recast relations with its surrounding communities on terms favorable to itself.[18] The HMO's prepaid population provides not only a laboratory

16. See American Federation of Labor and Congress of Industrial Organizations, "Policy Resolution on Collective Bargaining and Health," adopted October 1969, in *Physicians Training Facilities and Health Maintenance Organizations,* Hearings before the Subcommittee on Health of the Senate Committee on Labor and Public Welfare, 92 Cong. 1 and 2 sess., 6 pts. (GPO, 1971–72), pt. 2, pp. 481–82.

17. The Health Professions Educational Assistance Act of 1976 (Public Law 94-484) required that medical schools receiving federal educational aid have at least 35 percent of their first-year residents in programs in family medicine, general internal medicine, or general pediatrics by mid-1978, and that this rise to 40 percent by 1979 and to 50 percent by 1980.

18. I. S. Falk, "Academic Medical Center–HMO Relationships: Sponsorship or Affiliation?" *Journal of Medical Education,* vol. 48 (April 1973), pp. 53–59. Apropos is Aaron Wildavsky's comment that if the idea behind neighborhood health centers "was to bring services to the people, the idea behind the HMOs is to bring the people to the services." "Doing Better and Feeling Worse: The Political Pathology of Health Policy," *Daedalus,* vol. 106, no. 1 (Winter 1977), p. 112.

for teaching primary care but also a stable, predictable source of clients for the teaching hospital. A contract with an HMO that corners a portion of the community market and enables the hospital to count on twenty or thirty beds occupied each day as a direct result of the arrangement is attractive to any but a severely overused hospital. So, too, most teaching hospitals will encounter the community—often a poor community—daily in their inpatient departments and emergency rooms. Visits that end up as bad debts, or are reimbursed only in part by Medicare and Medicaid, may be paid in full if the patient is a member of an HMO.

Besides the inevitable logistical complexities, the major costs to a medical school in setting up an HMO lie in antagonizing its own constituencies, its own valued contributors. Teaching faculty, usually part of the academic medical world and seldom devoted to the private practice of fee-for-service medicine, may nonetheless oppose an HMO on philosophical grounds. "Salaried faculties really resist the notion of salaried doctors," one professor observed sardonically. And because these faculty will not be numerous enough, or willing, to staff the HMO themselves, conflicts may arise over the faculty affiliation, teaching role, and hospital status of the general practitioners, internists, and pediatricians who make up the HMO staff.

A second source of opposition is a medical school's alumni, resentful that a portion of their donations is used to subsidize a mode of practice to which they are ideologically and economically opposed. In only a relatively few liberal schools can the administration fail to think twice about such objections. But even if all 126 medical schools in the United States launched HMOs, their progeny would be largely urban, would often compete with one another, and would not begin to blanket the nation. In short, medical schools are likely to remain significant, but far from dominant, forces for HMO development.

Fee-for-Service Physicians

Whenever HMOs are launched, whatever the source, fee-for-service physicians usually respond by sponsoring similar organizations of their own. For example, when the state of California passed legislation in 1971 to encourage the growth of HMOs for Medicaid recipients, fee-for-service physicians serving inner-city poor neighborhoods saw, as one of them explained, that the law "would result in the loss of the medical practice that I had worked all those years to build."[19] Thus threatened, these physicians set up prepaid plans of their own.

19. *Prepaid Health Plans,* Hearings before the Permanent Subcommittee on Investigations of the Senate Government Operations Committee, 94 Cong. 1 sess. (GPO, 1975), p. 82.

When HMOs arise under private auspices to serve the community at large, the threat is more diffuse but hardly less worrisome. Whereas in fee-for-service practice, patients move among doctors in fairly fluid referral networks, those enrolled in a closed-panel practice are confined within the much narrower circles of the group itself. Moreover, an HMO will often seek to import physicians from outside the community—ironically, in good part because local physicians refuse to deal with it. Some of these newcomers will maintain fee-for-service practices too and competition for a fixed supply of patients increases.

The most familiar response to these anxieties is an attempt by the medical society to deter or crush the nascent plan. If this fails, the society will then move to establish an independent practice association.[20] Obviously, participating in such an association entails important costs for a physician; in particular, his fees are cut back for a portion of his patients and he must submit to review by the medical director. On the other hand, the IPA attracts new patients and retains old ones by combining the financial advantages of prepayment with the appeals of having a personal physician or maintaining accustomed relations with him. By establishing an IPA, physicians meet the local competition and prove to the "feds" and other critics that they are capable of moving toward cost-containment without governmental intervention.

Physicians form such groups to deal with the threat of an HMO, which explains both their limited number and their disproportionate concentration on the West Coast. An IPA will follow an HMO in a community only a little less automatically than night follows day and indeed by the late 1970s, physicians had begun establishing IPAs to preempt competition from HMOs that had not yet been launched or even planned, making IPAs the fastest growing type of prepaid group plan.

Health Insurance Plans

Insurance companies, meaning both Blue Cross and Blue Shield plans and commercial health insurance plans, have sponsored HMOs more than any other single source. Insurance interest in these plans, all-but-non-existent before, grew rapidly in the late 1960s and early 1970s. At that time, a national health insurance program seemed imminent, and talk of bypassing or even eliminating conventional health plans was common. At that time, too, national health insurance and health maintenance organi-

---

20. See, for example, Steven B. Enright, "Beating H.M.O's at Their Own Game," *Medical Economics,* vol. 55 (July 10, 1978), pp. 97–111, for details of the formation and development of the Physicians Health Plan in Minneapolis–St. Paul.

zations were frequently discussed in the same breath, both considered waves of the future. Anxious about their own futures, stung by charges that they were mere conduits for providers' bills, and bent on participating in a coming thing like HMOs, Blue Cross and commercial insurance plans began to give serious thought to sponsoring such plans. Offices of "alternative delivery systems"—the industry's euphemism for HMOs—began to spring up.

By the end of the 1972 presidential campaign (in which, surprisingly, national health insurance had been scarcely mentioned and by which time the Nixon administration had grown cool toward HMOs), the insurance industry's fears of being excluded from the future financing of health care had largely subsided. The preceding three or four years, however, had convinced many executives that the financing arrangements of the past were not immutable, that cost-containment would loom ever larger as a federal issue, and that HMOs (then under consideration by both the House and Senate) would figure in some way in federal policy. On all three counts, HMOs promised benefits: they allowed the insurers to diversify their product lines by exploring a direction in which consumer taste might be moving, they might save the companies some money, and they allowed the industry a more flexible response to federal cost-containment measures that might tamper with established financing patterns. By 1977 Blue Cross and Blue Shield plans had become involved in some way in fifty-five operational HMOs. Twenty-two private insurance companies were involved in fifty operational projects and fifty-five companies were involved with seventy-nine developing ones.[21]

These benefits are counterbalanced by costs, however. The traditional function of insurance plans is to indemnify subscribers against risk, which means paying the medical bills of subscribers and dependents after care has been sought out by the individual and rendered by his chosen provider. By contrast, HMOs involve insurers in the delivery as well as the financing of services. As the companies began feeling their way, they learned a number of painful lessons. Marketing an HMO is very different from marketing health insurance, those with some experience in the enterprise agree. An HMO cannot be presented as one option among others, for unless the HMO is pushed with enthusiasm, employees will look at the sizable payroll deduction they often must incur to belong to one, neglect to compute the likely dollar value of HMO benefits, and opt for or continue a traditional plan. Agents, however, were not accustomed or inclined to

21. Jeffery Cohelan, "An Update on HMO's," address before the Washington Conference on Legislative Update of the International Foundation of Employee Benefit Plans, May 25, 1977, p. 16.

single out one of several presumably equal options for special endorsement. (Their sales pitch, an insurance executive recalled, was, "We know how good Blue Cross is, but there is this other option.")

Moreover, to choose an HMO is not to select insurance benefits alone, but also to choose a delivery system and medical staff. Location matters. Officials attempting to market the Harvard Community Health Plan in its infancy, for example, discovered to their dismay that a major potential source of subscribers—employees who lived and worked near the Route 128 suburban ring around Boston—simply did not want to travel downtown for care. Wives' and children's opinions and allegiances proved important. "We saw time and again," an executive recalled, "how we'd sign up a worker only to have him go home and tell his wife, who'd cry that she wouldn't leave old Doc Jones down the road. He'd march in next day and take his name off."

In addition, HMO sponsorship raised a variety of internal political difficulties for insurance companies. The companies looked nervously at provisions of federal (and some state) laws that required a publicly funded or certified HMO to devote a substantial fraction of positions (usually one-third) on their policymaking board to members. Some Blue Cross executives found that relations with their Blue Shield counterparts grew frosty whenever plans to develop HMOs were mentioned. Most executives understood too that although theoretically an HMO works by means of incentives for cost-consciousness, in practice the sponsor of an errant group might have to do precisely what the companies found so distasteful in relations with fee-for-service providers—police, cajole, and threaten— in order to make the group work correctly. For each company that moved toward sponsorship, another backed away.

As the learning process stumbled along, some insurance-sponsored plans surmounted their early difficulties and thrived. Others languished, enrollment far smaller than anticipated. Still others died ignominiously. Failures became "paradigms" among insurance executives concerned with alternative delivery systems. In January 1974, for instance, Connecticut General opened an HMO in Brooklyn at the cost of $1.5 million. A little more than a year later, when only four hundred enrollees instead of the expected twelve thousand had signed up, the plan closed. Looking on from the sidelines, an Aetna executive concluded that HMOs were an idea "whose time has not yet come,"[22] and the company disbanded a large staff working on plans for HMOs in other parts of the country. Throughout

22. Joann S. Lublin, *Wall Street Journal*, February 11, 1975.

the insurance world, and especially in the commercial sector, which is understandably more sensitive to the uses of shareholder funds and to involvement with nonprofit organizations than is Blue Cross, these trials and errors produced ambivalence. On the one hand, the companies were reluctant to launch programs whose development they could not easily control and which threatened to cause them embarrassment. (The dollar sums are tiny; the stakes in reputation and managerial self-esteem are large.) On the other hand, the companies believed that they could not endlessly raise premium rates without threatening their competitive position. Some means had to be found to police doctors and hospitals, and HMOs looked like a promising means of self-policing through incentives instead of continuing battles between companies and individual providers. Moreover, by diversifying their product line, the companies could internalize a piece of the cost-effective competition they feared.[23] And, of course, governmental and public expectations that the insurers do something about health bills continually forced HMOs onto their organizational agenda. One insurance executive explained: "Our company has no real interest in doing anything with HMOs. The Connecticut General experience left bitter memories. Still we get letters all the time from people asking, 'What are you doing about the high costs of health care?' It's not enough to write back and say 'We're doing the best we can.' Maybe HMOs are an answer."

Government

At various times, each of the three levels of American government has sponsored HMOs. The Health Insurance Plan of Greater New York (HIP) came about largely as a result of Mayor Fiorello H. La Guardia's determination to build a prepaid plan for New York City employees.[24] The HMOs for Medicaid recipients grew in large numbers in the early 1970s at the behest of the state government of California. And since 1970 the federal government has been actively involved in sponsoring HMOs across the nation.

Before the enactment of Medicare and Medicaid, no practical politician seriously expected state or federal governments to promote HMOs; the American Medical Association's distaste for this approach was well known

23. As one Blue Cross official argued in an interview: "Why do we get into this? Because we recognize that the Blue Cross concept is only thirty years old and may not last forever. General Motors offers Cadillacs and Oldsmobiles too. It's the same for us with HMOs."

24. See Robert E. Rothenberg and others, *Group Medicine and Health Insurance in Action* (Crown, 1949), for background on HIP.

and that settled the matter. As the extent of the financial misadventures of Medicare and Medicaid grew clearer, however, state and federal governments took a fresh look at HMO development. No state authorizes large sums of money to develop HMOs. A state's commitment shows up, if at all, in its willingness to negotiate contracts for the care of Medicaid recipients by prepaid plans. A few states are willing and eager to do this, some are opposed, and most are indifferent.

The federal government, by contrast, has been actively encouraging development of HMOs since 1970.[25] Between 1970 and 1972 a number of flexible project grant programs—section 314(e) of the Comprehensive Health Planning and Public Health Services Amendments of 1966 (the so-called Partnership for Health legislation), the Office of Economic Opportunity, and others—were used to launch HMOs. With passage of HMO legislation at the end of 1973, the government required that its support be confined to grants under Public Law 93-222. The act, amended in 1976 and 1978, makes available modest sums for feasibility studies, planning activities, and the initial development of HMOs. Organizations that meet the requirements for federal qualification may receive loans (a maximum of $1.5 million in 1973, raised to $4 million in 1978) to cover start-up costs and operating deficits.

The benefits of HMO development to the federal government are straightforward. Federal planners believe that HMOs—well-designed ones at any rate—save money, provide care of high quality, and make care (especially primary care) more accessible to their members. They rely on economic incentives that work on local providers in local markets, thus circumventing the need for direct federal regulation. They also put competitive pressure on providers to contain costs. For all these reasons, they appear to be excellent answers for politicians expected to do something about a health cost crisis.

The costs the federal government faces in encouraging HMOs are essentially the same as those of other sponsors. It will lose its investment and credibility if the sponsored organizations go bankrupt, provide too little access, or poor quality care, or otherwise fail to work well. The government has reduced these risks by adopting a reactive posture. Whereas other sponsors typically feel impelled to go out and search for the raw materials with which to construct an HMO, and typically become involved

25. Since 1960, however, beneficiaries of the federal employees health benefits plan have been able to elect to receive care from HMOs certified by the Civil Service Commission (since 1978 called the Office of Personnel Management).

with continuing planning and operations, the federal government in effect gives notice that money is available, waits for applicants to appear, wades through the applications, rejects those that do not appear to be promising, insists that potential recipients conform to detailed statutory and administrative provisions, and confers money only on those who survive this review. Moreover, it reserves its largest sums and its official seal of approval—qualification—for those plans that have passed these tests at several sequential stages of development.

As might be expected, the federal effort to minimize risk has made the government a tight-fisted sponsor—so much so that by the middle of 1980 only about 115 HMOs had qualified under federal provisions, a far cry from the hundreds the government expected when it began its sponsorship a few years earlier. On the other hand, federal rhetoric about the virtues of HMOs and about its own intention to promote and reward them has probably done more than anything else to create the impression that HMOs are the wave of the future, to confer legitimacy on them, to publicize the arguments for them, and to galvanize other sponsors to create them.[26] For this reason, largely unquantifiable, the federal contribution to sponsorship far exceeds the results suggested by the number of federally qualified HMOs or the amount of federal money spent.

THE LIMITED volume of activity and small scale of support for HMOs in the United States accurately reflect the stakes—the ratio of benefits to costs—of would-be and actual sponsors. Most HMOs depend on limited financial and organizational support from one sponsor. These groups must usually of necessity begin life as islands of prepayment in a sea of fee-for-service. The occasional, fortunate organization that enjoys large-scale support from one or more enthusiastic sponsors is a vivid example of the type and magnitude of sustenance required if HMOs are to be launched successfully and in large numbers in the United States. The Rhode Island Group Health Association (RIGHA) in Providence, for example, began life in the early 1970s under the auspices of the state's AFL-CIO. Financial aid from this organization, several constituent unions, and the Group Health Association of America was insufficient to put it on a stable footing. The Prudential Insurance Company, however, took an interest in the plan and loaned it several million dollars and a full-time management team to put its affairs in order. Prudential funds and management enabled the

26. Richard McNeil, Jr., and Robert E. Schlenker, "HMOs, Competition, and Government," *Milbank Memorial Fund Quarterly/Health and Society*, vol. 53 (Spring 1975), pp. 203–04.

group to qualify under the federal HMO law in 1975—it was one of the first plans in the country to do so—and qualification, in turn, brought it $1.5 million of federal loan money.[27]

New Haven's Community Health Care Plan benefited from the political support of state and local unions; services, staff, and facilities of the Yale–New Haven Medical Center; land provided by New Haven's redevelopment agency; and funds from HEW, the Ford Foundation, and local banks.[28] In Rochester, New York, an alliance between the city's top industries and the local Blue Cross plan (which dominates the market in Rochester) led to creation of two HMOs.[29] The Harvard Community Health Plan in Boston put together about $3.5 million for planning, start-up, and construction costs from foundations—the Commonwealth Fund, the Ford Foundation, and the Rockefeller Foundation—as well as from the federal government and Harvard University, which loaned the plan money on "a very favorable arrangement . . . a Harvard University thing, within the family."[30] These plans are comparatively pure, with most of their subscribers prepaid and many of their physicians working full time for the plan.

The importance of a wealthy, generous, and committed sponsor is well illustrated by the Winston-Salem Health Care plan. A plan official recalled in an interview with reporter Harry Schwartz that "the chairman's instructions when we decided to take this route were spend whatever you need to within reason." The planner then spent $1.2 million on a building and another $1.5 million on decoration and equipment. The facilities, which reminded Schwartz "much more of an art museum or a top executive suite than of conventional doctors' offices," were intended to avoid that "antiseptic cold hospital emergency room of the sort our patients know and hate." The Reynolds Company's generosity probably also explains the extremely low monthly deduction—a mere three dollars in 1977—for an employee and his family. Furthermore, as the center's administrator observed: "We purposely overstaffed for each phase of our development here . . . so that people who come here don't have to wait. We don't want this to be just another doctor's office." The planners could also afford to

27. See the account of RIGHA's early history in *Congressional Record*, daily ed., April 12, 1978, pp. S5447–50.
28. Community Health Care Center Plan, *Report to the Plan's Enrollees, 1976*, p. 1.
29. For background on the Rochester efforts, see "HMOs are Coming, But Will They Last?" *American Medical News*, vol. 19 (February 25, 1974); reprinted in *Medical Care Review*, vol. 31 (March 1974), pp. 323–29.
30. *Physicians Training Facilities*, Hearings, pt. 2, p. 613.

be selective about physicians. Advertisements produced over a thousand applicants; for every ten flown to North Carolina to look the plan over and be looked over, one was hired. Moreover, the plan could offer salaries that were "over the going rate of $35,000 annually."[31]

The experience of most recent HMOs differs dramatically from the Winston-Salem plan's experience. Most of them plan under stiff fiscal pressures, do not resemble art museums, must struggle to avoid high monthly payroll deductions, are under-, not over-, staffed at each phase of development, oblige some patients to wait, cannot be too choosy about physicians, and cannot compete for them strongly on monetary grounds. A major reason, of course, is that sponsors like R. J. Reynolds are few.

The limited commitment of sponsors reflects a simple but very significant fact: for most of them the likely benefits of developing an HMO outweigh the likely costs only slightly if at all. This calculus, in turn, rests mainly on the complexities of building and maintaining a health maintenance organization. As noted earlier, each type of sponsor sees in the HMO an opportunity to gain control over processes that are, or threaten to become, uncontrollable. Industry hopes to slow the rising costs of employees' health benefits. Labor unions seek to gain a larger measure of control over both the members' benefit package and the delivery (as well as the financing) of care. Medical schools look for a controlled and stable setting in which to train students in preventive and primary care, stabilize hospital occupancy rates, and interact with the community. Fee-for-service physicians view independent practice associations as a means of retaining patients who might otherwise succumb to the temptations of prepaid closed-panel plans. Insurers work to gain control over the forces of price escalation more readily then their traditionally weak monitoring and review of fee-for-service physicians permits, and to assure the federal government, the public, and themselves that they are flexible, innovative, and cost-conscious, thereby reducing the chance that they will be roughly handled by federal efforts at cost-containment. The federal government expects that HMOs will enhance its control over the costs of health care that it supports. The HMO, an organized *system* for both financing and delivery of care, promises to introduce predictability, rationality, and control into otherwise fragmented, decentralized, and nonresponsible processes. The HMO is an organizational answer to the problems of large formal organizations.

If these benefits were the whole story—if HMOs could be brought into

31. *New York Times,* August 7, 1977.

being without friction, and with high assurance that their potential would be realized—sponsors would no doubt blanket the nation with them. The cost side of the equation is also prominent, however. One cost is simple fear of the unknown—in this case, fear of entering into direct delivery of complex and intimate human services. Even more important, however, is anxiety over the organization-building process itself, for a successful HMO rests on the commitment of many more contributors than sponsors alone. Sponsors know this and know too that these commitments are frequently unattainable or in doubt.

Physicians

A basic requirement for a workable HMO is of course an adequate stock of physicians. A familiar rule of thumb recommends one physician for each thousand enrollees,[32] and ideally the physicians should embrace three or four important specialties from the start. For physicians, as for other potential contributors, an HMO is a mixed package of benefits and costs. Unless the benefits of working for HMOs can be made to outweigh the costs for a sufficient number of doctors, the organizations cannot grow, and intensive efforts to develop HMOs as a policy strategy cannot succeed.

Proponents of HMOs have extolled a long list of benefits supposedly inherent in this mode of organization.[33] It is said, for example, that the HMO physician can specialize, concentrating on what he likes and does best instead of attempting to reach beyond his competence, as solo practitioners may be tempted, or obliged, to do. In the multispecialty group, appropriate consultants and ancillary personnel and facilities are just down the hall. Moreover, group practice is a continuing educational process. The benefits of innovation and experience combine as younger and older doctors interact. In addition, the group provides time off and funds for study. Among the tangible benefits are fixed schedules and dependable rotation of hours; immediate income (the HMO doctor need not worry about building up a practice slowly); fringe benefits, including malpractice insurance, life insurance, and a retirement plan; and relief from business and administrative burdens. To these may be added such intangible goods as a collective stake in the quality of care offered by the group (poor performance by any group member threatens the reputation

32. MacColl, *Group Practice and Prepayment of Medical Care*, p. 197.
33. Ibid, pp. 89–93.

of the group as a whole, so standards are kept high), and a sense of unity between physician and patient, their relation "uncontaminated by any financial negotiations."[34] These, at any rate, are the major advantages attributed to HMOs by their proponents.[35] The degree to which they do in fact motivate physicians to join these organizations, and with what relative weights, is unknown.

The pull of the HMO's native advantages is said to be reinforced by the push of solo fee-for-service headaches. The solo practitioner's lot is not an entirely happy one. He must meet the start-up costs of acquiring and maintaining office space and equipment, an increasingly expensive task; find and retain suitable office staff (nurses, bookkeepers, receptionists); and supervise administrative tasks and paperwork, including a growing flow of public and private insurance forms. Moreover, he may lack dependable coverage for his patients on evenings, weekends, holidays, and vacations, and has relatively little interchange with colleagues in the workplace, other than in the hospital or in informal consultations.

If the choice lay solely between the advantages of an HMO practice and the headaches of a solo practice, HMOs would no doubt have won the day long ago. In fact, however, physicians enjoy options that enable them to enjoy most of the advantages of HMOs while eliminating most of the problems of a solo practice, without accepting the costs of the former and without giving up the benefits of the latter. A young physician contemplating practice patterns faces five major opportunities. He may choose to become a solo, fee-for-service practitioner, to join a partnership with one or two other fee-for-service physicians (usually of the same speciality as his own), to join a multispecialty group of fee-for-service physicians, to combine one of these options with a part-time commitment to an independent practice association, or to join a prepaid group practice or mixed HMO. Many of the advantages of HMOs may be enjoyed, and many of the disadvantages of solo practice avoided, by options two and three. In short, HMOs compete not simply with solo fee-for-service practice but also with fee-for-service partnerships and groups, a fact that sharply limits the number of physicians attracted to HMOs.

Solo practice, despite its problems, has its compensations. The practitioner is his own boss, enjoys the pleasure of feeling that he has been chosen

34. Herman Weiner, "Organization and Responsibilities," in Somers, *Kaiser-Permanente Medical Care Program*, p. 95.

35. Obviously, this list of advantages applies mainly to physicians working "in" an HMO, either on salary to it or as members of a group under contract with it. Independent practice associations offer few of these benefits.

on his professional merits by patients and referring colleagues, and may make a great deal of money. Partnerships and fee-for-service group arrangements compromise these advantages to some extent, but nowhere near so much as an HMO does. Equally important, almost all of the advantages of HMOs may be obtained in nonprepaid group practices. It is therefore not surprising that about one-quarter of all physicians now practice in some form of group, and that prepaid groups are a small fraction of the total number.[36]

Four major disadvantages specific to HMOs limit their ability to compete with solo practice and with nonprepaid groups. First, because prepaid physicians are salaried employees of the prepaid plan, or of their own corporation under contract to the plan, their freedom to schedule work tasks and manage patient care as they see fit is limited to some extent by organizational procedures. Second, because review by peers and by the organization's medical and executive directors is thought necessary to reconcile quality and cost properly, the HMO practitioner must be willing to practice medicine "in a goldfish bowl." Third, because prepayment gives members a contractual right to comprehensive care, the HMO physician must be tolerant of patients who present themselves as "bureaucratic clients," to demand their rights to treatment even for trivial complaints.[37] Fourth, the HMO doctor will probably make less money than his fee-for-service counterpart. For general practitioners, internists, and pediatricians, HMO salaries are generally close to those in the fee-for-service sector, but for more specialized categories of physicians—for example, obstetricians, gynecologists, dermatologists, neurologists, urologists, and most types of surgeons—an HMO can seldom compete with the very high incomes possible outside the group. Each of these disadvan-

36. The AMA, using a definition of group practice as three or more "formally organized" doctors, counted 8,483 groups in the United States in 1975. These encompassed 66,842 physicians, or 23.2 percent of all active nonfederal patient-care physicians. In 1980, there were 10,762 groups, including 88,290 doctors—25.8 percent of the total. In 1975, only 662 groups, including 13,534 physicians, received revenue from some form of prepayment plan. Within five years, the number of such groups had nearly tripled (1,884 in 1980), but the rise in the number of physicians reporting prepayment activity was more modest (20,441 in 1980, a 51 percent increase from 1975). In 1975, about 71 percent of groups with some prepaid activity received less than one-quarter of their income on a prepaid basis, and fully 40 percent received less than 5 percent of their income in this way. In 1980, the latter figure had fallen to 23 percent, but 62 percent of groups with some prepaid activity still received less than 25 percent of their income from prepayment. Larry J. Freshnock and Lynn E. Jensen, "The Changing Structure of Medical Group Practice in the U.S., 1969–1980" (American Medical Association, Center for Health Policy Research, 1981), especially tables 1, 3, 6.

37. Eliot Freidson and Buford Rhea, "Processes of Control in a Company of Equals," *Social Problems,* vol. 11 (Fall 1963), pp. 119–31; Eliot Freidson, *Doctoring Together: A Study of Professional Social Control* (Elsevier, 1975).

tages eliminates some doctors from the ranks of HMO recruits. The four together probably eliminate most doctors from those ranks.

Moreover, an HMO physician must be prepared to cope with a fifth problem, inherent not in the nature of HMOs but instead in the local medical politics surrounding them. An HMO physician may acquire a pariah status among his fee-for-service peers, who tend to take umbrage at a mode of practice that cordons off its members from the general flow of referrals within the medical community, that threatens to increase competition for patients by recruiting physicians from outside the community for its staff, and that bases itself squarely on the view that fees tied to medical services are, if not immoral, at least inefficient. Thus aroused, local medical communities may employ several unpleasant devices to persuade would-be prepaid practitioners to restrain wayward impulses.[38] The prepaid physician can expect to be harangued by colleagues at medical society or hospital staff meetings. He may be called a substandard and unethical physician, and a socialist or communist. (Local medical politics are among the few areas of contemporary American life where these quaint allegations are still flung with abandon and enthusiasm.) His patients' medical records may mysteriously disappear from files. He may receive threatening and abusive phone calls and mail. He may be ostracized at medical gatherings. ("When I came in, they just got up and sat on the other side of the room," an HMO medical director recalled.) He and his family may be excluded from social gatherings sponsored by other physicians and their families and ignored at the country club or on the golf course.

If these social pressures do not deter effectively, guardians of the fee-for-service sector may resort to two more formal devices. First, specialists may be told in clear terms that any relationship with—indeed any public endorsement of—the HMO will bring an end of referrals to them by physicians in the fee-for-service mainstream. Unless a specialist is very well established, or the only one in the community, these are potent threats. Needless to say, this pressure often makes it difficult for HMOs to develop satisfactory part-time arrangements with community fee-for-service specialists in the years before the groups can afford to recruit full-time specialists to their staffs. Second, the fee-for-service doctors who dominate the medical staffs of local hospitals may refuse to grant staff, admitting, or

38. See, for example, Shadid, *Crusading Doctor,* chaps. 11–14, 17–18, 23; Charlotte L. Rosenberg, "LMDs Versus HMOs: The Battle Is Joined," *Medical Economics,* vol. 50 (January 22, 1973), pp. 132–49; Edwin W. Reiner, "Colleagues Did Their Best to Torpedo my H.M.O," *Medical Economics,* vol. 55 (August 7, 1978), pp. 84–98.

even courtesy privileges to HMO doctors. For physicians who already belong to the hospital staff, this threat is unimportant. But precisely because local physicians may boycott the new enterprise, HMOs frequently find it necessary to import doctors to the community. Then the issue of hospital privileges arises and the recalcitrance of the medical staff can make life miserable for any HMO but those few lucky enough to own or control their own hospital.

These political obstacles exert greatest impact on the first HMO in a community. An HMO that survives usually reaches accommodations with its antagonists. Moreover, a second HMO reaps some of the rewards of its predecessor's struggles. Every community with an HMO goes through such struggles once, however. In many communities—the exact number is obviously unknown—the prospect or result of these conflicts has precluded development of HMOs and will probably continue to do so.

These obstacles vary in force not only with HMO "generation" but also with location. In a small town or medium-sized city, where physicians spend most of their time in the private practice of medicine, are united in a strong and vocal medical society, and control the local hospital with little internal dissent, an HMO will find infertile soil. In reasonably large cities, however, the medical community is apt to be heterogenous and may contain a fair number of medical "liberals," the medical society may not be authoritative and united, a hospital whose administration values the assurance that an HMO will admit patients to it more than it fears medical staff opposition is likely to exist somewhere in town, and the organization may find allies—organized labor, for instance—to ease its way. In some areas too the continuing legacy of the cooperative movement appears to smooth the way for HMOs.[39] Finally, as noted above, once an HMO has gone to the mat with its opposition and survived, the area may be made safe for others—including, typically, a competing group sponsored by the medical society itself.

Even when these exceptions are given their due, however, the fact remains that at most times and in most places, an HMO physician lets himself in for sacrifice and perhaps even abuse. Understandably, HMOs tend to be small. The prevailing image of HMOs as vast medical complexes, based on large, multispecialty, wholly prepaid plans like Kaiser does not describe the norm. A study in the mid-1970s found that three-quarters of HMOs employed eight or fewer physicians. If very large plans were

39. This probably explains in part the large numbers of HMOs in Wisconsin (16, second to California's 32) and Minnesota (10). HHS, *National HMO Census of Prepaid Plans, June 30, 1980,* p. 6.

excluded, the average number of physicians per HMO was five.[40] To what degree the figures reflect inability to attract physicians and to what degree deliberate limitation geared to small sponsor commitments or small subscriber populations is difficult to judge.

Three types of motive, involving three types of benefits distinctive to *prepaid* group practice, may offset the political and other costs of HMOs. First, some physicians are philosophically opposed to fee-for-service medicine. The medical director of one plan explained that "the main advantage of a prepaid group is that you avoid putting a price on all services, as happens in fee-for-service. What exactly makes an X ray worth $15 or an appendectomy worth $300? The prices are illogical—they have little to do with supply and demand and all the rest. They're arbitrary and subjective and it's a hard thing to live with." Another medical director recalled: "I went into prepaid group practice because I don't like to charge for services. The patient always wonders if you're telling him to come in or have a test because of the money. It's a better psychological climate if you don't have this."

Second, some physicians are attracted to the conditions of work in HMOs. They may have no taste or gift for business and therefore for the incorporation strategies, tax deductions, stock options, dissolvings, corporate purchases, and the rest that medical partners and groups must work out collegially. Separation of financial management from medicine in an HMO appeals to physicians who want to devote their working time to medical tasks alone. For some, HMOs offer an attractive chance to allocate their professional hours in rewarding ways—"a chance to practice 75–80 percent of the time and devote the rest to something else," as one executive director explained. "For instance, one loves the computer, another likes working with medical students, and so on." One medical director praised the "denominator effect" in HMOs, explaining that "having a large defined group allows epidemiological analysis and planning and targeting for needs." Some groups give their physicians time—perhaps half a day each week—for teaching, enabling them to maintain faculty appointments at nearby schools. The HMOs affiliated with medical schools allow physicians an even larger role in teaching. Some physicians relish too the interchange with colleagues of their own and other specialties that the prepaid group can provide. As one medical director put it: "An HMO is more like

40. Raynald Pineault, "The Effect of Prepaid Group Practice on Physicians' Utilization Behavior," *Medical Care,* vol. 14 (February 1976), p. 135.

academic medicine than fee-for-service. It leaves time for auditing, quality control, peer review." And some physicians, including many women, find the group's predictable schedules more conducive than a fee-for-service practice to a stable home life.

A third motivation for employment in an HMO is economic. In some parts of the country, especially the metropolitan areas, general practitioners, internists, and pediatricians may fare better financially—or at least more predictably—on salary in an HMO than in fee-for-service competition. In some areas too, HMOs can be speculative enterprises offering a doctor a chance to get rich quick, as an advertisement in the *Los Angeles Times* suggests: "Los Angeles–based HMO requires 30 physicians . . . profit sharing, stock options, malpractice, and other fringe benefits. Starting salaries $40,000 to $50,000."[41] For young physicians, recently out of medical school, unsure of themselves, and reluctant to invest thousands of dollars to start their own solo practice or to join a group, part-time work for an HMO may offer a dependable income while they build up their private practice on the side. Some established physicians not working at full capacity may work part time for an HMO to put away some extra income. Foreign medical graduates may apply to an HMO because they hope to find a warmer reception than they would find elsewhere.

As might be expected, physicians attracted to HMOs by philosophical and professional motives often find themselves clashing with those attracted for economic reasons. Medical directors of new HMOs are generally of the former types: unless they feel strongly about the moral or professional superiority of HMOs they are unlikely to bear the costs associated with developing one, and they will try to surround themselves with a staff of physicians of similar outlook. In the early years, when the number of members and physicians is small, and financial, political, and social pressures are intense, this small group of ethically and professionally motivated men may resemble a "fighting organization" of sympathetic, mutually supportive comrades.[42] As the organization grows, however, they find that many of the applicants for positions are motivated mainly by the career and economic appeals of HMOs. Recruitment then becomes an organizational problem that takes enormous time and creates considerable tension. (See chapter 3.)

41. Quoted in Spencer Klaw, *The Great American Medicine Show* (Penguin, 1976), pp. 170–71.
42. The term is taken from Robert Michels, *Political Parties,* trans. Eden Paul and Cedar Paul (Free Press, 1962), p. 78.

It is possible that the attitudes of present and future generations of medical students will be more favorable to HMOs than has been the case in the past. According to Dr. Richard Nesson, former medical director of the Harvard Community Health Plan, "in the next decade we're going to get a bonus from the decade of the late sixties and early seventies. . . . We're going to see people coming out of medical school and finishing up their residencies who want to deliver their services in the best way possible, who want to have reasonably stable hours and a reasonably stable income, and who want to work with bright colleagues."[43]

Dr. George Silver, in an interview in 1978, took a more skeptical view. He noted that in their first year, medical students "tell you in large numbers they want to do family practice and group practice. Ask them in their fourth year and it'll be 30 percent family practice and 60–70 percent group practice. Ask them in their residencies and you'll get 10 percent family practice and 30–40 percent group practice. It's not just money. It's a matter of professional image."

There is no way of knowing precisely how many physicians will be attracted to HMOs if the benefits and costs of this and other modes of practice remain approximately as described here. Officials in HMOs sometimes offer 20 percent as a rough estimate. Some believe that the growing surplus of physicians in the United States will make prepaid group practice more attractive to many doctors and will even force a sizable number to flee the perils of fee-for-service competition for the stability of the HMO. Between 1965 and 1979, however, the number of active physicians grew from 285,000 to 422,000[44] without triggering such an exodus, and no one knows how large the surplus must become to do so. Clearly, few solid HMOs are likely to die for lack of physicians alone. Yet for the foreseeable future most will depend heavily on general practitioners, internists, and pediatricians for full-time staff; will depend too on physicians, generalist and specialist, who spend much of their time seeing fee-for-service patients; and will have difficulty for financial, professional, and political reasons in recruiting full-time specialists and even in negotiating arrangements on acceptable terms with specialists for part-time services. These constraints will continue to pose problems of morale, motivation, and money.

43. Klaw, *Great American Medicine Show*, p. 179.
44. Robert Gibson, "National Health Expenditures, 1979," *Health Care Financing Review*, vol. 2 (Summer 1980), p. 4.

Subscribers

For most of the American population, prepaid group practice has not achieved the status of a household word. The population does not appear strongly favorable to HMOs. Although the sample of a 1971 Harris poll said by a 74–15 percent margin that physicians' groups (presumably both prepaid and fee for service) were a good idea, a survey by Stephen P. Strickland in the same year, which asked directly about HMOs, found that only 33 percent of respondents thought them a good idea; 58 percent believed that it was better to stick with one doctor.[45]

A supportive nucleus of one-third of the population is probably enough to launch a sizable number of large HMOs, and that nucleus may have grown after a decade of federal encouragement. However, for a number of reasons, only a small fraction of those favorably disposed toward HMOs are able or willing to subscribe to one.

The literature on HMOs provides little basis for generalizing about who joins and why. There is a substantial literature on the degree of satisfaction HMO enrollees feel with the care they receive, but these enrollees are, of course, a self-selected group. Unfortunately, not much is known about why they joined or about how outsiders feel or might be led to feel about prepaid plans. A few surveys classify subscribers according to highly general reasons for joining (financial reasons, convenient location, and the like).[46] These surveys, however, do not explore the trade-offs subscribers perceive in reaching these decisions, and therefore give no clear picture of how the larger population might view HMOs as a concrete choice.

Each HMO must plan around a break-even point, an enrollment level that permits spreading of risks and receipt of revenues adequate to meet costs. There is no precise agreement on the average or optimum break-even point. Apparently a Kaiser-like plan (which usually aims to own its hospital and provide a balanced set of medical specialties) must be capable

45. *U.S. Health Care: What's Wrong and What's Right* (Universe Books, 1972), pp. 72–81. See also the more recent survey evidence reviewed in chapter 8, below.

46. See David Mechanic and Richard Tessler, "Consumer Response in Varying Practice Settings," in David Mechanic, *The Growth of Bureaucratic Medicine: An Inquiry into the Dynamics of Patient Behavior and the Organization of Medical Care* (Wiley, 1976). A more recent review concludes that answers to the questions who enrolls, in what, and why, "are at best tentative." S. E. Berki and Marie L. F. Ashcroft, "HMO Enrollment: Who Joins What and Why: A Review of the Literature," *Milbank Memorial Fund Quarterly/Health and Society*, vol. 58 (Fall 1980), p. 603.

of enrolling at least 50,000–60,000 to break even.[47] A spokesman for the Harvard Community Health Plan argued that HMOs in urban settings should aim for at least 35,000 members.[48] Some observers believe that less ambitious plans may be feasible with as few as 5,000 members.[49] The most widely cited average figure is about 20,000.[50] Judged against these benchmarks, the enrollment figures reported in the 1980 census of HMOs are not wholly encouraging. Of 236 plans enumerated, 61 percent had fewer than 15,000 enrollees, half (50 percent) enrolled fewer than 10,000, and about one-quarter fell below 5,000.[51] Perhaps consumer acceptance of HMOs will increase dramatically in the future. It is likely, however, that means must be found to make HMOs not only more available, but also more acceptable, if they are to achieve a prominent place in public policy.

Before would-be subscribers can join one, an HMO must, of course, be present in the area—an option that is limited mainly to residents of good-sized cities. Moreover, not every resident of an HMO's service area is eligible to join. Prepaid group plans fear that throwing enrollment open to the population as a whole leads to adverse selection, that those with the poorest health and the greatest need for care tend disproportionately to join. Even a requirement that individual applicants be screened for preexisting conditions may be circumvented by falsified applications. To avoid the clustering of high risks that individual enrollment may invite, most plans market only to employee groups, whose members' health is in the nature of the case good enough to enable them to hold full-time jobs, and whose medical risks are more typical of the population at large. Thus, the enrollment option is usually limited to full-time workers whose employers offer health benefits as part of the employment agreement. This fact effectively removes the HMO option from the unemployed, most of the part-time employed, and those workers whose job benefits do not include medical care. (In some states, Medicaid recipients are exceptions to this generalization.) Moreover, not all employers who offer medical benefits willingly offer an HMO option. McNeil and Schlenker found that three-

47. James Vohs, "Considerations in Establishing New Programs," in Somers, *Kaiser-Permanente Medical Care Program*, p. 157.

48. *Physicians Training Facilities*, Hearings, pt. 2, p. 611.

49. Richard C. Auger and Victor P. Goldberg, "Prepaid Health Plans and Moral Hazard," *Public Policy*, vol. 22 (Summer 1974), p. 357.

50. Paul M. Ellwood, Jr., "Restructuring the Health Delivery System—Will the Health Maintenance Strategy Really Work?" in *Health Maintenance Organizations: A Reconfiguration of the Health Services System* (Graduate Program in Hospital Administration and Center for Health Administration Studies, Graduate School of Business, University of Chicago, 1971), p. 4.

51. HHS, *National HMO Census of Prepaid Plans, June 30, 1980*, pp. 1, 19–33.

fourths of HMO administrators considered access to employers and other potential sources of membership to be the biggest problem they faced in attempting to form and expand their organizations.[52] In short, the combination of four objective factors—the limited number of HMOs, their focus on employee groups, the limitations of work-related health care benefits, and the unwillingness of some employers to complicate their lives administratively by offering an HMO option—severely limits the universe of HMO enrollees quite apart from and in advance of problems of consumer acceptance.

These limitations seriously affect major underserved segments of the population about whom public policy has been highly concerned in recent years. Specifically, they rule out an HMO option for most residents of rural areas (where HMOs are especially hard to form and where large employers are few), the unemployed, the elderly, and the urban poor—in short, those parts of the population that are medically, socially, and economically disadvantaged. There is no logical reason why HMOs could not market to individuals in these categories at (or below) prevailing community rates and make up the difference between their premiums and the cost of service by raising the premiums of the majority of better-off members. Most HMOs, however, appear to agree with Kaiser's position that subscribers pay taxes for the support of the poor and ought not to be asked to pay twice (that is, again) by serving the poor out of premium increases.[53]

An exception to this generalization are the so-called Medicaid HMOs in several cities, notably Los Angeles, Detroit, and Baltimore. In these organizations, plans comprising groups of inner city physicians, or set up by medical schools in or near the inner city, encourage Medicaid recipients to exchange their Medicaid cards for HMO membership. Not all states that contain HMOs are willing to work out Medicaid contracts with them, however, and not all states that allow Medicaid recipients to join HMOs allow them to join any HMO they please. The many obstacles in the way of Medicaid contracts between states and HMOs are reviewed in chap-

52. McNeil and Schlenker, "HMOs, Competition, and Government," p. 200. An observer of an effort to start an HMO in a four-county area around London, Kentucky wrote: "Local employers were uniformly opposed to the HMO plan. Small employers (under 25 employees) were hesitant because of increased bookkeeping that would be necessary and the belief that not enough employees would be interested to make it worth the trouble. Many of these smaller firms had borderline profitability at best and they employed the majority of the working population." Bonnie Tadlock, "Response to Job Start Proposed HMO," unpublished memo, p. 2.

53. "Discussion of Basic Philosophy and Organization," in Somers, *Kaiser-Permanente Medical Care Program*, pp. 46–47.

ter 7. Here it suffices to cite two major obstacles. First, it often proves impossible for state Medicaid officials and HMO executives to arrive at mutually agreeable reimbursement rates. Because Medicaid recipients tend to be in poorer health and to use more care than the population at large, HMO officials usually seek reimbursement levels that take these differentials into account. In practice, this often means payments—either prospective capitation or retrospective reimbursement—close to what a fee-for-service practitioner would receive. Medicaid officials, on the other hand, become interested in such contracts precisely because HMOs are said to be able to serve a given population at costs below those of the fee-for-service sector. Frequently, negotiations break down over unreconcilable estimates of true costs and fair reimbursement. On occasion, state and HMO officials will collaborate on lengthy and statistically complex efforts to estimate use and costs for Medicaid and control populations, and to predict costs with rigorous methodologies, but these efforts involve so many debatable assumptions that they rarely produce agreement.[54] For all of these reasons, HMOs tend to fear that they will be exploited by state Medicaid officials and, as a result, lose money on their Medicaid members, whereas state officials tend to fear that they will be shortchanged by HMO officials charging them more than the true organizational costs of serving their clients. Second, some HMOs are reluctant to market to, or even to accept, Medicaid recipients because numerous Medicaid recipients threaten to produce a "clinic atmosphere" that interferes with marketing to better-off groups.

Even those few HMOs that make a sincere effort to recruit Medicaid enrollees usually fail to attract them. A major reason is that the facilities' location itself discourages the poor. Most HMO sponsors want to set up business in an area that will appeal mainly, if not exclusively, to consumers

54. In Maine, for example, after sporadic and inconclusive talks between 1972 and 1976, state Medicaid officials and one of the state's two HMOs exchanged lengthy letters and held numerous meetings between December 1976 and June 1977 to arrive at a reasonable HMO capitation figure for Medicaid recipients in the HMO's service area. Despite countless man-hours, heroic efforts, and sophisticated statistical techniques, the effort foundered on such questions as the comparability of Medicaid recipients in the HMO's service area with Medicaid recipients in the state as a whole; the appropriate predicted rates of utilization of services by this population; the applicability of HMO cost estimates based on its own enrollees' characteristics and utilization to cost estimates for the new Medicaid population; how to arrive at a capitation figure that captures true costs when the HMO's cost figures were based on a range of services broader than and different from those permitted under the law and regulations of Medicaid; the degree to which prepayment itself induces utilization patterns different from those under fee-for-service care and how this might affect costs and therefore reasonable capitation levels; and more. In June 1977 the negotiations finally wound down, no agreement concluded. (File, Health Planning and Development Agency, Augusta, Maine.)

in and above the stable working class. A location convenient to their preferred constituency is often inconvenient or inhospitable to lower-class consumers, especially black consumers. In short, if an HMO is situated amidst the poor and black, it can give up hope of attracting many of the nonpoor and white; if it is located among the nonpoor and white, it will seldom attract many of the poor and black. Sponsors seldom agonize over which course to choose; as a result HMO care is decidedly stratified by class and race.[55] The few inner city Medicaid groups are exceptions that merely confirm the rule that HMOs are an option offered almost exclusively to full-time employed city dwellers of working class status and above.

Those within the favored universe of individuals enjoying an HMO option may have several strong reasons for declining to join. First and most important, individuals and families who like and trust a personal private physician outside the plan are very often unwilling to give up this physician to join an HMO. Moreover, even those not completely satisfied with their personal physician may like the idea of having "their own doctor." Not all consumers welcome the idea of receiving primary care from a "system." Many apparently prefer to come as close as possible to a face-to-face, personal relationship with one man; expect him to guide them through a system that works for him, not vice versa; and do not like to think of "their" doctor as an employee of a medical care bureaucracy. Attitudes on this subject tend to be basic, firmly held, and deeply embedded in personal experience and taste.

Consider, for example, this dispassionate description of the operations of prepaid health plans (PHPs) by Auger and Goldberg:

> The closed panel is built around medical clinics whose physicians and related health personnel are employees. The PHP may also own and operate other health-care facilities, such as laboratories, x-ray facilities, pharmacies, and even hospitals. Organizationally, this type of health plan often consists of two or three corporations tied together through contracts, ownership of stock, and interlocking directorates. There usually is an 'umbrella' organization to manage the entire health plan, provide administrative and support services (in some cases including ancillary health services), handle the marketing of the plan, and collect and disburse funds. Physician care is rendered through a professional corporation made up of the plan's doctors. The physicians are paid a salary and may have some sort of profit-sharing or other incentive to control costs. There is an internal peer review system or a close control procedure by the medical director (in the case of a relatively small organization). If the plan uses its own

55. Andreas G. Schneider and Joanne B. Stern, "Health Maintenance Organizations and the Poor: Problems and Prospects," *Northwestern University Law Review*, vol. 70 (March–April 1975), pp. 99–101.

hospitals, these may be owned and managed by a third organization. The corporations together constitute the PHP.[56]

Not all Americans have grown so removed from the ideal of the family physician that they find this picture of the medical setting congenial. Such attitudes are very difficult to tap properly on questionnaires. Nevertheless, aversion to "bureaucratic medicine"—especially if the consumer suspects that the economic incentives of the bureaucracy may encourage its employees to skimp on medical care—doubtless deters some potential HMO subscribers.

Third, some consumers may find the HMO facility inconveniently located. Fee-for-service doctors can be found in many sites, whereas an HMO facility (even if it is one of several satellite centers) must obviously be located in one place. Wherever this may be, a certain number of potential subscribers will prefer to visit a more accessible practitioner for routine office visits.[57]

Fourth, some potential enrollees may not like the hospital to which the HMO would send them for inpatient care. Hospitals tend to have higher or lower community reputations that potential subscribers may take as a proxy for the group's reputation. The HMO's need to economize on inpatient care and therefore to prefer cheaper hospitals to more costly ones may aggravate the problem.

Fifth, some subscribers are quite content with their present modes of conventional medical insurance. In some areas, to be sure, the HMO option may entail lower overall costs or even lower premium payments than Blue Cross–Blue Shield or commercial insurance. Sometimes, however, the saving that comes of joining an HMO is realized by the employer, not the employee, which deprives the latter of a positive economic incentive to join.[58] In other areas, joining an HMO means higher premiums than conventional options, which means extra deductions from the employee's paycheck. Experience has shown, Birnbaum notes, that "a $15–20 per

56. "Prepaid Health Plans and Moral Hazard," pp. 358–59.

57. For this reason, some single-site HMOs branch out to satellites in surrounding areas and others, especially independent practice associations, begin life with a network of delivery points. For details of the Group Plan of Northeast Ohio, an eleven-group network of physicians funded by capitation payments instead of by a fee schedule, see Arthur Owens, "An H.M.O. Setup Where Doctors Pay Doctors," *Medical Economics*, vol. 55 (March 6, 1978), pp. 131–40.

58. Between 1976 and 1977, for example, a Brookings Institution employee's premium for an individual membership in the George Washington University Health Plan fell approximately $2 below the cost of an individual Blue Cross–Blue Shield policy. Brookings followed its policy of paying the HMO "the same amount it would have paid" for Blue Cross–Blue Shield and retained the $2 saving, thereby reducing the employee's incentive to join the cheaper plan. When the HMO premium jumped above the Blue Cross–Blue Shield premium in the following year, the employee in the HMO was obliged—as usual—to make up the full difference between the former and the latter with a payroll deduction.

family per month differential between HMO premiums and prevailing levels represents the threshold beyond which significant market resistance is likely to set in."[59]

The employee who studies the fine print of alternative contracts may conclude that the broader benefits offered by the HMO are worth the additional costs. For maternity services and ambulatory benefits, including well-baby and well-child visits, for example, HMO coverage may clearly beat the competition. Many employees do not read the fine print, however, and many of those who do may conclude, on reflection, that the extra cost is not worthwhile. For example, if the cheaper conventional plan offers adequate coverage for expensive inpatient care and if the employee and his family expect to use little ambulatory care during the year, he may decide to keep the money (that is, avoid the payroll deduction) and take his chances on ambulatory care. Or if the HMO's improved pediatric benefits require leaving old Doc Jones, their value is much reduced. If, finally, conventional coverage entails a major medical option, under which the employee can buy most of the coverage of the HMO for equal or only slightly higher cost, while retaining his personal physician and freedom to choose another, the perceived advantages of HMOs again decline.

Frequently, large national corporations with many local units purchase health insurance from commercial companies that compute premiums on an experience-rated system (that is, they tailor rates to the utilization experience of the group, charging more for those groups that have used more care); the monthly deduction for membership in an HMO can be enormous by comparison and a major obstacle to HMO success. On the other hand, members of small employee groups with families appear to fare especially well under HMOs.[60] Marketing to such groups, however, can be a giant headache.[61]

Because packages of medical benefits are extremely diverse in the United States, it is difficult to generalize about benefit-cost analyses. It is safe to say, however, that the thoroughgoing spread of work-related third-party payment health insurance and, equally important, the reduction of employees' out-of-pocket contributions to these insurance premiums, have undercut the appeal of HMOs to subscribers as surely and strongly as the

59. Roger W. Birnbaum, *Health Maintenance Organizations: A Guide to Planning and Development* (Spectrum, 1976), p. 53.

60. *Medical Care Review,* vol. 17 (February 25, 1974), p. 326.

61. Joseph Axelrod, in *Setting Up a Group Practice: Headaches and Opportunities* (Yale–New Haven Medical Center, 1971), p. 18. Marketing to Medicaid recipients is a still larger headache, for it requires individual, door-to-door appeals. This fact goes far toward explaining why many HMOs prefer to avoid such subscribers and why those that seek them out sometimes pursue high-volume enrollment by means of high-pressure tactics.

growth of group practice has limited the attractions of HMOs to physicians. In sum, the pool of potential HMO subscribers, limited sharply by availability factors, is limited still more by satisfaction with private nonprepaid physicians, by aversion to corporate medicine, by considerations of access, convenience, and hospital reputation, and by several economic and subjective variables that influence the choice between HMOs and conventional plans.

The variables that work against choice of HMOs also explain why, mutatis mutandis, an HMO may be chosen. First, some subscribers may be attracted to the professional qualities of the group itself. They may be newcomers to a community attracted by the group's high reputation, or their personal physician may become part of the plan. Second, they may be attracted by the organizational character of the plan. They may value the opportunity to receive a wide range of services, including perhaps emergency care available around the clock, under one roof. Third, they may find the plan (and perhaps its affiliated hospital) conveniently located. Fourth, the plan's hospital affiliate may be one they prefer or find acceptable. Fifth, they may find that the benefits the plan offers in relation to its costs are a good economic bargain. The advantages and disadvantages of competitive plans lie entirely in the eye of the beholder, as David Mechanic discovered when he explored the choices, shown in table 2-1, made by a sample of City of Milwaukee employees between a Blue Cross–Blue Shield option and a prepaid group plan.[62]

It is crucial to emphasize the asymmetry of the choice. Presumably, a consumer must be at least reasonably satisfied on all five counts before he will join an HMO. If he or his family do not like either the physician staff at the plan, its organizational patterns, its location, the hospital it uses, or the benefit-cost bargain it offers, he will opt for the conventional alternative. Because conventional plans are neutral with respect to the first four of these factors, they are likely to be rejected on their merits only as a result of displeasure with the fifth. Clearly, an HMO faces a marketing task quite different from and much more difficult than that of its conventional competition. An experienced observer explained that in marketing an HMO "you are selling health care, not health coverage. You are selling a group of physicians. You are selling a location. You are selling attractive facilities. As a result, initial market penetration is often very low."[63]

62. Mechanic, *Growth of Bureaucratic Medicine*, p. 128.
63. John D. Valiante, "Start-Up Problems and Health Maintenance Organizations," in *Health Maintenance Organizations: A Reconfiguration*, p. 47.

Table 2-1. *Percent of Respondents Giving High Ratings to Various Factors in Evaluating Prepaid Group Practice*

| | Respondents enrolled in | | | |
| | Blue Cross–Blue Shield[a] | | Prepaid group practice[b] | |
Factor	Very important	Most important	Very important	Most important
Location of clinic	37	25	28	8
Clinic's association with specific hospital	16	2	22	3
Provision of all the family's medical care in one place	24	7	58	24
Family physician a member of the group	48	34	27	12
Medical care available at night and on weekends	22	9	56	18
Cost of medical care for the year known in advance	18	2	45	19
Size of member's family	19	7	24	3
Chance that a member of family might need a lot of medical care	29	14	40	14

Source: David Mechanic, *The Growth of Bureaucratic Medicine: An Inquiry into the Dynamics of Patient Behavior and the Organization of Medical Care* (Wiley, 1976), p. 128.
a. Sample of 165 enrollees.
b. Sample of 168 enrollees.

To complicate matters further, one might expect much of this low early market penetration to consist of individuals and families expecting to need unusually large amounts of care. After all, this is the group for whom the bargain is most favorable. Much attention has been given in the literature to this danger—known as the "risk vulnerability hypothesis"—with conflicting and inconsistent results.[64] It has been found that HMOs are more likely than conventional plans to attract enrollees with pre-existing chronic conditions, those who are hypersensitive to symptoms, and those who value preventive care highly.[65] On the other hand, they also tend to enroll substantial numbers of young single people and young couples with children, the latter presumably attracted in part by broader coverage for maternity care and outpatient services for children. These members tend to be healthy. In short, the danger that HMOs appeal disproportionately

64. For a succinct summary of findings, with references, see Mechanic, *Growth of Bureaucratic Medicine*, pp. 123–25.
65. Milton I. Roemer and others, *Health Insurance Effects: Services, Expenditures, and Attitudes Under Three Types of Plan*, Research Series no. 16 (University of Michigan, Bureau of Public Health Economics, 1972), pp. 14–17.

to those who use more care than the norm may be canceled out by their appeal to the young and healthy who use less.[66] Besides, most of the population with unusually poor health and atypically high rates of utilization—the poor, the unemployed, and the elderly—never enjoy an HMO option at all.

In sum, the calculus of benefits and costs that, hypothetically, a consumer constructs in deciding whether or not to join an HMO includes seven conditions that must be met before membership will occur. Three define availability: there must be an HMO in the consumer's area, he must receive work-related health care coverage, and his employer must offer an HMO option. Four define acceptability: the consumer must be satisfied with the professional reputation of the group (and its hospital affiliate), its organizational procedures (one man's "comprehensive, under-one-roof" care is another's "clinic medicine"), its location, and the economic bargain it offers. If any of the three objective conditions is not met, membership cannot occur. If any of the four subjective conditions is not met, membership is unlikely to occur.

Thus seven objectives must be simultaneously achieved if enrollment in HMOs in the United States is to grow appreciably. First, the number of HMOs must increase. Second, the scope of health care benefits (work-related or government-provided) must grow. Third, employers and government programs such as Medicare and Medicaid must offer HMO options more frequently. Fourth, the professional reputations of the groups and of their hospitals must be assured and enhanced. Fifth, consumer acceptance of bureaucratic medicine must increase. Sixth, the locations of new HMOs must be accessible and convenient to large numbers of people. Seventh, the economic bargain offered by HMOs must appear more favorable over time than that offered by the competition.

Some progress has been made in meeting the three objective conditions. The federal government and other sponsors have created new HMOs, work-related benefits are increasing, and the "dual choice" provision of Public Law 93-222 has increased the options open to employees.[67]

The subjective factors present a mixed picture. Well-publicized scandals involving abuses in some of California's prepaid plans in the early and

66. According to Berki and Ashcraft, "Although in its totality the evidence appears to indicate that those who enroll in HMOs are not sicker . . . than those who opt for the fee-for-service sector, there is no reason to believe that in fact they are healthier." "HMO Enrollment," p. 614.

67. Section 1310 of P.L. 93-222 requires all employers who are subject to the Fair Labor Standards Act, employ twenty-five or more workers, and offer health benefits as part of the employment contract to offer a federally qualified HMO if one exists in the area and if the plan asks to be offered.

middle 1970s did considerable harm to HMOs' reputation for professional quality and access to care,[68] despite protestations that these plans were not "true" HMOs. On the other hand, the spread of satellite HMO facilities is bringing prepaid plans closer to many consumers, allowing them to consider and judge HMO care for themselves. Perhaps most important, however, is the success of HMOs in many areas at keeping premium increases low in the face of rapid annual growth of the premiums of Blue Cross–Blue Shield and commercial plans. Whereas it was formerly argued that HMOs cost more but also offered more, in some areas these plans now offer broader benefits at lower costs than their competition. The trick, however, is to make lower HMO premiums serve simultaneously as a force for sponsorship and for membership. Insofar as employers pocket the savings on lower HMO premiums, their incentive to sponsor an HMO rises at the expense of the employee's incentive to join one. Insofar as employees reap the saving, their incentive to join an HMO increases at the expense of the employer's incentive to sponsor one.

On balance, HMO membership is likely to grow over time, probably steadily, but almost surely slowly. There is no reason to expect an abrupt shift in popular attitudes and calculi, producing a mass rush to membership. An estimate by the Arthur D. Little Company that 10 percent of the population will be enrolled in an HMO by 1988 is probably as good a guess as any other.[69]

Hospitals

A successful HMO must use hospital services carefully and economically. It must draw as sharp a line as possible between medical procedures for which the hospital is an appropriate setting and those for which it is not, and it must then insist to physicians and members that procedures in the latter category be performed on an outpatient basis. It must do this in spite of very different expectations and practice patterns in the fee-for-service sector around it. In short, the HMO stands in opposition to a basic historical trend in the American health care system: increasingly to

---

68. The abuses are detailed in *Prepaid Health Plans and Health Maintenance Organizations,* S. Rept. 749, 95 Cong. 2 sess. (GPO, 1976). This report of the Nunn subcommittee, so called for Senator Sam Nunn (Democrat of Georgia), chairman of the Permanent Subcommittee on Investigations of the Senate Committee on Governmental Affairs, deals mainly with California plans.

69. *New York Times,* June 5, 1977.

concentrate in the hospital a wide range of general medical activities, making it a community center for a wide variety of care, including nonacute care.

Over time, hospitals have absorbed more and more medical functions, going well beyond their theoretical role of providing secondary care. This expansion reflects both the declining availability of general practitioners and a growing tendency for the poor and others to resort to hospital emergency rooms for their medical needs. Probably most important, however, has been the growth of the *physician's* incentives to hospitalize patients.[70] A hospitalized patient eases the application of medical school training in optimal patient management; is more convenient to visit; is easier to supervise, control, and monitor; may be tested more easily; and may receive emergency treatment more rapidly than if he is treated outside the hospital. Inpatient care is of course more expensive than outpatient treatment, but the growth of third-party payment has insulated most patients and physicians against concern about cost. By challenging these attitudes toward hospitalization, an HMO runs counter to important consumer expectations and physician norms.

Advocates of HMOs have long condemned the social costs of separating the financing of ambulatory and hospital care and have pointed to prepaid group practice as a means of integrating and rationalizing the two. Ownership or control over, or, at a minimum, a cooperative relationship with, a hospital in its service area is vital to an HMO both because it needs a place to treat seriously ill patients and because it must be able to practice its own distinctive brand of "cost effective" medicine if inpatient service, the most costly component of care, is to be held within the limits of the annual budget.

In most of the Kaiser plans, "the ownership and operation of a hospital has been considered essential to assure the availability of beds."[71] It is also a basic principle at Kaiser that inpatient and outpatient facilities should be integrated in one medical center so that resources may be used rationally. In these Kaiser plans the area medical director is also the hospital chief of staff. The chiefs of services of the medical group are also the heads of the hospital departments, with "direct responsibility for, and authority to set and control, the level of outpatient and inpatient medical care."[72] Where

70. Victor Fuchs, *Who Shall Live? Health, Economics, and Social Choice* (Basic Books, 1974), pp. 96–97.
71. Vohs, "Considerations in Establishing New Programs," p. 157.
72. Irving N. Klitsner, "Style of the Permanente Physician," in Somers, *Kaiser-Permanente Medical Care Program,* p. 107.

controls are weak, economy suffers. For example, the Health Insurance Plan of Greater New York estimates that its economies are but half those of HMOs that control their own hospital.[73] Thus, because it is important both to the quality of care and to the organization's ability to remain solvent, an HMO approaches the problem of its hospital links with the same anxiety and deliberation that it brings to recruiting physicians and marketing to subscribers.

Very few HMOs are supported by sponsors wealthy and enthusiastic enough to stake them to their own hospital. Therefore, most HMOs must be content to negotiate with existing community hospitals as best they can. Negotiations can be highly frustrating for an HMO for two reasons: first, the hospitals are often dominated by medical staffs and service chiefs who are the same local fee-for-service physicians vehemently opposing the group. Second, a new HMO usually bargains from weakness, having little to offer hospital board members and administrators that might induce them to do battle with their medical staffs. In a small town, served by one general hospital, an HMO usually finds it very difficult to establish a working relationship. Opposition from the fee-for-service medical staff is one reason; another is that the hospital's administrators know that diversion of some of the area's population to an HMO and the realization of inpatient economies by the HMO mean a decrease in hospital business. To live within its budget an HMO will try to avoid or defer elective surgery, admit patients only when necessary, discharge them as quickly as possible, and perform laboratory and X-ray tests on an outpatient basis. These economies spell trouble for hospital administrators who know that "the name of the game," as one of them put it, is to "make sure you have the heavy admitters on your staff."[74] As a hospital administrator, feeling the pressure of an HMO in one small New England town, put it: "From the standpoint of a business manager of a hospital with a four million dollar budget and a mortgage and the rest, these economizing pressures are a threat. There are all kinds of outpatient functions an HMO must perform that directly cut into a hospital's business. From the philosophical standpoint there's a good bit to be said for HMOs. But from the hospital's viewpoint, they present real problems. They complicate the budgetary side of life."

If another hospital is added to the picture, however, the balance of

73. Ira G. Greenberg and Michael L. Rodburg, "The Role of Prepaid Group Practice in Relieving the Medical Care Crisis," *Harvard Law Review*, vol. 84 (February 1971), p. 911, n. 53.

74. *Wall Street Journal*, September 11, 1979.

inducements can shift markedly. In a community with two hospitals, both of which may be underused in some, and perhaps in all, respects, the possibility that an HMO will contract to do all its inpatient business with one, thus guaranteeing it predictability and a monopoly over part of the community's hospital use, sometimes awakens sympathetic understanding in administrators. The outcome in this competitive case depends on the balance of power within the hospitals. Mobilized medical staffs may preempt friendly gestures by a timid administration and lethargic board; on the other hand, administration and board may ignore or take on the medical staff and open negotiations with the HMO.

The larger and more heterogenous a community, and the larger the number of hospitals it contains, the better is the prospect that an HMO will find one on which to rely or several among which to shop for services. This is another reason why HMOs are likely to be feasible mainly in urban areas. In the early years, however, opposition of the medical staff and the hospital's determination to wait and see if the HMO takes off and gains enough enrollees to be worth bidding for causes friction and dissatisfaction. Still, pressure from the local HMO medical core and the occasional threat of HMO lawsuits against restraint of trade usually induce hospitals to enter into some type of arrangement serviceable to even a new and small HMO.

Serviceable arrangements are almost always less than ideal, however. It should be borne in mind that hospital utilization (rates of admissions and lengths of stay) and hospital expenditures (dollars spent or saved on hospital services) are two different things.[75] An HMO may be extremely frugal with utilization but be unable to reap proportionate dollar savings if it lacks control over important aspects of how the hospital it uses is run. For one thing, the per diem rate charged to the HMO is usually a product of negotiation between the group and the hospital; if the group needs the hospital more than the hospital needs the group (as is often the case in the group's early years), the hospital may charge higher than normal rates (as defined, say, by the rate charged Blue Cross subscribers). Even at normal rates, the HMO will pay in some measure for cross-subsidies among hospital departments needed to offset inefficiencies in overbuilt, underused, overstaffed, or poorly run units. The HMO rate embraces beds, equipment, and staff it might never have built or hired for itself. Nor can it do much

75. As Herbert E. Klarman remarks, this basic point is almost entirely ignored in the HMO literature. "Analysis of the HMO Proposal—Its Assumptions, Implications, and Prospects," in *Health Maintenance Organizations: A Reconfiguration,* p. 28. See also chapter 4 below.

to influence the costs of personnel, drug purchases, laundry, maintenance, and food purchasing and preparation. The hospital may refuse to accept preadmission X-rays and lab tests performed at the HMO (less expensively than at or in the hospital) and may insist on duplicating them regardless of discomfort to the patient and cost to the HMO. Some hospitals insist that their physicians observe norms that prolong hospital stays beyond what an HMO physician may think necessary. As one observer remarked: "Take cataracts. The hospital rule is often no discharge before five days, although the whole procedure could be done on an ambulatory basis. This is pure gold for the hospital. There are lots of subtleties like this."

Confronted with these difficulties, an HMO generally shops around for a comparatively "cheap" hospital at which to purchase all or some of its inpatient needs. There are important limits to this strategy, however. For one thing, a hospital with a reputation as "a place where your grandmother went to die" (as one HMO affiliate was described in an interview) interferes with image-building, marketing, and organizational growth. It may also interfere with physician recruitment and morale. Good physicians prefer to use good hospitals; they argue, plausibly, that in an HMO, where only the truly ill are hospitalized, the best facilities are none too good. For all of these reasons most HMO administrators dearly wish that they might own or control their own hospital, but few are in a financial and political position to do so. They must therefore muddle through in the hope that one day their enrollment and staff will be large enough to become (in the words of one HMO administrator) the tail that wags the dog in hospital decisionmaking.

Conclusion: Contributions and Expectations

When one contemplates the basic organizational elements of an HMO—those contributors who must be induced to support the organization if it is to succeed—the great difficulties and complexities of developing such organizations in the United States grow evident. Prepaid group practice plans run sharply counter to deep and fundamental trends in the organization and financing of care in this country. In particular, the need to unite financing and delivery of both outpatient and inpatient care in one organized system runs against the organizational and financial separation of these two types of care that has become traditional. The constraints of prepaid group practices contravene both the deeply rooted attractions of physicians to solo practice and the movement toward fee-for-service group practices, which give physicians most of the advantages but few of the problems of their prepaid competitors. The spread of third-party payments to protect most of the population against the most expensive and worrisome medical expense, hospital care, encourages consumers to remain within the fee-for-service sector and take their chances on outpatient bills. Finally, HMOs must attempt to reverse the trend toward concentrating on hospitals more and more functions beyond care of the severely ill, passing the costs to third parties. In short, each of the key contributors is apt to think long and hard before embracing an approach to care that is, in its broad implications, radical. Many conclude that the benefits—to society or to themselves—are not worth the costs of the organization-building effort. Furthermore, even contributors who think that HMOs are a good idea in general, or who may anticipate some personal advantage if one were formed, may be deterred from contributing by the difficulty of inducing adequate support from other contributors—by the complexities of the organization-building process itself.

The benefit-cost calculus is not inevitably negative, however. When willing contributors in all four categories can be found in, or brought to, a would-be service area, HMO development may become feasible. Conditions favorable to HMO formation are indeed increasingly present in some areas of the country and may well grow stronger over time.

It is reasonable to expect that HMOs will be launched in larger numbers and will grow larger in the future than they have to date. Yet the constraints on organization-building suggest that this forward movement will be slow and halting, not rapid and explosive. The policy implication is that the distribution of contributors' stakes is simply not suitable to sustain an intensive effort, launched by a federal administration or by others, to develop large numbers of HMOs in a short time. Health maintenance organizations are not machines to be assembled by master plan with interchangeable parts; rather they are artifacts in need of careful hand-crafting.

CHAPTER THREE

The Political Economy
of Management

In the history of the HMO field . . . a relatively limited number of people [came] into it, both on the physicians' side and the side of the people organizing it.

Their views were kind of crusade-oriented, they were doing a socially useful thing. And that wasn't limited to the board members; there was a certain kind of physician who was attracted to this kind of practice, because in the early days this was not a popular thing to do.

I think that now we're getting beyond that . . . because of the size and expansion of the HMO concept, into a different layer of physicians as well as a different layer of patient. Probably a lot of rethinking has to be done on a number of issues that were more or less sacred up to this point, on a number of positions that were the true faith.

Louis J. Segadelli, former executive director of the Group Health Association of Washington, D.C., quoted in B. D. Cohen, *Washington Post*, May 4, 1978

ONCE THE FOUNDERS of a health maintenance organization have enlisted contributors adequate to sustain their venture, they may congratulate themselves but also recognize that they have taken only the first steps in building a workable and desirable health care organization. In an HMO, as in any organization, the efforts of contributors, members, and employees must be transformed into a stable and "consciously coordinated" system of activities,[1] a task that falls to the organization's executives or managers.[2]

In the eyes of many executives in and observers of HMOs, the essence of a successful prepaid health plan may be captured in this single word "management." The term has never been and by its nature cannot be

1. Chester I. Barnard, *The Functions of the Executive* (Harvard University Press, 1938), p. 73. This chapter, like the preceding one, follows Barnard's usage: the term " 'contributor,' though including those whom we would ordinarily call 'members' of an organization, is a broader term and may also include others." Throughout this study the term "members" denotes persons enrolled in an HMO; "contributors" includes members and also sponsors, providers, and other (nonprovider) employees.

2. Although for some purposes it is useful to distinguish between "managers" and "executives"—see James Q. Wilson, *The Investigators* (Basic Books, 1978), p. 9—this chapter follows the everyday usage of the HMO field by including the organization's chief executives—usually an executive director and a medical director—under the heading "management," and in general by making no sharp distinction between the two terms.

defined precisely. The fate of an HMO depends partly on objective conditions and partly on strategic choice or management. Objective conditions are neither wholly malleable by management nor wholly beyond its reach; the precise degrees of malleability and independence are never entirely clear and appear to be so only with the simplification of hindsight. But if it is certain that the wisest and best-informed strategic choices cannot make a success of a plan facing highly unfavorable objective conditions, it is no less certain that the most beneficent objective conditions will not produce a successful plan in the absence of sound management. Management, in other words, mediates between the raw contributory materials with which a plan is constructed (the subject of the last chapter) and the organization's performance or output (the subject of the next chapter). This chapter examines the nature of management tasks in HMOs, the major difficulties these tasks entail, and the diversity of managerial approaches pursued in three of the most famous HMO "prototypes."

Organizational Costs of Comprehensiveness and Responsibility

Health care services comprise a set of very diverse and highly complex tasks. In the mainstream fee-for-service, third-party-payment system these tasks are entrusted to a range of separate, specialized individuals and organizations. Physicians of different specialties deliver care, hospitals provide an institutional setting for the more intensive modes of care, and insurers (private nonprofit, commercial, governmental, or other) design insurance coverage, market their plans, and pay medical bills. The system (or, as some critics prefer, nonsystem) comes together mainly by way of interorganizational and interpersonal relations mixing negotiation and deference—deference especially to the professional judgment of physicians.

By its very nature as a comprehensive and responsible organization, an HMO pulls within its own organizational framework virtually the whole range of services performed by discrete fragments of the fee-for-service, third-party-payment system. The HMO designs its coverage and markets it. It hires or contracts with its own physicians to provide care and contracts with (or owns or controls) a hospital for the more specialized services. This comprehensiveness is at once the essence of an HMO and the source of its peculiarly severe management difficulties. Functions performed in the larger system by means of interorganizational relations are transformed in the HMO into an intraorganizational agenda. Three consequences follow.

First, management of the HMO demands coordination of a number of highly diverse substantive tasks, each with a very different "technology." Failures of coordination are visited directly on the organization itself, not diffused throughout the system as a whole, as in the mainstream. The combination of highly complex and highly interdependent tasks is not unique to HMOs, of course; the traditional principles of organizational hierarchy were devised largely to manage this combination.[3] But a second aspect of an HMO, inherent in its mission as a medical care system, limits the application of this traditional response. This aspect is the coexistence and interdependence within the organization of administrators and physicians. As organizational analysts have often pointed out, extensive participation of professionals in an organization—especially professionals with highly developed codes of ethics external to the organization, esoteric skills and expertise, and a strong sense of autonomy of professional judgment, all features that physicians display in abundance—impairs formal hierarchical controls in many ways.[4] In short, the truly distinctive feature of the HMO as an organization is that it combines in one structure a collegium of professionals—highly trained scientists delivering intimate human services—and a business—competitive, entrepreneurial, preoccupied with the "bottom line," and therefore absorbed in all the traditional problems of hierarchical organization of corporate authority. Both elements must somehow be made to mesh.

The incorporation of many highly complex and interdependent tasks within an ambiguous and vulnerable, professionally dominated hierarchy produces a third consequence: in an HMO, conflicts arise easily but are difficult to resolve. Again HMOs are not unique. In universities, for example, similar combinations of organizational qualities produce "organized anarchy."[5] The costs of anarchy are lower in a university than in a health care organization, however, precisely because task *interdependence* is smaller in the former than in the latter. Hospitals too face similar

---

3. A classic statement is Luther Gulick, "Notes on the Theory of Organization," in Luther Gulick and L. Urwick, eds., *Papers on the Science of Administration* (New York: Institute of Public Administration, 1937), pp. 3–45.

4. For example, Mark Abrahamson, *The Professional in the Organization* (Rand McNally, 1967); Frederick C. Mosher, *Democracy and the Public Service* (Oxford University Press, 1968); Eliot Freidson, *Doctoring Together: A Study of Professional Social Control* (Elsevier, 1975), especially chap. 1 and the studies cited therein.

5. On universities see Michael D. Cohen and others, "A Garbage Can Model of Organizational Choice," *Administrative Science Quarterly*, vol. 17 (March 1972), pp. 1–25. The three "general properties" of organized anarchies, these authors contend (p. 1), are "problematic preferences," "unclear technology," and "fluid participation."

problems. Unlike an HMO, however, hospitals can usually take a generous and open-handed approach to the resolution of conflict by giving major contenders, especially the medical staff, autonomy within broad limits. Hospitals are at liberty to follow this "irresponsible" course precisely because they need not finance care—they pass its costs along to third parties—as well as deliver it.

The argument to be developed in this chapter is that HMOs achieve their comprehensiveness and responsibility at the price of great organizational fragility. Managing an HMO is an unusually trying exercise in conscious coordination. Viewed from an economic standpoint, the task should be virtually self-executing: for any HMO, information about facilities, staff, members, premiums, competitors, and other variables should define a set of equations that could (in theory) be solved to yield the proper value of each variable. Presumably policy analysts who describe the HMO as a self-regulating mechanism responsive to the economic logic of market competition have something like this in mind. But although the economic discipline of the market does impose some imperatives, it does not also impose uniquely determined responses on the plan that confronts them. The HMO is not merely, indeed not mainly, a bundle of economic laws, an economic system, but also, and more important, a complex of personal and professional relations, the workings and management of which are highly contingent. The HMO, in short, is a system of *political economy*, a point given short shrift in the vast economic and policy analytic literature on prepaid group practice plans. As managers respond to economic imperatives, they must be constantly sensitive to organizational politics. These organizational politics are not simply the sum of the economic interests and perspectives of the organization's participants. They draw life from the organization's ideology, its constituency, its structure, and its sense of mission, all of which coalesce to create the nebulous but pervasive presence of "organizational character."[6] Once it has become settled and valued for its own sake, organizational character may complicate organizational change—including changes that would rationally address changing economic or other environmental conditions that beset the HMO. Of basic importance at any time and over time, organizational character often holds the key to explaining HMO behavior that cannot begin to be understood in economic terms alone. It may therefore be useful to proceed to a brief description of the nature of the

6. The term and much of its application in this chapter are taken from Philip Selznick, *Leadership in Administration* (Harper and Row, 1957), especially pp. 38–42.

economic imperatives HMO managers face and then to explore at length the ways in which organizational politics influence managers' strategic choices.

Economic Imperatives of Management

The economics of HMO management have elicited much learned attention. For present purposes all that is possible—and, fortunately, all that is needed—is a brief and superficial overview of the subject. It may be postulated that the economics of management consist of three main *stages*—here termed planning, structure, and operations—and that the central managerial problem at each stage is to reconcile or balance the competing demands of each member of a distinct pair of *tasks*.

The first pair of tasks, fundamental to the *planning* stage (when the organization's resources are initially put in place and deployed) requires what may be called a resources/marketing balance. The managers of an HMO must design the size and location of its facilities and the number and specialty mix of its staff optimally in light of the size of its membership and the rate of growth of that membership (actual, expected, or desired) over time. Facilities and staff should be large enough to accommodate the plan's target enrollment, but not so large that the plan suffers the costs of waste. The location must be suitable to the numbers and types of members sought. In the early years, of course, enrollment generally falls below the break-even point, failing to bring in enough premium revenues to maintain operations and repay borrowed funds, and thereby pull the plan into the black. This is to be expected, but no plan may remain in the red indefinitely. The first basic managerial task, therefore, is to balance facilities and staff with a marketing strategy so as to yield an enrollment that will neither swamp the plan's resources nor prove too small to make the plan financially self-sustaining within a few years.

The second pair of managerial tasks, crucial to the plan's *structure* (those formal relationships among its participants that will govern the plan's use of resources over time) requires what might be termed a productivity/access balance. A well-managed HMO uses facilities and staff to the full, or nearly so. Efficiency in planning and deploying its resources implies a relatively small number of staff and facilities used intensively to serve a relatively large and growing membership. To the degree that resources are larger and productivity lower than optimal, efficiency suffers and the organization's financial position is weaker than it need be. But the optimal supply of services and staff and their optimal scheduling cannot be defined in a vacuum; hypotheses about optimality must be tested (balanced) against demand, against the size of the membership and the access to services it seems to require. Conversely, however, the needs of the membership and the operational meaning of desirable access must be defined (balanced) against the capacity of the plan's resources.

If resources and numbers appear to be properly balanced (the main task at the planning stage) and if scheduling appears to be geared to optimal productivity, then by process of elimination of managerial variables access must be adjusted and channeled in order to maintain balance in the organizational structure. If the membership's demands for service overburden a staff of reasonable size working at full steam, providers may feel strained and members may grow alienated. Managers of HMOs therefore try to channel access, by such expedients as limiting the number of switchboard operators and the number of calls they are expected to handle per unit of time, waiting times for an appointment, ease of access to drop-in clinics, and hours of operation; by requiring payment for certain routine services; and by "educating" members in the proper use of the plan.

A managerial principle crucial to balancing scheduling requirements with demands for access in the HMO may be termed channeled access. That is, members should be carefully guided along a hierarchy of specialization of providers. Generalist personnel—general practitioners, internists, pediatricians, and paraprofessionals—cost the organization less in salaries and in expensive procedures than specialists do. For a given dollar, more members can receive outpatient care from a generalist than can receive inpatient care from a specialist. Therefore the organization tries to ensure that a patient's first contact is with a generalist and that he is referred to a specialist only after generalists have done all they could. Likewise, outpatient care is the norm; hospitalization takes place if and only if one and sometimes more generalists affirm that it is necessary. (See chapter 4.)

The third pair of managerial tasks, essential to the successful *operation* of an HMO over time, requires what may be called a control/satisfaction balance. The productivity that is expected from a set of fixed resources does not flow automatically. Managers of an HMO must see to it that the staff neither under- nor over-provides, and that the product offered is of suitable quality. Therefore, they must install systems to monitor and control both utilization and quality of care. Overprovision generates immediate financial costs to the plan, but underprovision can result in longer term and worrisome costs in the coin of members' disaffection, loss of enrollment, and perhaps even malpractice suits.

In seeking to achieve balance between controls on providers and satisfaction among members, HMO managers employ a number of institutional devices. They monitor and seek to control the use and quality of care in a variety of ways—through review of charts and printout profiles, peer review, hierarchical authority, socialization, and in other ways. But the preferences of an HMO member can no more be taken as given than can those of providers. Members' preferences must be not only honored but also shaped to fit the distinctive operating characteristics of an HMO. In particular, members who may have believed that they had a right to immediate and unlimited access to specialists in the fee-for-service sector must be persuaded to be satisfied with channeled access that uses generalist care as a first resort.

Balance is seldom so stable that strains fail to arise. Although economies of specialist and inpatient care permit relatively large additions to generalist staff and outpatient resources, the organization's need to conserve resources may lead to queuing and rationing of contacts. When this happens, members must be "educated," cajoled, or co-opted into accepting a measure of delay and even of confusion. When these measures fail, formal grievance mechanisms must be available to restore satisfaction. Faced with delays, unpleasantness, confusion, or uncommunicative personnel at times when the organization's supply and the member's demand do not meet optimally, the member must be able to vent his displeasures within the organization lest negative word-of-mouth and even disenrollment restrict the organization's ability to grow or maintain an adequate base of subscribers. Thus HMOs establish public relations offices, consumer representatives or liaisons, formal grievance committees, and devices for representing members on the policymaking board—all designed to elicit information about their encounters with providers, redress members' grievances, and provide an internal safety-valve for relief of organizational stress.

This highly simplified and schematic account of HMO management suggests the main dimensions of the job. Managers begin with (and return to) a set of planning tasks centered on objective conditions—the size and location of facilities and the size and specialty mix of staff designed in relation to a membership base of a certain size and growth rate. They then seek to design a proper structural balance between the productive use of resources and the access needs of members. Finally, they try to achieve an operational balance between the qualitative and quantitative aspects of providers' use of care and members' satisfaction with both quality and quantity of care. Good management consists in producing a proper balance between two somewhat conflicting objectives at each stage. In a well-managed HMO each of these tasks (see table 3-1) is in balance both horizontally (with its counterpart) and vertically (with those at different stages).

In theory, balancing and trading off may be viewed as essentially economic, even mathematical, processes. Given the known values of some variables and reasonable postulates of the values of others, the HMO manager could manipulate the numbers to learn the value of unknown variables. In theory, if he knows the size of the HMO facility, its location, and the size and specialty mix of its medical staff, he could derive the number of members it is suited to serve. Given knowledge of the size of the membership (and therefore of the revenues it generates), of the HMO's payroll and debt service obligations, and the like, he could compute the number of days of inpatient care and the number of referrals to outside specialists the plan can afford.

Although no HMO manager can maintain indifference to such calculations and hope to succeed, the actual process of balancing managerial tasks does not remain within economic confines. The account offered in this section has touched on HMO management tasks in general. To consider the practical content of these tasks is to see that the principal tasks of HMO management involve not only calculations of optimal economic efficiency but rather, and more important, negotiations with individuals and organizational subunits with highly heterogenous backgrounds, interests, and inclinations. Far from being the self-regulating economic systems they are sometimes said to be, HMOs are highly dependent on managerial politics.

The Political Economy of Management

The top management tasks in an HMO are generally divided between two chief executives, an executive director and a medical director, the former at the head of a hierarchy of subordinates including financial, personnel, marketing, legal, and other managers, and the latter at the head of a "hierarchy" of physician colleagues. In a large HMO—one that embraces several separate plans serving several regions, as does the Kaiser

Table 3-1. *HMO Management Tasks*

Stage	Task affecting providers	Task affecting members
Planning	Determining size and location of facilities Determining size and mix of staff	Forecasting number and rate of growth of enrollment
Structure	Determining level of productivity	Channeling access to care
Operations	Reviewing and controlling utilization and quality of services	Promoting satisfaction with services

program, for example—these hierarchies are reproduced at various lower levels too—in each region and at each center within each region, for instance.

Successful chief executives of an HMO generally require three attributes: an understanding of various specialized skills that transcend those usually involved in running a business and practicing medicine; an intimate knowledge of local conditions and attitudes; and an ability to negotiate and get along well with other employees and with contributors to the organization. These skills are also important in their subordinates. Individuals combining these attributes are not in abundant supply, at least not at the salaries most HMOs are able to offer, and probably not at any price.

Planning the size, design, and location of an HMO's physical facilities requires a thorough understanding of construction costs and schedules, patient flow patterns, parking, land costs, the contents of local fire, building, and zoning codes, residential patterns (including trends in changing neighborhoods and metropolitan population shifts), traffic patterns, and more. Planning therefore requires an understanding of architecture, the construction trade, aesthetics, the logistics of health service delivery, land values, demographics, and law. It also demands an ability to negotiate with architects, contractors, doctors, and local government officials. Seemingly small mistakes may prove very costly. For example, facilities that are too large and expensive when judged against actual enrollment trends may push an HMO's break-even point higher and into the future, delay the repayment of debts, and perhaps require further borrowing or subsidies. A facility in the wrong place—in a neighborhood changing for the worse, too far from a hospital, or too removed from major roadways—may prove to be unpopular. According to one HMO executive, experience proves that "an HMO sells three things: location, location, and location." Yet the best location will rarely be the most economical one, and the most economical one may be neither best nor most conveniently accessible to the hospitals the HMO plans to use for inpatient care. The difference between making a necessary or inescapable trade-off successfully and making a damaging miscalculation lies mainly in an understanding of the attitudes, customs, and preferences of the local market—the local populace. These trade-offs extend to the smallest detail. Parking, for example, should be adequate but not overabundant ("dropping in" should not be too easy, after all). Even this trade-off, however, cannot be made entirely on the basis of ratios of square parking footage to number of members. It will depend partly on whether the demand for access may be expected to distribute itself fairly evenly over the day or whether it will peak, say, before and after work and at lunch hours. Successful chief executives must understand the issues inherent in these choices. More important, they must be able to identify and recruit employees endowed with the specialized skills the planning tasks demand.

Every HMO requires a marketing director—indeed, some observers believe that this position is equal in importance to that of the executive and medical directors—but no handbook or job description defines for all incumbents and all occasions the nature of the task. Marketing involves a sophisticated blend of analytical insight into demographic trends and persuasive skills in face-to-face negotiation. Marketing strategies vary both with the attributes of the plan—its location, premium levels, benefit packages, community reputation, hospital affiliation—and the attributes of subscribers—the size of employer contributions to employees' health coverage, the costs and benefits of existing conventional coverage, residential patterns (distance between the HMO and work places and homes), the attitudes of employers and unions. An HMO cannot be successfully marketed simply by identifying the potential market and then calling attention to the existence and features of the plan. As a first step, employers must agree to offer it. Some will agree on request; the resistance of others must be overcome. Some employers will devote a perfunctory sentence or two to announcing a new HMO option. Others will allow the HMO's marketing staff to set up displays on company grounds or to make a presentation to employees on company time. Still others will instruct company benefit managers to discuss the HMO option in favorable and encouraging terms.

However enthusiastic the employer may be, collective bargaining representatives may respond in very different ways, ranging from opposition to informal discouragement of the option to strong support. Some employers and union officials may prove to be intractable; in others skillful advocacy may spell the difference between begrudging acceptance of the option and aggressive promotion. The same applies to the subscriber's decision: the marketing presentation (written, verbal, or both) may be his first encounter with the plan. For some it will be the last; others may be curious to learn more. Marketing efforts cannot determine these reactions but they can influence them.

A good marketing director must first of all recruit a good marketing staff. To do this he must be a sound judge of quickness, energy, persuasiveness, tact, and other sales skills in job applicants. He must then instruct the staff in the particulars of the HMO "product" and in the attitudes and questions of potential subscribers, then monitor each staffer's performance in concrete settings, and correct mistakes and give advice. He must then decide whom to retain and whom to let go. The staff must grasp the nature of the local situation and the meaning of effective advertising and public relations in the heterogenous employee markets at hand. It must then go about patiently, tirelessly, and courteously, explaining to employer representatives, worker representatives, and workers themselves the merits of the HMO. The staff must be ever mindful of the difference between selling insurance and selling an HMO, a distinction said to be lost on many HMO marketing staffs recruited from the ranks of Blue Cross. Finally, the marketing director must have the rare ability to make realistic evaluations of his own ability to fulfill marketing targets over time, and to adjust them, for balanced decisions about the size and use of facilities and expansion of staff depend heavily on the plan's rate of growth.

The services of skilled financial personnel are important to an HMO's fiscal strength. Unless a new or expanding plan is very well endowed by its sponsor, it will seek access to local credit markets to finance its activities. Access to credit and, equally important, the terms on which it is extended turn in good part on the right local connections and on the success of the plan's financial spokesmen in persuading lenders that their money will be in responsible hands.

As a plan's enrollment builds, the monthly income generated by subscriber premiums constitutes a handsome nest egg which, if invested astutely even for a short time in an account or enterprise with a high yield, can enrich the plan's reserves and speed repayment of debt. The financial manager's acumen in recognizing such opportunities is again partly a function of financial intelligence and partly a function of connections. By the same token, inept or shady investments can lead to impoverishment or scandal.[7] Finally, the financial manager must grasp the relation between the plan's general financial health and other variables such as premiums and payrolls, which are of paramount concern to other parts of the organization such as the marketing and medical staffs. Analyzing and explaining the trade-offs demands a mix of financial wizardry and negotiating skill.

The importance of executives able to combine within themselves and in interaction with each other unusual economic and political skills is no less evident in the managerial tasks associated with designing an organizational structure than in those involved in planning. The heart of an HMO lies in the interaction between members and physicians. The optimal structure of schedules and procedures gives due regard to the sentiments of both groups. Drawing the line between due regard and undue deference demands sensitive coordination between the executive and medical directors and a careful balancing of the dictates of productivity and those of medical morale and professional integrity. If either side claims too much, efficiency or morale suffers.

Adapting the tools of management learned in business schools and practiced in the corporate world to the idiosyncrasies of medical practice strains the temperament and intellect of many otherwise exemplary administrators. Likewise, imposing hierarchical controls on physician colleagues is a task that many potential medical directors find intolerable or otherwise alien to their personalities and abilities. Moreover, the close daily interaction required of these executives in the highly interdependent medical-business world of the HMO may add personal strains to tasks that are difficult enough in their own right. As more than one HMO executive director remarked in interviews, employment at any level of an HMO requires a high capacity for negotiation. But this skill is often equally foreign to business administrators taught to honor clear, responsible, and hierarchical lines of corporate authority and to physicians accustomed to the unfettered exercise of their professional and personal judgments in deciding how they will practice medicine.

The tensions inherent in shared lay-physician management are perhaps most severe in the operation of utilization and quality reviews and controls. The executive director may first see signs of trouble in printouts of the

7. For instance, the 50,000 members of the Georgetown University Community Health Plan of Washington, D.C., could hardly have been reassured to read in the *Washington Post* of October 6, 1979, that the plan "had apparently lost at least $250,000 in an alleged investment fraud scheme," and that the plan's chief financial officer had resigned over questions concerning the investments.

physicians' utilization of services, but he will work through the medical director if he expects his concerns to be sympathetically transmitted and received. Thus his strength as a cost controller and financial planner is contingent on the strength and receptiveness of the medical director, an abridgment of hierarchy and concentrated executive control many administrators cannot accept gracefully. Two types of overutilization especially threaten an HMO's financial stability: excessive hospital admissions and excessive referrals to fee-for-service specialists in the community. The greatest danger to a plan's fiscal health, as one executive director put it, occurs when the chief executives lose track and control of what is "out there"—in the hospitals and on referral. In the words of another: "It depends on constant attention to little variables. For example, we allow no fee-for-service referrals now. You've gotta turn down some claims and watch the doctors constantly. You can't let any variable get away from you." In a plan with carefully controlled utilization, growth is the road to financial security, but in one where controls are weak, rapid growth may spell disaster: the more members the plan enrolls, the more money it loses. To steer the proper course, the medical director must be informed about and influential with his medical staff.

Monitoring and, still more of course, controls naturally sow the seeds of conflict. Physicians must be watched; those who deviate substantially from the group's norms must be "talked to" and "educated."[8] An effective medical director must be at once liked and respected, both sensitive and firm, if he is to achieve changes in behavior without hurting physicians' feelings, causing a sense of persecution, and spawning defensive alliances among the medical staff. Under a weak medical director, variables may begin to get away. If the recruitment process itself is flawed, allowing poorly socialized doctors with no taste for negotiation, peer review, and control to join the plan, even a strong medical director may find monitoring and controlling to be onerous, unpleasant, and ultimately ineffective processes. In sum, effective monitoring and control presuppose a gifted medical director and a receptive medical staff, both of whom must be adept at intraorganizational negotiation and dialogue and sympathetic to the administrative aspects of maintaining the plan. It is doubtful that physicians with these qualities exist in large numbers in the United States today.

Establishing suitable structures and procedures to give members chan-

8. On peer processes in prepaid group practice see Eliot Freidson and Buford Rhea, "Processes of Control in a Company of Equals," *Social Problems,* vol. 11 (Fall 1963), pp. 119–31; Freidson, *Doctoring Together.*

neled access to care and working to keep them satisfied with the care the plan supplies also require uncommon insight, foresight, and skill. The plan's management must persuade consumers who are accustomed to the norms of third-party-payment, fee-for-service medical care to modify their expectations to fit the distinctive practices of an HMO, and then insure that the plan itself meets those expectations. This educative enterprise calls for political skills of a high order.

Management of access and maintenance of member satisfaction rest on shared understandings among doctors, administrators, board members, consumers, consumer representatives, and others. A proper balance between the plan's supply of service and members' demand for it begins with the receptionist, a critical access point who encourages or discourages drop-ins and appointments, weighs the gravity of symptoms, and may give advice about what to do for the moment in emergencies. Balancing continues with the generalist of first resort, the nurse practitioner, paraprofessional, or general practitioner who evaluates the member's condition, may prescribe medication, and must decide whether to counsel rest and recovery, a repeat visit, a visit with a more specialized member of the plan's medical staff, or a referral to an out-of-plan specialist. It means instructing consumer representatives and those who handle grievance procedures in the fine print governing the plan's approach to reimbursement for out-of-plan services obtained in an emergency, real or imagined, and for out-of-area coverage, and in how to dispose of unsanctioned claims firmly but politely. It involves educating members of the board of directors not to rush to judgment when they are contacted directly by constituents disgruntled by a long wait for an appointment, a brusque or discourteous doctor, or a claim denied for outside service. An HMO thrives on efficient allocation of care; it also thrives on favorable word-of-mouth reports. Lest the former interfere too greatly with the latter, public relations skills must be implanted and diffused all along the hierarchy, from receptionist, to provider, to consumer representative, to board member. All must come to share a common understanding of plan philosophy and an ability to translate that philosophy clearly and firmly, but also sympathetically, to confused or disgruntled members. These skills entail both a sharp legalistic eye for the details of a member's contractual entitlement and a generous feeling for the spirit of medical care, two qualities seldom found together.

In sum, the precarious balancing act of which sound HMO management consists may go astray in many ways; failures of economic acumen are but one. Even experienced managers highly knowledgeable in the academic lore of managing businesses or even other health care institutions may be defeated in an HMO by an inadequate grasp of local particulars. Even well-trained managers with a sound understanding of the local HMO market may run into trouble because they lack the interpersonal negotiating skills, essentially unteachable, that almost every facet of HMO operations demands. The importance of these skills, which range from relatively hard (economic adeptness) to softer (localistic insights) to very soft indeed (negotiating ability), in particular cases and situations is usually clear only in retrospect. "If you talk to some of these new managers," said one observer with long experience in the Kaiser program, "you find that a lot of them think they have problems they don't really have, and that a lot of them have problems they don't know they've got." Considering the highly interdependent mix of very diverse and scarce skills on which successful HMO management depends, it is naïve to contend that well-managed plans can be built rapidly and in large numbers across the United States at the behest of the federal government or of any other sponsor.[9]

The Dynamics of Management: Organizational Growth and Bureaucratic Development

Although a snapshot of management problems and tasks frozen in time is useful for identifying actors and tasks, it oversimplifies the nature of HMO management in important ways. It is therefore helpful to take a brief third cut at HMO management, supplementing the economic and political perspectives with attention to organizational dynamics, to the ways in which managerial roles and tasks change over time as the HMO and its administrative structure develop, and as this development imposes stress on an organizational character established by a younger and smaller plan.

Unfortunately, it is difficult to generalize about the process of organizational development in an HMO or about its effects on the political economy of management. One reason is that HMOs differ markedly in their attributes and behavior. Another is lack of information. Most of the literature on HMOs is statistical, not descriptive; most of the descriptive literature is anecdotal and impressionistic, not highly analytic; and most

9. A useful discussion is Roy Penchansky and Sylvester E. Berki, "Evaluating HMO Development: Contributions from the Experience of the Community Health Network Program," paper prepared for the annual meeting of the American Public Health Association, October 17–21, 1976.

of the tiny body of analytic and descriptive studies offers snapshots of individual HMOs at fixed points in time and therefore at one point in their development. Few studies carefully follow individual HMOs through successive stages of growth and development and attempt to identify and explain major sources of change over time.

There is reason to believe that there are important organizational differences between generations of HMOs. The sociological literature on the older groups, especially the Health Insurance Plan of Greater New York, gives details of tension and strain, especially between physicians and administrators. Officials in the emerging generation of HMOs, however, often argue that these difficulties apply only to the "old and tired" generation. Their newer groups, they contend, are small enough to be consensual and harmonious and in any case are too busy struggling to take root to afford the luxury of bitter internal divisions. This viewpoint may be the result of youthful optimism or it may reflect some objective differences between generations. The more plausible explanation, however, is that the organizational growth of an HMO—*any* HMO—entails internal dynamics of its own. These dynamics are often unanticipated and sometimes unwelcome, but always vital to assessing the organization's ability to accomplish the goals it sets for itself or that others—including federal policymakers—set for it.

The central fact of organizational life for most young HMOs is the struggle for life itself. The major problem, as the previous chapter argued at length, is to induce key contributors to lend their efforts to the organization on a scale sufficient to maintain it as a going, and growing, concern. Because these contributors often conclude that the benefits they will reap from such efforts do not exceed, or only slightly exceed, the costs, an HMO's early years may be very lean indeed.

In most places and times, an HMO is conceived when a sponsor makes contact with one or more local physicians who are willing to shoulder the burdens of staffing such an organization. The next step is usually to procure from a foundation, a government, or some other source a small sum of money for feasibility planning. A staff aide, usually someone with a master's degree in business administration or in health planning or administration, is hired, and the protagonists assemble to examine data on the projected service area's population characteristics (age, sex, residential distribution), number of physicians, insurance coverage, identity of large employers, and so forth. They must satisfy themselves that the population density is adequate to support an HMO, that physicians are not already too numerous to support a new group practice, that work-related benefits are sizable and widespread—in short, that an effort at organization-building is not quixotic. If they are reassured, two or three more doctors, preferably locals known to and respected by the medical director, will be recruited. The sponsor and founding physicians also take care to search for a suitable executive director, the lay counterpart to the physicians' medical director.

Once this core staff is in place, attention turns to assembling a board of directors, that is, a collection of laymen from the community who oversee the group's corporate affairs. The choice of the board is highly important because it will be expected to ease the group's way toward capital from financial institutions, to reassure the community that persons of sober judgment keep their eye on what may be viewed as a suspect or even wacky experiment, and to provide valuable contacts with members of Blue Cross and hospital boards, on which an HMO's board members often sit also. Not surprisingly, HMO boards tend to consist, in the words of one observer, of businessmen, bankers, lawyers, civic leaders, union leaders, and a minority of well-meaning housewives. Constructing a suitable board usually requires a sustained effort at persuasion and cultivation. As one medical director explained: "There are always people in a community who can make things happen. You go to them and hope you can get four or five of them on your board. They'll recruit the rest." If it proves impossible to recruit four or five of these local notables, an HMO's financial and political situation may remain precarious.

With these assembled rudiments of the organization, work turns from planning to the difficult jobs of establishing the details of internal structure and of moving the plan from conception to operation. The sponsor's representatives, having committed their organization's funds to a contro-versial and risky venture, may wish to keep a close eye on, and retain a say in, management. The founding physicians will have learned that their effort makes them pariahs among their fee-for-service colleagues. The directors risk the sarcasm of their physician friends and other community stalwarts, and stand eagerly by awaiting results that vindicate their judgment. Meanwhile the executive director, conscious of sunk costs, daily operating losses, and the need to build up the number of members quickly, endures the hostility of employers who seldom wish to complicate their lives by redefining the health options they offer employees, the indifference of the employees who seldom set up a grass-roots clamor for an HMO option, and the contempt of local hospitals which rarely deign to discuss, much less conclude, agreements on terms favorable to an HMO with, say, two thousand members and much red ink. All the while local fee-for-service doctors, orchestrated by the county medical society, maintain a steady chorus of criticism and stand eager to pounce on the organization's slightest mistake.

Few physicians or staff involve themselves with an HMO primarily in hopes of money or prestige. In the early years little of either attaches to the enterprise; most participants could have more of both, with fewer headaches, in another line of work. Their commitment is based on a combination of what James Q. Wilson calls "purposive" and "solidary" incentives.[10] That is, they continue their contributions because they are dedicated to the ethical and professional superiority of the cause and to each other, to the group itself, their common undertaking. Rallying together for mutual support in pursuit of a good cause, but denigrated by their larger reference group, the original participants take on the attributes of a cohesive, egalitarian fellowship. Internal differences tend to be reconciled quickly under pressure of the daily struggle to take root in an inhospitable environment. The organization is small—physicians number perhaps a dozen at most—and most of the principal participants are known to, and interact often with, one another. Differences are resolved by face-to-face discussion or by consensus developed at a round table of major participants. In the early lean years the HMO is frequently a small, besieged group of idealists bound together by allegiance to their common ideals and to their common idealism.

Needless to say, a prepaid group plan set up by physicians intent on preempting or meeting competition from another sponsor's HMO faces a distinct set of problems. Because these HMOs are a response from within the fee-for-service sector to its critics in the HMO community, they do not suffer the same environmental obstacles they put in the path of others. The threat to their survival comes from within, not from without.

For most of the physicians who belong to it, an independent practice association (IPA) is a necessary evil, grudgingly supported in order to protect themselves against defections of benighted patients and to show the government and other meddlers that the fee-for-service community itself can organize to offer the advantages of prepaid care. Because their commitment is strictly instrumental and because their individual financial

10. *Political Organizations* (Basic Books, 1973), chap 3.

rewards come mainly from their fee-for-service practices, not the small prepaid practices in which they participate on the side, the physicians may be loath to alter their practice patterns—their readiness to order tests, to make referrals, to hospitalize patients, and to prescribe drugs, for example—in more economical directions for the sake of the financial health of the prepaid plan. Despite the difference in source of threat, however, the managers of an IPA face organizational problems similar to those of a "purer" prepaid plan: they must offer over time an attractive package of benefits at a premium low enough to induce a growing number of subscribers to select them instead of the conventional or HMO competition, and to stay with them over time. In the IPA, internal threats to success—physicians' unwillingness to restrain their utilization of services—are the functional equivalents of the external problems of the pure plan; for IPAs too, the early years tend to be lean, and failures are common. The dynamics of the political economy of management may be seen in both types of plan.

Within five years or so of its founding, an HMO either sinks or swims. It either acknowledges failure, closes its doors, and goes out of business or it grows to the point where it nears, meets, or surpasses the enrollment figure required in order to break even financially. If it achieves the latter condition, it has succeeded, at least on this tangible criterion. Yet, precisely because many early contributors view business success as a means to the accomplishment of larger goals, growth often brings changes within the organization that take these contributors by unwelcome surprise.

That growth in the scale of an organization's operations brings changes in the organization's internal control systems and character will surprise no student of organizational analysis. The literature on formal organizations repeatedly explains how increases in the scale (or size or scope) of operations generate increases in the number of staff and the size of facilities (that is, organizational growth), how staff and facilities become more specialized as they grow larger and more numerous, and how advancing specialization among interdependent units triggers new efforts at central control and coordination by the organization's executives. This is the bureaucratization process. Most of the literature on bureaucratization, however, draws on the experience of business firms and (to a lesser extent) government agencies and voluntary associations, giving little attention to bureaucratizing organizations that started life as small nonprofit enterprises engaged in delivering complex human services and bound together by purposive and solidaristic ties far more than by concern for material gain. Thus it is not surprising that the bureaucratic consequences of growth and market success take many of the original contributors by surprise, or that they worry about the future of their system of "bureaucratic medicine."

In an HMO, as in most other organizations, bureaucratization proceeds in step with growth in the scale and scope of operations. The first and basic imperative of a workable HMO is growth, the balancing of its resource commitments and its marketing strategy so as to recruit enrollees up to and beyond the break-even point within a reasonable period of time. Breaking even is the sine qua non of success, the one tangible indicator of how well the group is doing. Unless it is very generously supported, an HMO cannot afford to wait indefinitely to break even. As a rule, the sponsor's HMO specialist has superiors to account to and therefore limited patience. The organization's own board will want to know whether the group is catching on and why or why not. Payrolls must be met. Typically, therefore, an HMO sets out not simply to build enrollment, but to build it rapidly. Recognizing that aggressive marketing and thorough canvassing of employers and their employee groups are required, and that it cannot afford to shoulder the whole task itself, the young HMO often concludes a contract with Blue Cross or occasionally with private insurance firms to handle marketing for it.

As marketing proceeds, the executive director finds that the organization is in many ways at the mercy of forces beyond his direct reach. Growth often lags disturbingly—sometimes alarmingly—behind early planning projections, themselves based on guesswork and optimism. Only by trial and error do those entrusted with marketing an HMO discover that their task is much more complicated than selling health insurance. As HMO officials begin to question whether the Blue Cross staff is pushing the plan with adequate sincerity and enthusiasm, relations become strained.

Marketing energy is only part of the problem, however. The key to building enrollment is gaining access to large groups of employees by adding an HMO option to their work-related health benefits. Yet for many reasons—philosophical resistance, aversion to administrative complications, a wait-and-see attitude toward federal regulations, for instance—employers may be slow to add an HMO option, or to urge it on workers if they do adopt it.

Equally worrisome to the executive director is the possibility that mistakes by the HMO itself will damage its marketing effort in the community. Not only may growth fall short of initial projections, but the aggregate membership rolls conceal myriad enrollment patterns that may shift gradually or suddenly. Some early members remain with the group and mention it favorably to relatives, friends, and coworkers. Virtually all HMO marketers agree that word-of-mouth promotion is a potent force for growth[11] and therefore worry continually about how to make and keep comments favorable. While many members remain and others join, other members leave, however; they move outside the service area, change jobs and lose eligibility for membership, or grow dissatisfied with the plan. The executive director usually lacks a detailed picture of the motives behind these movements in and out. It takes time and a large enrollment to accumulate enough knowledge about geographical patterns, social characteristics, use, services, and growth trends to permit detailed planning and prediction.[12] In the meantime, the executive director may fear that he presides over a house of cards.[13] Because important elements of the marketing effort—the skill and enthusiasm of the marketing staff and the receptiveness of employers and workers, in particular—are difficult to control in the short term, he redoubles his effort to strengthen internal management variables.

It seldom takes an executive director long to recognize that most of his managerial levers are contingent on the performance of the medical staff. "Control," therefore, means controlling physicians' behavior, which is difficult because it depends on complex balances between productivity and access and between utilization of services and member satisfaction. If potential enrollees are to be attracted to the group, they must be persuaded that it offers them a good deal. If to join they incur an increase in monthly out-of-pocket costs or suffer other inconveniences, such as leaving their personal physicians, they must be convinced that the HMO offers them more for their money than conventional plans do. Potential consumers

11. "In urban, inner-city communities," said Fred Prime, marketing director of Detroit's Michigan Health Organization Plans, Inc., " 'word-of-mouth' is perhaps the strongest single tool for gaining acceptance; but it can also work in a negative way." Quoted in "HMO: It's Working in Detroit," *Urban Health,* vol. 4 (April 1975), p. 56. The Kaiser plans too have long depended on word-of-mouth as a major recruitment device. See, for example, Ernest W. Saward and Merwyn R. Greenlick, "Health Policy and the HMO," in John B. McKinley, ed., *Politics and Law in Health Care Policy* (New York: PRODIST, 1973), p. 387.

12. See John J. Boardman, "Utilization Data and the Planning Process," and Walter K. Palmer, "Finances and Planning," in Anne R. Somers, ed., *The Kaiser-Permanente Medical Care Program: A Symposium* (New York: Commonwealth Fund, 1971), pp. 61–80.

13. An official of a relatively young East Coast HMO expressed these anxieties in an interview: "We have 23,000 members now—probably not more because of rate increases. We do get new members, but the disenrollment rate is too high. In any given month maybe 300 join, but 250 leave; so the net increase per month is maybe 50–60 members. We used to say it's because too few companies offered us. Now we tend to blame it either on our delivery system or the rates. We don't really know; the rate of return on the questionnaires we give subscribers is poor."

may suspect—as a result of their own reasoning or at the prodding of local fee-for-service doctors—that a prepaid plan faces formidable incentives to discourage the use of services. To assuage such suspicions, the marketing staff often tends (as one HMO executive put it) to "promise the world," stressing both the plan's emphasis on preventive care and its continual readiness to provide medical treatment as need arises. (For example, an advertisement for a Sacramento HMO, which stresses that the group concentrates on keeping enrollees well, pictures a woebegone housewife, a metal object resting against her sneakered foot, and announces: "Your son's got the flu. Your daughter needs her allergy shot. And you just dropped the iron on your foot. Wow! Do *you* need HealthCare!")[14] Having raised expectations that the plan stands ready to meet enrollees' every need, the executive director—and the membership[15]—expects the plan's providers to live up to them.

The executive director also fears, however, that if physicians prove too responsive and services—especially expensive referrals to specialists and hospital admissions—are made too accessible, the organization will exceed its budget and be obliged to cover costs with an increase in premiums the next year, which might slow enrollment. He therefore expects physicians to balance responsiveness and accessibility with cost-consciousness and parsimony.

Reconciling these conflicting imperatives is an inherently difficult task and the dynamics of growth complicate it considerably. The group's very success in rapid growth raises four difficult managerial questions whose resolution raises new, troubling questions about the plan's future organizational character and strains its organizational cohesion.

One question involves physical expansion. As enrollment grows, the group's facilities become overtaxed. Parking becomes scarce, reception areas get crowded, phones go unanswered or callers are placed on "hold," waiting time for an appointment grows longer, records get misplaced, and so forth, producing irritation. At this point the directors and managers raise for explicit debate the relative merits of a single site and a strategy of decentralized expansion. By adding to its present facility or by acquiring or building a new, larger one elsewhere, the HMO can remain "one

14. *Sacramento Bee,* August 12, 1975.
15. "HMO members appear to have high expectations for what they perceive as high quality care. . . . They do feel themselves part of 'something new' and have internalized much of the marketing emphasis on ease of access to and continuity of care," concludes Jane M. Zapka, "Assessment of Member Satisfaction in an HMO: Understanding the Interaction of Variables and Their Implications," *Journal of Ambulatory Care Management,* vol. 2 (November 1979), p. 43.

organization, under one roof." On the other hand it may set up satellite centers in outlying areas, with decentralized staff, service units, and records-keeping.[16] The founders often argue the case for unity and integration of services and personnel, and the need for extreme caution in taking new physicians' groups into the plan, whereas newcomers, systems analysts, and consultants frequently argue that decentralized facilities will make the plan convenient to new population groups and thereby aid not only in management but also in marketing. All, however, understand that the organization has reached a turning point and that the close personal relationships of the small and lean years will be attenuated.

A second question involves staff expansion. The managers know that new physicians as well as ancillary personnel must be added, but how many? A growing HMO is not, by virtue of growth alone, out of the financial woods. Growth can slow to the point of stagnation or may even decline, and most HMO executives are acquainted with at least one horror story in which these misfortunes actually happened. A major operating cost in an HMO is of course salaries and a rapid expansion of staff may trigger a premium increase, especially if many new physicians unsocialized in the ways of prepaid group practice carry the freewheeling ways of the fee-for-service sector into the plan. The executive director is therefore likely to argue for modest increases in staff, continuing the policy of the lean years when staff were stretched as far as possible and accepted the burdens as part of the collective struggle. He is also likely to seek techniques to bolster the productivity of the medical staff, to monitor their use of services, and to persuade them of the ominous implications of excessive utilization. At the same time he will seek to assure himself that physicians' efforts at productivity and economy have not compromised access and responsiveness unduly.

In short, driven by the logic of organizational maintenance and growth and by the fear of financial instability, the executive director seeks to become more of a controller over time. His success in strengthening his role, however, depends on answers to two further questions. One concerns the role of the plan's board of directors. Expansions of staff and facilities may be viewed mainly as management issues, best left to the executive director and his staff; or they may be viewed as basic policy issues on

16. For independent practice associations, which rely on solo practitioners working in their own offices, and for networks of physician groups, growth poses the reverse problem. They are apt to consider the economies of scale the plan might reap from a central clinic at which X rays, lab tests, and other specialized services would be performed and to debate the implications of such a centralizing move for the decentralized practice patterns they cherish.

which the board should reserve to itself a detailed and authoritative voice. If the executive director is lucky, the board will gratefully acknowledge the group's success, declare its confidence in the management team, and withdraw to the sidelines. If he is unlucky, however, the board—which may well have expanded to include representatives of important employee groups who do not recall or share the ethos of the formative years, and whose original members may have been set to quarreling with one another by strains of growth itself—will assert its prerogatives to the full and insist on controlling both the pace and the purse strings of such expansion as it decides to allow.

Finally, the executive director's strength depends heavily on the emerging role of his managerial counterpart, the medical director. Expansion presents problems not only of the numbers but also of the type of new physician to be hired. On these matters the medical director and medical staff often hold strong views and expect to take the lead. As they interview potential colleagues, the founding physicians frequently worry about what they see. They discover that the pool of applicants with philosophical and professional (that is, purposive) commitments akin to their own is limited. Moreover, in the nature of the case, the applicants do not remember the lean years and what solidarity in defense of the group meant to those who lived through them. In the eyes of the core staff, applicants may display a motivational mix disturbingly slanted toward economic and career orientations. Some may be "tired of the rat race and eager for the tranquillity of the Maine coast"[17]—or the sunshine and life-style of California or Florida. Others may be seeking a stable income or an apprenticeship or may apply for other suspect reasons. To the founders the HMO is a noble edifice constructed in a moral pursuit; to the newcomers it may simply be a useful place to work for a time. As the founders' calling becomes the newcomers' career, pioneers are joined or replaced by employees or shareholders. To its founders it becomes ever clearer that the organization's character will change substantially, an ironic byproduct of the success of their efforts.

In the early years, an HMO usually contains a core of full-time general practitioners, internists, and pediatricians and, beyond this core, resorts to a miscellany of arrangements. Some members are seen by fee-for-service physicians paid by capitation, by negotiated rate, or by their customary

---

17. Jefferson D. Ackor, "The Rural Hospital and the HMO," in *Rural Health Care Delivery*, prepared for the Subcommittee on Rural Development of the Senate Agriculture and Forestry Committee, 93 Cong. 2 sess. (U.S. Government Printing Office, 1974), p. 99.

fee for service. Some of these community physicians come to the HMO facility for limited times; others insist on seeing HMO patients in their private offices. Some special services are hard to obtain anywhere. As the group grows it not only expands its core generalist staff but also finds that it can afford to begin hiring full-time specialists. This happy development gives it much more control over the terms of practice and remuneration and therefore more organizational autonomy. But it increases the number of newcomers whose motives for joining the organization often differ from those of their first-generation colleagues.

Growth creates anxiety not only for the medical director, who worries whether the newcomers have the right philosophical and professional orientations for an HMO, but also for the executive director, who tries to strengthen his mechanisms of control over an increasingly skeptical and resistant medical staff. The executive director's concern with balancing organizational imperatives is nothing new; he has worried about this balance from the day the plan opened its doors, and is accustomed to a measure of tension with the physicians being monitored. In the lean years, however, the precariousness of the HMO's economic situation, the hostility of its environment, and the purposive and solidary commitments of its staff led them to accept the need to resolve or repress their differences for the common good of the enterprise, and in a small group, face-to-face negotiation was feasible.

Infusion of a sizable number of new, full-time physicians with a different motivational mix alters the organization's political economy significantly. The newcomers may be unimpressed with the need for a united front against a hostile external world. After all, they joined the group in good part because it had become a going concern. Their status as employees or partners makes them directly interested in and sensitive to the organization's standard operating procedures and norms. Yet their relatively weak philosophical and professional commitments to the HMO and their detachment from the struggles of the lean years make them suspicious and resentful of the administration's efforts to constrain, by means of its various control mechanisms, the autonomy of professional practice and judgment. To the administration, insuring a proper balance among responsiveness, productivity, and frugality is the very essence of good management and a basic precondition of continued organizational stability and growth. The physician staff, however, may feel alienated and misunderstood: trying to practice good medicine and to follow their best professional judgment, they find themselves dominated, harassed, and exploited—as well as underpaid—by "the bureaucracy." As growth brings expansion, the binding force of purposive and solidary commitments weakens; as these incentives weaken, tensions between the administration and the medical staff increase.

The medical director and the founding physicians, many of whom now occupy chief-of-service or other administrative posts, find themselves in a disturbing crosscurrent. No longer first among a small body of equals dedicated to a cause, the medical director stands at the head of a sizable body of doctors, with whose backgrounds, outlooks, and practice patterns he is increasingly unfamiliar, and who insist that he represent them effectively and protect their rights and professional prerogatives zealously against a cost-conscious administration. Having lived through the lean years, the medical director generally shares the managerial concern for balancing conflicting imperatives. As head physician, however, he must protect his medical staff and he readily understands the doctors' resentment of lay interference with medical practice. As the motivational mix shifts toward career incentives among the medical staff, as purposive and solidary commitments decline, and as impatience with the bureaucracy grows, the medical director increasingly finds himself speaking "for" the staff "to" the administration in defense of high-quality care, which the latter appears to undervalue. What in the early years had been relatively harmonious, overlapping, and interpersonal activities increasingly become separated, specialized, and even adversarial tasks.

The executive director's first and major concern—the overall fiscal health and market appeal of the organization—implies insuring that members regard the plan as a good deal; that physicians' productivity remains high; that staff salaries remain reasonable; and that physicians do not overprovide services. Clearly, the medical staff is the key to sound executive management, and the executive director, in continual fear of losing track of what goes on in there (during scheduled hours and in the course of patient encounters) and out there (on referral to specialists and in the hospital), seeks means of influencing these factors.

The medical director's first and basic concern, by contrast, is with maintaining both the professional reputation of the group and a core of physicians able and willing to provide high-quality medical care. He too wants members to remain and the organization to grow, but his vision of the best operational means to these ends is different. Whereas the executive director seeks to install and monitor grievance procedures that encourage members to speak up about unsatisfactory features of the organization (including its physicians), the medical director must protect his troops against demanding and overbearing patients claiming a long list of contractual rights to service. Whereas the administrator wants to be sure that the HMO gets the maximum return for each dollar spent on physicians' salaries, that physicians hold office hours when and as they should, and that they see a steady flow of patients, the head physician must insist that the proper organization and pace of medical work cannot be reduced to contractual stipulations but must be left largely to the judgment of the physicians themselves. Whereas the executive is determined to keep a careful watch, by means of comparative profiles and computer printouts of physicians' services, in order to identify and deter wasteful use of specialist and hospital care, the medical director must argue that the physician is the best judge of what is medically necessary and appropriate, and that the quality of care must take precedence over concern for cost.

To repeat, there is nothing generically new about these conflicting perspectives or about the trade-offs they entail; they are inherent in an HMO. The change lies in the organizational climate in which they arise and clash. In the formative years, the importance of internal unity in a hostile milieu leads each "side" to restrain its wish to limit the power of the other. The resulting compromises express the group's collective will in a Rousseauian sense; they are, in effect, laws each participant willingly gives to himself. In the larger, mature HMO, each side is less willing to concede the legitimacy of the concerns of the other; resolution takes the form of standard operating procedures worked out among representatives of competing sides, conscious of their interests. These routinized procedures amount to (to paraphrase an apt title) the governance of strangers.[18]

Managing the conflicting imperatives of growth in a manner consistent with early valued images of organizational character becomes over time a major organizational problem for an HMO, an ironic price of success. The early harmony of administrative and medical interests and functions grows jangled; the interests of the two sides of the organization bifurcate in distinct representative roles. The group's success comes then progressively to depend on the solution of a new, internal problem: that of reconciling medical and bureaucratic perspectives and functions in a stable framework. The executive director is wont to emphasize bureaucratic controls. As he sees it, both the opportunities and motives for indiscipline increase with organizational size, calling for an enhanced effort to exert formal control

18. Hugh Heclo, *A Government of Strangers* (Brookings Institution, 1977).

and discipline. The medical director, however, is likely to argue the importance of "socialization": the balancing of HMO imperatives should be translated into practical norms that physicians are led to adopt by persuasion and example. As the organization grows, efforts at bureaucratic control and professional socialization increase simultaneously. Some physicians accept this tension and remain as good team players. Others rebel and leave. Still others, remaining in the group for reasons of their own, act as if they accept group norms, or tolerate them grudgingly, or subvert them. If resistance is high, and the distinction between medical and administrative authority sharp, the group may, like the one studied by Freidson, find itself deficient in norms indispensable to its proper workings.[19] In the large and stable HMO, the proper mix of bureaucratic and professional controls and their impact on staff performance remain central management concerns, for the balancing act among the conflicting imperatives these controls embody remains a key determinant of the organization's health.

Three HMO Prototypes

Nothing in the nature of the problems posed by organizational growth and bureaucratic development in HMOs determines or generates preordained, logical, and correct managerial strategies. Managerial decisions are taken in the complex context of organizational character, itself a product of organizational structure, history, environment, ideology, and power.

The great diversity of organizational context and managerial strategies—and the great difficulty of making these strategies achieve successful outcomes—evident in the experiences of three so-called prototypes refutes any notion that prepaid group practices constitute a neat logical set, a universe of plans of demonstrated success whose skeletal features may be emulated and whose differences are of little practical moment. It will be argued here that the so-called prototypes differ extensively from one another in their structure, managerial experience, organizational stability, and other important ways; that these organizational differences, far from being incidental variations on common themes, are fundamental to the plans' character and performance; that two of the three plans are

19. Freidson, *Doctoring Together*.

perhaps better examples of how not to than of how to build stable and durable HMOs; and that the one plan that seems to offer a desirable management model probably cannot be emulated feasibly by most HMOs developed in the 1970s and 1980s.

The Group Health Association (GHA) of Washington, D.C., the Kaiser-Permanente Medical Care Program, which has its headquarters and most of its members in California, and the Health Insurance Plan (HIP) of Greater New York were founded within a decade of one another. The GHA was organized in 1937 when a group of employees of the Home Owners Loan Corporation, worried over the direct connection in the Depression between the high costs of illness and mortgage defaults and other indebtedness, sought a means of spreading risks and stabilizing medical costs. The result was the GHA—a consumer cooperative to finance and deliver medical services to its members.[20]

The Kaiser program had its roots in industrialist Henry J. Kaiser's search in the 1930s for a stable, efficient means of providing medical care to his employees in remote or underdoctored settings such as the deserts of Southern California, the Grand Coulee Dam site, and the California shipyards during World War II. Securing the agreement of an insurance company to prepay a few cents per day per worker for medical care and the agreement of Dr. Sidney Garfield to provide care in exchange for a salary thus secured, Kaiser offered prepaid health care to his workers. After the war ended, the plan maintained its facilities and opened its doors beyond the Kaiser community.[21]

Like GHA, the Health Insurance Plan owed its origins to the perceptions (in this case of the New York Municipal Credit Union) of the close connection between illness and debt. But whereas GHA was the response of a small band of federal employees to their common problems,[22] HIP arose from the determination of New York Mayor Fiorello H. La Guardia

20. For the origins of GHA see William A. MacColl, *Group Practice and Prepayment of Medical Care* (Washington: Public Affairs Press, 1966), pp. 25–29, 190–92; Frank C. Watters, "Group Health Association, Inc. of Washington, D.C.," *Group Practice*, vol. 10 (September 1961), pp. 661–74.

21. For the origins of Kaiser see Cecil C. Cutting, "Historical Development and Operating Concepts," in Somers, *Kaiser-Permanente Medical Care Program*, pp. 17–22; Greer Williams, "Kaiser: What Is It? How Does It Work? Why Does It Work?" *Modern Hospital*, vol. 116 (February 1971), pp. 69–71.

22. At the outset GHA membership was limited to Federal Home Loan Bank Board employees and those in "affiliated agencies," such as the Home Owners Loan Corporation, the source of loan money for the plan. At the end of 1937 the plan's board of trustees voted to extend services to employees of the Federal Reserve Board, the Farm Credit Administration, the Rural Electrification Administration, and the Social Security Board. The board also noted that "numerous other Federal employee groups and individuals had applied for membership, but unrestricted expansion was not contemplated." Watters, "Group Health Association, Inc.," p. 663.

to put in place a citywide health care plan for the city's public work force. Working with Dr. George Baehr, an early and enthusiastic experimenter with prepaid plans for the poor, La Guardia rejected proposals for both an indemnity approach in the fee-for-service sector and a compulsory health insurance approach and opted instead for a prepaid group plan as a compromise. The plan opened its doors in 1947.[23]

All three plans encountered instant, bitter, and prolonged opposition from the fee-for-service sector. Doctors were censured by, expelled from, or denied membership in local medical societies, ostracized by their colleagues, accused of unethical practices, and denied hospital privileges. By a combination of formal legal redress—of particular importance was a landmark suit in which the federal Department of Justice brought antitrust charges against the American Medical Association and the District of Columbia Medical Society for their anti-GHA efforts, a suit which was upheld by the Supreme Court in 1943, and which led to fines imposed on both defendants—and informal negotiations, the plans gradually achieved something between an uneasy truce and a lasting peace with their critics. Memories of the bitterness and invective of the early years did not soon fade, however.[24]

The plans' shared plight in combat against a hostile fee-for-service environment and their common purposive allegiance to prepaid group practice should not obscure their very different missions and ideological roots—missions and roots that would branch out over time in very different directions. The GHA, a product of the consumer cooperative movement, with the character of a "social welfare membership organization," was "consumer-oriented" and "democratically controlled."[25] The Kaiser plan was the corporate product of a leading industrialist with a personal interest in health care and a conviction that the managerial techniques of private industry could furnish a solution to health care problems and therewith a private antidote to socialized medicine.[26] The HIP was a bold politician's

23. For the origins of HIP see George Baehr, *A Report of the First Ten Years* (Health Insurance Plan of Greater New York, 1957), pp. 1–7; MacColl, *Group Practice and Prepayment*, pp. 32–36. For an early, extended discussion of the plan's origins and structure, with special emphasis on one Brooklyn group, see Robert E. Rothenberg and others, *Group Medicine and Health Insurance in Action* (Crown, 1949).

24. On organized medicine's opposition to the plans see MacColl, *Group Practice and Prepayment*, chap. 7; Raymond Munts, *Bargaining for Health: Labor Unions, Health Insurance, and Medical Care* (University of Wisconsin Press, 1967), pp. 163, 195, 293, 294, n. 18, 296, n. 32. The landmark court case was *American Medical Association* v. *United States*, 317 U.S. 519 (1943).

25. Frank Watters, "An Overview of the Group Health Association, Inc., Washington, D.C.," paper prepared for a Forum on Health Delivery Systems in Pennsylvania, sponsored by the Pennsylvania Department of Insurance, March 18, 1971, p. 6.

26. William McAllister, *Wall Street Journal*, April 26, 1971, writes that "Mr. Kaiser's mother died

means of doing something big and important for New York City's municipal employees.

These diverse missions were faithfully reflected in the plans' organizational structures. The GHA has always taken its cooperative spirit seriously. Its "basic structure was established for consumer sponsorship of an organization managed by a Board of Directors from its own membership, providing its own financing for both capital and operating income, and arranging with a medical staff organized as a group for the provision of services, with this staff on a salary rather than a fee-for-service basis."[27] All power and most major decisions rested with a nine-member board elected by and from the membership for staggered three-year terms. So set was the plan on self-government that for many years it appointed a medical director, but no executive director. Doctors, salaried employees of the plan, occupied a third level in the hierarchy, responsible directly to the medical director and ultimately to the board. The hand-to-mouth method of raising all revenue from the membership itself endured until the 1960s.[28] The plan was housed in one major rented center, supplemented by a suburban satellite clinic, until it built its own central facility in 1962. The board established early on that its formal powers would be exercised vigorously and fully. No managerial issue—premium levels and structures, building plans and locations, admission of new groups to the plan, disposition of individual grievances, staffing patterns—fell outside its purview and prerogatives or was immune from prolonged and often spirited debate.

By extreme contrast, the Kaiser plan has the character and structure of a large medical care corporation. Although it began as a partnership between the managerial authority of Henry Kaiser and the medical authority of Dr. Garfield, this arrangement did not long survive the strains of institutionalization and growth after the plan went public in 1945. Observers recall that both Kaiser and Garfield were strong, indeed imperious, personalities contending for control over what each considered his show. Unwilling to remain salaried employees under the direct authority

---

in his arms when he was 16 years old, and his father later went blind. Had they had better medical care, both would have lived longer, happier lives, he believed." He quotes Edgar F. Kaiser's recollection that "these events left my father with a desire he expressed many times: to do something so that people could afford the costs of medical and hospital care." See also Edgar F. Kaiser, "Henry J. Kaiser's Legacy," in Somers, *Kaiser-Permanente Medical Care Program*, p. 3; and the unsentimental chronicle in Judy Carnoy, Lee Coffee, and Linda Koo, "Corporate Medicine: The Kaiser Health Plan," *Health PAC Bulletin,* November 1973; reprinted in abridged form in David Kotelchuck, ed., *Prognosis Negative: Crisis in the Health Care System* (Vintage Books, 1976), pp. 366–67.

27. MacColl, *Group Practice and Prepayment*, pp. 28–29.
28. Ibid., p. 191.

of either of them, the physicians in the late 1940s staged a coup, insisting that they be permitted to establish a structure that would give them both powers of self-government and an arm's-length relationship with the plan. Thus S. R. Garfield and Associates was between 1946 and 1948 transformed into the Permanente medical groups, profit-making corporations (or partnerships or associations, depending on the laws of individual states) of physicians which set their own standards and terms of recruitment of their members and which worked under contract to the Kaiser plan.

Despite these changes, Henry Kaiser's "aggressive actions . . . filled the medical group leaders with grave concern about 'unilateral decisions,' " bringing the plan to the "verge of disruption." After a series of meetings in 1955, the physicians were reassured that they could "live, work and stick together" with management, and, their autonomy intact and confirmed, have worked contentedly with it ever since.[29] Some Kaiser executives grumble privately that the price of stability was allowing doctors to run the plan. Most, however, prefer to think of the arrangement as "duality of management."

The physician groups recruit their own members, explore their compatibility over a three-year probation period during which recruits have the status of salaried group employees, and then, if group and recruit prove mutually acceptable, elevate them to the status of partners. The groups negotiate annually with the plan a capitation payment (that is, a sum per member served that the group will be paid) and allocate these payments (as well as any bonus payments allotted to the group from savings during the year) among their members as they choose.

The two administrative arms of Kaiser's three-part structure are the Kaiser Foundation Health Plan and the Kaiser Foundation Hospitals. The former, "basically an administrative and contracting organization," enrolls members, maintains records, collects dues, markets the plan, and contracts with the medical groups for the provision of services. The hospitals corporation provides all facilities, for both hospital and outpatient care.[30] The two organizations have identical corporate officers and work closely together. The board of the Kaiser program, for years composed entirely of Kaiser Industries representatives, now includes some high-status "public" members, but few representatives drawn from the membership.[31]

29. The details and quotations in this paragraph come from Williams, "Kaiser," p. 71.

30. Scott Fleming, "Anatomy of the Kaiser-Permanente Program," in Somers, *Kaiser-Permanente Medical Care Program*, pp. 24, 25.

31. Directors of the Kaiser Foundation Health Plan, Inc., and Kaiser Foundation Hospitals are listed in the 1978 annual report of the Kaiser Foundation Medical Care Program, *Organized Health Care Delivery Systems: A Historical Perspective*.

Uninhibited by the cozy, small-group ethos of a consumer cooperative, Kaiser has expanded when and where the market for its brand of prepaid care seemed suitable. In 1945, the plan consisted of three regions— Northern and Southern California and Portland, Oregon. It entered Hawaii in 1958, and Cleveland and Denver in 1969. In 1979 Kaiser joined with the Prudential Insurance Company to launch a plan in Dallas, and in 1980 it took over the faltering Georgetown University Community Health Plan in Washington, D.C. Although the structure of its eight regions differs in some particulars, all share most of the features outlined above, and all come under the general sponsorship and governance of the Kaiser program headquarters in Oakland, California.

The structure of HIP directly reflects its mission to deliver services to hundreds of thousands of city employees throughout the five boroughs of New York City. To make services conveniently accessible, the plan (governed first by a medical director, and later by a president) originally contracted with willing and available medical groups around the city. The groups varied from well-established multimember group practices to two or three physicians gathered together on the spur of the moment to take advantage of HIP's offer. The plan began life in 1947 with 22 groups embracing 423 doctors.[32] Foreshadowing the Kaiser arrangements, the HIP groups were for-profit partnerships under contract to the Health Insurance Plan and reimbursed by capitation. Unlike Kaiser, however, HIP physicians owned or leased their own offices and equipment; used hospitals wherever they had admitting privileges, not plan-owned hospitals (there were none); and in most cases worked only part time for HIP, while carrying on fee-for-service practices, too. A medical control board of HIP and community physicians set quality and other standards and (in theory) monitored the groups' medical behavior. Finally, unlike the member-dominated GHA board of directors and the industry-dominated Kaiser board, the HIP board was composed of a multiplicity of eminent and interested parties but dominated by representatives of the plan's major source of membership, the city unions.

The three plans confronted growth and institutionalization with settled and very different organizational characters. In each case the formative experiences, mission, ideology, and—a living testament to all of these variables—the structure of the organization strongly predisposed its responses to the challenges of growth and constrained sharply the strategies managers could employ in meeting the challenges. Two of the plans—

32. Baehr, *Report of the First Ten Years*, p. 7.

GHA and HIP—have wrestled continually but unsuccessfully to compress the forces of change into time-honored organizational structures and norms. In Kaiser alone have organizational structures proved consistent with both stable and steady growth and effective management.

The Group Health Association

For GHA, the consumer cooperative "family," growth has been an unceasing organizational trauma. Policymaking based on internal democracy and consumer participation worked tolerably well for the small cohesive group of founders, providers, and members of the first generation but proved quite unequal to managing the larger and less cohesive membership of the plan in its second generation. To abandon or modify these policymaking modes is to abandon or modify the plan's organizational character; not to do so is to imperil its organizational health. The GHA has yet to achieve a successful choice between evils.

Beginning in 1937 with a mere 6,000 members, GHA grew slowly. Membership was gradually opened beyond the small core of founders to new federal agencies, but by the late 1940s, the plan had only 15,000 members, all of them federal employees. The nuclear family, extending very gradually by choice, looked on growth ambivalently. Some of the cooperative consumers, believers in prepaid group practice and proud of their organizational accomplishment, wanted GHA to become a prominent force in Washington's health care system and a widely respected national model. A plan of 15,000 members was obviously too small to achieve this recognition. On the other hand, new members meant new consumer elements, new interests and stresses within the board, overtaxed facilities—and therewith disturbing decisions about physical expansion, and therewith worrisome questions of how growth was to be financed—and the recruitment of new physicians, who might not fit in or identify with the cooperative spirit of the plan. Although it set a membership target of 30,000 to be achieved by the end of World War II, the forces of intimacy and cohesion won out in practice. The plan barely grew: in 1950 membership stood at 18,000, in 1958 at 23,000.[33] Meanwhile, costs rose steadily and had of course to be shared among the relatively small membership, a new program of health benefits for federal employees was imminent, and conventional health benefits in both the Washington public work force and the private sector were growing rapidly. By the late 1950s the plan

---

33. Watters, "Group Health Association, Inc.," pp. 666–67.

had to choose between entering the larger world of health care coverage or reconciling itself to the status of a small sect. A considerable body of opinion favored the latter course. As one former administrator recalled: "The plan grew slowly because it was like a club. The people in control didn't want it to grow. But it was clear by then that the plan had to grow in order to succeed financially. Some of the more farsighted board members sold growth as the only way to survival."

In 1959, after extensive debate and negotiation, the GHA agreed to admit its first nonfederal group, the D.C. Transit Workers, whose leadership then brought its entire 10,000 members into the plan.[34] The following year the new federal employees health benefits plan went into effect and brought 13,000 new members to GHA. Thus in a mere two years the plan's membership doubled, standing in 1960 at 46,000.

These sudden and dramatic expansions put severe strains on the plan. As go-slow proponents had feared, new consumer elements sought representation on the board, and the old ways of conducting business seemed increasingly unsuited to the organization's new scale. After much debate the plan decided to move from its original facilities to a newly constructed center of its own, an option that its new revenue sources finally enabled it to afford. No sooner was this decision made than debate turned to the possibility that GHA might build or buy its own hospital. But the new center was expensive and a new hospital would be more so. The plan was therefore obliged to give up its cooperative practice of relying on interest-free loans supplied by members and to enter the world of commercial credit. The board found itself increasingly dependent on the counsel of an executive director. Equally important, as new doctors were recruited to serve the (doubled) membership and as the first generation of plan physicians passed from the scene, the medical staff was increasingly composed of newcomers to whom the early days of struggle and exhilaration were beyond memory and to whom the consumer cooperative spirit was an abstraction.

The GHA had from the start been beset by recurring family quarrels: in the nature of the case a board that thought itself positively obligated to get involved in any and every issue and that was determined to reach decisions by means of internal democracy and majority rule was subject to sporadic and sometimes bitterly sustained divisions. Under these conditions, management was difficult. As a former GHA manager put it: "GHA is like a

34. For details of the negotiations see Munts, *Bargaining for Health,* pp. 184–88.

church. The governing body just can't resist interfering in management. In a church someone'll write a letter to the governing body complaining about the organist's music: he doesn't like the hymns she selected. An executive director must be like a clergyman and a politician mixed together—and find ways of getting the job done in spite of the board."

Over time this strategy ceased to work. By the early 1970s, when membership stood at about 75,000, family quarrels had hardened into feuds. Those discontented with the plan and of a mind to change it had a ready strategy: seek election to the board by running against the plan, by broadcasting its shortcomings to the membership at large with a promise that new representation would cure them. For example, in 1972 a would-be spokesman for "the younger members," citing a list of their hardships—pediatrics "is one of the hardest departments in GHA to get appointments in"; obstetrics and gynecology "is a disaster area"; "out-of-area benefits are terrible"—proposed as solution: "please mail your ballot *now*."[35] Recomposition of and deliberation within the board thus became the plan's main response to the stress of growth and generational change.

Members were not the only disconsolate members of the growing and increasingly fractious family. In the early years, physicians with personal and ideological allegiance to the plan had worked in comparative content-ment as employees of the consumer-run organization. The expanded ranks of newer, younger physicians in the late 1960s and early 1970s had very different ideas, however, and organizational structures that had proved satisfactory in the 1940s and 1950s were no longer so. Finding their status as salaried workers under the control of a lay board to be incompatible with their professional attainments and self-image, many members of the medical staff became resentful and determined to have either a larger direct say in running the plan or a degree of separateness and autonomy within it.

The first major innovation took place in the 1960s when the physicians, with full support from the plan's executive and medical directors, elected from their ranks a medical council to act as an in-house bargaining group to negotiate with the board over salaries and working conditions. For a time the arrangement worked well. "For many years," one physician recalled, "GHA physicians felt very much involved in running things. It was a matter of the trustees working things out amicably with a few strong

35. Letter from Jan M. Lodal to "Dear Group Health Association Member," March 8, 1972. (Emphasis in original.)

personalities among the doctors. But as the plan grew, times changed, and our troubles began."[36]

Trouble began in earnest in 1975 when the plan, trying to avoid large increases in premiums, but damaged by the inflation that followed the end of wage and price controls in the Ford administration, suffered large financial losses. To recoup, GHA laid off 15 percent of its staff, including several doctors, and began relying for hospitalization less on well-regarded George Washington University Hospital and more on Doctor's Hospital, a cheaper institution with a "mixed reputation."[37] This crisis greatly raised the physicians' job-consciousness and gave new life to an interest in a Kaiser-like corporate structure, a for-profit, self-governing corporation under contract to GHA. In particular, it was argued, a corporate structure would overcome the alienation and indifference that were said to prevail among the salaried medical staff. One physician decried "a 'we-they' outlook: We only work here. They—management—have the responsibility for handling the finances."[38] Another noted "a civil service, nine-to-five mentality. . . . The physician becomes very concerned with what he is supposed to do with his hours. . . . At GHA . . . the physician who was nasty to a patient was rewarded. He got home earlier. He had fewer appointments."[39] The proposal had the strong support of Louis Segadelli, the plan's executive director, who argued that professionals work better in a corporate setting than as "employees on a production line."[40] Its fate, however, rested entirely with the board.

The board was divided and by early 1977 it was clear that that year's election of three trustees would settle the fate of the corporation. The arguments in its favor were advanced, of course, but the opposition forces countered with a variety of angry rejoinders. One trustee declared: "The only thing I could see the doctors getting from incorporation was profit. . . . They wanted us to give them a profit-making present of more than 100,000 patients."[41] Another, "unalterably opposed to abdicating the idea of a member-owned and operated organization," found it "galling" that physicians "would take over the prerogative of hiring and firing staff."[42] Still another feared that the corporation "might whittle away at

36. Richard L. Peck, "The H.M.O. That Drove Doctors to Strike," *Medical Economics,* vol. 55 (September 18, 1978), p. 143.

37. Lawrence Meyer, *Washington Post,* January 2, 1978.

38. Peck, "The H.M.O. That Drove Doctors to Strike," p. 146.

39. Meyer, *Washington Post,* January 2, 1978.

40. Lawrence Meyer, *Washington Post,* March 24, 1977.

41. Peck, "The H.M.O. That Drove Doctors to Strike," p. 146.

42. Meyer, *Washington Post,* March 24, 1977.

the scope of services offered to members," and noted, "Some of us are not totally impressed with the way corporate medicine has operated in other parts of the country."[43] As it happened, the anticorporation forces emerged from the balloting with a one-vote majority and promptly killed the proposal. Segadelli and about a dozen physicians then tendered their resignations.

Left with neither a corporation nor the older medical council (it had been disbanded in 1976 when the National Labor Relations Board suggested that it was probably an illegal form of company union), the physicians turned to a third mechanism. Late in 1977 more than half of the plan's doctors won NLRB recognition as a union. Early in 1978 they began difficult bargaining with the board over malpractice coverage, working hours, and their right to engage in medical practices outside GHA. Spring arrived with no progress and on April 14 the unionists voted overwhelmingly to strike. Although the plan managed to muddle through with the services of about one-third of the staff—thirty physicians who did not belong to the union—the twelve-day walkout attracted national attention to "the H.M.O. that drove doctors to strike"[44] and did little to promote harmony and fellow-feeling among the plan's members, providers, and administrators.

In May a second strike was barely averted and the two sides settled down to an uneasy truce. The next months then brought additional problems. A nurses' strike (which the physicians' union had pledged to honor) was avoided at the eleventh hour. In 1979 Doctor's Hospital suddenly went bankrupt, leaving GHA to make new and generally more expensive inpatient arrangements. By the end of 1979 the plan was rumored to be heavily in the red, its membership, once expected to rise to 300,000 by 1982,[45] stagnant at about one-third that number.

Some close observers shared the view of a GHA physician planning to leave in 1978 that "G.H.A. will be finished in three to five years."[46] Few doubted that anything less than "massive changes"[47] would allow the plan to recover from its ills. Although opinions differed on what changes ought to be made, many weary veterans agreed that the fundamental flaw lay in the plan's organizational structure, in the anachronistic arrangements that

---

43. Ibid.
44. This of course is the title of Peck's article.
45. *Health Maintenance Organizations,* Hearings before the Subcommittee on Public Health and Environment of the House Committee on Interstate and Foreign Commerce, 92 Cong. 2 sess. (GPO, 1972), pt. 1, p. 219.
46. Peck, "The H.M.O. That Drove Doctors to Strike," p. 160.
47. A former board member and president quoted in Meyer, *Washington Post,* January 2, 1978.

empowered a nine-man, member-selected board to run the show for 110,000 members in 1979 as its predecessors had for 10,000 in the early 1940s. So insistent and active a board was widely thought to preclude both the institutionalization of strong executive leadership and the design of satisfactory arrangements for the medical staff.[48]

Former executive director Segadelli conjectured that such improvisations as a joint committee of trustees and doctors to give the doctors more voice would not solve the basic problem, which he termed "a bad setup." He observed that "The doctors still have no real say on the issues that produced the tensions—budget, space allotment, and enrollment, for example—because these are still the province of the board. The union has become the only forum the doctors have."[49]

To an executive of another highly successful HMO prototype, the GHA setup is a wasted opportunity: "In a market like Washington, with all those federal employees, GHA should have a million members. Instead they have 100,000. The reason is simple: bad management. The board keeps interfering with the administration."

The GHA has continued to wrestle with organizational changes in a structure that had proved ill adapted to the needs of a large plan in the 1970s but which retained powerful ideological support among vocal consumer activists who self-selected themselves into the electoral process and onto the board. Late in 1979, the board was considering a change in the bylaws to allow the claims committee rather than the board itself to make final disposition of members' questions about reimbursement for out-of-plan services. It was trying to write new language to clarify the respective powers of the board and the executive director. It even contemplated allowing the executive director to appoint the medical director (a prerogative it had heretofore reserved for itself) and an assistant executive director (on the appointment of whom the bylaws were unclear).[50] Whether these efforts gradually to shift power from the board to newly strengthened managerial structures will bear fruit remains to be seen. Whether such steps, if taken, can rescue the plan from its current difficulties is entirely unclear.

48. Ibid. Said one former board member: "The board ought to show more confidence in its executive director, whoever that is. . . . If they don't like what the executive director is doing in a basic sense, they ought to get a new one. If they do like what he is doing, they ought not to nitpick every little individual managerial and administrative decision that he takes. The board had a tendency to do that. And it still does." The resulting "fragmented management . . . upsets the physicians as well as upsetting management, it leads to management problems—so they're all tied together."
49. Peck, "The H.M.O. That Drove Doctors to Strike," p. 160.
50. GHA News, vol. 42 (September–October 1979), pp. 1–2.

The Health Insurance Plan of Greater New York

For the Health Insurance Plan, growth and development posed a set of problems very different from, but no less severe than, those facing GHA. Whereas GHA's mission was to provide medical care for a small cooperative band of federal employees in a few agencies, HIP's mission was to care for as much of the New York City public work force as chose to enroll. Whereas GHA started small and grew slowly, HIP started big and quickly got bigger. Whereas GHA employed a small staff of salaried physicians working in a central facility, the logistics of moving rapidly and with less than $1 million in start-up capital to establish a citywide medical-care system obliged HIP to identify and affiliate with willing physicians, most of them practicing in their own offices and only part time for HIP, throughout the five boroughs. Two years after it opened its doors, HIP served about 200,000 members with about 700 doctors in 26 medical groups.[51] The physicians were a haphazard collection of the ideologically committed and returning servicemen in search of a stable practice and a stable source of income while they built up their own practices.[52] Because HIP could afford neither its own hospitals nor its own outpatient medical centers, the medical groups were for-profit partnerships that supplied their own offices and facilities and made hospitalization arrangements at preferred and convenient hospitals or, as was often the case at the outset, at those hospitals willing to grant admitting privileges to a HIP physician. The HIP marketed and administered the plan and paid the medical groups a capitation sum based on the number of members they served. It was understood by both plan and physicians that because HIP could not afford capitation rates adequate to support many physicians full time, a part-time

51. George Baehr, "Introduction," in Rothenberg and others, *Group Medicine and Health Insurance in Action*, p. xxii.

52. Rothenberg and others, *Group Medicine and Health Insurance in Action*, chap. 1; MacColl, *Group Practice and Prepayment*, p. 35. The medical director of HIP's Yorkville medical group and chairman of the HIP medical control board recalled: "During the three years I was in the army in World War II I was assigned as a chest physician to a large army hospital, an 1800 bed hospital, which was mostly for chest disease. But we had a full complement of all specialists. . . . We had top-notch men from all over the country. . . . I had the best medical experience of my life. When I got out of the army and went into solo practice I found myself completely away from the group practice experience I had in the army hospital. There we discussed cases, worked as a team, had conferences, and brought all of our experiences together to help the patient. It was real group practice and very exciting. I missed that excitement in my solo practice. One day I noticed in the Times that Mayor LaGuardia and Dr. Baehr were organizing HIP and they said they were welcoming physicians into HIP. I said this was great. And that's how I got into HIP." Dr. Hyman Bass, quoted in Health Insurance Plan of Greater New York, *HIP: The Health Plan New Yorkers Created for New Yorkers* [1976], p. 6.

commitment to HIP would be the norm. Moreover, uncertain of the costs and implications of placing itself at financial risk for its members' hospital care, HIP chose to require that members make their own arrangements (paid in part by city financial contributions) for hospital coverage. The HIP offered both inpatient and outpatient medical *services*, but the member was perfectly free to take his Blue Cross or other benefits and go outside the system for hospital care should he wish to do so.

Explosive growth in HIP's first decade strained these helter-skelter arrangements. By 1957, when HIP served 500,000 members with more than 1,000 physicians dispersed among 32 groups,[53] the structural flaws persisting from the formative years had grown increasingly clear and worrisome to member and administrator alike. The medical groups had uneven levels of commitment and quality, and individual physicians within them were still more variable. Some physicians retained the ideological and professional motivations of the early years, but as time passed and physician ranks expanded, these individuals, probably always a distinct minority, grew proportionately fewer. For many physicians, administrators and members remarked despondently, HIP was a hobby, a sop to charity medicine, a means of assuring a stable income while launching a private practice, an attractive side income, or something untaxing to do while easing into retirement. Rumors of second-class care made their way along various grapevines. A familiar anecdote told of physicians who insisted that HIP patients sit in their private waiting rooms until all fee-for-service patients had been seen, but who agreed to move the HIP enrollees ahead in the queue in exchange for a fee of, say, ten dollars.

No shrinking violets, HIP enrollees made their grievances known to their union representatives, who in turn made clear their dissatisfaction to the plan's board and executives. But although the president and the Medical Control Board might cajole, implore, plan, and promise, HIP's severely undercentralized structure gave them little bargaining leverage with the medical groups. The plan was not the primary source of most of its physicians' incomes and it owned neither the office facilities nor the hospitals in which most of them practiced. If the central administration made life unpleasant for them, individual physicians, and for that matter whole groups, risked little by withdrawing their affiliation. In the succinct words of one administrator: "HIP was simply not in the driver's seat." Moreover, as member complaints about long waits for appointments,

<hr/>

53. Baehr, *Report of the First Ten Years*, pp. 5, 7.

second-class treatment, and dingy facilities increased, city union officials grew ever less willing to support premium increases, thereby reducing both the plan's overall financial strength and the amounts it could pay its physicians. The result was a vicious circle of member disaffection and physician detachment.

By the early 1960s these strains threatened to become critical. Recognizing the high degree of negotiating skill required of administrators who would find terms of trade among the unions, the doctors, the city, the state, and other major interests with a hand in the plan's finances, the board offered the presidency to James Brindle, director of the United Auto Workers' social security department for ten years, and an important figure in establishing a plan in Detroit. Brindle and his vice-president, Martin Cohen, another UAW official with long experience in union health plans and prepaid group practice, saw clearly the severity of HIP's congenital defects and soon devised a strategy to put the central administration more squarely in the driver's seat. First, they would increase the number of full-time HIP physicians (about 20 percent of the total in the early 1960s) to overcome the transparent problem of divided loyalties. Second, because a large number of mostly small medical groups was conducive both to indifferent medicine and to making HIP a hobby, they would regionalize the plan by consolidating small groups into a few large ones, ideally one for each of the five boroughs. Third, the plan would acquire its own hospitals wherever possible. If full-time physicians practiced in a few centers owned by HIP and in HIP hospitals, the providers' commitment to, and dependence on, the plan would of course be greatly increased, and this in turn would enhance the administration's bargaining power.

Throughout a stormy ten-year tenure Brindle and Cohen pursued these goals with little success. Although a few medical groups were receptive to the idea of working full time for HIP, most, frightened and offended by the prospect of moving from their familiar private offices to huge HIP-owned centers, had no intention of trading the comfort of a limited commitment to and dependence on HIP for a career commitment and dependence. By means of negotiation, persuasion, and financial incentives—notably a bonus of several thousand dollars paid by HIP to a medical group for each new full-timer the group hired—Brindle and Cohen pursued their strategy, but by the early 1970s full-timers had risen only to about 30 percent of the total, and the number of groups had fallen only from about 32 to 28. Clearly, attainment of these goals waited on the death or retirement of a generation of HIP physicians content with their accustomed operations and prepared to fight to defend them.

In 1968 HIP did acquire a hospital for its (newly merged) La Guardia medical group in Queens, but this proved to be a unique success. The major obstacle to purchasing HIP hospitals was less the doctors than the unions. Buying hospitals meant raising large sums of money, which meant increasing premiums, which meant greater union contributions to HIP, which meant harder collective bargaining with the financially strapped government of New York City. The unions resisted and, as spokesmen for the plan's major constituency, had the power to prevail. There ensued a frustrating Alphonse-Gaston routine. As one participant recalled: "The unions were constantly unwilling to give us the money to fix the plan. They'd always say, 'Fix up the plan and then we'll give you the money.' And we'd always say, 'Well, Goddamnit, if you want the plan fixed, then you'll have to give us the money to fix it.' And it would go on like this, back and forth." In short, the fixing strategy was blocked by a coalition of conservative physicians opposed to full-time HIP practice and regionalization and city unions opposed to the cost increases required to buy HIP hospitals. The same extensive decentralization of managerial power that had caused the plan's problems now blocked solutions to them.

By the early 1970s antagonisms had multiplied, the plan's membership was beginning to drop (from almost 800,000 at the end of the 1960s to 750,000 in 1972), and the financial situation was more ominous than ever. In a final burst of negotiating energy Brindle and Cohen secured what they took to be a union commitment to premium increases, which would have paved the way for what one former HIP official described as "fairly rapid and major structural change," and went to the state insurance commissioner in 1972 seeking approval for a rate increase of 36 percent. To their surprise and chagrin the request was publicly and hotly opposed by a coalition of conservative doctors and city unions; the latter made it clear that if the increase were approved, they might have no choice but to take their business elsewhere.[54] The state approved a 29 percent increase, but the city would go no higher than 15 percent. This decision put an unmistakable period to the long-negotiated reforms. Repudiated, Brindle

54. According to Harry Schwartz, *New York Times,* April 30, 1972, a spokesman for many of the HIP medical groups made it clear in testimony and in private comments that "many HIP doctors fear the changes are really a power play intended ultimately to reduce physicians to salaried employees who must do as they are told by HIP administrators," and that the 36 percent increase, if adopted, "would drive away a large fraction of HIP members." New York City Personnel Director Harry L. Bronstein was said to have assailed HIP's description of the proposed changes as "distressingly vague," to have accused HIP of failing adequately to consult with the city, "its major contractor," to have asserted that "the regionalization program by itself does not appear to offer any substantial improvement in services to city subscribers," to have demanded an "independent medical audit system" to evaluate HIP, and to have issued an "implied threat" that the city might take its business elsewhere if the rate increase was approved.

and Cohen resigned amidst much acrimony, and the plan's presidency was entrusted to the interim superintendence of its legal counsel while the search for new leadership began.

As the 1970s proceeded the plan's problems worsened. Critics charged that HIP was living on the very edge of bankruptcy, sustained financially only by Medicaid contracts, in exchange for which it returned care alleged to be "scandalous."[55] Angry consumers insisted on changes both in their formal representation in the plan's management and in the delivery of services. The former would probably antagonize physicians ("Physicians won't accept the idea of consumers in decision-making roles on clinical matters," Brindle argued shortly before his resignation) and the latter— for example, a 24-hour emergency "drop-in" service in East Harlem, which the plan established after "about 40 angry adults and children affiliated with the Committee for Accountability stormed uninvited into a directors' meeting" in October 1971—would surely cost money.[56] The plan addressed representational demands by establishing new consumer councils and service demands by creating several new programs, but the management remained as enfeebled as ever to guide the plan between the demands of insistent members and the constraints of refractory contributors.

By 1974, enrollment stood stagnant at about 760,000. The aging population, unreplenished by younger, healthier members, generated rising utilization rates and with them, of course, rising costs. In 1974–75 HIP, like GHA, felt the force of rapid increases in medical costs following the removal of federal wage and price controls. Unlike GHA, however, HIP's major bargaining partners, the city unions and city government, fell victim to a severe financial crisis of their own, ending hopes of a major rate increase. (Finally in 1976 the plan won a small 12 percent increase.)[57] The unhappy coincidence of rising costs and declining resources with which to meet them in the middle and late 1970s aggravated still more severely HIP's congenital defects. As one HIP official, interviewed in 1979, explained:

> We're facing higher utilization. If the person's not turned off by HIP, and knows it's advertised as having no out-of-pocket costs, and has seen his wage increases held down, he'll be looking for health benefits, so they're taking advantage in terms of greater utilization. It's sort of a social thing, and this goes along with the naturally higher utilization of our aging membership. We have

55. Howard Levy and Oliver Fein, "Crippled HIP," *Health PAC Bulletin*, October 1972, pp. 15–22, especially p. 16.

56. Grace Lichtenstein, *New York Times*, February 20, 1972.

57. *HIP: The Health Plan New Yorkers Created for New Yorkers*, p. 1.

trouble providing for it, because we have a problem with doctors. As a PGP our salaries tend to be lower, especially when you take account of inflation, so we have lots of trouble attracting good doctors and then we have trouble keeping them. And this is the nitty-gritty, because the doctor controls matters. That's our central problem now. We offer family doctors a decent basic salary plus malpractice insurance and a chance to become a shareholder, with a portion of the group's profits, after two years. But this still comes to less than fee-for-service. And our specialist pay is way below the six-figure incomes possible in fee-for-service. So it's hard to keep them. So we have a lot of doctors in their late fifties and sixties—the shareholders—and lots in their early thirties—because of the economic climate. They're out of medical school and it's all there—malpractice, office, salary, and so on. So they come, get their feet wet for two years or so, and then leave. This trend has dramatically increased in the last few years and we can't stop it. And the main area of turnover is the family physicians, the main providers, the funnel for referrals, and all the rest. With the turnover here, patients are wandering around without an identity; they've had four or five of these family doctors in the last few years, and they float to the soonest available doctor, which upsets continuity. It also leads to greater use of the emergency room, because they can't get the care they want in the group centers.

In 1978, after a prolonged search for a new president to take over what was widely termed the "mess at HIP," the board announced the appointment of Robert Biblo, a highly respected executive with long experience in prepaid group plans in Detroit, Cleveland, and Boston. Biblo set about pursuing the goals that Brindle and Cohen had established almost two decades earlier and added some of his own. One was to promote HIP in suburban and private-sector markets in order to bring in younger members. The HIP qualified to be offered by major employers under the state's dual choice law and also sought the "good housekeeping seal of approval" accompanying federal qualification. To meet the federal requirement that qualified HMOs be at risk for hospitalization, it created an option called HIP-HMO, in which it severed its relation with Blue Cross. That for thirty years Blue Cross, not HIP, enjoyed the savings from HIP's lower inpatient rates had struck many plan officials and observers all along as an absurdity. As a practical matter, however, union leaders were said to fear the wrath of their constituents if they should agree to end the member's right to seek hospital care outside the HIP system—a right that HIP's accumulating misfortunes only made more valuable. The compromise adopted allowed existing members and groups to retain their accustomed flexible arrangements, but offered only the HIP-HMO option to new, principally suburban and private sector groups. Medicaid members had yet a third, separate contract.

It is too soon to know whether these measures will succeed in transforming HIP's organizational structure and in restoring its strength. It seems probable, however, that HIP, like GHA, has reached a crisis: unlikely simply to malinger longer, it will either get gradually healthier or will become severely, perhaps critically, ill.

The Kaiser Program

Of the three prototypes examined here, only the Kaiser-Permanente Medical Care Program has stood up well under the strains of growth and institutionalization. This accomplishment is the more remarkable for the unique scale of its growth and of its bureaucracy. Its complex division of labor among plan, hospitals, and medical groups serves almost four million members at hundreds of sites in eight regions of the United States.[58] No other HMO begins to approach this size.

A thorough explanation of the Kaiser-Permanente success awaits an intensive, detailed organizational study by a scholar with both the first-hand information of an insider and the objective detachment of a critic. For the modest purposes of this chapter it suffices to highlight factors of clear importance with respect to which Kaiser has differed from GHA and HIP. Three stand out.

First, whereas GHA and HIP have struggled for decades to confine the forces of growth and generational change within their original organizational frameworks and have suffered especially from their inability to make these frameworks embrace satisfactory arrangements for physicians, Kaiser underwent early a major organizational transformation that met the needs of the physicians and has, on the whole, served the plan exceedingly well. As long as the plan appeared to be a temporary expedient for serving Kaiser employees, physicians were willing to tolerate the status of salaried employees, but when it was decided that the plan would stay in existence and recruit beyond those ranks, the physicians grew restive. Fearful of being caught between two imposing personalities, they insisted, in the course of exchanges that generated more than "considerable heat,"[59]

58. Like HIP's, Kaiser's membership grew rapidly. By 1955 the Northern California region had just over 300,000 members, Southern California served almost 200,000, and Oregon served 23,000. Somers, *Kaiser-Permanente Medical Care Program,* p. 197. As of mid-1980, Kaiser's Northern California enrollment was 1,672,154, Southern California 1,565,634, Oregon 233,600, Hawaii 116,022, Cleveland 122,151, Denver 113,256, and its total enrollment 3,822,817. U.S. Department of Health and Human Services, Office of Health Maintenance Organizations, *National HMO Census of Prepaid Plans, June 30, 1980,* DHHS Publication no. (PHS) 80-50159 (HHS, 1980), table 26, pp. 19, 20, 21, 29. Kaiser created its seventh region by taking over the Georgetown University Community Health Plan in Washington, D.C., in August 1980. Dallas became the eighth region in March 1982.
59. This decorous phrase is used by Cutting, "Historical Development and Operating Concepts," p. 19.

on separateness (from the Kaiser plan itself) and on incorporating as a self-governing, profit-sharing group of partners, who would define their own leadership and recruitment arrangements and would negotiate capitation rates with the plan, with which they contracted. The outcome of this rebellion was Kaiser's highly prized "duality of management."

Second, as a result of this transformation, the structural relations between Permanente physicians and the Kaiser plan differ greatly from those at GHA, where salaried physicians sought to emulate the Kaiser approach in the mid-1970s but were overruled by the plan's board. Kaiser's approach differs too from that of HIP, where the physicians are also members of medical partnerships under contract to the plan, in two vital respects. Unlike HIP, Kaiser has generally insisted that Permanente physicians work full time for the plan, with no fee-for-service practices on the side; it has thus overcome HIP's perpetual problem of divided loyalties. (At the launching of its Hawaiian region, Kaiser tried to rely on part-time physicians and, finding the experiment unsatisfactory, soon moved to the full-timers who are, with the exception of some physicians serving drop-in clinics at various sites, its norm.)[60] And the plan has succeeded in providing the Permanente physicians a full-time Kaiser career by retaining its own control over medical centers, hospitals, and other facilities. (The principal exception is the Denver region, which had an excess of beds when Kaiser entered it and in which Kaiser relies on community hospitals.)[61] The HIP has generally exercised no such control, in good part because it could not afford its own centers and hospitals. Kaiser commitments and funding and the advantage of the Kaiser name and managerial reputation when the plan sought commercial loans gave the plan a distinctive, indeed unique, advantage in its early years.[62] Thus secured, the plan's reputation for excellent management and performance—exemplified by its AA Standard and Poor rating, unusual among nonprofit organizations—continued to attract long-term financing.

60. National Advisory Commission on Health Manpower, *Report* (GPO, 1967), vol. 2, app. 4: *The Kaiser Foundation Medical Care Program*, p. 206.

61. Wilbur L. Reimers, "The Denver Program: Development of a Kaiser-Permanente Program from Scratch," in Somers, *Kaiser-Permanente Medical Care Program*, p. 172. Neither do the Kaiser HMOs in Dallas and Washington, D.C., own hospitals.

62. See Carnoy, Coffee, and Koo, "Corporate Medicine," pp. 368–69. It has been argued that "the Kaiser operation, while self-sustaining, owes much of its capital expansion success to measures not available to other groups." Judith M. Carnoy argues that much of the money for capital expansion has come from Kaiser Family Foundation funds, the income of which derives in large part from ownership of stock of various Kaiser industries. "Kaiser: You Pay Your Money and You Take Your Chances," *Ramparts*, vol. 9 (November 1970), pp. 28–31; cited in John M. Glasgow, "Prepaid Group Practice as a National Health Policy: Problems and Perspectives," *Inquiry*, vol. 9 (March 1972), pp. 3–15. As Glasgow notes (p. 10), "Obviously, access to long-term, low cost loans and/or outright gifts have significant implications for plan expense and for subscriber premiums."

Although it is often said that Kaiser's ownership of its hospitals is a very important element in its financial success, the degree to which ownership, as distinct from the inpatient economies customary in well-run HMOs, is a source of savings is disputed. Perhaps more important than the economic are the political and organizational consequences of ownership, that is, the ways in which these structural arrangements have helped define the plan's organizational character and have promoted a shared organizational outlook. Although the hospitals "belong" to Kaiser Foundation Hospitals, whose officers and directors also manage the Kaiser Health Plan, they are staffed and used by the Permanente physicians. The service chiefs and department heads of the medical groups are also the chiefs and heads of the hospitals. This arrangement embodies both specialization and interdependence among the three units, and thereby makes coordination—that is, negotiations between "sides" aimed at achieving those mutually acceptable agreements without which neither could get on with its work—plainly necessary. The need for close operational coordination is as evident to the physicians as it is to the administrators. In-patient economies are a major source of Kaiser's savings—and therefore of funds for expansion, modernization, premium stability—and of higher capitation payments and physician bonuses. Inefficiencies in hospital planning and use redound directly and tangibly to both sides and both sides know it.[63]

From this acutely perceived interdependence of specialized partners has grown a complex set of institutional structures, procedures, and norms that pervade the Kaiser program and that differ greatly from those of GHA and HIP. From the central headquarters in Oakland to the leadership of the regions to the management of individual centers, administrators and medical directors work closely together, and take great pride in doing so. A capacity for reasonable negotiation is highly valued, indeed is thought to be as essential a quality in an administrator or physician-manager as managerial or medical expertise. Administrators and physicians unwilling to work together in this way are generally not recruited. If they should be recruited, they tend not to stay. If they do stay, they tend not to rise. Both the program's norms and its personnel patterns honor and reward administrative and medical managers with an appreciation of the importance of one another's roles and a capacity for negotiation and compromise. And the program's specialized yet interdependent structure tests and refines these skills in daily operations.

63. See Herman Weiner, "Organization and Responsibilities," in Somers, *Kaiser-Permanente Medical Care Program*, pp. 92–93.

The famous reasonableness and cohesion of relations between administrators and physicians in the Kaiser plans are a product neither of a sophisticated socialization process alone nor of mere good fortune. The pattern has been sustained and encouraged by early strategic choices that began by defining formal organizational structures and gradually nourished within these structures a strong organizational character.

Kaiser's successful functional division of labor has lent itself well to the search for a suitable areal structure. Avoiding both the overcentralization of GHA and the undercentralization of HIP, the structure of the Kaiser plans may be with equal accuracy described as both strongly decentralized[64] and unified.[65] This effective synthesis of decentralization and centralization has proved highly conducive to extensive but stable growth. Unlike GHA, for which growth has been traumatic, and HIP, which grew only by weakening further its already feeble central controls, Kaiser transposed its organizational arrangements, mutatis mutandis, to many new regions and markets. Extending the structure to dozens of individual centers within regions, it has reached out to growing suburban population centers and thence to younger populations to supplement its aging first generation of members. Moreover, individual centers offset somewhat the inevitable impersonality of service in the giant Kaiser system.[66] As the contrast with GHA and HIP makes clear, Kaiser's growth is not simply the result of its ability to offer a good product. It is also a result of its successful solution to the problems of organizational, and therefore managerial, structure.

Third, Kaiser management has benefited from its stubborn unwillingness to open its boards of directors to elements that might paralyze or bully management. Whereas GHA has always been constrained by the internal democratic norms of the consumer cooperative movement, norms that favor dominance of the organization by small bands of atypically interested and active elites with ideologies and axes of their own to grind,[67] and HIP by the "interest group liberalism"[68] incorporated in its board, the Kaiser

64. Fleming, "Anatomy of the Kaiser-Permanente Program," p. 32.

65. James A. Vohs and others, "Capital Requirements and Capital Financing in a Hospital-Based Group Practice Prepayment Plan," paper prepared for Conference on Capital Financing for Health Facilities, University of Pittsburgh, November 1976, p. 19.

66. Weiner, "Organization and Responsibilities," p. 94.

67. The vigor of the plan's member participation may be gauged from the observation in a GHA publication of 1971 that the board president's plea to "Get involved!" had not fallen "on deaf ears." The 1971 GHA annual meeting and institute had attracted a whopping 242 of the plan's roughly 75,000 members, said to be quite an increase over the 150 attendees of the previous year. GHA News, vol. 34 (June 1971), p. 2.

68. The term is taken from Theodore J. Lowi, The End of Liberalism (Norton, 1969), p. 71.

program has been above all a business enterprise. Henry Kaiser's attitude was that "you don't ask your corner grocer to share his ownership with people who buy at the store."[69] Resisting the view that representation on the board is indispensable to member satisfaction, the plans have pointed to the dual choice arrangements on which they insist for any group joining them and to the consequent right of any dissatisfied member to take his business elsewhere at regular intervals. The plan's central board of directors was for many years composed entirely of representatives of Kaiser Industries and interests. When it was finally opened up in the late 1960s, the new directors were a former medical school dean, the president of Radcliffe College, an attorney, and Art Linkletter, an "entertainer and businessman."[70]

Since becoming federally qualified in 1977, the Kaiser groups have expanded membership representation on their boards of directors, but no union representatives sit on the central board. Some unions have of course objected strongly to this rebuff, complaining that the plan is in this respect "still an overgrown company medical care program," recommending that Kaiser emulate the HIP board which "does represent the community in a broad sense," and contrasting the "candid and articulate public discussion of problems and goals by HIP spokesmen" with "the rather icy public relations of Kaiser."[71] At times unions have organized commissions and task forces to investigate alternatives to their heavy involvement in the Kaiser plans. The begrudging conclusion of these inquiries, however, has generally been that although Kaiser is far from perfect, it is clearly the best option the unions have or are likely to have available.[72] Few dispassionate students of the evolution of GHA and HIP will be inclined to deny that, unprogressive though it may seem, the Kaiser position, that an HMO should be run as a business and managed by men skilled and trained at management, has served the plan and its members well.

Conclusion: Prototypes and Management

The management of health maintenance organizations, far from being one property among others in a self-regulating organization that runs itself according to external and internal economic laws, is a highly fragile and

69. Quoted in Carnoy, Coffee, and Koo, "Corporate Medicine," p. 380.
70. Arthur Weissman and Richard Anderson, "Characteristics of Health Plan Membership," in Somers, *Kaiser-Permanente Medical Care Program,* p. 43.
71. Munts, *Bargaining for Health,* pp. 191, 196.
72. Ibid., p. 195. Asked in 1971 why unions, upset over lack of voice in Kaiser decisionmaking, do

thoroughly political process—one that can become more, not less, difficult over time. In two of the three major HMO prototypes reviewed here, organizational growth, bureaucratic development, and generational change have taxed the groups to the verge of disintegration. Yet management, trapped between conflict and inertia, has been powerless to set matters right. It would be cheerful (at least for new plans) to argue that these problems could have been averted or solved by more prescient, timely, and forceful strategic choices. The central point of this chapter, however, is that managerial choice in these HMOs is not invested solely in the hands of economic-minded managers; instead it is embodied in bits and pieces of highly durable and highly valued, yet very confining and sometimes dysfunctional, organizational structures, which both reflect and reinforce distinct organizational characters. Under the pressure of growth and generational change, these organizational characters may prove to be at once much in need of and highly resistant to renewal and transformation.

None of these plans has lacked perceptive management. In both GHA and HIP, managers have at times diagnosed the plans' problems astutely and worked aggressively to solve them. In the mid-1970s, for example, GHA's executive director Segadelli recognized the merits of the physicians' incorporation proposal. In HIP, Brindle and Cohen worked for years for a regionalized, hospital-based structure employing full-time physicians. In both cases the managers were effectively checked by internal organizational politics—in GHA by the board and in HIP by a coalition of unions and doctors—that is, by nonmanagerial actors whose power rested on enduring structural features of the organization which in turn reflected the organization's original mission, ideology, and formative experiences. Workable managerial structures, problem-solving powers, and choices presupposed organizational changes that lay beyond the powers of management itself to effect. Kaiser alone had the foresight and good luck to begin life with organizational arrangements—full-time physicians, Kaiser-owned facilities, and a management-oriented board, in particular—that proved to be both workable in themselves and supportive of organizational change where and when it turned out most to be needed—in the relationship between the physicians and the plan when the plan began to grow large. In this sense, Kaiser is indeed a desirable prototype. But GHA and HIP could have followed the Kaiser example only on pain of abandoning major elements of their organizational identities.

---

not simply walk out, Thomas G. Moore, executive director of the California Council for Health Plan Alternatives, replied: "We have no place to go. . . . What are we going to do? Throw our people out on the street?" Quoted in McAllister, *Wall Street Journal*, April 26, 1976.

Younger, growing plans today are also likely to face the difficulties of compressing the forces of organizational growth and generational change into cohesive structures that were adopted in the early years of smallness, purposive commitment, and struggle for survival. They too will probably face painful choices between continuing down the road to disintegration as new forces clash with old structures and ways and transforming their organizational arrangements in ways that require some abandonment of cherished character and values. They too will probably not escape the hard choice between management structures and powers adequate to effect a timely transformation and structures and powers strong enough only to extend managers a forum from which to argue for changes they cannot implement.

It is not likely that many plans founded in the 1970s and 1980s will find it possible to emulate Kaiser, the one prototype that can be judged a clear managerial success. Industrial sponsorship of HMOs is comparatively rare, and rarer still are firms with the commitment to launch a plan, endow it with facilities, help it secure generous financing, transfer top managerial talent from firm to plan, retain a keen proprietary interest in it, and insist against consumer, union, and other voices that the plan shall be run as a business and by a firm-dominated board of directors. Although some of the new HMOs own their office facilities, few own their hospitals, and few can now support a full-time complement of physicians on HMO business alone. Few, therefore, now enjoy the structural underpinnings of Kaiser's prized duality of management. Probably few will escape the effects of vigorous representation of consumer or special-interest groups on their boards of directors; few will dare to appear "anticonsumer" in the 1980s; most plans need union acceptance more than unions need the plan; and the federal government requires that one-third of the governing boards of federally qualified HMOs be plan members. To grow large and to avoid bad publicity, most plans will be obliged to make major concessions to members, unions, and other interests and these concessions will permeate all facets of management—premiums, location and design of facilities, staffing patterns, and more.

Nor is it possible to disassociate Kaiser's accomplishments from its status as the preeminent citizen of the HMO world—a position that, in the nature of the case, only one plan can occupy. The Kaiser program began life in a rapidly growing part of the country with a mobile population and many attractions to mobile physicians; before private indemnity insurance for health care was widespread; under the auspices of the famous Kaiser name; with a core of well-qualified physicians bent on surpassing their fee-for-service critics and thereby disproving slanders against themselves; and with adequate facilities and capitalization. Over time, the plans benefited from the concerted, cumulative advantages of quality, reputation, security, money, and location. It is very likely that Kaiser, long surpassing all other plans in these respects, has long attracted the best of that atypical subset of managers and physicians that is attracted to prepaid group practice, and that the self-selection of much of this top talent into the Kaiser plans has perpetuated and reinforced Kaiser's strengths over time. Nothing succeeds like success. Most plans founded in the 1970s and 1980s will enjoy neither Kaiser's initial advantages (which derived from time and place as well as from the human element) nor the formidable self-sustaining dynamic that arose from Kaiser's extraordinary beginnings.

To point out the many misleading aspects of the casual talk about the Kaiser prototype is not to argue that the plans launched in the 1970s and 1980s are predestined to be managerial failures. However, management of an HMO is an inherently fragile enterprise, one that cannot be neglected once the rigors of organization-building have been overcome, and one that will not automatically follow the basic economic laws often taken to be the heart and soul of prepaid group practice. Three lessons are of particular importance. First, a successful plan must design balanced organizational arrangements for physicians, arrangements that neither unduly subordinate physicians to other organizational elements nor allow them too large a measure of autonomy and detachment. In GHA, physicians chafed and finally struck against salaried-employee status. In HIP, part-time physicians, shareholders in profit-making medical partnerships, needed the plan far less than the plan needed them. Kaiser's duality of management is indeed exemplary, but insofar as it depends on separate full-time, high-quality medical groups it may prove hard to replicate in many places. Even Kaiser executives sometimes voice concern that their plan concedes too much to the physicians and discuss ways of strengthening nonmedical administrators as the powerful physician leaders who instituted the changes of the 1950s pass from the scene.

Second, in a well-run HMO the board of directors must recede from the front lines of decisionmaking once the plan has begun to take root and must refrain from meddling in managerial work. Needless to say, one man's minor administrative detail is another's central policy concern. Unless the board shows a definite taste for deference to management, however, the delicate balances of which HMO management consists are likely to be upset. Both GHA and HIP have suffered severely, financially, structurally, and otherwise, from domineering boards. The Kaiser plans avoided this centrifugal activism first by keeping the board largely within the family of Kaiser interests, and, lately, by refusing to allow member or union interests to dominate it. Younger plans, few of which will be in a position to emulate Kaiser in these respects, may nonetheless find suggestive the painful experience of GHA and HIP.

Third, an HMO with a successful political economy must achieve an appropriate balance between decentralization and centralization of its service sites. A plan with one central facility and staff, like GHA, may preserve its identity and sense of family at the expense of its ability to tap younger, healthier populations in growing suburbs, or to appeal to many of the residents in major urban markets for whom the plan's central facility is inconveniently located. A plan diffused among many medical groups relying on many hospitals, like HIP, may expand at the expense of organizational cohesion and central control. The most appealing model is again the Kaiser plan, which has transported its tripartite structure and dual management ethos into eight regions and into numerous sites within them, losing in the process neither identity nor control. Again, however, it is doubtful that the conditions of Kaiser's success can be duplicated extensively in the emerging generation of HMOs.

CHAPTER FOUR

Organizational Performance: Quality, Access, and Cost in the HMO

There was no end to the questions it was possible to ask about them and no end to the answers it was not possible to frame.   Henry James, *The Aspern Papers*

A DESIRABLE SYSTEM of health care would provide consumers with easily accessible care of high quality, at reasonable cost. Just as critics have long deplored the trade-offs—especially between quality and access on the one hand and cost-containment on the other—that fee-for-service medicine allegedly enforces, so they have found the principal appeal of prepaid group practice in its presumably unique ability to avoid these trade-offs. The organizational logic inherent in the union of prepayment and group practice, advocates contend, leads providers to keep quality high and access open while holding the line on costs all the while. Needless to say, the prospect of such an innovation close at hand appealed greatly to policymakers in search of solutions to the cost crisis of the late 1960s and the 1970s. Indeed, when he introduced HMO legislation to the Congress and the public in 1971, President Richard M. Nixon recited the advocates' traditional arguments almost verbatim.[1]

The purpose of this chapter is to evaluate these arguments about organizational performance. No definitive or all-purpose evaluation is possible, for, as the previous two chapters emphasized, HMOs differ significantly from one another in their organizational characteristics. Nonetheless, an overview of what is known and suspected, both in the literature and by practitioners and observers of HMOs, can promote understanding of what policymakers may realistically expect HMOs to accomplish.

1. See "Special Message to Congress Proposing a National Health Strategy, February 18, 1971," *Public Papers of the Presidents of the United States: Richard M. Nixon, 1971* (U.S. Government Printing Office, 1972), pp. 171–75; also see chapter 5 below.

Quality of Care

Proponents of HMOs often confidently advance the contention that such plans offer their members higher quality medical care than fee-for-service competitors provide. Among the reasons cited in support of this view are that the HMO physician works under an economic incentive to do a good job lest mistakes bring members back later with serious illnesses that the organization finds costly to treat; that the HMO physician "simply practices medicine," freed from petty, money-oriented distractions that come between the fee-for-service physician and his craft; and that the HMO physician is better informed, educated, and monitored because of the easy flow of communication and consultation in the prepaid group and because peer review within it enables physicians to observe and correct one another's errors. Unfortunately, these propositions have received little careful empirical examination.

It would be strange indeed if much could be said in general about the quality of HMOs versus that of fee-for-service medicine. For one thing, the phrase "quality of medical care" is extremely hard to define. Few medical conditions yield a list of actions against which physicians' behavior may be unambiguously monitored and which implies, computer-like, a verdict of good or poor quality. The concept of medical necessity is "highly elastic,"[2] and in the crucial area of standards of practice, medicine is in a "muddle."[3]

Furthermore, the art or science of quality assessment is not well developed. It is widely agreed that it is desirable and ought to be possible to develop methodological tests of data on physicians' contacts with patients that would with some precision mark the quality of the care rendered. Observers may compile an endless list of input measures—the educational achievements of physicians, the type of diagnostic or therapeutic equipment available to them, and others—but no one pretends that more of these inputs guarantees better medical care or even that there is a strong unequivocal correlation between larger inputs and higher quality.

2. Eliot Freidson, *Doctoring Together: A Study of Professional Social Control* (Elsevier, 1975), p. 248.

3. David Mechanic, *The Growth of Bureaucratic Medicine: An Inquiry into the Dynamics of Patient Behavior and the Organization of Medical Care* (Wiley, 1976), p. 275. For a very useful discussion with primary emphasis on the operational aspects of quality see Leonard Rubin, *Comprehensive Quality Assurance System: The Kaiser-Permanente Approach* (Alexandria, Va.: American Group Practice Association, 1975), especially pp. 17–22.

So too physicians may observe one another, or reconstruct a course of treatment from charts and records, and thereby draw conclusions as to whether, in their professional judgment, the observed physician behaved in a fashion likely to produce high quality care. Such "process" evaluations, however, are generally thought to be too limited and custom-bound.

Input and process measures of the quality of care face the same problem: one wants to know what difference a certain set of inputs or the application of certain medical procedures makes to the health of the patient—how care affects "health status outcomes." But morbidity and mortality measures capture the relation between health and all the independent variables on which health depends, and a satisfactory way of distinguishing and examining closely the contribution of medical care (inputs and processes) within the entire range of variables that affect health has so far eluded medical analysts. Input and process indicators are the easiest to devise and the most straightforward on which to gather data, but they are also least rigorous and least appealing scientifically. Outcome measures of quality are methodologically desirable, but murderously difficult to construct and use. These problems, which plague the pursuit of quality assessment in HMO and fee-for-service medicine alike, largely explain Greenlick's observation that quality assessment linking inputs, processes, and outcomes "has never been systematically attempted."[4]

Measurements of Outcome

Because HMOs offer a wide range of services to a large, defined membership about whom many data are gathered, some proponents have argued that HMOs are uniquely able to study the cost-effectiveness of various medical techniques and to generate sophisticated measures of the outcome of care. In fact, HMOs seldom conduct (or at any rate seldom publicize) such studies, and arguments for the superior quality of HMO care generally fall back on a series of studies of members of the Health

4. Merwyn R. Greenlick, "The Impact of Prepaid Group Practice on American Medical Care: A Critical Evaluation," *Annals of the American Academy of Social and Political Science*, vol. 399 (January 1972), p. 104. Paul M. Ellwood, Jr., "Restructuring the Health Delivery System—Will the Health Maintenance Strategy Really Work?" in *Health Maintenance Organizations: A Reconfiguration of the Health Services System* (Graduate Program in Hospital Administration and Center for Health Administration Studies, Graduate School of Business, University of Chicago, 1971), p. 4, suggests that "in the future, it might be possible to treat the medical care system as a 'black box'—to borrow the jargon of the systems analyst—where interest centers on the kinds of patients who go in, and what they are like when they come out the other side. Our present reliance on input measures and process control systems has developed in the absence of measures to evaluate the results of medical care. A 'black box' approach will require outcome measures." On some of the complications with the outcome approach see Rubin, *Comprehensive Quality Assurance System*, pp. 27–31.

Insurance Plan of Greater New York conducted in the 1950s and 1960s by Shapiro and his colleagues, who found lower rates of prematurity, infant mortality, and mortality of the aged among HIP enrollees than among a control group outside HIP.

The first study compared pregnancies among HIP members with those in a sample of New York City residents.[5] Prematurity rates among the HIP members were "appreciably lower" than those among the general sample.[6] When HIP births were compared only with those taking place under the care of private physicians, however, the prematurity rates were virtually the same, which suggests that the crucial difference may have been care versus no-care rather than a difference in medical care setting. The HIP enrollees had significantly lower perinatal mortality rates, however, even when the comparison was confined to patients of private physicians[7] and even when the HIP members were compared only to nonmembers in high-income areas.[8] The possibility remained that "other social (including attitudinal and behavioral) attributes of the two groups" might explain the differences.[9]

In a follow-up study that extended the data base to three years,[10] the HIP prematurity rate fell below that of the general sample, and below that of a sample of women under private physicians' care by a "small but statistically significant" margin.[11] The perinatal mortality rate in HIP remained below that of the general sample for the three-year period, although in one of the years it rose high enough to eliminate that year's difference—a fact the authors were unable to explain.[12] Problems of control remained serious—measures of social class and income were crude, and no indicators of differences in health status between the samples were available—and again the authors remarked on the need to gather information about "cultural and attitudinal attributes of population subgroups and their influence on health practices prior to and during pregnancy."[13]

5. Sam Shapiro and others, "Comparison of Prematurity and Perinatal Mortality in a General Population and in the Population of a Prepaid Group Practice, Medical Care Plan," *American Journal of Public Health,* vol. 48 (February 1958), pp. 170–87.
6. Ibid., p. 176.
7. Ibid., p. 179.
8. Ibid., p. 182.
9. Ibid., p. 183.
10. Sam Shapiro and others, "Further Observations on Prematurity and Perinatal Mortality in a General Population and in the Population of a Prepaid Group Practice Medical Care Plan," *American Journal of Public Health,* vol. 50 (September 1960), pp. 1307–17.
11. Ibid., p. 1307.
12. Ibid., p. 1309.
13. Ibid., p. 1315.

A third study compared utilization and mortality rates of recipients of old-age assistance before and after they enrolled in HIP, and also compared their rates with those of a sample of recipients of old-age assistance who remained outside HIP.[14] The pertinent "outcome" finding is that whereas in the first six months of the experiment the HIP group and the outsiders had virtually the same mortality rates, over the next year and a half the HIP group's rate fell 14 percent below that of their counterparts.[15]

Shapiro and his colleagues, scrupulously respecting the limitations of their data, methods, and findings, repeatedly called attention to the possibility that factors other than the quality of HIP care—such factors as culture, attitudes, and social class, for example—might have been of major importance. These differences of social selection—that is, the possibility that people "with greater health consciousness and interest in maintaining health, when given a choice, may have been more likely to select a prepaid plan"[16]—may explain the results.

There has been little other research on the relative impact of HMO and fee-for-service care on health outcomes. A research team from Johns Hopkins University that examined twenty-five studies incorporating eighty-six separate measurements of quality judged sixty-nine to be valid[17] and only seventeen to pertain to outcome.[18] Five of these seventeen are measurements contained in the HIP studies. Seven more are measures of consumer satisfaction, which probably ought to be excluded because they do not deal specifically with health status. One of the studies uses number of days of disability as a measurement of the quality of outcome; this the investigators consider inadequate. Two deal with immunization status and the provision of vaccines and tests, and these might be said to measure processes as much as outcomes.[19]

One of the two remaining studies used tracer methods to test for anemia,

14. Sam Shapiro and others, "Patterns of Medical Use By the Indigent Aged Under Two Systems of Medical Care," *American Journal of Public Health*, vol. 57 (May 1967), pp. 784–90.

15. Ibid., p. 787.

16. Mechanic, *Growth of Bureaucratic Medicine*, p. 37.

17. John W. Williamson and others, "Quality of Health Care in HMOs as Compared to Other Settings: A Literature Review and Policy Analysis," paper prepared for the Office of Health Maintenance Organizations, Department of Health, Education, and Welfare (April 1979), p. 2; see also Frances C. Cunningham and John W. Williamson, "How Does Quality of Health Care in HMOs Compare to That in Other Settings?" *Group Health Journal*, vol. 1 (Winter 1980), pp. 4–25.

18. Williamson and others, "Quality of Health Care," table 3, based on measures reflecting acceptable indicators of quality of care, lists 15 outcome measurements. Table B.1, less restrictive, lists 17 such measurements. The latter is used for the discussion here because this table matches measurements to study, as table 3 does not.

19. Ibid., table 3.1. On the exclusion of disability see table 2, "Executive Summary."

middle-ear infection, hearing loss, and visual disorders in children receiving care from different types of medical organizations; it found that "between 80 and 90 percent of those children attending the prepaid group practice and the Neighborhood Health Center had at least one screening test for anemia, compared with less than 25 percent of the children attending hospital outpatient departments," but that "the prevalence rates for the tracer conditions did not vary by statistically significant margins when children of comparable social status in different provider organizations were compared."[20] The final study compared perinatal mortality rates in a medical care foundation (the San Joaquin Foundation in California) and two other delivery settings—namely, "a conventional private practice county and a county with a well developed county hospital outpatient department and a strong health department with well developed maternal and child health policies." It found that "rates were virtually identical in the medical care foundation and private practice counties, while the rate for the third county was half that observed elsewhere."[21]

In short, the evidence on the relative effects of HMO and fee-for-service care on health outcomes is very limited. Such evidence as exists is equivocal and does not necessarily suggest that HMO care is better than fee-for-service care; rather HMO care may be better than no care or very limited care in the fee-for-service sector. Moreover, much of the evidence that does seem to support the proposition that HMO care produces better health outcomes than does fee-for-service care may involve spuriousness, for it may be open to explanation by variables that have little to do with the distinctive properties of HMO care.

Some theorists have called for extensive studies of the relations among inputs, processes, and outcomes. Although such efforts are worthwhile, there is no reason to expect that they will produce a clear understanding of the causal relationships between the quality of care and health outcomes. Given the omnipresent problem of controlling for the numerous and various determinants of health, even a well-designed study of a very large population sample would have to be content with macro-level correlations (between smoking, say, and lung cancer) not the micro-level causal links

20. Williamson and others, "Quality of Health Care," summarizing D. M. Kessner and others, *Contrasts in Health Status*, vol. 3 (Washington: Institute of Medicine, National Academy of Sciences, 1974).
21. Williamson and others, "Quality of Health Care," pp. 24–25, summarizing J. Newport and M. I. Roemer, "Comparative Perinatal Mortality under Medical Care Foundations and Other Delivery Models," *Inquiry*, vol. 12 (March 1975), pp. 10–17.

(between the behavior of an individual physician, say, and the survival rate of a patient who has undergone treatment for lung cancer) that the outcome school of quality assessment requires.

Even if the inquiry is scaled down from the impact of the quality of care on health to its impact on the progress of specific disease episodes, the control problem still precludes rigorous scientific judgments. As David Mechanic has observed, "it is often extraordinarily difficult to differentiate the consequences of the disease from those that result from the physician's intervention. Since we can never scientifically determine what might have occurred had the physician not followed the course chosen,"[22] objective determinations of cause and effect are never likely to be more than suggestive.

Apart from correlations of suggestive variables with health status outcomes, the only available hard (quantitative) measures that deal with the quality of HMO outcomes describe malpractice experience. Alas, for both HMO and fee-for-service practitioners, malpractice data are few and inconclusive. Administrators of twelve very prominent HMOs interviewed by Curran and Moseley thought that their organizations had more favorable malpractice records than non-HMO physicians around them, but the evidence is ambiguous. Supporting their view was the experience of the Aetna Insurance Company in the state of Washington, which handled about 80 percent of the state's malpractice insurance; the company paid $1.45 for every $1.00 in malpractice insurance premiums paid by physicians in the state in 1972 but only $0.89 on each $1.00 paid by Group Health Cooperative of Puget Sound.[23]

Other data suggest a different pattern. The Department of Health, Education, and Welfare's Malpractice Commission found that 12,600 malpractice claims were filed in 1970—about one for every 16,700 persons in the United States. In Curran and Moseley's sample of HMOs there was about one claim for each 11,400 members. Moreover, this figure may understate the true difference, for some HMOs keep records only of court actions, not of settlements out of court. In 1970 about 40 percent of the malpractice claims in the United States led to a payment. In 1972, Curran

22. *Growth of Bureaucratic Medicine*, p. 271; see also Robert H. Brook and others, "Assessing the Quality of Medical Care Using Outcome Measures: An Overview of the Method," *Medical Care*, vol. 15 (September 1977), supplement, pp. 1–84; William E. McAuliffe, "Studies of Process-Outcome Correlations in Medical Care Evaluations: A Critique," *Medical Care*, vol. 16 (November 1978), pp. 907–30.

23. William J. Curran and George B. Moseley III, "The Malpractice Experience of Health Maintenance Organizations," *Northwestern University Law Review*, vol. 70 (March–April 1975), p. 80.

and Moseley's sample of twelve HMOs paid 55 percent of claims, and their median payment was $8,000, much higher than the 1970 national median payment of about $2,000.[24]

The meaning of these figures is far from clear. Perhaps they reflect the disproportionate presence of HMO membership in California and New York, two states with heavy legal action in the malpractice field. Perhaps the number of inept or unlucky physicians in these HMOs was slightly higher than in the nation as a whole. Apart, however, from the great difficulty of assessing physicians' skill, and the consequent tendency for malpractice juries to decide cases on grounds of "breach of the duty of care," because "it is extremely difficult to show lack of skill or knowledge or failure to use best judgment,"[25] a fair interpretation should take account of the tendency for malpractice claims to arise from cases of hurt feelings, abrasive exchanges, and financial disagreements.[26] These frictions may be somewhat more common in the bureaucratic atmosphere of the large, well-established groups in Curran and Moseley's sample than they are in fee-for-service practices or in smaller, younger HMOs. Moreover, as one executive director put it, HMOs "invite trouble" by establishing grievance mechanisms, making their existence known to members, and encouraging complaints, practices that are uncommon in the fee-for-service sector. In short, these data may reflect more directly on the organizational character of HMOs than on the competence and care of their physicians.

The problem is a general one: efforts to make hard assessments of quality usually meet the problem of spuriousness either on the surface (as in the case of outcome correlates) or just below it (as in the case of malpractice data). Until much more is understood about the qualitative dimensions of physicians' behavior, which can be illuminated only by means of extensive interviewing, efforts at elaborate quantification of quality and its correlates are likely to confuse issues, not clarify them.

Clearly, it is necessary to use less than ideal methods and data to evaluate the case for a superior level of care in HMOs. The most useful approach is to identify the incentives that are said uniquely to lead HMO physicians to maintain high standards and then consider whether the conclusions based on these incentives do seem to follow from them.

One quality incentive is said to be budgetary, deriving from the economic

24. Ibid., pp. 80–81, note 54.
25. Randall Bovbjerg, "The Medical Malpractice Standard of Care: HMOs and Customary Practice," *Duke Law Journal*, vol. 1975 (January, no. 6), p. 1385, note 26.
26. Mechanic, *Growth of Bureaucratic Medicine*, p. 273.

logic of an HMO. If the doctor does less than his best—if he fails to practice health maintenance and prevention for a well enrollee or fails to deal properly with a patient who has symptoms of illness—he may have to treat that person later on when he is in poorer health, at greater cost to the organization (and therefore in some measure to the physician) than if he had taken earlier, timely action.

The image of the encounter between patient and physician that is implicit in this logic assumes a discernible and predictable relation among patient complaints, physician behavior, and health outcomes. In this image, the encounter begins when a patient appears before a physician with a complaint or set of symptoms. The physician listens and examines, applies his skill in making a diagnosis, and then applies his skill further to match a therapy to the diagnosis. Therapy, in turn, alters the patient's health status. The quality of care depends on whether the diagnostic and therapeutic judgments are correct or incorrect. If they are incorrect, the patient's health is assumed to suffer.

This image misconstrues the nature of contacts between patients and physicians in several ways. Most complaints brought to a physician fall into one of three categories: those that appear to originate in stress and anxiety, and personal, emotional, and environmental—but not somatic— causes generally; those that have a somatic basis but usually get better by themselves without medical intervention—flus, colds, bruises, upper respiratory infections, and sore throats, for example; and congenital, chronic, or even terminal illnesses that do not improve no matter what medical intervention takes place.

No one knows precisely what proportion of patient-physician contacts falls into each of these three categories, and the proportion has become the object of an extensive guessing game in recent years. Skepticism about the influence of medical care on health[27] has broadened of late to embrace doubts about the degree to which physician-patient contacts involve physical illness at all, and some guesstimators believe that the number of nonorganic complaints is very high. A Kaiser psychologist told a Senate subcommittee that fully 60 percent of patients seen in his plan have no "demonstrable organic etiology."[28] Another estimate conjectures that

27. See Victor Fuchs, *Who Shall Live? Health, Economics and Social Choice* (Basic Books, 1974); but also Karen Davis and Cathy Schoen, *Health and the War on Poverty: A Ten-Year Appraisal* (Brookings Institution, 1978), pp. 23–25, 219–24.

28. Nicholas A. Cummings, in *Physicians Training Facilities and Health Maintenance Organizations,* Hearings before the Subcommittee on Health of the Senate Committee on Labor and Public Welfare, 92 Cong. 1 and 2 sess., 6 pts. (GPO, 1971–72), pt. 6, p. 2451.

nationwide the figure might be 75 percent.[29] A physician wrote in a letter to *Medical Economics:* "Fully 80 percent of illness is functional, and can be effectively treated by any talented healer who displays warmth, interest and compassion regardless of whether he has finished grammar school. Another 10 percent of illness is wholly incurable. That leaves only 10 percent in which scientific medicine—at considerable costs—has any value at all."[30] If these estimates are correct, in very few of the cases that constitute the vast majority of medical contacts does the diagnostic and therapeutic judgment and behavior of the physician have any significant impact on outcome—on the health of the patient.

Only in a small number of cases, apparently, is good medical care of the essence. Such cases, in which the accuracy of a physician's diagnosis and treatment makes the difference between worsening illness and cure, are not unimportant. The medical chief of a Kaiser group in the Northern California region gave two examples: "In the community hospitals you sometimes see uncontrolled diabetes producing a diabetic coma. I haven't seen more than two or three such cases in the ten years I've been here. The reason is here they're taken care of early enough. Another example is hypertension. Pulmonary edema is rare here. Again, we don't see it because we identified it early on." Presumably it is manageable conditions like diabetes and hypertension that HMO advocates have in mind when they offer their familiar argument that early care makes good economic sense for an HMO. One may grant that HMOs are more likely to manage such conditions favorably than are fee-for-service practitioners, but this proposition cannot support the weight of the generalization that the inherent economies of HMOs produce superior health care outcomes, for, if the numbers cited above are to be believed, relatively few conditions are amenable to yielding positive outcomes as a consequence of early intervention.

Moreover, this preventive orientation may have little to do with financial incentives. The physician who emphasized early control of problems explained that it "saves time and work later on. Yes, you keep the specialists uninvolved and all that, but it's not mainly a matter of economic self-interest. Rather it has to do with the management of the work day. If you can get diabetes under control in half an hour, you won't be seeing that member in the hospital over the weekend. The economic issue has been

29. According to Jeremy Bernstein, "It is estimated that seventy-five percent of the visits to doctors and clinics are by people who do not have anything organically wrong with them. They go to seek reassurance and psychological comfort." "Profiles: Biology Watcher," *New Yorker,* January 2, 1978, p. 28. Note also the remarks of Dr. Lewis Thomas, ibid., p. 34.

30. Fuchs, *Who Shall Live?* p. 64.

overplayed. It's not mainly the cost of the admission that concerns the doctor here. It's the time, which is worth more than the money to him."

In short, the likelihood that a physician, prepaid or other, will actually confront the theoretical situation in which a stitch in time is needed to save nine is fairly remote. He may attempt to manage those conditions that lend themselves to early management, or to make a patient more comfortable on the road to recovery. He may unwittingly make a patient's health worse than it would otherwise be by misdiagnosing or mistreating an ailment. The argument under consideration, however, is that HMO physicians are continually led to make accurate diagnoses and prescribe beneficial courses of therapy by their knowledge that care of less than high quality will bring patients back to them, sicker and more expensive, at a later date. This argument does not correspond to a realistic picture of medical practice. There is therefore little reason to conclude that a strong allegiance to this prospect and a powerful fear of the organizational and personal evils that it entails are a dominating, much less distinctive, motivation for high quality care among HMO physicians.

An HMO's approach to the relation between members' health and the organization's fiscal soundness is addressed most appropriately at the level of general organizational policy, not routine physician behavior. The common understanding of this relationship produces in HMOs and in conventional third-party insurance plans alike a quite straightforward policy, namely, to keep sick persons out in the first place insofar as feasible. A plan's most powerful tool for securing this result is marketing to employee groups, but not directly to individuals who may seek out the plan precisely because its broader benefits are the answer to their larger needs—that is, who "select against" the plan. The plans' frequent reluctance to enroll groups whose health is poorer and whose use of care is higher than those of the society at large—Medicare and Medicaid beneficiaries, for example—is part of the same policy.

If "sickees" (as they are sometimes called in the endearing vernacular of both HMOs and third-party-payment plans) are admitted or do find their way into an HMO, the organization's response is not necessarily to concentrate care on them in hopes of restoring, or at least preventing degeneration of, their health. From a strictly economic viewpoint, such a policy makes no sense at all. The economically rational course is instead to withhold care from the sickest members in order to encourage them to leave the organization at the next reenrollment period and in the meantime to seek care outside the plan. In certain California plans, set up mainly to serve Medicaid recipients, officials attempted to do just that, by refusing to answer emergency room phones, keeping patients waiting for appointments until they gave up and went to local hospitals' outpatient or emergency departments (which the plan then refused to reimburse), by administering tranquilizers to make patients feel better in spite of physical problems, and by several other infamous expedients.[31] Very few HMOs resort to these blatant tactics. The explanation, however, cannot lie in financial incentives alone, for the response of the California groups is precisely what an unvarnished economic analysis of the relationship between the organization's and the enrollee's health would suggest under the circumstances.

Insofar as an economic perception of the relationship between the organization's fiscal health and the member's physical health arises in the daily course of physician behavior, cost-consciousness is more likely to be encouraged than quality-consciousness. As noted above, the doctor usually has little reason to fear that the organization will incur high future costs as a consequence of his inaction. On the other hand, he knows that computer printouts of utilization profiles of the group's physicians easily identify those who exceed the norm for diagnostic tests, referrals, inpatient admissions, and the like, and that these decisions do directly affect the organization's financial situation. If a physician gains a reputation with the medical director as an overprovider, his bonus at year's end or his salary increase for the coming year may suffer. In short, both the technology of monitoring and the specificity of monetary stakes in an HMO favor cost-consciousness, not quality-consciousness. Of course, if the poor quality of care provided by a physician leads to a malpractice suit or to a number of disgruntled subscribers leaving the group, the plan's budget suffers. These economic incentives to maintain quality are not distinctive to HMOs, however, for they operate with equal strength on fee-for-service practitioners.

A variant of the economic argument that HMO physicians face distinct inducements to practice high quality medicine maintains that a plan must retain a high reputation within the community if it is to gain credibility and enjoy a growing market share of consumers. "The secure group does not want any sub-par performance to mar its reputation and the insecure

31. For a thorough catalogue of abuses see *Prepaid Health Plans and Health Maintenance Organizations*, S. Rept. 749, 95 Cong. 2 sess. (GPO, 1978). See also Victor P. Goldberg, "Some Emerging Problems of Prepaid Health Plans in the Medi-Cal System," *Policy Analysis*, vol. 1 (Winter 1975), pp. 55–68.

cannot afford to have any incompetent members to threaten its success."[32] Those who accept the widely held proposition that consumers are inadequate judges of the quality of the medical product with which physicians supply them will raise the obvious objection that the community seldom has the data or the expertise to judge the quality of an HMO physician's behavior, much less the quality of the group as a whole. Consumers decide whether or not to join an HMO on many grounds—financial advantage, location, accessibility, and so forth—but the quality of care appears to be a comparatively nebulous consideration.[33]

On the other hand, just as favorable reports within employee groups are considered a major source of growth in HMO enrollments, unfavorable comments and high rates of disenrollment among disaffected subscribers may be expected to deal a plan a palpable hit. An HMO—including its physicians—may be expected to recognize and guard against the danger that enrollees displeased with the plan's care may move back to the fee-for-service sector and may tell their friends and coworkers what they think.

Although this type of consumer sovereignty may influence some aspects of organizational behavior, it is doubtful that it extends to quality care defined as a positive change in health outcomes as a consequence of a physician's intervention. In a given year the average HMO member may have three or four contacts with the organization's providers (some of them with paraprofessionals). Many of the conditions triggering these encounters will abate whether the doctor does something or nothing. Others will remain severe for reasons for which the doctor cannot plausibly be blamed. A few cases get either better or worse as a direct result of medical attention or the lack of it. Only these cases raise the quality issue in the outcome sense employed in this chapter so far. Most of these cases can be handled properly by any physician—prepaid or not—of average training, competence, and attentiveness. There are a small number of cases in which a deterioration of condition seems linked to the physician's failures of omission or commission. Even in these cases, however, patients usually feel unqualified or otherwise disinclined to dispute a professional judgment, however poor they may suspect it to have been. In Freidson's term, they find ways of "normalizing" the error.[34]

32. William A. MacColl, *Group Practice and Prepayment of Medical Care* (Washington: Public Affairs Press, 1966), p. 112; also p. 237.

33. S. E. Berki and Marie L. F. Ashcraft, "HMO Enrollment: Who Joins What and Why: A Review of the Literature," *Milbank Memorial Fund Quarterly/Health and Society,* vol. 58 (Fall 1980), p. 623.

34. The term is from *Doctoring Together,* pp. 134–35.

Occasionally, a patient will refuse to normalize an error and will take a formal complaint to HMO officials. But even if the complaint is moved along, physicians, as Freidson found, will usually have little difficulty in finding grounds of their own on which to normalize what they may admit was a colleague's error. If several patients repeatedly have problems with one doctor, if they all elect to press their complaints to the organization, if their claims are not dismissed as the result of grousing or misunderstanding, and if the medical group is persuaded that an incompetent is in their midst, the physicians may make an effort to talk to the doctor in question. Tenure provisions may make formal sanctions difficult, however, and physicians will usually be very reluctant to impose the sanctions the bylaws of the organization do support.[35] In short, the road between consumer dissatisfaction and physician behavior is long and tortuous.

Of course if a sizable employee group—a union, say—monitored physician care, found it wanting, and elected to move out of the HMO en masse, market discipline would be much stronger. Apparently this rarely happens, either because the representatives of enrolled groups seldom get deeply involved in monitoring the quality of care or because HMOs, anticipating this problem, make sure that quality is high. The former is the more plausible hypothesis: most members drift out of plans for reasons such as a job change that makes them ineligible to continue or movement from the service area that can rarely be interpreted as a judgment on the quality of care in the group.

Many HMO proponents argue that the ability of voluntarily enrolled subscribers to impose financial costs on a plan by voting with their feet (that is, leaving it) if they are dissatisfied with its care is the best assurance that quality will remain high. Probably no HMO advocate would contend, however, that the patient's ability to impose financial costs on one physician by giving his business to another is a sufficient guarantee of quality in the fee-for-service world. Why should the choice between HMO physicians and fee-for-service physicians be a better guarantee? No one would argue that typical HMO rates of penetration where a choice is available—20 percent HMO enrollment is considered quite a success—prove that the quality of fee-for-service care is better by a factor of five or more than HMO care. Yet this is what the "voting with the feet" argument implies.

Moreover, the plans' own behavior belies the argument: few HMO proponents would think well of a plan that failed to make painstaking internal efforts to monitor and improve the quality of care entirely apart

35. Ibid., pp. 209–22, 235–36.

from the budgetary discipline of enrollment patterns. That subscribers enroll in and remain with a plan and perhaps even express strong feelings of satisfaction with it on questionnaires says *something* about the plan, of course. That the subscribers are able to judge, and that these expressions of satisfaction do indeed reflect judgments on, the quality of care in the plan must be demonstrated empirically, not postulated, however.

Examining the Process

If quality of care is defined against outcomes, neither logic nor empirical evidence leads to a conclusion that HMOs enjoy an innate superiority over fee-for-service medicine. Although the view that outcome measures alone yield true evaluations of quality has become fashionable, there are other ways of explicating the concept. A process definition, which denotes a style or orientation toward care and toward the patient, fails to yield direct answers to the question "what objective difference does care make?" yet this is the conception of quality that the language and expectations of the average man appear to endorse. Moreover, most efforts at peer review that physicians establish to monitor and evaluate the quality of their care rely on procedural criteria.[36] As a Kaiser physician who has worked to develop a quality assurance scheme in California put it, the view that quality of care can only be judged against outcomes is mistaken: "Outcomes are a research question. Quality is something different. What we do today, what everybody today thinks is right—that's quality."

Understood as a process, quality care means careful care, physician behavior that is "full of care." A physician rendering such care listens closely to the patient's description of his condition, speaks courteously and tries to put the patient at ease, looks attentively for symptoms, considers reasonable diagnostic possibilities that cannot be ruled out prima facie, resorts to pertinent tests, asks discerning questions, takes pains to counsel a patient against unknowingly aggravating his condition, prescribes safe means of easing discomfort (ranging from bed rest to medication), and follows closely the patient's progress over time.

Care of high quality requires a physician with what philosopher Karl Jaspers called "a feeling for situations."[37] These processes and this feeling are essential to a sound operational definition of quality; probably very

36. See, for example, Rubin, *Comprehensive Quality Assurance System*; James D. Shepperd and others, "A Quality Assurance System for Prepaid Group Practice," *Journal of the National Medical Association*, vol. 68 (September 1976), pp. 404–08; and, more generally, Richard Greene, ed., *Assuring Quality in Medical Care: The State of the Art* (Ballinger, 1976).

37. *Philosophy and the World: Selected Essays*, trans. E. B. Ashton (Chicago: Henry Regnery, 1963), p. 161.

few observers would agree that the care given by a doctor who failed in these respects was of high quality, no matter what the patient's health outcome. Whereas the outcome definition of quality emphasizes curing (a result often beyond the physician's influence), the process definition stresses caring.

The literature offers two quite different approaches to assessing the procedural aspects of HMO care. One attempts to devise various measures of procedural quality and then applies these measures to statistically significant and carefully matched samples of patients in both HMO and fee-for-service settings. The Johns Hopkins researchers who reviewed this literature concluded that HMOs scored favorably on many measures addressing the procedural aspects of care. They summarized studies showing that HMO enrollees were more likely to get early prenatal care, Pap tests, and periodic health examinations than fee-for-service counterparts; that the elderly and the elderly sick were more likely to see providers in HMOs than outside them; that HMO physicians performed better on indexes of physician performance measuring the quality of diagnostic testing and therapy than fee-for-service counterparts; and more.[38]

Although these findings are impressive, the studies on which they rest are not problem-free. The reviewers noted that "definitions of quality, selection of measures, and the use of quality criteria . . . were as varied as the papers themselves," and almost one-fourth of the measures were, in their judgment, "not valid indicators of quality." The studies offered little information on the reliability and validity of their data, and the Hopkins researchers cautioned that relatively few of the studies "indicated that systematic checks of the reliability and validity of their questionnaires or encounter forms were made." "The adequacy of criteria applied for matching HMOs and non-HMOs" was open to question. "Patient sampling, including adequacy of sample forms, sampling procedures and sizes, and use of substitutions in case of no response" were of concern. The "validity of data abstracted from medical records" raised problems. The reviewers noted that "evidence of the efficacy of medical care interventions utilized was rarely mentioned." They also offered caveats on generalizing from the studies examined. The authors of a "landmark" study, they remarked, were "extremely guarded in claiming generalizability to the universe they sampled," and "most other projects are case studies of limited populations in limited geographic areas." Finally, generalizability is limited by the emphasis of the studies on "large metropolitan centers and well established HMO programs in California, New York, Washington, D.C., and Hawaii."[39]

The second approach forgoes quantitative measures of services provided to matched samples of patients in different settings in favor of case studies and direct, intense, sustained observation of individual HMOs as a means of discovering the peculiar features of the HMO work setting and their implications for medical care. In contrast to the favorable findings of the first approach, the major studies of this second school suggest that structural characteristics of the HMO can (which of course is not to say must) lead to important deficiencies in the caring components of medical encounters. As the previous chapter pointed out, the HMO physician usually serves two organizational masters, one professional, the other bureaucratic, whereas the fee-for-service practitioner generally serves neither. As a rule, one of these masters, the executive director, must find methods of living within a fixed annual budget and a competitive market milieu without controlling in detail the practice patterns of physicians, who remain under the purview of the other master, the medical director. The major strategy available to the administration is one of stretching, of holding down the number of inputs (employees, and therefore payroll, hospital beds, and so forth) and managing as well as possible the queuing and rationing—and friction—that result as patients are distributed among providers.

Thus stretched, HMO physicians may come to feel exploited and overworked, and, as a result, alienated and resentful. If they are salaried employees of the plan itself (as at the Group Health Association) or perpetually at odds with administrators, with whom they share little sense of common allegiance and fate (as at HIP), the problem may be especially severe. Obliged to improvise means of managing a steady flow of patients within what seems to be an unrealistically tight schedule, they may come to deplore the "trivia" they are asked to treat. This attitude, David Mechanic conjectures, may express the physician's frustration at being forced by the structure of the work place to treat patients as if their complaints were indeed trivial.[40]

Among the disturbing evidence on this point is a study that found group practice physicians in the 1950s believed that "their patients were worse off economically than the population average, that the prepaid members

39. Ibid., pp. 29–32.
40. *Growth of Bureaucratic Medicine*, p. 105. It may also be that physicians, who often dislike treating sore throats, intestinal ailments, and other such "garbage" (as they sometimes put it) assume a priori that in an HMO lower fee barriers increase the volume of garbage brought to them.

Table 4-1. *Reports on Trivial Consultation by Physicians in Varying Practice Settings*

| Type of practice | Number in sample | Percent reporting trivial consultation with | |
		50 percent or more patients	10 percent or less patients
British general practitioners	722	24	12
U.S. primary care physicians			
All nongroup[a]	1,148	7	36
All group[a]	310	10	36
U.S. general practitioners			
Nongroup	604	9	33
Group	113	13	27
Prepaid[b]	108	32	7
U.S. pediatricians			
Nongroup	136	9	31
Group	43	9	33
Prepaid[b]	154	29	14

Source: David Mechanic, *The Growth of Bureaucratic Medicine: An Inquiry into the Dynamics of Patient Behavior and the Organization of Medical Care* (Wiley, 1976), p. 106.
a. Includes general practitioners, pediatricians, internists, and obstetricians.
b. Includes physicians whose practices involve 50 percent or more prepaid activity.

were much more abusive of their medical services than were private patients, and that prepayment itself was perceived as a constraining influence upon the doctor." Yet, as the study demonstrated statistically, "the group health patients had, on the average, higher incomes than the general population and requested physicians services at about the same rate."[41] A later study, summarized in table 4-1, found that prepaid practitioners and pediatricians in the United States were far more likely than nonprepaid physicians in various practice settings to report that 50 percent or more of their patients were "trivial."[42]

Freidson's study of a prepaid group, in which overload was the physician's major complaint, suggests that these attitudes carry over into the conduct of medical practice. "Under circumstances perceived as overload," he found, they gave care that "was often impersonal, lacking

41. D. C. McElrath, "Prepaid Group Medical Practice: A Comparative Analysis of Organization and Perspectives" (doctoral dissertation, Yale University, 1958), summarized by E. R. Weinerman, in *Proceedings, 13th Annual Group Health Institute, Detroit, Mich., May 9–11, 1963* (Washington: Group Health Association of America, 1963), p. 10; and in Raymond Munts, *Bargaining for Health: Labor Unions, Health Insurance, and Medical Care* (University of Wisconsin Press, 1967), p. 213.
42. Mechanic, *Growth of Bureaucratic Medicine*, pp. 105–06.

amenities, and, on occasion, virtually mechanized."[43] One "efficient physician," describing "how the consultation could be organized when time was short," reported: "I sit and write when a patient is getting dressed. I sit and talk on the phone while writing, and I'm checking off lists and working on all those things. I don't let a patient relax. I keep him going. It's tense, that's all, and it's true, if I have a day where I get a couple of cancellations I enjoy myself tremendously."[44] Another physician conjectured that the main loss under these conditions was "supportive therapy," but "if there is anything organically wrong, they are well taken care of."[45] Some doctors took a different view, arguing that "the personal quality of care was essential to high technical quality."[46] As one put it: "I'm continually irritated at the lack of time, that I don't have enough time to do the kind of work that I want to do. I like to talk to people and I don't have time to do that unless I cut corners. . . . I cut corners by cutting out talking and cutting out the social history, and the social history, for an internist, at least, gives a key to at least half his diagnoses."[47] Freidson himself reached similar conclusions, observing that adaptations to keep the flow of patients moving may have had "some bearing on the technical quality of care, for occasional skipping of elements of medical routine may have led to missing conditions at an early stage, when their treatment might have been easier and surer"[48]—an ironic commentary on the traditional arguments about "health maintenance" in the HMO.

In this respect the circumstances of HMO and fee-for-service doctors may be quite different. The fee-for-service practitioner is often harassed, overbooked, and "constantly on call," but he believes that these problems arise from the confidence of a loyal and growing body of patients and the esteem of referring physicians. Moreover, his income increases in direct proportion to his workload. The HMO physician, in contrast, may trace his feelings of harassment to the exploitation of the administration and the contractual rigidities of an HMO practice. Nor does he receive a direct financial reward for increased effort. Mechanic's data suggest that "physicians in nongroup practice respond to practice pressure by increasing their hours seeing patients, while prepaid physicians process their patients more quickly." This in turn suggests "that fee-for-service physicians, if

43. Freidson, *Doctoring Together*, pp. 41, 60.
44. Ibid., p. 60.
45. Ibid.
46. Ibid.
47. Ibid., pp. 60–61.
48. Ibid., p. 86.

they wish, are probably in a stronger position to maintain the substantive integrity of a patient visit."[49]

Proponents of HMOs who acknowledge the potential for or the occurrence of these problems believe that peer review is an adequate mechanism to detect and deter them. They contend that HMOs not only monitor and correct substandard care by means of peer review but also, by applying it to both ambulatory and hospital care, surpass the norm of quality assurance in the fee-for-service sector, where peer review is usually confined to inpatients. As an HMO's physicians interact, converse, observe, refer, and consult, it is said, they evaluate—that is, they form opinions of each other's strengths and weaknesses. Evaluation in the course of systematic interaction offers the best vehicle for mutual education and improvement in skill and judgment. Moreover, HMO physicians have both the information and the will effectively to discipline each other if educational efforts prove to be too weak. In all these respects, the argument goes, HMO practitioners enjoy stable controls on quality not applied to their professionally isolated fee-for-service colleagues.

Unlike most of the claims on behalf of HMOs, this one has been subjected to sustained empirical examination. In *Doctoring Together,* Eliot Freidson took a close look at interaction and discipline among the physicians of a well-known and highly regarded prepaid medical group in the early 1960s and found that the standard arguments about peer review did not fit the facts. For one thing, the actual range of interactions among physicians and therefore the number of opportunities for interchange and evaluation were much smaller than might be expected. In particular, specialists seldom had occasion to review the work of specialists in other areas of medicine. In general, the circle of those with enough information to permit defensible judgments about a colleague's work was surprisingly small.[50]

Equally important, the will to evaluate and discipline was as lacking as the information. Freidson discovered that his physicians, like their fee-for-service colleagues, had no taste for conflictual exchanges and were positively averse to anything connoting collective discipline. The group physicians "seemed to share a very special conception of themselves. They assumed that the physicians were essentially ethical, conscientious and competent, these qualities being organized into an individually expressed

49. Mechanic, *Growth of Bureaucratic Medicine,* p. 90. As Mechanic remarks, "research is clearly necessary on this point."
50. *Doctoring Together,* pp. 138–85.

but stable pattern of behavior. From this followed the fundamental rule that one owed one's colleagues (and was owed by them) respect, trust, and protection unless overwhelming evidence pointed to the contrary."[51] Errors might, of course, occur, yet every physician knew that bad luck or routine oversights could "happen to anyone" and they were prepared to "normalize" all but the most egregious blunders. Emphasizing the autonomy of professional judgment, the physicians viewed their knowledge of a colleague's error as an embarrassing bit of information that ought to be kept secret. Colleagues should avoid criticizing one another—especially within earshot of outsiders like the administration or a patient. To look into a colleague's charts for the sole purpose of evaluating his competence was regarded both as a breach of etiquette and as superfluous—"they check them before they get in the group here."[52]

Even when unambiguously confronted with mistakes or poor work, the physicians had a high threshold for adopting even a weak reaction. Freidson found that "in the medical group a very large number of offenses did not seem to be followed by a [physician] complaint. Insofar as it was possible to tell, many were completely forgotten shortly after they occurred."[53] To be sure, repeated offenses were not overlooked. As one doctor explained: "The first time this happens, you sort of remember. The second time you begin to look around. The third time you do something about it."[54] But the offenses in question had little to do with the quality of medical care. "Collective forms of professional control were brought into play primarily when the issue was that of intercollegial relations, not that of patient relations or relations with the administration."[55]

Before the group would apply discipline, a physician had to antagonize a number of his colleagues on repeated occasions. As a disciplinary device, peer review proved largely ineffectual; it was scarcely more useful as an educative tool. In sum, "technical performance goes generally unobserved, and even if observed, uncommunicated, and, even if communicated, uncontrolled."[56]

On balance, it seems fair to conclude that there is nothing inherent in the financial or organizational nature of an HMO that assures high quality

51. Ibid., pp. 121–22.
52. Ibid., pp. 160–85, 213, quotation at p. 175.
53. Ibid., p. 211.
54. Ibid.
55. Ibid., p. 232; emphasis deleted.
56. Eliot Freidson and Buford Rhea, "Processes of Control in a Company of Equals," *Social Problems*, vol. 11 (Fall 1963), p. 128.

care. In other words, the inner dynamics of prepaid group practice per se—in particular, fear that neglected symptoms will blossom into expensive illnesses, the need to maintain a high community reputation in order to attract subscribers, and peer review processes in the group—cannot be expected automatically to produce higher quality care than the fee-for-service system provides. Indeed if one attributes the unflattering findings of Freidson and Mechanic to the innate structural features of an HMO, the literal theory is stood on its head: far from guaranteeing high quality care, the basic nature of the HMO seems to obstruct it.

There is, however, no more reason to inflate these findings into a model of HMO behavior than there is to accept the deterministic metaphysics of the literal model. As chapter 3 shows, HMOs differ substantially in their organizational properties, and although no one has yet studied systematically the connections between organizational character and quality in a range of plans, it is possible that a well-organized HMO is in a position to practice medicine not only superior to that of a less-well-run HMO but also better than that found in much of the fee-for-service sector.

Judging the Medical Staff

Even if HMOs do not embody automatic guarantees, the HMO setting may offer certain distinctive opportunities to practice medicine of high quality. Whether or not these opportunities are realized, however, is contingent on the organizational character of individual plans, and on the strategic choices of their managers. Four variables related to physical behavior may be important to the quality of care.

First, physicians bring certain *personal qualities*—attributes of individual character and temperament—to bear on their work. Some fee-for-service physicians would never succumb to the temptation to overprovide for the sake of a fee; others would succumb without a pang of remorse. It would never occur to some HMO providers to withhold care because more care meant less money for them; others would take financial considerations very much to heart. These are predispositions attached to physicians' personal and professional self-image. Second, physicians acquire and act on the basis of *academic training*. In medical school they are taught the meaning of a physician's calling and learn basic practical techniques. Third, they work within a *professional culture*. Norms of practice derive not only from medical school but also from peers in the local community. Indeed, community standards define the legal meaning of good practice (as distinct from malpractice). Doctors, in short, become socialized in local practice cultures, which set expectations about fees, hospital use, and more. Fourth, a physician may or may not be subject to an *organizational environment,* a subgroup within—and perhaps deviant from—the broader medical culture of the community. Solo fee-for-service practitioners stand largely outside such an environment; HMO practitioners necessarily work within one, and there is reason to believe that the organization's culture may cause a reconsideration of the norms of the local professional culture, the lessons of academic training, and the inclinations of individual temperament.

To enter the fee-for-service system a physician must pass various examinations and must meet licensing standards set by doctor-dominated medical boards in the states. If these hurdles are surmounted, the physician goes abroad in the community subject to few additional criteria and little evaluation over time. Recruitment into HMOs, by contrast, sets up additional criteria within this general community framework. As the previous chapters noted, well-working HMOs depend on the leadership and example of a medical director and a group of colleagues, with a professional, philosophical, and interpersonal commitment to the group. Such leaders are continually at pains to recruit new staff who practice their brand of medicine and view practice as they do. This amounts to peer review *at the point of entry* and its effectiveness cannot be inferred from evaluations of everyday peer review processes.

A well-run HMO will screen candidates with utmost care. Indeed, some groups devote more collective administrative time and effort to hiring physicians than to any other task. Although the number of doctors attracted to them is limited, most HMOs today have more applicants, including many foreign medical graduates, than they have positions open. The problem, executives tend to agree, is not quantity, but quality of candidate, which must be measured not only by conventional criteria of experience, certification, and academic background, but also by indications of commitment to and suitability for prepaid group practice.

Peer review at the point of entry, however, means little unless the behavior of the recruit can be monitored and influenced over time. "The system depends upon recruiting into it properly socialized workers—workers not merely well-trained, but also responsive to the values of their colleagues,"[57] and much of this training must take place on the job.

The major limitation of Freidson's study as a source of generalization about HMOs is that, like most case studies, it does not address the significance of its own setting in time and place. Its findings may reflect

57. Ibid., p. 129.

attitudes toward medical practice and peer review that were current in the early 1960s, but that are changing. They may also derive from the peculiar organizational properties of the group he studied, which cared for about 25,000 enrollees with about 50 salaried physicians, about 20 of them working for the group part time. This experience may fall midway, so to speak, between that of the very differently institutionalized Kaiser plans and that of the younger, newer HMOs developed in the late 1970s. Several possible differences are worth pursuing.

First, the lack of interest in peer review and contempt for administrative constraints found in Freidson's group may reflect its status as a large group with many salaried specialists with private practices, who worked for it on the side. Would a group of Permanente physicians working full time for the Kaiser program and practicing in a Kaiser hospital show the same indifference? As might be expected, Kaiser officials do not think so; some described at length, in interviews for this study, their extensive and creative efforts to develop and improve peer review among their (carefully selected) physicians.[58] Still, a study of peer review in Kaiser comparable in sophis- tication and depth to Freidson's study—that is, a study not of what physicians say for public consumption about peer review but rather of how they themselves react to it—might turn up comparable findings. The question cannot be answered because no such study has been done.

The organizational properties of Freidson's group also differ from those of most of the newer, younger HMOs. For one thing, the younger plans tend to be much smaller. Interchange and communication may be easier among one or two dozen physicians than among the fifty in the group studied. A small, young group, in which about half the physicians are a founding core that picks the other, newer half, may be in a strong position to realize the quality potential of recruitment, socialization, and peer review. The younger groups are also less specialized. (The lack of oppor- tunities for specialists to evaluate one another was a major obstacle to peer review in Freidson's study.) In smaller, newer groups young physicians expect to take cues from older ones. One HMO official observed that in his group, which cannot afford its own specialists and has trouble making improvised arrangements with fee-for-service specialists, physicians with subspecialties are expected to take the lead in educating their colleagues in the handling of various complaints and ailments. In such a group, the need to control use and costs is evident, and the problem of deciding where fee-

58. See also Rubin, *Comprehensive Quality Assurance System* for details.

for-service norms can be compromised without cutting quality is fresh and challenging. This stage of organizational development seems to foster communication and exchange of ideas, and this is the organizational stage that many HMOs today have attained.

A second difference is that the professional status of cost-consciousness in the 1980s has changed from what it was at the time of Freidson's study. In the early 1960s it was considered at least tacky and probably downright immoral to admit that money had some connection with care; a provider should act as if cost was truly no object.[59] Today cost-consciousness is a watchword that physicians must act as if they honored.[60]

Third, there appear to be generational differences in physicians' willingness to pass judgment on their fellows. A survey by *Physician's Management* found that only 13.6 percent of doctors who had been in practice for twenty to thirty years criticized their colleagues, and only 8.5 percent would call a colleague's error to the attention of patients. For doctors in practice five years or less, however, the corresponding figures were 32.6 percent and 14 percent. The figures for large groups were 35.1 percent and 29.7 percent as against 12.3 percent and 5.6 percent for solo practitioners. In short, younger doctors and those working in large groups may be substantially more willing to identify and discuss their colleagues' errors than are their older, solo practice counterparts.[61]

In sum, organizational differences among HMOs and general attitudinal and environmental changes surrounding peer review suggest that generalizations from Freidson's account of the early 1960s might be unduly pessimistic. Yet the small, young, struggling plans of today may exhibit some troublesome features in the future. The physicians working in many of these plans will retain fee-for-service practices too and it is this situation, many observers believe, that most erodes organizational loyalty and discipline. As time passes, the core of founders who embarked on HMO-building for philosophical and professional reasons will give way to or be supplemented by new ranks of economic and career-minded physicians who—especially if they are part-timers—may resist review and control.

59. Freidson and Rhea, "Processes of Control," p. 122.

60. According to Dr. Robert B. Hunter, chairman of the American Medical Association's board of trustees, "the most important thing doctors can do is to keep cost uppermost in their minds. Consider the cost-benefit ratio every time you order anything." "The Real World of Hospital Finance," *Medical Economics*, vol. 55 (May 1, 1978), pp. 98, 102.

61. "Physicians Judge Colleagues Harshly," *Physician's Management*, October 1977, p. 56. Legal changes extending immunity from slander and libel suits for persons reporting errant doctors to state medical disciplinary boards also appear to be leading to more criticism and discipline. *New York Times*, December 2, 1978.

Many plans will establish satellite centers in order to build their markets; these facilities may become (as one HIP administrator put it) "little empires," resistant to central control. Few of the plans will own their hospitals, and HMO physicians will therefore be caught between the need, urged by HMO officials, to economize in the interests of the plan, and the need, emphasized by hospital officials and governmental reviewers, to treat all patients alike in conformity with prevailing norms. For all of these reasons the problems of peer review that Freidson found are likely to afflict the growing generation of HMOs at least to some extent in the future. Independent practice associations may be expected to be severely afflicted with all of them.

Of the two types of quality control discussed here—"entry" peer review at the point of recruitment and "practice" peer review on a continuing basis—the former is less vulnerable than the latter to organizational processes of erosion. A plan with recruitment processes aimed at selecting better-than-average physicians may perhaps provide better-than-average care, even in trying and strained organizational circumstances. These entry controls constitute the major—perhaps the only—clear, qualitative advantage of HMOs over fee-for-service care.

There is evidence that mature and well-established HMOs maintain at the entry stage a very high level of concern for quality, defined in terms of both technical medical skills and personal fitness for HMO work. All twelve of the well-established HMOs that Curran and Moseley surveyed had "quite elaborate" programs of recruitment. At the Group Health Cooperative of Puget Sound the whole medical staff screened applicants and a personnel committee conducted interviews. As many as twelve staff physicians in Detroit's Metro Health Plan (renamed the Health Alliance Plan in 1979) may interview a candidate. At the Group Health Plan in St. Paul an independent medical board composed of doctors unassociated with the group screened potential recruits. Equally important, these groups usually put new physicians on carefully supervised probation during their first years with the plan. At Puget Sound, specialists and generalists evaluated one another, and evaluation questionnaires were even sent to nursing and administrative personnel. If the doctor was to stay with the group after two years, he had to be approved by a two-thirds vote of the medical executive committees and the entire medical staff and about 15 percent of new physicians left during or after the probationary period.[62]

62. Curran and Moseley, "Malpractice Experience of Health Maintenance Organizations," pp. 85–86.

The Kaiser program has similarly rigorous entry standards. One Kaiser physician with a special interest in peer review explained in an interview that "intake is the key. The initial selection process is even more important than ongoing surveillance as a quality control. Here a candidate must bring three references, go through interviews, be board-certified or -qualified, be interviewed by the department head; the chief physician must approve of him, and more. It leads to weeding out." The chief physician of a Kaiser facility, speaking of the new recruit's probationary period, explained that "for these first years there's a very elaborate evaluation every six months. There's constant review. If the partners see a problem they'll take it to the chief. So over the course of the three-year evaluation you really scrutinize a newcomer. If he survives these reviews for the first two years, he becomes a 'participant' for the third year. After that he may become a partner." This physician estimated that 10–15 percent of new recruits left the plan in these first three years.

Under such rigorous entry conditions, the excuse offered by the HIP physician who preferred not to examine his colleagues' charts—"they check them before they get here"—is not absurd. A consumer choosing among competing medical plans and practitioners probably has a better chance of ending up with a high quality physician when selection procedures such as these have been employed than he has if he simply consulted an omnibus list of local practitioners, or let himself be shuttled along the referral networks of the fee-for-service community.[63] A powerful indicator of HMO quality, then, and one that any government or individual reviewer should study carefully in the course of assessing quality, is the rigor of the HMO's policies for physician recruitment and promotion. Curiously, however, HMOs seem seldom to publicize these procedures in their marketing appeals, consumers seem seldom to ask about them, and reviewers (including the federal government) seem seldom to investigate them. All appear to give more attention to continuing peer review than to entry standards and procedures.

One should not claim too much on behalf of these entry standards. In the first place, the degree to which young HMOs follow the examples of the mature plans is not known. Second, even if all HMOs observed very elaborate entry standards, this would not prove that HMOs were staffed by high quality physicians, but only that they tended to select the highest

63. Almost half of the doctors in the survey reported in "Physicians Judge Colleagues Harshly," p. 57, admitted to knowing one to three doctors whom they would not let near their own patients because of incompetence. Only 28.5 percent said that they know no physicians in this category.

quality physicians from among those who apply to them. No one knows whether there are systematic differences among HMOs or between HMOs in general and fee-for-service practice in the skills and attainments of physicians seeking work. Third, even if one granted that all HMOs recruited physicians of high technical skill, the possibility remains that the work setting of the HMO enforces some compromise of the "spirit" (Freidson's term) and, for all one knows, the quality of care. Research is needed on all of these questions. Finally, even if one grants that the entry and review processes of the HMO setting offer a potential for consistently high quality care that is missing from the more haphazard and easily-entered fee-for-service sector, judgments about the actual quality of care provided are likely to remain soft, impressionistic, and resistant to confident generalization. The medical director of a mid-Atlantic group, for example, claimed he could tell something about the quality of care in an HMO

> just by hearing who's involved. There are some names in prepaid group practice that'll make me suspicious right away; others inspire confidence that it's a first-rate operation. The checklist approach—organization chart, benefit schedule, etc.—won't tell you. It really should be peer review; you've gotta have this done by somebody who knows what the ballgame involves. For example, the on-site audits that GHAA uses for its accreditation rating. For example, I and some others went to Albany for one and a half full days to talk and review operations at an HMO there. We came away persuaded that this was a good HMO. What did we look at? The number of doctors per enrollees. Scheduling of time—are too many patients wedged into an hour? Amount of time a doctor spends with each patient. Information flows—if a lab test is done, what mechanisms assure that the doctor gets it and sees it, what arrangements are made for specialist consultation, and so on. Just talking awhile with the medical director gives you an idea of the style and procedure, and some of the evaluators went into the waiting room and asked the patients direct questions about waiting time, their opinions of the plan, and so forth.

This director described the quality of care in his own plan in words very similar to those of other medical directors interviewed on the subject for this study: "We don't practice the best medicine in the world. We won't compete with the Mayo Clinic this year. But we're better than the community norm."

This approach to quality review, which one critic derided as "flying one HMO medical director up to spend a day or two talking with another medical director," strikes some observers as almost laughably unrigorous. But although efforts continue to develop scientific measures, it is doubtful that any will entirely replace the "feeling for situations" of interested parties, physician peers and consumers alike. A highly sophisticated HMO physician who had invested much effort in developing a peer review system, for example, defended his high opinion of the care provided in his plan without a trace of facetiousness: "My children were delivered here. Would I have let that happen if I didn't think the quality of care was good?"

The arguments developed here suggest a "self-perpetuation hypothesis" about quality of care in HMOs. In the best case, medical directors and founding physicians, deeply committed for philosophical and professional reasons to the success of prepaid group practice in general and of their organization in particular, establish meticulous procedures to select physicians who are not only excellent by technical standards, but also sympathetic to, and easily socialized in, HMO norms. These recruits are carefully monitored and are promoted only if the permanent staff agrees that their professional skills and their tolerance for the frustrations of prepaid group practice are both high. The values and expectations of these committed and skilled physicians permeate the organization's daily life and produce high quality care.

In the worst case, entrepreneurs concerned mainly with making a quick dollar or with protecting their share of the local market from HMO competition might be expected to hire like-minded and similarly motivated colleagues, who ask and are asked few questions. In this case, technical skill may be high, but tolerance for the distinctive frustrations of prepaid group practice is likely to be low. Compromises with the human, procedural dimensions of care, including a general willingness to cut corners, would be expected. The result would be indiscipline and indifference among physicians—in Freidson's words, a "delinquent community" of physicians.[64] If such HMOs become numerous, they could "actually have a profoundly adverse effect on the quality of health care in the country."[65]

Access

The goal that medical care should be easily, if not indeed equally, accessible to consumers includes three basic elements: care should be conveniently located, timely, and within the financial capacities of consumers. These three components of access are sometimes captured colloquially in the dictum that "you should be able to get a doctor when you need (or want) one."

64. *Doctoring Together*, p. 244.
65. Lester Breslow, in *Physicians Training Facilities*, Hearings, pt. 5, p. 1878.

The question whether HMOs can make significant contributions to improved access has in turn, two parts. The "macro" facets of the question—whether HMOs are likely to take root in large numbers and in many states and localities in the United States and whether a sizable majority of the population may soon enjoy an HMO option—are addressed in chapter 2. Discussion here concentrates on the "micro" facets: whether HMOs, whatever their number and geographical distribution, are organized internally so as to provide accessible care to their members.

The standard arguments betray no doubt that HMOs promote access to care in ways that fee-for-service plans find impossible. The HMO offers one-step care under one roof—the member need not piece together by trial, error, and repeat visit the benefits of modern medicine. The HMO offers, by contractual obligation, a comprehensive range of services—preventive, primary, specialist, inpatient care, and more—and twenty-four-hour-a-day, seven-day-a-week emergency care. Finally, prepayment and prepayment alone effectively eliminates the main financial deterrent to a timely resort to care, the fear of a hefty fee for each service. Prepayment, the argument goes, not only insures that enrollees may resort to care without fear of inability to pay for it; it also positively induces them to use access to this timely care in a timely way, thereby encouraging prevention and early detection and treatment of symptoms. In all these respects, proponents believe, HMOs provide far more access to care (of higher quality) than does the fee-for-service system.

Regulating the Flow of Patients

Even as they propound this theory of access, HMO administrators are well aware that if all or even many members pressed the theory and the claims it confers to the full, the HMO system would be paralyzed. As Heyssell and Seidel put it, "a closed-end budget . . . can be constructed and met only if an appreciable number of people joining the prepaid group practice do not claim their due."[66] To reduce the danger that once financial disincentives to care are removed, a flood of "worried well" patients (as Dr. Sidney Garfield of the Kaiser program termed them) will rush into the system demanding their rights and by doing so both sink the budget and block access to care for those acutely ill people who truly need it,[67] HMO

66. Robert M. Heyssel and Henry M. Seidel, "The Johns Hopkins Experience in Columbia, Maryland," *New England Journal of Medicine,* vol. 295 (November 25, 1976), p. 1231.
67. Sidney R. Garfield, "The Delivery of Medical Care," *Scientific American,* vol. 222 (April 1970), pp. 15–23, especially p. 19.

executives seek means of regulating the flow of patients. These means compromise, but do not wholly invalidate, the standard arguments about access.

To some degree, of course, the flow of patients regulates itself along lines that have little to do with organizational policy. Even if financial obstacles to care are removed, other costs remain salient—transportation costs, time lost from work or leisure activities, and the aggravation of encountering the medical care system and dealing with its personnel, for example. Moreover, the notion that the elimination of fees for service inevitably increases trivial demands may apply faulty psychology to some consumers. In American society, payment of a fee is one means of achieving legitimacy for a demand. The patient who makes his complaint, receives his service, and pays his bill puts his money where his mouth was. When the fee is removed in an HMO, some members may find themselves caught up in a Schelling-like game:[68] believing that the doctor believes that he (the member) believes that his prepaid premium entitles him to run to the plan with every little ailment, the member may be inhibited from "bothering" the physician.

There is little evidence about the nature and consequences of these logistic and psychological aspects of demand, and there is much disagreement among HMO officials about the problem of the worried well. Although Dr. Garfield's position is sometimes taken to be the Kaiser position, Kaiser officials disagree sharply on the relationship between financing mechanisms and patient characteristics. One administrator, who declared that Garfield's views on the subject were strictly his own, sarcastically attributed the worries about the worried well to "the conceit of the medical profession, thinking that people just love to come to the doctor." Greer Williams noted that Garfield offered no data beyond "Permanente doctors' clinical impressions that 50 to 70 percent of their patients appear well," and that a medical economist at Kaiser had stated he was "unfamiliar with any data to support the contention that—there is an 'uncontrolled flood' of patients." However, Williams also noted that the executive director of the Permanente Medical Group of Northern California had remarked that "one of our big problems is developing an

---

68. The complex interpersonal games based on estimates of another's stakes and intentions were elaborated in Thomas C. Schelling, *The Strategy of Conflict* (Oxford University Press, 1963). For remarks on other ways in which physicians occupying a "gate keeper" role on behalf of a formal organization may deviate from fundamental assumptions of doctor-patient trust, see Deborah A. Stone, "Physicians as Gatekeepers: Illness Certification as a Rationing Device," *Public Policy*, vol. 27 (Spring 1979), pp. 227–54, especially pp. 236–40, and 245–50.

appointment system that will screen members so the sick can get in for service and yet the well and 'worried well' can be appropriately taken care of without swamping our physicians."[69] Be all this as it may, many HMO officials share this concern (or conceit) and therefore adopt a variety of formal and informal mechanisms to regulate the demand for care.

One technique is blunt admonition. "We just tell them, 'Don't waste the doctor's time,' " said the executive director of a small HMO in New England. "We say 'There's 15 minutes set aside for you, and it could be for someone else, so use it wisely.' " Another basic and obvious deterrent is to restore some fees. No HMO is entirely prepaid. All impose at least nominal charges for at least some services, and they do so at least partly as a deterrent to excessive use. Most require small copayments for doctor's visits, eye examinations, drugs, laboratory tests, X rays, home visits, or allergy shots. Over time, the sum of these costs can be substantial, though seldom as large as the out-of-pocket costs the enrollee would incur in a conventional plan. To some unknown degree, these costs deter access to HMO care, just as fees deter access to fee-for-service care.

No HMO is content to let a combination of intangible costs and modest fees make the difference between overuse and appropriate access, however. A more stringent allocational device is simply to let the political economy of management take its course. An HMO attempts to use its staff with high productivity and to keep the number of employees (and therefore its payroll) limited to what is demonstratively justified by organizational growth. Likewise, it plans facilities—especially hospital beds, insofar as it is in a position to plan them—with an eye toward forcing choices and, therefore, economies. If beds are scarce, physicians will decline to hospitalize those who do not really need it and will delay elective surgery until beds become free. If staff is limited and facilities are used to capacity, those seeking services may have to wait for them, or may even have to give up. In sum, if allowed free play, the political economy of management generally leads to some degree of queuing.

Officials of HMOs generally think that some queuing is desirable: by raising the price of utilization it discourages trivial users from pressing their claims. On the other hand, extensive and badly managed queuing may make care unavailable to some who need it and runs the risk that members will be inconvenienced and otherwise alienated from the organization. Therefore, the political economies of management cannot be

69. Greer Williams, "Kaiser: What Is It? How Does It Work? Why Does It Work?" *Modern Hospital,* vol. 116 (February 1971), pp. 86, 89.

given full rein. Access must be carefully managed so as appropriately to balance economies with member satisfaction.

An HMO's major approach to managing access is to set up a fairly rigid set of standard operating procedures that require that contacts between members and providers be channeled along a hierarchy of specialization. Higher (more specialized and expensive) skills are engaged only after significant medical need for them has been demonstrated. Encounters begin when the member makes an appointment with, or recites symptoms to, a receptionist, continue with examination by a paraprofessional or general practitioner, and often proceed to a return visit to these generalists, who monitor symptoms. "The family doctor," as the founding physician of HIP put it, "is the quarterback of the team."[70] Unless something serious is at hand, a visit to a specialist may not be set up before the patient's second or third visit, and then only if the generalists think it necessary. The HIP, for example, counsels members wondering "If I think I need to see a specialist, what should I do?" to "see your family physician first," and warns that "patients who try to diagnose themselves and decide what kind of specialist they need are too often mistaken. They may do themselves real harm by wasting time and delaying proper treatment."[71] Hospitalization is a last resort, reserved for emergencies and for the acutely ill who cannot be treated as outpatients.

When he wishes to enter the system, a member's first contact is usually a telephone call that will be answered by one of the health center's receptionists. Members of HMOs regularly complain of delays in getting their call answered and of the amount of time spent on "hold" once the call has been taken. An administrator in Kaiser's Northern California region, who remarked that "access is Kaiser-Permanente's only Achilles heel," noted that "complaints do come in, especially about the telephone. It may take awhile to get through, then they're put on hold, then they learn it'll take two or three months to get an appointment. People can get mad, especially if it's a toll call. Some bring in the phone bill and say we ought to pay it!" Less common but not insignificant are complaints about the brusqueness of the receptionist once they finally have his or her undivided attention. Remarking some years ago that these were the most frequent member complaints about prepaid group practice, MacColl counseled that "a smoothly functioning reception and appointment system" is crucial.[72]

70. George Baehr, *HIP: A Report of the First Ten Years* (Health Insurance Plan of Greater New York, 1957), p. 3.

71. Health Insurance Plan of Greater New York, "Your HIP Questions Answered," p. 2.

72. *Group Practice and Prepayment of Medical Care*, p. 124.

No HMO administrator wants entry to proceed too smoothly, however, for these initial delays perform a crucial screening function. As an interviewer concluded after discussions with several HMO physicians in California, it is " 'common knowledge' that the small switchboard is the most efficient way of separating the patients with 'real problems' from the 'crocks.' "[73]

The caller who, having made contact with the receptionist, expects to be connected immediately with "his" physician is likely to be disappointed. The physician with whom he generally schedules his appointments will probably be otherwise engaged on or off the premises. The receptionist will listen to the caller's request and general description of the problem and then decide whether he should wait for a scheduled appointment with his doctor or be told to drop in to see those members of the group who are on duty that day.

A routine appointment may be disturbingly far off. Judged against the standard promulgated by HIP, that "the maximum amount of time a patient should need to wait for a non-emergent medical problem is a week for an appointment with a primary care physician and two weeks for an appointment with a medical specialist,"[74] HMOs appear to fall short. One study found that at Kaiser-Portland, members who were not acutely ill waited between six and eight weeks to see a doctor; more than half of the plan's membership thought it took too long to get an appointment.[75] Officials in Kaiser's Northern California region, interviewed in 1978, stated that the wait for a routine appointment with a busy physician could be two to three months, although, as one put it, "if you're running a 104° temperature we'll have you with a doctor in 15 minutes." Washington, D.C.'s GHA was reported to have required a member complaining of a lump in her throat—"one of the classic warning signs of possible cancer"— to wait ten weeks for an appointment, and routine obstetric and gynecological appointments in GHA may entail a wait of more than twelve weeks.[76]

Even as they regret these delays, HMO officials are quick to defend them as an unavoidable means of matching scarce resources to needs. "To fully respond to the demands of every member," the executive director of the GHA declared, "would create costs that would be unacceptable to the

73. Jeff Brown, "What are H.M.O.'s?" (unpublished seminar paper).
74. Health Insurance Plan of Greater New York, *Accountability in HIP: 1974 Financial Report*, p. 14.
75. Spencer Klaw, *The Great American Medicine Show* (Penguin, 1976), pp. 171–72; Greenlick, "Impact of Prepaid Group Practice," p. 106.
76. B. D. Cohen, *Washington Post*, October 3, 1979.

majority of members."[77] Similarly, the director of the Group Health Cooperative of Puget Sound argued that "we can't be immediately accessible to everyone who would like to see a doctor without a big rise in our dues."[78] The medical director of the George Washington University Health Plan linked the need for limitations on access to both the removal of the fee barrier and the danger of the trivial patient:

> "If you were going to have to pay $25 to see Joe Miller, you might just wait to see if your cough was going to get worse, or was just a common cold. But if you have open access to care" and don't have to pay, "you're not going to wait" to go in unless it's impossible to get an appointment.[79]

Dealing with Drop-ins

Because delays for routinely scheduled appointments tend to be long, HMO officials must reconcile themselves to some aggressive insistence that members be allowed to drop in. These requests pose obvious problems. Physicians facing a solid phalanx of scheduled appointments resent it when their day is littered with unanticipated drop-ins, many of whom, they decide, bring trivial complaints that could have waited. Members obliged to wait an hour or two for a very few minutes of a harried physician's time share in the frustration. One means of soothing the frictions inherent in this process is to reserve some time in each physician's daily schedule for drop-ins. Another is to screen requests; a Kaiser plan, according to one of its administrators, does so by urging its members to call before dropping in.

> We *say* it's so we can get their medical record, but the real reason is to keep some of them from coming in. For instance, the guy with the flu—he might do better to take an aspirin and call his own doctor in the morning. Some of our centers have periods set aside for short scheduled appointments. For instance, you might call at 6:00 P.M. and they'll tell you to come in at 8:45. But making this work depends a lot on telephone screening, usually by a nurse, and it can be a problem. If they just drop in, they'll tell them to go to a nearby phone and call and make an appointment just to break them of the drop-in habit.

The aggravations that drop-ins cause for both physicians and members can be reduced somewhat if, on arrival, members are checked by a nurse

77. Ibid.
78. Klaw, *Great American Medicine Show*, p. 172.
79. Cohen, *Washington Post*, October 3, 1979. It is noteworthy that HMO physicians apparently do not give themselves highest marks for access—a sample of salaried doctors in group practice rated their mode inferior to both individual and group fee-for-service practice for "availability of M.D. to patient" (23 percent rated prepaid practice best, while 29 percent and 30 percent selected the group and individual fee-for-service practices). These doctors believed that the distinctive advantages of prepaid group practice were lower costs and more preventive care, not improved access. Stephen P. Strickland, *U.S. Health Care: What's Wrong and What's Right* (Universe Books, 1972), p. 76, table 21.

practitioner, physician's assistant, or other aide. These paraprofessional personnel are trained to diagnose and treat common complaints and therefore may assume, in states that permit them,[80] and in plans that choose to employ them, a substantial share of the burden of giving primary care in HMOs. A paraprofessional may listen to the member's complaints, conduct a brief examination for symptoms, conclude that nothing serious is at hand, offer advice, and send the member home without a physician's examination. Sometimes—especially in states where the law allows paraprofessionals to treat patients only under a physician's supervision—the paraprofessional will do his work, and then leave the room to explain his findings quickly to the doctor, who then talks with the patient very briefly and (as a rule) sends him home.

If the aide or generalist physician whom the member first encounters decides that the symptoms are not serious, nonexistent, or impossible to diagnose, he may prescribe medication, order tests, and tell the patient to go home and take it easy and to call again if problems persist. If the trouble (or merely the member) does persist, he will have to call the receptionist again and confront again the option of an appointment or dropping in. If he chooses to drop in again, he will wait to see the generalist again, and perhaps go through it all yet again before another physician is called in for consultation or referral to a specialist is arranged.

This recitation of steps in HMO care is not meant to suggest that the fee-for-service sector necessarily compares favorably in avoiding delays and frictions. The major differences, however, are: first, that a fee-for-service physician is more likely than his HMO colleague to feel obliged to speak directly to the patient in the course of first contact; second, that the fee-for-service physician is more likely to see the patient himself or to arrange to have him seen by another physician; and third, that in fee-for-service practice, there are fewer obstacles in the way of a patient who decides that he wants to see a specialist—he can call one directly or insist that his physician arrange a referral, and he will usually encounter little resistance.

The Emergency Room Problem

The more specialized the care, the more expensive it tends to be to provide. It is therefore a basic rule in HMOs to try to resolve matters at

---

80. For an account of state limitations on paraprofessionals see Philip C. Kissam, "Physician's Assistant and Nurse Practitioner Laws: A Study of Health Law Reform," *Kansas Law Review*, vol. 24 (Fall 1975), pp. 1–65.

the generalist level whenever possible. Most costly, of course, is hospitalization. Thus HMOs may deliberately put organizational obstacles in the way of access to specialist and inpatient services. One large California plan, for instance, requires advance authorization by one general practitioner and two physicians working under his direction in all nonemergency hospitalization decisions and in all referrals to outside specialists.[81] Not all groups are so stringent, but most adopt some form of deterrent.

Members who prefer not to move patiently through the channels of the organization sometimes adopt a familiar expedient: avoid the crowds by going at an off hour. They call or show up at the plan's emergency room or that of the hospital that handles the plan's emergency business. "Not only in group clinics but all over the country," MacColl lamented in 1966, "the number of people coming to emergency rooms for the treatment of non-emergency conditions has created problems of management. . . . apparently many patients find it more convenient to choose the off-hours for a visit, rather than to avail themselves of the regular services."[82] This practice, HMO officials believe, is bad both for patients (it leads to "episodic" care which is the opposite of the "comprehensive, continuous" care they think desirable) and for the organization (it wreaks havoc on scheduling and budgeting). They therefore try to discourage it.

Most plans attempt in one way or another to educate members to distinguish between proper and improper uses of emergency services. For example, the George Washington University Health Plan in Washington, D.C., devoted half of the front page of the second issue of its newsletter to this chronicle:

> Over recent weeks the following have been received through the telephone answering service (so help us!):
> 3:00 A.M.—Man called having been bitten by a cat. The bite just scratched the skin. Turns out he is not even a member of the Health Plan, but his girl is—and it's her cat.
> 1:30 A.M.—Man called having been stung by a bee that afternoon. It is red and irritated. What should he do?
> 8:00 P.M.—Saturday—Woman is out of her birth control pills. When asked why she hadn't gotten them refilled earlier in the week, she replied she really hadn't expected to need them, but then she went to this marvelous party . . .

81. Andreas G. Schneider and Joanne B. Stern, "Health Maintenance Organizations and the Poor: Problems and Prospects," *Northwestern University Law Review*, vol. 70 (March–April 1975), p. 48, note 41.

82. *Group Practice and Prepayment of Medical Care*, p. 104. The medical director of a New Mexico HMO estimated that "about half of the emergency room care we review is really not emergent or urgent." *Health Scope* (Mastercare–New Mexico Health Care Corp.), vol. 1 (July 1, 1978), p. 3.

9:00 P.M.—Man setting roach traps spilled roach powder on the floor and accidentally stepped in it in his bare feet. What would happen? He was advised that roaches would not likely eat his feet.

4:00 A.M.—Sunday—Man called complaining of rash of 10 days duration. There is music in the background and obvious sounds of a party in progress.

Reminding subscribers, in italics, that "We know of no other health system that provides unlimited [sic] access to a physician 24 hours a day at no [sic] cost," the newsletter went on to explain to readers that the emergency service is for plan members only, that patients should call before coming to the emergency room, and that the room should not be used for nonemergencies. It drove home its lessons with appeals to guilt ("You are not calling the hospital; you will be getting one of our physicians out of bed") and to self-interest ("Inappropriate use of the emergency room or use without prior consent of a Plan physician is not covered").[83] Fee-for-service physicians exchange anecdotes about "crocks" constantly, of course, but few ridicule them in stories they circulate to their patients.

Education alone is seldom adequate to the task, so an HMO typically regulates the emergency room shortcut directly by urging that patients telephone a special emergency number (printed on their membership card) before arriving.[84] A receptionist screens the call, takes the caller's phone number, and then phones the plan physician on call for the night. Thus rudely awakened, the physician telephones the member to discuss the situation. The member may be urged to make an appointment or arrange to drop in the next day, or if the symptoms appear to be actually or potentially serious, he will be told to go to the emergency room used by the plan, where a physician will examine him and perhaps arrange admission to the hospital.[85]

These orderly procedures are meant to screen out members who would use emergency services for routine matters. They may, however, provoke anger and alienation in worried people who must negotiate them. For

83. *Vital Signs*, vol. 1 (Fall 1976), p. 1.

84. Large plans—Washington's GHA, for example—usually maintain "minor injury" and emergency services at which a member may drop in at any time and be treated by a physician or other health worker on duty. See the account of the development and difficulties of GHA's system in Raymond W. Turner, "Urgent Care in the HMO: Evolution of a System in Washington, D.C.," *Medical Care*, vol. 16 (May 1978), pp. 361–71.

85. Most plans instruct members who become seriously ill while out of the plan's service area to proceed to the nearest source of care and then notify the plan at the earliest possible moment so that it might be apprised of, and discuss the course of, treatment. Some set explicit limits on the number of hospital days or the dollar value of care for which a member may be reimbursed in such circumstances. Few plans agree to reimburse other providers for nonemergency care rendered to a member, and the precise definition of an emergency may become an object of controversy between member and plan when the out-of-area provider or the member approaches the plan for reimbursement.

example, a medical school dean recalled the incident that led him to disenroll from a prominent midwestern HMO to which he and his family subscribed some years ago. "One night my wife started coughing up blood. I couldn't make a diagnosis myself and I called the plan's emergency number. This high school girl answered the phone, listened to me, and kept asking, 'is this really an emergency?' I know they have to protect the doctors and all that, but what really bothered me was the sense of doubt she conveyed. After a little of this I got mad and started to sound like a husband. 'I want to talk to a *doctor* and I want to talk to him *now*,' I said. I did, and things worked out, but the incident left a sour taste. Soon after that I left the plan."

Costs of Channeled Access

From the organization's standpoint, procedures to channel access carefully along a hierarchy of specialization make excellent sense. From a financial standpoint, an HMO that insists on using generalist care unless the need for more specialized care is clearly established can serve its members with fewer specialists and hospital beds than can a fee-for-service system, which permits easier access to specialists and which allows or even encourages hospitalization for minor as well as for major medical procedures.[86] The HMO's substitution of generalist and outpatient care for specialist and inpatient care permits it—ceteris paribus—to pass savings along to subscribers in broader benefits or lower premiums. Proponents of HMOs believe that the professional argument for channeled access is equally impeccable: the member is best served when the degree of specialization conforms closely to the nature of the medical problem.

Although there is much to be said in support of these arguments, channeled access does impose costs, mainly pertaining to the spirit of care. It can make the system "a complex maze to patients";[87] the multiple layers of organizational structure along which members are channeled may be "infuriating." As David Mechanic points out, "bureaucratic barriers are exaggerated in large, prepaid group practices and contribute to patient perceptions that they are not fully responsive or caring."[88] There also is danger that negotiating the system may put a premium on skills and

---

86. Mechanic, *Growth of Bureaucratic Medicine*, p. 39; Herbert Klarman, "Analysis of the HMO Proposal—Its Assumptions, Implications, and Prospects," in *Health Maintenance Organizations: A Reconfiguration*, pp. 27–29.

87. *Accountability in HIP*, p. 10.

88. *Growth of Bureaucratic Medicine*, p. 96. See also, Eliot Freidson, *Patients' Views of Medical Practice: A Study of Subscribers to a Prepaid Medical Plan in the Bronx* (New York: Russell Sage, 1961).

attitudes more readily found in higher than in lower social classes, and more common among the worried well than among the "inarticulate ill."[89] Each of the stages described above is both an entry or access point to care and also a stopping point. Because the organization's interests demand that problems be handled at generalist stages as close to the point of entry as possible, the tendency of the system is to hold back, urging the patient back and along to later stages only if need is clear. In these circumstances, skill at "playing the system"—demanding rights, arguing the possibility of problems that tests alone can rule out, being pushy and aggressive—may be necessary to make the system move.

There is reason too for concern about physicians' attitudes and behavior when for any of several reasons—the sudden emergency, the demanding patient who successfully jumps the queue, shorthandedness in the office that day, and others—the highly organized, tightly scheduled, and meticulously budgeted system fails to work smoothly. In a young and struggling HMO, an unpredictable and sometimes burdensome workload is viewed as one of several collective burdens to be shared in service of a good cause. In the Kaiser plans, too, which emphasize duality of management and negotiation of work patterns between the plan and self-governing physicians' groups, these problems seem to be kept in hand. But in the large and growing universe of in-between cases, physicians may regard themselves as exploited professionals, not as combatants in a noble cause, or coequal plan managers, and resentment may deepen.[90]

Clearly, there is a fine but very important line between providing appropriate but not extravagant access to care and obstructing access. Access is obviously a precondition of high quality care and it is noteworthy that the "worst case" HMOs have generated scandals not because—or at any rate, not only because—they delivered poor quality care but rather because they built indefensible barriers to access to care. In general, the worrisome dark side of HMOs is not that they will hire hacks and incompetents, providing technically inferior care, but rather that economic logic could lead them to erect obstacles to access and to pollute the spirit of care.

89. Conrad Rosenberg, "Who Delivers Primary Care in Group Practice?" *Bulletin of the New York Academy of Medicine*, vol. 53 (January–February 1977), p. 106.

90. Asked about the comment of a GHA physician that "the physician who was nasty to a patient was rewarded. He got home earlier. He had fewer appointments" (Lawrence Meyer, *Washington Post*, January 2, 1978), a Kaiser physician speculated that such attitudes could well be present "in a plan like GHA where the doctors have no voice" but he denied that it was an important problem at Kaiser, "where the doctors participate in management."

Notorious worst cases came from California's MediCal program in the early 1970s. Seeking ways to save money on Medicaid, Governor Ronald Reagan's administration aggressively encouraged creation of prepaid health plans for the state's MediCal recipients. The organizations that grew out of the MediCal Reform Act of 1971 varied considerably from one another, but some unquestionably denied access.

In the worst plans, members found many promised services unavailable. Emergency service numbers went unanswered. Emergency rooms were found closed or "not yet" opened. Sick people waited in line at emergency facilities for specialists who failed to appear. These unfortunates were therefore obliged to seek care in the emergency rooms of local hospitals, but when the plan was billed for these services it declined to pay on the grounds that it had not authorized them. Disgusted, some subscribers sought to disenroll. The organizations would then delay their disenrollment papers for several months, continuing to collect state money while enrollees were unable to recover their MediCal cards for use elsewhere. Of course, by the time disenrollment papers were processed, a fresh set of members had been recruited by a variety of questionable appeals.[91]

The MediCal scandals had done serious harm to the emerging HMO cause, HEW Under Secretary Hale Champion observed in 1977. Taking a familiar proponent's position, he denied that these were "real" HMOs.[92] Yet they certainly meet a reasonable definition. They were group practices promising voluntarily enrolled subscribers a defined range of medical services in exchange for a prepaid premium. Unfortunately, real HMOs do face real incentives to place obstacles in the way of members' access. Fortunately, most HMOs appear to counterbalance these incentives, not follow them to their unsavory conclusion.

91. See *Prepaid Health Plans*, S. Rept. 749; Goldberg, "Some Emerging Problems," pp. 55–68. Schneider and Stern, "Health Maintenance Organizations and the Poor," p. 132, note 210, list some of the major solicitation methods: "appearing at the doorstep in doctor and nurse uniforms claiming they were representatives of the Welfare Department and telling recipients that unless they switched over to the new HMO their Medicaid coverage would be terminated; (b) telling recipients they could still continue to see their own doctor, but by signing up for the HMO they would be entitled to an additional new 'transportation' service or other medical benefits not otherwise available to them under the regular Medicaid program; (c) offering free chicken dinners for every member of the household who enrolled; (d) telling frightened Mexican-Americans who neither spoke nor understood much English that unless they enrolled they would receive no more medical care; (e) telling people they were state representatives coming to verify their Medicaid numbers and, having elicited it from the recipient and put it down on the form, requesting the recipient's signature to verify the number and insure continued eligibility; (f) claiming that they were going door-to-door to get signatures for a petition to oust Governor Reagan."

92. "Remarks by Under Secretary of Health, Education, and Welfare Hale Champion before the Group Health Association of America," Los Angeles, California, June 20, 1977, p. 8; reprinted in *Congressional Record*, September 26, 1977, p. 31013.

Somewhere between the best and worst cases presumably lies the HMO norm. Unfortunately, there is very little agreement on what that norm is. No good studies have documented systematic underutilization of physician or inpatient services in HMOs,[93] and studies of HMO utilization give very different answers to the question whether inpatient economies are balanced by access to outpatient services equal to or greater than those of the fee-for-service sector. In a comprehensive review of the literature, Luft found that studies of prepaid groups were "evenly split between those showing more and those showing fewer outpatient visits." (Studies of enrollees of independent practice associations, however, showed "consistently more visits" than in the fee-for-service sector.)[94]

These objective data are inadequate indicators of access both because they fail to address the distribution of access among members (do these rates conceal a situation where the worried well overconsume opportunities for care at the expense of the inarticulate ill, for example?) and because they give no sense of whether members feel subjectively that the access they enjoy conforms to their needs. For this reason, investigators have amassed data on members' satisfaction with various aspects of HMO care. These findings too vary significantly.

For example, Mechanic found that a sample of HMO enrollees in Milwaukee had to travel longer to get to their doctor than Blue Cross–Blue Shield members and had to wait longer to get an appointment, but spent less time waiting in the doctor's office after arriving for the appointment.[95] Gaus and others, on the other hand, found that their sample of HMO members had an easier time contacting the doctor than did their fee-for-service controls and waited the same length of time to get an appointment, and the same length of time in the office. Their fee-for-service group, however, found it much easier to reach a doctor on a weekday.[96] MacColl cited two older studies that showed that 7–8 percent of subscribers were frankly dissatisfied, and between one-quarter and one-half had used out-of-plan doctors at some point, often because of some specific dissatisfaction (delay in forming new relationships, inconvenient appointment systems, transportation problems, dislike of "clinic" atmosphere, dissat-

93. Schneider and Stern, "Health Maintenance Organizations and the Poor," p. 87.

94. Harold S. Luft, "How Do Health-Maintenance Organizations Achieve Their 'Savings'?" *New England Journal of Medicine*, vol. 298 (June 15, 1978), p. 1342.

95. Mechanic, *Growth of Bureaucratic Medicine*, p. 150.

96. Clifton R. Gaus and others, "Contrasts in HMO and Fee-For-Service Performance," *Social Security Bulletin*, vol. 39 (May 1976), pp. 11, 13.

isfaction with the group doctor, and more).[97] Dozier found that HMO enrollees were satisfied with their care in general, highly satisfied with its financial aspects, but significantly less satisfied about the time needed to get a doctor's appointment, about time spent waiting in the doctor's office, about information given them on their condition, and about the number of doctors and places they had to visit to get care.[98] Similarly, Roemer and his associates concluded from a study of enrollees in certain California HMOs, Blue Cross plans, and commercial insurance plans, that the HMOs elicited the highest overall consumer satisfaction, in large part because of the financial aspects of the plan; satisfaction with the medical care received was "more often moderate than high."[99] Mechanic's study, by contrast, found that "although prepaid practice participants were on the whole satisfied with their medical care, Blue Cross participants indicated significantly higher levels of satisfaction on most items."[100]

One explanation for these discrepant findings is that investigators seldom ask the same types of questions of closely similar samples. Yet even when questions and samples are reasonably similar, findings vary significantly, sometimes sharply. The only justified conclusions are that "most people report that they are very satisfied with their health care, regardless of which plan they are enrolled in," that "the existing evidence on relative satisfaction with prepaid group practice is inconsistent," and that "differences in satisfaction are often a product of varying expectations, experiences, and personal attributes as well as a feature of the actual services provided."[101]

Advocates of health maintenance organizations often point out that no study has found evidence of massive or even substantial dissatisfaction among HMO members with their plans. This finding means less than meets the eye, however, because of self-selection factors; it may mean only that those who find no reason to object to the distinctive features of HMOs do not object to the distinctive features of HMOs. These findings, therefore, cannot be taken as evidence that non-HMO members would move in large

97. *Group Practice and Prepayment of Medical Care*, pp. 232–33.

98. Dave Dozier and others, "Survey of Consumer Experience," Report of the State of California Employees' Medical and Hospital Program, 1973, pp. 104–10.

99. Milton I. Roemer and others, *Health Insurance Effects: Services, Expenditures, and Attitudes Under Three Types of Plan*, Research Series no. 16 (University of Michigan, Bureau of Public Health Economics, 1972), p. 58.

100. *Growth of Bureaucratic Medicine*, p. 139.

101. Ibid., p. 138.

numbers to HMOs if these groups became more numerous in the United States[102] or that they would be satisfied with them if they did enroll.

In sum, it cannot be accurately said that access to care in an HMO is either better or worse than access in fee-for-service systems, but only that it is different. The HMO establishes a hierarchical channel of contacts between providers and enrollees and attempts to make access more difficult—as compared to the fee-for-service sector—to care thought inappropriate to the condition at hand. But just as they try to complicate access to expensive specialist and inpatient care, HMOs attempt to provide easier access than does the fee-for-service system to generalist and outpatient care. Here too, however, certain structural obstacles may be imposed in order to discourage worried-well patients from clogging the flow and interfering with the system's ability to treat the truly ill. In short, any evaluation of the accessibility of HMO care depends on an evaluation of the merits of the channeled access HMOs provide.

Cost of Care

The argument advanced most frequently and confidently by HMO proponents and embraced most readily by policymakers is that HMOs are far more economical than fee-for-service systems, by which it is meant that they provide care at lower cost than their competitors. Although the question of costs, unlike those of quality of care and access to it, lends itself readily to quantification, analyses of the relative economies of HMOs and fee-for-service systems tend to be less sophisticated and rigorous than might be expected.

Semantic and conceptual confusion plagues both the literature and popular discussions about HMO costs. Use of the term "HMO savings" is often unclear. For example, whereas Victor Fuchs attributes undefined "savings" of 15–30 percent to HMOs,[103] Herbert Klarman concludes that "at best . . . little that is definitive can be said" on the subject but suggests that "the *saving* in hospital *use* . . . may be appreciably lower than widely estimated." "Of course," he continues, "even a savings of 10 percent, realized in perpetuity," has huge value.[104]

As used in these examples and in most discussions of the subject, the term "savings" might have one or more of three different meanings. It

102. Ibid., pp. 38–39.
103. *Who Shall Live?* p. 140.
104. "Analysis of the HMO Proposal," p. 29; emphasis added.

might mean that HMOs *use less* of some resource or service, such as hospital care; or that HMOs *save money* (as compared to fee-for-service systems) on some service such as hospital care; or that HMOs save money *on their total operation,* presumably by conserving on such resources as hospital care, although the precise source and distribution of economies are seldom presented. In short, the first meaning of "saving" refers to utilization rates, the second to the dollar costs of specific services, and the third to the dollar costs of providing all covered services to an HMO population, as contrasted with the cost of providing the same services in a fee-for-service system. Unfortunately, writers seldom make clear exactly which meaning of the term "HMO savings" they intend to employ.

Rates of Utilization

Most studies of HMO savings document utilization rates. Though various investigations have found widely differing outpatient rates of utilization, almost all agree that HMOs make much less use of inpatient services than do fee-for-service plans. Many analysts assume that reduced inpatient services translate directly into organizational economies, troubling themselves neither about the dollar value of these savings nor about possible confounding variables. Health maintenance organizations economize dramatically on inpatient care; ergo, HMO care "costs less." This inference is simplistic. If all the other components of HMO and fee-for-service costs could be disregarded or held dependably constant, the distinctions among rates, specific service costs, and total organizational costs could be collapsed and the equations implied in much of the literature could be accepted. Unfortunately, the distinctions must be maintained and the equations should be scrutinized carefully.

The lower use of inpatient care in HMOs (as compared to fee-for-service, third-party plans) is both well documented and impressive.[105] Inpatient economies take many forms and appear at several organizational levels. If the HMO is fortunate enough to own its hospital, it can control the number of its beds. It may, like Kaiser-Permanente, maintain about half the number available in the larger system (that is, about two beds per thousand people as against more than four), thus obliging its physicians to ration beds by making hard decisions about who is most in need.[106] Because most HMOs lack this direct control over their environment, utilization

105. Luft, "How Do Health-Maintenance Organizations Achieve Their 'Savings'?" pp. 1338–39.

106. For an argument singling out "the control exercised through bed supply" as perhaps the major source of economies, see Klarman, "Analysis of the HMO Proposal," p. 29.

controls are their major source of economies. They repeatedly remind their physicians about the evil effects of wasted hospital resources, for even a plan with low rates of hospital use may run into financial trouble if its hospital charges are high.[107]

Some prepaid group medical plans, as Auger and Goldstein found, have elaborate review procedures to ensure that patients are not admitted unnecessarily and do not stay in the hospital longer than is justified. "For all but emergency admissions, most plans require that the medical director or senior medical consultant approve any hospitalization before it actually occurs." To limit the patient's stay to the time that is medically necessary, "the plan's medical director bases his admission authorization on a given number of days; should a longer stay appear appropriate, the admitting physician must receive approval for it." Some plans have a system for monitoring the progress of hospitalized patients. In smaller plans, the medical director may "periodically review the patients' charts or visit the patients himself." In larger plans, "health professionals (typically nurses) are stationed in hospitals to make daily reviews of patients and patient charts. Questionable in-patient status is then referred to the medical director of the utilization review committee."[108]

Prepaid groups take a dim view of admitting members to the hospital for diagnostic tests that could be done more safely, quickly, and cheaply outside the hospital. The medical chief of a facility in Kaiser's Northern California region remarked that he believed this to be the single most important source of savings in his organization. The HMO tends also to take a skeptical view of the need for surgery; it typically retains fewer surgeons than are found in the fee-for-service sector and uses their time more intensively. Frugal staffing, in combination with the organization's aversion to unjustified elective surgery, lowers surgical rates considerably—

107. A case in point is the Group Health Association in Washington, D.C. In 1975 the plan used only 420 days of hospital care per 1000 members, but these days were spent mainly at George Washington, a very expensive teaching hospital. Federal Trade Commission, *Staff Report on the Health Maintenance Organization and Its Effects on Competition* (FTC, 1977), pp. 67–68.

108. Richard C. Auger and Victor P. Goldberg, "Prepaid Health Plans and Moral Hazard," *Public Policy,* vol. 22 (Summer 1974), pp. 381–82. The certified hospital admissions plan developed by the Sacramento Medical Care Foundation combines preadmission certification with in-patient monitoring. The plan's nurses "thoroughly monitor a member's progress from the time of his admission to that of his discharge, working with the admitting physician and, as necessary, bringing circumstances that do not appear to warrant in-patient care to the attention of the reviewing physician. The latter, if he feels that continued in-patient status is inappropriate, may request the attending physician to discharge the patient or else to explain the need for continued hospitalization. Disputed cases go to the peer review committee of the Foundation." Ibid., p. 382. See also the account of the cost control techniques of the Physicians' Association of Clackamas County (Oregon) in FTC, *Staff Report on the Health Maintenance Organization,* pp. 96–97.

in 1970 the average ratio of general surgeons to population was one to 12,471 in HMOs and one to 7,573 in the nation as a whole.[109] Fewer surgeons mean less surgery, which in turn means less hospitalization, fewer risks of iatrogenic injury and death, and lower costs.[110] The HMOs perform more surgery on an ambulatory basis than their conventional competitors.[111] They also attempt to get patients out of the hospital or into less expensive beds and settings as soon as possible and experiment with paraprofessional aides and other comparatively inexpensive sources of home care for recuperating patients and the chronically ill. Whereas the patient who wishes to stay an extra day at third-party expense to enjoy a holiday from home and work often finds the fee-for-service doctor acquiescent, the HMO doctor may argue and insist on a timely discharge. Admissions are arranged with speed of treatment in mind: thus Friday admissions, with weekend layovers, are avoided if possible. Preadmission laboratory and X-ray tests are ordered in the HMO's own outpatient units if possible, saving inpatient time and costs.[112]

The precise causes of these inpatient economies have never been adequately explained. True to the literal model of prepaid group practice, HMO critics and many proponents alike have assumed that the explanation must lie in the changed economic incentives physicians encounter in the HMO setting. To the proponents this means that HMO physicians find no financial reward in prescribing unnecessary treatment. To the critics it means that HMO physicians enrich themselves by underproviding. But this line of reasoning oversimplifies the sources of human (in this case physicians') motivation, attributing behavior simply to economic self-interest. Ironically, the fee-for-service critics of HMOs exempt themselves from their reductionism by refusing to follow their argument where it leads, to the conclusion that their own presumably optimal degree of service derives solely from the monetary force of their fees. Nor do they proceed to the logical corollary: that the effect of financial incentives on their own behavior may be waste and extravagant overprovision.

Equally ironic, the HMO defense and counterattack usually join in the economic reductionism. Fee-for-service physicians, it is said, evaluate and

109. Erwin A. Blackstone, "Misallocation of Medical Resources: The Problem of Excessive Surgery," *Public Policy*, vol. 22 (Summer 1974), pp. 343–44.

110. Auger and Goldberg, "Prepaid Health Plans and Moral Hazard," p. 385.

111. Fuchs, *Who Shall Live?* p. 59.

112. Prepaid plans also make sustained efforts to find and implement economies in purchasing and prescribing drugs. See ibid., pp. 97–98, 123, 126; and Auger and Goldberg, "Prepaid Health Plans and Moral Hazard," pp. 386–87.

deliver services only in light of the fees they command, but HMO providers, proud participants in a system that "eliminates fee barriers" and "allows the physician to deal with the patient freed from cost concerns," refuse to acknowledge that money might play a role in their own behavior. Each camp is convinced that economic motives are effective in—indeed solely determinative of—the behavior of the other and play no role whatever in their own. The economists' preoccupation with financial incentives has unintendedly lent legitimacy and energy to an illogical and self-serving debate.

Recently, these narrow arguments have come under critical scrutiny. As Mancur Olson, Jr., and others have pointed out, behavior that may seem rational for an individual considered in isolation may prove not to be rational for him in a collective context, especially one in which his own contribution to the general outcome may be very small or imperceptible.[113] "The larger the firm, the more likely the physician will ignore the effects of his behavior on the well-being of the group."[114] Thus "there is no theoretical reason to expect HMO's to be more efficient than fee-for-service providers. Solo practitioners recognize that they bear the costs of their own ineffectiveness, whereas physicians in groups face a dilution in incentives."[115] A recent discussion of the usual explanations offered for lower HMO use of inpatient care—restricted access to hospital beds, structural arrangements that accompany the union of prepayment and group practice, financial risks borne by HMO doctors, favorable socio-demographic characteristics of HMO enrollees, broader ambulatory coverage in the HMO, and relative ease of consultation and referral among members of the multispecialty HMO staff—concluded that none was adequate,[116] and singled out as "particularly misleading" those " 'rational' explanations which argue that financial rewards or penalties per se induce desired physician behaviors."[117]

The problem is that the traditional economic emphasis on the direct financial incentives of the HMO physician has obscured the importance of the organizational environment in which he works and has nourished a preoccupation with one organizational process and one level of analysis. As chapter 3 argues, the essence of HMO management—and of HMO

113. *The Logic of Collective Action* (Harvard University Press, 1965).

114. Auger and Goldberg, "Prepaid Health Plans and Moral Hazard," pp. 379–80.

115. Luft, "How Do Health-Maintenance Organizations Achieve Their 'Savings'?" p. 1337.

116. George B. Strumpf and others, "Health Maintenance Organizations, 1971–1977: Issues and Answers," *Journal of Community Health*, vol. 4 (Fall 1978), pp. 42–46.

117. Ibid., p. 46.

fragility—lies in striking a satisfactory, stable balance between economic efficiency and professional and member satisfaction. An organizational perspective invites attention to the ways in which this balance is struck not merely in the financial calculi of the individual provider but, more broadly, at and between two distinct organizational levels—the policymaking level of the medical and executive directors (managers) and the behavioral level of the individual providers. The problem, for both analysts and organizational executives, is to understand how incentives at work on the managerial level may be brought to bear on providers.

As Herbert Klarman has observed, incentives deriving from capitation payment—by *subscribers* to the *organization*—work on the policymaking level, but not directly on the providers. It is seldom made clear "how capitation payment to the HMO will change most existing arrangements for paying providers."[118] Indeed, as Freidson's study and the daily exigencies and occasional failures of prepaid groups show, cost-consciousness can be easily blotted out by physicians who prefer the simpler rule that more is better. The proper workings of an HMO depend crucially, therefore, on satisfactory resolution of the level-of-incentive problem.

The constraints of prepayment should be examined not at one level ("the provider") but at two. First, the HMO leadership makes a series of policy decisions about levels of staffing and facilities and about relative emphases among services. "The medical director," as one described his job, "is like a portfolio manager; he takes the group—the investor's stock, so to speak—and invests it where he thinks it'll do the most good." The views of the HMO's leadership and the decisions the leaders make and defend about the relative payoffs of investing the marginal dollar in various medical activities, and in alternative staff patterns and facilities, set a general framework for organizational policy.

The organization's executives must then bring policy to bear on the individual providers. Relations between providers and managers—and the incentives felt by the former—are a subtle mix of autonomy and constraint, highly variable from group to group, and quite uninferable from unaided economic reasoning. A manager obliged to appeal to the providers' immediate economic self-interest, which managers may be able to influence very little in the short term, is in a precarious position indeed. A far more valuable managerial resource is the provider's loyalty to and sense of identification with the group effort. Having reviewed and dismissed the

118. "Analysis of the HMO Proposal," p. 27.

usual economic explanations of HMO economies, Strumpf and his associates arrived at precisely this hypothesis:

> Group dynamics motivate the physician to behave in ways consistent with professional norms of medical practice and the objectives of the organization. . . . The specific techniques used in the operation of a group, e.g., peer review, prehospital admission programs, utilization review, and risk sharing, contribute to existence of individual commitments and identification with short- and long-term objectives of the HMO. Group dynamics, the result of organization pressures and control from peers, from medical group directors, and from the interplay of a group organization combined with a capitation-based system, are believed to determine utilization patterns.[119]

The intertwined effect of organizational policy and of the commitment of providers is to define within the HMO a distinctive context for medical decisionmaking, a distinctive professional-organizational culture, resting on a complex synthesis of values and interests. The HMO physician is not divorced from the norms of fee-for-service medicine; he goes to the same medical schools, receives the same training, and faces the same licensing requirements as other doctors. Like his fee-for-service colleagues, he remains influenced by professional training and norms, the technological imperative, fear of malpractice suits, and eagerness to please patients. Unlike his fee-for-service colleagues, however, he finds these mainstream influences challenged and balanced by questions whether the benefits of routine or new procedures are really worth the cost, by the examples and expectations of his HMO colleagues, and by concern for the effects of his behavior on the well-being of the organization and therewith on his own salary and career. The decisions reached in this environment may not always or even often vary from those a fee-for-service physician would make, but there is a higher probability that trade-offs will be recognized and hard questions posed and explored in the HMO setting. This is perhaps the central appeal of HMOs. They appear to be the best organizational mechanism available with which to reconcile cost-consciousness and professional norms in the daily practice of medicine.

The point, then, is not to dismiss the force of economic incentives in the HMO but rather to view them in their organizational context—a point sometimes overlooked by those who properly emphasize the force of nonmonetary incentives in medical practice. For example, Harvey M. Sapolsky argues that the main problem with the HMO concept is that it overrates the importance of markets and underrates the role of professional

---

119. "Health Maintenance Organizations," pp. 46–47.

pressures in medicine. Indeed, "physicians practicing in organized settings are even more likely than solo practitioners to bow to professional influence in the selection of treatments."[120]

One frequently encounters this either-or formulation. *Either* HMOs run on economic motives, so that they have incentives to underprovide, *or* they respond to professional norms, in which case they have no effective incentives to contain costs. "One cannot have it both ways." But perhaps one can. A more accurate picture is that HMO practitioners, like their fee-for-service counterparts, respond to a combination of economic and professional influences. Whereas the economic camp commits a fallacy of reductionism, the professionalists impute an equally fallacious determinism to professional norms. Their image is apparently that for each medical problem there is a clear and correct, professionally prescribed, answer. In fact, medical practice is replete with gray areas. In many areas of diagnosis and therapy, medical necessity is an unclear or inapplicable concept, the verdict on established or experimental procedures is not yet in, professional judgments may and do differ, and reasonable and conscientious physicians may reach decisions in alternative, equally legitimate ways.[121] Therefore, as economic and professional norms interact, neither must necessarily negate or eclipse the other; instead each may cast the other in an illuminated context.

The fee-for-service physician faces a powerful combination of incentives to treat gray areas as if they were unproblematic. By proceeding with "the best"—that is, the most—care medical technology offers, he reassures his patient, protects himself against malpractice claims, maximizes his own income, and, often as not, sends the bill along to the insurance company. The HMO physician, by contrast, has some motivation to explore the light and shading of the situation with which he is presented; he may wrestle with and ponder the ambiguities of evidence and the ambivalence of professional judgment in the gestalt. Neither economics nor professional

120. "A Solution to the 'Health Crisis,' " *Policy Analysis*, vol. 3 (Winter 1977), p. 117.

121. See Lorrin M. Koran, "The Reliability of Clinical Methods, Data and Judgments," *New England Journal of Medicine*, vol. 293 (September 25, 1975), pp. 642–46, and (October 2, 1975), pp. 965–701; and John E. Wennberg, "PSRO and the Relationships among Health Need, Elective Surgery and Health Status," in *Preadmission Certification and Elective Surgery*, Perspectives on Health Policy, no. 2 (Boston University Medical Center, 1975), pp. 3–15. Wennberg suggests that "there is no consensus *even among the specialists themselves* on how to use the technologies of a particular medical specialty"; that "there are important ideological and behavioral aspects to current patterns of choice of therapies"; that "process standards and guidelines for care which are developed by group consensus techniques" are "hypotheses rather than established truths"; and that consensus will vary greatly both with "the speciality composition and individual preferences" of physicians and with time and place. Ibid., pp. 9, 12, 13; emphasis in original.

training, nor the two in combination need *determine* his behavior; ideally, the interplay between the two clarifies, not forecloses, his options.

Ideally, HMO balancing should work to reinforce (in Freidson's terms) the craftsman orientation in its physicians, as distinct from the entrepreneur (who responds mainly to money) or the official (who gives clients their rights regardless of professional need). It is difficult to say whether HMOs (or fee-for-service systems) attain this happy state in practice. There is no agreement in the scholarly literature on the relative importance of, and the nature of the interaction between, economic incentives and professional norms as sources of physicians' behavior,[122] and the careful, intensive interviewing of physicians needed to explore the question properly has not been done.

In the absence of sound empirical research, one must make do with conjecture. An organizational perspective generates some counterintuitive hypotheses, one being that the stronger the level of general policy and the stronger the sense of provider commitment, the less will the HMO be obliged to rely on specific monetary rewards to motivate balanced behavior. The Kaiser program, for example, which owns its facilities, has a high degree of managerial autonomy, and contracts with full-time physicians who have made a career in the Permanente medical groups, tends to play down the importance of economic incentives operating directly on providers. Long defensive about the effects of the bonuses that some Permanente groups divide at year's end, Kaiser spokesmen deny that bonuses have an important impact on physicians' behavior or on utilization.[123] A veteran Kaiser physician and administrator argued that "good quality care is less expensive in the long run, but this isn't the paramount consideration. Financial incentives are quite different from quality incentives. The bonus is basically a help to management to remind the doctors about utilization and the rest. It's a reminder, not a primary thing. A good doctor won't

122. Interviews disclosed ambivalence among HMO officials on this point. A Kaiser administrator declared: "Philosophical commitment is the key to a well-functioning physicians group," but immediately added, "but you've got to pay the going rate." An administrator at HIP declaimed enviously on the bonuses Kaiser pays its physicians from savings on hospital use, but then noted that HIP's hospital days are well below conventional third-party-payment plans despite peculiar arrangements that give Blue Cross most of the savings. "The commitment is one of principle," he explained. The executive director of a young HMO in New England said that in his plan "doctors are made acutely aware of what services cost. If they make a referral they get a copy of the bill. And we can put pressure on them, asking questions about procedures." But shortly afterward, the medical director of the same plan emphasized that "there are no financial incentives to influence practice here, so the physicians' environment, which leaves a wide latitude for professional life, is the whole picture."

123. "Discussion of the Health Plan—Business Aspects," in Anne R. Somers, ed., *The Kaiser-Permanente Medical Care Program: A Symposium* (New York: Commonwealth Fund, 1971), p. 85.

skimp. He'll do what's needed or he'll quit. And group practice is a fishbowl environment: all see what the others are doing, and how good they are. Doctors here take a pride in quality care. The only competition within the groups is for respect. The incentive is pride, and this overrides skimping." Skeptics may consider such statements to be merely public relations tools carefully honed to reassure the public (and perhaps the providers themselves) that Kaiser physicians do not profit by withholding care. On the other hand, these statements, and the attitudes they purport to reflect, may faithfully reflect Kaiser's remarkable organizational characteristics.

Conversely, an HMO with relatively weak policy controls and relatively detached physicians may be expected to make strenuous efforts to bring financial considerations and rewards to bear on providers. Plans that do not own or control their hospitals, that must rely heavily on fee-for-service specialists in the community, that are uncertain of their planning techniques and utilization controls, and that are staffed by physicians whose income derives primarily from fee-for-service practices and whose attraction to the HMO is mainly pragmatic and economic rather than philosophical and professional may dearly wish to rely predominantly on the rationality of their strategic choices and on the loyalty of their providers. But they will find in practice that they must continually try to establish links in the physician's mind between utilization and the shared financial well-being of plan and provider. The extreme case is the independent practice association struggling to convince indifferent physicians that the plan cannot survive unless they modify their normal fee-for-service behavior sharply.[124]

Newer HMOs, recognizing that the bonus system allows critics to charge that their physicians get rich by holding back services, sometimes opt to do without it. Annual salary increases at the discretion of the medical and administrative leadership serve much the same function, however. In the succinct words of one executive director: "The general corporate situation has a direct impact on salary increases, and they know it."

Nor should the limitations of peer review be taken to mean that administrators and medical directors lack information with which to fine tune their discriminations. Review of hospital admissions and general familiarity gained over time allow the medical director to identify physicians who are too free with hospital care. Computer printouts also identify doctors who significantly vary from the norm for various services, especially

124. For an account of the travails of an IPA, see Steven B. Enright, "Beating H.M.O.s at Their Own Game," *Medical Economics*, vol. 55 (July 10, 1978), pp. 97–111.

referrals. The degree of detail to which a plan resorts in seeking to inculcate cost-consciousness depends on the plan's organizational character, that is, on the combined strength of its managerial controls and its physicians' commitment. The executive director who explained the importance of salary increases (and who heads a younger, struggling plan) noted: "Our doctors are all made acutely aware of what services cost. As bills come in to us, a copy is sent to the doctor, with items itemized. They see that it all comes out of our pocket." An administrator in a similar plan remarked: "Here we pound it into the doctors' heads—*think* about a referral before you make one." By contrast, doctors at a Kaiser facility, according to the medical chief, "don't know how much a service costs. If someone's overdoing it, giving tests or whatever with no patient benefit, that's bad practice and the chief of the department will question it and talk to him about it."

In sum, by means of a mixture of specific reviews and diffuse organizational loyalties, HMOs try to socialize physicians into adopting cost-effectiveness thinking as a way of life. The ratio of review to loyalty will vary with the strength of the plan. The stronger the organization, the less it is likely to exhibit the theoretical preoccupation with direct monetary incentives to providers; the weaker the organization, the more likely it is to display this concern and to adopt practices aimed at manipulating monetary motives.

Dollar Savings

If the HMO's lower use of inpatient care were the whole story, one could readily endorse the proponents' assertion that HMOs are "more efficient systems" whose diffusion cannot fail to save the nation large sums of money. Unfortunately, utilization rates and total dollar savings are two different matters. Although the term "savings" is tossed about with abandon in discussions of HMOs, the evidence on the subject is scanty and unable to support the argument that large numbers of HMOs of diverse origins and structures will necessarily bring great savings to society as a whole.

Harold Luft concluded from a review of the literature on HMO savings that there is "clear evidence that total medical-care costs are lower for HMO enrollees than for comparable people with conventional health insurance."[125] The evidence, however, rests on five studies, of which none

125. "How Do Health-Maintenance Organizations Achieve Their 'Savings'?" p. 1342.

includes HMOs outside of California, all include a Kaiser plan, only three include non-Kaiser HMOs (Ross-Loos, IPAs, and, in one study, the Family Health Plan), three were done before the enactment of Medicare and Medicaid, four are more than ten years old, and the most recent examined the costs of California state employees in 1970–71.[126] Insofar as Kaiser, California, or the HMO enrollments in California ("self-selection may be an important factor," Luft acknowledges)[127] are "different"—and all three may well be—the conclusion that total costs in the Kaiser plans fall 10–40 percent below those of the competition cannot be automatically extrapolated.

The superior economies of the Kaiser plans allowed them to charge premiums that were below those of the Blue Cross competition in three of the studies, equal in another, and higher by only one dollar in the fifth. This advantage, coupled with significantly lower direct out-of-pocket costs, gave the Kaiser plans a consistently lower total cost. So closely competitive a premium is not the rule among HMOs, however, and a true reading of the "cost savings" of the universe of HMOs will await careful studies of non-Kaiser plans.

A useful reminder of the complexities is a recent study that tried to measure systematically the actual costs of providing a wide range of services to members of an HMO in St. Louis as compared to a fee-for-service population.[128] Perkoff and his associates began by gathering data on utilization rates in an HMO and in a matched fee-for-service population. They found, surprisingly, that the two groups had similar rates of surgical utilization, but the HMO used much less nonsurgical care.[129] However, even leaving out of consideration pre- and post-natal visits, obstetrics, and the laboratory services that go with them (an omission that overstates HMO economies), the HMO's utilization rate for all ambulatory services was more than twice that of the controls.[130] Then, after constructing a complicated set of "fee equivalents" for the HMO and the controls, they compared costs. Measured by cost per person per year, the HMO proved more costly for all services except surgery and hospital charges.[131] Posing a logical question—if HMO hospital savings are so sizable, why are HMO

126. Ibid., p. 1337.

127. Ibid., p. 1342.

128. Gerald T. Perkoff and others, "The Effects of an Experimental Prepaid Group Practice, *Medical Care*, vol. 14 (May 1976), pp. 432–49.

129. Ibid., pp. 437–38.

130. Ibid., p. 439.

131. Ibid., p. 441.

premiums generally higher than those of their competitors?—the investigators concluded that much higher rates and costs of ambulatory care
contained the explanation.[132] "Even though the reduction in hospital
utilization was significant, the savings from that reduction did not make
up for the increased costs of providing ambulatory services in a setting
which emphasized preventive care and which made consultant's services
available and paid for them as needed. . . . Organization of medical care
into an effective group with prepayment did lead to reduced hospitalization
and increased ambulatory services utilization, but in and of itself did not
lead to reduced medical care costs."[133]

As Perkoff's work suggests, inferring from inpatient utilization rates the
dollar savings that HMOs realize as compared to fee-for-service systems
is far from simple. Unfortunately, all the relevant complexities are seldom
considered. The usual approach—that of the five studies cited by Luft as
clear evidence of lower HMO costs, for example—begins by looking at
the relative *premiums* paid by subscribers to HMO plans and to the
competition. Usually (the Kaiser California plans are of course major
exceptions), HMO enrollment costs more, although the differentials are
narrowing in some parts of the country.[134] The next step is to compute the
out-of-pocket costs—expenses not covered by the plan—incurred by
members of the different modes. Generally, HMO out-of-pocket costs are
far lower than those required by conventional plans. When premiums and
out-of-pocket costs are summed, it often turns out that HMOs offer wider
benefits for a smaller total cost than their fee-for-service competitors.
A source of special complexity, however, is out-of-plan use—the number
and the dollar cost of services the membership seeks outside the plan.
Estimates of this variable differ widely. For instance, Roemer found that
in Kaiser's Southern California plan, 7 percent of hospitalizations and 12
percent of ambulatory visits took place outside the plan.[135] Greer Williams,
however, cited a consumer satisfaction survey in the same plan at about
the time of the Roemer research, in which 44 percent of a random sample

132. Ibid., p. 444.
133. Ibid., pp. 444–47.
134. Data from the federal employees health benefits plan in the mid-1970s showed that "for the first
time the impact of escalation of inpatient care costs has become so great as to put the *price* of HMO health
care below that for Blue Cross/Blue Shield high option coverage and essentially equal to that for Aetna
high option coverage." (The average price per family per month for 40 HMO plans was $86.20, an
increase of 20.0 percent from 1975 to 1976; for Blue Cross–Blue Shield, high option, $93.47, an increase
of 35.6 percent; and for Aetna, high option, $83.33, an increase of 34.0 percent.) Jeffery Cohelan, "An
Update on HMO's," prepared for Washington Conference on Legislative Update of the International
Foundation of Employee Benefit Plans, May 25, 1977, p. 9. Emphasis in original.
135. Roemer and others, *Health Insurance Effects*, p. 40.

of plan members replied yes to a consumer survey that asked if "you or any member of your family had occasion to see any other doctor or used any other medical services" since joining the Kaiser plan. Williams observed that in a similar study in 1961 one-third of old members and one-half of new ones claimed to have used such outside services at some time.[136] In still another survey, 55 percent of respondents had used outside medical services since joining Kaiser and 78 percent of these members had had to pay for them.[137]

Ideally, costs of entering HMO and fee-for-service systems should be taken into account too. For example, HEW Under Secretary Hale Champion proclaimed that in a study of 1,000 Medicaid recipients enrolled in the GHA of Washington, D.C., the annual prepaid costs per capita for 1972, 1973, and 1976 were $282, $232, and $282, respectively, compared to Medicaid fee-for-service costs per capita of $373, $435, and $465 over the same period.[138] Benefit *packages* are one thing; benefits *received* are another. The gap between entitlement and services no doubt varies considerably among plans. The GHA may be exemplary; some of California's MediCal groups were not. No one knows what the norm is. As one federal Medicaid official remarked: "Our data system should allow us to objectively compare HMO utilization data with fee-for-service. But we can't even show today that Medicaid people in HMOs get services! We should know. We should be comparing units and prices. But we don't know about the units, the services. Maybe they're getting less care than in fee-for-service, maybe they're getting all kinds of health maintenance services they don't get in fee-for-service—we just don't know."

Summing up premium costs, out-of-pocket costs (including out-of-plan costs), and possible access costs deriving from the logistics of entering HMO systems to yield an HMO total is a complex endeavor. Comparing this total with one derived for comparable services delivered to comparable fee-for-service populations is, of course, even more complicated. If, as the General Accounting Office (GAO) contends, the federal government "has not demonstrated that it can accurately determine average fee-for-service costs for Medicare and Medicaid enrollees," then obviously one cannot

136. "Kaiser," p. 83.

137. Cited in Judy Carnoy, Lee Coffee, and Linda Koo, "Corporate Medicine: The Kaiser Health Plan," *Health PAC Bulletin*, November 1973; reprinted in abridged form in David Kotelchuck, ed., *Prognosis Negative: Crisis in the Health Care System* (Vintage Books, 1976), p. 376.

138. Cited in a speech by Congressman Paul Rogers, Democrat of Florida, in *Congressional Record*, daily ed., March 10, 1978, p. H1921.

accurately *compare* such costs with average HMO costs in order to determine which is cheaper.[139]

Ironically, at about the time that Under Secretary Champion was flailing the Nixon administration for having dared to call the federal HMO effort a demonstration and for having failed to share his view that the superiority of HMOs was an indisputable fact, the department over which he presided took a different view. "At this time there are very little data to permit comparison of HMOs with alternative forms of health care delivery," an HEW report remarked. "Data on total fee-for-service health costs and utilization are virtually nonexistent."[140]

Social Costs

Even if all these complications were taken fully into account and even if all proved consistent with the case for large HMO dollar savings, these calculations capture only what may be termed the *subscriber* costs of HMO membership. Attention should also be given to two *social* costs relevant to the savings hypothesis. One such cost is that of organization-building. Health maintenance organizations are often expensive to launch and sustain through the break-even point. For example, the Kaiser Family Foundation gave $3.5 million in grants and interest-free loans to the Kaiser Cleveland plan,[141] and the red ink incurred by the plan, which grew slowly, was said to be many times that figure. Other examples were given in chapter 2. Like Blue Cross and Blue Shield plans, but unlike commercial insurance plans, HMOs are usually tax-exempt too. These various subsidies carry opportunity costs of social capital and should be factored into calculations weighing the costs of HMO versus fee-for-service care. (The costs of repaying loans also add to subscriber premiums, of course.) As one federal HMO official put it: "It's not like opening a boutique. If you look at the experience of Kaiser, the Harvard Community Health Plan, and some others, you see it requires really *heavy* investments—not the $4 million the feds make available, but well over $10 million." (Independent

139. U.S. General Accounting Office, *Can Health Maintenance Organizations Be Successful?—An Analysis of 14 Federally Qualified 'HMOs'* (GAO, 1978), p. 22. See, however, Mildred Corbin and Aaron Knute, "Some Aspects of Medicare Experience with Group-Practice Prepayment Plans," *Social Security Bulletin*, vol. 38 (March 1975), pp. 3–11.

140. U.S. Department of Health, Education, and Welfare, Division of Health Maintenance Organizations, *Health Maintenance Organization Program Status Report: December 1976*, DHEW Publication no. (HSA) 77-13022 (HEW, 1977), p. 41. This study also notes that its own inpatient data comparing HMOs with Blue Cross "are not adjusted for age, sex, or any other characteristics."

141. Sam Packer, "The Cleveland Program: Merger of An Independent Plan with Kaiser-Permanente," in Somers, *Kaiser-Permanente Medical Care Program*, p. 170.

practice associations are, of course, much less expensive to launch and maintain.)

It may be argued that the savings engendered by an HMO's efficiencies handsomely repay such largesse. There is little hard evidence to support this contention or to estimate the magnitudes involved, however. One study estimates that a typical HMO does not begin to reduce total community costs until its fifth year, when it has reached an average enrollment of 25,000 members, and that a plan that enrolls 50,000 members over ten years of operation may be expected to save the community about $1.6 million.[142] Although this study calculated the annual costs of physicians' services, hospital care, and administration in HMOs and in the fee-for-service system, the weight it assigns to organization-building costs is unclear, and it is unclear too how their inclusion would affect the estimate of savings.[143] Of course, plans that go out of business, fail to reach 25,000 or more members, grow more slowly than expected, or encounter higher costs than anticipated will realize smaller savings, if any.

A second social cost may be termed adaptive costs. For example, a study of the competitive effects of HMOs conceded that "it is possible that hospitals may raise rates to compensate for reduced utilization" introduced by HMOs.[144] Moreover, as Alain C. Enthoven pointed out, another important response to HMO competition—an expansion of benefits by Blue Cross or other plans—"would have the effect of reducing consumer cost-sharing and, by inducing greater utilization of services, increasing per capita spending."[145] Thus HMO savings might be lost to society at least in part because of the reactions they triggered in the fee-for-service sector. Very little is known about these important possibilities.

If the argument that HMOs now in existence cost less than other modes is debatable, still more so is the contention that HMOs generalized in large

142. ICF Incorporated, *Selected Use of Competition by Health Systems Agencies, Final Report* (Washington: ICF, Inc., December 1976), pp. III-35–III-36.

143. See ibid., pp. III-25–III-31, and app. B.

144. FTC, *Staff Report on the Health Maintenance Organization*, p. 117, note 1. In a similar vein, John E. Wennberg observed that "not only is the regional cost superiority of HMO's still unproven by the data" but there also are "plausible mechanics" by which HMOs might raise costs. He gave this example for his state, Vermont: "A profit maximizing and cost minimizing operation by an HMO would . . . require that it enroll the nonpoor Vermont native and that when their enrollees require care, they be placed in less expensive hospitals if at all possible. This procedure will raise the cost for the nonenrollees. The end result is that the price to non-enrollees rises, . . . and the total costs to the region may rise." *Physicians Training Facilities*, Hearings, pt. 1, pp. 203–04.

145. "Competition of Alternative Delivery Systems," in Warren Greenberg, ed., *Competition in The Health Care Sector: Past, Present, and Future* (Federal Trade Commission, 1978), p. 339.

numbers to the population as a whole are a promising—indeed *the* most promising—cost-containment strategy. For one thing, as noted above, the true incidence and extent of subscriber, organization-building, and adaptive costs have not been carefully calculated over a representative range of plans.[146] Furthermore, the current crop of HMOs has benefited from favorable natural selection—they have grown up where their founders had reason to think they could take root, compete, and thrive, and they have enrolled few rural, poor, or unemployed people, and few of the elderly.[147]

Another basic question, then, concerns extrapolation costs: how would HMOs fare if the strategy were transported to less favorable areas and less "desirable" populations? To answer that question demands first that data on the utilization of HMOs be adjusted by age and sex to show what the rate would be for a population comparable to that of the nation as a whole or some specified part of it. For example, it was estimated that Kaiser-Permanente's 488 days of hospital stay per year per 1,000 members in 1969 would have risen to 613 days if they were so adjusted (this was still below the Blue Cross rates for the same area, however).[148] The organization-building costs of making HMOs take root in areas less ripe for them than those in which they now exist might be high too.

If the national government or other sponsors choose to help the new groups meet these costs, they may also require them to provide additional services. Kaiser-Permanente's savings over the costs of fee-for-service care can hardly serve as an example if HMOs are expected to offer significantly broader benefits than Kaiser. John M. Glasgow argues that data on neighborhood health centers raise questions whether "we can have significantly more services, of a significantly different nature, for everyone including those presently medically indigent, at essentially no increase in

146. In Canada, William A. Glaser observes, the concern in the United States over "health center organization and multidisciplinary teamwork for primary care" has generated much discussion and, at least in Quebec, some concerted efforts to create health centers. But, he notes, "when one adds to the operating costs capital and overhead costs supplied by the local government, they prove more expensive than predicted." *Paying the Doctor under National Health Insurance: Foreign Lessons for the U.S.*, 2d ed. (Bureau of Applied Social Research, Columbia University, 1976), p. VI-6.

147. The mortality rate for HMO-type projects is in fact quite high. Of 79 organizations that received aid from HEW before the enactment of P.L. 93-222 in 1973, 37 terminated their effort to develop HMOs. In fiscal 1975, HEW awarded feasibility grants under the HMO law to 108 organizations. Within about one year, 41 of the grants expired. For the data and a discussion of reasons for these terminations see George B. Strumpf and Marie A. Garramone, "Why Some HMOs Develop Slowly," *Public Health Reports*, vol. 91 (November–December 1976), pp. 496–503. The data cited here are taken from pp. 496, 498.

148. Arthur Weissman and Richard Anderson, "Characteristics of Health Plan Membership," in Somers, *Kaiser-Permanente Medical Care Program*, p. 41. The data came from Kaiser's Northern California region.

total expenditures."[149] In short, a valid, policy-oriented judgment on the cost-saving potential of HMOs requires that three dimensions of the question—subscriber costs, social costs, and extrapolation costs—be disentangled and explicated individually with much greater refinement than has so far been evident.

Even if one granted, finally, that every question raised above could be answered in ways entirely favorable to the proposition that HMOs realize impressive total dollar savings over the fee-for-service sector, it is important to be clear about exactly what these savings mean and where they go. The usual image conjured up by the talk about "savings"—that HMOs manage to rescue sizable sums of money from the bloated national health care budget—can be misleading. The image may be accurate when dollars saved from HMO utilization economies are devoted to bringing premiums below those of conventional plans and then stabilizing or reducing them further. They need not be, however. Even if savings on inpatient care are not consumed by higher outpatient use, the plan's management may devote them to higher salaries or bonuses for physicians, to building up reserves or contingency funds, to expanding or renovating facilities, or to launching a new plan or aiding a faltering one. Management bent on getting rich quickly may devote savings to administrative overhead. (A study of fifteen plans in California found that an average of 52 percent of the budget went for administration, leaving less than half for health services; these and other figures led the GAO to conclude that California's program for MediCal recipients may have cost more than fee-for-service care in that state.[150]) In these cases, savings are not diverted from the health care budget, but rather redistributed within it.

Conclusion: Contingencies of Performance

This chapter took as its point of departure a set of arguments that distinctive features of prepaid group practice enable HMOs to offer more accessible care, of higher quality, and at lower cost, than fee-for-service systems. Inspection of these arguments suggested that there is little reason to accept their premises, and much reason to question the conclusions they deduce. There is no logical and little empirical basis for concluding that

149. "Prepaid Group Practice and HMOs: Separating the Rhetoric from the Reality," *Connecticut Medicine*, vol. 37 (November 1973), p. 589.
150. Schneider and Stern, "Health Maintenance Organizations and The Poor," pp. 129–30.

quality of care in HMOs is, in general, better or worse than in the fee-for-service sector. Few data on outcomes address the question; those that do are vulnerable to various forms of spuriousness, including the omnipresent possibility that HMO subscribers are largely self-selected and therefore "different." Malpractice data are in similarly short supply and are similarly open to disputes of interpretation. On procedural dimensions the comparative picture on quality of care is again cloudy. Certain features of HMO life—notably, intensive scheduling and harried and resentful physicians—can lead to hurried and even careless, not to mention abrupt and brusque, care. On the other hand, HMO physicians can be screened by a watchful medical director and group at the point of entry, monitored over time, promoted to full partnership in the group only gradually, and made subject to at least some scrutiny in the outpatient as well as inpatient aspects of practice. All this suggests that a well-run HMO offers its enrollees a higher chance of receiving treatment by well-trained and conscientious physicians than do the laxer processes governing fee-for-service practice. Whether positive or negative potential predominates in HMOs, or whether they tend to cancel each other out, cannot be judged in general; the answer depends on specific organizational traits that can be discerned only on close inspection of individual groups.

It is also unjustified to argue that HMOs offer more or less access to care than do fee-for-service competitors. Accuracy permits little more than the judgment that HMO access is different. For both professional and economic reasons, HMOs attempt to establish a clear hierarchy of providers, along which a patient is channeled in a set sequence of contacts. The intent is to reserve specialist and inpatient care for those who truly need it, making such care less accessible, but more appropriately accessible, than it is in fee-for-service systems, and to encourage complaints that are not serious to be handled by generalists (paraprofessionals, general practitioners, internists, pediatricians), on an outpatient basis, thus making this type of care more accessible than it is in the more specialized and hospital-oriented fee-for-service sector. This division of labor seems to match provider to need and task more efficiently than the mainstream system does. However, there is a risk that organizational procedures may, willfully or by inadvertence, make it difficult for members, particularly the least aggressive, to initiate contacts within the hierarchy of providers or to move from one stage to the next in timely fashion.

Finally, the familiar contention that HMOs provide care at dramatic savings over fee-for-service systems runs up against several semantic and empirical ambiguities. Beyond question, even HMOs that do not own or control their own hospitals have inpatient utilization rates well below those of conventional plans. These economies in the rate of hospital utilization cannot be automatically translated into dollar savings, however, because other facets of the organized system that is an HMO should be, but seldom are, taken into account. For example, one of the few studies that examine rates in the light of dollar costs found that one HMO's inpatient efficiencies were offset by a vastly higher rate of ambulatory visits that consumed most of the dollar savings and left the HMO about as costly as comparable fee-for-service care.

Even if one grants that the sum of HMO premiums, out-of-pocket costs, and out-of-plan use yields a cost lower than fee-for-service plans, it would capture only one aspect of cost important to public policy. Social costs must be considered along with subscriber costs. Health maintenance organizations typically require large public or private subsidies in their early years of operation, capital that could be otherwise invested. The arrival of an HMO on the local medical scene has repercussions for other providers; if, for example, local hospitals compensate for the HMO's inpatient thrift by raising per diem charges for other patients, and local insurance competitors respond by expanding coverage, encouraging higher utilization, society may not reap the benefits of the HMO's frugality.

Finally, even an accurate reading of the individual and social costs of current HMOs will not automatically yield an estimate of the savings possible if HMOs expand to new areas and enroll new population groups. Today HMOs take root more or less naturally, where there is thought to be a promising potential for growth and stability. Large outlays will be needed to make them take root in less naturally hospitable milieus and large operating subsidies may be required to keep them in business over time. Today HMOs usually avoid enrolling the poor, the unemployed, rural residents, and the elderly. If they begin to do so, their population mix, utilization patterns, and costs will change. On balance, then, Freidson's suspicion that the federal government's decision to encourage HMOs was based "far more on fiscal and ideological grounds than on grounds of empirical evidence"[151] is well founded.

151. *Doctoring Together,* p. 13.

Part Two

CHAPTER FIVE

Prepaid Group Practice
Goes to Washington

'That is not what I meant at all;
That is not it, at all.'
T. S. Eliot, "The Love Song of J. Alfred Prufrock"

IN 1970, prepaid group practice abruptly entered the federal agenda, and in the following year it came, much to the amazement of its proponents, to occupy a prominent place among federal health care initiatives. The concept, incorporated in legislation in 1973 after three years of debate, has been alternately pushed into the wings and pulled back to center stage. Because most of the intermittent theatrics and silences have centered on the Health Maintenance Organization Act of 1973 (Public Law 93-222), amended in 1976 (Public Law 94-460) and again in 1978 (Public Law 95-559), the first step toward understanding the progress of the federal HMO assistance effort is to understand the politics that brought the law into being between 1970 and 1973—the subject of this chapter.

Even when judged against the customarily undisciplined and freewheeling style of legislative-executive cooperation in the United States, the politics of the HMO program may appear confusing, counterintuitive, even whimsical. A quick synopsis of events surrounding the passage of the law seems to sustain this impression. In enacting Medicare and Medicaid in 1965, the administration of liberal Democratic President Lyndon B. Johnson and a strongly liberal Democratic Congress agreed that it was prudent to reassure organized medicine that the new federal venture in financing would in no way interfere with the organization and delivery of care. They therefore wrote into the law: "Nothing in this title shall be construed to authorize any Federal officer or employee to exercise any supervision or control over the practice of medicine or the manner in which medical services are provided, or over the selection, tenure, or compensation of any officer or employee of any institution, agency, or person

195

providing health services or to exercise any supervision or control over the administration or operation of any such institution, agency, or person."[1] Later that year they wrote a similar pledge into the statute providing for a regional medical program.[2]

Most observers were caught by surprise when, five years later, Republican President Richard M. Nixon, a moderate conservative, skeptical of growing federal involvement in the private sector, and the American Medical Association's (AMA) preferred candidate in 1968, proposed to a Democratic Congress that the federal government launch a coordinated reorganization of both the delivery and financing of care by sponsoring those sworn antagonists of fee-for-service medicine, prepaid group practices, newly christened health maintenance organizations (HMOs). The initiative, which relied almost entirely on the literal theory of prepaid group practice (PGP) explored in part 1 of this book, was the product of a fragile coalition among planners in the Department of Health, Education, and Welfare (HEW), assisted by Dr. Paul Ellwood, a physician and policy analyst; the Office of Management and Budget (OMB); and the White House. Coalitions formed quickly. The AMA reacted with predictable displeasure and appealed to conservative and moderate members of the House of Representatives to contain the proposal. Spokesmen for and officials of established prepaid group practices reacted with unpredicted distaste for the proposal and approached liberal Democratic friends in Congress in hopes of improving the administration bill.

During 1971 and 1972, both House and Senate considered HMO legislation but failed to reach agreement. Beset by partisan and ideological disputes, the House failed to report a bill in either year, while the bill passed by the Senate in 1972 strained the coalition between liberal Democrats in that body and PGP spokesmen. In 1972 the coalition in the executive branch broke down too, leading Nixon to reconsider his position on federal aid to HMOs and to temper publicly his administration's previously enthusiastic support for its own proposal. In 1973, Congress finally passed legislation quite different from what either the president or the PGPs wanted. Nixon signed the bill and called it "another milestone" in the administration's health care strategy.[3] Many HMO advocates, however, denounced the act, which came to be derided as the "anti-HMO act of 1973."

1. Social Security Amendments of 1965, P.L. 89-97, sec. 1801.
2. Heart Disease, Cancer, and Stroke Amendments of 1965, P.L. 89-239, sec. 900(c).
3. "Statement on Signing the Health Maintenance Organization Act of 1973, December 29, 1973," *Public Papers of the Presidents: Richard M. Nixon, 1973* (U.S. Government Printing Office, 1975), p. 1029 (Hereafter *Public Papers: Nixon, 1973*).

In some quarters, a simple explanation for this political chaos has taken hold. The HMO proposal, it is argued, was a simple and good idea complicated to the point of ruin by certain legislators, most especially Senator Edward M. Kennedy, the Massachusetts Democrat, who would not rest content with allowing HMOs to face a competitive, fair market test with the fee-for-service system, but instead stubbornly insisted on saddling HMOs with numerous social goals that made them, in effect, a stalking horse for national health insurance. This is not the view that will be taken here. This chapter will argue that the HMO proposal was not the simple, self-evident, and self-regulating strategy its generalist supporters took it to be, and that once the full complexity of the issue became clear, the comprehensive range of policy issues it raised naturally and appropriately attracted a very full list of disagreements of value, opinion, and interest about the proper design of the health care system and its reform. These disagreements raised many more issues than merely the merits of a fair market test versus a social goals approach to HMOs and divided not only congressmen but also executive branch officials, policy analysts, interest group spokesmen, and the PGP community itself. In short, the keys to explaining the peculiarities of HMO politics between 1970 and 1973 are the strategy's peculiar combination of high complexity and low consensus, and the shifting and unsettled coalitions this combination produced.

From Anathema to Initiative

Followers of the prepaid-group-practice movement have extolled the merits of their mode of medical organization since it first appeared in the United States in the late 1920s and 1930s.[4] Their arguments gained an audience among scholars and New Dealers when the Committee on the Costs of Medical Care, in the course of a massive research inquiry in the early 1930s, argued that the union of prepaid financing with physicians' group practice was the most rational response to the economic uncertainties

---

4. Prepaid medical plans established by employers for the benefit of their workers date to the late nineteenth century in the United States. The first independent prepaid group practice plans were founded in 1929—the Community Hospital of Elk City, Oklahoma, a medical cooperative, and the Ross-Loos plan of Los Angeles, a group practice clinic which contracted to provide health care to employees of the city water and power departments. For a succinct review of early industrial sponsors and "contract medicine," see Kaiser Foundation Medical Care Program, *Organized Health Care Delivery Systems: A Historical Perspective*, 1978 annual report, pp. 7, 9; for an account of the early PGPs see William A. MacColl, *Group Practice and Prepayment of Medical Care* (Washington: Public Affairs Press, 1966), chap. 2.

of the Depression and to powerful forces of specialization and technological development in medical science.[5] The physician minority of the committee dissented from this view, as, of course, did the majority of solo fee-for-service physicians represented by the AMA. As it turned out, the need for prepaid medical coverage, dramatized by the Depression, was met by arrangements that interfered minimally with the established system of medical delivery and that even separated coverage of hospital care (Blue Cross) from coverage of physicians' services (Blue Shield).[6] The committee's plea for a comprehensive approach—one that addressed the financing of both hospital and physician care and combined these financing reforms with appropriate changes in the delivery system—went unheeded. Spokesmen for organized medicine deplored it outright; many New Dealers agreed that the argument made sense on the merits, but they made little effort to incorporate it in public policy.

The political logic of the situation was straightforward. Those most impressed with the merits of prepaid group practice were also those whose chief concern was national health insurance, meaning a large and direct federal role in paying for medical care. Their fight for national health insurance pitted them against the AMA, which represented the dominant fee-for-service solo-practitioner sector. Advocates of national health insurance saw no point in doubling their troubles by proposing to use federal power to upset the prevailing delivery system along with existing private payment plans. Because the liberals generally viewed the financing problem as more pressing and important than the delivery question, they tacitly agreed to avoid talk about prepaid group practice in order to narrow the range of conflict and fight one battle at a time. The fight for national health insurance dragged on until 1965, and the fight for prepaid group plans never began.[7]

The enactment of Medicare and Medicaid changed American medical politics significantly, indeed fundamentally, by unsettling what had been

5. *Medical Care for the American People: The Final Report of the Committee on the Costs of Medical Care*, Committee Publication 28 (University of Chicago Press, 1932).

6. For the minority views see ibid., pp. 152–88; also, I. S. Falk, "Medical Care in the USA—1932–1972: Problems, Proposals and Programs from the Committee on the Costs of Medical Care to the Committee for National Health Insurance," *Milbank Memorial Fund Quarterly/Health and Society*, vol. 51 (Winter 1973), pp. 1–4; and I. S. Falk, "Proposals for National Health Insurance in the USA: Origins and Evolution, and Some Perceptions for the Future," *Milbank Memorial Fund Quarterly/Health and Society*, vol. 55 (Spring 1977), pp. 165–71.

7. The Federal Employees Health Benefits Act of 1959, P.L. 86-382, did, however, authorize payments on behalf of federal employees enrolled in "comprehensive medical plans," of which "group-practice prepayment plans" were one type and "individual-practice prepayment plans" the other.

stable ideological and partisan political configurations. Once the battle for this modest form of national health insurance had been won, liberal Democrats were obliged to consider both the limitations of the policies they had enacted and their undesired side effects. Likewise, conservative Republicans were compelled to acknowledge that a costly program of medical benefits legislated and financed by the federal government was here to stay; the market might play a role within these government programs but it was no longer a feasible alternative to them. In the post-Medicare era, in short, liberals and conservatives, starting out from dissimilar positions about newly given facts, converged on the practical problem of rationalizing federal health care programs. For reasons to be developed as this chapter proceeds, the search led first of all to prepaid group practice.

Following the enactment of Medicare, liberals were of course delighted that the federal government at last participated in paying the medical bills of many of its neediest citizens. On the other hand, they were disturbed that so much of the federal effort would consist of picking up the pieces, of assuaging the suffering of the elderly, victims of largely irremediable conditions, and of the poor, whose illnesses might have been prevented if their symptoms had been addressed earlier. The need to supplement hospital benefits and treatment of disease with preventive and primary care—to encourage comprehensive care—seemed compelling. At the same time, conservatives, worried about the fiscal implications of open-ended federal reimbursement of medical bills on a retrospective, fee-for-service basis as Medicare and Medicaid spending rose immediately beyond its projections and continued to soar year by year, began to entertain second thoughts of their own. Prepaid group practices, it was pointed out, offered comprehensive preventive, ambulatory, and inpatient care; faced incentives to serve patients before illnesses developed; and operated with budgets and costs fixed in advance each year. Among liberals and conservatives alike, interest in PGPs was newly piqued.

Prominent Medicare officials in HEW's Social Security Administration might have been expected to seize the opportunity to launch a policy drive for prepaid group plans. Some of them, after all, had led the fight for Medicare, were unenamored of traditional fee-for-service medicine, remembered the arguments of the Committee on the Costs of Medical Care, and saw the analytical case for improvements in the delivery system. In fact, these officials, eager to get Medicare off to a good start and wary of antagonizing the AMA further, continued to approach the question gingerly.

In 1966, political executives in the HEW secretary's office worked to secure legislation offering federal mortgage insurance for construction of facilities for physicians in group practice.[8] In doing so, they rode a tide that was rapidly bringing more of the physician population into some form of group arrangement. Wilbur Cohen, a master legislative tactician who was well aware of the arguments on behalf of prepaid group practice, may have been employing his accustomed "salami tactics," intending that *prepaid* group practice would be the next, or at any rate a future, legislative slice. But when HEW executives were asked to devise administrative arrangements that would permit prepaid group practices to receive their familiar prospective capitation payments for Medicare beneficiaries, they were firmly rebuffed. Many HEW officials had a high opinion of prepaid group practice and expressed open admiration for the Kaiser plans' success in providing good care at reasonable cost. The merits of the Kaiser plans had little to do with the realities of Medicare, however. Adjusting the detailed, highly complex Medicare law, drafted with retrospective cost-based reimbursement in mind, would require a tremendous investment of agency time and effort on behalf of the 2 percent or so of the population who belonged to PGPs. The old political obstacles remained too: special administrative exceptions would anger the AMA at a time when Medicare and Medicaid were new and fragile, and conciliation in the interest of a harmonious start was the order of the day. Picking a new fight with the massive fee-for-service sector for the sake of the tiny group of PGPs made no political sense. Thus, ironically, the liberals within the federal bureaucracy who had been and continued to be quickest to see the substantive merits of prepaid group practice were now slowest to perceive their growing political appeal.[9]

Elsewhere, however, interest grew steadily stronger. In 1967 a report prepared by HEW's assistant secretary for program coordination had kind words for PGPs; a National Advisory Commission on Health Manpower extolled the virtues of the Kaiser system at length;[10] the department awarded a grant to the Group Health Association of America (GHAA)

8. The Demonstration Cities and Metropolitan Development Act of 1966 (P.L. 89-754), which established the model cities program, authorized, in title XI, federal mortgage insurance for group practice facilities.

9. Judith M. Feder, *Medicare: The Politics of Federal Hospital Insurance* (Lexington Books, 1977), pp. 82–94. On reaction in the social security administration to the Nixon HMO proposal, see pp. 130–33.

10. William Gorham, "A Report to the President on Medical Care Prices" (Department of Health, Education, and Welfare, February 1967), especially p. 4 ("Group practice, especially prepaid group practice, should be encouraged"), p. 34; National Advisory Commission on Health Manpower, *Report* (GPO, 1967), vol. 2, app. 4: *The Kaiser Foundation Medical Care Program*, pp. 197–228.

to study the feasibility of launching PGPs in new locations; and the Office of Economic Opportunity (OEO) awarded a grant to Kaiser-Portland to enroll disadvantaged residents in its service area.[11] Throughout 1968, the terms "prevention," "ambulatory care," "primary care," "community health centers," "group practice," and even "capitation" percolated in academic pronouncements and congressional speeches. Many speakers noted approvingly that prepaid group plans combined most or many of these desirable elements. In 1969, organized labor announced that it would launch a major drive for national health insurance, and spokesmen made it clear that their proposals would actively encourage PGPs.[12] Early in 1970, Senator Jacob Javits, New York Republican, introduced his proposal for national health insurance, which would depend on "comprehensive health service organizations" to deliver care under prepaid arrangements.[13] In 1970 and 1971 Senator Kennedy, Democratic Congresswoman Martha Griffiths of Michigan, and others joined with organized labor to introduce the health security plan, in which a wide set of cradle-to-grave benefits would be federally financed and administered.[14] A host of more modest proposals followed, all but one of which—the AMA's medicredit plan—explicitly included prepaid groups as recognized health plan options. None of these bills, however, proposed a prepaid group practice *strategy*—that is, a federal effort that would directly encourage the rise and growth of such plans.

Initiative by Elimination

Considering the diffidence of the friends of prepaid group practice, many observers were surprised, indeed shocked, when President Nixon, as part of his legislative program for 1971, called for federal financial aid

11. Merwyn R. Greenlick, "Medical Service to Poverty Groups," in Anne R. Somers, ed., *The Kaiser-Permanente Medical Care Program: A Symposium* (New York: Commonwealth Fund, 1971), pp. 138–48.

12. See transcript of a broadcast by the AFL-CIO social security director, Bert Seidman, in *Congressional Record*, March 18, 1969, pp. 6769–71; reprint of an article by Seidman, in ibid., August 13, 1969, pp. 23935–37; excerpt from an AFL-CIO publication quoting its president, George Meany, calling for national health insurance, in the development of which "pre-paid group practice plans would be integral," in ibid., December 8, 1969, pp. 37760–61.

13. *Congressional Record*, April 14, 1970, pp. 11521–36.

14. Kennedy introduced his labor supported Health Security Act (S. 4297) in August 1970; *Congressional Record*, August 27, 1970, pp. 30142–67. On provisions for "comprehensive health service organizations," see especially pp. 30149 (sec. 47) and 30162 (sec. 87). Congresswoman Griffiths and numerous cosponsors introduced the counterpart measure (H.R. 22) in the House a few months later; ibid., January 26, 1971, pp. 490–94. About a year earlier, Mrs. Griffiths had given high praise to Kaiser and two medical care foundations on the West Coast when introducing her own plan; ibid., February 9, 1970, pp. 2783–85, especially p. 2784.

to build a network of health maintenance organizations, by which he meant prepaid group plans and independent practice associations (IPAs), both nonprofit and for profit, across the country. Nixon too had his national health insurance bill, and he, like the other sponsors, expected PGPs to play a role in it.[15] Unlike the others, however, Nixon proposed a separate and distinct federal program to encourage what were now being called HMOs.

At first glance it surprised many that an ambitious initiative to extend the federal role in the delivery of health care should come from Richard Nixon. As the nation's top Republican, the president enjoyed the support of the AMA, a political spender second only to organized labor and an organization whose official coolness toward prepaid group practice barely disguised its members' deep hostility to it. As a moderate conservative on most domestic issues, Nixon tended to resist greater federal intervention in the private sector. Several facts of political life, however, made it clear that the administration could not go indefinitely without exerting leadership in the area of health care.

By all available indicators—percent of the gross national product devoted to spending on health care, absolute dollar amounts spent, cost increases over time, increases in hospital costs relative to those in the consumer price index—the cost of health care in the United States was rising steadily, rapidly, and "alarmingly." By 1970, large cost overruns in Medicare and Medicaid had become chronic and worrisome—so much so that they were considered "uncontrollable."[16] It was widely taken for granted among politicians, union leaders, health planners, and (apparently) the general public that the delivery system should be improved, health care benefits expanded, and costs contained. That the federal government should take the lead in fashioning these reforms, and in striking the trade-offs they required, seemed equally evident.

Many approaches had been identified, but none captured the attention of the media and the public more fully than the growing list of bills to

15. Nixon's employer-based National Health Insurance Standards Act and its publicly funded companion for the poor, the Family Health Insurance Plan, were unveiled along with the administration's HMO assistance initiative in the president's health message to Congress on February 18, 1971. "Special Message to the Congress Proposing a National Health Strategy, February 18, 1971," *Public Papers: Nixon, 1971*, pp. 182–85.

16. An uncontrollable program is one in which the authorizing legislation requires the government to pay certain costs that cannot be reduced by means of the annual budgetary and appropriation processes. Reductions and limitations could come about only by a change in the authorizing legislation itself. See Murray Weidenbaum, "Budget 'Uncontrollability' as an Obstacle to Improving Allocation of Government Resources," in Joint Economic Committee, *The Analysis and Evaluation of Public Expenditures: The PPB System*, 91 Cong. 1 sess. (GPO, 1969), vol. 1, pp. 357–68.

introduce national health insurance, of which the Kennedy-Griffiths health security plan was by far the most ambitious. It seemed that health care policy in general and national health insurance in particular would be key items of contention in the 1972 presidential election. Many observers believed that the enactment of some form of national health insurance was nothing short of imminent. Many such proposals, especially those offered by Democrats in Congress, and most especially that offered by Kennedy and Griffiths, would be very costly to the federal treasury. On the other hand, they promised to reduce much of the risk and insecurity with which limited and shallow coverage and rising out-of-pocket costs and insurance premiums burdened consumers and employers, and they promised firm federal controls on medical care budgets and charges. For all these reasons, White House aides and top health care officials in HEW understood that the administration had to have a program. They therefore began casting about for policy options that would restore the administration's initiative in the field, steal the Democrats' thunder, and—equally important— produce appealing policy outcomes at modest cost to the federal treasury.

The administration's ideological conservatism was decisively offset by the political conviction that in policy matters the best defense was a good offense. This philosophy had been articulated by presidential counselor Daniel P. Moynihan in July 1969. Noting that he was "pretty discouraged about the budget situation in the coming three to five years," Moynihan had cautioned Nixon:

> I fear you will have nothing like the options I am sure you hoped for. Even more, I fear that the pressure from Congress will be nigh irresistible to use up what extra resources you have on a sort of ten percent across-the-board increase in all the Great Society programs each year. This is the natural instinct of the Congress, and it is hard for the president to resist. If your extra money goes down that drain, I fear in four years' time you really won't have a single distinctive Nixon program to show for it all.[17]

Coming to the point, Moynihan wrote that he was "doubly interested" in seeing the president send to Congress a "family security system," which later became known as the family assistance plan.[18] Not only could the United States afford the plan, but it would be a "genuinely new, unmistakably Nixon, unmistakably needed program, which would attract the attention of the world, far less the United States." He concluded: "Once

17. Quoted in Richard P. Nathan, Assistant Director, Office of Management and Budget, "Memorandum for the Director," July 14, 1969.
18. See Vincent J. Burke and Vee Burke, *Nixon's Good Deed: Welfare Reform* (Columbia University Press, 1974); Daniel P. Moynihan, *The Politics of a Guaranteed Income: The Nixon Administration and the Family Assistance Plan* (Random House, 1973).

you have asked for it, you can resist the pressures endlessly to add marginal funds to already doubtful programs. . . . This way, in 1972 we will have a record of solid, unprecedented accomplishment in a vital area of social policy, and not just an explanation as to how complicated it all was."[19]

This logic applied with equal force to the problem of health care costs and the threatening pressures from Congress for a national health insurance program. In 1969 and early 1970, however, two problems stood in the way of a sustained effort to develop a health policy. First, the top White House, OMB, and HEW generalists who would fashion a "genuinely new, unmistakably Nixon" health care program were preoccupied with the design of and fight for the family assistance plan. Second, these officials and their top aides knew, and knew that they knew, very little about health care policy. "We were in no man's land in health policy," one of them remembered in an interview. "We'd gone for six months without an assistant secretary for health while the AMA and Congress blocked Knowles. Egeberg was named real quick, and he wasn't beloved at the White House. Everything was in chaos. None of us knew much about health care policy and neither did anyone at the White House."

Frustrated, administration officials saw that the problem could neither be grasped nor made to recede. For one thing, the family assistance plan itself kept pushing thorny health care issues into view. Well before the plan was proposed to Congress in August 1969, a former Budget official recalled in an interview, its architects had recognized that the new program would create a "disconnect" with the public-assistance-based Medicaid program, and that the latter could not be left intact. Thoughts turned to a supplementary Medicaid program incorporating health care benefits for the poor to supply the connection. But the problem did not end there. Questions of equity between the poor and the working near-poor, the continuing headache of uncontrollable costs, and—not least—the persisting danger that Kennedy and other congressional Democrats would seize the initiative or outbid and inflate any administration plan for limited health care financing argued for a general and rounded health care strategy, one that addressed the special problems of the poor, the needs of the better-off population, and the problem of cost-containment in a coordinated, consistent policy package. With resignation and little enthusiasm, administration officials conceded that these tangled issues would have to be addressed when time permitted.

19. Quoted in Nathan, "Memorandum."

As the family assistance plan made its way through the House and into the Senate, discussion of the ingredients of an administration health care strategy proceeded at a leisurely pace. Early in 1970, however, a legislative event abruptly forced the administration's hand. When Wilbur Mills, chairman of the House Ways and Means Committee, announced that he would hold hearings in March on amendments to Medicare and Medicaid, the administration grew worried. Political executives in HEW and the White House, newly in charge of costly programs enacted under Johnson and run by officials of suspiciously Democratic loyalties, feared that the hearings would degenerate into a Democratic insiders' dialogue between the programs' congressional patrons and the bureaucratic specialists who ran them. The administration's silence would look unpresidential and would extend an invitation to congressional-bureaucratic collusion and initiation. Yet the generalists were still, as one of them put it, "swamping around" in the health policy options and had no concrete idea whatever to offer as their own.

None of the obvious initiatives meshed politics and policy in a way the administration could accept. A logical and economical approach to cost-containment in Medicare and Medicaid was to reduce benefits or to expand beneficiaries' share of medical expenses, but this course was politically risky.[20] An equally logical means to the same end—governmental regulation of costs or services—was ideologically distasteful. And as yet the administration's plans for a national health insurance package that would do justice to the family assistance plan, the poor, and the nonpoor were incomplete.

Work on a distinctive, politically feasible Medicare strategy, now pursued with mounting urgency, centered in the office of HEW Under Secretary John Veneman, a former member of the California state legislature. As it happened, Veneman's special assistant Tom Joe, a welfare policy expert who had worked in the California bureaucracy and as a long-time aide to Veneman, had recently been negotiating with the staff of the American Rehabilitation Foundation over details of a study that organization was carrying out under contract with HEW. At one meeting the foundation's executive director, Dr. Paul Ellwood, accompanied the staff and impressed Joe strongly and favorably. Ellwood, Joe recalled, was not only a physician but also a policy analyst with pronounced views on the

20. In 1971 the administration did propose increased cost sharing by Medicare beneficiaries, but Congress was unenthusiastic. Indeed, Democrat Russell Long of Louisiana, chairman of the Senate Finance Committee, remarked that he had been persuaded not to pursue the idea by Social Security Commissioner Robert Ball, "who felt that the idea departed too sharply from social insurance principles." Feder, *Medicare*, pp. 133–34.

very issues he and other HEW generalists were thrashing out. Not only did Ellwood share their concern about the problematic incentives of existing Medicare and Medicaid reimbursement arrangements, but he also appeared to have some appealing ideas about what to do about them. Surprised and delighted to encounter this rare combination of qualities, Joe in turn surprised Ellwood by asking if he would be willing to join a small group of high HEW officials to discuss health care policy. Shortly thereafter the two men arranged a meeting, on the evening of February 5, 1970, at Washington's Dupont Plaza Hotel. Joe prevailed on Veneman, Lewis Butler, HEW's assistant secretary for planning and development and also a Californian, and Dr. Thomas Georges, a former Pennsylvania state official on the Temple University medical faculty, to attend.

None of the participants knew Ellwood well and each was skeptical of Joe's promise that an unstructured session devoted to conceptualizing and education would prove beneficial. Ellwood, however, who could be (in the words of one participant) "inspirational" and "evangelical" was both that night, and a sense of revelation quickly replaced disbelief. Ellwood's arguments about the need to develop, by means of public policy, organizational forms to encourage prevention, timely primary care, and economies of hospital care tied together the fragments of the generalists' own thinking. Ellwood wanted a shift in the *incentives* that governed medical treatment under existing fee-for-service arrangements and was pointing out the kind of leverage the federal government might apply with the billions of dollars it spent each year on Medicare and Medicaid. Veneman, Joe, and Butler were, of course, well acquainted with the Kaiser plans and admired them, but they knew that Kaiser's operations were highly distinctive, if not unique. No plan to sprinkle the nation with Kaiser plans was tenable. Kaiser might be a prototype, in the sense that it suggested general organizational features and patterns, but an organization-building initiative would have to include other approaches too—such as the San Joaquin County Medical Foundation, the nation's first, with which the Californians were also familiar.

Drawing and embroidering on the literal theory of prepaid group practice, Ellwood now suggested precisely this: that the famous PGP model be broadened and made flexible so as to accommodate a wide variety of organizational types—medical foundations, plans launched by medical schools, variants of neighborhood health centers, and more—whose common defining feature would be contractual acceptance of responsibility to provide a comprehensive range of services to members in exchange for prepaid premiums. The organizations, Ellwood explained, would be "health maintenance organizations," for their incentives would lead them to practice preventive medicine, offer primary care before inpatient care was needed, and in general do everything possible to keep or make their members healthy. Budgetary incentives would also lead them to search for the most efficient means of caring for their members consistent with quality. The organizations would be, in essence, self-regulating systems: their innate economic logic would keep them cost-conscious, accessible, and careful. Moreover, the economies realized by these organizations would put competitive pressure on indemnity plans and revitalize market processes throughout the health services industry, making it in turn more self-regulating, and averting the need for greater governmental regulation. The HMO option, moreover, would be purely voluntary: it would take nothing away from anyone and would be in no sense required.

For all these reasons, Ellwood argued, the federal government should take steps to help HMOs get started and to make them more widely available. If the government merely acted as catalyst, offering the infant industry both its stamp of approval and some modest start-up aid, private capital newly attracted to a growing "health maintenance industry" would flow in to carry the plans to the break-even point, whereupon subscriber premiums would finance their operation. In sum, the HMO strategy would allow the government to use very small sums as leverage for large results.[21]

Veneman and the others listened with keen interest, for Ellwood had packaged their major analytical themes and pointed out a way to carry them into public policy. All admired the general concept and each was especially drawn to particular aspects of it. One participant recalled that Veneman and Joe, who had been grasping for means to use the government's authority and purchasing power as leverage to bring about greater cost-effectiveness in Medicare and Medicaid, seemed especially pleased that HMOs would mean reduced hospitalization and a fixed set of benefits purchased at a known, fixed premium in advance. If the federal government could prepay its Medicare and Medicaid expenses and budget in advance its annual costs for those beneficiaries in HMOs, it would take an important step toward controllability. Dr. Georges agreed that had HMOs been

21. This account of Ellwood's arguments draws on interviews with participants at the February 5 meeting and on "Plans for a Health Maintenance System" (HEW file folder), which includes a paper by Paul Ellwood, " 'The Health Maintenance Plan': Health Reform," February 25, 1970 and a paper called "The Health Maintenance Strategy," March 9, 1970. The main ingredients of the argument were later published in Paul M. Ellwood and others, "Health Maintenance Strategy," *Medical Care*, vol. 9 (May–June 1971), pp. 291–98.

available in Pennsylvania, buying Medicaid services at fixed cost would have made his job much easier. Butler was delighted that HMOs offered an alternative to regulation. He recalled later in an interview:

> Ellwood took an old idea—PGP and Kaiser-Permanente—and said, this ought to be part of a very different policy strategy, one that avoids regulation. The point was to take a close look at the incentives, to set up a self-regulating system. Kaiser has the right incentives, and it's much easier to regulate quality than costs. As they say, the FAA approach is easier than the CAB. The idea was consistent with Republican ideology and fit well with our general ideas. Ellwood spelled it out and our reaction was "Hey, that sounds good," and "We don't have any better idea." As a lawyer I'd worked on regulating the phone company and I knew something about public utility regulation. It's hard to do. I knew that if you're talking about regulating not ten phone companies but thousands of hospitals, it's going to be a lot harder. My only quibble with Paul's model was that it was too detailed. I said, why not allow solo practitioners to produce these services, as long as they did so with the right incentives? There must be fifty different arrangements. Don't specify the number of doctors and all that. Just set up the framework and the incentives and let them do their work. I didn't call this by the name "IPA," but that was the general idea.

The group readily agreed on the merits of the proposal. "Consensus," one participant recalled, was "instantaneous." The real question—indeed the only question—they concluded, was how to sell it politically. One thing seemed clear: entrusting the transition from concept to initiative to the bureaucracy would be fatal. Ellwood had presented very similar ideas to officials in the Health Services and Mental Health Administration (HSMHA) late in 1969 only to have them sniff that prepaid group practice was nothing new. Asking Social Security and Social and Rehabilitation officials to reconcile prospective capitation payments with the language of the statutes and regulations of Medicare and Medicaid would elicit endless niggling questions, cavils, and complications, and the program specialists, distressingly experienced and adept at such nitpicking, would exhaust everyone's goodwill and patience. As a practical matter, the generalists agreed, if the health maintenance initiative was to be saved from drowning in the bureaucracy and prepared for the next month's Ways and Means hearings, they would have to work it up themselves, with help mainly from their personal staffs. Then they would have to sell the concept to the White House.

As the meeting adjourned, Veneman asked Ellwood and Butler to work up a position paper as the basis for the administration's proposal to Ways and Means. Ellwood soon submitted a detailed exposition of his plan, which Butler edited. When, as a matter of bureaucratic politesse, the HMO document was circulated to appropriate people in the department for comment, most reactions were politely skeptical. Ruth Hanft, an aide to the assistant secretary for planning and evaluation, observed that one of the paper's major shortcomings "is the lack of description of how we move from the current system to the proposed one." Would providers cooperate? Could the pertinent licensure laws be changed, and the necessary utilization review systems be set up? "What are the incentives for sponsoring Health Maintenance Organizations and at what level?" "There is no definition as to what is included in comprehensive health maintenance plans." Hanft's opinion was that even assuming it was possible, many years—perhaps twenty—would be required to "develop enough new organizations within communities to develop competitive situations."[22]

Arthur Hess of the Social Security Administration wrote that the principal problem he found in the plan was "how you get from here to there in any reasonable period of time." Hess added that he knew of "no organizational or societal structure in our Nation on which to predicate the widespread development of contracts of this kind." Nor was he persuaded "that the complex system of incentives and arrangements needed to subject such plans to 'market influences' will guarantee cost control."[23] Nor was it clear that Kaiser was an appropriate prototype. Indeed, Kaiser executive Scott Fleming cautioned Ellwood that "a similarly conceived program starting afresh in 1970 would almost inevitably produce a significantly different economic picture by the time it had become reasonably well established. . . . Whether that significantly different picture would reflect markedly higher or markedly lower costs or similar costs would depend upon the unique development of that particular program. Hence, although we desire to cooperate with you in your search for generalization, we can only be most skeptical of attempted generalizations."[24]

Although these warnings were important, indeed fundamental, they made little impression on the HEW generalists. Butler recalls reassuring Ellwood after a meeting with some of the skeptics, who "had all dumped on him." "He thought it had been a disaster," Butler noted. "I admitted there had been no cheering, but politically the important thing was that they had commented. We controlled the process. They had no vote."

22. Ruth S. Hanft, Office of the Assistant Secretary for Planning and Evaluation, to Lewis H. Butler, Tom Joe, "The Health Maintenance Plan," March 3, 1970, pp. 1–3.

23. Arthur E. Hess to Mr. Tom Joe, Mr. Lewis Butler, "The Health Maintenance Plan—Draft of 2/25/70," March 2, 1970, pp. 1–2.

24. Letter from Scott Fleming to Dr. Paul Ellwood, March 4, 1970, p. 2.

The White House, of course, had not a vote but a veto. Yet to the generalists' surprise, the job of selling HMOs at the White House went smoothly. The AMA had not yet caught wind of what Veneman and the others were contemplating (in any case, one of the HEW protagonists later recalled, the prevailing view was that the AMA had "shot its wad" on the Knowles affair), and the program specialists in the Social Security Administration and the Social and Rehabilitation Service had neither the ear nor the confidence of top White House aides, who fully shared the HEW generalists' view that the department was divided between "us" (the administration) and "them" (the suspect specialists).

Butler was a personable and persuasive man, an observer later remarked, and he used all the right arguments: HMOs cost little, were optional, took nothing away from anyone, emphasized markets and competition, and were self-regulating. The argument, this observer recalled, was always "at least it's better than x." This was one argument in favor of the HMO option; another was that the White House could think of no x better than it. Few alternatives were both politically feasible and ideologically compatible, and most of these few had yet to be worked out in detail.

A deeply involved participant summed up in an interview the decision-making process that led to White House endorsement of the generalists' plans:

> By sheer luck and ineptness the one presidential message we had that sounded anything like pro-incentive was HMOs. . . . We were out to lunch on FHIP [the family health insurance plan]. We had no ideas about national health insurance—we didn't even like the sound of it. There was no money for new programs. There was nothing resembling a health message that was worth a damn except HMOs. Ehrlichman had said to come up with the outlines of a presidential health message and an option paper setting out the pros and cons. We did it—an eleven page paper on HMOs, with three options. First, the president could say it. Second, nobody could say it. Third, the secretary of HEW could say it. We recommended option three. For one thing it wasn't presidential and we didn't really have a message. The president had no business making a big statement about HMOs when we really had no health policy. For another thing, this option left us in charge.

To the generalists' delight, the White House approved option three and on March 20, the Friday before the Monday on which the Ways and Means hearings were to start, HEW program specialists were told that the proposals on which they had been working would not be needed. The administration, they learned to their surprise, would propose that a part

C option embracing HMOs be added to Medicare. None of them had any idea what part C was, an official later recalled.[25]

As offered by the administration, Medicare part C would combine the hospital benefits of part A and the physician coverage of part B and add to them new preventive services and prepayment of coinsurance and deductibles. The committee rejected this approach, however, and the administration reduced its request to new statutory language permitting beneficiaries to receive then-covered services from HMOs. When it came time to complete action on the bill, Veneman, one of the few administration officials whom the committee honored by admission to closed mark-up sessions, feared that the measure might be lost, for the committee had discussed it very little. At the end of a long day, however, Chairman Mills inquired whether anything remained to be resolved. Veneman reminded him of part C, whereupon Mills asked if there was any opposition to it and found none. "No one knew what they were doing," an observer remembered, but part C was on its way to the House floor. The generalists were elated. One recalled:

> Our reaction was "We got it made! We have our own statement plus instant legislation!" We kept asking Mills if a statement would be okay and when he said yes, Butler started writing one for Finch, who hadn't been in on the details. Egeberg was out of town. Hess and Ball [of SSA] were running around. We gave Finch the statement and asked him to "read fast please." Veneman put out the word to the press office. Someone called Egeberg and told him, "You're for HMO's. We just put out a statement." We were thrilled: we were in the HMO business!

Health maintenance organizations had cleared their first hurdle in the House, but the question now before the generalists was what to do for an encore. They knew that the option they sought would be limited by the small number of existing HMOs and their concentration on the West Coast. The idea of creating more HMOs in order to bring the option to more people, one of them later recalled, "just fell into place as the logical next step." There was no consensus, however, about whether an effort should be made to broaden the role of HMOs under Medicare and, by means of negotiations with and demonstrations in the states, Medicaid; to develop pilot HMOs by means of project grants under HEW's control; or to persuade the White House to ask Congress to authorize a major effort

25. Beverlee A. Myers, "Health Maintenance Organizations: An Illustration of Federal Health Policy Development," prepared for the Massachusetts Public Health Association, April 13, 1972, p. 5.

to develop HMOs. The month-and-a-half blitz that sold first the White House and then the Ways and Means Committee on part C had succeeded beyond the planners' hopes; the next step, it was clear, would take more time and preparation. In May, therefore, Secretary Robert H. Finch set up a small project group in his office, chaired by Veneman, and staffed by officials from various HEW units.[26] In June the House passed the Medicare amendments, with part C intact (the Senate would not do likewise until 1972), and Elliot L. Richardson replaced Finch as secretary of HEW. Meanwhile, the study group's research and debate continued.

One major finding was that a federal HMO development effort would be an extremely complex endeavor. By August, the group had identified fifteen major unresolved policy issues, raising such problems as consumer involvement in HMOs, levels of capitation payments, risk-sharing by physicians and hospitals, size of HMOs, and number of HMOs to be developed. As it turned out, however, resolution would have to wait, for about the time these issues were being identified, HEW found itself entrusted with a much larger agenda—examining and refining options for a major health message the president planned to deliver six months later.

An Ambiguous Understanding: HEW and OMB

Although the explorations earlier in the year had been whittled down to an HEW statement on the part C option added to Medicare, the larger policy issues could not be deferred much longer. In the summer of 1970 the Nixon administration, nearing the end of the first half of its first term in office, had said next to nothing about health policy. Edward Kennedy and labor leaders were intensifying the pressure for a broad national health insurance program, and health care costs continued to rise. In the media and on the political stump, somber warnings of a deepening crisis had become commonplace. Each week saw new proposals introduced in Congress, and Republicans were increasingly supporting Democratic health bills for want of an administration alternative.[27] The administration would have to act, and a presidential health strategy announced in a well-publicized presidential health message early in 1971 was the chosen approach. Now the administration had six months to decide what it wanted to say.

26. Ibid., pp. 6–8.
27. Eric Redman, *The Dance of Legislation* (Simon and Schuster, 1973), p. 165.

Within HEW, two task forces were quickly established, one to deal with changes in the health care delivery system, the other to address financing. Identifying options was no problem; in fact, within a month the delivery task force had found two hundred and fifty of them. One was HMOs. As the bureaucrats sifted through the options and developed the pros and cons, however, HMOs did not stand at the head of the list. In fact, they were, in the delicate phrase of one participant in the process, "not necessarily prominent."[28]

In October, however, the generalists again rescued HMOs from the rough hands of the program specialists. Richardson, who had grasped the substantive and political appeals of the HMO strategy immediately upon taking office in June, and had become an articulate and energetic advocate, upset the planners' work by asking them to remove HMOs from the miscellany and present him with a well-developed HMO option. Working under something like the forty-eight-hour deadline that seemed inevitably to accompany such requests, the staff concluded that it might be reasonable to assume that thirteen hundred HMOs of various types could be in existence within five years provided that about one billion dollars were invested in development grants and loans.[29]

If the staff's projections—and especially their price tag—were to be believed, Richardson would have no easy time persuading the White House that important new forces for cost-containment could be placed on the health care scene with a few million "catalytic" dollars of federal aid. Nor did a solution draw closer when economists and lawyers in the secretary's office set about revising the staff's analysis and helpfully concluded that ten thousand HMOs could be started within five years at no additional federal investment if all the nation's hospitals were converted into HMOs![30] The HMO concept was so amorphous and experience with it so limited that the contours of policy kept expanding precisely when they should have been narrowing.

Soon, however, OMB narrowed HEW's options for it. As planning for the president's message continued, it became clear that even if the HEW generalists were prepared to argue for a billion dollar—or even a multi-million dollar—budget figure, OMB officials would oppose them strenuously. From the outset OMB officials had viewed skeptically HEW's enthusiasm for HMOs. As a part C option in Medicare, HMOs posed little

28. Myers, "Health Maintenance Organizations," p. 9.
29. Ibid., p. 10.
30. Ibid.

risk—and little cost. Indeed, a high OMB official had noted about two weeks before Mills accepted the proposal that one advantage of the part C approach was that it would "enable us to make many of the points in the Butler paper without committing ourselves—until we have had more experience—to the corporate form for health maintenance providers."[31] The growing talk of a federally sponsored development effort without the benefit of such experience was another matter, however. One OMB official later remembered sardonically how the HEW generalists made HMOs sound like "the greatest thing since sliced bread." Another recalled the office's disappointment with the "endless and not very useful materials HEW kept dredging up about HMOs." The proposals, he concluded, "lacked conceptual and analytic integrity." The OMB's traditional role was to cast a jaundiced eye at departmental enthusiasms, and HEW's vague and shifting thoughts on HMOs allowed it to play this role often. What good were inferences from Kaiser data if the organizations to be encouraged would unquestionably differ from Kaiser in major respects? If HMOs were so good, why could they not develop on their own? Why did they need federal money? The reply, that HMOs were an infant industry facing heavy start-up costs and many political and legal obstacles that deterred private funding sources, was admittedly plausible. But, to avoid vociferous OMB objections, direct federal costs must be kept modest and in particular must not extend to federal subsidies of HMO operations. The OMB took a dim view of subsidy programs generally, and it also considered the prospect of federal "supply-side" subsidies for HMOs offensively reminiscent of such Great Society enterprises as neighborhood health centers which, at the time, it was trying to lead to financial self-sufficiency. "Demand-side" subsidies, meaning support for consumer purchasing power under a national health insurance program, were more equitable, staff argued, and more in line with the administration's philosophy. The OMB conceded the need for supply-side reorganization, and it followed that HMOs might be a useful companion piece to the administration's health insurance plans—but only if they could be launched with modest federal investments and could then support themselves in the competitive marketplace.

The OMB officials recognized that HEW had awakened considerable interest in HMOs at the White House and they would not try to alter the broad outlines of this agreement. They were determined, however, to ask hard questions and to trim back the government's financial commitments—

31. Memorandum from Richard P. Nathan to Lewis H. Butler (copies sent to members of the Health Project Group and ex officio), "Listing of Major Health Reform Proposals," March 10, 1970, p. 3.

at least until the president himself made a decision. Knowing that OMB's fiscal reservations were shared at the White House and that HMOs had all along been sold there as a modest, low-cost initiative, HEW had no choice but to accede to OMB's fiscal constraints.

The HEW generalists were not left entirely without resources, however. While the administration's basic policy decisions were still pending, Secretary Richardson decided that HEW's own commitment to the effort need not wait. In December he established a small project grant group in his office (a location that dramatized its importance to him and protected it from foot dragging and jurisdictional disputes in the bureaus), whose job was to identify provisions of existing law that might be used to promote the development of HMOs. Four days after the president officially committed the administration to HMO development, Richardson explained to a Senate subcommittee the reasoning that had led him to make that commitment on behalf of HEW three months earlier. Noting that the contribution of the incentives in Medicare's reimbursement patterns to inflation was "not too difficult to discern," he characterized "at cost" payments to providers as "a euphemism for a blank check," and continued:

> I intend to see that my Department puts together "packages" of resources, negotiating with a single instrument and permitting advance payments to be made—with later adjustments, if necessary—to enable HMOs to get as rapid a start as possible. I am convinced that the frustrating experience of those who earnestly wish to implement national purposes but are blocked by the compartmentalization of Federal funding can be ended, and will be ended—in HEW.[32]

As it turned out, Richardson and the other generalists had little to fear. The interaction of policy analysis and political strategy that had narrowed the administration's strategy to a new HMO option in Medicare early in 1970 now elevated HMOs to high prominence in the larger plans contemplated later that year.

Once an aggressive federal effort at regulation and a firm insistence on reduced entitlements or substantially increased consumer cost-sharing were dismissed, the "urgent need for organizational reform"[33] of the supply side of the health care system followed readily. Late in 1970, two approaches had strong advocates within the administration: Donald

32. *Examination of the Health Care Crisis in America*, Hearings before the Subcommittee on Health of the Senate Committee on Labor and Public Welfare, 92 Cong. 1 sess. (GPO, 1971), pp. 79, 91.

33. Memorandum, "Decision Issue: What Should be the Relative Role of Health Maintenance Organizations and Family Health Centers in Achieving Reorganization of Service Delivery?" (n.d.), p. 2, in Office of Management and Budget files (OMB, Legislative Reference Division, Legislative Information Center, File R5-10/73.1 [R5-10/71.3]), vol. 1. (Hereafter OMB files.)

Rumsfeld, head of the Office of Economic Opportunity (OEO), argued for a network of one thousand family health centers, while HEW leadership, of course, made the case for HMOs. The HEW generalists viewed Rumsfeld's proposal as a barely concealed power play—"He'd have OEO running the nation's health program," one of them later snorted—and were anxious to counter it. Health maintenance organizations, they pointed out, were distinctly Nixonian, stood a better chance than family health centers (another term for Johnson-launched neighborhood health centers) of becoming financially self-sufficient, and because they would attract large sums of private capital, would cost much less. These arguments fell on receptive ears at OMB, where concern to derail Rumsfeld's expensive proposal ran as high as at HEW, and strengthened the fragile HEW-OMB agreement on HMOs. The nature of the appeal, however, consistent with the planning process of a year before, was thin and inferential: the administration was committed in general to "reorganization," not regulation; its supply-side reorganization efforts needed an "organizing theme";[34] and HMOs were better (that is, less objectionable) than the alternatives.

At about the time that Richardson was unilaterally committing the federal government to HMO development, a Domestic Council review group began meeting to explore policy options, and discuss the major pros and cons of each, in order to guide preparation of the president's message, now only two months away. To their pleasure, the HEW representatives on the review group found that HMOs fit very nicely into the emerging line of argument.

In its report, issued on December 8, the group recommended that the administration's health strategy follow two principles. The first was the need for prevention, "that is, avoiding the need for medical care." The second was that when medical care was required, "equity" should be combined with "efficiency." As for the federal government, it "should play a leadership and catalytic role in health" and "must make maximum use of its leverage," the report argued. It noted too that the administration's "political challenge in 1971 will be to redirect the growing debate on National health insurance into a proper debate on the entire subject of National health and to demonstrate that those who are concerned only with financing are not dealing with the fundamental problem."[35]

The report then pointed out the pros and cons of various options pertaining first to the "supply and efficiency" aspect of policy, and then to

34. Ibid., p. 15.
35. "Report of the Domestic Council Health Policy Review Group," December 8, 1970, pp. 6–7.

financing. Under the first heading, it reviewed six options: training more medical manpower, overcoming legal obstacles to reform, taking new measures to benefit underserved areas, increasing research and education for prevention financed by a tobacco tax, creating a new oversight body for health research and—number two on the list—developing HMOs.

The report observed that HMOs directly honored the prevention and efficiency principles it had recommended, and did so by means of incentives. The approach, it argued, "is well suited to the concept of trying to limit direct federal intervention and using our leveraging devices to the maximum." References to HMOs were also scattered throughout the observations on other options: bonuses might be added to federal aid to medical schools to encourage them to undertake "additional functions (e.g., sponsorship of HMOs)"; loans to medical students might be written off if their recipients practiced in an HMO; among the major legal obstacles to reform that the government might try to overcome were state laws restricting HMOs; HMOs might be viewed as a useful innovation to bring health care resources to underserved areas.[36] Finally, looking forward to the prospect that the administration's financing proposal, a family health insurance plan, might go into effect in fiscal 1973 or 1974, the review group remarked that the "acid test of health policy in 1971" would be the nation's ability to "increase the supply of health care services in the short-run so that this time a new financing system will not just be dissipated in higher prices."[37] Here too HMOs would obviously play a central role.

The prominence of HMOs in the review group's synthesis, and their apparent consistency with the administration's principles, meant that HEW was on the verge of winning its case. However, the report made it clear that OMB's determination to trim the department's budgetary expectations was prevailing too. The report listed three approaches to federal aid to HMOs. One was a loan guarantee program, OMB's preferred approach. "Loan guarantees use substantially less federal funds than direct federal loans or grants for a given investment level," the report pointed out, adding that "the discipline of having to go to the private capital market would help screen out programs which are unlikely to become financially viable within a reasonable period." A direct loan program, a second option, might be used for *public* HMOs in need of a substitute for private risk capital, to carry them through a two- or three-year period until they were self-sustaining. Loans could also be limited to HMOs in "health service

36. Ibid., pp. 9, 10, 15, 18.
37. Ibid., p. 23.

scarcity or poverty areas," the report pointed out. Finally, in a single terse sentence, the report listed a third option: "A grant program could be provided as well, to subsidize start-up costs and initial operating deficits of HMO's in selected under-served areas."[38]

By the end of 1970, HEW and OMB had reached a general and superficial agreement. The department might extol the virtues of HMOs all it pleased and indeed it might be a good thing if the president did so too. The OMB had its doubts, but the conceptual appeals of HMOs were undeniable, the commitment of HEW's top leadership was apparently unlimited, and the interest of the White House in a bold new health initiative that substituted self-regulation for public regulation, gave doctors incentives to keep patients well, injected competition into the health care system, and all the rest, was unmistakable. Thus, OMB accepted the HMO initiative as a political decision with which it ought not to tamper and concentrated on the budgetary dimensions of the decision.

For its part, HEW would have to live with a "catalytic" federal role in HMO development and a very small dollar contribution. Health maintenance organizations were supposed to save the government money, not spend a lot of it; on this point, the White House and OMB clearly were at one. The same political logic that had once led the president—reportedly in a "light vein"—to authorize Agriculture Secretary Clifford M. Hardin to say that "this Administration would have the first comprehensive, far-reaching attack on the problem of hunger in history, *provided it doesn't cost money*"[39] now applied to HMOs.

Having reached this general agreement, neither HEW (development commitment in hand) nor OMB (reassured that costs would be small) had an incentive to press the other on particulars. The question of how to get from here—a few million federal dollars devoted to HMOs—to there—an HMO presence large enough to have an important impact on the cost and delivery of health care—would wait for another day. But even if the protagonists had been inclined to press each other on specifics, neither had the time. With the date of the message drawing near, truly thorny issues on a truly major program—the administration's national health insurance plan—remained to be resolved. These issues required extensive HEW and OMB staff work and the president's ear. Simple, attractive, and consensual, HMOs would stand tall among the administration's supply-side initiatives.

38. Ibid., p. 14.
39. Richard P. Nathan, Assistant Director, Office of Management and Budget, "Memorandum for the Director," April, 8, 1969; emphasis in original.

Under the circumstances, it hardly seemed to matter that the president's own understanding of and involvement in the HMO deliberations was, as an observer recalled, "virtually nil."

The President Delivers

Nixon's State of the Union message, delivered on January 22, 1971, contained no reference to HMOs per se, although the president did call for "new programs to encourage preventive medicine by attacking the causes of disease and injury, and by providing incentives to doctors to keep people well rather than just to treat them when they are sick."[40] In the special health message sent to Congress on February 18, however, the president left no doubt that HMOs were a top priority in his health care strategy. The message made it clear that escalating costs were the immediate source of Nixon's concern and the consideration uppermost in his mind. It opened with the statement that "in the last twelve months alone, America's medical bill went up eleven percent, from $63 to $70 billion," and proceeded with several other statistics to the same effect. The message made it equally plain that Nixon had accepted the economic theory of prepaid group practice in its classic and literal form and had come to view HMOs as a means of realizing the goals of cost-containment, equal access, and quality care simultaneously and in one program.

"We *cannot* simply *buy* our way to better medicine," the president declared, adding that "we have already been trying that too long." The need, he said, was to "organize a more efficient" system of care. The "two particularly useful ways" of doing so, he continued, were emphasizing health maintenance and preserving cost consciousness. Nixon defended the virtues of a pluralistic health care system, but emphasized the need to introduce incentives into it to promote cooperation and coordination. He then articulated a six-point program, point A of which consisted of "reorganizing the delivery of service" by means of HMOs.

"The most important advantage" of HMOs, Nixon argued, is that "they increase the value of the services a consumer receives for each health dollar." But, by the same token and by the same logic, HMOs enhance the quality of care too.

40. "Annual Message to the Congress on the State of the Union, January 22, 1971," *Public Papers: Nixon, 1971*, p. 53.

Under traditional systems, doctors and hospitals are paid, in effect, on a piecework basis. The more illnesses they treat—and the more service they render—the more their income rises. This does not mean, of course, that they do any less than their very best to *make* people well. But it does mean that there is no economic incentive for them to concentrate on *keeping* people healthy.

A fixed-price contract for comprehensive care reverses this illogical incentive. Under this arrangement, income grows not with the number of days a person is sick but with the number of days he is well. HMO's therefore have a strong financial interest in preventing illness, or, failing that, in treating it in early stages, promoting a thorough recovery, and preventing any recurrence. Like doctors in ancient China, they are paid to keep their clients healthy. For them, economic interests work to reinforce their professional interests.

At the same time, HMOs are motivated to function more efficiently. When providers are paid retroactively for each of their services, inefficiencies can often be subsidized. Sometimes, in fact, inefficiency is rewarded—as when a patient who does not need to be hospitalized is treated in a hospital so that he can collect on his insurance. On the other hand, if an HMO is wasteful of time or talent or facilities, it cannot pass those extra costs on to the consumer or to an insurance company. Its budget for the year is determined in advance by the number of its subscribers. From that point on it is penalized for going over its budget and rewarded for staying under it.

In an HMO, in other words, cost consciousness is fostered. Such an organization cannot afford to waste resources—that costs more money in the short run. But neither can it afford to economize in ways which hurt patients—for that increases long-run expenses.

After summing up the HMO's advantages, he declared: "Patients and practitioners alike are enthusiastic about this organizational concept. So is this administration."[41]

Noting that the administration had already urged an HMO option for Medicare recipients, Nixon went on to spell out a simple legislative proposal aimed at encouraging HMOs. To help plan new HMOs, $23 million would be authorized for grants, and an additional $22 million of direct federal grants and loans would be made available to launch HMOs in medically underserved areas. This direct federal investment would be supplemented with loan guarantees adequate to enable HMOs to raise $300 million in private loans to help support themselves after they had been launched. Other legislation would discourage "archaic" state laws that prohibited or impeded HMOs and would preempt them entirely in contracts with federal beneficiaries. His national health insurance plan, Nixon remarked, would require insurance plans to offer an HMO option when an HMO was available.

41. "National Health Strategy," *Public Papers: Nixon, 1971*, pp. 170–71. Quotations are from pp. 172–75; emphasis in original.

The bill the administration sent to Congress in March was simple, short, and straightforward. In fourteen pages it set out a general definition of an HMO, defined certain stages of development, and attached a few conditions to the organizational features of an HMO eligible for federal aid.[42] Two months later, HEW issued under Richardson's direction a White Paper explaining in detail the merits of this and other of the administration's health care proposals. The president's speech had avoided predictions of how many HMOs might be established within a given period of time. The HEW White Paper, by contrast, was extremely specific about "the administration's" intentions. By the end of fiscal 1973, the document declared, the administration hoped to develop 450 HMOs, 100 of them in scarcity areas. By the end of fiscal 1976 it expected to see 1,700 HMOs in existence, enough to serve 40 million Americans. By the end of the decade it hoped to have enough HMOs to enroll 90 percent of the population if they wished to join.[43]

At OMB, the White Paper caused some unease over what seemed to be another of the "disconnects" that troubled the administration's health care policy. This time the gap, the analysts thought, was between the figures the president had "signed off on" and those HEW was promising. Nevertheless, the White House in its wisdom had elevated HMOs to a central position in its health care strategy, and the OMB's role, which called for it to be "hard as nails" before a presidential commitment, now required it to be "soft as mush." For the time being at least, HEW was riding high—and so were HMOs.

The Administration's Political Game

Between the winters of 1970 and 1971 the interplay among Ellwood's policy analysis, the HEW generalists' promotional zeal, and OMB's skepticism and cost-consciousness had produced an ambiguous compromise—a generally, but superficially, shared understanding about the administration's position on the relations between means and ends. The administration, in a word, had committed itself to a political "game,"

42. The bill, S. 1182, may be found in *Physicians Training Facilities and Health Maintenance Organizations,* Hearings before the Subcommittee on Health of the Senate Committee on Labor and Public Welfare, 92 Cong. 1 and 2 sess., 6 pts. (GPO, 1971–72), pt. 1, pp. 84–98.

43. U.S. Department of Health, Education, and Welfare, *Towards a Comprehensive Health Policy for the 1970's: A White Paper* (HEW, 1971), pp. 31–37. The predictions, which returned to haunt the administration, appear on p. 37.

whose "rules" were expected to enforce conceptual and political discipline on its "players." Because the administration's game would soon be challenged by other players, intent on changing the rules and, indeed, the nature of the game itself, it is worth reviewing briefly here the core political and policy logic on which the administration's position rested.

At the heart of the administration's game lay three central premises. First, and basic to the original and continuing appeal of the HMO strategy, was that the strategy not cost much money and that the federal government's role be indirect and catalytic. This premise was of first importance to the White House, and OMB was vigilant in protecting it; HEW had no choice but to tailor its proposals to it. Yet this premise was not merely a cost constraint applied to proposals left otherwise substantively intact; instead, the constraint dictated major elements of policy substance. The least-cost premise could be honored only if the capital requirements and start-up costs of most new HMOs were low. A second premise, therefore, was absolutely essential to the administration's game: that independent practice associations and profit-making HMOs be encouraged. Independent practice associations did not depend on the full-time medical staffs, central office facilities, and separately owned hospitals of the Kaiser plans; their start-up costs were therefore comparatively small. And unless for-profit HMOs were encouraged, the all-important flow of private capital needed to launch HMOs on a large scale would probably remain at a trickle.

These propositions implied in turn a third: that requirements imposed on HMOs by the federal government be minimal. The more detailed the list of federally required services or organizational specifics, the more complex, arduous, and costly the HMO-building task became, and the more likely it was that private physicians would be deterred from forming IPAs and that private sources of capital would decline to invest in HMOs. It was therefore crucial to emphasize that (in Richardson's words) HMO legislation was not "designed for or even appropriate for the prescription of benefit packages" or other specifics. Instead it should aim simply to get HMOs off the ground.[44] These three propositions defined the essence of the administration's HMO policy proposal. Protecting them together and intact was the essence of its political game.

The three-step logic produced by the internal compromise left the administration's game playable but highly vulnerable to criticism. Critics

44. *Physicians Training Facilities*, Hearings, pt. 5, p. 1801.

would point out, as indeed OMB had already, that it made little sense to push for a national network of seventeen hundred HMOs unless the concept was proven. Yet the proof (such as it was) vindicated Kaiser-like plans, with full-time salaried doctors, control of their own hospitals, and hundred of thousands or even millions of members. The administration was obviously not proposing to develop seventeen hundred Kaiser-like plans; that would be unthinkably expensive. On the contrary, to honor its cost constraints, it was bound to insist that HMO was *not* synonymous with prepaid group practice and to argue for flexibility to permit a wide variety of organizations to qualify for federal aid. Ellwood's arguments were appealing precisely because they gave the assurance of a policy analyst that such a course was both desirable and feasible. Critics would then reply that the result would be seventeen hundred organizations whose characters could only be guessed at and whose performance was not only unproven but indeed undescribable and unpredictable even in gross terms. The charge would have to be faced, however, for the price of logical rigor—a large increase in federal budgetary commitments—was unacceptable.

Luckily for the administration, the literal economic theory of prepaid group practice, now elaborated at length by Ellwood for HMOs, again saved the day with a plausible justification. Understandably, the administration grasped it tightly and flung it forth whenever challenged. Flexibility, diversity, and pluralism were more than desirable, the planners argued; they were necessary, because local medical markets differed and local consumer preferences differed too. Nor need one fear that the federally aided organizations might take the money but cut corners on quality or accessibility of care. If members got sick, logic demonstrated, the plan's costs would rise; they would therefore do everything possible to practice prevention and early care. After all, HMO physicians had an incentive to keep plan members well. Moreover, if the local subscribers grew dissatisfied with the plan, they would take their business elsewhere. Thus, market logic both implied and vindicated the administration's call for a vague, general, and inclusive statute.

No one in the administration knew whether, or how far, this logic was valid in the real world, and, in truth, few cared. The important thing was that the same appealing policy analysis that had inspired the HMO strategy in the first place now could be invoked to defend the administration's political game. For the inevitable expansionists and doubters, the administration had its ever-ready, all-purpose rejoinder: the economic logic of HMOs would find a way to transform a few million federal dollars into seventeen hundred HMOs and would then insure that the new organizations behaved in a manner of which the federal government might be proud.

The Gathering Storm

Among liberal Democrats in Congress and old hands in the established PGPs, in their trade association, the GHAA, and in organized labor, the Nixon initiative was greeted with derision. When Nixon announced his plan, a Kaiser spokesman recalled, "we were just as shocked as the AMA." At a GHAA meeting shortly after the president's proposal the conferees, he remembered, were "snickering" at the prospect of seventeen hundred inchoate HMOs launched with such minuscule sums.

As legislators and plan executives scrutinized what few details the Nixon plan offered, snickers turned to disappointment, incredulity, and anger. The vaunted flexibility on which the Ellwood-HEW project rested struck them as both dangerous and insulting to the concept of prepaid group practice. "Our basic disagreement with the Administration bill is that it is nebulous and does not define specifically what an HMO is going to be," said Brian Biles, legislative aide to Democratic Congressman William Roy of Kansas, who took a keen interest in HMOs.[45] A GHAA official phrased the basic disagreement in less diplomatic terms, growling indignantly that the Nixon bill would "allow any amorphous piece of shit to call itself an HMO." An aide to Senator Javits noted that the bill would give "absolute discretion" to HEW—and therefore to the White House and OMB too— to decide what entities were and were not eligible for federal HMO funds. Whereas Ellwood and the HEW generalists thought that their plan's inclusiveness of a wide range of sponsors and its appeal to private sources of capital were among its central virtues, purists in the PGP "movement" and in the AFL-CIO objected strongly to amalgamating IPAs with "true" PGPs under the artificial rubric "HMO," and complained even more strongly about federal support for profit-making HMOs. In sum, the "community" of HMO advocates sharply split into camps of Ellwood eclectics and PGP purists, the former allied with the administration, and the latter with congressional Democratic health leaders. The latter coalition rapidly reached general agreement that all three basic tenets of the

45. Quoted in, "Health Maintenance Organizations," *Medical World News*, October 29, 1971, p. 40.

administration's political game were untenable. Much larger sums, they concluded, should be devoted to carefully defined organizations subject to a variety of standards and safeguards.

Once they overcame their initial surprise that Nixon made his HMO proposal at all, Democratic health policy leaders in Congress set out to "perfect" it. Given the nature of congresssional health care politics, any proposal, good or poor, advanced by any administration, Republican or Democrat, was likely to be changed significantly by the legislature. The Nixon administration's ill-received HMO initiative was predestined to be changed fundamentally. By 1971, congressional activism in health care policy had been well established for over two and one-half decades; congressional Democrats had refused to confine themselves to mere oversight of the executive's health care proposals, offering instead aggressive and frequently independent leadership, often enjoying strong bipartisan support in the full Congress. John Fogarty of Rhode Island and Lister Hill of Alabama, chairmen respectively of the Labor-HEW subcommittee of the House Appropriations Committee and the corresponding Senate subcommittee during most of the 1950s and 1960s, had used their positions to influence federal policy on biomedical research and hospital construction pervasively.[46] In the early 1960s congressional hearings on the plight of the elderly helped build grass-roots support for what would become Medicare,[47] and Democrat Robert Kerr of Oklahoma and Wilbur Mills designed a program of medical assistance for the aged, Medicare's means-tested forerunner. In 1965, Mills and John Byrnes of Wisconsin, ranking Republican on the House Ways and Means Committee, took a major hand in shaping both Medicare and its companion, Medicaid.[48]

The HMO proposal, which dealt primarily with the delivery, not the public financing, of care, fell to yet a third pair of committees chaired by yet a third set of health policy leaders. In 1971, Paul Rogers of Florida had newly assumed the chair of the health and environment subcommittee of the House Interstate and Foreign Commerce Committee and Edward Kennedy was at the head of the Senate Labor and Public Welfare Committee's health subcommittee. Kennedy's strongly liberal convictions about health policy were evident from his ambitious health security proposal, and Rogers, though in many ways conservative, was actively

46. Stephen P. Strickland, *Politics, Science, and Dread Disease: A Short History of United States Medical Research Policy* (Harvard University Press, 1972), especially chaps. 5–10.

47. James L. Sundquist, *Politics and Policy: The Eisenhower, Kennedy, and Johnson Years* (Brookings Institution, 1968), chap. 7.

48. Theodore R. Marmor, *The Politics of Medicare* (Aldine, 1973), pp. 62–70.

seeking new and progressive ideas in the health field.[49] No one could doubt that the Nixon initiative would undergo close scrutiny by these leaders and that it would emerge much changed.

The traditional activist inclinations of Congress in the field of health care were reinforced in the early 1970s by relations between the legislative and executive branches that were generally poor and far poorer than average in this policy area. The protracted struggle over the appointment of Dr. John Knowles as HEW's assistant secretary for health, whom the Nixonites first promised to nominate and then betrayed in the face of AMA opposition; sporadic battles over Nixon's vetoes of bills dealing generously with the National Institutes of Health and the Hill-Burton program of hospital construction; frustration with the administration's indifference to the newly established National Health Service Corps; and the administration's seeming indifference to national health insurance caused it to appear antihealth in the eyes of many Democrats and some Republicans. These legislators approached HMOs with mingled suspicion and fascination. On the one hand, the proposal was suspected to be a bold ploy to shift debate away from national health insurance and other primarily Democratic measures. On the other hand, the prospect that the federal government would make far-reaching changes in the delivery system by encouraging organized alternatives to fee-for-service care contained exciting possibilities.

Kennedy Takes Aim

In the Senate, Edward Kennedy, whose legislative thunder the new Nixon initiative was in part designed to steal, naturally looked on with considerable interest. Kennedy had been hard at work promoting his health security plan as the answer to what he was convinced had become a spreading, worsening health care crisis. By 1971, however, it was apparent that he could do little to get his bill reported favorably from the Senate Finance Committee, that the administration would not endorse anything faintly resembling it, and that the Congress as a whole, internally divided on national health insurance, could not generate from within an ad hoc coalition to pass it. National health insurance might become a

49. Redman, *Dance of Legislation*, pp. 89, 99–100.

major issue in the 1972 election; Kennedy certainly intended to try to make it one. In the meantime, however, it would have to wait.

When Nixon's proposal placed HMOs on the federal agenda along with, and perhaps ahead of, financing reforms, the executive's agenda necessarily became Kennedy's too. The significance of the president's move only six years after the dutiful assurances to the AMA in the Medicare and regional medical program laws was not lost on him. As an aide recalled, "Kennedy saw that for the first time the federal government would become directly involved in the organization and delivery of medical care in this country and he was determined to have a hand in it."

Kennedy had little experience with HMOs (in 1971 the two-year-old, struggling Harvard Community Health Plan was the only HMO in Massachusetts) and no fascination with the idea per se. His preferred policy approach combined a large federal role in financing care with broad federal regulatory powers—precisely the combination the administration hoped to head off by means of HMOs. Kennedy was familiar, however, with the standard arguments for prepaid group practice—the emphasis on prevention, the reduced hospitalization, the beneficial effects of peer review, and the rest. He also appreciated that PGPs represented a critique of and alternative to the fee-for-service system cherished by the AMA, a system and an organization that, in Kennedy's eyes, were major elements in the health care crisis.

Although Kennedy had not yet developed a firm position on HMOs, the general philosophy on which his reformist views rested carried some definite implications for them. Kennedy's first and basic premise, as he later put it, was that "in order to qualify for federal support . . . an HMO should offer a real alternative for the consumer of health services." He saw no justification for making federal funds available to "those who wish to retread the same old ways of delivering health services under different names, or to continue the unparalleled dominance of providers and the absence of public accountability in the health care field."[50]

The rules of Kennedy's game held that federal funds should be used to encourage HMOs only if they offered more care and better care than did the fee-for-service mainstream. This premise, in turn, implied further propositions sharply at odds with the administration's approach. Kennedy saw no reason to extend federal aid to IPAs, for they were mere associations

50. *Physicians Training Facilities*, Hearings, pt. 5, p. 1677.

of fee-for-service practitioners. They could spring up on their own initiative and with their own funds, he said, and there was no case for subsidizing them at taxpayers' expense. Likewise, if HMO benefits were no broader than those in conventional commercial or Blue Cross insurance plans, why should the government make a major effort to launch them?

Kennedy and his staff were attracted by the cost-containment record of prominent PGPs, but in their view, nothing followed directly from it. It was obvious, that the new HMOs would differ extensively from Kaiser and the others, and they had no faith whatever that innate economic incentives would keep the new organizations on the road to high quality, accessible care. Prepayment, Kennedy declared, was a "double edged sword," fully as capable of leading to corner-cutting abuse as to appropriate and timely care.[51] Consumers always had a hard time judging the quality of the care they received, economists and other experts agreed, and Kennedy had long been deploring the lack of quality monitoring and regulation in the fee-for-service sector. He was not about to endorse HMO legislation that lacked specific safeguards for quality and access.

The short, vague, inspecific statute the administration sought was unacceptable to Kennedy for another reason, too. Behind the talk about flexibility and responsiveness to local markets lay the bald political fact that such a program would establish a project grant program that the Nixon administration would be at liberty to define, shape, and direct as it pleased. To acquiesce struck Kennedy as an abdication of partisan principle, congressional prerogative, and sound policy judgment. Neither Kennedy nor many other Democrats thought it prudent to hand the administration a blank check to launch over a thousand HMOs of unknown description without firm legislative guidance, and few of them trusted HEW, dominated by an "anti-health" Republican White House and OMB, to get the HMO program off to a good start and see it through to a satisfactory conclusion. The extraordinarily wide discretion the administration sought would allow it to turn HMO funding into a subsidy for local fee-for-service providers and profitmakers if it chose, or would equally allow it to slow down or even effectively stop the program if that was its inclination. Instead of defining HMOs loosely and agreeing to promote them largely by federal encouragement to private capital, Kennedy and his staff, it was clear from the outset, would spell out the characteristics of an HMO eligible for federal aid in detailed statutory language and then,

51. Ibid., p. 1894.

having satisfied themselves about the nature of the entity to be promoted, authorize federal funds sufficient to do the job. Of course, the price tag for well-designed HMOs equipped with safeguards would be high, perhaps a billion dollars or more. To Kennedy and his staff, however, the ciphers the administration was proposing were not worth even the modest sums it sought, whereas a properly designed HMO effort would be well worth a high price, and they were prepared to pay it.

An Early Skirmish

After Nixon's message, Kennedy hastily added to a bill to expand medical training facilities a section offering federal aid to medical schools to set up HMOs. This measure was but a stopgap, that differed significantly from the Nixon measure only in the size of the authorization it proposed, $337 million.[52] Kennedy knew that a well-designed HMO bill would require a great deal of time, information, and effort. It would also require that the administration's simplistic approach be exploded and the many major points of difference between the Nixon and Kennedy viewpoints be sharpened and publicized.

As an aid to both publicizing and drafting, Kennedy began a round of hearings in July to explore HMO issues at length with the administration and other witnesses. The first witness before Kennedy's subcommittee was Dr. Merlin D. DuVal, HEW's newly appointed assistant secretary for health and scientific affairs. Kennedy immediately made it clear that he took strong exception to—indeed that he took positions diametrically opposed to—all three premises at the heart of the administration's political game.

First, although the Nixon bill defined an HMO as an organization that received prepaid premiums in exchange for medical services, it would allow the organization to reimburse its physicians on a fee-for-service basis if it so chose. In other words, it would make IPAs eligible for federal aid. In Kennedy's view, this inclusion simply reinstated the wasteful features of fee-for-service care, and he pressed DuVal to justify it. Preserving fee-for-service arrangements, Kennedy declared, seemed to offer no incentives for doctors "to reduce the numbers of occasions of treatment" and amounted to "giving a blank check to the doctors and hospitals." DuVal

52. For the bill, S. 935, see ibid., pt. 1, pp. 5–27, especially pp. 13–24.

replied that "under the HMO principle, whether the physician was paid on a fee-for-service or a salary would not make any difference because the total amount of capital flowing into the organization is fixed." Kennedy countered that "more payments" to physicians must necessarily lead to higher premiums for consumers in the following year. DuVal replied: "The physician has a stake in the total amount of money expended through the organization. If there was a fee-for-service provision and it was abused, the regulations would come into force or a competitive HMO would take the business away." What regulations, then, did the administration have in mind? "We are part way into it now, Senator."[53]

Second, noting with displeasure that the administration bill did not spell out a specific set of medical services that a federally supported HMO would be required to provide, Kennedy challenged the administration's flexibility premise. Observing that dental care is a "very important feature" lacking in some well-known prepaid group practices, Kennedy wanted to know if the administration would require that eligible HMOs offer it. To DuVal's "They could," Kennedy objected, "Do you have anything that will tell us what will be included?" DuVal reminded him that the bill would require as a minimum "four parts . . . outpatient, inpatient, physicians services, and preventive care." Specifics would be decided by the groups themselves. Kennedy pressed again: "If we were to pass the administration's program, what would be the services that would be provided in any particular HMO?" DuVal rejoined again: "We think that there should be room for variation." To Kennedy's query whether some sponsors "would exclude certain services to their subscribers," DuVal replied that "it will be the consumer who . . . will end up . . . describing the market that he needs." Kennedy persisted. The four minimum parts of the administration's package were "rather general boilerplate descriptive words"; he wanted to know whether there would be "family planning services available, for instance." They then went through it all again: "Yes, there could be." "Is it always 'could be.' Will they?" Kennedy's view was that "it would be better to say that there will be certain medical specialties provided in every HMO that is developed, and this is the list that will be provided." The secretary of HEW might have "flexibility to make a determination that it is impossible to provide 'X,' 'Y,' and 'Z,' " he added, and the secretary "could find under certain circumstances, that they would not be included."[54]

53. Ibid., p. 111.
54. Ibid., pp. 116–18.

Third, Kennedy made it clear to DuVal that he found the proposed authorizations inadequate to the organization-building task ahead. DuVal acknowledged that "HMOs are expensive to start and will require a large amount of capital." "But," he continued, "the financial structure of the HMO is such that this capital need not be in the form of large amounts of equity or grant funds." He explained that "based upon our discussions with successful HMOs," the administration estimated that it would take $100,000 to $500,000 to plan an HMO, and $1 million to $2.5 million to carry the plans through the early start-up period. Finally, excluding hospital construction, HMOs would require up to $2.5 million in capital "for health center rehabilitation or construction." Kennedy then disputed these estimates with DuVal and Vernon Wilson, director of the Health Services and Mental Health Administration. Were not the HMOs cited as successful prototypes "enormously costly in terms of startup costs, up to $5.5 million roughly?" Wilson replied that the "average cost" anticipated fell somewhere between the "maximum cost" of a "fully freestanding HMO of the Kaiser-Permanente variety," and the much lower cost of plans "who can build on a group practice or on an existing activity." Kennedy then reconstructed, question by question, the arithmetic behind the administration's estimate that in fiscal 1972 a total of 163 HMOs, 118 of them in medically underserved areas, would be funded: $250,000 for planning and $2.5 million for the start-up; for construction, up to $2.5 million. "That is approximately $5 million, which seems to be the average cost. . . . If they cost approximately $5 million, and we talk about getting 160 started by the administration, that is $815 million." "Senator, we are talking about fiscal 1972 with these figures, and we are still in the planning stage," DuVal rejoined. "We would not reach the expensive end of that scale. Secondly, of course, you have used our upper limitation and that is true that that may be what experience will show. We are not planning that they will." "Where do you think the cuts will come," Kennedy asked, "in the number of HMOs developed or the increase in the money?" To which Dr. Wilson responded: "In the utilization of present facilities."[55]

Having demonstrated that the administration's plans contained no careful assessment of the cost-saving potential of IPAs, no clear picture of the services HMOs would provide, and no firm estimates of start-up costs for a given number of organizations, Kennedy extended and sharpened his critique of the Nixon bill. Noting that the bill's development grants would

55. Ibid., pp. 118–20.

suffice to launch five or six HMOs at most, he observed that loan guarantees would have to do most of the job. DuVal acknowledged that as far as he knew "no HMOs started with loan guarantees," and he was unable to resolve Kennedy's doubts that such guarantees would bring an adequate flow of private capital to would-be HMOs, especially in underserved areas.[56]

Remarking on the high priority the Nixon bill assigned to developing HMOs in underserved areas and on the "constant references" to the Kaiser model, Kennedy wondered how DuVal expected to make the latter relevant to the former. Kaiser, Kennedy noted, serves those employed in "a recession-resistant industry, with steady work records, and incomes of from $8,000 to $12,000." Observing that inner cities and rural communities met none of Kaiser's criteria for a suitable "atmosphere" for HMO development, the senator asked how the administration proposed to bring an HMO option to those too poor for private, but excluded from public, medical insurance. DuVal's reply—that they would receive this option under the administration's national health insurance bill—was, needless to say, less than satisfactory.[57]

Noting that "the HMO concept . . . lends itself comfortably to the concept of peer review," Kennedy sought to learn how the administration would monitor quality of care in HMOs. DuVal's aide replied, "Unequivocally it will be done and I think the specifics [are] still under discussion." Kennedy wanted as precise a statement as possible about the administration's intent in the near future.[58]

Kennedy wanted to know what provisions the administration would make to allow HMO subscribers to participate in running the organizations. DuVal's reply—that it expected to make no such provisions, lest they antagonize providers—antagonized Kennedy. ("You mean we might have to develop the legislation to see what the providers want?") He was also skeptical about including for-profit HMOs in the program.[59]

At the start of the next day's hearings, Kennedy expressed a low opinion of the administration's presentation, declaring that "the subcommittee was distressed at the lack of specificity and precision in the administration's recommendations." For good measure he condemned "its continued reliance on an inadequate and discriminatory national

56. Ibid., p. 120; see also pp. 123–24.
57. Ibid., pp. 127–29, 137.
58. Ibid., pp. 133–34.
59. Ibid., pp. 136–38.

health insurance proposal."[60] Then Kennedy and a series of friendly witnesses, many of them purists and other old hands in the PGP movement, continued to demolish the administration's bill. Although they recognized that IPAs could not be excluded from the program altogether, spokesmen for the American Public Health Association (APHA) and the GHAA insisted on the differences between "real" PGPs and fee-for-service doctors dabbling in prepaid practice on the side and hoped that legislation would be sensitive to the differences.[61] No punches were pulled in behalf of for-profit HMOs, however; spokesmen for the United Auto Workers (UAW), the AFL-CIO, and the GHAA strongly condemned them and recommended that they be kept out of the program.[62] The GHAA, which a few months later would raise loud cries about the excessive specificity of emerging HMO legislation, now argued that "the most disturbing" aspect of the administration bill was "the lack of a clear and specific definition as to what a health maintenance organization is, how it is structured, what services will be provided, who will provide them, and in what manner." Legislation, the GHAA's executive director argued, "should establish definite criteria . . . which will insure that the health maintenance organization concept does that which it is designed to do—provide a more efficient system of health delivery with the most effective utilization of every dollar spent." The GHAA wanted to see some "rather firm standards" to make sure that a group of doctors did not "band themselves together, draw up a prepayment scheme, offer limited services labelled 'comprehensive,' charge regular premiums, set excessively high fees and call themselves a health maintenance organization."[63] A spokesman for the APHA urged the subcommittee to require eligible HMOs to provide at least six "absolute minimum" services—health education and preventive services, primary physician care, specialist care, hospitalization in short-term general hospitals, diagnostic studies, and ambulatory mental health services.[64] As for the latter service, soon to become controversial, Kennedy learned that the Harvard Community Health Plan covered short-term psychiatric services for its members, and that on one estimate PGPs could provide ambulatory mental health benefits for as little as 70 cents per member per month.[65]

---

60. Ibid., p. 148.
61. For example, ibid., pp. 192–95 (GHAA); pt. 2, p. 541 (APHA).
62. For example, ibid., pt. 1, pp. 157–61 (UAW), 192–93 (GHAA); pt. 2, pp. 466, 471–72 (AFL-CIO).
63. Ibid., pt. 1, 192–93.
64. Ibid., pt. 2, pp. 556–57.
65. Ibid., pp. 600, 800.

Kennedy's skepticism about the number of HMOs the administration's authorizations would create was supported by the director of medical planning of the Harvard plan, who said that the sums were "clearly too low." Melvin Glasser of the UAW likened the administration to "a corporation executive who proposed to bring about a major redesign of an enterprise which spends $70 billion annually with the investment of $23 million, that is with 0.03 percent of annual operating income to produce change." The AFL-CIO offered a detailed estimate, based on GHAA experience, of what it would cost to bring 820 new HMOs simply to the initial development stage over a six-year period. The price tag was just over $1 billion. The "full treatment" for 820 HMOs would cost over $4 billion.[66]

The APHA argued that in the development period "the reliance has got to be on grants," not on loan guarantees, and the Association of American Medical Colleges (AAMC) urged that HMOs "be fully funded . . . until enrollment is at a level that provides sufficient premium income to finance operations."[67] Dr. Ellwood, the architect of the administration's HMO strategy, acknowledged that "we have to face up to the fact that the incentive for HMO's to underserve their enrollees is there, and that some sort of regulatory steps should be taken to prevent this underservice." Ellwood argued that quality should be assessed in relation to health outcomes and recommended that Congress establish an "independent quality regulation agency for HMOs right now, and give it operating responsibilities as well as R. and D. powers."[68] (The administration, of course, wanted nothing of the sort.) In short, Kennedy found consistent confirmation of his reservations about the administration's approach from individuals with long and extensive experience in the field. Convinced that the HMO bill would in some respects be "the most important piece of legislation that may come out" of his subcommittee[69] in the Ninety-second Congress, Kennedy and his staff set about writing a better bill of their own.

In May 1972 Kennedy introduced his new HMO bill, a broad and detailed measure seventy pages long. The bill envisioned about $5 billion over five years, about $1 billion of which would promote development of HMOs "narrowly" defined. Kennedy's HMOs would be required to offer virtually the full range of services that a desirable national health insurance

66. Ibid., pt. 1, p. 149; pt. 2, pp. 614, 474–75.
67. Ibid., pt. 2, pp. 544, 501.
68. Ibid., pp. 512, 514–15.
69. Ibid., p. 460.

plan would offer, and they would be complemented by institutions needed to reform the delivery system, including area health education centers in underserved areas, and a national quality control commission. The ambitious bill he introduced was a bargaining chip, hardly likely to be enacted intact, and Kennedy probably shared Javits's view that it was "not a finished legislative product," but rather "an extremely valuable working paper, a springboard for serious congressional consideration." Kennedy declared that it had been "drafted in an attempt to describe the type of health care the American people deserve and should have."[70] Congressional action on HMOs would receive much attention in coming months and Kennedy recognized an invaluable opportunity to educate the public, the administration, and the Congress on the condition of the health care system and the need for far-reaching reforms. He would not achieve all of his agenda, perhaps not most, or even much, of it; yet he was determined to fulfill what Polsby has called the policy "incubation" function, the forwarding of ideas whose time has not yet come.[71]

Roy, Rogers et al.

As Kennedy's hearings and drafting proceeded, the health and environment subcommittee of the House Interstate and Foreign Commerce Committee was the site of yet a third political game. First-term Democrat William Roy, a physician who had also acquired a law degree and a taste for public service, viewed the HMO initiative as a highly exciting opportunity to do something about the health care crisis. Many of the shortcomings and inconsistencies of the administration's proposal evident to Kennedy were also apparent to Roy, who saw at once that the administration had begun with a least-cost premise and then asked how one got from here to there (seventeen hundred HMOs). The logical implications—a dominant role for IPAs and profit-making groups and a refusal to include carefully defined safeguards and standards—seemed to carry the program

---

70. Ibid., pt. 5, pp. 1788, 1678. The huge authorizations, often cited by critics as evidence of Kennedy's irresponsible and utopian approach to HMO legislation, also contained a large element of symbolism. One legislative aide explained: "Remember in those days everybody said, 'What's the difference what you authorize, it's not an appropriation.'" Another recalled: "This was the end of the Great Society period. The view had been that authorizations reflect need and appropriations resources. So we wrote *big* authorizations."

71. Nelson W. Polsby, "Policy Analysis and Congress," in Subcommittee on Economy in Government of the Joint Economic Committee, *Analysis and Evaluation of Public Expenditures: The PPB System,* 91 Cong. 1 sess. (GPO, 1969), vol. 3, p. 947.

in precisely the wrong direction, away from, not toward, the proven prototypes.

Roy resolved to pursue what he considered to be a more rational approach to planning. As his health policy aide at the time explained:

> Our first reaction to the Nixon bill was that it was very general. So we visited Kaiser and some other well-established PGPs and asked, "How do we know it'll look like you?" And they said, "You don't." So we discussed it with them and asked about their key defining features—comprehensive care, a basic set of services, and so on. And we put it in the bill. Then we asked, "What does it cost to start a plan like you?" And they went over their figures for Cleveland and Denver and Boston with us. And we said, "My goodness; expensive, isn't it?" So we basically took what they looked like and what they cost and multiplied. Then we added some provisions to insure that they wouldn't skim and underprovide, and so forth.

After several evening drafting sessions over beer and cold cuts at GHAA headquarters, Roy's bill, which presupposed an authorization of about $1 billion, was ready.

Subcommittee chairman Rogers looked on Roy's work with the predictable ambivalence of a solidly conservative legislator from a Florida Gold Coast district who nonetheless sought to use his new leadership position to launch progressive health care measures.[72] He, too, found the administration's bill seriously deficient and was, moreover, extremely angry that HEW had already committed over $6 million in project grant funds to HMO development without explicit congressional guidance or approval. He therefore endorsed Roy's determination to assert Congress's will in HMO policy and to introduce specifics and safeguards into the legislation.

On the other hand, Rogers's conservative instincts told him that the administration's hopes for seventeen hundred HMOs were premature and that Roy's projected $1 billion authorization figure was "really out of sight."[73] At Rogers's request, Roy deleted the figure, leaving the draft bill silent on the funding level. Rogers then joined Roy as a sponsor of what quickly came to be called the Roy-Rogers bill, a thirty-three-page measure introduced in November 1971. In tempering Roy's original plan, Rogers consulted his sense of his subcommittee environment as well as his own conservative instincts. He knew that even if he wanted to launch a broad

72. See Redman, *Dance of Legislation*, p. 89.
73. John K. Iglehart, "Democrats Cool to Nixon's Health Proposal Offer Their Own Alternatives," *National Journal*, November 20, 1971, p. 2313.

HMO effort, his subcommittee colleagues would not agree. As Roy's aide put it in 1978:

> In explaining what happened to Roy's bill, you've got to consider the nature of the subcommittee. This is the House *Commerce* committee. Most of these guys were lawyers who went for the committee assignment and got put on the subcommittee. They were basically a conservative bunch interested in serving on a *regulatory* committee. The Senate was very different. The Senate committee is the *Labor* committee. It deals with Taft-Hartley and Landrum-Griffiths. The labor people make sure their friends get on to protect them. So you get a very liberal group.
>
> Over here, Roy was the most liberal member of the subcommittee and the most vigorous for HMOs. He pushed it along. Rogers was in the middle. The Democratic majority then was small—six to four, not two-to-one like it is now. And one of the Democrats, Satterfield, was a constant opponent, who had to be brought along. The Republicans were all moderates or conservatives, no liberals there. Rogers was trying to steer a bill through. He's a legislative craftsman. Some people make tables; Rogers makes bills.

In almost every respect pertinent to building a committee coalition, the Senate and House bodies were strikingly different. The Senate Labor and Public Welfare Committee, which encouraged policy partisanship, individual position-taking,[74] policy incubation, and "education," offered an ideal forum within which Kennedy, a liberal Democratic leader with strong personal views on health care policy, might wage battles against a Republican administration whose health care strategies he considered backward. The House subcommittee members, by contrast, were well aware that their personal positions and educational efforts would attract few television cameras. To make itself felt, their political influence must be exercised within the House itself; and in Fenno's words, in the House, "the individual member's influence on chamber decision is exerted, almost wholly, within and through his committees."[75]

The atypically liberal cast and decentralized structure of the Senate committee meant that subcommittee chairman Kennedy could proceed with little fear of being hamstrung by conservative Republican colleagues. Javits, the ranking Republican on the committee, tended to be more of a health policy activist than the ranking Republican on the subcommittee, Richard Schweiker of Pennsylvania, and Javits was an unusually liberal Republican. No subcommittee conservatives were bent on fighting Kennedy for control of the HMO bill and only Republican Peter Dominick of

74. The term is taken from David Mayhew, *Congress: The Electoral Connection* (Yale University Press, 1974), p. 61.
75. Richard F. Fenno, Jr., *Congressmen in Committees* (Little, Brown, 1973), p. 147.

Colorado showed much interest in it. In the House subcommittee, on the other hand, Tim Lee Carter, Kentucky Republican and himself a physician, Ancher Nelsen of Minnesota, the ranking Republican, and David Satterfield, Democrat of Virginia, were all relatively conservative and eager to have a hand in the legislative product.

In the Senate, the bill that cleared the subcommittee would almost surely pass the full committee without difficulty. Nor was the subcommittee's handiwork much constrained by concern for eventual Senate action, much less by concern for positions of the House or the administration. Much given to position-taking, yet also strongly practical, Kennedy understood that he might end up with half or less of the loaf he originally sought. His political style and game called for him to fight tenaciously for his cause and then compromise, drastically if need be, in order to preserve the chance of securing some legislative victory.

In the House, the subcommittee's work would face scrutiny and possible revision by the full committee, whose members and chairman, Harley Staggers, West Virginia Democrat, were by no means antipathetic to the AMA or burning to launch broad legislative reforms of the health care system.[76] Kennedy and his liberal subcommittee colleagues could work their will in subcommittee and then compromise when and as necessary on the Senate floor or in conference. But if Rogers failed to anticipate correctly the mood of the full committee, the bill he reported might never make it to the House floor. His fundamental concern, therefore, was to write a bill that would leave the subcommittee and reach the full committee "invulnerable,"[77] to reach a compromise that would bring the subcommittee as close to unanimity as possible. The task would plainly require many more hours and much more legislative craftsmanship than would be demanded in the Senate subcommittee. The respective legislative products were also certain to bear everywhere the traces of these important institutional differences. In short, the HMO bills produced by these two very different legislative institutions would inevitably differ sharply not only from the administration's, but also from one another. And of course the difficulty of reaching agreement within and between each chamber would increase directly with the number of controversial issues and the degree of controversy. Because the HMO proposal raised a great many controversial issues, agreement would not come quickly or easily.

76. For a good general overview of the politics, see Patricia Bauman, "The Formulation and Evolution of Health Maintenance Organization Policy, 1970–1973," *Social Science and Medicine*, vol. 10 (March–April 1976), pp. 129–42.

77. Ibid., p. 137.

Three Games, Three Bills

The different motives, premises, and environments of the three political games were fully evident in the content of the three bills under consideration in 1971–72. They ranged from short and elliptical (the administration bill) to very long and detailed (the Kennedy bill); the Roy-Rogers bill, in these respects as in others, took middle ground. A full summary of the bills and of the differences among them would be pointless here; a succinct HEW synopsis ran to forty-two pages.[78] Nevertheless a selective overview of major issues is useful, indeed indispensable, to understanding the compromises that eventually produced Public Law 93-222.

Organizational Type

Each of the bills relied originally on the same general concept of an HMO—an organization related to a physicians' group that provided a wide range of medical services to voluntarily enrolled subscribers in exchange for prepaid premiums. The language and intent of the bills differed significantly on the type of physicians' group that would be permitted to deliver services in a federally qualified HMO, however. The Nixon bill allowed services to be provided by employees or partners of an HMO, or by physicians' groups, including IPAs, under contract to the HMO. Physicians' groups had to be reimbursed by the plan "primarily on the basis of an aggregate fixed sum or on a per capita basis," but the groups could reimburse their individual members on a fee-for-service basis if they chose to do so.[79]

The Roy-Rogers bill appeared to exclude IPAs by defining a medical group as a partnership or association of practitioners who "as their principal professional activity and as a group responsibility engage in the coordinated practice of their profession." It also required that they share medical records and "substantial portions" of equipment and staff, that they utilize additional health personnel "needed to provide comprehensive health services," and that they arrange for the continuing education of their members. Although he later acknowledged that this language had led

---

78. Health Services and Mental Health Administration summary in OMB files, vol. 1.

79. The three bills are conveniently assembled in William R. Roy, *The Proposed Health Maintenance Organization Act of 1972* (Washington: Science and Health Communications Group, 1972). See especially pp. 99–102 (the administration bill); pp. 62–96 (the Roy-Rogers bill); pp. 128–61 (the Kennedy bill). For the specifics on organizational type and the quotations in the text see pp. 68, 99, 129.

most readers to assume that IPAs were excluded from federal aid, Roy denied that this was his intention.[80] Kennedy, whose distaste for federal aid to IPAs was well known, and who certainly did intend to exclude them, used language almost identical to that of the House bill. However, his bill defined a medical group to consist of "not less than four persons," to insure that actual group practices, not single-specialty partnerships, provided the services.

The bills also disagreed on the status of profit-making HMOs. The Nixon bill would aid public, private nonprofit, and (private) for-profit groups. The Roy-Rogers bill excluded profit-making HMOs from any type of aid. Kennedy's bill made for-profit groups eligible for loan guarantees, but for no other form of aid.

Organizational Features

The three bills differed too on other organizational criteria that eligible HMOs must meet. First, the bills spelled out in varying detail the range of services the HMOs would be required to provide. The administration bill required only that four broad types of services be offered: "emergency care, inpatient hospital and physician care, ambulatory physician care, and outpatient preventive medical services."[81] The Roy-Rogers bill spelled out physicians' services explicitly to include "consultant and referral services," and also required inpatient *and outpatient* hospital services, home health services, diagnostic laboratory and diagnostic and radiologic services, rehabilitation services (including physical therapy), and out-of-area emergency services. Kennedy included the list of services in the House bill and added vision care and podiatric services, mental health services (including drug abuse and alcoholism services), dental services (including preventive dental services for children), and prescription drug services.

Second, the three bills prescribed the way federally aided HMOs would set premium rates and recruit members. Whether the plans should be required to practice community rating and to hold an open enrollment period raised ethical questions of equity and need more directly than any other provisions of the bill. If open enrollment was not included, HMOs would be free to exclude those with an unfortunate medical history; in the

80. *Health Maintenance Organizations*, Hearings before the Subcommittee on Public Health and Environment of the House Committee on Interstate and Foreign Commerce, 92 Cong. 2 sess., 4 pts. (GPO, 1972), pt. 1, p. 88. Also, John K. Iglehart, "House Panel Moves Toward Compromise HMO Plan Despite Strong AMA Opposition," *National Journal*, May 6, 1972, p. 779.

81. On benefits see Roy, *Proposed Health Maintenance Organization Act*, pp. 67–68, 99, 129.

absence of community rating, they could tailor premiums to past medical experience, thereby pricing many of the sick out of the new plans. But including both provisions threatened to flood HMOs with sick persons, who would use large amounts of care and drive costs and premiums up for all subscribers. The result might be to make HMOs uncompetitive with more selective—that is, discriminatory—plans, which typically practice experience rating and do not hold an open enrollment period.

The administration's bill required each plan to hold "an open enrollment period at least every year under which it accepts up to the limits of its capacity and without restrictions, except as they may be authorized by regulations of the Secretary, individuals in the order in which they apply for enrollment."[82] Because the bill made no mention of community rating, however, the plans would be allowed to tailor the premiums of the open enrollees to their past medical experience. This approach was equally unacceptable to the prepaid group practice plans, which typically use a community rate but do not have open enrollments, and to congressional liberals, who objected that HMOs could exclude the poor sick by charging high premiums.[83] The Roy-Rogers bill required open enrollment in language very much like that of the administration, but it also required that the plans charge rates that are "uniform for all its members," that is, that they community rate. Kennedy's bill also included both provisions and allowed no exceptions by HEW.

Third, the three bills subjected HMOs to different forms of quality assurance monitoring. The Nixon bill simply required that HMO services "meet quality standards which it establishes in accordance with" HEW regulations.[84] The Roy-Rogers bill went further by insisting that HMOs have "organizational arrangements established in accordance with regulations of the Secretary, for an ongoing quality assurance program which stresses both health services processes and outcomes; and assures that health services provided meet quality standards established in accordance with regulations of the Secretary." The Kennedy bill used similar language, but instead of relying on HEW, followed Ellwood's recommendation by

---

82. On rates and recruitment see ibid., pp. 64, 66–67, 99, 128–29.

83. Kennedy was convinced that "experience rating, the practice wherein low-risk persons are sold health insurance at preferential rates, has been extraordinarily damaging to the entire health industry and to the patterns of availability of services. This practice of 'skimming the cream,' of leaving those people most in need of health services to pay the highest bills—often without the assistance of adequate insurance, cannot and should not be encouraged by any program utilizing Federal funds." Ibid., p. 108.

84. On quality assurance provisions see ibid., pp. 65–66, 99, 128.

establishing in a separate title a national commission on quality health care to set standards.

The bills also disagreed on several less fundamental organizational criteria. The Roy-Rogers bill required HMOs to make reinsurance provisions, the Kennedy bill set limits on the extent of allowable reinsurance, and the administration bill simply required that HMOs demonstrate that they were financially sound. The legislative bills called for HMOs to include members on their policymaking boards, and to set up grievance mechanisms; the administration bill did not. The congressional bills called for health education for members and staff of HMOs, but the Nixon bill did not.[85]

Program Costs

In their estimates of the cost of the federal aid effort the three bills differed dramatically. The Nixon measure contained no specifics, but the president had declared that he looked to $45 million in grants and loans and $300 million in loan guarantees over a five-year period. The Roy-Rogers bill authorized unspecified sums for an unspecified period of time. Kennedy's bill combined some specific figures with "such sums" provisions, leaving the total cost unclear (but likely to exceed $1 billion) for HMO development and perhaps as much as $5 billion in total.[86]

Types of Aid

The structure and approach to federal aid contained in the three bills were broadly similar. All authorized eligible HMOs to receive aid in four sequential stages: feasibility assessment and planning, initial development, construction, and early operations. Within each stage, however, the three differed significantly on details.[87]

All three bills awarded *grants* to HMOs for feasibility planning, the earliest stage of development. The Nixon bill offered grants to cover initial development costs only to HMOs dealing with underserved areas. The Roy-Rogers and Kennedy bills awarded grants for this purpose to any HMO, although they instructed the secretary to give priority to applicants enrolling 30 percent (Kennedy) or 40 percent (Roy-Rogers) of their members in underserved areas.

85. Ibid., pp. 65, 99, 128–29.
86. Ibid., pp. 147–61; "National Health Strategy," *Public Papers: Nixon, 1971*, p. 175; Iglehart, "Democrats Cool to Nixon's Health Proposal," p. 2313.
87. Roy, *Proposed Health Maintenance Organization Act*, pp. 70–74, 78–79, 84, 100, 130–31.

All three limited federal aid for HMO construction to ambulatory facilities. The Nixon bill confined its construction support to loan guarantees to private HMOs. The Roy-Rogers measure offered three types of construction aid: grants to cover construction costs of serving an underserved area, construction loans for any eligible HMO, and loan guarantees and interest subsidies for private, nonprofit HMOs. The Kennedy bill reflected its sponsor's skepticism about the availability of private capital for HMO development by simply authorizing construction grants and loans for any eligible HMO.

For initial operating costs, the Nixon bill awarded grants to cover the losses of HMOs operating in underserved areas. The Roy-Rogers bill contained the same provision, to which it added loans for any eligible HMO. Kennedy offered grants and loans to any eligible HMO to cover early operating costs.

Medically Underserved Areas

All three bills offered special incentives to HMOs setting up in or expanding into medically underserved areas.[88] The Nixon bill confined grant awards to the planning phase of HMOs unless they entered a medically underserved area, whereupon they became eligible for grants to cover initial operating costs. Whereas private HMOs were to be eligible only for loan guarantees, public HMOs in underserved areas could receive federal loans. Moreover, in approving planning grants and loan guarantees, the secretary was to give priority to applicants who would provide new or expanded services to these areas.

The Roy-Rogers bill required that planning and initial development grants be targeted on HMOs expected to enroll at least 40 percent of their anticipated total membership from medically underserved areas. Moreover, whereas the construction costs and initial operating costs of other HMOs would be supported only by loans, construction and initial operating costs incurred in serving such an area could be offset by federal grants. The Kennedy bill contained similar distinctions among the terms on which grants and loans would be awarded; it, however, required only 30 percent enrollment in underserved areas. This bill also placed an upper limit of 50 percent on the proportion of underserved enrollees an eligible HMO (except those in rural areas) could enroll. These provisions, Kennedy

88. Ibid., pp. 71–75, 100, 102, 129.

explained, were "intended to prevent the perpetuation of the dual-class system of medical care."[89]

Kennedy's bill also contained three provisions, not found in the other two bills, intended to encourage the growth of HMOs in underserved areas.[90] Title II of his bill would stimulate growth of "health service organizations," which were essentially variants on the HMO theme, for rural population groups with few medical services. Title III would establish "area health education and service centers" in rural areas to help medical schools or health centers attract a wider range of resources. The latter proposal, advanced by the Carnegie Commission, had been endorsed by President Nixon in his health message but did not appear in the administration's HMO measure. Finally, to encourage HMOs to enroll poor persons who could not afford private insurance but were for some reason ineligible for public assistance, Kennedy's bill included still another type of aid: the secretary of HEW was authorized to make grants to HMOs to cover the difference between these subscribers' premiums and what they could afford to pay.

In short, the seemingly tractable question of how federal aid to HMOs ought to be defined readily turned into a problem of truly scholastic complexity. Four mechanisms (grants, loans, loan guarantees, and subsidies) were to be allocated in some combination among three objects of aid (public, private, and private nonprofit HMOs) for five purposes (feasibility and planning, initial development, construction, initial operations, and meeting the costs of enrolling the disadvantaged), and the specific combinations would vary according to the type of area (medically underserved or not) the organization served. The permutations and combinations arising from arranging these fourteen different variables within these four categories were both numerous and strongly conducive to nitpicking and ideological disputation.

External Advantages

The three bills were in general agreement on the external advantages a federally qualified HMO would enjoy. The Nixon bill did not address the problem of state laws that inhibited development of HMOs, but the administration promised to override such laws in other legislation. The

89. Ibid., p. 109.
90. Ibid., pp. 131–34, 137–38.

Roy-Rogers and Kennedy bills enumerated a list of inhibiting state practices and declared them invalid for HMOs as defined in their bills.[91]

None of the three HMO bills included what would later come to be seen as the major advantage of federal qualification—the dual choice requirement that employers of twenty-five or more employees at the minimum wage or above who offer health benefits to workers must offer an HMO option if a federally qualified HMO exists in their area and seeks to be offered. Almost all national health insurance proposals (including those of both the administration and Senator Kennedy), however, included the requirement, and it was clear that it would be available in some piece of legislation.

In sum, comparison of the three bills reveals an almost infinite range of disagreements on details beneath a general and superficial veneer of agreement. All three measures contained a broadly similar definition of an HMO, but they differed on the proper role of IPAs and for-profit groups. All three required open enrollment and the two congressional bills—but not the Nixon bill—called for community rating. All three defined a required set of services, but the three sets were quite different. All three required quality assurance monitoring, but again the three mechanisms differed greatly. The three bills envisioned roughly the same stages and sequence of federal aid to HMOs, but they differed extensively on the proper mix of grants, loans, loan guarantees, and subsidies at each stage. Each bill took several special steps to encourage HMOs in medically underserved areas, but they differed on specifics. Estimates of the cost of aid, which were naturally based mainly on what would be required of the plans and what type of plans would be permitted, differed dramatically. Moreover, much of Kennedy's bill had no counterpart in the Roy-Rogers and Nixon measures.

Viewed side by side, the three bills demonstrated vividly the chimerical quality of HMO politics. The bills' presence, and the hard work that had gone into them, testified to the broad appeal of the HMO concept. Their content, and their differences in detail, proved that their sponsors pictured HMOs very differently and were drawn to them for very different, often incompatible, reasons. The Nixon and Kennedy bills stood worlds apart, founded on entirely contradictory premises and political assumptions. That the Roy-Rogers bill fell somewhere between the two pointed out a

91. Ibid., pp. 95–96, 105, 137.

road toward compromise but, by the same token, dramatized its distance from the other two measures. Clearly, the politics of compromise would be long, painful, and precarious.

Collapsing Coalitions: Congressional Liberals and PGP Purists

In the spring of 1972, the Rogers subcommittee held its first round of hearings on HMOs and Kennedy's subcommittee continued those it had begun in 1971. For the most part the hearings were devoted to "ventilating"[92] the usually predictable views of affected interest groups—the AMA's argument that HMOs were experimental and should be approached slowly and cautiously, that requirements should be numerous and federal subsidies assiduously avoided; the American Hospital Association's proposal for health care "corporations"; the American Pharmaceutical Association's emphasis on drug benefits and the American Psychiatric Association's on mental health benefits.[93] From one source, however—the "community" of prepaid group practice officials and supporters—came arguments that were neither stale nor obvious. Between spring 1971 and spring 1972 these interests had oscillated from bemused disdain—for the administration's wish to create seventeen hundred nebulous HMOs with a few million federal dollars—to hope—that congressional friends such as Kennedy, Javits, and Roy would improve the substance of HMO legislation and expand its authorization—to a severe case of nervous tension over the contents of the Kennedy and Roy-Rogers bills. As the legislators—or, more accurately, their staffs—constructed a hybrid from the bits and pieces of their newly acquired knowledge about PGPs and IPAs, the insiders feared not only that their own expert advice would go unheeded, but also that the requirements the congressional bills would impose on a federally qualified HMO would prove alien and perhaps damaging to their own organizations.

Despite their unconcealed skepticism of the merits of IPAs, most purists recognized that they could not be entirely excluded from a federal HMO program. The proper approach, their spokesmen argued, was to treat PGPs and IPAs in separate parts of the legislation. None of the three bills did so. The Nixon bill included virtually anything as an HMO, the Roy-Rogers

---

92. This description of the hearings is taken from GHAA director Jeffery Cohelan, in *Health Maintenance Organizations*, Hearings, pt. 2, p. 332.

93. Ibid., pp. 333–62, 537–67, 685–737; pt. 4, 1168–85.

bill was ambiguous on the status of IPAs, and the Kennedy bill excluded them altogether. So too, the purists—especially those in organized labor, but many also in the GHAA—strongly objected to federal support of for-profit HMOs. Yet both the Nixon and Kennedy bills offered some forms of aid to such groups.

The purists feared that confusion of IPAs and for-profit operations with "real" prepaid group plans would taint the movement and themselves by unsavory association. Their objection to the organizational features of HMOs required by the congressional bills was, on the other hand, rooted in concrete fear for the future of existing HMOs (their own) and HMOs yet unborn. As they reacted not to the offensiveness and vagueness of the Nixon bill but instead to the worrisome rigor of the Kennedy and Roy-Rogers bills, the purists articulated positions quite different from those they had advanced in 1971. Whereas GHAA executive director Jeffery Cohelan had criticized the lack of specificity of the administration bill and argued for some "rather firm standards," he and his colleagues now emphasized the need to preserve the HMOs' flexibility and to limit what the government would require of them. Required benefits, they argued, should be limited to emergency care, inpatient hospital and physician care, ambulatory physician care, outpatient preventive care, and diagnostic laboratory and diagnostic and therapeutic radiological services. To demand that HMOs offer further services would drive costs up, raise premiums unreasonably, and make the plans uncompetitive in local markets.

The community rating requirement in the Roy-Rogers and Kennedy bills was acceptable, for it conformed to their general practice, but the proposed open enrollment period, required in all three bills, evoked angry protest. Forcing HMOs to accept individual applicants on a first-come, first-served basis would inflict "compulsory adverse selection" on them and drive their costs up if they were required to serve the open enrollees at community rates. James Brindle, president of the Health Insurance Plan of Greater New York, warned the Senate subcommittee: "If you mandate open enrollment for HMO's without mandating it for the whole insurance system, which would be very difficult to do, then you put HMOs at a serious disadvantage." The HIP's experiment with open enrollment in the late 1950s had resulted in "an enrollment that was substantially more expensive to handle."[94] At most, the spokesmen urged, the law might

94. *Physicians Training Facilities*, Hearings, pt. 6, p. 2616.

include language obliging HMOs to market to groups so as to achieve a balanced cross-section of the community.

The plan spokesmen also recommended that quality monitoring be left flexible and subject to community norms rather than carried out, as Ellwood had suggested, according to federally devised "outcome" standards. The conceptual merits of currently available outcome measures were doubtful, they said, and, as a practical matter, if HMOs were required to follow elaborate procedures not required of their fee-for-service competition, costs and premiums could rise so dangerously as to imperil the plans' competitive position and survival.

In one respect, however, the PGP community's line remained consistent with their 1971 position. The spokesmen were certain that the funding levels in the administration bill were far too low.[95]

If the plans' new emphasis had been unpredictable (or at any rate unpredicted), congressional reactions were not. Kennedy was perplexed and annoyed by the repeated plea that no more be required of HMOs than was demanded of their competition. After all, he pointed out, HMOs were said to be a more efficient, cost-effective system, capable of great internal economies and much more rational patterns of service delivery than fee-for-service practice permitted. Largely in recognition of these virtues, the federal government now proposed to give HMOs millions of dollars of aid, exemption from troublesome state laws, a market advantage under dual choice, and other advantages. Considering that HMOs would enjoy both native internal economies and federal support, was it unreasonable to require that they earmark a portion of their "surplus" to expand services and enroll the disadvantaged? Kennedy, like any experienced politician, knew that affected interests always seek to shape federal programs in ways that will require as little deviation from standard operating practices as possible. He knew too that the fundamental purpose of a federal grant-in-aid was to extract a quid pro quo—funds in return for institutional change—and as he had said all along, it made sense to offer federal aid to HMOs only if they did more than, and better than, the fee-for-service mainstream. Kennedy and his staff had no intention of allowing the HMO community to have its cake and eat it too.

As they contemplated the unforeseen turn of events and Kennedy's obdurateness, the PGP spokesmen felt betrayed by their friend. Obviously, they concluded, Kennedy and his staff did not understand the way an

95. *Health Maintenance Organizations*, Hearings, pt. 1, pp. 179, 229–30, 238.

HMO worked, meaning the way they thought it best for their HMOs to work. Equally serious, they were convinced that Kennedy and his staff were determined to saddle a full complement of social goals on the small, vulnerable HMO community and even to use it as a tool in the national health insurance game Kennedy was playing. Observing that Kennedy was immovable, that he appeared to have Javits's support, and that no other subcommittee member was both interested in HMO legislation and influential, the nervous insiders hoped to find a more receptive hearing in the House. The Roy-Rogers bill, after all, contained many fewer objectionable provisions than did Kennedy's.

The Rogers subcommittee listened patiently to the experts, but kept its own counsel. In part this noncommittal stance reflected the complex character of the political game its members played. Kennedy turned a deaf ear not only to the pleas of the PGPs but also to those of the administration and the AMA. In the Rogers subcommittee, by contrast, the PGPs took their place in line along with the administration (ranking Republican Ancher Nelsen saw to it that the administration's lobbyist had ample opportunity to ask questions and inject comments during committee deliberations), the AMA (whose views would be entirely disregarded by no member and were of considerable interest to several), and others, to receive a respectful hearing.

In part, however, the committee's refusal to jump to the support of the plans' arguments reflected an understanding very like Kennedy's of the nature and proper terms of federal aid. Disturbed to hear the good guys sounding more and more like the average recipient of federal aid—that is, articulating self-serving positions that boiled down to the usual request for maximum federal aid with minimum federal strings—the members held fast to the view that a federally supported HMO would be a hybrid, fashioned from desirable bits and pieces of HMO theory and practice, whether or not the product fully resembled or pleased existing plans. The politicians' view was summed up succinctly by James Hastings, New York Republican, after he had been told for the umpteenth time that federally aided HMOs should not be obliged to play by rules more stringent than those of their conventional competitors: "One slight difference. If we are being asked to invest as much as $6 billion of Federal money in the creation of HMO's, I don't know that we are going to be required to subsidize the health insurance programs."[96]

96. Ibid., p. 309.

By mid-1972 the PGP insiders had concluded that the growing HMO momentum had ironically led the legislators to perfect the administration's bill to the point where a set of unworkable requirements now filled an earlier, equally deplorable vacuum. The insiders would work hard to persuade sympathetic legislators and their aides, especially in the House, that the bills should conform more closely to how HMOs work in the real world, but none could be highly optimistic. Clearly, the future of HMO legislation now depended mainly on the terms of trade that would prove acceptable within the subcommittees, their parent committees, each chamber, and then between chambers. Political games were being played out on their own internal logic in sharply different environments. No external force, however expert and deeply affected by the outcome, could now hope to control the process or to guide it very far toward a happy ending.

Action in the Senate

In July 1972 the Labor and Public Welfare Committee reported Kennedy's bill with few changes.[97] The bill carried a total authorization of $5.2 billion for fiscal years 1973, 1974, and 1975, although only about $1 billion would have gone to planning and starting HMOs per se. Aid would be allocated according to a detailed combination of planning grants and loans, subsidies for initial operating costs, and loan guarantees and interest subsidies. Title I of the bill defined an eligible HMO narrowly, but in an important departure from Kennedy's original measure, it permitted limited funding of so-called supplemental HMOs, intended mainly for small communities, rural areas, and other areas where comprehensive HMOs were infeasible. The provision would allow "indirect provisions of services, permitting solo practice forms of organization to qualify for support."[98] The bill mandated a detailed and extensive list of services that HMOs receiving federal support must offer, authorized premium subsidies for the medically indigent, and required both community rating and open enrollment. Losses as a result of open enrollment would be subsidized, and the secretary of HEW might even waive the requirement for three years or more if a plan could demonstrate that meeting it would damage its financial well-being. It also called for mandated dual choice, but resistance of

97. *Health Maintenance Organization and Resources Development Act of 1972*, S. Rept. 978, 92 Cong. 2 sess. (GPO, 1972).
98. Ibid., p. 22.

employers and unions to creating a new unfair labor practice in a health bill threatened to trigger a major battle, and Kennedy moved that the provision be deleted from the bill as soon as it reached the floor.[99] The bill, which would also override state legislation inhibiting the growth of HMOs, won the committee's unanimous approval, although Dominick appended dissenting views to the report.

When the measure came up for debate in September, Kennedy and Javits led an ostentatiously bipartisan effort to pass it. As expected, the opposition was led by Dominick, who argued that it made little sense to contend that HMOs would promote pluralism and innovation in the delivery of care while excluding IPAs, the most prevalent type of prepaid plan. Kennedy replied that it was precisely the predominance of individual practice that made federal endorsement of multispecialty group practice necessary. Moreover, the bill made medical care foundations eligible for support as health *service* organizations in rural areas and, as supplemental HMOs, for all benefits except subsidies for start-up costs in urban areas, where (Kennedy contended) such subsidies were not needed. Nor did Kennedy see the case for subsidizing medical societies, the status quo which, after all, ran the IPAs. Javits, too, reminded the Senate that Title I would allow supplemental HMOs, which included solo practice elements, to be funded if money was not used up by HMOs more exclusively defined, and noted that he himself had worked out that compromise with Kennedy in hopes of placating Dominick. Dominick's amendment to broaden the definition of an HMO was defeated 37–40 (with 23 senators not voting), but his proposal to earmark 25 percent of appropriations for supplemental HMOs was then accepted on a voice vote.[100]

Dominick made it clear that he continued to object to many other facets of the bill. When Kennedy attempted to answer doubts that HMOs could provide such services as mental health care, preventive dental treatment for children, and prescription drug services within a competitive marketplace with the argument that "each of these services is being delivered by HMOs at the present time," Dominick replied that "even the HMO prototypes such as the Kaiser-Permanente . . . do not provide the range of services that his bill would mandate."[101] Whereas Kennedy was prepared to authorize subsidies to HMOs to cover premium increases required by the combined effects of community rating and open enrollment, Dominick

99. *Congressional Record*, September 20, 1972, p. 31563.
100. Ibid., pp. 31570, 31580–90, 31590, 31599.
101. Ibid., pp. 31565, 31581.

deplored both the anticompetitive consequences of the combination and the subsidies proposed to offset them. Kennedy strongly defended the proposed quality control commission and Dominick sharply attacked it. With the exception of the earmarking of appropriations for "supplemental" HMOs, however, Dominick found few allies, and S. 3327 passed by a margin of sixty votes (including Dominick's) to fourteen.[102]

Although the Senate had committed itself to an expensive and ambitious program, the prospects that this measure would make its way into public policy were slight. Danger signals were present in the Senate itself. Dominick's amendment to redefine HMOs had been rejected by a very narrow margin. The high number of senators absent from the debate (twenty-six failed to vote on the final roll call) suggested a relative lack of interest. More important, many senators seemed attracted to the bill by extraneous provisions. Richard Schweicker saw the quality control commission as "clearly the most significant feature of this bill"; Democrat Jennings Randolph of West Virginia, a legislator from a rural state, was especially interested in the health service organization variant of HMOs;[103] Democrat John Tunney of California offered an amendment to add standardized recordkeeping to the quality commission's functions; and Republican Glenn Beall of Maryland suggested similar functions for the National Institute of Health Care Delivery, a favorite proposal of his own.[104] Kennedy's bill, as he had intended, had become an open invitation for position-taking, a legislative vehicle with which to compile and endorse publicly as the will of the Senate an omnibus list of progressive reforms in the health care delivery system. The fact was, however, that none of these new institutions and HMO subtypes was contemplated in the administration's bill or in the Roy-Rogers measure, and the senators knew it.

Collapsing Coalitions: HEW, OMB, White House

In the rush to assemble the presidential health message of February 1971, the extent to which the federal HMO program would be an ambitious development effort (the HEW generalists' preferred approach) as distinct from a limited demonstration effort (OMB's view) was left ambiguous.

102. Ibid., p. 31603.
103. Ibid., p. 31584.
104. Ibid., pp. 31596–97.

The department had its vigorous presidential endorsement of HMOs, the budget makers had kept the dollar commitments small, and, considering that HMO issues appeared elementary in contrast to those raised by the impending financing measures, no one then thought it necessary or wise to explicate the federal role in HMOs further. The problem, of course, was that the compromise was highly vulnerable to the charge that the administration's promises could not be met with the resources it proposed. Indeed, once the president's speech had been delivered and draft HMO legislation introduced in Congress, Richardson and his aides gave the administration's HMO proposal more leisurely scrutiny, concluding that the proposal was too modest to support an important development effort. They therefore resolved to work to expand the limits of federal aid to HMOs.

Two limitations particularly worried Richardson—the paucity of federal financial support for HMOs, and the danger that unless the federal government firmly checked state laws that blocked HMO development, progress would be seriously stifled. In the summer of 1971, therefore, he asked Assistant Secretary Bruce Cardwell to identify new approaches to federal aid and also asked lawyers within the department to explore ways of incorporating a federal override of troublesome state laws into the administration's bill. Under the tutelage of Scott Fleming, a high-ranking Kaiser-Permanente executive who joined HEW as a deputy assistant secretary for planning and development late in 1971, Richardson decided to seek other changes too in the administration's plan. The most important were deletion of the open enrollment requirement (the provision was "quite unrealistic," Fleming advised[105]) and a change in language to require that one-third of HMOs' governing boards be composed of public, not subscriber, members. Late in the year the secretary sought clearance from OMB for the changes, and a decision whether they should be presented as formal amendments, informal but public suggestions, or mere private recommendations to the committees.

Richardson's initiatives reopened debate within the administration about the nature of its HMO commitment and, as 1972 wore on, produced results quite different from those he sought. The OMB readily assented to the deletion of open enrollment, and a few months later Richardson argued for deletion in legislative hearings on the grounds that the adverse impact of open enrollment on HMOs was "self-evident."[106] (Why it had not been

105. "Issue Paper: Open Enrollment" (n.d.), p. 2, in OMB files, vol. 1.
106. *Physicians Training Facilities*, Hearings, pt. 5, p. 1820.

so a year earlier was not explained.) Nor did OMB object to the change in board composition. (An OMB reviewer did, however, change Richardson's draft language from "and we will propose an amendment to the Administration bill to reflect this approach" to "We would have no objection to a requirement.")[107]

New funding sources and a state override were far more touchy issues, for the former meant more money and the latter evoked New Federalism and states' rights themes. When, having studied Cardwell's memorandum and having opted for a federal direct loan fund for public and private nonprofit HMOs, Richardson sought approval from OMB director George Shultz around Christmas of 1971, he won approval for the "concept," but not the "details."[108] An OMB official noted in a memorandum that "HEW now feels that loan guarantees, by themselves, will not be adequate to attract diverse sources of private capital" and observed that Shultz had given his general approval. First, however, the reviewer reported, HEW must fix the "deficiencies" in its proposal. Specifically, it would have to demonstrate a strong policy rationale for a federal direct loan program (had HEW checked out savings institutions, for example?) and it must refine and describe the many technicalities the proposal entailed. Who, for instance, would manage the fund, make the loans, guarantee them, and how?[109] The department returned to the drawing board.

For the first few months of 1972, HEW had reason to hope that its plan for incremental additions to the federal HMO commitment would eventually succeed. In his State of the Union message of January 20, President Nixon reaffirmed his support, then nearly one year old, for HMOs, calling them an "essential tool" for making the delivery of medical care more efficient and effective. In his health message of March 2 he reiterated that making HMOs "everywhere available," so that the whole population might have an alternative to fee-for-service care, stood high among his legislative priorities.[110]

When the Labor and Public Welfare Committee unanimously reported

107. "Issue Paper: Consumer Participation" (n.d.), in OMB files, vol. 1; first draft of Richardson's statement to the Kennedy subcommittee, pp. 16–17, in OMB files, vol. 2.

108. Memorandum from Wilford J. Forbush, Director, Division of Budget, to Thomas P. Reutershan, Executive Secretariat, OS, "Status Report on HMO Capitalization," December 29, 1971, in OMB files, vol. 1.

109. Memorandum from Martha Blaxall to Mr. William Fischer, HRPD/Health, "HMO Direct Loan Fund," December 30, 1971, in OMB files, vol. 1.

110. "Annual Message to the Congress on the State of the Union, January 20, 1972," *Public Papers: Nixon, 1972*, p. 56; "Special Message to the Congress on Health Care, March 2, 1972," ibid., p. 389.

the Kennedy bill in July, however, OMB moved to clarify—meaning, scale down—the administration's commitment. The agency found itself confronting a concrete legislative product that embodied precisely the features it found most offensive. An OMB official recalled:

> The Kennedy bill scared us. It forced us to decide the limits of our commitment. The question, "Where are we vis-à-vis the Kennedy bill?" led us to work out a lot of our specifics.
>
> We kept asking, "What exactly is a federal commitment to HMOs a commitment *to?* To launch and expand HMOs by means of government subsidies? To develop market alternatives to compete on their own merits? A permanently subsidized program?"
>
> The OMB emphasis was on developing institutions that could compete in the marketplace. This was the big difference between us and Kennedy. The Kennedy bill had subsidy programs in many places. It didn't aim at a demonstration of what HMOs could do in today's competitive environment.
>
> The White House view, as we saw it, was to get HMOs started and to subsidize purchasing power by way of national health insurance, giving people a choice. That would be all. This approach was more equitable and more in line with our thinking on the "federal role" kind of issues—which was important to the Nixon administration.

Equally important, OMB executives feared the political implications of Congress's HMO activism. The committee had reported Kennedy's $5.2 billion package unanimously and the Senate was very likely to pass it. The Rogers subcommittee was hard at work on its own bill and might report it in time for action before the Ninety-second Congress ended. Although the House measure would surely be more modest than Kennedy's, there was no telling what a conference committee might do, especially in a Democratic Congress a few months before the 1972 elections. If the House did complete work on its bill and did compromise with Kennedy, a high OMB official later recalled, "we were afraid we'd be in a very bad situation. Congress would give us the choice of accepting a monster or vetoing in an election year a health bill we had started rolling."

Thus even if HEW could be kept in line, Congress was another matter altogether. As they reviewed the unsatisfactory drift of HMO legislation, OMB officials concluded that the best antidote to the philosophical and political problems posed by both Congress and HEW was repeated and unambiguous White House reiteration of what had been the OMB position all along: the administration sought a modest financial commitment to a short-lived demonstration program designed to launch a variety of flexibly defined HMOs and see if they could become self-sustaining in the competitive marketplace.

As OMB officials rethought the limits of the federal HMO commitment, their thoughts naturally turned to the elastic limits of HEW's own commitment. The prolonged ambiguity surrounding development versus demonstration, it seemed in retrospect, readily invited precisely the incremental expansion HEW was then seeking. And the department could not always be held properly in line. For example, in April 1972, when asked at a legislative hearing how far Congress should go to override state laws that inhibited HMO development, Richardson had replied, "in effect . . . as far as the traffic will bear."[111] At a time when the administration was pushing its revenue-sharing packages and wished to leave no impression of encroaching on lower levels of the federal system, this seemed like inappropriate guidance for the HEW secretary to be giving Congress—especially because, as Richardson well knew, OMB had not approved this position. A high-level OMB official recalls setting up a meeting among Richardson, a White House staffer, and himself to discuss the matter.

Eagerness to establish firmly the limits of the administration's HMO commitment and fear that HEW would continue to press against these limits naturally influenced OMB's reception of the department's revised loan fund plans. In June, HEW submitted a set of proposed amendments that would allow the department to make direct loans for construction purposes; authorize it to sell direct loans on a guaranteed, taxable basis; authorize the Government and Federal National Mortgage Associations (GNMA and FNMA) to purchase HEW's loans; delete a provision in the administration's bill that guarantees could amount to no more than 90 percent of the loss of principal and interest on a loan; authorize financing of guaranteed HMO loans by bonds backed by GNMA mortgages; and authorize HEW to guarantee outstanding loans to HMOs.[112] The OMB set about analyzing the proposals and solicited comments from affected agencies.

By the middle of June, comments had arrived. Treasury raised a multitude of complex objections to the proposals and recommended that OMB not clear them. A FNMA executive replied crisply: "FNMA and GNMA are corporations established for the purpose of financing residential mortgages. While the providing of financing for Health Maintenance Organizations is certainly a worthwhile goal, it has no relevance to the residential mortgage market. . . . It is our view that the provisions applicable

---

111. *Health Maintenance Organizations*, Hearings, pt. 1, p. 124.
112. Draft of proposed HEW amendments, June 5, 1972, especially pp. 4–18, in OMB files, vol. 2.

to FNMA should be deleted." Housing and Urban Development Secretary George Romney replied that his department had no objection to authorizing GNMA to guarantee securities backed by loans made to health maintenance organizations and guaranteed by HEW, but he recommended against provisions authorizing GNMA to purchase such loans.[113] Late in the month an OMB analyst added his own negative views to the chorus.[114] On July 7, HEW was informed of OMB's refusal to approve its proposals and decided not to pursue the matter further.[115]

As the summer of 1972 wore on, skeptics in OMB received independent but highly effective outside support in their effort to trim and define the limits of federal HMO aid. In mid-1972 an impending HMO law coincided with a presidential election campaign, a coincidence of which the AMA was of course well aware and which it was determined to exploit in its fight against HMO legislation. As noted above, when HMO plans were taking shape throughout 1970, administration officials had felt that the AMA had "shot its wad" on the Knowles affair. In mid-1972 organized medicine had a new wad to shoot, and it was determined to shoot it hard—preferably at the president himself—while it was of maximum value.[116] Dr. Malcolm Todd, a Californian who had been personal physician to Nixon when he was vice president, and was now both a member of the AMA House of Delegates and chairman of the Physician's Committee to Reelect the President, laid out the cold, hard facts at the White House. Todd told *National Journal* reporter John Iglehart that he had made it clear to the president that "this HMO thing" kept coming up whenever physicians were approached for contributions to the Nixon campaign.[117] Nixon was losing money and support among good friends, Todd argued. And, he pointed out, in an argument that must have struck a responsive chord at the Nixon White House in 1972, HMO supporters—the "Wilbur Cohenites"—had never been Nixon supporters anyway. Reinforcing the

113. See letters from Roy T. Englert, Acting General Counsel, Department of Treasury, June 16, 1972; Oakley Hunter, Federal National Mortgage Association (FNMA), June 20, 1972; George Romney, Secretary, Department of Housing and Urban Development, June 22, 1972, in OMB files, vol. 2.

114. Memorandum from Lynn Etheredge to Paul O'Neill, June 28, 1972, pp. 1–4, OMB files, vol. 2.

115. Memorandum from J. Stimpson to Files, July 7, 1972, in OMB files, vol. 2.

116. As an AMA official told John K. Iglehart, "We're in the driver's seat now, but once the election is over it will be a different story. Any commitment we get from the White House to curb HMOs must be made before Nov. 7." John K. Iglehart, "Intense Lobbying Drive by Medical Group Dims Prospect for HMO Legislation," *National Journal,* September 2, 1972, p. 1405.

117. Ibid.

very themes OMB was articulating—that the president seemed to intend a small-scale experiment, not a major development effort, and that HEW had exceeded White House intentions—Todd apparently won his point.

The main political question was how the White House could reassure the AMA without embarrassing itself. The opportunity arrived late in July, in the form of a memorandum from the chief of OMB's division of human resources programs to James Cavanaugh, a White House staffer who specialized in health issues. The Rogers subcommittee was working hard on an HMO draft, and HEW wanted to push their proposal for overriding state laws while there was still time. "We asked HEW not to discuss any specifics until an Administration position could be developed," the OMB official explained.[118] A few days later, Cavanaugh, who was known to be deeply sympathetic to the AMA in general and highly useful to the organization's spokesmen in pressing the case against HMOs, replied to another OMB official, whose notes in OMB files recorded the fate of the override:

    1. Cavanaugh wants HEW directed to STRONGLY *oppose* ANY override of state laws.

    2. His view is *absolutely no discussion of a compromise.* Any override provision would make the HMO bill a prime candidate for a *veto.* He . . . would be willing to see a bad override provision in the bill and use this as grounds for a veto. In fact, he sounded enthusiastic about vetoing an HMO bill before November.[119]

On August 10, OMB informed HEW's deputy assistant secretary for legislation of the decision.[120]

The cold winds blowing from the White House, added to OMB's already frosty position, finally froze HEW's hopes that the administration would enhance its HMO development effort. Richardson denied that he had received instructions from the White House to back off on HMOs, but he acknowledged that his own enthusiasm for HMOs was not necessarily

118. Memorandum from C. William Fischer, Chief, Human Resources, Program Division, to Jim Cavanaugh, July 25, 1972, in OMB files, vol. 2.

119. Memorandum from Lynn Etheredge, HRPD/Health, to Paul O'Neill, "Federal override of State laws that hinder the development of HMOs," August 9, 1972, p. 4, in OMB files, vol. 2. Emphasis in original.

120. Memorandum from HRPD/Health to Jim Stimpson, "Override of State laws that hinder HMO development," August 11, 1972, in OMB files, vol. 2; it notes that HEW had been informed of the decision the day before. About one week after the decision Veneman, unrepentant but practical, told a news conference that "The Department is committed in principle to an override provision, as previously stated by Secretary Richardson. However, due to the lateness of the Congressional session and the Administration's desire to get an HMO bill this year, the Department is willing to accept a bill with no state override provision." Note by Jim Stimpson to the files, August 18, 1972, in OMB files, vol. 2.

shared there. By September 1972 it was clear that the original coalition had fallen apart, and that OMB and White House skeptics, not HEW enthusiasts, would write the administration's future HMO script.

The Senate, which had shown equally little interest in the administration and the AMA positions on HMOs, and now had its bill in hand, cared very little about the administration's wavering. In the House, however, hearings had ended in May and the laborious work of developing partisan and ideological consensus was under way. With a shift in the position of the administration's spokesman "literally overnight," as a legislative aide recalled, one more complication was added at a delicate time by encouraging the committee's many skeptics to reassess the limits of their own commitment. As it happened, the subcommittee reported its bill very late in the session and it joined the customary end-of-session logjam. Facing a packed agenda, chairman Staggers exercised his prerogative to pick and choose the bills his committee would complete; other measures struck him as both more pressing and less likely to require extensive committee discussions and a long and difficult conference with the Senate. Consequently, the Ninety-second Congress ended without enactment of HMO legislation. The year's efforts had not been without accomplishment, however: the Senate had gone off in one unexpected direction and the administration in an opposite, equally unexpected direction, leaving their erstwhile allies in the prepaid group practice community and HEW, respectively, confused and friendless and the coalitions of 1971 in shambles.

Reassembling the Fragments

When the Ninety-third Congress began work in 1973, a chastened HEW, now headed by former OMB Director Caspar W. Weinberger, a firm believer in a short-lived, competitive, demonstration approach, spelled out the administration's revised thinking tersely and unambiguously. Frank Carlucci, the department's new under secretary, explained to the Rogers subcommittee on March 6 that "we have . . . taken another look at HMOs. We have taken another look at all Federal programs in light of the President's directive to us this year in connection with the budget and we have decided it would be more appropriate to go the demonstration route to try and determine whether this is feasible as a nationwide option."[121]

121. *Health Maintenance Organizations—1973*, Hearings before the Subcommittee on Public Health and Environment of the House Committee on Interstate and Foreign Commerce, 93 Cong. 1 sess. (GPO, 1973), p. 84.

The following day he told an appropriations subcommittee: "The basic difference is that last year it was envisaged as an operational program. This year we have decided it would be better to have it as a demonstration program so we can thoroughly test the viability of the concept."[122]

The administration's revised thinking called for clear emphasis on medically underserved areas, not on the population at large; leaving state legislation governing HMO development to the states themselves; clear limitation of federal support to start-up costs; an adamant refusal to consider subsidies for operations—and deficits—over time; explicit focus on the need for economically viable and competitive HMOs; and repeated assertions that the federal government was merely testing the feasibility of HMOs, not endorsing them as appropriate for all, or any, of the population. Chairman Rogers congratulated Carlucci and the administration, adding that "I think you have pretty much followed the action of this subcommittee and have modified your positions accordingly."[123]

Meanwhile the Senate was modifying its own position. As action in the House grew imminent, Kennedy and his colleagues on the health subcommittee in the Senate set aside their earlier concern to educate the public in the desirable elements of health care reform and began trimming their bill down to something with which the House would be able to compromise. The Kennedy bill (Senate 14) introduced in the Ninety-third Congress on January 4, 1973, was identical to the HMO bill the Senate had passed the year before. In considering the bill, however, the committee made several major changes designed to bring it closer to the Rogers subcommittee's viewpoint and sharply reduced the three-year authorization from $5.2 billion to $1.5 billion. (Of this, HMOs per se would receive about a third.) It also allowed HEW to waive some of the required services if manpower were unavailable to an HMO, limited federal subsidies for individual premiums and open enrollment losses to the first three years of an HMO's operation, and deleted the proposal for a national institute of health care delivery, which it reported as a separate measure. In other respects the measure remained much as it had been.[124]

When Senate bill 14 was called up for consideration by the full Senate on May 14, it seemed at first that the debate would be little more than a reprise of the arguments of 1972. Kennedy opened by calling attention to

122. *Labor and Health, Education, and Welfare Appropriations for 1974,* Hearings before a subcommittee of the House Committee on Appropriations, 93 Cong. 1 sess. (GPO, 1973), p. 99.

123. *Health Maintenance Organizations—1973,* Hearings, p. 84.

124. *Health Maintenance Organization and Resources Act of 1973,* S. Rept. 129, 93 Cong. 1 sess. (GPO, 1973).

the reduced authorization level and to other changes in the bill. He noted that the sums provided would furnish HMO care for about 3 percent of the American population at most, and that an investment of $1.5 billion over three years in changing a health industry that spent $80 billion per year was "minuscule." He then pulled out and delivered with few changes his speech of the previous year. Dominick repeated his now-familiar objections. Hubert Humphrey, Democrat of Minnesota, rose to support the bill, saying it met the test of "fiscal responsibility," whereas the administration's $60 million request for HMOs in fiscal 1974 was "totally inadequate." He did think, however, that the basic benefit package should be broadened to include mental health, extended care, and other services.[125] The Senate then turned to consideration of amendments.

The first proposal came from Republican Robert Taft of Ohio, who offered the administration's bill (Senate 972) in place of Kennedy's. This measure would authorize $60 million for the program and give HEW very wide discretion over its allocation. Kennedy observed that the administration's skimpy budget figure fit strangely with HEW's original projection that 90 percent of the population would enjoy an HMO option by 1980 and objected strenuously and at length to giving the secretary carte blanche to "say anything is an HMO." Taft replied that an experimental program ought to be flexible and that he would "rather have $60 million carte blanche than a $1.5 billion blue-plate special cooked up by a bunch of apprentice cooks who have just come on the line." This view, however, was not shared by the Senate which rejected Taft's amendment on a voice vote.[126]

Dominick then made the case for the set of amendments he was again about to offer. Unlike the previous year, an HMO law was a strong possibility. Holding out for highly ambitious legislation, he argued, would reduce the prospect of finding a compromise with the House in conference and would invite Nixon's veto—one the Senate could probably not override. Even if the two chambers compromised and a veto was avoided, the appropriations committees would not agree to sums many times higher than the administration had sought. The result could only be "the usual fancy language" in which the Senate promises "in broad, sweeping terms, that we are going to take in half the Treasury, and by so doing cure the problem."[127]

125. *Congressional Record*, May 14, 1973, pp. 15497–504.
126. Ibid., pp. 15507, 15509.
127. Ibid., p. 15514.

Arguing that his amendments were both reasonable and politically essential, Dominick moved that subsidies for initial operating costs and for premiums be removed from the bill, quality control provisions be deleted, health service organizations for rural areas be eliminated, and the percentage of appropriations earmarked for supplemental HMOs be increased to one-third. The Senate, however, rejected his modifications by a 37–50 margin (with 13 senators absent). Dominick next moved simply that capitation grants (premium subsidies for the medically indigent) be stricken, which would decrease the authorization by one-third and remove pressure on HEW to "keep on going forever and ever" as HMO premium costs inevitably proved uncompetitive. Moreover, it would avoid backing into national health insurance which, he argued, was properly the province of the Finance Committee, not Labor and Public Welfare. Kennedy noted in reply that his bill limited capitation grants to three years and that this would overcome economic barriers to HMO membership until national health insurance was enacted. The amendment was defeated 37–49, with 14 senators absent. Finally, Dominick moved to delete the title that established the quality control commission and was again defeated, 40–47, with 13 senators absent.[128]

Participants had expected a freewheeling struggle on the floor ("all bets are off on this one," a Kennedy aide told Congressional Quarterly before debate began),[129] and despite the defeat of Dominick's amendments, the danger that absent senators might be recruited in support of further amendments the next day, and, most important, the disadvantage of going into conference with the House with a clear record of minority disaffection and thin majorities on key provisions all troubled Kennedy. His concern increased appreciably when Javits, a steadfast ally and guarantor of bipartisan support despite fierce Republican criticism, concluded that the bill was in trouble and suddenly intimated that he saw some merit in the minority view and was prepared to offer an amended version of his own that would come much closer to the administration bill. "When Javits changed abruptly," a Kennedy aide recalled, "Kennedy saw that compromise was necessary in order to get the bill passed at all. And he was determined to pass it."

In what the GHAA's legislative lobbyist later described as "the most dramatic development in the entire legislative process of the HMO act,"[130]

128. Ibid., pp. 15501–05, 15519–22.
129. "Senate Passes Kennedy-Javits Health Maintenance Bill," Congressional Quarterly Weekly Report, May 19, 1973, p. 1234.
130. James F. Doherty, "A Brief Account of the Legislative Peregrinations of the Health Maintenance

Kennedy suddenly offered a substitute measure designed to placate Javits and the bill's critics. "While I feel that the bill as reported is an excellent, strong piece of legislation," Kennedy explained, "I am mindful of the desirability of consolidating the Senate's position with respect to this important issue to the greatest extent possible." The amazed Dominick, who declared that he had "never heard of this substitute until just this second,"[131] found himself confronted with a proposal that would broaden the definition of eligible HMOs to include IPAs; cut authorizations in half to $865 million; delete both supplemental HMOs and health service organizations; and eliminate the area health education and service centers.

By the time debate resumed the next day, Kennedy had conferred with Javits and Schweiker and had decided in essence to adopt as his own the compromise Javits had drafted. The revisions reduced authorizations to $705 million, transformed the quality control commission into an HEW agency, deleted malpractice reinsurance provisions, and strengthened HEW's power to issue waivers and exemptions for HMOs having difficulty in meeting provisions of the bill. The compromise got around the appearance of separate authorizations for capitation grants to cover HMOs' costs in enrolling poor and high-risk individuals by earmarking for these purposes 15 percent of the appropriations for support of HMOs.

Kennedy hoped that his explicit concessions to the minority would secure a broader base of support than had been evident the day before. He had viewed Senate bill 14 as a "bare minimum proposal," but, he concluded, "we are dealing with legislative realities this afternoon." Dominick complained that the measure still overrode state laws, contained capitation grants, and included quality control measures, and declared that he would vote against it. The Kennedy-Javits compromise succeeded, however, as the revised measure passed 69–25, with only six senators absent.[132]

Meanwhile, the Rogers subcommittee was putting the finishing touches on a bill that it hoped would prove uncontroversial in the full committee and find its way easily to passage on the House floor. Most of the hard and

Organization Act of 1973," paper prepared for the American Bar Association meeting, August 12, 1975, p. 10.

131. *Congressional Record*, May 14, 1973, p. 15531. According to a veteran lobbyist and Kennedy-watcher, "this isn't unusual behavior when he sees his bill threatened. Nor is it unusual for Javits. They work something out and then both take credit for coming up with a compromise. Of course there's some risk that the whole thing will fall apart, but on the other hand, nobody has much time to study the terms. And Kennedy gets to make his pitch before having to compromise."

132. Ibid., May 15, 1973, pp. 15673, 15678, 15684. The final authorization returned to $805 million when Democrat William Hathaway of Maine sought and won an amendment adding $100 million specifically earmarked for HMOs in nonmetropolitan areas (p. 15677).

detailed work of compromise had been completed the year before and, had it not been for Staggers's unwillingness to take up the long, detailed, and controversial HMO bill at a time when other end-of-session measures were pressing and a long and difficult conference with the Senate seemed inevitable, the bill might well have made it to the House floor then.

As one subcommittee draft followed another, the compromise process trimmed Roy's original bill very considerably. As noted earlier, a projected $1 billion authorization had been deleted at Rogers's request even before the bill had been introduced. All evidence for and bold declarations of the merits of HMOs had been deleted.[133] The bill had been broadened to permit loan guarantees to for-profit HMOs (Roy had at first adamantly opposed their inclusion) and rewritten to make it clear that IPAs were eligible for aid. The benefit package had been reduced. Open enrollment was no longer required. Instead, the bill authorized "demonstration grants and contracts" to a maximum of eight HMOs to test the feasibility of enrolling high-risk members. Sixteen HMOs could also receive special funds to test the feasibility of serving the indigent, and twenty to experiment in rural medically underserved areas. Community rating was retained, but it could be offset by "nominal" copayments.

The administration, which had endeavored to supply its sympathizers with evidence, arguments, and moral support, thought that the modified Roy bill was substantially improved. Whereas in 1972 it had worked up and submitted fully three dozen disagreements with the Roy-Rogers bill,[134] in 1973 it made little effort to influence the outcome. In two parts of the bill, however, it happened that the administration's reservations were shared by conservative members of the subcommittee, and these threatened to generate controversy in the full committee too. One part contained the subsidies to cover the costs of experimenting with enrollment of high risk and indigent persons and serving medically underserved rural areas. These subsidies were extended only to a few HMOs, ended after three years, and served explicitly the demonstration purposes the administration itself emphasized, but they *were* subsidies and this fact alone led the administration to oppose them strongly. The other controversial section overrode state legislation inhibiting HMO formation or operations, a provision the White House of course opposed and insisted that HEW oppose too.

Afraid that the skeptics on the full committee would insist that the sixty-seven-page bill be read in its entirety and then join with subcommittee

133. Bauman, "Formulation and Evolution of Health Maintenance Organization Policy," p. 135.

134. Notes on meeting at OMB on the administration's response to the Roy-Rogers bill, August 23, 1972, in OMB files, vol. 2.

conservatives in an attack on these provisions, Roy listened receptively to a compromise offered by James Hastings in August. Subcommittee Republicans wanted language in the bill that would explicitly limit the number of federally aided HMOs under the new law to one hundred. If Roy would give up the state override, Hastings suggested, he and his Republican colleagues would settle for language in the report stating that the committee intended to aid about one hundred HMOs, but establishing no actual limit in the statute. Moreover, he pointed out, if Roy would also agree to delete the demonstration subsidies (which aided fewer then two dozen HMOs and took many pages to spell out) and the construction funds, he would at once placate the minority and cut the length of the bill in half. Roy agreed and in September the bill (trimmed almost by half) made it through committee in about half an hour.

The bill (House bill 7974) authorized $240 million for a five-year program (fiscal years 1974–78) to bring approximately one hundred HMOs to the operating stage. The committee recommended that support for feasibility studies, planning, and initial development be authorized through June 30, 1976, with funds for initial operations authorized until the end of fiscal 1978. At this point the five-year program, and all federal HMO assistance, would come to an end. There would be no need, the committee carefully declared, to renew or extend HMO legislation to meet outstanding or continuing commitments.[135]

In a message to Congress on September 10, President Nixon endorsed the committee's approach. The president complained that the bill passed by the Senate "calls for a full-scale development effort rather than a limited demonstration program. A national development effort would require funding levels far beyond what is needed or what we can afford." He viewed the bill reported by the House committee, however, as a "fiscally responsible demonstration effort," and stated that he would sign such legislation.[136]

Two days later, the full House took up the committee's measure. In the course of a short, repetitive, and lackluster debate, committee members emphasized the modest, experimental, and finite nature of the program; the absence of capitation grants for enrollees; the lack of preemption of state laws; the conformity of funding levels and substantive provisions to the administration's wishes; and the possibility that HMOs might make

135. *Health Maintenance Organization Act of 1973*, H. Rept. 451, 93 Cong. 1 sess. (GPO, 1973), p. 16.

136. "Special Message to the Congress on National Legislative Goals, September 10, 1973," *Public Papers: Nixon, 1973*, p. 776.

an effective stab at containing high and escalating health costs. The consensus was that the committee had reported a good bill, and it passed, without amendment, 369–40.[137]

Despite these efforts to reach common ground, the House and Senate bills were so different that, as Staggers observed in explaining the results of the conference to the House in December, the conference report contained "an entirely new draft of the legislation." The draft, he explained, "generally follows the format of the House bill with the addition of Senate provisions."[138] The amount authorized—$375 million over fiscal years 1974–78—was closer to the House than to the Senate figure, and the managers followed the House approach by emphasizing a sequence of planning aid in the first three years followed by development support in fiscal 1977. Three House provisions absent from the Senate measure were accepted—dual choice, continuing regulation of HMOs by HEW, and periodic reviews of HMO progress by the secretary and by GAO with periodic reports by them to Congress. Three elements of the Senate bill not contained in the House version were eliminated—construction assistance for HMOs, capitation subsidies for the medically indigent, and subsidies to HMOs suffering the consequences of open enrollment. On many other points the managers compromised—for example, 20 percent of appropriated funds would be spent in nonmetropolitan areas, certain types of state laws discouraging HMOs would be preempted but only in the case of organizations supported under the new legislation itself, and HEW would carry out research into the quality of HMO care and report its findings to Congress. The managers also compromised on two of the most controversial features of the legislation, omitting from the final basic benefit package the Senate bill's vision care, prescription drugs, and physical therapy, but adding to the House package emergency medical care, treatment for alcohol and drug abuse, and aid during mental health crises. (Preventive dental services for children appeared on both lists of basic benefits.) The conference report also required HMOs to observe both community rating and open enrollment. However, it permitted HMOs to levy nominal copayments to offset the costs of the former, and allowed a three-year renewable HEW waiver of the latter.[139]

On December 18 the House approved the conference report quickly and with little discussion. The next day the Senate did the same.[140]

137. *Congressional Record,* September 12, 1973, pp. 29353–70.
138. Ibid., December 18, 1973, p. 42228.
139. See *Health Maintenance Organization Act of 1973,* S. Rept. 621, 93 Cong. 1 sess. (GPO, 1973) for details.
140. *Congressional Record,* December 18 and 19, 1973, pp. 42228–30, 42504–12.

A week later, OMB Director Roy Ash transmitted the customary enrolled bill memorandum to the president, incorporating the comments of affected agencies and the office's own analyses and recommendations on Senate bill 14. Describing the bill as "a compromise between Congress and the Administration," Ash noted that although "the enrolled bill goes beyond the Administration's HMO proposal in a number of respects . . . it embraces much of the Administration's bill." Some provisions ran "contrary to a limited demonstration program." For one thing, the sections calling for continuing HEW regulation of assisted HMOs, overriding obstructive state laws, and setting up a revolving loan fund might make the program hard to terminate, for "congressional and other pressures will undoubtedly seek its 'extension.' " Furthermore, the broad benefit package and community rating requirements might put HMOs at a competitive disadvantage and therefore "necessitate even longer term subsidies to Federally-assisted HMOs." The OMB's conclusion, however, was that "most of the objectionable provisions can be ameliorated through prudent administrative actions and that the original purpose of an HMO demonstration program can be maintained. On balance, therefore, we recommend approval of S. 14."[141]

On December 29, Nixon signed the bill at San Clemente "with great pleasure," calling it "another milestone" in the administration's health strategy. Meeting with reporters, Weinberger remarked that he considered the legislation "a very good bill and an excellent example of the results of a cooperative approach with the congressional leaders and patient negotiations and all the rest." Asked by one kibitzer whether the administration had not at one point talked about having 90 percent of the population covered in a short period of time, Weinberger replied: "I don't really know. The Administration is a very large organization."[142]

Conclusion: The Politics of Disappointment

Far from viewing it as a milestone, the HMO lobby quickly let it be known that they viewed Public Law 93-222 as a millstone around their collective neck. The chorus of complaint, orchestrated by the GHAA,

141. Roy L. Ash (Director), "Memorandum for the President: Enrolled Bill S. 14, the Health Maintenance Organization Act of 1973," December 26, 1973, in OMB files, vol. 3.

142. Office of the White House Press Secretary, "Press Conference of Caspar W. Weinberger, Secretary, Department of Health, Education, and Welfare, and Charles Edwards, Assistant Secretary, Health," December 29, 1973, p. 8, in OMB files, vol. 4. It was perhaps a harbinger of things to come that the name of the largest prepaid group practice was misspelled "Keiser" throughout this transcript.

began at a conference held in February 1974, where administrators of prepaid group plans and would-be applicants for federal aid were told in no uncertain terms that few HMOs could offer the benefit package required, conjoin community rating and open enrollment, and still hope to market their plans at competitive premiums.[143] Irritated that (as they saw it) their supposed ally Kennedy had led the political process to ignore their experienced voices, spokesmen in well-established PGPs and other old hands in the field served notice that they intended to work for amendments at the first feasible moment.

Their displeasure was widely shared among academic and other observers. Pointing to the administration's waffling, Kennedy's reformist dreams, and a general misunderstanding of the workings of HMOs among politicians, they concluded that the political system had failed, this time or as usual, depending on the commentator's ideology. Obviously, the critics proclaimed, a single law and program could not be expected to bear the burden of incorporating both a market-oriented, cost-containment approach and a development-oriented, social goals design. The political system, they concluded, had taken up a sound, straightforward policy strategy and distorted and complicated it over three years of work into an unworkable law.

The critics seldom distinguished between two senses of "unworkability." One meaning is that the law effectively prevented new HMOs from developing and would prevent both new and older HMOs from marketing required services at competitive premiums. Another meaning, however, is that the law displeased existing HMOs because it failed to conform to their established organizational practices and offended their sense of justice and sound business judgment. In the latter sense, the law could be called "unworkable" because established plans refused to "work" with it. Chapter eight will develop the argument that although the law was admittedly unworkable in the latter sense, it was not necessarily so in the former sense too. Here it suffices to note that after the law was enacted, critics were content to cite the plans' objections as unquestionable evidence that the law was unworkable in both senses.

Prima facie, the argument that the political process failed the HMO strategy is convincing. The legislative-executive politics that produced the law were no model of rational problem-solving. Three aspects of the process in particular held the HMO strategy hostage to considerations

143. See, for example, Nancy Hicks, *New York Times*, February 14, 1974; "HMOs are Coming But Will They Last?" *American Medical News*, vol. 19 (February 25, 1974), pp. 323–29.

that bore little direct relation to the workings of HMOs: the nature of the executive's initiative, the tense and deteriorating state of legislative-executive relations between 1970 and 1973, and the institutional differences between the Rogers subcommittee in the House and the Kennedy subcommittee in the Senate.

Executive Initiative

The administration's HMO proposal may fairly be described as a textbook example of how an executive initiative ought not to be constructed. Health maintenance organizations entered the federal agenda abruptly when, in early February 1970, they were grasped by a small group of HEW generalists, who lacked background in health policy issues, knew little about HMOs, were attracted in large part by what HMOs would *not* entail, and were content to rely on a highly abstract analytic model of HMOs' "proincentive" and "self-regulating" properties. Ignoring pertinent questions and reservations of specialists and PGP officials, the generalists convinced the House Ways and Means Committee of the merits of adding an HMO option to Medicare a little over a month after they first saw the light themselves.

Shortly after this victory had been won, new HEW generalists, led by Secretary Richardson and equally lacking in familiarity with the world of prepaid group practice, began attempting to convince the White House that an aggressive effort to develop HMOs would save money, reinvigorate competition in the health care system, avoid regulation, and meet the needs of medically underserved areas. All of these claims were conjectural and unsubstantiated; some were farfetched indeed. When yet another set of generalists at OMB sought to limit the budgetary implications of HEW's plans, an ambiguous compromise between development and demonstration resulted. The OMB appeared never to consider that its insistence that federal aid be limited to a few million dollars essentially dictated the substance of the administration's HMO proposal. The least-cost premise implied inclusion of many kinds of groups and flexibility in their operation, a policy package that could be defended only by heavy and often implausible reliance on the literal model. In consequence, Congress was obliged to start from scratch, devoting two and a half years to detailed sifting of options and information—tasks for which the executive's superior staff capacities and expertise theoretically suited it better.

After the president had enthusiastically endorsed HMOs and an administration bill had been sent to Congress, HEW finally gave the proposal some detailed thought. Richardson came to the view that the contemplated federal financial support was too small, that a strong override of obstructive state laws was needed, that open enrollment should be dropped, and that the bill should be amended in other ways. In the course of the legislative clearance process, OMB's substantive involvement grew (spurred by Kennedy's bill) and interest at the White House grew too (spurred by the AMA). By the late summer of 1972 the ambiguous compromise, which had never made much sense, had collapsed, as had the uneasy HEW-OMB coalition on which it rested. The administration would now, a year and a half after the president's speech, rethink and define its commitment. A sound executive initiative engages department, OMB, and White House in careful thought and definition of the nature and limits of the administration's commitment *before* the president endorses a proposal and recommends legislation embodying it to Congress. Reversing this order, the Nixon HMO proposal grew out of HEW entrepreneurship, with little discussion and less clarity. After the commitment was made and the legislation introduced, institutional involvement grew and deliberation proceeded. The blunt fact, in the words of more than one administration participant in the HMO initiative, was that no one knew what he was doing.

Legislative-Executive Relations

Ironically, the poor and deteriorating state of legislative-executive relations between 1970 and 1973 guaranteed that each increment of clarity and definition in the administration would be met met by a corresponding increment of congressional indifference to the administration's views. No matter who the executive happened to be, the legacy of congressional activism in the health field and the quest of new health policy leaders Rogers and Kennedy to make their mark would have given the legislature views of its own on HMOs. The minority party's control of the White House while the majority party held the Congress, and the growing bitterness between the parties and branches over the administration's allegedly antihealth attitudes, further incited congressional activism. The Watergate incident and the strident partisanship surrounding the 1972 presidential election further insured that Democratic health leaders in Congress would go their own way. By the time the administration finally decided what it wanted to say about HMOs, Congress had no desire to listen. Communication, a legislative aide recalled, "had completely broken down." That the administration secured some of its objectives in the final bill stemmed not from its influence but from the presence on the Rogers subcommittee and the parent House committee of several moderates and conservatives of both parties who happened to share the administration's views for reasons of their own. The climate, in short, was not conducive to smooth, sympathetic legislative-executive harmony in defining and launching new, fragile HMOs.

Institutional Differences between House and Senate

Finally, internal congressional differences, superimposed on the administration's internal difficulties and the hostility between the branches, inevitably complicated the work of agreeing on one widely acceptable HMO measure. Kennedy's game and Rogers's were not the same, and in view of the large differences in the institutional environments of their respective subcommittees and parent committees, could not be the same. The predominance of internal congressional terms of trade over the internal coherence of the HMO strategy was bound to produce a legislative hybrid HMO that frustrated and perplexed both devotees of innovation and those familiar with the real article.

A Different Interpretation

Although the view that the political process badly failed HMO policy between 1970 and 1973 is not unpersuasive, it is not a completely satisfying explanation. The political failures that dogged the evolution of HMO policy—administration wavering, legislative-executive tension, and discrepant congressional agendas—were constants of political life in the Nixon years and are to be found in some measure—at times in large measure—in all administrations. The theory of political failure between 1970 and 1973 does not explain why similar political dynamics produced a sizable number of laws which, while no doubt less than perfect, were not greeted as flatly unworkable and remediable only by immediate amendment.

The administration's wavering over HMOs was part of a fairly common pattern. In such policy initiatives as the "war on cancer," national growth policy, and the family assistance plan, similar confusion reigned. In each case, a set of administration generalists, suspicious and even contemptuous of largely Democratic bureaucratic specialists, developed among themselves bold initiatives which they then sold to the president, who then publicly endorsed them. As time went on, another set of generalists gained the upper hand, took a dim view of their brethren's earlier work, and successfully urged retrenchment on the president, thereby at once clarifying the administration's position internally and throwing it into confusion for onlookers in Congress and elsewhere. At times this pattern stifled legislation (the family assistance plan, for example); at other times, progress went haltingly forward in spite of it.[144]

Strained and worsening legislative-executive relations were also a constant of 1970–73. Nonetheless important legislation emerged—amendments to Medicare in 1972, for example, which, among other things, established the professional standards review organization program; a general revenue-sharing act in 1972; and a manpower block grant measure in 1973. Some important legislation emerged from that odd couple, the House Commerce and Senate Labor Committees, too—important health manpower legislation in 1971, and significant organizational changes in the government's fight against cancer, for instance. And a few months after enactment of the HMO law, these committees finished work on a new health planning act. None of these measures emerged free from conflict and none was judged ideal. None, however, was surrounded by the aura of pervasive misunderstanding and failure that assailed the HMO law.

A more persuasive view is that the apparent unworkability of the HMO law had more to do with the nature of the HMO policy strategy itself than with the ever-present inadequacies of the political process. The strategy's peculiar, perhaps unique, combination of qualities helps explain this unusually poor fit between politics and policy. First, even by the unsimple standards of contemporary policymaking, an attempt by the federal government to design, launch, and regulate new, small business organizations that integrate both financing and delivery of health care was an extremely complex undertaking. In the nature of the case, designing these comprehensive organizations was bound to elicit a comprehensive range of disagreements about how health care should be financed and delivered.

Second, the complexity of the HMO concept naturally acted as a lightning rod, drawing to itself and into the political arena what had before been mainly private-sector, in-house disputes among purists and Ellwood

---

144. Richard A. Rettig, *Cancer Crusade: The Story of the National Cancer Act of 1971* (Princeton University Press, 1977); Strickland, *Politics, Science and Dread Disease*, pp. 273–75, 288; James L. Sundquist, "A Comparison of Policy-Making Capacity in the United States and Five European Countries: The Case of Population Distribution," in Michael E. Kraft and Mark Schneider, eds., *Population Policy Analysis* (Lexington Books, 1978), pp. 71–72; Burke and Burke, *Nixon's Good Deed*; Moynihan, *Politics of a Guaranteed Income*. Energy policy seems to be still another case in point. See Harmon Zeigler and Joseph S. Olexa, "The Energy Issue: Oil and the Emergency Energy Act of 1973–74," in Robert L. Peabody, ed., *Cases in American Politics* (Praeger, 1976), pp. 196–201.

eclectics, the AMA and the AFL-CIO, liberal reformers and conservative market experimenters. It attracted a too wide range of quality monitors, benefit expanders, and others who were confident that any comprehensive health care system worthy of federal endorsement and support should embrace their particular priority. In short, the nature of the concept agitated an unusually large number of intensely interested and deeply dissentient organized actors. Inevitably, the lack of consensus on how that hybrid, the federally supported and qualified HMO, should be constructed brought into pitched battle a preexisting set of political tensions.

Third, unlike institutions either created out of whole cloth by the federal government or involved only marginally with it, HMOs faced a perplexing bottom line: marketability. In particular, the omnipresent objection that any requirement that HMOs offer more services or enroll riskier members than their competition would make them uncompetitive grated harshly against the fundamental premise of the U.S. grant-in-aid system: that in exchange for federal funding and recognition, the government should extract as a quid pro quo a measure of institutional change and social progress. Warned that in *this* case, federal grant politics as usual would surely destroy the program's goals, legislators responded with skepticism, annoyance, and disappointment that the PGP community had learned so rapidly to play the game of insisting that its established ways of operation were the best, indeed the only workable, ways. The persisting tension, produced by the marketability issue, between the politicians' grant politics as usual and the plans' business as usual introduced a precision and precariousness into program design that does not afflict so greatly programs and institutions whose success is less defined by the rules of market competition, or ones merely regulated by government, as distinct from ones created and defined by government.

Fourth, the complexity of the HMO proposal was initially, and occasionally later on, concealed by the literal model, a piece of highly abstract policy analysis that unashamedly built reasoning about self-regulating organizational incentives into a full-blown theory of reorganization of the U.S. health care system. Rarely has so complicated a political proposal been so credulously concealed behind so simplistically satisfying a piece of policy analysis. Understandably, this analysis appealed strongly and immediately to the HEW generalists, busy men with a powerful need for an initiative and with a weak background and interest in the complexities of health care reform. Inevitably the literal model would be challenged and the hard work of organizational design, complete with standards and safeguards against the double-edged sword of prepaid group practice incentives, would have to be undertaken in Congress. An abstract model was no permanent substitute for a flesh-and-blood model; yet the fact was that the proven Kaiser plans were too costly and ambitious to be a model and that IPAs offered too little to constitute an attractive model in their own right. Inescapably, the legislators would fashion a synthetic HMO, a hybrid, from bits and pieces of desirable experience and practice; that model would fall somewhere between Kaiser and IPAs. That few real-world HMOs occupied that intermediate terrain might have been taken as a caveat against the strategy itself; instead, it merely complicated the synthetic process the legislators were determined to pursue and served to demonstrate that the political process is not an appropriate form for elaborate, improvised exercises in concept-formation.

As the legislators went to the drawing board, the interaction between complexity and lack of consensus soon caused heads to spin and positions to shift. Contending factions in the ever-expanding community of affected interests scrambled to press their arguments with friendly legislative and executive factions whose friendship often proved fickle. The only clear datum was that no actor or faction could control the process. The only certain predictions were that the federal HMO hybrid would fall somewhere between what the administration and Ellwood had proposed and what the experienced plan spokesmen knew and loved, and that both camps would therefore disown it. Whether the political invention could sustain the policy promises that had kept the inventors hard at work for three years only time would tell. The HMO community lost no time, however, in making clear its own conviction that the clumsy inventors had succeeded only in transforming an administration mouse into a legislative monster.

To most of the legislators who painstakingly fashioned the compromise that finally led to the act, however, process and outcome alike appeared reasonable. On a very long list of very wide disagreements, they had reached middle ground time and again. "Health maintenance organization" still meant both prepaid group practice and independent practice association, and important safeguards and standards had been written into the law. The benefit package called for more than the administration had proposed, but much less than Kennedy had sought. Community rating was required, but copayments were permitted. The open enrollment requirement remained, but HEW could grant a three-year waiver, and subsequent waivers, for plans that would be damaged by it. A modified scheme for overriding state laws had been adopted. The sums authorized were substantially more than the administration had asked, but much smaller than what Kennedy had proposed. The discretion granted to HEW was not, as the administration had proposed, almost unlimited, yet it seemed large enough to support those "prudent administrative actions" of which OMB Director Ash had written and which any complex law demands. On each of the many controversial provisions, accommodations had been reached by careful, patient, repeated applications of the politician's art. To be sure, the individual compromises, and the hybrid HMO that constituted the sum of these many parts, deviated in important ways from what both the Ellwood eclectic and the purist factions of the HMO community had recommended. But this too was inherent in the political process. All laws are complex amalgamations; no group ever gets, or should expect to get, all of what it seeks. To the weary politicians, the HMO community's constant plaint that an HMO was in essence a Swiss watch, so intricate that the displacement or imperfection of a single tiny part would cause the whole to break down, seemed self-interested, apolitical, and finally tiresome.

CHAPTER SIX

HMOs in HEW: The Frustrations
of Administrative Prudence

This is the story of America. Everybody's doing what they think they're supposed to do.
Jack Kerouac, *On the Road*

THOSE WHO looked to the Department of Health, Education, and Welfare (HEW) for those "prudent administrative actions" required to smooth the implementation of the Health Maintenance Organization Act of 1973, were soon disappointed by the bureaucracy's performance. Sharp critiques of the program's administration, which quickly appeared in HMO trade association conferences, newspaper and journal articles, and legislative hearings, made three points in particular. First, they charged, the department had left the entire exercise in limbo by failing to issue timely, clear regulations on a variety of important provisions. Second, it had been lamentably slow in certifying that HMOs that met the standards of the act did indeed qualify to receive federal loans and be offered under the dual choice provisions of the law. When the House subcommittee chaired by Paul Rogers met in July 1975 to consider amendments to the act, only four health maintenance organizations (HMOs) had qualified for federal loans and none had qualified under the dual choice provisions—not surprising, critics noted, considering that final regulations on these vital subjects had not yet been published. Third, and in good part as a consequence of the first two problems, HEW had allowed large portions of appropriations to revert, unspent, to the treasury—the Rogers subcommittee learned that the department had managed to spend only 55 percent of funds appropriated for the program in the previous fiscal year.[1] A little over a year later,

---

1. *Health Maintenance Organization Amendments of 1975*, Hearings before the Subcommittee on Health and the Environment of the House Interstate and Foreign Commerce Committee, 94 Cong. 1 sess. (U.S. Government Printing Office, 1975), p. 46. (Hereafter Rogers Subcommittee Hearings, 1975.) Three months earlier, the acting administrator of the Health Services Administration had testified that the department had managed to obligate only $9 million of the $40 million available to it in grant funds and had made only $1 million in loans. *Appropriations for 1976*, Hearings before the Subcommittee on Departments of Labor and Health, Education, and Welfare of the House Appropriations Committee, 94 Cong. 1 sess. (GPO, 1975), p. 138.

the General Accounting Office (GAO) reported that through fiscal 1977, the department had requested only $70 million of the $250 million authorized for grants and contracts, hardly a sign of departmental enthusiasm and bold forward progress.[2] As the health care cost "crisis" continued, critics wanted to know why a program placed with great fanfare at the center of the Nixon administration's health strategy and enacted by overwhelming margins in both houses of Congress was languishing in the bureaucracy.

Critics divided predictably over the correct answer. A widespread congressional view—especially strong among Democrats hostile to the conservative domestic policies of the Nixon and Ford administrations—was well summarized by Senator Edward Kennedy's aide, Philip Caper: "HEW seems to be doing as well with HMOs as it is doing with anything, and that is not very well."[3] On this view, indifference, perhaps indeed downright sabotage at high political levels of the administration, deprived the program of the top-level support needed to rescue it from HEW's customary bureaucratic fumbling. The executive branch blamed the legislators who had torn up the flexible Nixon initiative and passed instead a complex, detailed bill filled with supposedly unworkable provisions—an excessively rich benefit package, an anticompetitive community rate-setting requirement, an inequitable open enrollment provision, and more—and had added insult to injury by denying HEW the discretion it needed to set matters right. Academics, equally predictably, cursed both legislature and executive for the stultification that had beset what some now wittily dismissed as the anti-HMO act of 1973.

In short, the debate over the sources of the slow implementation of the law basically continued the legislative debates that had preceded its enactment. This chapter examines the nature of these bureaucracy problems and evaluates the competing theories of their origins.

For the analytical purposes at hand, the administrative process is decomposed into three subprocesses: organization (setting up institutional and staff structures to house the program); rule-making (writing and issuing the regulations and guidelines that program participants will be obliged to obey); and implementation (applying—and modifying—the rules in concrete cases). After a brief discussion of the program's administrative climate, each subprocess is considered in turn.

2. Comptroller General of the United States, "Factors that Impede Progress in Implementing the Health Maintenance Organization Act of 1973" (U.S. General Accounting Office, September 3, 1976), pp. ii, 2.

3. John K. Iglehart, "Heralded HMO Programs Beset by Unexpected Problems," *National Journal Reports*, December 7, 1974, p. 1825.

Administrative Climate: Unsettling Cross Pressures

After its long-awaited, much delayed birth, the infant HMO program met an uncertain reception at HEW for two simple reasons. First, major elements of the department and its political environment disagreed about what the program was, or was meant to be, or should be. Second, those elements of the program's character that were reasonably plain were unfamiliar, sometimes alien, to the department's experience. This section addresses the first of these points; the following section takes up the second.

In early 1974 the department housed three major HMO factions. The officials in the big-spending Social Security Administration (SSA) in charge of Medicare and in the Social and Rehabilitation Service (SRS) that ran Medicaid were unfamiliar with prospective capitation reimbursement and for the most part skeptical of HMOs as a federal policy. Their view was both shared and reinforced by one of their parent committees, Senate Finance, which had long taken a dim view of the prospects for HMO participation in the Medicare and Medicaid programs, based as they were on reimbursement of costs and reasonable charges.[4]

The department also housed a Health Maintenance Organization Service (HMOS), which had begun life as the small project-grant group set up by Secretary Richardson in 1970 and had come formally to life in the Health Services and Mental Health Administration (HSMHA) in 1971. This agency, the program's natural home base, had fallen on hard times. Having begun support for about one hundred HMO projects in various stages of development under flexible project grants, it had been sharply rebuffed in 1972 by Congressman Rogers, who thought it very forward of HEW to make HMO policy on its own while Congress was considering legislation on the matter. When Rogers made his irritation clear,[5] new starts abruptly ceased, leaving the HMOS to tend to its existing projects.

---

4. See Judith M. Feder, *Medicare: The Politics of Federal Hospital Insurance* (Lexington Books, 1977), especially pp. 130–33.

5. *Health Maintenance Organizations*, Hearings before the Subcommittee on Public Health and Environment of the House Interstate and Foreign Commerce Committee, 92 Cong. 2 sess., 4 pts. (GPO, 1972), pt. 1, pp. 69–84. Rogers, described by some observers as extremely angry, declared: "I think this committee is going to have to face up to whether we have given authority that is too broad. I admit it is very broad. I think you could almost do anything—and have. . . . Under the interpretation you have previously used from the general authority of the law on experimental work . . . you could go ahead and get $27 million from the Appropriations Committee for this program without this committee giving any initial approval." (Pp. 77, 84.)

Although the passage of Public Law 93-222 promised to start the flow of grants-in-aid once more, the role of the HMOS in the new program was not yet clear or secure. Throughout 1973 the Nixon administration, led by the Office of Management and Budget (OMB), had refined its demonstration rationale for the program. Personnel in HMOS sensed a high-level betrayal of the HMO cause, and, by the same token, the HMOS advocates impressed some administration officials as entirely too aggressive and ready to spend money. Early in 1972, HMOS's patron, Elliot Richardson, had been replaced as HEW secretary by Caspar Weinberger, a prime architect of the demonstration emphasis. In 1973 HSMHA had been eliminated in a departmental reorganization. With the passage of the law, HMOS personnel anxiously awaited major decisions about organizational placement of HMO activities, which of course meant major decisions about leadership and the chain of command, in short about bureaucratic prominence.

The administration's HMO policy had been developed and guided into the legislative process by a third group, a shifting cast of political executives in and around the secretary's office. These generalists had deliberately insulated themselves from bureaucratic pressures and advice elsewhere in the department. Between 1970 and 1972, the Richardson-centered generalists had carefully avoided the SSA and SRS faction, whose skepticism toward a federal HMO policy had been made evident. In 1973, the Weinberger-centered generalists had tried to insulate themselves from the HMOS faction, whom they suspected of wanting a large, continuing federal HMO development effort. Separated by choice from the other two departmental factions, the generalists also found themselves steadily and involuntarily separated from administration policy. As chapter 5 explained, the brief burst of energy leading to the president's endorsement of HMOs and the bill sent to Congress in the spring of 1971 gave way to a more leisurely reappraisal of the initiative within HEW early in 1972. Over the course of the year, the issues raised by the department progressively involved OMB and the White House staff. By August, when James Cavanaugh forbade the department to compromise on or even to discuss a statutory provision overriding states' laws that inhibited development of HMOs, it was evident that the HEW generalists could not speak for—or indeed about—the administration's HMO policy without advance approval from OMB or the White House.

Another, equally painful separation had also become clear. By the summer of 1972 it was apparent that the administration's position, however composed, would be largely rejected by the House and ignored by the Senate. The legislative outcome would reflect bargaining not between Congress and administration but rather between House and Senate, as the administration stood on the sidelines and awaited the news.

As HEW took charge of the HMO program early in 1974, it worked under a statute that bore little relation to what the guardians of its big-money programs deemed desirable, to what its HMO specialists had been doing under the flexible project grants, or to what its generalists had asked Congress to enact. The program's most enthusiastic and skillful advocate, Richardson, had departed HEW. His successor, Weinberger, understood the program to be a short-lived demonstration that would select its plans carefully and systematically and, above all, cost little federal money.

The program's external environment was as unsettled as the internal. Congress had committed itself to a demonstration approach, but there was no agreement about what that meant. The Senate had accepted the demonstration rhetoric as a price of agreement with the House, but the closest Senate observers of the program—Kennedy and his staff—had never endorsed that view. They had worked hard to enact the law and they wanted to see significant results fast. The House, on the other hand, had indicated that it expected to see at most one hundred HMOs launched under the program. It had said so only in the committee report, however, in a compromise between committee liberals, notably Roy, who did not accept the demonstration rhetoric, and committee conservatives and moderates, who insisted on it.

In sum, there was no consensus either in the executive or in the Congress as to the character and appropriate pace of the program. Some congressmen and some departmental enthusiasts hoped for quick promotion, development, and qualification of large numbers of HMOs. Whereas the congressional enthusiasts tended to support the law, however, the executive enthusiasts generally deplored it. Other congressmen and the top HEW leadership understood the law to call for a carefully targeted, short-lived demonstration. These officials tended to occupy a middle position on the law itself, viewing it as more flawed than the congressional supporters did, but less disastrous to the HMO movement than the HMOS advocates took it to be.

These cross pressures were an extreme variation on an age-old bureaucratic theme, namely, how an agency may be at once *responsible* to the meaning and intent of a law and *responsive* to the needs of those affected interests that must live under it.[6] In this case the law was alien both to the department's general experience and to its particular experience with HMOs. It was, moreover, crafted in good part from distrust of the department's administrative capacity and responsibility. In this case too, the affected interests to whom the department would try to respond included entrepreneurs of would-be HMOs; executives and other officials of established prepaid group practices (PGPs) and independent practice associations (IPAs); the Group Health Association of America (GHAA), the trade association representing many (but not all) PGPs; and officials in the insurance industry, the corporate world, organized labor, and other potential institutional sponsors of HMOs. Most of these interests made it plain that they considered portions of the law unworkable and that they would look to HEW for administrative relief from onerous provisions. If a happy solution to these tensions was possible even in theory, the unsettled state of internal and external expectations of the program's nature and pace all but guaranteed that no such solution would emerge in practice, and, as this chapter will show, none did.

Organization: An Uncomfortable Fit

The cross pressures at work on the HMO program were not unusual, much less unique. They are the constant raw materials of bureaucratic politics and are perhaps especially common to new programs, where, in the nature of the case, shared informal understandings have not yet been evolved by trial and error.[7] Congressmen often differ about the intent and spirit of the laws they pass and they may, especially if they serve on key committees or come from heavily affected localities, put pressure on a department to adopt their personal interpretations of what was said and meant. It is part of the Washington political game that legislators stand ready to blame bureaucrats for failing to clarify provisions and rationalize consequences of laws that the politicians themselves could not or would not clarify or rationalize. Nor is it unusual that departmental factions

---

6. See James Q. Wilson, "The Bureaucracy Problem," *The Public Interest*, no. 6 (Winter 1967), pp. 3–9.

7. For case studies of both newer and older programs see *Policy Sciences*, vol. 7 (December 1976), pp. 399–518, especially Drew Altman and Harvey M. Sapolsky, "Writing the Regulations for Health," pp. 417–37, which deals with the HMO program.

disagree on the pace and emphasis of a program. That affected interests look to the administrative process for modifications in burdensome legal provisions is equally commonplace. These generalizations simply delineate the perpetual tension between administrative responsibility and responsiveness. The tensions can be more or less acute, however, and the complexities of improvising bureaucratic solutions to these cross pressures can be more or less vexing. In the HMO case all major variables tended to aggravate tensions and compound complexity.

The fundamental administrative problem from which many others flowed was the sheer unfamiliarity and "technical" difficulty[8] of the HMO-building task. The 1973 HMO act transformed a small, highly flexible grant-giving operation into a rigorously defined effort to launch new but comprehensive health care enterprises. By 1974 HEW's Public Health Service (PHS) had acquired some experience with direct delivery programs to clients other than merchant seamen; neighborhood health centers and the National Health Service Corps were the major cases in point. But it had no experience whatever in launching, supporting, monitoring, and regulating comprehensive health care organizations that combined delivery and financing mechanisms in one intricately interdependent system and supported themselves in competitive local health insurance markets.

To be sure, the department had some limited experience in organization-building with grant and loan combinations under the Hill-Burton program. Yet the hospital construction program, like most such HEW programs, worked through the states. State health agencies did most of the planning, submitting their work to HEW for review. The HMO program did not work this way. Officials in HEW would have to come to terms face-to-face with HMO officials on a wide range of complex, controversial issues, without benefit of mediation by state or local agencies. Nor was it clear that the PHS's experience with Hill-Burton loans—its only important loan program—could be transferred to the HMO loan program.

Direct relations between the department and fund recipients were not unknown; indeed, in medical manpower training and the research programs funded by the National Institutes of Health this was the standard procedure. These programs, however, involved support for a mere subset of the continuing activities of established institutions; the department was not asked to bring the institutions into being, ensure that their organiza-

---

8. The terms "technical" and "technology" are used here and throughout this chapter not in a scientific sense, but rather in the sense familiar in organization theory. See Charles Perrow, *Organizational Analysis: A Sociological View* (Wadsworth, 1970), pp. 75–80.

tional nature met myriad detailed criteria, and then follow them down the road to financial health. Again, the nearest analogy was the neighborhood health center program, and the analogy was not reassuring. Since the early 1970s the Nixon administration had been trying to transform these centers from subsidized wards of the federal government into self-sustaining enterprises, with little success. In the HMO program, federal support would be smaller and the requirements greater.

Finally, the requirement that HEW carry out continued regulation of the entities it aided was new and alien. Public Health Service officials were not sure what this requirement meant; they were quite sure, however, that they did not like the sound of it.

In several respects, then—the comprehensiveness and complexity of an HMO's services and structure, the ambitiousness of the organization-building job, the central importance of market survival without continuing subsidies, the direct relation between agency and recipient, the lack of state or local mediation, the ambiguous position of the loan program in the aid package, and the substantial, permanent regulatory role—the technology of the PHS's administrative task was unusual, perhaps unique.

Nowhere in HEW did such a program fit naturally, yet of course it had to be placed somewhere. As HEW officials contemplated the new units created after the dismantling of HSMHA, they deduced that the program's logical home was the Health Services Administration (HSA), newly created to house the federal government's ventures in promoting new modes of delivering health care.[9] The program's exact location within HSA was a more troublesome question. Gordon MacLeod, head of the lingering HMOS unit, thought that the program should enjoy separate bureau status and report directly to the HSA administrator. The program might be small, he argued, but the president had singled it out for special priority within his legislative program, and bureau status was necessary to honor that priority. Harold Buzzell, the HSA's new administrator, took a different view. Many independent-minded bureau chiefs reporting directly to the agency head was precisely what had made HSMHA unmanageable, he believed, and he did not want HSA to repeat that unfortunate precedent. Moreover, on taking office Buzzell had been distressed to find most of the bureaus under him filled with "advocates" unwilling and unable to document their programs' effectiveness in economic terms. He wanted

9. See George D. Greenberg, "Reorganization Reconsidered: The U.S. Public Health Service 1960–1973," *Public Policy*, vol. 23 (Fall 1975), p. 497.

HMOs placed with other grant programs aimed at changing community delivery systems and he wanted them run by someone who shared his commitment to strong management. Both considerations argued for placing the program in the Bureau of Community Health Services (BCHS), under the direction of Dr. Paul Batalden, who had impressed Buzzell with his managerial skill and was eager to acquire the program.

To MacLeod and some of his HMOS staff, Buzzell's decision seemed an inauspicious start, indeed a reproach. Instead of enjoying equal status with other bureaus reporting to the head of HSA, the position they had occupied in HSMHA, they now stood a level farther down, merely one of a half dozen programs within BCHS, which itself was one of several bureaus within HSA. Offended that the program should lose administrative stature precisely when it finally gained legislative sanction, MacLeod and several of his staff resigned.

The decision to make the HMO program a division within BCHS did not exhaust the organizational questions at hand. For one thing, section 1312 of the act required that continued regulation of HMOs be conducted in the Office of the Assistant Secretary for Health. The legislators evidently were determined to see that a high and visible level within the department was responsible for ensuring that HMOs, once qualified, did not lapse into noncompliance with the law. As he pondered the matter, however, Buzzell recognized a related problem not addressed directly in the law. True, the HMO advocates would be under Batalden's control, but Buzzell nonetheless had a nagging suspicion, fueled by the advocates' resistance to cost-effectiveness thinking, by questions raised by the GAO and by Congress about misuses of pre-act HMO grant money in South Carolina,[10] and by his visits to some "wholly impractical" sites the HMOS had funded in the South, that the grantsmen might prove to be less than fully expert and dependable. A background in financial management had taught Buzzell to appreciate the distinction between treasury and audit functions, and he thought it dangerous to allow the same officials who promoted HMOs by means of grants to make the final decision whether, once they became operational, they qualified under the law to receive federal loans and to be offered under the dual choice provision. Development and qualification, he concluded, should operate at "arms length," subject to a "check and balance" arrangement. He therefore informed Frank Seubold, the new

10. Comptroller General of the United States, *Review of Grants to Health Maintenance Organization of South Carolina, Inc.* (GAO, 1974), and *Grants for Development of Health Maintenance Organizations in Region IV* (GAO, 1975).

head of the newly named Office (later Division) of Health Maintenance Organizations (OHMO or DHMO) in BCHS, that he would split off the qualification function from the development function.

The remaining organizational decision concerned allocation of staff among development, qualification, and continued regulation, now three distinct functions. The answer seemed straightforward. There were as yet no qualified HMOs continually to regulate and there was hope among some top administration officials and OMB that this function might yet be turned over to the states, which regulated other health insurers. As for qualification, most of the established HMOs were loudly proclaiming their distaste for the "unworkable" law, and their unwillingness to seek qualification under it. Plans newly developed under the law might take two or three years to become operational and qualifiable. The short-term volume of qualification activity would be small. It would also be distasteful, for it would mean forcing established plans to conform to the details of legislation both they and most of HEW despised. Not until summer 1974 was the qualification function staffed, when William J. McLeod, president of a PGP in California, became Buzzell's special assistant for qualification. It seemed reasonable to expect that McLeod and a few assistants would have no trouble processing the meager flow of applications while developing regulations in their bailiwick—those that spelled out the details of the qualification process, the requirements of continued regulation, and the specifics of dual choice.

The development function, on the other hand, seemed from the first to require all the staff it had and more. Batalden, a "hard-charger," wanted to get the program off and running. Many of the groups the HMOS had supported before passage of the law now hoped to win new awards and wanted advice and technical assistance. New and would-be HMO entrepreneurs sought counsel and feasibility funds in varying combinations. Some plans and founders had urged their congressmen to help them make their way to the head of the line for aid and some congressmen had let the bureaucrats know of their interest. Unlike qualification, an uncharted terrain, development was an extension, though highly modified, of what HMOS had been doing before the act passed—that is, giving out money. Some of the HMOS staff remained and these advocates, pleased that the pipeline was flowing again, albeit through a highly imperfect mechanism, were eager to resume promotion. Seubold, one of his HSA superiors recounted, was "like Ellwood, an advocate, anxious to get as many HMOs started, and enroll as many people as possible as soon as possible." Thus organized, HEW's HMO staff confronted the pressing task at hand: issuing regulations to inform interested parties of the rules of the game.

Rule-Making: An Impossible Fit

The technical complexities of HMO-building, compounded by the intricacy of the new HMO law, insured that rule-making for the program would be a difficult substantive task. The law specifically required the secretary to issue regulations on twenty-seven subjects and conferred discretion to do so in forty-seven more areas.[11] Many, indeed most, of these areas raised the most nettlesome substantive and political questions, those that Congress itself had found most ticklish and had been most averse to grasping. Now it waited and watched impatiently for HEW to resolve these conundrums.

The department's methods of devising regulations guaranteed that the task would be procedurally cumbersome too. In 1974 the rule-making process contained about a dozen distinct steps, each offering opportunities for questions, disputes, and delay. First, task forces combining outside experts, consultants, and HMO program officials in HEW drafted issue specification papers, so-called specs, to define and outline the issues that regulations should address. Then, a policy work group composed of Batalden and other in-house personnel went over the papers and devised proposed regulations. Next, the head of the Health Services Administration reviewed the proposals and concurred. The draft rules then went to the Office of the Assistant Secretary for Health for comment. After this stage, a notice of proposed rule-making was drawn up and submitted to HEW's General Counsel's Office for clearance. Next, the Bureau of Community Health Services and the HSA reviewed and approved the notice as revised by the general counsel, after which the assistant secretary for health cleared the revisions. Then the notice went to the secretary's office where it was reviewed by HEW's Office of Regulation Coordination and by the secretary or his staff. If the regulation was new or controversial, the secretary would discuss it with key congressmen and their staffs. If all went well, the secretary then signed the notice and sent it to the *Federal Register* for publication. At the next stage, all interested parties were invited to comment. Then the comments—often hundreds of them—were considered

11. "HMO Regulations: Timetable" (n.d.) in Department of Health, Education, and Welfare files; Altman and Sapolsky, "Writing the Regulations for Health," pp. 419–22.

and the notice was revised. Then the revised regulations went again for clearance to BCHS, HSA, the assistant secretary for health, and the secretary. Finally, the secretary signed the regulations—now called final rules—and the *Federal Register* published them.

Like all procedures, these carried both benefits and costs. Chief among their benefits was their capacity to protect important values often summarily described as those of administrative accountability—that is, they aimed to hold administrators responsible to the law, political superiors, and the public (both general and special) in some, often conflicting, combination. Some of these steps—for example, the requirement that proposed rules be published, that the public be allowed to comment, and that the comments be taken into account before final rules are published—are contained in the federal Administrative Procedure Act.[12] Other steps ensure, at least in theory, that a mix of skills and roles comes into play in rule-making, and that these roles come into play in a hierarchical sequence of approval.

The process entails the vices of its virtues, however. The most obvious—and perhaps least serious—problem is that the process is unwieldy and time-consuming. Three more serious costs are that indifference or confusion at higher levels can nullify good staff work at lower levels; that serious problems developing at lower levels may sit unresolved unless higher levels actively intervene to impose a solution, something that busy men with multiple duties may have neither the time nor the inclination to do; and that the creative synthesis of perspectives that defines administrative accountability may strike affected parties, who expect administrators to rationalize their troubles away, as bureaucratic inconsistency. The inevitable blending and clashing of views may appear to compound the follies of legislative politics with new ones born of bureaucratic politics. The benefit-cost puzzle is well illustrated in microcosm by the HMO program's experience with rule-making.

Burcaucratic outputs are in some sense a joint function of tasks, procedures, and organization. When, as in the HMO case, a highly complex task was addressed by means of cumbersome procedures in an unsettled and controverted organizational setting, the department could hardly have been expected to arrive at polished regulatory outputs with effortless grace. The BCHS was not slow to set to work on rule-making; indeed, it convened eight task forces on different facets of HMO operations even before the

---

12. 60 stat. 239, sec. 4. "Loans, grants," and some other matters are exempt from these provisions, however.

legislative conference committee finished its work on the law. It immediately became clear, however, that speed and thoroughness were incompatible. Scrutinizing Public Law 93-222, the task forces perceived, as had the legislators, that writing a defensible and consistent set of rules for HMOs was little different from drafting a national health insurance measure. A staff memorandum of January 21, 1974, observed that federal standards would govern provision of minimum benefits; financial viability; quality of services provided; open enrollment; the mandatory enrollment period; a mandatory community rating system; consumer participation on policy boards; marketing, advertising, solicitation, and mandatory disclosure; financial audits; data collection (both financial and medical); grievance procedures; malpractice protection; standards for disenrollment (initiated by both enrollees and HMOs) and refusals to reenroll; period of enrollment; coordination of benefits; limitations on capital expenditures; and confidentiality of medical records.[13] Under each heading, dozens of subordinate issues arose, and this list pertained only to operating features of the HMO itself. Dual choice, the measure overriding state law, and continued regulation raised equally complex questions.

The immediate need, it seemed clear, was to try to answer the questions uppermost in the minds of new and developing plans and those who wanted federal funds to start a plan: how would HEW refine the complex statutory definition of a health maintenance organization and what must entrepreneurs do to enter the sequence of aid leading from feasibility studies to an operational plan and qualification? Most staff energy in 1974 was devoted to these questions; regulatory issues that would arise later—notably those governing dual choice, qualification, and continued regulation—were entrusted to McLeod to be worried over by higher levels after the so-called subpart A regulations had been completed.[14]

As the task forces began drafting their issue specification papers, it grew apparent that virtually every term used in the law was in some way ambiguous. The community rating requirement, for example, demanded "equivalent charges for families of similar composition." But exactly what

13. Memorandum from Bill Kopit, Work Group IV, to BCHS HMO Task Force, "Federal Regulation Under the HMO Act of 1973," revised, January 21, 1974, in HEW files, p. 2.
14. These regulations, which spelled out subpart A (requirements for a health maintenance organization), also addressed subparts B (general conditions on federal financial assistance), C (grants and contracts for feasibility surveys), D (grants, contracts, and loan guarantees for planning and for initial development costs), E (loans and loan guarantees for initial operating costs), and G (restrictive state laws and practices). Reserved for explication in later rules were subparts F (employees' health benefits plans, or dual choice), and H (continued regulation of health maintenance organizations). *Federal Register,* vol. 39 (May 8, 1974), pt. 2, p. 16422.

was a "family?" (The act gave no definition.) What was its "composi-tion"—age, sex, marital status, or all of these? How did an "equivalent" rate differ from an "identical" rate or a "roughly equivalent" rate? How large could the copayment required of members be before it violated the law by constituting a "significant barrier to care?" These ambiguities were, from one point of view, a headache: they opened the door to endless scholastic memos and to continued squabbling with lawyers in the General Counsel's Office over what the law meant or seemed to mean. From another point of view, however, ambiguities were opportunities: the department might fashion regulatory language that would give HMOs relief from objectionable portions of the act. As the process wore on, however, hopes that regulations could resolve the conflict between the language of the law and the preferences of the HMO coummunity were dashed. Efforts to improvise regulations that were both responsible and responsive proceeded differently from case to case. However, the striking and important point—illustrated by a review of five most troublesome cases—is the similarity of the cases in their outcomes and in their effects on the HMO community.

Alcoholism Benefits

When the HMO benefits task force began meeting a month before the conference committee completed work on Public Law 93-222, its members expected that alcoholism and drug abuse services would appear on the list of supplemental, not basic, benefits.[15] To the group's surprise, section 1302 of the act, which defined the basic health services an HMO had to provide, included "medical treatment and referral services (including referral services to appropriate ancillary services) for the abuse of or addiction to alcohol and drugs." The terms "medical treatment," "referral services," and "ancillary services" were all susceptible to various defini-tions, and the HMOs, few of whom offered such services and fewer of whom wished to labor under a detailed, expansive requirement, would watch closely to see what HEW would do.

Just after New Year's Day of 1974, Dr. Joseph Dorsey, medical director of the Harvard Community Health Plan, who was in charge of developing the task force's position on alcoholism benefits, set down his thoughts in a

15. Basic health services were those with which "each member is to be provided . . . for a basic health services payment," supplemental services those to be provided for additional payment if the necessary manpower was available to the HMO and if the member chose to contract for them. P.L. 93-222, sec. 1301(b) (1)–(2).

short memo. "The precise intent of the Senate lawmakers in adding this section . . . is not self-evident," he remarked.[16] From this ambiguity he inferred that the requirement should be interpreted "in the context of current arrangements for handling patients" with alcoholism problems. "Medical treatment as distinguished from referral services," he argued, should mean "the diagnosis and treatment of organic complications which arise from the abuse of alcohol or addiction to drugs." In the case of alcohol abuse, such conditions included gastrointestinal bleeding, nutritional deficiencies, and cirrhosis. Such a definition posed few problems for the plans: "the HMO would meet this part of the definition if it did not exclude from its covered services the medical services needed to handle problems arising from the abuse of alcohol." As for referral services, Dorsey argued that HMOs should try to "secure help" for the patient, either within the HMO itself or in the community. But "since the obligation is only to conduct the initial screening evaluation and to make the referral, the HMO is not obligated to payment for the actual services provided." Providers might range from doctors and psychiatrists to Alcoholics Anonymous. In any case, the HMO's emphasis should be on screening and on establishing "linkages," not on "the direct provision of services" to deal with alcoholics' problems. He added a warning: "Services for dealing with alcohol abuse and drug addiction require highly specialized resources which cannot be developed within most HMOs." Therefore, he concluded, "it is much more appropriate to develop linkages to existing community programs rather than to require their direct provision by the HMO."

A few days later the head of the benefits task force heard another point of view. The National Institute of Alcohol Abuse and Alcoholism (NIAAA), HEW's major spokesman for stronger alcoholism components in health care programs, deplored the usual short shrift given to alcoholism by physicians, and had been delighted to learn that Congress had honored alcoholism treatment with a place on the HMO basic benefits list. A NIAAA spokesman now argued that a proper definition of the benefit must include "medically supervised withdrawal from prolonged or acute intoxication and other accepted therapies."[17] Both that view and Dorsey's were summarized in the task force's report, which ended with a warning:

16. Memorandum from Joseph L. Dorsey, M.D., to Mr. Ron Jydstrup, "Re: Section 1302 (1) (E)—'Medical Treatment and Referral Services (Including Referral Services to Appropriate Ancillary Services) for the Abuse of or Addiction to Alcohol and Drugs,' " January 3, 1974, in HEW files.
17. "Report of HMO Task Group 5 on Services and Benefits," January 11, 1974 (Revised: 1/16/74), in HEW files, p. 28. The account of relations between BCHS and NIAAA draws heavily on David Alexander, "The HMO Case: The Reimbursement of Chronic Alcoholism," HMO Case (B) Section III, Kennedy School of Government, Harvard University, 1977.

This is an unresolved issue with obvious differences in the points of view. The primary difference of opinion centers around the NIAAA language which would have the HMO responsible for "medically supervised withdrawal from prolonged or acute intoxication. . . ." Consultants of Task Group 5 suggest that the NIAAA approach to this part of the legislation would not be workable "in the real world."[18]

In the following weeks, positions hardened. A NIAAA staffer wrote an eight-page memo developing the case for an extensive set of alcoholism treatment services. The task force itself, meanwhile, rallied behind Dorsey's position. Even Dr. Harold Hunter, a staff member of the American Public Health Association (APHA), who was strongly supportive of alcoholism treatment, agreed that the NIAAA definition "can be broadly interpreted to include the most expensive portion of treatment and could result in inordinate costs to HMOs in areas of high incidence."[19]

As the regulations threatened to bog down in an interagency dispute, BCHS director Batalden grew impatient. Recognizing the incompatibility between thorough and speedy regulations, Batalden followed his straightforward formula for resolving conflicts in such cases—quote the language of the statute in the regulations when in doubt and worry about details later in guidelines.[20] The language of the notice of proposed rule-making published in the *Federal Register* on May 8, 1974, was therefore succinct and little more explicit than the act. An HMO, it said, must provide:

> Medical treatment and referral services (including referral services to appropriate ancillary services) for the abuse of or addiction to alcohol and drugs. The diagnosis and medical treatment of alcohol and drug abuse and addiction shall be provided to health maintenance organization members. Screening, referral, and followup of patients with alcohol or drug abuse problems to appropriate ancillary resources shall be provided.

The proposed rule also stated explicitly that, except insofar as this definition required it, an HMO was not obliged to provide, as a basic health service, "treatment for chronic alcoholism and drug addiction."[21]

This solution was temporary at best, however, for the department would have to issue final regulations and hoped also to publish guidelines to interpret legal requirements in greater but more flexible detail. The minimalist language of the proposed rules dealt NIAAA a setback, but the skirmish soon resumed. As the HMO staff turned its hand to guidelines (which it planned to issue simultaneously with final rules), it discovered

18. "Report of HMO Task Group 5 on Services and Benefits," p. 29.
19. Harold R. Hunter, Dr. P. H., "Comments on January 16 Report of HMO Task Group 5, Services and Benefits" (n.d), in HEW files, p. 2.
20. Alexander, "Reimbursement of Chronic Alcoholism," p. 13.
21. *Federal Register*, May 8, 1974, p. 16426; pt. 110.108, (A)(5), (b)(6).

that it had very little to say. The staffer assigned to draft the alcoholism guidelines was no specialist on the subject and had no doctor or alcoholism expert on the staff. Obliged, therefore, to turn to HEW's resident specialist, NIAAA, for help, the staffer could not avoid offering the institute an invitation to try to win in the guidelines—what it had failed to achieve in the proposed rules. Institute staff responded with a draft that would, in the HMO staff's judgment, ask far too much of the HMOs. Positions hardened once more.

Unwilling to hold final rules hostage to this (and other) disputes, Batalden put pressure on the combatants to reach at least some minimal common ground. The final rules reflected a tenuous compromise, explicitly requiring detoxification, but allowing the plans discretion as to how (and how often) it would be provided: "Diagnosis and medical treatment shall include detoxification for alcoholism or drug abuse on either an outpatient or inpatient basis, whichever is medically determined to be appropriate, in addition to treatment for other medical conditions." The rules added new concessions to the HMOs' concerns by distinguishing between referrals for medical services (which were to be treated as a basic service) and those for nonmedical services (which need not be so treated) and dropped the reference to screening in response to comments that the law did not require it.[22] The exclusion of treatment for chronic alcoholism and drug addiction remained.[23]

This carefully crafted compromise yielded the language of a final rule but its sparseness merely intensified the continuing battle over the language of the guidelines. Caught between Batalden's pressure to expedite the guidelines and NIAAA's seemingly unreasonable demands, the HMO staff called for help from the HMO community. Dr. John Smillie, for many years the head of a Kaiser Foundation hospital in San Francisco, combined the expertise of a physician with the practical experience of a long-time and highly respected participant in prepaid group plans. Brought in as a consultant, Smillie scanned the guidelines, found them "entirely too prescriptive"[24] and otherwise flawed, and began meeting with NIAAA to

22. For example, the executive vice-president and director of research of Seattle's Group Health Cooperative of Puget Sound commented: "We suggest deletion of the word screening. . . . The act is silent on screening. To mandate that all members must be provided a screening for alcohol or drug problems appears both unrealistic and unwise. The methods available are largely unproven and costly." Letter from Harold F. Newman and Richard Handschin to Charles C. Edwards, Assistant Secretary of Health, May 24, 1974, p. 9; in HEW files, HMO Comments folder N; emphasis deleted.

23. *Federal Register*, October 18, 1974, p. 37313; pt. 110.102(a)(5), (b)(6).

24. Alexander, "Reimbursement of Chronic Alcoholism," pp. 18–20.

"educate" them about the real world of HMO economics. The institute, however, proved to be a slow pupil. By December 1974, a year after the signing of the act, neither side had changed the other's mind, memos continued to sail back and forth, and the guidelines had not been issued. Batalden then decided personally to mediate this and other interagency disputes that were delaying their issuance. At a meeting of the protagonists, Batalden rejected most of NIAAA's arguments; the HMO staffer then retired to draft three double-spaced, highly unspecific pages to insert amid the one hundred and twenty pages of draft guidelines.[25]

In March (1975) the HSA submitted the package to the Public Health Service's general counsel for review. The lawyers never got to study the alcoholism section. After reading twenty-two pages they concluded that the guidelines were poorly drafted and inconsistent both with the law and with one another. In June they wrote a detailed, five-page, single-spaced letter setting out some of their objections to the pages they had read and returned the package to HSA to rework.[26] The costs of the decision to sacrifice exegesis for speed by quoting the law in the regulations were becoming apparent. By now a repository of all the deliberate ambiguities, inconsistencies, perplexities, and conflicts the regulations had passed over, the guidelines proved impossible to rework.

In sum, HEW's pronouncements on alcoholism services responded to the concerns of the HMO community by resisting the pressures of the "categorical people" in NIAAA for an expansive set of required services. Although they conceded to NIAAA the addition of the word "detoxification" in the final rules, they avoided any mention of the number or frequency of required detoxifications, allowed the plans to opt for outpatient detoxifications when they thought them appropriate, and explicitly exempted them from the obligation either to screen for alcoholism or to care for chronic alcoholics.

It might be expected that the HMO community would have been pleased at the outcome. Some observers, who recognized and appreciated the flexibility the rules preserved, thought that HEW had indeed made the best of a bad statutory requirement. Others, however, were fearful that administrative reversals or reinterpretations might produce new and unsettling pronouncements in the ever pending guidelines. They preferred a statutory

25. "Regulations and Program Guidelines, Draft 2/13/75," in HEW files, pp. 36–38.
26. Letter from Mr. Sidney Edelman, Assistant General Counsel for Public Health, to Mr. Frank Seubold, Ph.D., Acting Associate Bureau Director, Office of HMOs, BCHS, "HMO Guidelines for 42 CFR Part 110, Subpart A—Comments on pp. 1–22," June 19, 1975, in HEW files.

exemption from alcoholism services to HEW's vague rulings accompanied by perpetual promises of clarification.

Preventive Dental Services for Children

Dental benefits sprung a second unpleasant surprise on the benefits task force. Despite the HMO spokesmen's repeated warnings, the conference committee required that HMOs offer as part of their basic benefit package "preventive health services (including . . . preventive dental care for children . . .)."[27] The law said no more on the subject. The conference report, however, declared that "the conferees intend that preventive dental health services for children shall mean at a minimum oral prophylaxis, topical fluoride application, and surface sealant services, as provided by regulations of the Secretary, to children under the age of twelve."[28]

Many HMO spokesmen viewed the provision as a "lousy benefit package" and did not hesitate to say so.[29] According to the conferees' declared intent, they argued, a dentist or dental hygienist could clean a child's teeth without performing a thorough dental examination or even establishing a medical record. But even if these omissions were corrected, the requirement for preventive services would fragment care. In some cases the HMO would have to identify problems and then refer the member to fee-for-service dentists in the community, who would impose an out-of-pocket charge. From the standpoint of both continuity of care and member satisfaction, they found the provision objectionable. The plans could solve these problems, of course, by offering a full, or at any rate a broader, range of dental benefits on their own initiative. However, as they had explained to Congress many times, most did not think that they could do so and still charge monthly premiums that would be competitive. Even those that could perhaps afford it faced other obstacles. A California state law, for example, prevented the two Kaiser plans in that state from organizing dental services in what it took to be the most cost-effective manner.[30]

27. P.L. 93-222, sec. 1302 (1)(H).

28. *Health Maintenance Organization Act of 1973*, S. Rept. 621, 93 Cong. 1 sess. (GPO, 1973), p. 30.

29. Testimony of Thomas O. Pyle, executive vice-president of the Harvard Community Health Plan, in Rogers Subcommittee Hearings, 1975, p. 87. The summary of the plans' objections to the provision follows Pyle's testimony and interviews. The American Dental Association commented that the regulations failed to meet "what is either professionally or commonly understood by 'preventive dental care,' " and that "the child will be meeting his dental needs from at least two sources, the HMO and his family dentist." Letter from Dale F. Roeck, Chairman, Council on Dental Health, American Dental Association, to Dr. Paul Batalden, June 7, 1974, in HEW files, HMO Comments folder R.

30. A Kaiser spokesman explained that a California professional practices law forbidding members of different professions to be members of the same professional corporation or partnership precluded

The benefits task force faced two alternative courses. It could use the regulations to require more than the law did in order to make the "lousy" benefit better, or it could say as little as possible in the regulations in order to minimize cost and aggravation to the HMOs. Unsurprisingly, members of the HMO community brought onto the task force as consultants argued strongly for the second approach. Even before it was known that preventive dental services for children would appear in the basic benefit package, Dorsey had argued that the most effective regulatory approach was "a general statement that preventive services be provided, without being specific as to details."[31] He and his HMO colleagues offered this argument with renewed force once the bad news reached them.

A few members of the task force, however, wondered whether many of the economic and professional objections to the benefit did not rest, at bottom, on organizational conservatism; few plans had experimented with prepaid dental benefits and few wanted to enter this unfamiliar area merely because the federal government said they must. These members argued for regulatory language that would make the benefit meaningful. In mid-January one of them suggested that regulations require a routine oral examination and the following preventive services at least yearly: explorer and mouth mirror examinations; prophylaxis if necessary; plaque control through demonstration of the use of disclosing materials, floss, and toothbrushing; diet counseling; topical application of fluorides or the prescription of fluorides for systematic use when not available through the community water supply; sealant treatment at three-year intervals or more frequently as conditions warrant.[32] Harold Hunter of the American Public Health Association found even this list too modest and in a memo suggested some additions. "I cannot understand the exclusions of dental x-rays," he wrote. At a minimum, "bite-wing x-rays are mandatory." Noting that "X-rays account for diagnosis of 30–40% of carious (decay) lesions," he warned that "if a patient is lured into a feeling of oral health without the benefit of x-rays, a disservice has been created bordering on malpractice." Observing that the cost of bite wings was minimal, he stated his own preference for "the radiographs . . . as opposed to the sealants which are

---

Kaiser's customary approach to staffing. The plans might contract for services with community dentists, but another state law, designed to curb dental "chains," prevented dentists from having more than two offices and thus prevented Kaiser from providing care with dental hygienists under dentists who supervised more than two of the plan's facilities.

31. HMO Task Group V, "Resume of Discussion of Sub-Task #1—Basic Health Services" (n.d.), in HEW files, p. 9.

32. "Report of HMO Task Group 5 on Services and Benefits," pp. 32–33.

not yet even accepted and approved by the ADA [American Dental Association] Council on Dental Products." He also hoped that the exam would include "a soft tissue examination." The definitions, he protested, gave the impression that dental care concerned only the "exposed hard structure—teeth," leaving out of account "the soft tissues such as the lip, buccal mucosa, soft palate," which might involve "cancerous lesions, cysts and abscesses, fractures, and might be covered under the basic services."[33]

The HMO spokesmen argued heatedly that such detailed requirements would keep many HMOs from attempting to qualify under the law and might even drive those that attempted to offer the services out of the market altogether. It soon became clear that no amount of debate about costs per member per month or about desirable dental practice could make the HMO spokesmen feel less hostile toward dental benefits, and in the end, the minimalist approach prevailed. Both the proposed and final rules restated the language of the statute and conference report. The reference to sealants (which appeared in the conference report, not the law, and which Hunter had questioned) was dropped. Nothing new was added.[34]

As in the case of alcoholism services, a long debate had brought the department back full circle to the language of the law and (in this case) the conference report. No in-house dental lobby had pushed for an expansive requirement, as had the NIAAA in the alcoholism case, and no mediation between conflicting agencies had been necessary. The outcome in the two cases, however, was the same: HEW ended up conceding to the HMO community's instructions as to how to make the best of a bad situation. It did so, in essence, by saying as little as possible. And the HMO community's response to the department's handiwork was similar in this case too. A few plans resolved to try to qualify even if it meant providing the required services. Others, especially Kaiser, whose California plans purportedly could not provide these services, resolved to work to strike the requirement in legislative amendments.

Community Rating

The HMO act required that HMOs offer basic health services, as well as whatever supplemental health services they chose to provide, on a prepaid basis at premiums "fixed under a community rating system." The law defined community rating as "a system of fixing rates of payments for

33. Hunter, "Comments on January 16 Report," pp. 2–3.
34. *Federal Register*, May 8, 1974, p. 16426; pt. 110.108 (a)(8)(iii); and October 18, 1974, p. 37313; pt. 110.102 (a)(8)(iii).

health services. Under such a system rates of payments may be determined on a per-person or per-family basis and may vary with the number of persons in a family, but . . . must be equivalent for all individuals and for all families of similar composition."[35]

The act permitted three exceptions to these equivalences. First, rate differences to conform with the specific procedures of governmental health benefit programs were allowed. Second, the plans could set "nominal differentials . . . to reflect the administrative costs of collecting payments" from individuals and their families, from small groups of members, and from large groups of members. (The meanings of "small" and "large" groups were to be determined by regulations.) Third, and most important, the act allowed the community-rated premium to be "supplemented by additional nominal payments which may be required for the provision of specific services (within the basic health services), except that such payments may not be required where or in such a manner that they serve (as determined under regulations of the Secretary) as a barrier to the delivery of health services. Such additional nominal payment shall be fixed in accordance with the regulations of the Secretary."[36] In the conference report, the legislators gave the secretary some guidance as to what they expected. There they stated that the additional payments (copayments) imposed "may not exceed 50 percent of the total cost of providing any single service to any given group of members . . . and the co-payments charged by an HMO shall not, in the aggregate, exceed 20 percent of the total cost of providing basic health services to any given group of members."[37]

The HMO spokesmen were intensely interested in how HEW would use its discretion on these points. Most of them supported community rating in principle but thought it ill advised to require it in the law. Experience rating, which tailors premiums to the health experience of groups and individuals, made it hard for the neediest—the sick, and especially the sick poor—to buy health care coverage. As a moral precept, the subsidization of sicker persons by healthier ones inherent in a community rating system was appealing, and many of the established plans set rates in this way. Kaiser, for example, had long done so not only for ethical reasons but also—perhaps mainly—because it saw that the administrative costs a prepaid group incurred by "costing out" detailed records of the utilization experience of all its members were pointlessly high.

35. P.L. 93-222, sec. 1301 (B)(1)–(2).
36. P.L. 93-222, sec. 1301 (a)(2).
37. S. Rept. 621, *Health Maintenance Organization Act of 1973*, p. 32.

However, neither Kaiser nor the other established plans practiced community rating exactly as defined in the law. Most of these plans offered different combinations of premiums and copayments to different groups of subscribers. The various packages reflected the group's preferences and ability and willingness to pay for various mixes of services. Although detailed utilization experience was seldom factored into the computation, proxies such as the age and sex composition of the group somctimes were included. As a result, subscribers with similarly composed families within a given plan might well pay different premiums and be subjected to different copayments. Thus, viewed from the standpoint of the established plans, the act's definition was offensively pure.

Some plans that both endorsed community rating in principle and practiced it believed that the law might work a hardship on newer, smaller groups attempting to build their memberships. As Blue Cross, which had started life with community rating and was gradually driven by the competition of experience-rated commercial insurance plans to abandon it, had learned, community rating could encourage adverse selection.[38] If experience-rated conventional plans offered healthier groups a rate tailored to their low utilization and that rate fell much below the community (that is, cross-subsidized) rate the HMO offered, the healthier groups might well be lost to the HMO. The HMO, in turn, would be attractive mainly to sicker people. If the groups began to separate in this way, the process would snowball: over time the favorable experience of the conventional plans' members would permit steady or lower experience-based rates in future years, while the high utilization of the HMO's members would drive its community rate steadily higher over time. The gap between the two would therefore widen constantly and the competitive position of the HMO would erode steadily. Eventually a point would be reached where the HMO was an attractive buy only for very high users, at which point its financial survival would be in doubt.

Some HMO spokesmen used this straightforward economic logic unsparingly in their assault on the community rating requirement. Inevitably, however, proponents of community rating pointed to a confounding fact: a major appeal of the HMO strategy, after all, was precisely the ability of community-rated plans to offer wider benefits at rates below or close to those of their inflation-ridden, albeit experience-rated, competition and to maintain or improve this economic edge over time. As usual, the

38. Sylvia A. Law, *Blue Cross: What Went Wrong?* (Yale University Press, 1974), p. 12.

unadulterated economic logic overreached itself. In practice, decisions to join one or another plan are not made on the basis of premium levels alone, and premiums in turn reflect much more than members' health status. Other important variables include underused facilities to be maintained, utilization controls, substitutions of outpatient for inpatient care, and others reviewed in chapter 4. A well-designed plan, in short, was not necessarily at the mercy of the economic logic of adverse selection. Moreover, as the authors of the act recognized, a community-rated plan could improve its competitive position considerably by a judicious use of copayments.

The fact was that no one knew precisely what the effect of the requirement would be or how to disentangle its influence from all the other determinants of an HMO's financial workability. What was clear was that Congress did not intend to use federal funds to establish new delivery systems that discriminated against the sick. However, much more concerned to strike a blow against experience rating than to delve into the complexities of its opposite, Congress had included the requirement, appended three exceptions, and left it to HEW to make sense of it all.

The language of the law gave important discretion to HEW, whose staff was obliged quickly to school itself in the intricacies of community rating and copayments. As usual, schooling meant lengthy calls to and conferences with officials of established PGPs and the results were discouraging. Inquiries showed that there existed almost as many variants of community rating as there were plans. No two defined the term in precisely the same way and any definitions HEW might hand down would fail to fit at least some of the practices of most of the plans.

As the staff pushed bravely on, complexities multiplied. Soon the staffer assigned to explore the issue listed nine questions the department would need to resolve.[39] Some of these questions went to the heart of community rating. For example, should multiple copayment arrangements be permitted? "Nothing in the law," the staffer noted, "suggests that the co-payment level must be the same for all enrolled groups." On the other hand, "permitting an HMO to offer one level of co-payments to one employee group and another to a different employee group would be to encourage experience rating through actuarial finagling." The correct approach, he argued, was "to require that an HMO offer all of its co-payment options to each employee group, although not to each member of the group," and

39. "Community Rating and Copayments" (n.d.), in HEW files.

that individual (that is, nongroup) subscribers be permitted to choose among "one or more co-payment levels." He also raised questions about (and proposed solutions to) a number of other problems: whether copayments should be allowed to reflect cost-of-service differences by area; whether differences in "family size and composition" should be interpreted to include age and sex; whether the cost of collecting payments, which the act authorized rate differences to reflect, should include costs of marketing the plan; whether copayment levels should be allowed to vary with subscribers' incomes; and how copayment levels should be established to conform to the "barriers to care" language in the act and the percentage ceilings set out in the conference report.[40]

As the regulatory options were debated, HMO spokesmen, predictably, argued for language that would leave them as much discretion as possible. Thus, they tended to favor diverse copayment options, which they might offer to subscribers as the plans saw fit; the inclusion of cost-of-service differences by area; age and sex differences in rates; and so forth. To these suggestions, however, the General Counsel's Office had a simple reply: the act stated that rates must be "equivalent . . . for all families of similar composition," and many of the suggestions under discussion would allow the plans to charge similarly composed families different rates.

Stalemated between the preferences of the plans and the language of the law, yet under pressure to get the regulations published, the BCHS resolved to save the complexities for the guidelines and publish for the time being language that would be as undemanding and inoffensive as possible. Thus the proposed rules of May 1974 added to the statutory language on community rating in only three significant respects. First, the cutoff point between "large" and "small" groups was defined at one hundred members. Second, the rules dodged the many problems surrounding "nominal differentials" by declaring that differences reflecting administrative costs of collecting payments were permitted "upon demonstration to the Secretary" that they were justified. Third, the rules held that the "geographically distinct and separate" components of an HMO were permitted to set

---

40. These complications were soon compounded by others. A memo of January 31, 1974, in HEW files on "Screening in Underwriting Limitations in Group Enrollment" to Bill Kopit from Ron Jydstrup, pointed out that the paper on "Community Rating and Copayments" did not define community rating, did not spell out the meaning of the small groups and large groups the law required the secretary to define, did not address the ways in which waivers for preexisting conditions and maternity could undercut community rating, and did not deal completely with the problems of defining families and their composition for purposes of rate setting.

different rates upon meeting some criteria that would clearly pose no problem for Kaiser, which of course did not wish to see its six regional plans obliged to set the same rate.[41]

With one exception, the department's embroidery on the copayment provisions of the law was similarly sparse. To establish flexibility, the proposed rules allowed each HMO to "establish one or more copayment options." But to prevent actuarial finagling, the next sentence declared that "every copayment option so established shall be offered to each member, whenever enrolled individually or in the case of a voluntary association to that association." The proposed rules then restated the percentage ceilings on copayments in the conference report and—the one exception—added language forbidding copayments "in any calendar year, when the copayments made by each individual or family in such calendar year total 50 percent of the total annual premium cost" that they would have incurred under an option with no copayments. This provision was added at the insistence of lawyers in the General Counsel's Office, who noted that the law forbade copayments "that serve (as determined under regulations of the Secretary) as a barrier to the delivery of health services." Obliged to come up with regulatory language defining the "barrier," the staffer handling community rating pondered the problem and, as he later recalled, " pulled the 50 percent criterion out of my ear."

Cautious and undemanding though they appeared, the proposed rules on community rating provoked many agitated objections. Kaiser devoted nine of its forty-six pages of comments on the proposed subpart A rules to premium and copayment issues, mainly explaining the heavy burden of administrative work the rules would impose,[42] and HEW responded favorably to most of these points. The final regulations changed the term "members" to "subscribers" to make it clear that, for example, the employed head of the family ("the subscriber"), not his eight-year-old son (a "member") was entitled to select among copayment options; deleted the rule requiring the secretary to approve regional differentials; and added language assuring existing subscribers that their rates would not be changed

---

41. *Federal Register*, May 8, 1974, p. 16423, pt. 110.101(h); and p. 16424, pt. 110.103.

42. Letter from Jerry Phelan, Counsel, Kaiser Foundation Health Plan, Inc., to Director, Bureau of Community Health Services, June 7, 1974, in HEW files, HMO Comments folder P, especially pp. 10–19. Extensive comments were also offered by Blue Cross–Blue Shield of Michigan (on behalf of Metro Health Plan), Blue Cross Association and National Association of Blue Shield Plans, Mutual of Omaha, Ford Foundation, Community Health Care Center Plan, Inc. of New Haven, GHAA, and Group Health Cooperative of Puget Sound (HMO Comments folders R, B, M, K, F, C, N).

in mid-contract if and when their plan adopted a community rating system.[43]

The provision that every copayment option must be offered to each individually enrolled member proved very controversial. Kaiser explained that it would encourage the highest utilizers to elect the lowest copayments and would impose a great burden of paperwork and communication. The final rules dropped the provision. In response to many complaints about the paperwork required to keep and monitor individual records of copayments to insure that no member paid more than 50 percent of the total annual premiums he would have paid under an option without copayments, the rule was changed to put the burden of recordkeeping on the subscriber or member. Finally, at the plans' request, the rule writers added a paragraph to authorize HMOs to recover payments for services covered by third parties such as workmen's compensation or employer's liability laws.

The final rules on community rating and copayments passed over in silence most of the complex issues identified by the HMO staff and most of the even more complex issues explored in comments on the proposed rules. For the most part the rules restated the language of the law and conference report. All additions except the 50 percent ceiling defining a "barrier to care"[44] came at the request of the HMO community and were designed to meet its needs. In this case, too, then, a full identification of issues and wide-ranging discussions gradually led to the conclusion that the trade-off between responsibility and responsiveness was met best by quoting the law, adding to it only procedural measures designed to ease the HMOs' way, and avoiding hard questions of definition whose resolution could only tie the plans' hands. For the time being at least, the less said the better.

Although this minimalist approach preserved the plans' flexibility in the short term, program officials and HMOs alike knew that the questions begged would have to be pursued eventually. The plans would go to work and applications for aid under the various sequences, leading finally to operations and qualification, would flow in. Reviewers in HEW would study the specifics of the plans' rate-setting arrangements and pass judgment whether they did or did not conform to the law and regulations. Working with such unspecific regulations, the reviewer who approved

43. *Federal Register*, October 18, 1974, pp. 37308–09; p. 37312, pt. 110.101 (1); p. 37314, pt. 110.105.

44. In 1979, regulations raised the copayment ceiling to 100 percent. *Federal Register*, July 18, 1979, p. 42062.

some variant of the many options practiced by the plans might find himself under attack by Congress, the GAO, or departmental superiors for sanctioning practices deemed inconsistent with the statute. The plans might be required to revise their rate structures in midstream. The respite was only temporary.

Well aware of these anxieties, HEW staff invoked their all-purpose reply: unresolved issues would be addressed in the guidelines, now (that is, perpetually) in preparation. Yet the guidelines, which were steadily becoming a repository of unresolved, fiendishly complex questions, foundered on the same old dilemma: each step toward specificity was a step away from flexibility. The plans wanted to know where they stood. But what they really wanted to know, of course, was that they could stand wherever they then stood without fear of being held out of compliance with the law and regulations. The department could give them its sympathy and understanding but not the assurance they sought, for the administrators themselves feared that the lawmakers (whose staffs were ever vigilant for signs of subversion) or the lawyers in the General Counsel's Office would challenge them. Beneath all the complications, the problem was exquisitely simple, a lawyer in the General Counsel's Office pointed out: no language that sanctioned the wide variety of HMO rate-setting practices could also meet the law's requirement that premiums be equivalent for all families of similar composition.

In short, the same dilemma that made a tight-lipped policy attractive in the short run made a lucid and detailed set of guidelines necessary in the longer term. Yet the sharp trade-offs between flexibility and specificity, between responsiveness and responsibility, could not be dispelled administratively. Whatever the department said would be too much for some plans, too little for others.

The department did try to define community rating in the guidelines. After repeating parts of the law and regulations, the guidelines said this:

> A *community rate* is the rate per person which has been calculated and is used to determine the total revenue for the HMO. The *community rating system* is the procedure which uses that community rate to calculate the family rate variations. This procedure can produce the family rate arrangement necessary for meeting the competitive or administrative requirements of a particular group and still fulfill the requirements of the Act.

The guidelines then referred the reader to an appendix for further information.[45] The reaction of lawyers in the General Counsel's Office was

45. "Regulations and Program Guidelines," p. 19 and app. A.

predictable and terse: "We do not understand the description of community rating on page 19 and appendix A which produces different family rates for families of similar composition. We recommend further discussion of this question."[46]

The department did discuss the issue further from time to time, but without success.[47] In 1978, five years after the question first arose, it remained unresolved, and guidelines remained unissued.[48] In June 1978 the GAO published a study of fourteen federally qualified HMOs and found a wide variety of rate-setting practices. Seven of the plans, the investigators concluded, appeared to violate the law by charging unequivalent rates for couples. This was not strange, the investigators observed; after all, HEW had never defined community rating.[49]

Open Enrollment

No single provision of Public Law 93-222 united the HMO community more firmly and vociferously in opposition than the one requiring that qualified plans "have an open enrollment period of not less than thirty days at least once during each consecutive twelve-month period during which enrollment period it accepts, up to its capacity, individuals in the order in which they apply for enrollment."[50] Community rating, they worried, might induce adverse selection over time. Open enrollment, they were certain, would guarantee that HMOs, many of them new and struggling to break even, would be inundated with cancer and heart cases— the "Blue Cross rejects"—whose utilization rates for expensive services would exceed by many times those of normal members. These disproportionate rates would mean higher costs that the plan could cover only by charging higher community-rated premiums for all members; this would make the plan ever less competitive over time and set in motion the logic that led down the road from adverse selection to financial disaster.

46. Edelman to Seubold, "Comments on pp. 1–22," p. 5.

47. For example, in a memorandum, "Community Rating," of March 9, 1976, in HEW files, apparently intended for the staff of the qualification office, William McLeod noted that the language of the act on community rating had "haunted the implementation of the provision from the outset." The BCHS regulation writers merely quoted the statute, he pointed out. He added that the approach then contemplated and later adopted in amendments—to waive the requirement for a few years—merely postponed the problem. McLeod's suggestion was that the confusing language about equivalences be scrapped in favor of a definition that stated what was *not* permissible, namely differentials in rates attributed to historic or prospective use of services.

48. In June 1976, in the course of one of the intermittent exchanges of blame over who was responsible for the absence of guidelines, Seubold noted that the community rating issue in particular was holding them up. *Health Services Information,* July 19, 1976, p. 3.

49. Comptroller General of the United States, *Can Health Maintenance Organizations Be Successful?—An Analysis of 14 Federally Qualified 'HMOs'* (GAO, 1978), pp. 8–9.

50. P.L. 93–222, sec. 1301 (c) (4).

In an ideal world, the HMOs agreed, no citizen would be denied health care coverage because of prior illness. The world of American health insurance was not ideal in 1974, however, and the federal government was not about to make it so. The states, not the federal government, regulated conventional health insurers, and even if the authors of the HMO legislation had been willing to fight the insurance industry and its allies to preempt the states and impose a federal open enrollment requirement on all insurers (a prospect that was politically out of the question), the Senate subcommittee chaired by the strongest defender of open enrollment, Edward Kennedy, lacked jurisdiction in this area.

In the real world, the HMOs asserted, neither Blue Cross nor commercial insurance plans held open enrollment periods. What sense did it make to require the smallest and most vulnerable health plans—the "weak sisters"—to play by rules far stricter and more onerous than those imposed on their competition? The provision might be made workable—though no less distasteful—if the plans were allowed to tailor a rate to the unhappy experience of the open enrollees. The act's insistence on both community rating *and* open enrollment, however, closed the door to this possibility.

The authors of Public Law 93-222 had listened attentively to these arguments, but some remained unconvinced. They were conferring on HMOs advantages—money, recognition, access to markets under dual choice, and an override of inhibiting state laws—that their competition would not enjoy, and some thought it not so very unreasonable a bargain to ask the HMOs to extend themselves on behalf of the disadvantaged. Moreover, despite all the doomsaying, no one knew the true impact and costs of open enrollment—it had seldom been tried, after all. A few plans had experimented with limited open enrollment periods and did indeed find that the open enrollees used services at rates considerably higher than other members. These plans usually did not bother to publish data that addressed "the bottom line," however—the impact of this higher utilization on costs per member per month and on premiums. One plan that did hold open enrollment and did compute the premium increase it produced—the Marshfield Clinic in rural Wisconsin—found that such enrollees tended to raise subscriber premiums by about $1 per month. Marshfield spokesmen did not regard this increase as uncompetitive and thought it a small price to pay for an important redistributive principle.[51] Kaiser spokesmen replied

51. *Health Services Information*, December 15, 1975, pp. 1–2. Earlier the newsletter had reported Marshfield's finding that its individual enrollees used 25 percent more health care services than its group members, but that when the relative size of the two groups was taken into account, only 8 percent of the group subscribers' fees underwrote the individual enrollees' expenses (August 26, 1974, p. 3).

that rural Wisconsin was not Los Angeles or San Francisco. In the former, the number of "basket cases" was limited, whereas an open enrollment period in the latter cities could attract vast numbers of very expensive members.

The congressional proponents of open enrollment had found these disputes beside the point. If open enrollment was the right course to take, but it threatened to damage the HMO's competitive position, there was an obvious solution: subsidize the plans to cover the costs that open enrollment imposed. As may be recalled from chapter 5, Kennedy's bills had done precisely this. The 1972 version of the Roy-Rogers bill had been unwilling to go so far but it had contained subsidies to a few HMOs to demonstrate the effects of open enrollment. The presence of subsidies in the bill became a key point of argument between House Democrats and Republicans, however, and the ifs, ands, and buts contained in this tangential section of the bill ran to many pages, so when the bill was pared down in 1973, these subsidy provisions were deleted. In the conference committee, the managers struck a bargain by keeping the open enrollment provision, about which Kennedy felt very strongly, and substituting for the subsidies a waiver provision. The plans could be excused for three years, and for longer if they wished, from holding an open enrollment period if they could satisfy HEW that honoring the rule would damage their viability. Viewing this compromise as workable and fair, the legislative defenders of the provision grew impatient with the established plans' laments.

The grounds for a waiver set out in the act required that a plan demonstrate to the satisfaction of the secretary that "it has enrolled, or will be compelled to enroll, a disproportionate number of individuals who are likely to utilize its services more often than an actuarially determined average (as determined under regulations of the Secretary) and enrollment during an open enrollment period of an additional number of such individuals will jeopardize its economic viability." A second statutory basis for a waiver was that open enrollment would prevent a plan from enrolling membership that was "broadly representative" of the groups within the area it served.[52]

Rule-making for open enrollment proved to be a far less frustrating bureaucratic exercise than rule-making for community rating. In the latter case, the problem, which proved intractable, was how to define the

52. P.L. 93–222, sec. 1301 (c) (4).

requirement with enough specificity to be reassuring (that is, to let the HMOs know in advance that their particular rate structures were or were not consistent with the rules) without either diminishing their flexibility or publishing language that clearly sanctioned rate discrepancies prohibited by the law. In the former case, the problem was "simply" how to compose conditions for a waiver that would honor the statute but still permit any HMO with a halfway reasonable argument to win exemption.

In its proposed rules, the department cited, but did not define, the "economic viability" and "broadly representative" criteria, and then defined the "up to its capacity" provision as the HMOs had hoped it would. A waiver was in order, the proposed rules declared, if the plan "would be compelled to enroll a number of individuals which would exceed its capacity, *based upon a reasonable projection of new enrollments under existing group contracts.*"[53] The proposed rules then set down four procedural steps an HMO must take to qualify for a waiver:

(1) Submit a plan to (i) compute on a prospective basis an actuarially determined average of the utilization of services by current and/or potential enrollees, and (ii) collect data from potential enrollees and project patterns of utilization and costs in order to determine if open enrollment would jeopardize the economic viability of the organization;

(2) Indicate, upon the basis of reasonable estimates, that an open enrollment period would result in enrolling more than 50 percent Title XVIII and Title XIX beneficiaries . . . or

(3) Indicate, upon the basis of reasonable estimates, that an open enrollment period would result in the enrollment of more members than could be served within the capacity of the organization, considering the new enrollment anticipated under existing group contracts; and

(4) Provide an assurance that a waiver granted on the basis of the occurrence of certain conditions will not be utilized unless and until such conditions actually occur.

During the comment period, the HMOs expressed three major reservations about this language.[54] First, they pointed out the absurdity of the fourth criterion, which would allow a waiver to prevent damage to economic viability only after the damage had already demonstrably been done. Second, they pointed out that arguments based on data gathered from "potential enrollees" would be costly to gather and inconclusive at best. Third, they were uneasy with the general term "economic viability" and sought greater specificity.

53. *Federal Register,* May 8, 1974, p. 16425; pt. 110.107 (d)–(e) (emphasis added).
54. Eamon M. Kelley submitted comments on behalf of the Ford Foundation, Thomas O. Pyle for

The final rules met the HMOs' wishes on all counts. The offending fourth criterion was deleted. Acceptable sources of data were broadened and clarified by the following language:

[An HMO must] submit documentation that the health maintenance organization has prospectively determined on an actuarial basis, utilizing data available in the area or from similar organizations elsewhere, that the average utilization of services of potential individual members would so increase costs as to jeopardize the economic viability of the organization if it maintained an open enrollment period. The data concerning the prospective utilization of individual members need not be obtained by the health maintenance organization from actual individual cases in its area, but may be composite data from known experiences.

Finally, revised language made it clear that jeopardizing economic viability included, but was not limited to, situations "requiring an increase in rates which would make the health maintenance organization noncompetitive in its area."[55]

Some observers of the final rules argued that the department had done a masterful job of responding to the fears of the HMOs without violating the letter of the law. A rate increase that would make the HMO "noncompetitive in its area" was a basis for a waiver. The data to show that higher use of the plan would compel such an increase "need not be obtained from individual cases in its area," but could be "composite data from known experience," obviously including historical experience and the experience of plans in other areas. (To meet these terms "they could have all xeroxed the same Ph.D. thesis on the subject and sent it in," a former Rogers subcommittee aide commented later.) Moreover, the plan's capacity was to be judged by extrapolation from existing group contracts. Under such criteria, an HMO executive must be dull indeed not to qualify for a waiver.

Some plans sighed with relief at the broad language of the regulations and decided to seek a waiver in conjunction with their qualification applications. Others, however, remained suspicious. The rules looked good on paper, but the interpretation of the key terms still lay in the eyes of the beholders. Who would decide how large a rate increase made an HMO noncompetitive? Logically, any increase, even a few cents, made the plan somewhat less competitive than before, so HEW reviewers would have to decide how "significant" an increase must be to meet the terms of

---

the Harvard Community Health Plan, and Jerry Phelan for the Kaiser plan (HMO Comments folders K, pp. 5–8; P, pp. 3, 34–35).

55. *Federal Register,* October 18, 1974, p. 37315; pt. 110.107 (d)–(e).

the rule. Bureaucrats would likewise be the ones to decide just what the Ph.D. thesis on plan x implied about plan y, and they could similarly second-guess the plan's judgment as to what its growth trends implied about its true capacity. In very large plans—those of the Kaiser program, for instance—it would take some time before the effects of higher use under open enrollment diffused through the membership base sufficiently to influence rates. But by that time the plan might be stuck with a large number of very costly members and serious damage might be done. "We were not sure we could explain that to anyone," a Kaiser spokesman remarked. Considering the high stakes, many HMO executives concluded that "bureaucratic whims" were a poor foundation for the tight businesses they prided themselves on running. Moreover, they remained exasperated by what they took to be the sheer injustice of it all.

The plans understood that HEW understood their plight, shared their objections to the open enrollment requirement, and had shown its sympathy in the broad language of the final rules. Yet they also understood that departmental sympathies and interpretations were changeable—as changeable as congressional committee pressures, staff shakeups, reorganizations, and legal rulings. The only sound policy, these plans concluded, was to get open enrollment killed once and for all in amendments to the law.

Dual Choice

The so-called dual choice provision of the HMO act (section 1310) required all employers who employed at least twenty-five workers, paid the minimum wage or more, and offered a health benefit plan to their workers to include the option of joining a federally qualified HMO if such an organization existed in the area and asked to be offered. The provision, of course, was designed to improve HMOs' access to subscribers and was viewed by some onlookers as the single most important feature of the act.

As the previous chapter pointed out, the Nixon administration, the Rogers subcommittee, and the Kennedy subcommittee all had agreed on the dual choice principle, but they had differed on the proper legislative vehicle for it. The administration had preferred that it be enacted as part of a broader national health insurance package, not in HMO legislation. Both the Roy-Rogers and Kennedy bills had contained dual choice provisions in 1972, but when Kennedy's bill came to the floor conservatives had threatened to make a major issue of their objections to legislating changes in labor-management practices in a health care bill. Fearful that this issue would dominate debate about what was already a large and controversial bill, Kennedy had immediately moved to delete the provision and did not replace it in his scaled-down 1973 bill.[56] When the conference committee met in December 1973, most of their difficulties lay in finding compromises between expansive Senate provisions and modest or nonexistent House counterparts. Dual choice, contained in the House but not the Senate bill, was a happy exception. The House had passed it, the Senate was happy to have it; the provision presented no problems and was quickly included in the act, as the managers moved on to much more controversial issues.

The language of section 1310 was brief and elliptical. The section noted the universe of employers to whom it applied, required employers to offer *both* a qualified HMO and a qualified IPA if both existed in their area, stated that no employer was obliged to pay more for health benefits as a result of the requirement than he would otherwise pay under a prevailing collective bargaining agreement or other contract, and defined the term "qualified health maintenance organization" in reference to other definitions in the law.

The section itself and HEW's impending refinement of it evoked deep concern from a wide range of interests. Entrepreneurs thinking of launching new HMOs viewed dual choice as a crucial aid to marketing their plans. Existing HMOs were ambivalent: the new access to employee markets might help, but in order to be offered under the law they must first qualify on its terms. Many plans had decided that the costs of doing so were too high. On the other hand, if they disdained qualification, they might be obliged to stand by while a newly qualified plan raided their markets. To the existing plans, in short, dual choice was the major, indeed the only, incentive to participate in a program they disliked. Understandably, they wanted to know exactly what it involved.

Employers, affected across the nation, sought to learn precisely what their obligations—and their administrative costs—would be as a result of the provision. Labor unions, which represented employees in health benefits negotiations, were likewise curious about their role. None of their questions could be answered definitively from the sparse language of the act; answers would have to come from HEW.

The task of writing dual choice regulations plunged the department's HMO staff and general counsel straight into the arcane and complex issues attending the negotiation and administration of work-related health benefits plans in the United States. The staff, indeed the department, had

---

56. *Congressional Record*, September 20, 1972, p. 31563.

done nothing remotely like it before. In the course of a forty-page issue paper written soon after the law was signed, a staffer outlined seventeen complicated issues.[57] Some were both substantively important and certain to become controversial. For example, what was the status of part-time employees under the law? What was an employer's obligation when his contribution to an employees' health plan was confined to payments to a union-run health and welfare trust? How much and what type of marketing should an employer be obliged to permit an HMO to conduct, and how often, and how soon before a contract renewal date? What were the employer's obligations when some or most of his workers lived outside the qualified HMO's service area? If only a handful lived within the plan's service area, was he still obliged to offer it? Granted that no employer was required to pay more for an HMO than for another plan, could he properly elect to pay less? The law did not say no, yet if he did the cost to the employee would rise and the appeals of HMO membership would diminish. Could an employer count the administrative costs of making the offer in his calculation of the costs of offering the HMO? Would an employer be allowed to cancel alternative coverage and meet his obligation to the law by offering his employees *only* a qualified HMO? On these and several other points the law was silent or ambiguous.

To make matters worse, when the staff working on draft regulations began discussing various solutions with the General Counsel's Office it became clear that yet another question, unresolved in the law and its legislative history and unrecognized in the earlier forty-page memo, would assume greater practical importance than all other questions combined. This question concerned the specific prerogatives of organized labor— collective bargaining agents—in the dual choice process.

When, in December 1974, a year had passed and proposed dual choice rules had not appeared, Sidney Edelman, then HEW's assistant general counsel for public health, explained to Buzzell that the source of the delay was a question "whether the offer of the option of membership in qualified health maintenance organizations as required by the statute must, where there is a collective bargaining representative designated . . . be made (1) only to the collective bargaining representative which may accept or reject the offer on behalf of the employees whom it represents, or (2) only to the individual employees for acceptance or rejection by each of them."[58] The

---

57. "Section 1310: Dual Choice; Draft Issue Paper" (n.d.) in HEW files.
58. Memorandum from Sidney Edelman, Assistant General Counsel for Public Health, to Harold O. Buzzell, Administrator, HSA, "HMOs—Section 1310—Offer of HMO Option—Effect of Section 1310 on Employer's Obligations Under National Labor Relations Act," December 12, 1974, in HEW files.

law stated that the employer must include the HMO option "in any health benefits plan offered to its employees." The question, then, was if the HMO option was offered to a collective bargaining agent and rejected, must the employer then offer it to each individual employee?

Not surprisingly, opinions differed. Union spokesmen and lawyers in the Department of Labor, which the HMO act charged with enforcing the dual choice provision, had strong views on the matter. They pointed out that the National Labor Relations Act made it an unfair labor practice for an employer to refuse to bargain collectively with the representative of his employees, that designated collective bargaining agents under that law shall be "exclusive representatives of all the employees" for collective bargaining purposes, that the employer and employee are required by that act "to confer in good faith with respect to wages, hours, and other terms and conditions of employment . . . but such obligation does not compel either party to agree to a proposal or require the making of a concession . . . ," and that health benefits were clearly subject to these requirements. From this it followed, said the labor spokesmen, that any requirement forcing an employer to offer an HMO option rejected by a collective bargaining agent to his individual employees would violate the terms of the labor law.

Lawyers in HEW took a different view. In Edelman's opinion, Labor's arguments ignored "the evident intent of the statute [Public Law 93-222] to mandate the inclusion of an HMO option as an alternative mode of health care in existing health benefits plans and would add little, if anything, to the employer's existing obligation to bargain collectively on conditions of employment." Moreover, he contended that there was a clear legal basis for "accommodating" the NLRA to subsequent acts and court decisions and concluded that rules that exempted the employer from offering to his employees an HMO option rejected by the union were "legally questionable and would be difficult to defend if challenged in litigation."[59]

Embarrassed by the slow progress of the dual choice rules, the department attempted to negotiate with labor spokesmen. At the end of January HEW's general counsel reported to Secretary Weinberger on the results to date.[60] He explained that his counterpart in the National Labor Relations Board "basically accepts" the HEW position that "if the union declines

59. Ibid.

60. Memorandum from John B. Rhinelander, General Counsel, to the Secretary, "Health Maintenance Organization—Accommodation of the Dual Choice Provision in Section 1310 (a) of the HMO Act with the National Labor Relations Act (NLRA)," January 29, 1975, in HEW files.

the employer's offered plan with the HMO option and the employer insists upon it, the parties may reach a good faith impasse on the issue, after which the employer would be free, under NLRA principles, to institute his offered plan with the HMO option on the same terms and conditions as offered to the union." Unfortunately, he continued, the Department of Labor did not agree. That department's view was that under section 1310 "the employer is simply mandated to bargain periodically, with the union free to reject." His own view was that although the Labor position was "not untenable," the HEW position was "the better reading of the two statutes." He therefore recommended that HEW publish proposed rules that embodied the department's own legal views, but revise the preamble to the rules to "highlight" and "flag" the issue. The department could then see what comments came in, and make concessions to Labor if it seemed advisable to do so. The proposed dual choice rules published in the *Federal Register* on February 12, 1975, followed the counsel's advice.[61]

Upon publication of HEW's side of the argument, positions hardened and pressure on the department to back down grew. A lawyer in the HEW General Counsel's Office later recalled his depression when a NLRB spokesman took to a public forum to declare that the department's assertion that the board "basically accepted" the HEW argument was a misconstruction. Depression deepened when an AFL-CIO official proclaimed in effect that the proposed rules would become final over the dead body of the labor movement. Most of the 171 comments transmitted on the subject took labor's side. The HMO staff itself was overwhelmingly in favor of conceding the fight to labor. In the first place, they pointed out, labor was a proven and indispensable ally of the HMO cause, and, in the second place, few HMOs would find many subscribers among the individual members of groups whose union had rejected the HMO option.

In one very important part of the department, however, the original point of view prevailed. Secretary Weinberger had followed the legal arguments and was persuaded that HEW had a strong case.[62] (Three years later he said in an interview that he remained convinced that HEW would have defeated Labor if the issue could have been brought before the courts.) Moreover, as a conservative Republican who had no inordinate fondness

---

61. *Federal Register*, February 12, 1975, pp. 6602–05. The collective bargaining issues are flagged at pp. 6602–03.

62. The Weinberger-Edelman position was reinforced when Congressman Rogers declared in March 1975 at a conference on the act: "The intent is that the *individual* covered is to make the choice and nobody else for him. I hope we'll see it. If not we'll write it stronger." *Health Services Information*, March 24, 1975, p. 1; emphasis in original.

for organized labor and held strong philosophical views about individual free choice, he could not endorse the precept that only workers not in unions should have a personal say about their health care coverage. Despite the growing unpopularity of his stand and the inevitable leaks to the press by HMO advocates that he was out to sabotage the program, Weinberger refused to change his position.

At an impasse, the interagency argument dragged on through the summer of 1975 with no resolution in sight. By late summer it had become clear that the deadlock would be broken only by the intervention of the White House or OMB, and John Veneman, then serving on Vice President Nelson Rockefeller's staff, wrote to a White House staffer urging him to "get on top of" the dispute. Weinberger's adamant stand, Veneman argued, was simply impractical in the real world. "If labor and management cannot agree on an HMO, and management offers one to its employees anyway, all the union has to do is send a notice to its members telling them not to join. Chances are few, if any, union employees would join an HMO under these circumstances."[63]

In August 1975 Weinberger left the administration and the Ford White House summoned memorandums from both HEW and Labor explaining their points of view. The decision came back in favor of Labor and the final rules, signed by Weinberger's successor, appeared in the *Federal Register* on October 28. The preamble explained that the department had concluded "that the employer's obligation to offer the option of health maintenance organization. . . . membership to its represented employees is satisfied if the offer is made to such bargaining representative in accordance with the requirements of the NLRA."[64]

The prolonged dispute had been costly. When the final dual choice rules appeared, the HMO act was almost two years old. Employers had sat cautiously watching, reluctant to add HMO options to their benefit plans until the precise nature of their duties became clear; young HMOs found employers' reticence an important obstacle in their fight to reach a break-even point; growing HMOs reported a sag in the marketing momentum that federal recognition surrounding passage of the act had generated; some sponsors held up their plans to launch HMOs until the dual choice process could be factored into their market estimates. Many existing plans

63. Jack Veneman, "Memorandum for Jim Cannon; Subject: Health Maintenance Organization Policy Issues and Amendments" (n.d.) in Office of Management and Budget files (OMB Legislative Reference Division, Legislative Information Center, File R5-10/75.18), vol. 1.

64. *Federal Register*, October 28, 1975, p. 50212.

withheld their decisions about qualifying until they determined whether the benefits of dual choice would outweigh the costs of qualifying. Organized labor, HMO spokesmen, and some congressmen and their staffs criticized the department sharply for delay and political rigidity which, they concluded darkly, could only reflect the administration's determination to ruin the program. In this case too, the department's best efforts to reconcile responsibility with responsiveness left nearly everyone unhappy.

Implementation, Fragmentation

Although many established plans chose to approach the HMO program gingerly or to avoid it altogether until the law was amended, many proposed, new, and young plans enjoyed no such luxury. These plans usually needed at least some federal funds and usually considered the expanded markets that would open to them once they qualified under dual choice vital to their marketing efforts and therefore to their financial security. The muddled state of the regulations disturbed them. Rules on some important matters did not exist, others were vague, and still others were offensively specific. Everything, the department promised, would soon be clarified in guidelines. But whether the rules were published, proposed, or embryonic; acceptable, tolerable, or detested; clear, muddled, or indecipherable, the fact remained that three sets of HMO officials— developers in the regional offices and developers and qualifiers in Washington—would have to come up with answers at once for a growing flow of inquiries and applications for advice, money, and qualification.

Development

Of the two functions, development—the part of the program which made grants to bring HMOs into existence or to make young HMOs operational—proved much the simpler and smoother to implement. Development was an extension of an activity that had been carried on for three years before the act emerged. Development director Seubold and many of his staff had served in HMOS. The final sub-part A regulations appeared in October 1974. The developers were largely spared the established plans' discontents with the law and regulations, for these plans usually did not need federal money and were solely concerned with qualification. The developers' constituency was both eager and supplicant, heavily dependent on federal largesse. The task itself—giving out money—was not noticeably painful.

To be sure, the developers would have preferred to operate in the flexible style of the pre-act days. Many made no secret of their wish that the original Nixon plan, which would have given them virtually unlimited discretion to define and fund HMOs as they saw fit, had passed intact. Yet although the act guaranteed that the grant givers would be compelled to attach strings to aid and to say no oftener than they liked, the major problems it posed seldom rested heavily on their shoulders. From the standpoint of the development process, the cumulative body of legislative compromises and agency improvisations gave the HMO program a curious, even paradoxical, aspect. Viewed in toto, the law and regulations were a massive, intricate, formidable package. Yet the individual elements within the package were often surprisingly flexible; few of them would, by themselves, prevent a sophisticated HMO entrepreneur from obtaining federal aid to launch a plan.

In essence, the developers were asked to predict whether an applicant could build an HMO that would prove qualifiable when operational (or nearly so) within one, two, or three years. Nor must predications about qualifiability be constructed with this schedule in mind. The various waivers, exemptions, ambiguities, and silences in the law and regulations extended the time when full compliance would be expected. For example, a qualified plan could phase in the required benefits over three years, could take three years to meet the staffing requirements, could waive open enrollment for at least three years, and, so far as anyone could tell in 1974, could practice almost any version of community rating it chose. Thus, it might be five or six years after a feasibility or planning grant before an HMO would be held to the exacting standards of the law. Moreover, many observers hoped and expected that offending provisions would be amended from the law long before the day of judgment came. Despite the rigors of law and regulation, the fact was that the developers enjoyed a very wide range of discretion.

The uses of discretion typically began in the field. Most entrepreneurs or HMO executives interested in applying for one or another type of aid under the law called first on regional officials in one of HEW's ten regions. These officials reported to the regional administrator, who himself came under the authority of the assistant secretary for health, not the heads of OHMO, BCHS, or HSA. The blurred lines of authority made it difficult even to count, let alone account for, the number of regional officials working on HMOs. A few were assigned full time to the HMO program; many worked on it part time along with other duties. By one count, a list of regional officials working on HMOs in 1974 yielded thirty-six—twenty-two professionals and fourteen clerical staff. By another count, the same list yielded twenty-nine (seventeen professionals and twelve clerical staff).[65]

Few of these regional staffers knew much about prepaid group practice. Most of them, the GAO later reported, "were 'generalists' with expertise in health care delivery systems, hospital administration, disease control, or Federal grants management," and usually had only a "general knowledge" of PGP.[66] An HMO management consultant, less delicate, noted that the staff's theoretical grasp of HMOs ranged from almost nil to excellent and its operational understanding from almost nil to negligible.[67] Seubold himself doubted their capabilities and explained in a memo to Batalden that the regional situation was "rapidly approaching the crisis stage" because too many of the regional officials lacked experience with PGPs.[68] Although their expertise tended to improve with trial, error, and time, in the early phase of the development effort many of those entrusted with guiding HMOs along the road to qualification were at best one chapter ahead and often several chapters behind the applicants themselves.

Armed with copies of the act, the regulations, and a few memos from Seubold, acquainted only in passing with the workings of prepaid group practice, and besieged by eager inquirers or applicants, regional officials were obliged quickly to improvise decision processes that would look reasonable to central office superiors (who, despite the preferences of Nixon administration generalists for decentralization, were determined to review grant awards closely themselves) and, they hoped, to applicants. To their relief they soon discovered that advanced literacy in PGP was not a requirement of the job; a reasonably close reading of the law and regulations allowed them to assume the offensive by asking "hard questions"—for example: Have you identified your markets and what are they? What physician/member ratio do you anticipate for various specialties and how do you expect it to change from the first to the second year? Whom have you contacted about serving on the board of directors? What costs per member per month does your community-rated premium presuppose? If the applicant was reduced to incoherence, the officials could safely

65. List, "Health Maintenance Organization Service, Regional Positions" (n.d.), in HEW files.
66. Comptroller General, "Factors that Impede Progress," p. 13.
67. Rogers Subcommittee Hearings, 1975, p. 18. The consultant added, "Unfortunately, our experience with HEW headquarters indicates the same pattern."
68. Iglehart, "Heralded HMO Programs," p. 1826.

assume that he knew even less about HMOs than they did and was therefore a poor candidate for development funds.

In fact, the regional officials were approached by a sizable number of applicants, who, it soon became clear, did not understand the act and its requirements and could not respond intelligibly to its many concerns. Many spokesmen for the medically indigent, for example, had a dim conception of the program as a new source of federal funds with which to set up or shore up community health centers, rural health clinics, and the like. Interrogating them, the regional officials soon learned that many interested parties had no idea how to perform a marketing survey, had given no thought to where physicians would come from, had approached no hospitals with a contract in mind, could not so much as define community rating let alone do it, understood nothing about utilization controls, and in general failed to grasp the difference between a health center and an HMO. The officials therefore discouraged or rejected such applications and pointed proudly to their judicious selectivity.

Applicants versed in the workings of prepaid group practice and in the statutory specifics of an HMO were another matter, however. Many of these applicants matched or surpassed the regional staff's understanding of the subject matter, yet the latter were obliged to improvise criteria by which a rejection or approval of the former could be defended. The officials usually responded with lengthy checklists of variables—marketing plan, marketing staff, physicians, sponsor commitment, relations with a hospital, employer and union enthusiasm, site location, board of directors, community image, and more—attempted somehow to rate the adequacy of each, and finally arrived at an overall judgment of the plan's likely success.

Posing these questions was of course a good deal easier than answering them. For one thing, the "adequacy" of many of these variables—for example, marketing, staffing, and facilities—covaried in ways that could be predicted, if at all, only on the basis of extensive experience with PGP and extremely detailed analyses of the particular case. Second, the value of many of these variables could not be estimated without a very intimate understanding of the local scene. Third, some of these variables could hardly even be guessed at, for they were at the time of application still being discussed and negotiated among interested parties. Moreover, applicants varied in their command of written and spoken English, their grantsmanship skills, and their adeptness at statistics. Given the inherent uncertainty of the enterprise, even a highly knowledgeable reviewer would find it difficult to separate sound plans from the apparently promising yet seriously flawed. Although some regional reviewers learned fast (not all did), in the start-up years few could be described as highly knowledgeable.

Similar problems arose for the developers in the central office. Some of them had gained experience with HMOs in the pre-act grant program and felt rather confident that their experience had at least taught them to recognize a plan that would *not* work when they saw it.[69] By July 1975 the developers had evaluated 368 applications for grant funds and had funded about half of them—172 grants to 156 organizations.[70] The high rate of rejection, they argued, showed their determination to be responsible, astute, and selective. The problem, however, was the same as that faced by regional staff: once the cut had been made on grounds of basic literacy, the highly complex and intimately local covariation of key elements, many of which were indeterminate, made it possible that a certain number— perhaps a large number—of plans that did not appear flatly unworkable at the point of review would prove to be so for one reason or another as time went on.

The developers had, or at any rate expressed, little doubt that they knew what they were doing and that they were investing the public's money wisely. Others were less confident. In 1978 an HEW official summed up six years of close observation of both the central office and a West Coast regional office: "Developing an HMO is like designing an airplane: you don't really know if it's safe until it's up in the air. People used to ask me what I did and I'd tell them I felt like I was designing the allied air force for World War I. Some of these plans are held together with rubber bands, they all have different motors, some have two wings, some three, some four. Who knows how they'll work? But they'll sure make the sky look pretty."

Qualification

Judgments about which of the developers' vehicles were airworthy fell to the HMO program's qualification office, run by William J. McLeod and a small staff. The qualification office began life, as one former HEW staffer

---

69. At a meeting of the American Public Health Association in Washington, D.C., on November 1, 1977, HMO program staffer George Strumpf explained that despite Congressman Rogers' anger at the department, Secretary Richardson's decision to develop an HMO "strategy" while "policy" was still unformed was a good one, in large part because HEW's HMO staff gained experience in judging what types of HMOs would work and which would not. Strumpf's views on the correlates of a workable HMO may be found in George B. Strumpf and Marie A. Garramone, "Why Some HMOs Develop Slowly," *Public Health Reports*, vol. 91 (November–December 1976), pp. 496–503.

70. Rogers Subcommittee Hearings, 1975, p. 43.

put it, as the "stepchild" of the program. As explained earlier, those who gave the program its organizational character had three data in mind: the act's requirement that continued regulation of qualified HMOs be administered in the Office of the Assistant Secretary for Health; the conviction that HMO development efforts should be situated with similar efforts in BCHS, not in a separate bureau; and the belief that grant-givers ought not also to be qualifiers. These data implied nothing more about the qualification function than that it should be organizationally separate from grant-giving. It could be placed with continued regulation in the Assistant Secretary's Office, but early in 1974 that office had no enthusiasm for these responsibilities and hoped to delegate its statutory responsibilities to HSA.[71] But if it was not in OASH and not in BCHS, where was it? And, for that matter, *what* was it? Early in 1974, qualification floated in organizational and conceptual limbo.

Buzzell and other HEW managers viewed the qualification function ambivalently. From one point of view it was an important protection. Many of Seubold's superiors had doubts about some of the HMO projects funded in the pre-act days, knew that some of the same cast of characters were now awarding development grants under the new act, and feared that the advocates on the undeniably promotion-minded staff would, in their zeal to get the money out to large numbers of new HMOs, fund plans that would end in failure or, like the California prepaid health plans then receiving wide publicity, in scandal. The qualification office would apply institutional checks and balances to the advocates.

From another point of view, however, the process was a nuisance, a side issue that did not appear to require or repay careful attention. Early in 1974 qualification was not a pressing problem; how to get the money

71. An HEW staffer told *National Journal* reporter John Iglehart that Assistant Secretary Edwards's office "has shown absolutely no interest in regulating the HMO industry.... There is no desire to regulate; they are grantsmen. There is no hassle with handing out grants." ("Heralded HMO Programs," p. 1827.) At least as early as May 1974 Edwards contemplated delegating his authority under section 1312 of the act to the HSA administrator. In response to an "oral request" from the chief of the HMO program's financial division, an attorney in the General Counsel's Office explained that "the proposed delegations do not seem to recognize the need for a separate administrative structure consistent with the requirement that the administration of section 1312 of the PHS Act be 'in' the Office of the Assistant Secretary for Health," and that the delegation would "appear to constitute a failure to comply with the statute." Letter from David Benor, Attorney Advisor, Public Health Division, to Roger Gibson, Chief, Financial Division HMO, "HMO Act of 1973— Delegations of Authority," May 15, 1974, in HEW files. The issue arose again a few months later. In January 1975 the HSA administrator was advised that delegating the continued regulation function to him was "prohibited by the statute." Letter from Sidney Edelman, Assistant General Counsel for Public Health, to Mr. Norman E. Prince, Acting Chief, Organization Analysis Branch, DMPA/OOMS/OAM, "HMOs—Section 1312, PHS Act—Continued Regulation," January 31, 1975, in HEW files.

out was. Many existing plans were proclaiming that they very well might refuse to seek qualification until the law was amended. Plans launched or aided in an early stage by the new grant effort would not be operational and qualifiable for some time. The immediate pressures—from entrepreneurs, small plans, pre-act plans, Seubold and his staff, and congressmen advancing the interests of plans in their districts—focused on grant-giving. The development staff was enthusiastic and, not least important in bureaucratic politics, there in place. Qualification, which in essence meant rubbing the plans' noses in the details of a law both they and the department disliked, was by comparison distasteful and deferrable. The PHS tended to enjoy a close, supportive relationship with its grant beneficiaries, not a regulatory one, and independent, institutionalized review and nay-saying was not an arrangement to which it cared to become accustomed. In sum, the task was unsavory in general and forbidding in its particulars.

For all of these reasons few officials saw any urgency in the qualification process. In the rush to get the grant effort up and running, its counterpart was treated as an afterthought, an important protection whose institutional character could be addressed at leisure later on. Not until work on the subpart A regulations and guidelines that defined a qualifiable HMO was well under way did Buzzell bring in McLeod as his special assistant for qualification, and the Office of HMO Qualification and Compliance was not created until June 1975. To McLeod and three aides were entrusted the task of writing the regulations governing dual choice, qualification, and continued regulation, and the job of reviewing the (then limited) flow of applications for qualification.

Within a short time this seemingly peripheral part of the program moved to center stage. Within two years the qualifiers managed systematically and deeply to alienate Seubold and his staff, the regional office developers, young plans applying for qualification, and the most important established plans, notably Kaiser. By the end of 1976 an alliance of developers and the HMO community, joined by reporters and congressional aides seeking to explain why the HMO program was faltering, found in the qualification office the source and symbol of HEW's mismanagement of the HMO program.

McLeod assumed office with some definite ideas about how the qualification function should be handled. The very existence of the office as well as his instructions from Buzzell made it clear that qualification was to mean an independent, arm's-length review of plans seeking federal certification—a formal mandate that reinforced McLeod's personal predilections. Before and during his stint as president of a Los Angeles PGP he had seen enough of the developers to form some strong and unfavorable impressions of them. As viewed from the qualification office, Seubold and those in his shop were "bureaucrats and grantsmen," an associate of McLeod recalled. They used their discretion with the traditional "PHS mentality": "If we like you, you'll get the grant. As long as you fill out the forms halfway right, you'll get it. If we don't like you, you'll never get the grant, no matter how well you fill out the forms." McLeod, this observer continued, wanted to guarantee "integrity" in the qualification process. "The law is the law; do you comply with it or don't you?"

A bright (some said brilliant) man with a sizable ego, McLeod soon made it evident that he took a dim view not only of the grant-giving process and of the developers ("he thought they were a bunch of jerks," an aide recalled) but also of the merits of the plans they supported and encouraged to apply for qualification. As applications began trickling in, McLeod and his staff were astonished at the amount of "junk" they found in them. Many plans had a very limited understanding of the act, had not been much enlightened by the developers, and could not in good faith be certified. As one qualifier explained: "Our view was that we were entrusted with decisions affecting public money. There had to be some responsibility in this program. You just don't qualify a plan that puts out misleading marketing literature, where half the enrollees will never know where the doctors are, plans that would go broke and leave their subscribers in the lurch. We saw a responsibility to weed out the really bad. Maybe we didn't do enough."

As the qualifiers began sending applications back to the drawing board, they endeared themselves to no one. Rebuffed, plans communicated their pain and sense of betrayal to Seubold. Why had the rules of the game not been made clear from the start? Relations between the two offices rapidly deteriorated. In part, the tension reflected personality. McLeod, an observer recalled, was more "dynamic," whereas Seubold came across as "plodding." In part too, the conflict was a fight for bureaucratic prominence. Seubold and his staff, who were there first, were now subjected to the reproaches and even vetoes of a newcomer, who did not conceal his low opinion of their judgment. Moreover, McLeod, convinced that the program's center of gravity would inevitably shift in his direction, as the funded plans matured and the implications of dual choice became clear to the established plans, was determined to build his staff and his mission. Seubold could not help but feel threatened. Personality and prominence

merely aggravated the deeper conflict, however. At bottom, neither etiquette nor restraint could have disguised the fact that McLeod was, in
essence, paid to question Seubold's judgment, that regulation and promotion were functions fundamentally in tension, and that the HMO
program had, without full awareness of the implications, ambiguously
institutionalized both.

McLeod's reproaches to the developers hurt all the more because they
hit a sore spot Seubold himself had worried over since the start of the
program: how to impose consistency and control on inexperienced regional
staffs who worked for the regional administrator, not for him. Because
regional officials did much of the screening and gave much of the technical
assistance to developing plans, they tended to be taken as the source of
authoritative interpretations of the requirements of the act, and the plans
made many decisions based on their advice. As the plans became operational, or nearly so, and awaited qualification and the federal loan money
it brought, the central office developers frequently found themselves in a
painful dilemma in deciding how to handle problem cases. They could
send them along to McLeod, who would poke holes in their applications
and send them back, or they could attempt first to patch up the plans'
problems themselves, which risked exposing their own confusions, under-
cutting the regional officials, and antagonizing the plans, which had been
trying hard to do as they had been told. The former course often seemed
less painful, for it had one compensating advantage: when the application
was returned, central office developers, regional staff, and plan could unite
in deploring and denouncing McLeod's "arbitrary" judgments, thereby
disguising the implausibility of the advice the regions had given.

Some observers believed that a little conscious effort at coordination
among regions, central office developers, and qualifiers might have solved
the problem. If young HMOs were following the developers' advice on the
meaning of the law and the proper road to qualification only to apply and
learn that the qualifiers had a different understanding of the conditions,
why did developers, qualifiers, and applicants not sit down together with
the act and the rules and thrash out a reading that was acceptable to all
parties? The problem was that the act and the rules were all but worthless
for negotiating purposes. The subpart A rules, drafted before McLeod
arrived, and issued in October 1974, had deliberately left many debatable
issues unresolved in the interest of speed. The guidelines that the department
promised would resolve these problems remained on a shelf. To be useful,
guidelines would have to govern the expectations of regional staff, central

office developers, and qualifiers alike, but it was highly unlikely that they could. McLeod and his staff had drafted a set of subpart A guidelines in December 1974, but nothing had come of it; now they were preoccupied with drafting regulations of their own—dual choice, qualification, and continued regulation, all difficult and time-consuming. Nor were they inclined to try to find the time for interdivision negotiations. The developers and qualifiers were feuding, and McLeod did not think it his job to try to rescue the developers from conundrums they had created before he came on the scene. Besides, the qualification office was set up to provide an independent evaluation of the developers' work, untainted by sub rosa understandings.

Even if developers and qualifiers had been able to agree on a detailed set of guidelines, however, the General Counsel's Office might very well have marked them up and sent them back again. In practice, the guidelines, the distilled essence of the contradictions and dilemmas the regulations had passed over, could have been made legally acceptable only if the attorneys wrote them themselves. The lawyers were few and busy, however. They had many other programs to work with, the HMO program already took up an inordinate amount of their time, the dual choice battles were then raging, and they could not have shouldered such a task had they wanted to do so.

Even if the lawyers had written meticulous guidelines, however, and even if HMO officials in Washington had formed a united front at last, what was to prevent regional officials from ignoring, misinterpreting, or otherwise mangling the instructions? And even if everyone, in Washington and in the field, had agreed on the *letter* of the requirements, there was no way to avoid creeping subjectivity when it came time to apply them. Consider, for example, the statement of the "premise" behind guidelines for conduct of HMO marketing evaluations that a consulting firm designed for the benefit of the qualification staff in 1976:

> In evaluating a Plan's marketing forecast, consideration should be given (individually and in total) to the attractiveness of the product itself, the viability/appropriateness of the marketing strategy, the calibre of the personnel who will be selling the plan, the sales material/aids that will be utilized, and the dollars budgeted for the marketing effort. The marketing forecast itself reflects the *plan's* evaluation of future results based upon these various factors. The function of an *outside* reviewer is to conduct an *independent* assessment of these same factors and to estimate the effect (if any) of deficiencies and the forecast results.[72]

72. Charter Medical Development Corp., "Guidelines for Conduct of HMO Marketing Evaluations," presentation to DHEW Qualification Staff Personnel, November 4–5, 1976, in HEW files. Emphasis in original.

Some of these variables—for example, the "attractiveness" of the product and the "calibre" of sales personnel—would have remained matters of opinion no matter how lengthy and detailed guidelines might have been. Even the harder variables—the adequacy of sales material and the marketing budget, for example—could only be assessed against highly specific local conditions, on the import of which reasonable observers might well differ. The fact was that the state of the art did not—could not—permit all or even most disputes to be settled by appeal to a rule book. Subjectivity— that is, more or less educated guesses—was bound to play a part in the judgments of both developers and qualifiers. Institutionalized as they were, these subjectivities were bound to clash.

For the developers, the next best thing to guidelines—indeed perhaps a better thing—was an explanation of their absence that blamed McLeod. The real reason for the absence of guidelines, they suggested darkly, was that McLeod wanted to maintain maximum discretion to reject plans. The qualifiers, who recognized that a lengthy list of nondefinitive guidelines was not worth the time and effort required to draft them, took a different view. One might as well acknowledge the obvious, they argued—that the "process" leading from early development to qualification was highly imperfect—and then try to apply the admittedly flawed process as equitably and consistently as possible. To McLeod, equity and consistency meant applying the law thoroughly and impartially to all applicants, using discretion reasonably in the many areas where it could not be avoided, and then giving deficient plans ample opportunity to be reviewed again if and when they thought they had come into conformity with the law. When translated into review procedures, however, these protections proved extremely cumbersome. (Even the streamlined qualification review process constructed in 1977 took twenty-two pages simply to outline.) Inevitably these procedures antagonized the plans subjected to them.

Applicants for qualification initiated the process by filling out long and detailed forms providing data on all facets of their operations. After these data were submitted, a qualification case officer read them carefully. Frequently the application turned out to contain large areas of "junk," or to require extensive clarification. The case officer then drafted a letter describing in detail—often in five to ten single-spaced pages—the deficiencies of the application and requested either that the application be withdrawn or that additional information be supplied. The applicant then either gave up or replied and correspondence might continue. When the application itself was finally put in order, the qualifiers would arrange to spend a day or two at the plan on a site visit. Seeking to tap multidisciplinary skills in the evaluation, McLeod sent a team of reviewers on the visit—the generalist case officer who had handled the application and analysts who focused on marketing, health delivery, and financial aspects of the plan. After acquainting themselves firsthand with the plan, the team interrogated the plan's officials at length, probing for important weaknesses and for answers to questions left unclear in the written documents. After the visit they wrote up and submitted their reports—often long and highly detailed—to McLeod, who then met with his staff and studied and discussed them.

Frequently structural questions, especially ones bearing on the marketing and financial status of the plan, stood in the way of immediate qualification. Yet even properly structured plans were often out of compliance with various details of the HMO act. Although a plan might be qualified at this point, more typically it would receive another detailed letter explaining the deficiencies observed. The plan was then entitled to try to correct these deficiencies and request a redetermination, which meant a review of more supporting documents and another site visit by the qualification team. This time the plan might qualify, or again, deficiencies might remain and the process would drag on to still more documents and other visits.

Although the process was universally found to be frustrating and time-consuming, not all plans considered the time and effort wasted. Some executives appreciated the rigorous, multidisciplinary evaluation and explained in interviews that the planning discipline, goal clarification, and objective information they gained in the application process served them well. Some were pleased that the weeding process insured that marginal and fly-by-night operations would not receive the federal stamp of approval. Still others pointed out that the opportunity for redeterminations made it almost inevitable that well-designed plans run by committed executives would qualify eventually, so long as they had access to enough private or federal grant funds to stay solvent along the way.

Other plans—especially those that were weeded out or could not afford to stay the course—took a dim view of the process. The volume of paperwork and the amount of staff time and money required to complete it were enormous. The qualifiers often countermanded advice given to the plans by their "friends" in the regional offices. Delays were frequent—and much resented—as McLeod's small staff, attempting simultaneously to manage applications in various stages and regulation drafts, fell behind in their work. The most important source of resentment, however, was the humiliating process of being interrogated, cross-examined, lectured, graded, and, in some cases, flunked by the feds. Inevitably the qualifiers made enemies in the HMO community.

For some plans, qualification meant much more than a federal stamp of approval and expanded access to markets. These plans could remain fiscally solvent once operational only if they received the loan—up to $2.5 million—authorized by the act to cover initial operating deficits of *qualified* HMOs. The language of the law made it impossible for developers and qualifiers to remain at arm's length and still resolve loan questions. In these cases the tensions, always unpleasant, accompanying qualification grew rapidly into acute anxieties.

The HMO act authorized loans to HMOs to cover their early operating deficits. To obtain the loan, however, the plan had to be qualified as an HMO as defined by law and regulations. One criterion for qualification was that the plan be financially viable. But many plans needed the loan to attain that condition, and for many time was of the essence, for the $2.5 million could make the difference between survival and bankruptcy. The developers sat by nervously; as they saw it, the qualifiers were prepared to fiddle while their progeny burned. The qualifiers in turn were loath to trigger loans of many millions of federal dollars that would be lost if the plans failed (that is, if they turned out to be financially unsound for reasons other than lack of the loan). On the other hand, aware that some plans teetered near bankruptcy, they found themselves under strong pressure to set their reservations aside and qualify them, especially if the developers had promised a loan.

In some cases, the qualifiers stifled their questions and objections. In at least one, reported the GAO, the qualifiers "seriously questioned the fiscal soundness of an applicant but felt forced to qualify it since a loan had been approved."[73] On others they held firm. In September 1976, for instance, the developers were reported to have extended an initial development grant to a Madison, Wisconsin plan to which McLeod's office had denied qualification; "several sources" were quoted as saying "the plan hasn't a chance for survival, even with the extension."[74] As was their fate, the

73. Comptroller General, "Factors that Impede Progress," p. 23.
74. *Health Services Information*, September 13, 1976, p. 6. For a jaundiced view of the federal effort to keep the Madison plan alive, see Richard A. Justman, "The H.M.O. That Politicians Won't Let Die," *Medical Economics*, vol. 55 (December 25, 1978), pp. 41–46; about the time the article appeared, an HEW employee who had followed the plan's history closely said in an interview that the plan, which became qualified in June 1977, was "one of the clearest cases for denying qualification" the program had seen.

qualifiers were damned whether they went along or held firm. If they compromised their judgment and a plan went bankrupt or developed other problems, HEW superiors, Congress, the press, and others would want to know why the qualification office wasted $2.5 million of public money by approving it. If they held firm, they felt the wrath of the developers, whose judgments they questioned (on the two occasions when plans demanded an administrative hearing on their denial of qualification, an observer recalled, "the regional people marched right in and defended the plans"); of other HMO advocates, who blamed them for slowing down the progress of the program and for driving plans to the edge of bankruptcy; of the plans themselves, which complained that they had been given conflicting signals by HEW; and by congressional sponsors, who wanted to know why plans in their district were not good enough to qualify.

Although they had no need of federal money, the established plans, notably Kaiser, the Harvard Community Health Plan, and a few others, found the qualification process no less enervating than did their junior colleagues. Lacking an immediate financial stake in qualification, these plans resolved to wait until final regulations appeared before they weighed comprehensively the benefits and costs of attempting to qualify. As they waited and watched, they grew incredulous, for as McLeod and his staff went to work on the qualification-related regulations, they quickly hit a series of snags that insured that final rules would not be published for some time and that major questions would remain unanswered even when they did emerge.

The qualification office made no formal pronouncements for a full year after the law was signed. Finally, in December 1974 it issued proposed rules on the details of qualification. Established plans then learned with relief that the department would allow them a three-year grace period during which they could phase in the benefits a federally qualified HMO must offer. In August 1975 these rules were published in final form.

The *stakes* of qualification remained unclear, however, for not until February 1975 did the department publish its proposed rules on dual choice, and they languished in controversy until October, almost two years after the law was signed. The proposed rules on continued regulation did not emerge until December 1976, after the law had been amended, and the final rules did not appear until July 1978.

The developers had a simple explanation for the slow progress: McLeod preferred to run the office from his hip pocket and to rely on verbal communications because doing so maximized his discretion. The qualifiers, who viewed the matter differently, of course, pointed out that no one had tried to qualify HMOs according to the criteria contained in the law before and that through no fault of their own, endless sequences of complications kept arising. The clearest case in point, of course, was dual choice. And other difficulties, less volatile politically, yet extremely nettlesome conceptually and legally, arose constantly. Qualification was a regulatory function, subject to formal administrative procedures and legal review. The prospect of suits and embarrassment at administrative hearings bedeviled both the qualifiers and the PHS attorneys who would have to defend them, and threw them together in uneasy cooperation. McLeod was receiving a quick, intensive legal education. On inquiry by a plan about the consistency of some facet of its operation with the statute, he would give what he took to be a "reasonable man" reply. Listening to McLeod or reviewing correspondence, attorneys in the General Counsel's Office would then identify some hitherto unrecognized snafu and McLeod would be obliged to take back what he had said. The general counsel, the plans fumed, was a "strict constructionist." After a few such incidents, McLeod learned to check with the lawyers before answering questions that looked as if they might turn out to be extremely complex—for example, an attorney needed two and a half single-spaced pages to answer the question, "May an HMO impose copayment requirements on medically necessary health services provided other than through the HMO?"[75]—and other baffling questions arose in every application for qualification. This caution earned McLeod no new friends in the HMO community. "Why," the plans grumbled, "must he expect the general counsel to run his program for him?"

Whatever their origin, these delays and confusions had a chilling effect on the established plans. Conservative executives who prided themselves on sound, efficient business management, had never taken a nickel from the federal government, had received little but trouble from the public sector, and wished the federal government had never embraced HMOs in (as one of them put it) its bear hug, could not believe they were expected to make major changes in their organizations, benefits, rates, and more, on the strength of shifting verbal communications from Washington. Their contempt for the chaos, superimposed on their contempt for the act itself, made qualification an increasingly less attractive prospect, yet one they dared not finally reject.

No established HMOs were more unsettled by the prospect of qualifi-

---

75. Memorandum from Dave Benor, Attorney Advisor, Public Health Division, to Mr. William J. McLeod and Frank H. Seubold, Ph.D., Office for Health Maintenance Organizations, HSA, "HMOs—Issues Raised by Community Health Care Center Plan, Inc.—Your Memorandum of September 2, 1975," September 23, 1975, pp. 1–4, in HEW files.

cation than the six Kaiser plans, whose headquarters in Oakland, California had been laboring since the act passed to fashion a consensual position. Qualification would disrupt Kaiser's organization arrangements in many ways; no disruptions would prove fatal, but many would be highly annoying to doctors, administrators, and members. The prospect evoked many internal differences of opinion. At one extreme, militants urged that Kaiser turn its back on the process entirely; at the other, conciliators argued that the law was not the disaster its critics claimed and that Kaiser should make every reasonable effort to meet its terms. Many intermediate positions—"we might consider qualifying *if* HEW agrees to *x* or *y*"—were occupied between the extremes.

In 1975 a consensus developed that Kaiser should take at least preliminary steps toward qualification. A spokesman explained why:

> Kaiser didn't need federal money, and we really didn't need dual choice. So at first we thought to hell with it, we just won't qualify. But as we thought about it, we saw that this was a dangerous course. Here was a law written around Kaiser as a model and if we didn't qualify, we'd be in a position of repudiating the national government's effort to help HMOs. So if in the future Kaiser ever wanted to influence Medicare or national health insurance or whatever, we wouldn't be looked on with favor. And these were the big games in town, not the HMO bill. So we decided to delay as long as possible our qualification and in the meantime work hard for amendments to the law.

By the end of 1975, Kaiser had waited for two years, amendments had passed the House, and the Senate was expected to act shortly. Between January and June 1976 all six Kaiser plans submitted applications.

The decision did not mean that the plans were about to change their organizations without a fight. Quite the contrary; as a close observer in the GHAA put it: "Kaiser took the position that everything they did was legal and that HEW would have to take them down from there point by point." McLeod on the other hand recognized that the office's handling of Kaiser would be closely watched by smaller HMOs, would be the major test of his office's integrity, and would set a precedent. He therefore resolved to interpret the rules meticulously and hold Kaiser to them fully and impartially. The two positions set the stage for a lengthy, minor epic clash. Fortunately the range of disagreement could be narrowed quickly. The qualifiers soon established for themselves what they already suspected: the Kaiser plans were in fine financial shape and gave every appearance of being well run. The problem was "simply" that with respect to a wide range of details they appeared to be at variance with the letter of the law.

Determined to place his findings on firm legal ground, McLeod submitted to the General Counsel's Office a list of questions accompanied by his own interpretations and a request for legal opinions. Having received Edelman's replies, he felt obliged either to follow them or to persuade Edelman to change his mind. Kaiser, annoyed that McLeod was "hiding behind" the lawyers, promptly put its own legal staff to work on these questions and produced conflicting opinions. After some inconclusive exchanges, McLeod, Edelman, and the qualification staff began meeting with Kaiser attorneys and executives to narrow, point by painful point, the range of disagreement.[76] After much correspondence, repeated meetings, countless phone conversations, and many severely frayed nerves, the qualification of the Kaiser plans was announced in October 1977—one year and three months after the last of the six applications had been submitted.

The long negotiations had produced concessions by both sides, and both sides viewed them ambivalently. The Kaiser plans had qualified without accepting terms that did severe violence to their notions of responsible management; McLeod had qualified them without making endless ad hoc exceptions for the mighty Kaiser program. On the other hand, each side remained exasperated with the other. The qualifiers ruefully recalled Kaiser's view that, as one put it, "whatever Kaiser does is the way it should be done regardless of what the law says." The view of some Kaiser participants, transmitted widely by way of the GHAA and the HMO grapevine, was that McLeod was a poor manager who, instead of taking decisive stands himself, looked to the general counsel to run his office for him.

As the HMO program neared the end of its third year, the qualifiers had managed to alienate virtually everyone who cared to express an opinion about HMOs. Virtually every facet of the office had become

76. The issues separating Kaiser and the qualification office are too complex to be recounted in detail here. Among the most important were whether Kaiser could exclude from its benefit package services covered by an employer or by government programs; whether Kaiser could refuse to pay for normal child births that occurred outside its service area; whether Kaiser's service contracts could exempt the plan from liability for care in cases of strikes, riots, and the like; whether Kaiser was obliged to reverse voluntarily received surgical infertility procedures; and whether Kaiser could refuse to pay for out-of-plan emergency services received by a member within a thirty-mile radius of the plan's service area. In these cases, Kaiser spokesmen argued that the exemptions or refusals were necessary to sound management. The general counsel took the position that the terms of the act prohibited them and that the proper corrective was legislative amendments. McLeod and his staff were caught in the middle. After more than a year of correspondence and intermittent negotiations, a series of complex but mutually acceptable compromises was reached. For a list of the issues see memorandum from William J. McLeod to The Record, "Meetings with Attorneys from the Kaiser Foundation Health Plan," May 2, 1977; letter from Robert J. Erickson, Senior Vice President [Kaiser], to the Honorable Joseph A. Califano, Jr., Secretary, June 29, 1977, in HEW files.

controversial—the delayed qualification regulations, the even further delayed dual choice rules, the proposed-but-not-final continued regulation rules, the absence of guidelines, the lack of coordination between qualifiers and developers, McLeod's unwillingness to give regional staff a major role in qualification decisions, the lengthy and cumbersome application process, the humiliation HMO officials endured at being interrogated by feds, the cliffhangers while shaky plans awaited qualification before receiving a loan, the aggravations of established plans over McLeod's approach to the law and lawyers, and more. Moreover, the accumulation of complexities and delays had produced a backlog in the office; the rate at which applications arrived was accelerating and the qualifiers could not keep up with the flow. New applications sat on desks, unread, indeed unopened. Divergent theories of the true source of the backlog joined the crowded list of disputes between McLeod and the growing corps of critics. The backlog happened, McLeod argued, because his office, ludicrously understaffed, had too many things to do and too few people to do them. The backlog, his critics replied, was artificially created by McLeod, who allowed work to pile up in hopes of making a stronger case for more staff, an indicator of higher bureaucratic prominence.

To the critics, the backlog was merely a symptom of all that had gone wrong with the program since McLeod, with his devastating synthesis of power lust and bad management, had come aboard and tried to wrest control of the program from Seubold. McLeod's defenders saw the matter differently. It was not McLeod's fault, they argued, if the law was complex and demanding; if plans could not or would not live up to its terms; if HMOs insisted on submitting incomplete or junky applications to secure their place in the queue; if inexperienced regional officials gave them misleading advice; if central office enthusiasts, whose reach to the federal treasury exceeded their grasp of the intricacies of prepaid group practice, kept lavishing federal aid on flawed plans; if new and complex legal implications arose when the details of established or proposed plans were scrutinized closely; if the effort to give all applicants a fair and thorough review and a chance to mend their ways produced delays and frictions; if Kaiser was self-righteous; and if, as a result of the state of the art, none of these difficulties could be addressed without discretion, subjectivism, and improvisation.

Obliged to play a nay-sayer's role, McLeod made few friends. However, a lawyer in HEW, one of the few officials who both observed McLeod closely throughout his tenure and had no special ax to grind, defended his behavior:

The qualification office took strong stands; they did what was needed. McLeod had a clear vision of what he was supposed to do, and if he had greater problems than Seubold, it's because he was the cutting edge. It's not hard to give money away, but McLeod was in an uncharted area—what *was* fiscal soundness, really, and an acceptable rate structure, and all the rest? McLeod really knew his stuff, and he had lots of common sense. But he was out there all alone with no armor.

Most observers were far readier to deplore the slow rate of qualification than to explore the reasons behind it, and in the HMO numbers game, the number of qualified plans was the one relevant indicator of the program's progress. When the Rogers subcommittee met in July 1975, only five HMOs had qualified for loans under the act. Not until December were four of them (those that were operational) notified that they also qualified under the dual choice provision.[77] In mid-July 1976, when only eighteen plans had qualified, *Health Services Information* presented an interim evaluation of the program that read rather like an epitaph:

> "There is no federal HMO program," a source said. "There are at least two separate, independent and feuding HMO programs coordinated by an agency with no commitment to managing the effort."[78]

Conclusion: Management and Politics

The view suggested by the journalist's source—that what the HMO program mainly lacked was "good management," which presupposed a "commitment" to management hitherto missing in HEW—was a familiar one among critics of the federal HMO-building effort. The argument had at least prima facie plausibility in three areas—staffing, coordination, and organizational placement. The problems, however, were only partly bureaucratic and their solutions only partly managerial.

A seemingly simple managerial solution, one strongly urged by critics concerned about the backlog in the qualification office, was to correct the extreme imbalance in staff sizes between the developers and the qualifiers. Seubold began operations with and retained about fifty staff members (not all of whom worked on HMOs exclusively), whereas McLeod started out with a staff of only three. By the time his staff increased to roughly a dozen in 1976, delays were severe and growing worse. The understaffing of McLeod's office weakened the HMO effort at a very vulnerable point— the point where qualification, continued regulation, and dual choice rules

---

77. *Health Services Information*, December 1, 1975, p. 1.
78. Ibid., July 19, 1976, p. 1.

had to be devised and issued, where existing plans looked for advice on qualification, and where maturing plans looked for the qualification that would permit them to receive timely federal loans. McLeod made these points insistently and often. Why, then, did the department—meaning someone at the level of HSA administrator or above—not redress the imbalance?

The arguments for a larger qualification staff were well known to the HSA administrators and to their superiors because McLeod, the GAO, and various interdepartmental evaluations of the program made them repeatedly.[79] Upon consideration, however, those who addressed the problem (notably Robert Van Hoek, acting administrator of HSA from February 1975 to May 1976, and Assistant Secretary Theodore Cooper) found not only that the situation was far from simple but also that it was almost a textbook case of a problem that a manager finds a waste of time and political capital to try to resolve.

Experienced political executives quickly grow accustomed to subordinates' arguments that a larger staff is an indispensable condition of discharging their tasks and soon learn to approach such arguments skeptically. In the HMO case several specifics reinforce their natural hesitation. First, the qualification office, which performed a semiregulatory, nay-saying function, was antithetical to the PHS ethos. No one wanted to build up a large corps of regulators busy refining the details of an unpopular law. Second, until 1975 wore on and the complications of regulation-writing and application-processing became fully evident, no one saw the need for a large qualification staff. The office's burdens were expected to be relatively light. Third, by the time the size of the problem became clear, the bitterness of the interoffice fight between Seubold and McLeod had become clear too. Seubold would fight any diversion of staff from his office to McLeod's and any increase in the qualification office might damage the developers' morale. Fourth, it was not clear that more staff was the answer to the problems plaguing the qualifications office. Whatever his merits, McLeod was undeniably a casual manager and some observers suspected that he deliberately tolerated the backlog in order to dramatize his repeated requests for more staff. Fifth, the budget-minded Weinberger and OMB interpreted dissatisfaction with the pace of the

79. Three staffers in the office of the deputy assistant secretary for health planning and analysis in 1975 and 1976 recalled in interviews that they were well aware of the staff imbalance and kept writing memos to Assistant Secretary Cooper on the subject. One aide recalled meeting personally with Cooper to explain the problems to him and to warn that the deteriorating situation in the program threatened to become a scandal. All three were at a loss to explain why their warnings went unheeded.

program as a call to spend more money. That the HMO program was moving slowly and selectively was to them no reproach, and the urgency of adding staff to get the program moving (and spending) was lost on them.

Even if these problems had not existed, however, a sixth problem was virtually intractable: that of putting the right people with the right skills in the right job at the right time. Staff was not absolutely unavailable. Officials leaving the regional medical program, then being phased out, were present, and indeed, under the department's procedures had first preference for new slots. Social Security Administration staff could be detailed for a time to the qualification office, and so could regional office staff. Consultants could also be and were used for some qualification tasks. In McLeod's eyes, however, this borrowing approach only exacerbated his office's basic weakness: the lack of the full-time services of people knowledgeable about and experienced in the elements of prepaid group practice. He especially wanted top-quality, permanent staff to shore up the financing, marketing, and medical delivery facets of his multidisciplinary reviews. The nature of government personnel practices made it impossible simply to reach out and pick up such talent, however. McLeod was first obliged to describe the position in detail and to advertise it within the department, then, having received and reviewed internal applications, he was required to describe in detail the reasons why these applicants would not suffice, and then argue at length the need for an outside search. By the time the search was authorized and carried out there was no guarantee that the right people with the right skills would be between jobs or that they would be willing to trade a good job in the private sector for a middle management job in Washington at government pay. In short, McLeod was not content with what departmental managers had at hand to offer; this conflict, plus the other complications, gave the managers good reason to limit their own involvement in the issue and leave McLeod to fend for himself. Until 1976 they did so.

Even if McLeod's staff had been very large, however, none of the program's fundamental problems would have been solved. A larger qualification staff would have meant more federal officials finding more things wrong in more HMO applications more quickly, and a fuller agenda of disputes between the qualifiers and the developers.

A second managerial solution called for forceful, imposed interoffice coordination. Throughout 1975 and 1976 the developers and qualifiers were caught in a nasty, worsening feud and everyone around them knew it. Critics contended that a strong manager, having observed the problem, would have intervened with enough head-knocking to induce cooperation. What was needed, the argument runs, was an HSA administrator, or assistant secretary for health, or secretary of HEW, who was proud to be a hard charger and would never permit confusion or personal hostility to interfere with the steady implementation of programs. The department badly needed managerial types who would call subordinates in, bang their fists on the table, and make it clear in a string of lusty epithets that if problems were not resolved by noon tomorrow the troublemakers would be unemployed.

This managerial style is celebrated precisely because it is the exception that proves the rule. For better or worse, few political executives in the United States can or care to summon the imperiousness the style requires. Most, like those in charge of the HMO program between 1974 and 1976, are much too easy-going to engage in such aggressive behavior toward subordinate coworkers.

Even if managers had been willing, however, the table-pounding and head-banging would have had to be directed to some tangible purpose. The pertinent purposes in the HMO case were either drafting a set of mutually accepted *guidelines* to govern behavior or reaching agreement on each *application* for qualification. Head-knocking might have produced a set of guidelines, but they would not have been unambiguous, determinate, and capable of resolving case-by-case disputes. As a practical matter then, the aggressive manager would have had to become a permanent third participant in each particular case of disagreement between developers and qualifiers. But no hard-charging manager can be expected to immerse himself repeatedly in such minute details or to consider well spent the time it would take to do so. In reality, the general view of the assistant secretary's office, shared by most managers with an aversion to conflict, an observer pointed out, is that "the well-run bureau is the one that brings no problems to this office." Health maintenance organizations were but one of half a dozen major programs in BCHS, which was but one of four bureaus in HSA, itself one of six agencies under the assistant secretary for health.[80] A managerial solution that requires managers to act as if no other program existed or mattered is obviously no solution.

Coordination might have been improved if the HSA administrator or a higher-up had fired Seubold or McLeod and put two fast friends or at any

80. Office of the Federal Register, *United States Government Manual, 1974–75* (GPO, 1974), pp. 230–36.

rate two officials with dependably accommodating natures in their jobs. Yet this solution would work only if the development head internalized the qualifiers' norms or took his cues from them. Given the complexity of the law and regulations, this solution would limit development to a slow pace and a small scale. Moreover, in the very nature of the case, the qualifiers would examine plans with more of a track record than the developers could have seen; differences of judgment differed with the data base as well as the role and would be very hard to avoid. Alternatively, the qualifiers might be instructed to rubber-stamp the developers' work. Such a course would be good bureaucratic politics, however, only until the Congress, the GAO, the press, and other observers began asking why sizable numbers of federally qualified plans did not meet the standards of the law.

The proximate problem, in short, was neither one of staffing nor one of interoffice or interpersonal coordination; it was, instead, one of division of labor and organizational structure. The PHS's unfamiliarity with qualification-like activities and its readiness, in the rush to get the money flowing, to treat them as an afterthought produced a division of labor assigning what appeared to be coequal status to offices one of which in effect held a veto over the end product of the other. Despite the reassuring checks-and-balances imagery, the inherently conflicting missions of developers and qualifiers made any coequal arrangement unworkable.

If one accepts both the desire for checks and balances and the impossibility of a coequal division of labor, it appears in retrospect that the one workable arrangement would have vested overall control of the program in the head of the qualification office, placing the development function and its head under his authority. Had this been done, organization would have been consistent with the ultimate objective of the program—to develop qualified HMOs as defined in the act. The qualification office would have been organized and staffed first, not six months after the program began, and qualifiers, not developers, would have written the regulations that governed the qualification process. Whether guidelines subsequently proved feasible or not, the qualifiers would have settled disputed or ambiguous cases. This approach, completely alien to PHS experience, was apparently never considered, let alone discussed.

With these points in mind, it is possible to dispense quickly with a third managerial argument—that if the program had enjoyed separate bureau status instead of being buried within BCHS, its problems would have been avoided, or at any rate, more promptly and decisively handled. Separate bureau status would not, by itself, have avoided the problem of staffing or, more important, the inherent conflicts between developers and regulators that arose when the two functions were assigned equal status. The appeals of this solution were more symbolic than managerial.

The fundamental managerial problems in HEW's treatment of the HMO program were a failure to think through a basic question of division of labor between program functions and, after problems arose, a failure to impose what would necessarily have been a disruptive and controversial reorganization on the program. Such thinking and reorganizing ran deeply against the grain of accustomed PHS procedures; this is one reason why they did not happen. Yet there was no obvious reason why the secretary, the assistant secretary for health, the HSA administrator, or others (in the White House or OMB, for instance) could not have done such rethinking and reorganizing. Managers exist, after all, precisely because agencies like the PHS are *not* to be left to govern themselves according to their accustomed and comfortable procedures when they prove dysfunctional. A search for the key to the missing managerial commitment must explore managerial incentives. These are never purely or even mainly bureaucratic; instead they derive from the department's larger political environment.

One important explanation for the program's difficulties is simply that its managers did not know what they were doing. It is not a final explanation, however. Even if the managers had approached the program with expertise and élan (or with a determination to acquire them), the attitudes and actions of politicians in the Nixon and Ford White House and OMB would have led them—as in fact they did—to temper their enthusiasm rapidly.

It may be safely assumed that at any time most government programs suffer from managerial problems of one sort or another—some like those suffered by HMOs, some different; some more serious, some less. The attempt to solve such problems usually awaits the attention and intervention of what may be called a bureaucratic superior at the administrator, assistant secretary, secretary, or White House level. Yet this superior usually is in charge of at least half a dozen programs; the time and attention he can give to any one of them is limited. To repeat, in the period under discussion, HMOs were one program among half a dozen within BCHS, which was one bureau among four in the HSA, which was only one major unit among six within the PHS, which by no means exhausted HEW's health activities, excluding as it did Medicare, Medicaid, and more. In budget terms HMOs were a minor program. The $60 million anticipated for them in fiscal 1975, for example, were less than one-third of the budget of BCHS's community health centers, and less than one fourth of the budget for its maternal and child health program,[81] both of which had management problems of their own.

Addressing the problems of a program like HMOs means attracting the attention and winning the time of the bureaucratic superior, which means, in turn, making a program like HMOs stand out from the crowd. Which programs stand out, in turn, depends mainly on administration priorities— that is, the signals conveyed by the bureaucratic superior's political superiors. The signals transmitted by the Ford administration on the subject of HMOs in the period 1974–76 clearly were strong disincentives to managerial effort.

Most of HEW fared poorly in 1975. The fiscal 1976 budget composed by OMB and the Ford White House left program advocates howling in indignation and provoked the angry resignation of the assistant secretary for health, Charles Edwards. The HMO program suffered in the general onslaught.[82] In OMB, some of the same Nixon appointees who had elaborated the limited demonstration approach now pushed the demonstration logic harder. Replying to a letter from John Veneman, Budget Director James Lynn explained that OMB supported HMOs and remarked that the budget levels of 1974–75 had reflected "a limited demonstration strategy of supporting HMO demonstration in viable market and geographic areas in which no HMOs existed." This approach, he said, was better than an "extensive and expensive development strategy," for two reasons. First, one hundred and fifty HMOs existed and this showed the workability of the basic concept. Second, almost all of these HMOs had developed without federal assistance. On balance, he concluded, $18 million in the fiscal 1976 budget was quite enough for that year and the two following.[83] In short, a little pushing on the demonstration logic produced the conclusion that no further demonstration was needed; at OMB, the HMO program was a lame duck, whose life would expire with its budget commitments in 1979.

Late in the summer of 1976 HEW tried again. Fearful that the program was approaching the disaster stage, HEW Under Secretary Marjorie Lynch wrote to OMB Director Lynn requesting an extra $11,725,000 to fund

81. *The Budget of the United States Government, Fiscal Year 1975—Appendix*, p. 387.
82. See John K. Iglehart, "Ford Makes Personal Effort to Curb HEW in Asking Changes in Law to Cut Growth," *National Journal Reports*, February 8, 1975, p. 201.
83. James Lynn, "Memorandum for Jack Veneman," June 16, 1975, in OMB file RS-10/75.18, vol. 1.

new and continuing HMO projects and to add fifteen new positions to the qualification office. The OMB budget examiner who sifted the pros and cons acknowledged that HEW "had been conscientious in reviewing applications," and that this care had slowed the program and caused some funds to go unused. Yet there were arguments against the request too. Funding "all approvable grant applications," as Lynch had suggested, might signal a federal responsibility larger than a mere demonstration. Moreover, the examiner wrote, the workability of HMOs in urban and rural areas had already been demonstrated in all ten federal regions. The backlog of applications in the qualification office was "only" twenty-two, and once the grant activities ceased, fifteen staff could be moved over from that office. He added that one hundred and eleven federally supported HMOs were no better a demonstration than eighty-nine and recommended that the request be denied "with a strong reaffirmation that all Federal support will cease at the end of 1979. We believe that there is a danger of extending funding indefinitely; particularly where there are distinct stages of funding. If this reprogramming and supplemental or amendment are approved, there will be greater pressure to extend the program and authorize legislation beyond 1980."[84]

The OMB in the Nixon administration had embroidered the demonstration rationale to support its obsession with keeping federal subsidies for HMOs out of the law. The OMB in the Ford administration now embroidered the rationale further to support its obsession with ending the program altogether in 1979. Political executives in HEW were not slow to get the message.

Even if the Nixon and Ford administrations had been fully supportive of the HMO program, however, the result would have been at best a more timely and thoughtful response to its problems, not a solution to them. The technology, the technical complexity, of the administrative task guaranteed that even with exemplary administration, the program's early years would be filled with trials and errors.

A program that is not merely unfamiliar but positively alien to an agency's organizational character and routines is obviously very likely to bog down in its start-up period in delay, confusion, and controversy. The administrative task in the HMO program—to launch, nurture, bring to financial self-sufficiency, qualify, and then regulate large numbers of

84. Memorandum from Marjorie Lynch, Under Secretary of HEW, to James Lynn, Director of OMB, August 16, 1976, in OMB files R5-10/75.18, vol. 2; Budget Examiner to the Director, September 3, 1976, ibid., pp. 3–5.

comprehensive medical care enterprises, all in a period of time short enough to make a "real contribution" to containing the nation's health care costs, and all subject to a new and complex law—fell on HEW as from another planet. Understandably too, the most unfamiliar and alien elements of the job—qualifying and regulating balky plans in a PHS that valued close, harmonious relations with grateful grantees, administering loans in a PHS that rarely used them, evaluating in detail HMOs' marketworthiness in a PHS used to dealing with nonprofit or public enterprises, regulating collective bargaining and the administration of work-related health benefit plans—proved most difficult of all.

To observe that in 1974–76 HEW lacked familiarity with the technology of HMO-building is not to imply that quicker wit or deeper managerial commitment could have produced a technically correct answer. The technical problem—that no one knew how to build HMOs, especially with the machinery of the act—reflected a deeper, nontechnical problem, namely, the absence of political consensus on what HMOs were, or should be, and therefore on what an HMO-building process should look like. When Rogers, Roy, Kennedy, and their staffs parted company with the self-regulating approach to HMOs espoused by Ellwood and the Nixon administration and began fashioning a statute with safeguards and specifics, they plunged themselves willy-nilly into a rigorous exercise in rational planning, indeed an exercise not essentially different from designing a system of national health insurance. Issues that the Rogers and Kennedy subcommittees had not considered in detail before and on which wide disagreements separated many interested and attentive observers—benefit levels, staffing standards (numerical and qualitative), rate setting, enrollment practices, marketing procedures, quality review, reporting and accounting methods—had suddenly to be addressed and resolved in the HMO law. Health maintenance organizations were, by definition, comprehensive systems responsible for both the financing and the delivery of care. It followed that in attempting to write a federal HMO law, the legislators could either trust to self-equilibrating financial incentives to make the various elements cohere properly—a course they rejected—or take the elements up one by one and spell out as best they could within the limits of time, information, expertise, and agreement both the appropriate values of the variables and their appropriate relation to one another. Lacking time, information, expertise, and agreement on many key points, Congress left many issues undefined or ill defined.

When HEW's task forces began drafting regulations for the program, they were obliged to resume the work, part planning theory and part lexicography, the legislators had only begun. It soon became clear that virtually every word in the law—child, employer, health professional, community rate, medical group, dental care, and more—was subject to complicated and extended debate. Worse still, most of these terms had at least three different *types* of definition: a legal definition (what the wording of the act appeared to mean on its face), a political definition (what the legislative compromises underlying a given formulation seemed to imply), and a practical definition (what HMOs themselves meant by a term and wanted HEW to mean by it).

Left to fill in the blanks, the department tried to improvise a course of action that would satisfy both the HMO community and its political superiors. It gradually discovered, however, that its best efforts were bound to alienate both. Two general administrative approaches lay open. First, HEW could make a thoroughgoing, highly detailed effort to define terms and to answer major questions in the rules. However, leaving aside that no one knew how to define many of the act's terms or to answer many of the questions it raised, and that it would have taken virtually unlimited amounts of time and manpower to get it right, the problem remained that every step toward specificity would upset one or more HMOs whose practices or intentions were at some variance with the language HEW adopted.

On the other hand, the department could say as little as possible. But this course would anger entrepreneurs and established HMOs who wanted to know in advance the exact rules of the development and qualification games before they began to play them. In short, obliged to mediate between a heterogeneous community of HMOs and a new, confining federal statute, the department could not possibly have devised an optimal administrative solution. Highly codified rules and interpretations would have disturbed many HMOs with their lack of *flexibility*. Vaguely worded rules and interpretations would have offended many other (or indeed many of the same) HMOs by their lack of *specificity*. Like the statutes they refine, regulations are inevitably generalizations, and these generalizations inevitably presuppose and construct hybrids of real-world cases. These statutory and regulatory generalizations never fit affected interests perfectly; often they do not begin to fit well. Some interests bear up stoically as best they can. In the HMO case, by contrast, affected interests—established plans, the GHAA, Blue Cross, the AFL-CIO, and others—protested loudly, threatened to avoid the program, and insisted that the law be redrawn to conform to their various, though often highly discrepant, preferences.

Faced with this tension between specificity and flexibility, the department attempted to steer a middle course between Scylla and Charybdis. Not surprisingly, it sailed first into one, then into the other. In essence, the department attempted to say just enough to satisfy the literalists while stopping short of saying too much to antagonize plans in search of flexibility. When the HMO community's interests could be served without violence to the law, the department developed its regulations at length— open enrollment is the main case in point. When the language of the law foreclosed such discretion, HEW quoted the law and said little more—in the cases of community rating, dental benefits, and alcoholism services, for instance. This strategy allowed the subpart A regulations to appear quickly, but speed brought problems of its own. The most difficult aspects of each difficult issue were deferred to the guidelines, for which, as for Godot, the plans waited in vain. Thus HEW's strategy began by begging major questions and ended by returning to them in a vicious circle. Just as regulations that truly clarified the law could not be designed, so too guidelines to illuminate the regulations could not be, and for the same reason: no one knew how, within acceptable limits of law, expertise, staff time, and agreement, to write them.

Even if the department had somehow been able to please its heterogeneous HMO constituency, however, no conceivable administrative course would have pleased all, or even many, of its political superiors. The contradictions in the legislative product, imported into the administrative task, assured that the department would be damned whatever it did. There simply was no way to build large numbers of workable, well-designed HMOs all around the country in a short period of time under a new, selective, responsible, demanding demonstration program. Had the department charged hard ahead, playing the numbers game aggressively, it would have antagonized the general counsel (in whose favor a detailed law naturally tilts the balance of bureaucratic power and who was in this case concerned to protect the niceties of a highly detailed law), the secretary (a prime architect of the demonstration emphasis), the White House (eager to trim HEW's spending and commitments and mindful of the AMA), the AMA itself (hopeful that HMOs would progress slowly if at all), House conservatives (who remembered all the talk about a demonstration program aimed at one hundred HMOs), and the GAO (concerned about how all that money was being spent). Had it moved slowly, committing funds only to plans with a high probability of qualifying with little difficulty under the law, it would have displeased Kennedy and other liberals on his subcommittee, a fair number of House liberals, the GHAA, the trade and general media (eager to dissect another faltering program), and the GAO (wondering why the program got off to so slow a start).

The politics of the administrative process were inseparable from those of the parent political process. To attempt "goal refinement" in the administrative process—that is, to state unambiguously what the HMO effort meant—was to point to the need for "goal reconciliation"[85]—that is, the need to forge agreement among diverse constituencies with conflicting conceptions of the program. In sum, the administrative process was lengthy, cumbersome, and complex for the same reason the politics of the HMO law had been; no agreement existed among politicians and affected interests on what the federal HMO program was or should be, or indeed on what an HMO was or should be.

85. This terminology is taken from Lawrence D. Brown and Bernard J. Frieden, "Rulemaking by Improvisation: Guidelines and Goals in the Model Cities Program," *Policy Sciences*, vol. 7 (December 1976), p. 457.

CHAPTER SEVEN

The Continuing Quest
for an HMO Policy:
Consensus and Its Limits

Do you believe in evolution? Well, we got a monkey. It's evolving. The tail's a little shorter now. But it's still a young program with a long way to go.
HMO program official in HEW, interviewed early in 1979

LATE IN 1976 the ailing HMO program was born again—or so for a time it seemed. As the program lay at lowest ebb and began to be discounted even by its strongest proponents as a good idea gone hopelessly astray, three developments suddenly changed the situation significantly and—so for a time it seemed—decisively for the better.

First, on October 8, 1976, President Gerald Ford signed amendments to the Health Maintenance Organization Act of 1973.[1] These amendments (Public Law 94-460) eliminated or modified most of the provisions of the act that were most objectionable to the HMO industry. Second, in the presidential election held a month later, Democrat Jimmy Carter defeated Ford. Within a few months the two top jobs at the Department of Health, Education, and Welfare (HEW) were in the hands of Joseph Califano (secretary) and Hale Champion (under secretary), who made it clear that health maintenance organizations (HMOs) were a major priority of the executive branch at last. Whereas the Ford administration had insisted that the program was a demonstration worth no more than $18 million per year until its short life ended in 1979, the Carter administration was at pains to declare that it did not view HMOs as a demonstration, that it had no intention of calling for an end to the program, and that its budget requests would substantially exceed the tiny sums Ford had budgeted for the program.

1. The House passed its version in November 1975; the Senate acted in June 1976, and the conference committee reconciled the two measures in September.

Third, in December 1977, Califano reorganized the HMO program within HEW, moving all its components into the Office of the Assistant Secretary for Health. The secretary announced too that he would follow the advice of HMO insiders by appointing a "czar" to oversee the program. In the future the program's various divisions would all report directly to one man whose full-time responsibility was the HMO program. On March 1, 1978, Howard Veit became director-designate, that is, HMO czar.

These three developments—legislative amendments, changing political priorities, and administrative reorganization—were precisely what HMO advocates critical of the federal effort had recommended. Basking in the sudden and nearly simultaneous achievement of these gains after years of frustration, many observers hoped that the federal HMO program would finally live up to its promise. Even as these events occurred, however, old problems lingered and new ones arose. In 1980, ten years after HMOs first reached the federal agenda, and seven years after the 1973 law passed, the quest for a workable federal HMO program continued with no happy outcome in sight.

This chapter reviews the hopeful developments and the major problems, new and old, that plagued the program between 1976 and 1980. The argument, put simply, is that the power of political action and political change has proved far more limited in restoring the program to health than most observers expected. This argument in turn suggests the hypothesis, explored in the next chapter, that the program's difficulties are not, and have never been, fundamentally political. Instead, they may be inherent in the very nature of the federal HMO policy strategy.

Consensus and Amendment

As the two previous chapters explained in detail, the many compromises that were incorporated during 1971–73 in HMO legislation left the HMO industry widely and deeply depressed. As these chapters also made clear, however, the major factions within that industry were depressed for very different reasons. Paul Ellwood and his colleagues at InterStudy (the Minnesota-based research organization that had worked tirelessly to promote HMOs) were disturbed mainly by the law's disregard for the importance of flexibility and inclusiveness. The community rating requirement particularly offended them, for, as they saw it, it struck at the financial security of new, small plans. The prepaid group purists took very different positions on these questions. Community rating, most of them agreed, was both historically and morally intrinsic to the prepaid group practice (PGP) philosophy. Although they grudgingly accepted the presence of independent practice associations (IPAs) in the program, they were not happy about it and they certainly did not wish to make it easier for IPAs to join prototype plans as federally qualified HMOs. And their distaste for profit-making groups remained.

Kaiser executives, by far the most important actors in the community of established PGPs, tended to take a middle position on these issues. They definitely considered full-fledged PGPs superior to IPAs, but some of them believed that the growth of IPAs might induce greater familiarity with and acceptance of PGPs by physicians and consumers. They believed strongly in community rating, and would not oppose it outright, but they wondered if it should be required of new HMOs. As business executives who believed in sound management and preferred private to governmental capital and control, they did not dismiss the arguments for profit-making groups out of hand. But, heavily influenced by the humanitarian sentiments of the PGP movement, they worried over the connection between profits and health care.

To most of these executives, however, these arguments were largely abstract and secondary. Their major concern was with the many frictions, large and small, between the language of the law and regulations and their own long-standing, time-tested management practices. These concerns, in turn, were of comparatively minor interest to the Ellwood eclectics and the PGP purists, who were more concerned with designing and launching plans than with running them.

When one looked beyond these three factions within the HMO industry proper to the wide range of organizations with some ancillary interest in HMOs—Blue Cross, organized labor, the insurance industry, the medical schools, private medical clinics, fee-for-service group practices, and more—the list of quarrels with the law grew steadily longer. Moreover, because these positions were born of intricate admixtures of ideology and organizational self-interest, these groups tended to quarrel as bitterly with one another as they did with the HMO law.

The various factions readily agreed only on two major points: that the required basic benefit package should be trimmed, especially by deleting mental health, dental, and alcoholism and drug treatment services, and that open enrollment should be killed.[2] Thus although the entire HMO

2. The industry agreed on several less important issues, especially: that the requirement governing provision of supplemental services should be made more flexible; that the meaning and obligations of dual choice should be clarified; that the authorization ceilings for HMO grant and loan funds should be

industry agreed in general on the need for amendments and although it was collectively determined to work to secure them, the many disagreements of value and viewpoint set up grave political obstacles that complicated the design of a specific legislative agenda to fight for and bargain over. Amendments could not be limited to two areas of agreement, for each group would insist on expanding the list of amendments with one or more items of great importance to itself. Other groups would then take issue with these additional items before the impatient eyes of congressmen. Such bickering might sabotage the whole package, or, as in 1973, invite the legislators to fashion hybrids of conflicting positions that would leave matters worse off than before.

The industry's internal chaos was all the more exasperating to its leaders in 1974 and 1975 because they knew that some important legislators were overtly receptive to amendments. These congressmen could see that the established plans were snubbing the program until the law was changed, and they did not feel comfortable explaining the rationale for an HMO law with which the Kaiser plans, the prototype for the law and the source of care for about half of all HMO members in the United States, could not or would not comply. Congressman James Hastings declared that he and William Roy (who was no longer in Congress, having lost a bid for the Senate in 1974) "didn't think HMOs could ever float under this legislation."[3] Most of the other members of the House subcommittee chaired by Paul Rogers appeared to agree. Agreeing, after all, caused them no political embarrassment; most of the offending provisions had originated in the Senate and had survived the conference largely at Edward Kennedy's insistence.

If the political climate in the Rogers subcommittee offered a strong positive incentive to a unified, well-planned effort at amendments, the political climate in the Senate subcommittee chaired by Kennedy was such that nothing less than a unified, well-planned effort had the remotest hope of success. Unlike the obliging Rogers and Hastings, Kennedy and his aide Philip Caper maintained consistently that the slow progress of the law was explained by poor adminstration in HEW. The law, they argued, should have a fair chance before being judged unworkable. They would resist a

increased; that provisions of the Medicare law restricting reimbursement to HMOs for Medicare enrollees should be revised in the plans' favor; and that HMOs should receive statutory protection against planners in health system agencies and certificate-of-need regulators at the state and local levels.

3. Quoted in Elizabeth Bowman, "Changes Sought in 1973 HMO Legislation," *Congressional Quarterly Weekly Report*, August 9, 1975, p. 1772.

replay of the debates of 1972 and would resist even more strongly the reproach to their judgment and the abandonment of principle that amendments implied.

In sum, the legislative situation required, and probably would reward, a major political mobilization of the HMO industry, a well-orchestrated, one-time, all-out push to secure a package of changes in the law. Yet politics within the industry made it depressingly probable that such a concerted move would bring into the open the full range of lingering disagreements and produce a cacophony of spokesmen and suggestions that would sink the whole effort. The problem continued to be consensus.

The person most concerned with the problem was, understandably, the man whose job it was to bring politicians and HMOs together in harmony— James Doherty, legislative lobbyist for the Group Health Association of America (GHAA). One of the few HMO insiders with extensive political experience, having worked as a counsel to the House Committee on Banking and Currency and as a legislative representative for the AFL-CIO before joining the GHAA in 1970, Doherty was at once tantalized by the legislative possibilities and wryly resigned to the endless difficulties he met in constructing an agenda that his bickering constituents might all enthusiastically endorse. In the course of many meetings among what he described as "the fellowship of the persecuted" devoted to deploring the law and discussing possible administrative improvements, Doherty came to the view that HEW alone could not make the HMO act acceptable. Therefore, when he learned that the Health Insurance Association of America (HIAA) had an HMO subcommittee, Doherty suggested to its chairman that they compare notes on desirable amendments. Doherty later recalled in an interview that he had viewed amendments as a farfetched prospect: "I figured that the insurance industry and Blue Cross didn't want competition and wished HMOs would just go away. Other organizations had problems over the definition of eligible groups. Others had other problems. Even Kaiser kind of wished it would all go away—for example, they disliked the consumer board requirement." But then he compared notes with a spokesman for the health insurance industry and found, to his surprise, that the insurers' proposed amendments "were almost identical to ours. Then I asked about dual choice, which of course meant competition for the insurance industry. He said they took no position on it. I asked, what does that mean? He said, it means we'd leave it alone. Then I perked up. If we can agree on that, I figured, we can get somewhere. So we drew up an agenda."

Having constructed his preliminary agenda, Doherty set out to persuade as much of the HMO industry as possible to join as a "consensus group" to speak with one voice in support of it. Predictably, many balked. The American Group Practice Association wanted to eliminate the "principal professional activity" requirement that limited participation of fee-for-service group practices in the HMO program. Their suggestion inflamed purists in the GHAA and in the AFL-CIO. Doherty negotiated a compromise: the group would seek language requiring "substantial," but not "principal" involvement in prepaid care. InterStudy was determined to seek elimination of the community rating requirement. Obviously, the GHAA, an organization committed to community rating, and the purists, whose affection for community rating was, to put it mildly, greater than their affection for the Ellwood eclectics, could not go along. It was finally agreed that Walter McClure, InterStudy's representative, would join the group, but that his reservations about community rating (which the group sought merely to delay as a requirement for five years after a plan qualified) would be clearly labeled as his own, not the group's. Spokesmen for medical care foundations wanted a change in the language that required that a foundation establish a separate corporate entity called an HMO and then contract with it in order to qualify. Persuaded by Doherty that their preference could not be sold on Capitol Hill, they agreed on compromise language. Blue Cross strongly wished to eliminate the provision of the law requiring that one-third of an HMO's board of directors be members of the organization. After much discussion and some friendly teasing—"if you can't run the thing with two-thirds board membership, stay out of the business"—the organization agreed to withdraw the demand.

After months of negotiation and redrafting, Doherty had his battle plan in hand, and his troops assembled and rehearsed. A consensus group composed of spokesmen for Blue Cross, the American Group Practice Association, the Kaiser Foundation Health Plan, InterStudy, the American Association of Foundations for Medical Care, the Health Insurance Association of America, and others—every major organization with an interest in HMOs except, a participant chortled, the American Medical Association (AMA)—would appear before the Rogers and Kennedy subcommittees and speak with one voice on behalf of a list of amendments designed to make the federal HMO law workable at last.[4]

4. Bert Seidman, director of the department of social security of the AFL-CIO, explained that his organization supported the consensus group's package of amendments "fully . . . in their present form," but "with one exception." Seidman insisted on underscoring both his organization's unique concern with

While Doherty was pondering how to sell the package of amendments to the Congress, a casual inquiry about the feasibility of amendments came from Spencer Johnson, the aide of James Hastings, who had played a key role in designing the compromises of 1973. Doherty rushed across town to show them his package. Hastings, reassured that the HMO industry stood united behind the plan, then approached Rogers. Rogers agreed to cosponsor the amendments, and, when Hastings introduced them (House Resolution 7847) on June 12, 1975,[5] quickly put them high on the subcommittee's agenda.

One month later, the subcommittee held two days of hearings on the amendments.[6] Although some differences of opinion remained, the breadth and distinction of the consensus group's membership could not fail to impress the legislators, most of whom regarded HMOs as a promising, relatively painless approach to holding down medical costs, were concerned above all that the law be workable, and had neither the will nor the expertise to dispute in detail the insiders' definition of a workable law. Attending the hearings en bloc, but dividing their collective testimony into short individual presentations, the group explained the importance of trimming the basic benefit package, making the relationship between basic and supplemental benefits more flexible, delaying the community rating requirement, deleting open enrollment, softening the definition of an eligible medical group, and clarifying the meaning of the dual choice option. In most respects, their arguments were seconded by the General Accounting Office (GAO) and the administration.[7] Tim Lee Carter of Kentucky, a physician who had become ranking minority member of the subcommittee after Ancher Nelson of Minnesota retired in 1974, posed some sharp and lengthy questions about why, if HMOs were so desirable, they had so much trouble doing the praiseworthy things the 1973 act required of them, but his views did no more than ruffle slightly and temporarily the smooth and steady stream of consensus. By the end of July

the interpretation of the dual choice provision (see above, chapter 6) and—the one exception—its hope that the "principal professional activity" requirement, which inhibited participation of fee-for-service groups in the HMO program, would be retained. Thus, although Seidman emphasized his support for most of the consensus positions, he offered separate testimony at the hearings. See *Health Maintenance Organizations Amendments of 1975*, Hearings before the Subcommittee on Health and the Environment of the House Interstate and Foreign Commerce Committee, 94 Cong. 1 sess. (U.S. Government Printing Office, 1975), pp. 123–59, quotation at p. 124. (Hereafter Rogers Subcommittee Hearings, 1975.)

5. *Congressional Record*, June 12, 1975, pp. 18719–23.

6. Rogers Subcommittee Hearings, 1975; the volume is a modest 216 pages of testimony heard on July 14 and 15.

7. Ibid., pp. 16–41, 42–61.

the subcommittee had reached agreement on changes in the law and on September 26 the full Commerce Committee reported the amendments.[8]

The committee found three major defects in the law. First, the basic and supplemental service packages were too costly. Second, the open enrollment and community rating provisions were anticompetitive. Third, the dual choice option was confusing. To deal with the first problem, it recommended that HMOs be relieved of a requirement to offer supplemental health services to those who wished to purchase them at a cost beyond the basic benefit premium. It also deleted alcoholism and drug addiction treatment services and preventive dental care for children from the basic package and added some inexpensive prevention-oriented services to the list.[9] As a bargaining concession to Carter, who threatened to press myriad objections, the consensus group agreed to retain home health services, which they had originally hoped to delete but which, they decided, they could live with after all.

Second, the committee proposed that the open enrollment requirement be dropped altogether and that community rating be delayed for five years after an HMO became qualified. Third, it clarified the scope and the enforcement machinery of the dual choice provision. These and several other less important changes, the committee expected, would allow the program to get on track at last. Accordingly, it proposed that the program's authorization be extended by two years, and that $40 million of the sums authorized for each of fiscal years 1976 and 1977 be shifted to fiscal years 1978 and 1979, when HEW would (it was hoped) be in a better position to spend the money.[10]

The committee's views were not unanimously endorsed. Subcommittee members David Satterfield, Virginia Democrat, and Carter appended individual views to the report, arguing that it made no sense to tamper with a demonstration program so soon after it had begun, and that many of the suggested changes violated basic elements of the original HMO rationale. Carter noted that, "wisely," new preventive services had been added and home health services retained. Nevertheless he argued, "The amendments will make HMOs more profitable; unfortunately they will render the HMO concept almost unrecognizable."[11]

8. *Health Maintenance Organization Amendments of 1975*, H. Rept. 518, 94 Cong. 1 sess. (GPO, 1975).

9. Ibid., p. 23.

10. Ibid., pp. 1, 9–15.

11. Ibid., pp. 57–61, 63–64. The administration, too, reaffirmed its reservations. It would be preferable, HEW Secretary David Mathews explained, to delete community rating altogether. Mathews also objected that the committee's provision that the HMO program be administered in a "single

On November 7 the amendments came up for consideration by the full House. Satterfield and Carter restated their arguments, but the proponents' view—that ideal-type HMOs that could not be launched and could not compete were of little practical value—was widely shared. That amendments would make the difference between a stalled, unimpressive HMO effort and a vigorous vehicle of cost-containment appears not to have been doubted. After all, it was the consensus of experts and practitioners that the 1973 law was the principal villain in the piece. Hastings pronounced the benediction: "The most important factor regarding this legislation is that it is a result of consensus—consensus by those involved in HMO development, by labor, by business, by GAO, by medicine and even by the administration."[12] The House gave forth a fulsome amen as the amendments passed without major change by a vote of 309–45.[13]

The Senate, of course, would be a much more serious obstacle. Most of the offending provisions had originated there and the two principal offenders—Edward Kennedy and his staff aide Philip Caper—were still on the job, feisty and unrepentant. Kennedy and Caper refused to acknowledge that the 1973 law had been badly drafted. The reason for the program's slow start, they argued, was that the Ford administration and HEW had bungled its administration inexcusably. The executive branch would have to straighten itself out and give the law a fair chance, they warned, before Kennedy's health subcommittee would give serious attention to amendments.

In the hands of a stubborn, respected legislator a subcommittee chairmanship is a formidable resource, and Doherty soon concluded that renewed direct efforts to change Kennedy's mind would not work. The consensus group's only hope, he decided, was to work on Kennedy's subcommittee colleagues in an effort to surround him with supporters of the amendments, isolate him, and eventually wear him down by the steady application of peer pressure.

As in the Rogers subcommittee, recruits were not difficult to enlist. Richard Schweiker of Pennsylvania, apparently displeased that his position as ranking minority member of the health subcommittee was obscured by Jacob Javits's activism, and in search of issues that he might claim as his

---

identifiable unit" in HEW violated the department's need for organizational flexibility. Predictably, the administration protested an extension of the program's life and an increase in its funding. The original five statutory years, Mathews wrote, were enough, and the $18 million for each of fiscal years 1976, 1977, and 1978 quite sufficient (pp. 35–38).

12. *Congressional Record*, November 7, 1975, p. 35505.
13. Ibid., pp. 35504–15.

own before a wider national audience, recognized both that the cost of medical care was a prominent national issue and that the competitive, market-oriented HMO strategy was an appealing, positive Republican approach. He therefore readily agreed to take the lead on behalf of the amendments in the Senate. Javits, who prided himself on practicality as well as principle, was both prepared to support the amendments and highly impressed by the stellar lineup of HMO experts assuring him that amendments would get the stalled program moving. An aide at the time recalled in an interview:

> Our view the first time out was that if you press hard enough you can make the system respond. We did tend to view the HMO lobby as self-serving—and you do tend to discount a lot of what the affected organizations say. But in 1976, look at the constituency they lined up. It was Kennedy, with what he thought was right, versus the world, an impossible position to maintain. Our view (Javits' and mine) was that if what we required wasn't catching on in the real world, let's change the requirements.

Having secured the cooperation of these two crucial subcommittee Republicans, Doherty went after some prominent Democratic liberals. Ellwood and his colleagues at the Minneapolis-based InterStudy argued the case before Minnesota's liberal Democratic Senators Hubert Humphrey and Walter Mondale. Alan Cranston of California was of course solicitous of the interests of Kaiser and other plans in his state, which housed more HMOs than any other. With Schweiker, Javits, and (as Doherty later recalled with a chuckle) "all the S.3 [Kennedy's health security plan] supporters" in favor of amendments, Kennedy found himself isolated, with only the AMA for company.

Listening to the arguments of his colleagues, Kennedy conceded that he would not wage a major fight over the requested changes in the benefit package. On open enrollment, however, he refused to give an inch. In the first place, he noted, the Marshfield Clinic had found that open enrollment raised costs per member only slightly and apparently worked no adverse effects on its competitive position.[14] In the second place, plans that might be damaged by the provision could apply, under generous statutory and administrative terms, for an HEW waiver. As for very large and secure plans, like Kaiser, it simply made no sense to argue that their competitive position would be damaged by the requirement. Kaiser, needless to say, took a different view of the matter.

14. For the Marshfield plan's own account of its experience, see *Health Maintenance Organization Amendments of 1975*, Hearings before the Subcommittee on Health of the Senate Labor and Public Welfare Committee, 94 Cong. 1 sess. (GPO, 1975), pp. 224–307.

These and related issues, which of course had been discussed at length in 1971–73, were agitated again at length at subcommittee hearings in November and December 1975. The issue had become, as a GHAA official put it, "quite personal" with Kennedy and Caper, and although (as an aide related) Kennedy's colleagues were increasingly angry at him for "rubbing their noses in open enrollment," he refused to change his stand. Finally, in May 1976, aware that Kennedy's lonely resistance might go on indefinitely, Labor and Public Welfare Committee chairman Harrison Williams, Democrat of New Jersey, scheduled the amendments for a vote and suggested a compromise on open enrollment. Williams's proposal was to impose the requirement only on plans that had either been in existence for five years, or had achieved an enrollment of 50,000 members, and in the previous fiscal year had not incurred a deficit. Moreover, the plans would only be obliged to accept a number of open enrollees equal to 4 percent of the net increase in their membership during the preceding calendar year. The plans would not be required to enroll individuals institutionalized at the time of application and could delay the effective date of benefits for open enrollees for ninety days. The HEW waiver would also be retained.[15]

Kennedy strongly opposed the compromise, which would obviously emasculate the provision, but his was decidedly a minority view.[16] A Senate aide recalled that when he was outvoted, "Kennedy said with a sort of wry smile, 'Then I move that all insurers be obliged to open enroll.' The smile just acknowledged the political impossibility of what he was saying." On June 14 the amendments came before the Senate. Kennedy made an emotional speech in favor of retaining open enrollment and voted against the amendments. They passed nonetheless by a vote of 80 to 8, the opposition consisting of Kennedy, Democrat Gaylord Nelson of Wisconsin, and six conservative Republicans.[17]

In July the members of the conference committee met to discuss forty-four discrepancies between the two bills.[18] As in the conference of 1973, differences were numerous. This time, however, the disagreements on most provisions were small and compromises came, for the most part, swiftly and consensually. Soon the managers' staffs had reduced the list of

15. *Health Maintenance Organization Amendments of 1976*, S. Rept. 844, 94 Cong. 2 sess. (GPO, 1976), pp. 8–10, 13–14.

16. Kennedy and four other Democratic senators were outvoted by ten of their committee colleagues. Ibid., p. 12.

17. *Congressional Record*, June 14, 1976, pp. 17903–15, 18020–25. For Kennedy's statement see pp. 17909–10. The vote is at p. 18021

18. "Conference Agenda: The Health Maintenance Organization Amendments of 1976; House Bill H.R. 9019, Senate Amendment S. 1926."

unresolved issues to seventeen, of which only four were truly troublesome. The most important of these, of course, was open enrollment, which the House had simply deleted.[19] Senate subcommittee staff urged that the Senate managers insist on their version—it was "minimal, but finite" and would "reaffirm Congressional opposition to the practice of 'skimming.' "[20] The conferees compromised, retaining the Senate provision but reducing the required open enrollment from 4 percent to 3 percent of the previous year's increase. The conference committee then rapidly finished its work, which was endorsed by the Senate on September 16 and by the House on September 23.[21]

One last hurdle remained. The Ford administration's opposition to increasing the life and appropriations of the HMO program was well known, and the consensus group nervously wondered whether the president would sign amendments that authorized appropriations of $45 million for fiscal years 1977 and 1978, and $50 million for fiscal 1979. Fortune smiled on the group again, however, for prominent among White House advisers on health care were none other than John Veneman and Spencer Johnson. As aide to Hastings, Johnson had been instrumental to the group's success at the outset; now as the outcome neared, he patiently and knowledgeably explained the merits of the amendments at the White House. On October 8, Ford signed them.

The consensus group had won a very large percentage of its original aims. To be sure, mental health, home health, and alcoholism services remained in the basic benefit package, but the group's leaders had privately regarded these as loss-leader items all along. From the start it had decided against fighting the mental health provisions. An effort to eliminate them would trigger a bitter battle with the zealous mental health lobbies, and they knew that the objective was not worth the effort. Home health services had been retained as a concession to Carter in the House, and the leaders had refused to retain alcoholism services as another concession to Carter only because they were deliberately saving it to concede to Harrison Williams, a reformed alcoholic, in the Senate. Preventive dental services

---

19. The other three were a provision to exempt churches from the dual choice requirements, revisions in the conditions on an HMO's eligibility to receive Medicaid funds, and a provision authorizing grants to states to install water treatment programs. Memorandum from Phil Caper, Brian Biles, Cal Johnson, Senate Committee on Labor and Public Welfare, to Subcommittee Staff, "Subject: HMOs," July 21, 1976. The first and third issues reflected long-standing ideological battles having little to do with HMOs per se.

20. Ibid., p. 2.

21. *Congressional Record,* September 16, 1976, pp. 30759–60 (passed by voice vote); September 23, 1976, pp. 32110–13 (passed 298–29, with 1 member voting present, and 102 not voting).

for children were gone, however, and it was this service that Kaiser and the other large established plans most wished to see eliminated. Requirements governing the provision of supplemental services had also been made more flexible.

The amendments gave HMOs flexibility in contracting with community physicians for services and made it easier—though not too easy—for fee-for-service groups to qualify as HMOs by replacing the "principal professional activity" requirement with the provision that groups "as their principal professional activity engage in the coordinated practice of their profession and as a group responsibility have *substantial* responsibility for the delivery of health services to members of a health maintenance organization."[22] Community rating would be waived for four years after qualification (a compromise between the House's five-year and the Senate's three-year waiver). Open enrollment remained little more than a symbol of Congress's view that skimming was undesirable. The dual choice provision was revised explicitly to recognize the collective bargaining agent's right to reject the offer of an HMO option. The upper limits on federal support for the various stages of HMO development were increased to keep pace with inflation since 1973. Authorizations were extended, the sums were increased, and the period over which a qualified HMO was eligible for a loan was extended from three to five years. The language governing relations between HMOs and the Medicare and Medicaid programs was revised, and, as a response to scandals in California's MediCal contracts, a requirement was added making federally qualified HMOs the only HMOs eligible for Medicaid contracts. The consensus group and the HMO industry, in short, had brought off a major legislative coup.

A Rising Political Priority

A second pleasant surprise for HMO enthusiasts followed the presidential election of November 1976. Between January and June 1977 the Carter administration moved from guarded and hesitant endorsement of HMOs to a firmly articulated commitment to them. Although HMO proponents sometimes said despairingly that anything would be better than the Ford administration's HMO position, the attitude the new Carter administra-

---

22. Public Law 94-460, sec. 106(A). Emphasis added.

tion would take toward them was not immediately evident and indeed caused some anxiety. In the course of the campaign, Carter had offered the obligatory ode to HMOs as efficient modes of care worthy of federal encouragement. His advisers intimated that HMOs would play "a key role" in health care delivery and that Carter would "sharply increase" federal spending to develop them,[23] but HMOs were not central to his campaign rhetoric and he made no aggressive promises or firm budgetary commitments on their behalf.

The earliest signals from the new administration were in fact far from encouraging. For example, a twenty-six-page memorandum that assumed that cost-containment was "the most important immediate health policy issue facing the Administration," said not one word about HMOs.[24] Early in January, GHAA officials sent several memorandums to White House health staffer Joseph Onek urging that the administration declare its support for and reorganize the HMO program,[25] but the administration was unwilling to make immediate commitments. When Andrew Biemiller, director of the AFL-CIO's department of legislation, wrote to HEW Secretary Califano in February to urge additions to HMO funds in the budget about to be submitted, Califano's reply could have been ghost written by Caspar Weinberger:

> We agree that the program is a useful method of cost-containment and health care delivery. However, I feel that the funds requested in 1977 and 1978 are adequate to carry out the demonstration effort. There are no plans at this time to initiate new feasibility projects.
>
> At the end of the program's authorization it is anticipated that approximately 83 HMOs will have resulted from the Federal initiative and at maturity these HMOs will have a potential of 2,700,000 people enrolled. These results should provide an adequate nucleus for the demonstration of the HMO concept.[26]

About the time that Califano's reply was penned, the stock of the HMO program in HEW took a sudden turn for the better with the appointment of Hale Champion as under secretary. Amid a sea of HEW officials generally sympathetic but not deeply committed to HMOs, Champion was a passionate devotee. He had belonged to a Kaiser plan in California

23. Ken Rankin, "Jimmy Carter's N.H.I. Master Plan," *Physician's Management*, October 1976, pp. 38–47.

24. "Memorandum for Governor Carter—Priority Administration Decisions on Health" (n.d.), p. 1.

25. Memorandum from James F. Doherty to Mr. Joseph Onek, Carter/Mondale Transition Team, January 3, 1977; memorandum from Peter Brock to Joseph L. Onek, "Subject: HMOs," January 4, 1977.

26. Letter from Joseph A. Califano, Jr., to Mr. Andrew J. Biemiller, February 22, 1977. In a similar vein, letter from James E. Dickson III, M.D., Acting Assistant Secretary for Health, to Mr. Peter Brock, Director, Department of Education and Research, Group Health Association of America, Inc., March 4, 1977.

and was fond of pointing out that his son was born under Kaiser care. As a vice-president of Harvard University in the early 1970s, he had helped launch the Harvard Community Health Plan and had served on its board of directors. Like Veneman in 1970–71, indeed more so, Champion used his position as HEW's second-in-command to say a good word for HMOs whenever and wherever he could.

The Carter administration in 1977, like the Nixon administration in 1970–71, was urgently in search of cost-containment strategies. Unlike the Nixon administration, however, the Carter planners did not rule out regulatory approaches. In the first two months of 1977, before Champion arrived and when HMOs enjoyed no strong advocates within the administration, most HEW energies were devoted to developing a forthrightly regulatory approach, a hospital cost-containment bill that would limit to 9 percent the annual revenues hospitals could accrue and place an annual $2.5 billion ceiling on new capital expenditures for the nation's hospitals.[27] The plan, unveiled in April, showed Champion's influence by exempting HMO hospitals from the ceilings in recognition of their superior efficiency. Moreover, Champion later pointed out, the planners arrived at the specific limits contained in the bill by studying HMO experience as a model of efficiency.[28] The administration had yet to articulate an HMO strategy of its own, however.

In the spring and early summer of 1977, after the cost-containment plan was released and submitted to Congress, three forces turned HEW's attention toward HMOs. First, Champion was an ardent advocate. Second, Carter's HEW had inherited the Ford administration's problems with HMO regulations, problems considerably complicated by the amendments enacted six months earlier. In a memorandum to Califano, Assistant Secretary for Planning and Evaluation Henry Aaron pointed out the "urgent need" to get the regulations out in order to speed up HMO development grants and the qualification process. In order to avoid the lengthy delays brought on by complexity and understaffing, the department was thinking of issuing "interim" regulations that simply deleted from existing regulations language inconsistent with the amendments and replaced it with the language of the amendments themselves. This approach would suffice for the moment, Aaron reluctantly concluded, but other

27. See William L. Dunn and Bonnie Lefkowitz, "The Hospital Cost Containment Act of 1977: An Analysis of the Administration's Proposal," in Michael Zubcoff and others, eds., *Hospital Cost Containment* (New York: PRODIST, 1978), pp. 166–214.

28. Speech reprinted in *Congressional Record*, September 26, 1977, pp. 31013–14.

problems would remain. In particular, revisions would be needed in regulations governing the health systems agencies, which reviewed the need for HMO plans and facilities in the states and localities, and in the Medicare and Medicaid regulations, in order to make the department's HMO-related policies compatible at last. Aaron began chairing meetings to work on this agenda.[29]

Third, the strong opposition of hospital interests and organized medicine to the cost-containment bill, and the skeptical and even hostile reception it was encountering on Capitol Hill, especially in the House, turned administration minds, now unburdened of the cost-containment plan itself, to additional cost-containment techniques. In this respect HMOs had two important resources: Champion was a strong advocate and HMOs, unlike the proposed ceiling on hospital costs, did not require new legislation. While it awaited the fate of its major cost-containment strategy, HEW could work administratively to make the most of the HMO program and virtually everyone in and around the secretary's office thought this a good idea.

By June, Aaron and his deputy, Karen Davis, had surveyed the HMO scene in HEW and were ready to make recommendations. In a memo to Califano, Aaron explained that "the best of these organizations provide high quality care at costs far below those of conventional insurance plans," but that "the HMO format encourages abuse through 'self-dealing' by doctors, rejection of chronically ill patients, and cutting quality corners," which meant that they must be monitored rigorously. Aaron recommended that HEW move "from general support to strong affirmative action to promote high quality HMOs"—that the administration make a major public announcement of its HMO initiative, speed up the qualification process, promote HMOs more aggressively, give them more technical assistance, develop and promulgate regulations more quickly, modify Medicare and Medicaid to encourage HMO enrollment, establish the compliance monitoring function, seek legislative authority to reorganize the program, seek an extension of the duration and scope of HMO authorizations and appropriations, and modify the qualification requirements.[30]

Not everyone at HEW agreed. For example, Ellen Wormser, director of

29. Memorandum from Henry Aaron, Assistant Secretary for Planning and Evaluation, to The Secretary, "Subject: Interim Final Regulations for Health Maintenance Organizations (HMO)," April 29, 1977.

30. Memorandum from Assistant Secretary for Planning and Evaluation to The Secretary, "Subject: Health Maintenance Organizations" [early June 1977], pp. 1, 7–10.

the department's division of health budget analysis, opposed a major expansion of the program until its many lingering problems were solved and argued that "our current approach takes too long, and would appear to cost too much to justify the minimal impact achieved so far."[31] Hers was a minority view, however, and the move from "general support" to "strong affirmative action" on behalf of HMOs found strong support where it counted, that is, from Califano and Champion.

At about the time that Aaron was completing his memo, the administration made its commitment to HMOs unmistakably clear. In an emotional, flag-waving speech to a GHAA convention in Los Angeles, on June 20, Champion reassured the HMO industry that its well-being and future were executive branch priorities at last. Recalling his own credentials as an HMO supporter, Champion declared that "Secretary Califano and I don't think you are a demonstration project. We think you're for real, and we intend that you shall be treated that way." Lamenting that HMOs had often been "ill served" by HEW in the past, he promised that "we are going to try to do a whole lot better by you in the future." Deriding the Nixon administration's demonstration emphasis as "ridiculous," Champion proclaimed: "We are through with this nonsense about demonstration. We are going to get about the business of stimulating the development of more HMOs—and we're going to stay in that business!" He then spelled out the steps the department would take to prove its commitment, basically the same as those Aaron was recommending.[32] There had been no similarly enthusiastic, public statement of support for HMOs from a high executive branch official since Nixon's health message more than five years earlier, and the HMO community was understandably elated.

Califano and Champion proved their commitment to HMOs throughout 1977 and 1978. Whereas the first Carter budget, a rapidly constructed set of adjustments to the last Ford budget, retained that administration's request for $18 million for HMOs in fiscal 1978, the request for fiscal 1979 jumped to $32 million.[33] Recognizing that even substantially larger federal sums could be little more than seed money for a national HMO development effort, the HEW generalists concluded that it would be most

31. Ellen Wormser, Director, Division of Health Budget Analysis, "Note to Karen Davis; Subject: Memo from AS/PE to the Secretary, Health Maintenance Organizations," June 10, 1977, p. 1.

32. *Congressional Record*, September 26, 1977, pp. 31013–14.

33. *The Budget of the United States Government, Fiscal Year 1978—Appendix*, p. 311, and *The Budget of the United States Government, Fiscal Year 1979—Appendix*, p. 410. See also "HEW Deputy Assistant Secretary for Planning and Evaluation/Health Discusses HMOs and Health Issues," *Group Health News*, vol. 18 (June 1977), p. 2; and "President Requests $32 Million for HMOs," *Group Health News*, vol. 19 (March 1978), pp. 1–2.

productive to persuade business and labor, the major gatekeepers of capital and subscribers, to sponsor and encourage HMOs. In March 1978, therefore, Califano convened in Washington a highly publicized conference attended by "over 1200 key health figures from the public and private sectors" to celebrate the advantages of HMOs and to discuss how the private sector could support and encourage them. Califano paid humble obeisance to the notables assembled; whatever government could do to promote HMOs, he confessed, the private sector could do better. These appeals to the public interest and to corporate pride were reinforced by direct appeals to organizational self-interest. Health maintenance organizations could help hold down employers' health care premiums, it was noted, and they might well prove to be the last chance to stave off direct intervention in and regulation of health care costs and delivery by the federal government.[34]

The generalists' commitment did not flag. When the Office of Management and Budget cut $17 million for support of new HMOs from HEW's fiscal 1980 budget request, Champion was described as "outraged." The OMB, a New York Times reporter explained, was asking a "fundamental" question: "Inasmuch as Congress first authorized aid to H.M.O.'s in 1973, was it wise to commit Washington to another half-dozen years of support for a new generation of these medical groups?" Champion conceded that the question was legitimate but recalled that nonetheless: "I lost my temper. I couldn't believe it." After arguing his case at OMB, Champion prevailed: the deleted funds were restored. The administration's fiscal 1980 request called for $74 million, a 100 percent increase over the previous year. The argument that had clinched Champion's case was "that H.M.O.'s could help reduce by billions of dollars a year the cost of national health insurance."[35]

Reorganization

The amendments of 1976 and the elevated stature of the HMO program among generalists in the Carter administration "controlled for" and therefore turned a spotlight on bureaucratic performance in HEW. Unable any longer to blame the act and political indifference among its superiors,

34. "Whatever Government Can Do, Business Can Do Better: The Secretary's National HMO Conference," Group Health News, vol. 19 (April 1978), pp. 4–5; "Remarks of Joseph A. Califano, Jr., Secretary of Health, Education, and Welfare, at the National HMO Conference," Washington Hilton Hotel, March 10, 1978, especially pp. 3, 12, 15, 20, 23.

35. Edward Cowan, New York Times, December 28, 1978.

the department would have no excuses if the HMO program stayed mired in administrative confusion. Lack of coordination between developers and qualifiers, the qualification backlog, and the long delays in writing and issuing regulations were still the main problems in 1977 and the Carter administration was determined to solve them.

The Ford administration had made a few tentative efforts in 1976 to address those problems. This belated interest had followed from a political chain reaction. As the HMO spokesmen increased their pressure on Congress for amendments, and proved successful in the House, Kennedy repeatedly reaffirmed his view that HEW's poor performance, not the law, caused the program's woes. As the GAO joined Kennedy in finding fault with the administration of the program, HEW officials, especially Assistant Secretary for Health Theodore Cooper, felt obliged to protect themselves. In the spring of 1976, Cooper asked Eugene Rubel, a highly regarded official who had served as the first director of HEW's Bureau of Health Planning and Resources Department, to study the situation and report his findings and recommendations. After a month or so of shuttling back and forth between Seubold's development office and McLeod's qualification office, Rubel was astonished and appalled at the poor working relations between the two divisions and at the inconsistent advice the HMOs received. His eight-page report in June urged that the Health Services Administration finally "make a commitment to manage the program," that the regional health administrators take more interest in it, that a monitoring system be established to catch emerging problems, that clear guidelines finally be issued, and more.[36] Cooper then asked Under Secretary Marjorie Lynch to ask OMB for extra manpower for the qualification office, and he directed William Munier, head of the Office of Quality Standards in the Office of the Assistant Secretary for Health, to ride herd on the qualifiers. In the fall, Lynch made her request of OMB and Munier sent Cooper an "action plan" to reduce the qualification backlog, improve the qualification staff's skills, and implement a compliance system.[37]

Six months later, as the new administration surveyed the situation, it was clear that very little had come of Cooper's efforts. The OMB had rejected Lynch's appeal for new qualification positions.[38] Munier explained

36. Memorandum from Eugene J. Rubel, Special Assistant to the Assistant Secretary for Health, to Mr. John Kelso, Deputy Administrator, Health Services Administration, "HMO Study," June 17, 1976, quotation at p. 2.

37. Memorandum from William B. Munier, Director, Office of Quality Standards, to the Assistant Secretary for Health, "Subject: HMO Qualification and Compliance Plan—ACTION," November 15, 1976.

38. See chapter 6, above.

that despite Cooper's support, his action plan "was never implemented because of OMB budget and position cuts in the Office of the Assistant Secretary for Health and the Presidential order to eliminate all vacancies existing as of February 28." In fact, the situation had deteriorated because the qualification office had been "deluged" by new work brought on by the October 1976 amendments. The situation, Munier concluded in May 1977, could "best be summarized as an imminent disaster."[39] Thoughts naturally turned to reorganization.

Since taking office, administration health officials had been receiving advice from the GHAA on how the program ought to be reorganized. The root problem, most observers agreed, was not organizational placement or level. "I never cared *where* they put the program," Doherty recalled, adding that "they could put it in the South Richmond Postal Annex" for all he cared. What was needed, he explained, was to have "all the HMO staff reporting to one man with full-time responsibilities for HMOs." The existing situation, which had Seubold's shop reporting to the head of the Bureau of Medical Services in the HSA and McLeod reporting to the head of the Office of Quality Standards in the Office of the Assistant Secretary for Health, violated this principle twice over. Not only were the two components housed in two separate units, but the feuding Seubold and McLeod each reported to superiors who had many pressing duties besides HMOs. What was needed, the critics contended, was an HMO czar.

Califano's immediate response to these organizational difficulties was to appoint Milton Roemer, professor at UCLA, physician, and respected authority on HMOs, to study the program and recommend improvements. Roemer's report, presented in August, supported the czar theory. As a temporary measure, Roemer argued, Califano should establish a special office of HMO development in the Office of the Assistant Secretary for Health. The office should be headed by "a mature physician who commands wide respect for his knowledge and experience with HMOs," and both developers and qualifiers should report to him. Later, the entire program might be transferred to a major operating agency of the Public Health Service, preferably the Health Resources Administration, and preferably with bureau status.[40]

Roemer urged too that the new office contain a division of HMO promotion. Considering the number of local trade unions, general hospi-

39. Memorandum from William B. Munier to Consultant, Office of the Assistant Secretary for Health, "Subject: Status Report on the Health Maintenance Organization Qualification and Compliance (HMOQ&C) Activity—INFORMATION," May 17, 1977, quotations at pp. 2 and 4.

40. Milton I. Roemer, Consultant, "Moving Ahead with HMO Development," University of California, Los Angeles, August 1, 1977. pp. 11–12, 16–17.

tals, physicians in group practice, medical schools, Blue Cross plans, insurance companies, and industries, it seemed to him a waste that of these "thousands of potential sponsors, only a few hundred have been educated and stimulated by the HMO central and regional staffs to undertake the effort of planning an HMO."[41] Aggressive HMO promotion was in order; this would require "zealous," "energetic," "inspired" leadership.[42]

Persuaded by Roemer's report, Califano began searching for a prominent figure to become director of a unified program, but he was turned down by a series of "heavyweights."[43] In December, while the search for a director continued, the HMO program was both unified and elevated in the course of a departmental reorganization: a new Office of HMOs, consisting of a division of HMO development and a division of HMO qualification and compliance was created in the Office of the Assistant Secretary for Health.[44] In February, Califano announced that the long search for a director of the new office had ended in success: Howard Veit, a former executive of the Harvard Community Health Plan, then serving as assistant commissioner for health regulation in the Massachusetts Department of Public Health, had accepted the job. Those who had hoped that an eminent figure with national credentials would be named had some reservations about the thirty-five-year-old regulator. Nonetheless, the industry had, on balance, succeeded handsomely again: the HMO proponents had their reorganization, their elevated organizational status, and their czar.

One year after Champion's speech to the GHAA, Veit, then three months in office, went before a GHAA conference in New York City to recount his accomplishments and plans. He had proceeded with the reorganization of the HMO office, spinning off a new division of compliance from the division of qualification and complementing the division of development with a new division of promotion, which would make "aggressive efforts to sell the HMO concept throughout the nation."[45] Thirty-seven new positions had been approved for the program, and a "whole new" management team was being assembled. (This was interpreted, correctly, to mean that Seubold and McLeod were on the way out.) The qualification backlog was being reduced, several sets of regulations

41. Ibid., pp. 18–19.
42. Ibid., pp. 19, 21.
43. The term is taken from *Health Services Information*, January 23, 1978, p. 4.
44. *Federal Register*, December 2, 1977, p. 61320.
45. Howard R. Veit, "Revitalizing HMO Growth: A Report and a Challenge," in Group Health Association of America, Inc., *Proceedings of the 28th Annual Group Health Institute, June 18–21, 1978* (Washington: GHAA, 1978), p. 9.

had been published, a compliance plan was being developed at last, and officials on his staff were working with congressional committee staffs to increase the number of Medicare and Medicaid recipients in HMOs. Many obstacles remained, not least the very low recognition the HMO concept enjoyed with the American public.[46] Nonetheless, Veit expected the program to thrive at last, and many of his listeners, enspirited by the accumulated force of new legislation, rising political stature, and administrative reorganization, held similar hopeful expectations.

The Limits of Reorganization

Although the arrival of a new management team in charge of a reorganized HMO program gave considerable satisfaction to those who had observed or experienced the muddlings-through of Seubold, McLeod, and others in the Nixon and Ford years, major changes in personnel and structure inevitably produced problems of their own in a program with four years of complex, troubled history and an immediate need to prove that it had straightened out. Given the complexity of the law and the regulations; of accommodations and understandings, formal and informal, between HEW staff and more than one hundred HMOs; and, most important, of the organization-building process itself, the new occupants of the new high-level positions had to learn a great deal quickly. Unfortunately, very few of the new managers had deep practical experience with HMOs or with the federal HMO program.

It was not to be expected that the new managers would at once take firm command of the program, yet three impending tasks were especially urgent: issuing long-delayed regulations, developing the long-awaited subpart A guidelines, and writing regulations to take account of the 1976 amendments. The first two tasks had been long delayed precisely because they were extremely complicated, and the third was far from simple. Newly arrived managers could not hope to survey the situation and make quick, authoritative decisions that explained lucidly the obligations now binding on a qualified HMO, defined community rating in an acceptable fashion, set forth the criteria for the open enrollment waiver, and more.

Inevitably, the new managers delegated major portions of these tasks to the (now subordinate) "holdovers," those survivors of the Nixon-Ford

46. Ibid., pp. 9–10.

years who had the knowledge of the issues needed to draft technical language. Inevitably too, the newcomers distrusted the loyalties and capacities of the holdovers, who perceived, accurately, that they bore the stigma of having sabotaged the program in the past. This certainly was Champion's view and he was not reticent about broadcasting it—as he had in his speech to the GHAA in June 1977, for example, and to Veit. The holdovers resented these reproaches to their sincere best efforts, but they were in no position to fight back. Indeed, they knew that they were in danger of losing their jobs at any time. The bureaucratic chemistry between top-level newcomers bent on aggressively selling their program once they had rectified earlier blunders and suspect middle-level holdovers, lingering on, edgy about their reputations and job security, yet entrusted with much of the substantive work required for the selling and improving, was less than ideal.

Understandably, the new managers found themselves unable to deliver regulations and guidelines with dispatch. Before Veit arrived, the department had issued interim regulations, which, as noted above, simply deleted old regulatory language and replaced it with the text of the 1976 amendments. This action would speed up grant-giving and qualification, but it was a mere stopgap. Not until a year after the interim rules appeared, however—six months after Veit took office—did the department draft new proposed subpart A rules.[47] These rules, like the earlier version, raised many questions and elicited many anxious comments, and as of mid-1980, the final rules had yet to appear.[48] Despite feverish efforts to finish them at last, the fabled subpart A guidelines remained unissued too.

On July 25, 1978, the department at last published final rules on continued regulation of HMOs.[49] (The proposed rules had appeared in September 1976.) The text ran only to a page and a half, however, and left unanswered the major question about continued regulation: what type of compliance plan would the department impose on qualified HMOs? The absence of such a plan had been noted with ritualistic regularity in virtually every study of the program since the first HMOs qualified. The plain fact was that HEW still had very little idea whether the qualified HMOs were behaving as the law and regulations specified and what they were doing with their sizable federal loans, which under the 1978 amendments might

47. *Federal Register*, September 11, 1978, pt. 2, pp. 40376–84.
48. On July 18, 1979, the department published "interim" final regulations on subpart A. Ibid., pp. 42060–71. "Final" final regulations appeared on October 31, 1980. Ibid., pp. 72524–36.
49. Ibid., July 25, 1978, pt. 3, pp. 32254–56.

reach \$6.5 million per organization (a maximum of \$4 million for initial operation and a maximum of \$2.5 million for acquisition and construction of ambulatory facilities).[50] Nor did the department have much information whether employers were or were not complying with the dual choice requirement.

Three months after Veit took office the department announced plans for a comprehensive compliance program, which it hoped to have "fully implemented" by the beginning of 1979.[51] Unsurprisingly, the formulation of the plan proved to be highly complex and evoked nervous warnings from HMOs about the dangers of excessive reporting and overregulation. The January 1, 1979, deadline passed with no system in place. By March, the department had issued compliance regulations, transmitted an outline of a program, and developed a computer-based management information system to assemble data adequate to offer early warning signals of HMOs in financial trouble. A GAO report issued in May, however, made it clear that the program's compliance problems were not over. Some HMOs, the investigators noted, were not submitting quarterly reports containing the data the monitors needed, and "the data the division receives may not be reliable." Although compliance branch staff had been increased, the GAO thought it still might not be up to the workload. The HMO office "lacked uniform policy guidance by which to evaluate compliance," the study found, and it added that the compliance role of the regional offices had not been defined.[52]

If reorganization had little effect on the intrinsic difficulty of writing administrative language and instituting agency procedures that would at once honor the law and please the HMOs, it had even less effect on the continuing problem of bringing the behavior of HEW's regional officials assigned to the HMO program into line with central office goals. The problem was partly structural. Regional HMO personnel reported to the regional health administrators, who in turn reported to HEW's assistant secretary for health. The regional HMO officials could be brought directly under the control of the HMO central office only by disrupting the department's usual lines of authority or by constant interposition of the assistant secretary, a busy man, in the HMO activities of the ten regions.

50. Public Law 95-559, secs. 4(a) (1)-(2), 5(a).

51. *Federal Register*, June 27, 1978, pp. 27898–903; also, "HMO Compliance Plan Proposed," *Group Health News,* vol. 19 (August 1978), pp. 1, 3.

52. Comptroller General of the United States, *Health Maintenance Organizations: Federal Financing Is Adequate, But HEW Must Continue Improving Program Management* (U.S. General Accounting Office, 1979), pp. 31–36.

Structure was probably less than half the problem, however. Almost every outside appraisal of the program since its inception had pointed out that regional officials appeared for the most part to lack the background and skills needed to provide appropriate technical assistance to plans and to evaluate their potential accurately. Moreover, the time these officials devoted to HMO efforts, their understanding of the law and of the meaning of qualification, and their interest in and sympathy for the program all varied substantially from region to region.

Because the central office could not take each actual or would-be plan by the hand and guide it solicitously from planning to qualification, the regional staffs were obviously crucial to the program. They were the ports of first call for interested applicants, answered questions about the requirements of participation in the program, offered advice, and in general, represented central office to plan and plan to central office. For these reasons, despite the reorganization and the new management team, there remained a serious danger that inadequacies in the regions would undo the central office's diligence in rule-writing, in promoting new HMO development, and in monitoring compliance.

The December 1977 reorganization modified the regional role somewhat by concentrating HMO activities in a division of health care systems in each region.[53] But lack of technical expertise remained a fundamental problem. "Deficiencies in the evaluation letters to applicants in the areas of marketing and finance," were noted in almost every plan that the HMO office reviewed for qualification, an official admitted.[54] Citing such reports, the investigative staff of the House Appropriations Committee concluded in February 1978 that "in general, the regional offices lack the number and expertise of staff needed to provide good quality technical assistance to developing HMOs."[55]

The following month the GAO told the Kennedy subcommittee that as in 1976, when the agency had called attention to the problem, "few regions employ personnel with needed expertise." The same old problem remained: "few people with the desired expertise in marketing, actuarial analysis, and financial management and with a broad knowledge of prepaid health plans would work for the Federal government at the grade levels and

53. *Federal Register*, December 2, 1977, p. 61328.

54. Quoted in David A. Schmidt, Director, and C. R. Anderson, Chief, Surveys and Investigations Staff, House Appropriations Committee, "Memorandum for the Chairman, Re: Health Maintenance Organization Program Administered by the Department of Health, Education, and Welfare," February 21, 1978, p. 41.

55. Ibid., p. 42.

salaries offered."[56] These problems of knowledge, judgment, and attitude lay largely beyond the reach of reorganization and management, and by mid-1980 there was no evidence that they had been solved.[57]

If reorganization proved largely powerless to solve the deeper continuing problems of the HMO program, it also brought new problems in its wake. The most important was that the new integration of leadership under the czar was in some measure offset by a greater fragmentation of functional units within the program.

As HEW officials and HMO insiders contemplated the division of labor within the program, they increasingly saw more than the obvious need to coordinate development and qualification tasks, for both tasks were in important ways incomplete. Merely to sit back and wait to be contacted by plans in search of development funds was far too passive a posture to accomplish the HMO-building goals of Champion and other enthusiasts. The department should instead go abroad in the land and aggressively sell the HMO concept, especially to business and labor groups. In a word, large-scale HMO development presupposed the "aggressive, inspired, zealous" HMO leadership and promotion emphasized by Roemer. At the other end of the line too, it had become clear that qualification of a plan did not end its relationship with HEW. Qualification conveyed the federal government's "good housekeeping seal of approval," and, as Dr. John Smillie of Kaiser put it, "promotion of HMOs (by HEW) will have no credibility until an effective compliance program is in place."[58]

These reasonings led to the addition of divisions of promotion and compliance to the development and qualification divisions. Some observers, however, doubted that this organizational pattern, even superintended by a czar, would resolve the old interunit conflicts, and conjectured that the new fourfold division might well make matters worse. As promoters traveled about selling the HMO concept and working to stimulate the interest of labor, business, and other groups, they would find it hard to refrain from making representations as to the terms of federal aid and the probability that a group might be eligible for it. The developers must then either make good on the promoters' words or antagonize and embarrass

56. U.S. General Accounting Office, "Statement of Gregory J. Ahart, Director, Human Resources Division, Before the Subcommittee on Health and Scientific Affairs, Committee on Human Resources, United States Senate, on the Implementation of the Health Maintenance Organization Act of 1973, as Amended," March 3, 1978, pp. 10–11.

57. For an account of the problems of the regions as of mid-1979, see Comptroller General, *Health Maintenance Organizations: Federal Financing Is Adequate*, pp. 47–53.

58. Quoted in "HMO Compliance Plan Proposed," p. 3.

both them and the interested party by transmitting that nemesis of the HMO program, "conflicting signals." If the qualification process, in turn, was to retain integrity, that office must feel free to conduct independent-minded, careful reviews and to speak its piece candidly about the merits of expectant plans. If it did so, however, misunderstandings among developers, qualifiers, regional officials, and plans that had produced such antagonism under Seubold and McLeod might arise anew. Finally, the risk that the new compliance branch would interpret requirements differently from the qualifiers and try to enforce them on plans howling about changing rules of the game could not be eliminated. As before, each of the parties (now four in number) must either agree to support the understandings of the others, engage in ad hoc negotiations to reach compromises as the plans stood by waiting, or alienate one or more bureaucratic peers and infuriate the plans by offering independent, contradictory advice.

There were many theoretically appealing ways to mitigate these problems, but none was likely to prove stable in practice. Even the best and most carefully articulated regulations, for example, could not foreclose differences of opinion on matters so complex and inescapably soft as those surrounding the adequacy and future workability of an HMO, and in fact the department's HMO rules were anything but exhaustive and self-evident.

The czar might of course instruct each unit to perform its given task faithfully and take on himself the burden of coordination and negotiation. But unless the quartet worked together very harmoniously, he could expect to spend much of his managerial time resolving conflicts and soothing the egos of his deputies. Conversely, he might avert this problem by instructing the quartet to defer to one another up and down the line: developers would meet whatever pledges the promoters made, qualifiers would raise no major objections to the qualification of developing plans, and compliance monitors would inject no new or unsettling interpretations. But this course might purchase short-term peace at the price of medium- and long-term risk. Overseers of the program in OMB, the GAO, the Congress, and the media would soon be pointing out that the department had funded plans that ought never to have been developed, that its qualified plans did not meet the terms of the law, that the qualified plans were failing to remain in compliance with the law, and that HEW was doing little about all of this.

The root problem, an HMO program official suggested in 1979, was to be found in the multiple and conflicting roles the HMO office was expected to play. No office could embody simultaneously, successfully, and har-moniously the roles of promoter, developer, regulator, technical assistant, and creditor, and no conceivable reorganization scheme could avoid the tensions and trade-offs among roles. Indeed this official concluded dourly that the reorganization had in essence erected four uncoordinated offices on the foundations of two. The presence of the HMO czar did indeed place the responsibility for coordination in one place. But however much and however well the czar might embody these tensions and conflicts, he could not dispel them.

The Limits of Administration Support

The fission of divisions was symptomatic of the larger problem of the reorganized HMO program: HEW was attempting to take on new func-tions while continuing to grapple with old ones, under leadership often little familiar with the program or with HMOs, yet bent on straightening out the program and carrying it to new heights of activity and excellence in the very near future. Under the best of circumstances, these would have been difficult, probably impossible, goals to attain. In fact, the circum-stances were far from ideal. As the limits of reorganization as a solution to the program's administrative hardships grew clearer, it also became depressingly apparent that a new priority status in a new administration willing to give HMOs high-level executive support was not an automatic cure for the program's political problems, nor even a means of ensuring that other public, federally funded programs would cooperate in promoting HMOs. In the decentralized U.S. political system, characterized by sepa-ration of powers, a division of labor among three levels of a federal system, and extensive interdependence between the public and private sectors, no administration may unilaterally "set national priorities." As the first term of the Carter administration wore on, HMO proponents learned anew the lesson that Congress, state and local governments and agencies, and actions within the private sector could effectively neutralize or defeat the benefits of executive support.

Congressional and Media Oversight

In 1978, as the Rogers and Kennedy subcommittees greeted approvingly the Carter administration's efforts to reinvigorate the HMO program, a new congressional presence entered the arena with great force. In 1974,

Senator Sam Nunn, Georgia Democrat, vice-chairman of the Permanent Subcommittee on Investigations of the Governmental Affairs Committee, and an energetic staff had begun reviewing complaints against prepaid health plans in California's MediCal program. The committee's report, issued in April 1978 after extensive investigations, gave little comfort to those bent on promoting HMOs to an American public largely unfamiliar with or suspicious of them. "Almost all" of the fifty-four plans it had examined were nonprofit, tax-exempt entities "that subcontracted with for-profit corporations and partnerships owned or controlled by officers or directors of the non-profit organizations"—that is, they had "self-dealing" relationships. More important, "the quality of much of the health care—sometimes provided through non-accredited and substandard hospitals—was judged poor and even dangerous by State medical auditors." The report documented political influence by plan officials in obtaining MediCal contracts with the state; exorbitant payments for consultant services; marketing practices that were at times outlandish and "nothing more than a street hustle"; deliberate exclusion and forced disenrollment of the ill; closed clinic doors on evenings and weekends; inadequate physician staffing; indifference to these and other issues in the California state government; and costs that may have exceeded those of the fee-for-service system.[59] The subcommittee also harshly assessed HEW's monitoring of the program. Although 50 percent of the MediCal funds came from the federal government's Medicaid program, the department apparently had done little in response to a series of memorandums and reports that made it clear to HEW officials that abuses were widespread.[60]

Proponents of HMOs were irritated at several aspects of the Nunn report and most especially at its timing. Many of the abuses were old hat, they pointed out; the committee had been exploring and the press had been reporting these scandals since the subcommittee began its investigation in 1974. The committee's report acknowledged that the 1976 HMO amendments, which made only federally qualified HMOs eligible for Medicaid contracts, had done much to correct the situation. And, the proponents noted, the abuses had occurred in plans that had never been federally qualified. Thus the whole affair had little to do with the federal HMO effort. The release of the report and its revival of old horror stories,

59. *Prepaid Health Plans and Health Maintenance Organizations*, S. Rept. 749, 95 Cong. 2 sess. (GPO, 1978), pp. 3, 4, 13.

60. Ibid., pp. 29–34. Early in 1975 California began taking steps to banish shady operators from the program and improve it in other ways. The role of HEW in bringing about these changes is difficult to assess (see ibid., pp. 34–40).

they feared, could only damage the reorganized HMO program and retard efforts of its new leader to get the program on track and to promote the HMO cause.

These rebuttals did not dispose of the matter, however, for the Nunn report had some unflattering words for the federal HMO program itself. Declaring that many of the problems found in California "also exist in the Federal HMO program," it contended that the HMO law provided inadequate protection against "marketing, enrollment, and corporate structure abuses and problems," and that the program was not adequately organized and staffed to regulate HMOs so as "to assure the public of the quality medical service and fiscal integrity expected of Federally certified HMO's."[61] The report then recited the familiar litany of HEW shortcomings.

In May, Nunn, a legislator highly respected as knowledgeable and fair-minded, carried his findings to the Senate Finance Committee's subcommittee on health, then considering amendments to ease the way of Medicare recipients into HMOs. Summarizing the abuses in California and HEW's difficulties with the federal HMO program, Nunn argued that "building upon this foundation would be building on quicksand." Noting that the administration would liberalize Medicare and Medicaid reimbursement to HMOs and increase grant and loan awards to HMOs in the federal program, he quipped: "Based upon experience to date it seems as though HEW is rewriting that old saying 'double or nothing' to 'double and nothing.' For there is nothing—not a word—in the Administration's HMO bill that effectively responds to the evidence of HMO fraud and abuse."[62] Observing that the administration and HMO spokesmen sought a reimbursement formula for Medicare recipients that would pay HMOs 95 percent of the adjusted per capita cost of care in the fee-for-service system, Nunn posed an "interesting question": "Why should the Federal Government give organizations $2 million in grants and $5 million in loans to set up health maintenance organizations and then pay them an amount equal to fee-for-service for providing care to Medicare and Medicaid beneficiaries?"[63] He then reviewed a set of newly alleged abuses in the federal

61. Ibid., p. 41.

62. *Findings of Permanent Subcommittee on Investigations on Health Maintenance Organizations,* Hearings before the Subcommittee on Health of the Senate Finance Committee, 95 Cong. 2 sess. (GPO, 1978), p. 115.

63. Ibid., p. 93. Nunn's figures were those contained in the Kennedy subcommittee's report on the 1978 HMO amendments. See *Health Maintenance Organization Act Amendments of 1978,* S. Rept. 837, 95 Cong. 2 sess. (GPO, 1978), p. 2.

program, including involvement of some plan officials with organized crime, and recalled that HEW's HMO officials had conceded before his subcommittee in 1976 that they "cannot manage the HMO program properly." He then drew his conclusions: "These were the people who were really in the trenches. These were the people who managed the program. Basically, they said 'slow down' to us. Of course, that is not the official policy of HEW now. HEW is saying 'speed up.' Based upon what the people who manage the program told us, I am saying this morning that I think we ought to slow down." Subcommittee chairman Herman Talmadge, also a Georgia Democrat, thanked Nunn for "an excellent and most alarming statement."[64]

Later that day the subcommittee heard Val Halamandaris, special counsel to the House Select Committee on Aging, explain that his investigations into fraud and abuse in HEW programs had turned up many of the same problems that Nunn had described.[65] Confirmed in its longstanding opposition to the "95 percent" approach to reimbursing HMOs, the subcommittee laid the issue to rest. In June, the GAO concurred, recommending that Congress defer action on proposals intended to stimulate Medicare and Medicaid enrollments "until HEW demonstrates that it could effectively administer proposed changes in the reimbursement method and implement an effective compliance program."[66]

In July, Nunn carried his "go slow" message to the whole Senate, then considering amendments that would extend the authorization of the HMO program for five years and increase its funding to $400 million in grant authorities.[67] Fearful that the new HMO policy leader would lead a floor fight to trim the proposal and would almost certainly succeed, Schweiker and Kennedy agreed to offer jointly with Nunn an amendment reducing the length of the reauthorization from five years to three and cutting the funding levels from $400 million over the three years to $170 million. This figure, said Kennedy, was "the minimum amount needed over the next three years to maintain the program at its current pace, and to prevent HEW from defaulting on existing commitments to infant HMOs."[68] Nunn's message had effectively checked the expansionist hopes of the HEW officials and the HMO lobby.

64. Findings of Permanent Subcommittee on Investigations, Hearings, p. 109.
65. Ibid., pp. 138–47.
66. Comptroller General of the United States, Can Health Maintenance Organizations Be Successful?—An Analysis of 14 Federally Qualified "HMOs" (GAO, 1978), p. iii.
67. HMO Act Amendments of 1978, S. Rept. 837.
68. Congressional Record, daily ed., July 21, 1978, p. S11449.

Likewise, although the Senate agreed to raise the maximum grant allowed to individual HMOs for initial and continuing development from $1 million to $2 million and to raise the maximum loan sum per organization from $2.5 million to $5 million, in deference to Nunn and the GAO the legislators postponed these increases for one year to give HEW time to work out its management problems. To the new promoters, the new congressional overseers had formulated and delivered with the endorsement of the Senate a blunt message "that HEW should temper its zeal to promote rapid development of HMO's until it can prove that it can manage the program well."[69]

Three months later the media dealt the promoters' hopes yet another serious blow. On October 18, CBS newsman Dan Rather explored on the popular television show "60 Minutes" how Gunnar Frederickson, an HEW official who had supervised HMO grants in the Denver regional office, had allegedly seen "almost one and a half million dollars of taxpayer funds being misspent or siphoned off into private hands" in HMO projects in Utah and Wyoming. When Frederickson protested this "waste, perhaps even corruption" to his superiors, he became the victim of what an associate called "an administrative gang-bang" that led him to be "shunted" into a nonsensitive job in Washington, D.C., checking blueprints for hospitals on Indian reservations. Frederickson's superiors offered Rather a less than persuasive rebuttal ("Uh-hmm ... Uh-hmm ... I'm not going to get involved—I'm not going to discuss it"), and Rather closed the episode with a reminder to his national audience that "Congress has told the Administration it will not vote to expand this HMO program until scandals of the kind Frederickson was pointing to are stopped."[70] About the time of the broadcast Veit posted a small note on the office bulletin board alerting staff to it and urging them to inform him in coming weeks of any damage they thought the broadcast had done.

Finding a Place for HMOs in Other Federal Health Programs

During 1977 and 1978, the endless talk about improving coordination among the units of the HMO program was accompanied by only slightly less urgent discussions of the importance of coordinating the program with the federal government's own health care programs. The Carter administration, enamored of coordination, reorganization, and sound manage-

---

69. Ibid., p. S11454.
70. The quotations are taken from a transcript, furnished by CBS News, of the "Who Got Gunnar" segment of "60 Minutes," October 18, 1978.

ment, resolved to work out a coherent, governmentwide approach to HMO policy. As the planners set about trying to reconcile the HMO program with the federal employees health benefits plan (FEHBP), Medicaid, Medicare, and the health systems agencies apparatus set up in 1974, however, they learned that obstacles neither of their making nor in their power to eliminate prevented HMOs from finding a comfortable and supportive place in the larger federal programs.

FEHBP. The FEHBP went into operation in 1960 with 5,174,000 participants (subscribers and their dependents) and had nearly doubled its enrollment by 1978 (9,857,142, including annuitants). From the outset the plan offered PGP and IPA options—twenty-one in 1960—to federal employees in areas where such plans existed. Indeed, by the end of the decade the federal employees' experience had become a main source of data documenting the cost savings of prepaid groups.[71] However, the law and regulations governing participation of "comprehensive medical plans" (the generic term for PGPs and IPAs) in the program was at once much simpler and much more restrictive than those attached to the 1973 HMO act.[72]

This law, which contemplated such prototypes as Kaiser, the Health Insurance Plan of Greater New York, and the San Joaquin County Medical Care Foundation, excluded many organizations qualified under the terms of the HMO act. The Civil Service Commission (CSC) generally accepted mature, developed plans, not new, developing ones; seldom accommodated hybrid plans that mixed features of the PGP and the IPA; generally required that "physician specialists in group-practice prepayment plans . . . earn 75% or more of their professional income from the prepaid funds of the

71. For example, George S. Perrott, The Federal Employees Health Benefits Program: Enrollment and Utilization of Health Services, 1961–1968 (U.S. Department of Health, Education, and Welfare, Health Services and Mental Health Administration, 1971); reprinted in Health Maintenance Organizations, Hearings before the Subcommittee on Public Health and Environment of the House Interstate and Foreign Commerce Committee, 92 Cong. 2 sess. (GPO, 1972), pt. 1, pp. 244–72; George S. Perrott and Jean C. Chase, "The Federal Employees Health Benefits Program: Sixth Term Coverage and Utilization," Group Health and Welfare News: Special Supplement, October 1968; reprinted in Health Maintenance Organizations, Hearings, pp. 273–80.

72. The FEHBP statute defined a "group-practice prepayment plan" as one that offered benefits "in whole or in substantial part on a prepaid basis, with professional services thereunder provided by physicians practicing as a group in a common center or centers." A "group" meant doctors representing "at least three major medical specialties who receive all or a substantial part of their professional income from the prepaid funds." "Individual-practice prepayment plans" were defined as ones that "offer health services in whole or in substantial part on a prepaid basis, with professional services thereunder provided by individual physicians who agree, under certain conditions approved by the [Civil Service] Commission, to accept the payments provided by the plans as full payment for covered services given . . . and which plans are offered by organizations which have successfully operated similar plans before approval by the Commission of the plan in which employees may enroll." 73 Stat. 711.

medical group,"[73] which was seldom the case in the newer plans; and imposed other requirements that many newer plans did not meet. By the end of June 1976, when there were approximately 175 HMOs nationwide, 16 of them federally qualified,[74] only 40 plans were offered by the CSC,[75] and only four of these were federally qualified.[76]

In the 1976 amendments, Congress attempted to help federally qualified HMOs to gain access to federal employees (who were excluded from the scope of the dual choice requirement) by amending the FEHBP law to require that the CSC contract for a health benefits plan with "any qualified health maintenance carrier" that offered one. The definition of "qualified" came from the HMO law as amended.[77] Whether a federally qualified HMO offered "such a plan"—that is, a health benefits plan meeting the specifications set out in the FEHBP law—however, was a matter of CSC interpretation.

Throughout 1977 negotiations among the GHAA, the CSC, and HEW explored how regulations and interpretations might be broadened or softened to increase the number of qualified plans offered to federal employees. Although mindful of the limitations imposed by its enabling legislation and long-standing administrative rulings, the CSC (renamed the Office of Personnel Management in 1978) was receptive and the number of comprehensive medical plans offered increased to 64 in 1978 and 84 by mid-1980.

This willingness to add new plans was not matched by subscribers' willingness to join them. By mid-1980 only 10 percent of those covered had enrolled in a prepaid plan. Some HMO proponents pointed proudly to this figure—the HMOs offered by FEHBP enrolled more than twice the proportion of the general population enrolled in HMOs—as evidence of growth and consumer acceptance. They usually neglected to mention, however, that in 1972, when only twenty-four plans were offered, the enrollment figure had been 7.2 percent, and indeed in 1960, when the FEHBP began with twenty-one prepaid plans, 5.8 percent of its beneficiaries had enrolled in a prepaid option. Moreover, much of this enrollment is

73. Letter from Marie B. Henderson, Chief, Comprehensive Health Plans Office, to Mr. Jeffery Cohelan, Executive Director, Group Health Association of America, March 8, 1977.

74. Department of Health, Education, and Welfare, Division of Health Maintenance Organizations, "Summary of the National HMO Census of Prepaid Plans—June 1976," p. 1; *Federal Register*, February 8, 1977, pp. 8008–09.

75. U.S. Civil Service Commission, Bureau of Retirement, Insurance and Occupational Health, *Annual Report of Financial and Statistical Data for Fiscal Year Ended June 30, 1976*, p. 34.

76. Calculated from a comparison of ibid. and the list of qualified plans, with dates of qualification, in *Federal Register*, February 8, 1977, pp. 8008–09.

77. Public Law 94-460, secs. 112, 101–06.

explained by the presence of the Kaiser plans. In 1961, the Kaiser plans, then four in number, accounted for fully 50 percent of FEHBP enrollees in prepaid plans. In the 1970s, the share of the six Kaiser plans declined only slightly, reaching 44 percent in 1976, and 42 percent in mid-1980. In other words, HMO membership in FEHBP has grown more concentrated: whereas in 1961, 20 percent of the plans (four of twenty-one) accounted for 50 percent of the membership, in 1980, 7 percent of the plans (six of eighty-four) accounted for 42 percent of the membership.[78] To be sure, not all federal employees enjoy an HMO option and in some parts of the country penetration rates among those that do have risen well above these aggregate figures. Still, it can hardly be argued that HMOs have caught on among federal employees.

These trends must be all the more disheartening to HMO proponents because the government's payment system under FEHBP is often said to be ideally suited to favor the growth of HMOs. The CSC computes the average of high option subscription charges for a sample of participant plans (the Kaiser plans of Northern and Southern California represent comprehensive medical plans in the sample) and then contributes 60 percent of that average to the purchase of employee coverage. Because enrollees pay the balance of the premium, they face, in theory, a strong incentive to choose more economical plans, notably HMOs. The small increase in the HMO penetration rate—from 5.8 percent in 1960 to 10 percent in 1980 over twenty inflationary years—is a sobering measure of the efficacy of this incentive.

To those familiar with the daily details of marketing health coverage to federal employees, it was plain that however sympathetic and diligent FEHBP might be in accepting new HMOs into its ranks, the major obstacles to selling them to federal employees would remain. These obstacles had little to do with law, regulation, or coordination between HEW and CSC. They turned instead on "small" details of consumer psychology, preferences, and information. "The usual gripe," Marie Henderson, chief of the CSC's comprehensive plan division, observed in 1975, "is that these people did not realize that they would be locked into one source of care or would have a limited choice of physicians."[79] Three years later, after the amendments of 1976 and the negotiations among agencies, Robert Gettys, a close

78. Calculated from data in Civil Service Commission annual reports on the federal employees health benefits program, and summaries of enrollment, 1960–80, assembled and kindly made available by Joyce Gaynor of the Office of Personnel Management.

79. Marie B. Henderson, " 'As Others See Us': The Federal Employees Health Benefits Program," in *Proceedings of the 25th Annual Group Health Institute, June 23–25, 1975* (Washington: Group Health Association of America, 1975), pp. 249–50.

380   POLITICS AND HEALTH CARE ORGANIZATION

observer of the federal health plan, composed a long list of continuing impediments to HMO growth in the program. Federal employees tended to be poorly informed about HMOs and about how they differed from traditional health insurance. Brochures describing the plans were not sufficiently informative. The CSC's information and instructions about enrollment were slow and inefficient. Federal agencies seldom allowed HMOs to make verbal presentations to explain their plan to employees. Areas that offered HMOs usually also offered many alternatives, which complicated gathering information and making comparisons. Displays set up in federal buildings to publicize HMOs were seldom successful. Promoting HMOs in public or agency media proved costly and showed mixed results. Small plans serving only one local area suffered competitively from their inability to average higher against lower costs, as plans with larger numbers of members, and greater regional variation in costs, can do.[80] Few of these problems could be solved by interagency agreements.

Medicaid. Enrollment of the Medicaid population in HMOs has been far less impressive than FEHBP's record: in 1980 only about 270,000 of the roughly 21 million Medicaid eligibles—1.3 percent—were in HMOs. Problems between HMOs and Medicaid largely reflect the joint federal-state character of the Medicaid program. Under title XIX of the Social Security Act, states are permitted to contract with HMOs for Medicaid services, but they are not required to do so. In 1980, only sixteen states and the District of Columbia had Medicaid contracts with HMOs. Of 236 HMOs, less than one-quarter (53) had such contracts. Of 115 federally qualified HMOs in thirty-two states and the District of Columbia in June 1980, only 29 in sixteen states (including the District of Columbia) had Medicaid contracts. Although as a result of cancellations and nonrenewals of contracts with scandal-ridden plans the number of California plans under contract fell from 54 in 1974 to only 12 in 1980, these plans accounted for 41 percent of all Medicaid enrollees in HMOs.[81]

Many factors explain this unimpressive record. Financial obstacles are important: in some states Medicaid benefits and fee schedules are too limited to purchase a comprehensive range of HMO services and even in generous states, program officials and HMO executives may fail to agree on a fair capitation rate for Medicaid recipients. Federal and state laws

80. Robert Gettys, "Barriers to Effective Competition Among Health Benefit Carriers in the Federal Employees Health Benefits Program" (April 1978), in file on Federal Employees Health Benefits Program at Group Health Association of America library, Washington, D.C.
81. Health Care Financing Administration, Division of Alternative Reimbursement Systems, "Medicaid Experience Summary with HMOs and Other Prepayment Plans" (unpublished, 1980), table 4.

and regulations complicate enrollment. For example, the federal government long forbade a qualified HMO to enroll more than 50 percent of its membership among Medicare or Medicaid recipients,[82] and states generally determine Medicaid eligibility monthly, which greatly complicates bookkeeping and budgeting for HMOs accustomed to annual enrollment periods. Moreover, because few states give recipients an HMO option directly on enrollment, and Medicaid rules prevent states from releasing the names of eligibles to the plans, HMOs must shoulder an immense burden of individual marketing. "If HMOs faced this situation in groups," an executive explained, "their records would be as dismal as the Medicaid record." These obstacles need not always be decisive, but in some states the opposition of medical societies and the conservatism of politicians and civil servants inhibit negotiation. Some HMOs would avoid the Medicaid program even if there were no such constraints. Many plans, hoping to market to stable, employed, middle- and working-class groups who might be offended by a clinic atmosphere, are situated in areas inaccessible or forbidding to the poor, and few plans care to have their budgets thrown into chaos by annual political struggles over the role of Medicaid cuts in achieving a balanced state budget. But even if both states and HMOs were able and eager to pursue Medicaid enrollees, penetration might well remain small. Medicaid recipients, like the rest of the population, often view freedom of choice as a prime ingredient of a desirable health care system and are reluctant to lock themselves into one source of care.

There is very little that the federal government can do about these obstacles. A federal Medicaid official interviewed on the subject leafed contemptuously through a set of instructions he had just received from HEW higher-ups calling for an increase in the number of states with Medicaid contracts with qualified HMOs from twelve (as of May 1979) to sixteen. "Why not thirty-two? Why not forty-eight?" he asked rhetorically.

> These numbers and instructions mean nothing. The thing we have trouble explaining to people in the secretary's office is that our influence is limited. Medicaid isn't like Medicare, where you can *let a contract*. All we can do is talk

82. The 1976 HMO amendments allowed Medicare to reimburse only HMOs less than half of whose members were age 65 and over, but they also allowed HEW to waive the requirement for not more than three years. Public Law 94-460, sec. 201(a). The amendments restricted Medicaid participation to HMOs that had no more than 50 percent of their membership in Medicare or Medicaid, and allowed a three-year grace period. Sec. 202(a). In the rules published in *Federal Register*, February 10, 1978, pp. 5823–31, the department granted HMOs with Medicaid contracts an "indefinite" waiver (p. 5830) beyond the legislated three-year period, reasoning that it was "in accord with the intent of Congress that quality medical care be available to all persons" (p. 5826).

to the state Medicaid director, but he's not usually the one who makes these decisions. For instance, some states have problems reaching agreement with HMOs on a proper capitation. So we have a standing contract with an actuarial firm; if the state is interested we'll pay for them to go and consult with these actuaries. They don't have to negotiate feeling that they have to take the word of the HMO's actuary. Is there any interest in this? No. We have training sessions; the actuary comes and makes a presentation. The trouble is the technicians come and the damned decision is really political. It depends on the governor, the legislature, and interested groups getting together. The Medicaid director's influence is usually nil and so is ours. We're just kidding ourselves to think that we can suddenly change the way states view HMOs.

Medicare. Participation of Medicare beneficiaries in HMOs poses problems both less and more difficult than those presented by Medicaid. Because Medicare is a fully federal program, it need not be bound by the preferences and capacities of the states. The extreme complexity of Medicare financing tends to discourage participation in the program of plans based on prospective capitation, however.

Medicare offers retrospective reimbursement to a defined set of providers for a delimited set of services. Hospitals and other institutions are paid on the basis of costs, physicians on the basis of charges, which may be "customary" for the doctor in question and "prevailing" in the area. Both costs and charges must, however, be "reasonable."[83] Over time, Congress and HEW have spun out ever-more-elaborate definitions of these terms and ever-more-arcane techniques to measure what they denote. Program funds come mainly from three sources: social insurance contributions by employees and employers, general revenues, and out-of-pocket payments by beneficiaries.

Health maintenance organizations, by contrast, provide a wide range of services in exchange for a fixed monthly premium based on measures of costs per member per month. These costs are usually calculated under a community rating system that incorporates some degree of cross-subsidy among subscribers. Payment is prospective, not retrospective, and capitation payments supplant fees for services. Doctors are typically on salary, not paid piecemeal on the basis of prevailing, customary, reasonable, or otherwise-defined charges. The two approaches do not mesh easily.

The possible economies of HMOs and, equally important, the budgetary peace of mind derived from purchasing care for fixed sums known in advance each year have persuaded some policymakers since at least 1970 that HMOs should play a much larger role in the Medicare and Medicaid

83. For an introduction to these terms, see Robert J. Myers, *Medicare* (Irwin, 1970), chap. 7.

programs. Fully as clear as the policymakers' interest in inducing Medicare and Medicaid recipients to enter less costly modes of care, however, is the HMOs' interest in limiting the number of high utilizers, or ensuring that the plans receive a suitable compensation for taking them. This clash of interests has led to years of sporadic sparring among HMO officials, federal Medicare administrators, and legislators and their staffs. Although the debate has been waged in highly technical language, the issue, like most HMO issues, rests in fact on rather straightforward disagreements of value and interest.

The original Medicare law, tailored closely to the presuppositions of the fee-for-service, third-party-payment system, allowed HMOs to participate in the program only if they abandoned prospective capitation payments for fee-for-service, "actual cost" reimbursements for their Medicare enrollees. Officials in HMOs naturally protested that converting to fee-for-service arrangements for a subset of members was administratively costly and troublesome and that reimbursement at cost neither offered the plans incentives to recruit Medicare recipients, nor gave the recipients an incentive to join an HMO.

In 1970, the Nixon administration argued for a Medicare part C permitting prospective capitation payments to HMOs on behalf of Medicare recipients, and the House endorsed the proposal. The Senate Finance Committee, however, raised lengthy objections. Not until 1972 did the two chambers reach agreement, and the compromises enacted failed to please the HMOs.

The amendments of 1972 distinguished between established HMOs, with a track record suggesting that Medicare recipients would be in good hands, and newer, developing plans whose fitness to serve Medicare recipients could not yet be evaluated. The established plans were allowed to participate in Medicare on a "risk" or "incentive" basis—the government would make periodic capitation payments for their Medicare enrollees and later calculate each plan's allowable costs incurred for these members by comparing the HMO's costs with those incurred for comparable recipients in the fee-for-service setting. If a plan realized savings, it was rewarded by being allowed to retain up to 10 percent of them. If costs exceeded those of the comparison group, the plan would bear the losses itself. Developing HMOs, by contrast, would receive capitation payments retroactively adjusted to reflect allowable costs, with a share in neither savings nor losses.

The architects of this approach considered it a reasonable compromise.

It allowed HMOs to receive their periodic capitation payments, but protected both the government's interests and the well-being of members by insisting on retroactive payment adjustments and on separate arrangements for established and unproven plans. The HMOs objected, however, that by requiring negotiations over retroactive adjustments in payment calculated on the basis of actual costs the provision largely undid the administrative and accounting advantages of advance capitation. The essential problem, a Kaiser executive explained, was that Medicare might take two or three years to pay an efficient HMO the savings it earned. "Therefore, in order to use the 'savings,' an HMO must first estimate what they will be and then use its own funds, or funds it borrows, to finance the added benefits or lower rates it charges. To make matters worse, if an HMO's Medicare membership grew, it would never be able to catch up until the third or fourth year after it stopped growing. Thus, any significant expansion of Medicare membership by an HMO would require a substantial investment."[84] Moreover, reimbursement fine-tuned to costs offered no new incentives for the HMO to seek out Medicare enrollees and no new incentives for Medicare beneficiaries to join, for at-cost reimbursement left the HMOs no "extra" Medicare funds with which to improve their competitive edge by expanding benefits for recipients. In sum, the burdens of participation were hardly counterbalanced by the benefits,[85] and the plans largely avoided the Medicare program while continuing to argue for a reimbursement approach more consistent with their interests.

In essence, the spokesmen recommended that HMOs be paid by means of a prospective capitation rate computed as follows. First, the federal government calculates the average cost of delivering Medicare services in the HMO's service area to a population similar in composition to the Medicare beneficiaries expected to join the HMO. This computation yields the "adjusted average per capita cost" (AAPCC), 95 percent of which would be paid prospectively to the HMO. Next, using data supplied by the HMO, the government adjusts the HMO's community rate (for non-Medicare members) to reflect differences in Medicare benefits and the greater needs and utilization of the elderly. This figure is the "adjusted community rate" (ACR). The difference between the AAPCC and the ACR would go to the HMO.[86]

84. James A. Lane, personal communication, November 6, 1980.

85. Judith M. Feder, *Medicare: The Politics of Federal Hospital Insurance* (Lexington Books, 1977), pp. 131–32.

86. See "HMOs and Medicare Reimbursement," *Group Health News*, vol. 20 (March 1979), pp. 7, 9–10; James A. Lane, "Encouraging HMO Participation in Medicare and Medicaid," in *Findings of Permanent Subcommittee on Investigations*, Hearings, pp. 93–98.

Critics of this proposal raised a simple objection: if it happened that the true cost of serving Medicare beneficiaries in an HMO fell below 95 percent of the adjusted fee-for-service cost, why should the HMO enjoy a "windfall profit" at public expense? Although the data are poor and the conceptual bases for comparing HMO and fee-for-service costs unsatisfactory, the best estimate of a prepaid health research group in California, using the experience of recipients of aid to families with dependent children, is that HMO rates could reasonably be set at 83 percent of projected fee-for-service costs.[87] If this figure held for Medicare, the 95 percent rule would yield the HMOs a 12 percent "profit" on the program—an unwarranted windfall, critics contended, in a system based on reimbursement for actual costs. The HMOs argued that "the setting of the rate will involve a trade off between maximum expansion of Medicare and Medicaid membership in HMOs and minimum short-term costs to the Medicare and Medicaid programs,"[88] and held that the short-term costs are justified. After all, the Medicare program essentially entitles recipients to a claim on public funds; why should they not be allowed freely to choose to commit 95 percent of their entitled sum to an HMO?

Critics made several replies. For one thing, Medicare commits federal funds for specific and limited purposes, among which subsidizing HMO development is nowhere to be found. Subscriber premiums and contributions are only part of the Medicare fund base, and the program ought to be confined to its legislated purposes—meeting all or part of the costs incurred in the course of providing medical care to eligible persons. Furthermore, the federal government enacted a separate program to encourage HMO development. Why then, as Sam Nunn put it, should the government give HMOs millions of dollars in grants and loans to get started in hopes of realizing economies, and then pay them sums nearly equal to the fee-for-service system for caring for Medicare and Medicaid beneficiaries?[89]

In the eyes of many HMO spokesmen and not a few government officials, these arguments give excessive weight to abstract philosophizing at the expense of what should be the central point: Medicare incentives to encourage HMO growth and enrollment might save the Medicare program large sums of money over the long run. Not all critics consider this the central point, however. Although economy and efficiency are surely desirable, they acknowledge, the Medicare program should give due weight

87. Rigby Leighton, "State of California—Memorandum," in *Findings of Permanent Subcommittee on Investigations*, Hearings, p. 103.
88. Lane, "Encouraging HMO Participation," p. 95.
89. *Findings*, p. 93.

to access and quality considerations too. The fee-for-service system explicitly links individual services rendered to individual payments. Thus it is possible, at least in theory, to ensure that the beneficiary gets what he (or the government) pays for and pays for only what he gets. However, the government might pay an HMO a handsome prospective capitation fee and still wonder whether the beneficiary is receiving proper amounts and types of care. A study of prepaid plans in California noted succinctly that in such a situation "the possibility of profit maximization at the expense of quality of care exists." Of course, a properly working peer review system could reduce the risk, but in California, peer review in most of the plans studied "amounted to a system in name only."[90] The members and staffs of the committees in charge of Medicare had no wish to incorporate the errors of the MediCal program nationwide, especially when, as the GAO reported in June 1978, many qualified HMOs had only rudimentary programs of quality review and HEW had little idea what arrangements they had established.[91] The problem was really very simple, a Senate Finance Committee staffer explained: "These are public trust funds and the burden of proof is on everyone."

Spokesmen for HMOs protested that these criticisms misunderstood the nature of both their organizations and their reimbursement proposal. The problem of windfall profits used to subsidize the expansion or operations of a plan had, they pointed out, a simple solution: amendments to the Medicare law should require that HMO "savings" on Medicare be earmarked for increased benefits or lower payments for Medicare enrollees. They denied that such a requirement was "virtually unenforceable."[92] Translating savings into lower costs for supplemental Medicare coverage, an HMO executive explained, is "a dollar-for-dollar transaction and may be easily verified," and the conversion of savings into new benefits may be determined with "standard accounting methods." Earmarking also answered objections about over- and under-provision. An HMO that provided too much care to Medicare enrollees would reap no windfall profit; on the contrary, the increase in the adjusted rate would reduce or eliminate the new benefits or lower costs and therewith the incentives to induce recipients to enroll. And savings resulting from underservice would go to the Medicare enrollee, not the plan.

By 1979, the earmarking proposal and patient lobbying had won new momentum for the Medicare revisions. Although it differed with the plans

90. *Prepaid Health Plans and Health Maintenance Organizations,* S. Rept. 749, p. 34.
91. Comptroller General, *Can Health Maintenance Organizations Be Successful?* pp. 52–56.
92. Leighton, "State of California—Memorandum," p. 104.

on details, the Carter administration announced its strong support for their basic proposal.[93] The House, long supportive, remained so. In the Senate, the staff of the Finance Committee's Health Subcommittee, the main source of opposition for a decade, was increasingly isolated. Whether legislation finally would be adopted remained to be seen. Whether membership of Medicare recipients, often strongly attached to personal physicians, would increase much above its minuscule level (less than 2 percent) was uncertain.

Health Systems Agencies. Disturbed that the federal financing programs were reluctant to embrace HMOs, the plans' advocates were equally distressed that new federal regulatory programs seemed perversely intent on putting obstacles in the way of their development and growth. From 1975 on, serious conflicts arose between HMO proponents and officials of the health systems agencies (HSA) network established by the national Health Planning and Resources Development Act of 1974 (Public Law 93-641). The 1974 law built on the foundations of the comprehensive health planning agencies established in the 1960s, new, supposedly stronger, health systems agencies assigned regional jurisdiction and coordinated within each state by a state health planning and development agency and a statewide health coordinating council. The law also required that the states enact a certificate-of-need law, under which a state agency must formally confirm the community's need for new or expanded hospitals or other institutional facilities, before such projects could legally proceed. The HSAs were intended to, and often did, play an important role in certificate-of-need deliberations—a project's absence from or inconsistency with their planning documents was sometimes taken as strong prima facie evidence that the community did not need it. In the course of drawing up short-term and long-term plans that reviewed the needs of their jurisdictions and the appropriateness of existing and projected health resources, the HSAs were generally asked for their views on HMO development or expansion. Indeed, the 1973 HMO law required that HMO applications for federal aid be submitted to planning agencies for review and (if state law required it) approval.

The 1974 planning law handled HMOs ambivalently. It appeared to endorse them by listing third among ten national priorities "the development of medical group practices . . . health maintenance organizations and other organized systems for the provision of health care." It appeared to constrain them by explicitly including HMOs in the definition of "institutional health services" covered by certificate-of-need reviews. It appeared to resolve its ambivalence by requiring that HEW, HSAs, and state agencies establish review criteria that took account of the special needs and circumstances of HMOs.[94]

By 1976, HSAs in many jurisdictions were organized and at work and certificate-of-need reviews were increasingly common. No HEW regulations or guidelines defining the special criteria to guide HSA reviews of HMOs had been issued, and HMO advocates began to protest loudly that they were not receiving fair treatment at the hands of the planners and regulators. In many areas—probably most—it was clear that the staffs and boards of the planning agencies had little knowledge of, and less interest in, HMOs. Viewing them as irrelevant to their communities' needs, they failed to include them in their resource development plans and did not argue on their behalf.[95] In some cases, too, planning sessions and community meetings provided a convenient forum from which members of the local medical establishment and other critics could put in a bad word for HMOs in general or argue that the community did not need the facilities of an HMO.

Lack of HSA enthusiasm was but one among many dampers on the development of new plans, and rarely the most troublesome. Certificate-of-need reviews, however, posed a direct and tangible threat to the growth and management policies of established HMOs. Plans like Kaiser, accustomed to building their own hospitals when and where the membership base was adequate to justify them, sometimes found that certificate-of-need reviewers, in some cases abetted by HSA planners, refused them permission to build and thus artificially limited their growth. Other plans—the Group Health Association (GHA) of Washington, D.C., for example—which sought economies in building their own hospitals after years of costly reliance on community or teaching hospitals, discovered that Blue Cross and other local competitors used the certificate-of-need process successfully to oppose these projects. Newer plans too were thereby put on notice that, should they grow to the point where they could afford their own hospitals, or should they merely wish to develop new outpatient medical centers in other parts of the community, they might be thwarted by state and local planners and regulators. Equally important, certificate-of-need controls deprived all HMOs of a powerful bargaining resource—the credible threat that they would build their own beds and compete if local hospitals refused to negotiate acceptable arrangements with them.

94. Public Law 93-641, secs. 1502(3), 1531(5), 1532(c) (8).
95. See "HMOs and National Health Planning," *Group Health News*, vol. 20 (April 1979), pp. 6–7.

To the planners and regulators, all of this seemed only reasonable. Their job was to take an overview of the public interest and to evaluate proposals for construction and expansion in light of the needs of the community as a whole. Health maintenance organizations might depict themselves as self-contained, self-financed systems, but their supporters enthusiastically promised that their diffusion would have far-reaching competitive effects on the larger system. These effects—on hospital occupancy rates and charges, physician practice patterns, and more—were little understood and could not be assumed a priori to be for the better. Health maintenance organizations ought to be evaluated on the merits, exactly as others were. That someone believed that the community needed an HMO no more proved that it did than the eagerness of a hospital administrator to add a new service unit demonstrated the community's need for it. That, when viewed in perspective, the development or expansion of HMOs often appeared to be of low priority was not the planners' fault.

To the HMOs, however, the obstacles they met, and indeed the reviews themselves, often seemed absurd. Why should the federal government make a major effort to encourage the growth of cost-conscious, cost-cutting HMOs and then turn around and establish planning and regulatory bodies which, in the name of cost-containment, placed barriers in the way of HMO development? "We are part of the solution, not part of the problem," HMO advocates argued in exasperation. What the HSA and certificate-of-need regulators simply could not see, they decided, was that the internal operations and cost implications of an HMO differed radically from those of the fee-for-service, third-party-payment, cost-plus world in which the regulators worked. Many concluded darkly that the resistance they met could only be explained in one way: the planners had been captured by fee-for-service providers and the regulators were determined to exclude competition and the entry of new providers into the prevailing system. After all, the economists who proclaimed that HMOs were the proper market- and incentive-based answer to the medical cost problem also handed down the general law that regulation always worked in this devilish way.[96]

96. Evidence of HSA damage to HMO development was in much shorter supply than anecdotes. One study found that of 501 applications by HMOs for federal grant funds, 76 percent had been approved by HSA reviewers, and only 7.4 percent had been denied. (The rest were pending, waived, or otherwise uncertain.) Of 116 HSAs reviewing HMO applications, only 20 had ever recommended a denial. Of 88 applications by HMOs through the certificate-of-need process, only 8 had been rejected. The study could find "little evidence to support the contention that planning agencies have been hindering the development of HMOs." Analysis, Management and Planning, Inc., *Executive Summary: Evaluation of the Impact of Planning Agency Review Actions and Decisions on Health Maintenance Organization Development*, Contract No. 232-78-0080, Task Order No. 4 (Cambridge, Mass.: 1979), pp. 5–7, 19.

To counter opportunities for discrimination, HMO proponents urged that the 1976 HMO amendments explicitly exempt the plans from the "institutional health services" to which the certificate-of-need process applied. The Senate included such a provision in its bill, but the House did not, and at conference time a dispute arose over the proper course of action. Senate legislators and staffers favored a simple HMO exemption, but others objected to watering down the planning law in this way. It was preferable, they argued, to strengthen the law and preserve equity between HMOs and other institutions by broadening the scope of the certificate-of-need requirement to cover all outpatient, as well as inpatient services, for both HMOs and fee-for-service providers. A staff statement prepared for the conference contended that the certificate-of-need provision of the planning law was originally intended to do this, but that HEW's regulations had perversely subjected "only inpatient services (and outpatient services provided by facilities which also have inpatient services) to certificate of need." Thus, HMO outpatient services were subject to review, but "services of free standing outpatient facilities are not." An alternative to exempting HMOs from certificate of need was therefore to amend the planning law, soon coming up for reauthorization, to cover ambulatory services, "as originally intended."[97] With AMA supporters working hard to keep the unequal impact of the law intact and some legislators and staffers determined to wait and seek to expand the scope of the planning law, the simple exemption sought by the HMOs was not feasible. The 1976 HMO amendments therefore merely added some brief language to suggest that the special criteria for HMO review to be spelled out in HEW regulations "would be the responsibility of the HMO program rather than the health planning program."[98]

In May 1978 the Senate Human Resources Committee in reporting a package of amendments to the HMO act included major revisions in the certificate-of-need provisions of the planning law that would benefit HMOs.[99] Proponents of HMOs already faced a struggle with Sam Nunn over authorizations, however, and thought it risky to galvanize the opposition of the AMA and various states' rights legislators over revisions in the planning act, and therefore withdrew them. The Senate then passed HMO amendments that made no change in the planning act's treatment of HMOs.[100] One week later, however, Kennedy and Schweiker called up

97. "Conference Agenda: The Health Maintenance Organization Amendments of 1976," p. 26.

98. Ibid., p. 27; P.L. 94-460, sec. 117(a).

99. *Health Maintenance Organization Act Amendments of 1978*, S. Rept. 837, pp. 13–14.

100. *Congressional Record*, daily ed., July 21, 1978, pp. S11443–65. See p. S11445 for the proposed Health Planning Amendments and pp. S11451–52 for their deletion.

the certificate-of-need amendments separately and managed to pass them by a narrow margin.[101]

The revisions then fell victim to the vagaries of bicameralism. In the House a combination of controversy (to which the HMO-related provisions were a main contributor) and irritation over legislative tactics produced a surprise defeat for its planning act amendments[102] and the Ninety-fifth Congress closed without altering the act. The House did pass HMO amendments, however, which ironically required the conference to reconcile a Senate bill that stood silent on planning act issues and a House bill that amended section 1122 of the Social Security Act (which provided for review by state health planning agencies of capital expenditures proposed for health care facilities and HMOs) to state that "the establishment of an HMO will not be covered and . . . the development of outpatient facilities and services will be covered only to the extent that a health care facility would be covered for the same activity."[103] The Senate accepted this modest revision, the HMO industry's sole regulatory victory in the Ninety-fifth Congress.

The HMOs fared better in 1979. On April 2, HEW at long last issued final regulations that incorporated administratively many of the Senate-passed provisions of July 1978 governing certificate-of-need reviews of HMOs.[104] In September the House and Senate finally passed the health planning amendments. State certificate-of-need laws would no longer apply to the construction of ambulatory care facilities by qualified HMOs or others that met specified standards. Purchases by HMOs of major medical equipment would still come within the scope of the certificate-of-need process, but the reviewers would be required to confine themselves to limited, specific criteria that took account of the distinctive attributes and needs of HMOs. Large plans with mainly prepaid practice memberships could construct or expand their hospitals and buy equipment without undergoing review, and hospitals of smaller plans would be reviewed against special criteria.[105] In short, the HMO industry had fought free of most of the health planning process.

101. Ibid., July 27, 1978, pp. S11905–38. See pp. S11919–20 for votes on major HMO-related measures.

102. Elizabeth Wehr, "Health Planning Bill Suffers Surprise Setback," *Congressional Quarterly Weekly Report*, September 23, 1978, pp. 2542–43. A few legislators, apparently angry to see so complex and costly a bill brought up under the suspension of the rules procedure, whereby a yea vote by two-thirds of voting members might pass the bill without amendment, at the last minute voted nay, depriving the bill of the required extraordinary majority.

103. *Health Maintenance Organization Amendments of 1978*, H. Rept. 1784, 95 Cong. 2 sess. (GPO, 1978), p. 23. See P.L. 95-559, sec. 14(h).

104. *Federal Register*, April 2, 1979, pp. 19306–26.

105. Public Law 96-79, sec. 1527.

Some optimists believed that the new legislation would greatly protect and enhance the HMOs' local positions. Other observers argued, however, that even if regulators could be restrained from "discriminating" against HMOs, inducing a positive attitude toward them was quite another matter. Though the new provisions might alter or eliminate the prevailing vocabulary of indifference or opposition to HMOs, there was little chance that state and local planners and regulators would aggressively promote them, and little or nothing the federal government could do about it.

The Limits of Legislation

Severe as they were, the problems of managing and promoting the HMO program and of finding a place for HMOs in other federal programs paled in significance in the late 1970s beside the immediate problem of assuring that the federally qualified HMOs remained financially viable— that is, did not go bankrupt. In the early years of the program, it was all but universally agreed among HMO proponents that the requirements of the 1973 HMO law guaranteed that many, perhaps most, developing HMOs that dared to meet the terms of federal qualification would become uncompetitive and financially imperiled. In 1976 and 1978 the law was amended to reduce the requirements imposed on qualified plans and increase the financial aid available to them, thereby eliminating the major government-imposed risks. By 1979 it had become clear, however, that much as the federal government might try to lighten the tasks of HMO managers, it could not teach them how to run their organizations successfully, or save them from problems that fell beyond the boundaries of federal influence.

That HMO development is a precarious, risky business had been evident all along. By the end of 1976, about half of all recipients of federal development grants had fallen by the wayside for various reasons, most of which HEW officials lumped together under the vague heading of bad management.[106] At that time, only twenty-seven plans were federally qualified, in good part because the complex, controversial qualification process kept pointing to weaknesses in the applicants' financial and marketing plans. By the end of 1978, however, the new regime at HEW had raised the number of qualified plans to sixty-seven. As the qualified

106. See George B. Strumpf and Marie A. Garramone, "Why Some HMOs Develop Slowly," *Public Health Reports*, vol. 91 (November–December 1976), pp. 496–503.

plans developed track records, as HEW gathered fuller information about them, and as thoughts turned to repayment of millions of dollars of federal loans, it grew evident that many plans were struggling to make ends meet.

At about the time that Senator Nunn presented to the Senate Finance Committee, the full Senate, and the public his findings on mismanagement and abuse in California's prepaid health plans and was successfully urging Congress to insist that HEW slow down the federal HMO effort, the program was shaken further by the GAO's pessimistic estimate of the financial future of a sample of qualified HMOs. Examining fourteen federally qualified HMOs, the investigators cited many problems. None of the plans owned its own hospital, which deprived them of a source of savings some prototypes enjoyed. Most of the plans depended heavily on contracts with fee-for-service physicians for medical services, a costly way of doing business. Many appeared to be too optimistic about their future growth and about their ability to hold down costs per member. Taking advantage of federal support, some plans seemed to be underpricing their services in order to preserve a short-term competitive edge—an "ultimately disastrous pricing strategy," the GAO warned. Some suffered from combinations of inadequate planning, weak utilization controls, ineffective marketing, and weaknesses in financial management. The verdict was that only three of the fourteen plans stood a good chance of becoming financially independent within five operational years after qualification. Five had a fair chance and for six the chances were judged poor.[107]

One month later, in July 1978, the findings of the outside auditors were reinforced by an authoritative internal source, when the chief of the HMO loan branch wrote a pessimistic memo to the director of the division of development explaining the problems fifteen operational HMOs faced in managing their federal loans. One plan "may have used loan monies improperly for clinic expansion," some had fallen far short of their enrollment estimates, one was simply running out of money. Another had recently been the subject of a twenty-three-page management analysis—"mostly negative." One had projected an enrollment of 1,051 members through May 1978 but had enrolled only 112. In one, "there was no marketing data to support the estimates and hospital costs appear to be grossly underestimated"; the plan had a "grim marketing performance." In another, monitoring performance "is virtually impossible because of the lack of a realistic budget." One was about to have its qualification

107. Comptroller General, *Can Health Insurance Organizations Be Successful?* pp. 3, 27, 28–33, 34–38, 38–42, 24.

status revoked and the loan defaulted. Yet another had received notice of noncompliance because its financial projections were unacceptable and it would soon exhaust all the loan money HEW could legally provide. Two others showed apparent conflicts of interest. Moreover, some plans suffered from more than one of these problems.[108]

As the year wore on, the bad news continued. In the fall, even as Dan Rather recounted the misadventures of Gunnar Frederickson, it became unmistakably clear that the Sound Health Association of Washington, a plan that had benefited from the interest of Washington's Senator Warren Magnuson, chairman of the Senate Labor–HEW appropriations subcommittee, and one of the first plans to receive federal qualification, would fail financially despite its $2.5 million federal loan. In January 1979 the plan was taken over by Group Health Cooperative of Puget Sound, a Seattle-based prototype, and in March 1979 its federal qualification was revoked.[109]

At about the same time, the Health Alliance of Northern California, a rapidly growing, qualified HMO in San Jose, went into receivership under the direction of a state court after sustaining large losses. In June 1976 a senior case officer in McLeod's office had advised that the plan not be qualified because, among other problems, "the staff did not demonstrate that they fully appreciate the relationships among enrollment, facility staffing, and facility membership capacity."[110] The plan had nevertheless qualified in November of that year, only to run into the problems the reviewer had predicted. Another early qualifier, the Florida Health Care Plan, was also limping along, enrollment rates well below projections.

In some cases HEW had apparently allowed political considerations to prevail over substantive ones. More commonly, however, the plans ran into trouble for reasons such as inadequate utilization controls, rapid physician turnover, inaccurate market forecasts, inept marketing efforts, unattractive locations, indifferent receptions by employers or employees, and, most important, imperfect understanding of the ways in which change in one of these variables can lead to changes in others. The core problems, in short, were that HMO development is a complex, little-understood task and that both the plans' managers and the federal program's executives

108. Memorandum from Donald M. Perkins, Chief, HMO Loan Branch, to Director, DOD, "Subject: Operational HMO Loan Problems," July 17, 1978.

109. "GAO Finds HMO Program Improved But Cites Continuing Problems," *Group Health News,* vol. 20 (June 1979), p. 4.

110. Memorandum from Nancy A. Null, Senior Case Officer, to The Record, "Qualification Site Visit—Health Alliance of No. Calif., Inc.," Case No. 75-2-76, June 10 and 11, 1976, June 24, 1976, p. 10.

were frequently unacquainted with, and therefore unpleasantly surprised by, the twists and turns of the organization-building process.

Even if managers had been more experienced and better prepared to cope with variables under their control, however, other important variables lay outside it. Had the managers of the San Jose plan appreciated more fully "the relationships among enrollment, facility staffing, and facility membership capacity," the plan's course would no doubt have been smoother. On the other hand, managers could do little about its "direct competition with Kaiser of Northern California, which covered 18 percent of the local market and which maintains one of the lowest HMO premiums in the country."[111]

For all these reasons, the late 1970s found HMO staff in HEW boning up on the intricacies of bankruptcy and receivership law. Some weak HMOs will no doubt close their doors, pull the shades, and disappear. Some will probably be rescued and taken over by stronger plans, preferably as inconspicuously and quietly as possible. In any case, the perils of the qualified plans are likely to cause anxiety for some time to come and will probably ensure that the HMO program continues to appear "faltering" in spite of political and administrative efforts to steady it. The program's leaders may thus, like the hero of the film *Last Holiday,* learn the difficulties of simultaneously smiling and maintaining a stiff upper lip.

As the 1970s ended, the program could not be said to be prospering. Early in 1979 Veit wrote an internal memorandum containing the unhappy news that in the last quarter of 1978 the number of feasibility grants had fallen fifteen below projections. Only twenty-one applications had been received of the thirty-six anticipated, and of these six had been rejected. Some observers concluded that after nearly a decade of HMO momentum (albeit interrupted) most of the sponsors likely to try to launch HMOs with federal funds had made their move, and interest may simply have been exhausted. Others, however, attributed the slow rate of applications to a persistent bureaucratic problem: HEW's regional officials were not promoting the program.[112]

Despite these problems—or perhaps because of them—the program's leaders continued to concentrate energy and rhetoric on promoting and aggressively selling the HMO concept, but the prospect that uncontrollable

---

111. "GAO Finds HMO Program Improved But," p. 4.

112. Veit also remarked on a shortfall of four qualified plans below the number expected in the last quarter of 1978 and attributed it to "understaffing of trained personnel and a time delay to resolve technical problems." He pointed out too a "slight downfall in the number of enrollees in qualified HMOs," although overall enrollment in HMOs nationwide increased during 1978. *Health Services Information,* January 15, 1979, pp. 2–3.

events in the plans themselves would cast a skeptical light on the promotional effort remained strong. Even in the absence of a careful compliance-monitoring scheme, the department had by the end of 1978 sent out letters of noncompliance to sixteen of the eighty-one qualified HMOs. With a compliance scheme in place, many more problems would probably have been uncovered. The strongest evidence for this prediction came from the HMO program itself. In January 1979, a high-ranking program official noted in an interview that fully one-half of the qualified plans were expected to run into serious financial problems within two years if they did not improve their management practices soon.

Conclusion: The Limits of Consensus—and of Politics?

The first decade of the federal government's involvement with HMOs divides roughly into three periods: first, four years of debate, deliberation, and dissension on the content of HMO legislation (1970–73); second, two years of discontent with the law and its administration (1974–75); and third, four years of reconstruction, as conflicting members of the HMO industry finally reached agreement on what they wanted from the federal government and as top federal policymakers finally began following the industry's advice on most major issues (1976–79).

In response to those who argued that a short-lived demonstration program saddled with an unworkable law could never achieve its goals, Congress twice amended the law, striking most of the allegedly unworkable provisions of the 1973 act, extending the program's life, and increasing its budget. In response to those who contended that the low priority assigned to HMOs by the Nixon-Ford administrations was a major roadblock to effective implementation and program stability, the secretary and under secretary of HEW in the Carter administration, with White House support, made it clear again and again that the HMO program was here to stay and that they wanted HMOs to grow in number, size, and importance. In response to those who counseled that the program could not thrive without careful coordination between developers and qualifiers, especially the coordination imposed by a single full-time director of the program, the HMO program was reorganized and a czar position created and filled. If the bill of indictment against the federal government's role in the HMO effort was accurate, there was every reason to expect that this combination of amendment, reauthorization, increased funding, high-level executive support, and reorganization would at last make HMOs an important policy weapon, a major institutional presence, in the U.S. health care system.

Despite these efforts and contemporaneous with them, however, the HMO program was shaken by a series of heavy blows during 1978 and 1979. Both the damaging effects of these blows and the preexisting damage of which they gave evidence produced justified doubt that the program had finally found the road to success.

In February 1978, the investigative staff of the House Appropriations Committee completed a lengthy report that argued that most of the problems that had plagued the program all along—regional incapacity and confusion, lack of central office coordination, lack of central office staff with needed skills, absence of regulations and guidelines, lack of a compliance scheme, and more—continued without fundamental improvement. In the spring and summer, Congress, public, and press were educated at length (by way of a committee report, testimony before the Senate Finance Committee, and speeches on the floor of the Senate) by Senator Sam Nunn on abuses in prepaid health plans in California's Medicaid program and on the possibility that similar abuses were occurring or might occur in the federal HMO program. In June, the GAO added to its long and growing list of critiques of the program a study contending that only three of a sample of fourteen of the first twenty-seven federally qualified HMOs had a good chance of reaching financial independence within five operational years. One month later the loan chief of the HMO program described a lengthy list of serious problems in fifteen qualified HMOs. In October, a national television audience, many of whom were no doubt hearing of HMOs and the HMO program for the first time, learned not only that alleged abuses of federal funds in HMO projects in the Denver region had wasted taxpayers' money, but also that the regional official who tried to stop the waste claimed to have been punished by his superiors. In early 1979, an HMO program official acknowledged that no fewer than half of the eighty-odd qualified HMOs would develop major financial problems if lax management practices continued, thus raising the possibility that the program's promotional efforts would be offset by a series of bankruptcies and financial cliffhangers. These problems, considered alongside the equally serious difficulties of finding a place for HMOs in such federal health care programs as FEHBP, Medicaid, Medicare, and the planning process, gave realistic observers little reason to predict that even a decade of effort climaxed by three years of consensus and federal self-reform was sufficient to create the conditions in which HMOs would emerge as the vehicle of a major reorganization of the faulty incentives of the U.S. health care system.

The federal government's tenacious commitment to the HMO strategy, a commitment manifested in a remarkable capacity for political learning and change, offers an unusually fruitful case against which to examine the interplay between politics and policy. The extraordinary responsiveness of federal policymakers between 1976 and 1979 to complaints of HMO proponents about the early direction of the program in effect "controls" for the impact of politics on the federal government's ability to achieve its policy objectives. This test, imperfect but suggestive, is not reassuring to those who believe that fulfillment of the potential of appealing policy analyses such as the HMO proposal depends mainly on—indeed, only awaits—timely and wise political action. Many of the HMO program's most serious problems persisted and grew worse despite the hard-won consensus of the HMO industry and the new deference to that industry among federal policymakers. A reasonable inference is that, contrary to a common opinion, the problems of the HMO program are not now and have never been fundamentally political, that they do not result from political failures of the federal government, or from politics at all. Instead, it may be that large-scale development of HMOs as a means of system-reorganization and medical cost-containment has always been a highly implausible policy strategy, and that it lies beyond the power of political action, learning, and change, however sincerely motivated, wisely consti-tuted, and energetically pursued, to supply the plausibility the strategy intrinsically lacks.

Part Three

CHAPTER EIGHT

Politics and Policy:
The Federal Government
and HMOs

The architect, before building a large edifice, studies and probes the ground it is to occupy, to find out whether it is capable of supporting so great a weight. The wise legislator, similarly, starts out not by drafting laws good in and of themselves, but rather by finding out whether the people for whom he intends them is capable of bearing them.   Jean Jacques Rousseau

A FAIR appraisal of the first ten years of federal efforts to promote health maintenance organizations and to increase their prominence in the U.S. health care system must conclude that very little was accomplished. Two hundred and thirty-six HMOs were in operation by the middle of 1980, not the seventeen hundred once contemplated, and most of them were small. Only 5.5 percent (thirteen plans) had more than 100,000 members, 76 percent (one hundred eighty plans) had fewer than 25,000 members, and 61 percent (one hundred forty-four plans) had fewer than 15,000. Half the plans had fewer than 10,000 members.[1] Only one hundred fifteen plans were federally qualified.

The growth of HMO membership in the population at large has not been impressive. In 1973, before passage of the HMO act, a study identified one hundred HMO-like entities and gathered data on seventy-seven of them. The 4.5 million members of these seventy-seven plans constituted about 2 percent of the U.S. population. Almost three-fifths (59 percent) of these members belonged to one of the six Kaiser plans. Seven years later, when the number of plans had more than doubled to two hundred thirty-six, only about 4 percent of the population belonged to an HMO. More than two-fifths (42 percent) of these members belonged to a Kaiser plan.[2]

1. Calculated from U.S. Department of Health and Human Services, Public Health Service, Office of Health Maintenance Organizations, *National HMO Census of Prepaid Plans, June 30, 1980*, DHHS Publication (PHS) 80-50159 (HHS, 1980), pp. 13, 15–33.
2. Ibid.; Robert E. Schlenker and others, *HMOs in 1973: A National Survey* (Excelsior, Minnesota:

In 1980, HMO membership remained mainly a western proclivity—59 percent of HMO members lived in western states and 44 percent lived in California.[3]

Of the thirteen giants, with 100,000 members or more, seven were founded before 1950, two in the 1950s, and three in the 1960s. Only one plan founded since the federal government first embraced HMOs in 1970 has reached 100,000 members.[4] Although overall growth percentages may be made to seem highly impressive—for example, a newsletter of the Group Health Association of America (GHAA) proclaimed on page one "National HMO Enrollment Up 13.9 Percent" in 1978 from the previous year—closer inspection (page twelve) shows that most of this figure is explained by the growth of very young plans (an increase from 7 members to 707 is a "10,000 percent increase," after all). Although the average increase in membership between 1977 and 1978 for plans that had been in operation for two years or less was 710.9 percent, plans over ten years old (including the Kaiser giants) grew at a rate of only 2 percent, and those plans older than ten years that had fewer than 50,000 members had very low or negative growth rates.[5]

A decade of federal encouragement apparently had little effect on the attitudes and information of the general population about HMOs. Polls taken in 1971 and 1972 found that "only 33 percent of those interviewed felt that HMOs are a 'good idea.' Fully 58 percent said it is better to stick with one doctor and 9 percent didn't know."[6]

In 1975, two years after the passage of the HMO law, data assembled in HEW's health interview survey showed that 70.3 percent of persons twenty years of age or older had never heard of a prepaid group practice plan, and of the 19.9 percent who had, only 4.3 percent could name one

InterStudy, 1974), pp. 4, 93–97; U.S. Bureau of the Census, *Statistical Abstract of the United States: 1980* (U.S. Government Printing Office, 1978), p. 6. Earlier estimates vary widely and depend heavily on the definition of an HMO. Rhona L. Wetherille and others, "Growth Across the Nation," *Prism*, October 1975, p. 15, counted 41 HMOs as of 1970 but gave no estimate of their membership. Anne R. Somers, ed., *The Kaiser-Permanente Medical Care Program: A Symposium* (New York: Commonwealth Fund, 1971), p. vi, counted about 20 plans, "open to the general community and providing comprehensive care" (25 if Kaiser is counted as 6) serving less than 4 million members in 1971, but about 125 with about 8 million members if the count includes "all the plans serving special union or employee groups."

3. HHS, *National HMO Census of Prepaid Plans, June 30, 1980*, p. 2.

4. These calculations, derived from ibid., pp. 5, 19–33, exclude such units as MediCal plans that grew large in the early 1970s but failed before 1980. One of the giants—the Wisconsin Physicians Service Health Maintenance Program of Madison, Wisconsin, with 162,606 members—began operating about the same time that the federal effort began (ibid., p. 32).

5. *Group Health News*, vol. 19 (December 1978).

6. Stephen P. Strickland, *U.S. Health Care: What's Wrong and What's Right* (Universe Books, 1972), p. 75.

correctly.[7] A Harris poll taken in 1977–78 found that "by 78–16 percent, a very heavy majority say that they are not familiar with the federal government's plan to foster Health Maintenance Organizations. The ignorance is rather constant across the board." Although the "leadership community" did somewhat better—a mere 57–38 percent majority said that they "are not really familiar" with HMOs—the conclusion was that "HMOs have not made a strong impact on the consciousness of most Americans."[8] A 1978 survey conducted by the Health Insurance Institute found only 22 percent of the public familiar with the HMO concept. Although familiarity increased with education and income—64 percent of those with family incomes over $40,000 had heard of them, as had 44 percent of the college educated—the survey also discovered that eight in ten respondents proclaimed themselves satisfied with their current method of receiving care and supported only minor changes in the health care delivery system.[9] Finally, a Harris and Associates study published in mid-1980 painted a similar picture. Fifty-eight percent of the "eligible non-members" of HMOs identified in the Harris sample were "hardly or not at all interested" in joining one. Twenty-eight percent of the eligible nonmembers professed to be "somewhat interested," but only one in ten was "very interested." The survey found that 79 percent of the public was either not very or not at all familiar with the terms "health maintenance organization" or "HMO," and that 59 percent of the eligible nonmembers were unfamiliar with these terms. As for the federal government, 90 percent of the public did not know that it had a policy toward HMOs; indeed, only 15 percent of the HMO members in the sample knew that the federal government was encouraging them.[10]

Health maintenance organizations have not proved to be solutions to the health care problems of many poor, sick, old, unemployed, rural, or central-city underserved citizens, as some early enthusiasts hoped they would. They have been too few and too slow to develop to play a major role in containing the costs of health care. Nor is there reason to expect that the federal efforts of the 1970s will prove to have been a protracted prelude to explosive HMO growth. Even if the HMO penetration rate

7. Cited in George B. Strumpf and others, "Health Maintenance Organizations, 1971–1977: Issues and Answers," *Journal of Community Health*, vol. 4 (Fall 1978), p. 52.

8. Cited in Federation of American Hospitals, *Review*, vol. 11 (June 1978), p. 14.

9. Health Insurance Institute, *Health and Health Insurance: The Public View* (Washington: HII, 1979), pp. 34, 13.

10. Louis Harris and Associates, Inc., *American Attitudes Towards Health Maintenance Organizations: A Survey of the Public, HMO Members and Potential Members Nationwide*, Prepared for the Henry J. Kaiser Family Foundation (Louis Harris and Associates, Inc., 1980), pp. 17, 20, 100.

more than doubled, HMOs would enlist only about 10 percent of the population, and 90 percent would remain in the fee-for-service and third-party-payment systems.

The program has not been entirely devoid of accomplishment. It is probably better to have two hundred-odd HMOs, one hundred of them federally qualified, than to have fewer. It may be that these plans have offered their members high-quality and accessible care at costs below those of the fee-for-service system. The program has avoided major scandals and, as federal programs go, has not been very costly. Moreover, although the program's substantive accomplishments have been modest, its political and symbolic significance has been considerable, as chapter 10 explains. The program is neither a waste nor a boondoggle, but neither can it be termed a success. Hopes that HMOs would lead a major reorganization of the "illogical incentives" of the health care system and thereby avoid the need for ever larger measures of government regulation have been thoroughly disappointed. This chapter discusses and challenges the most familiar explanation of this outcome. The next chapter develops a more persuasive explanation.

An Unworkable versus an Unacceptable Law

Throughout the 1970s most HMO proponents gave a simple, straightforward explanation for the slow progress of the HMO-building effort: the federal government was at fault. Until 1977, their critique concentrated on the "unworkable" HMO law, the so-called anti-HMO law of 1973. The law, they argued, was a political miscarriage. Torn between lawmakers who sought a fair market test of HMOs' potential for containing medical costs and those who sought to sneak the social goals of comprehensive national health insurance into HMO legislation, between those who wanted flexible market competition with no subsidies and those who wanted detailed requirements imposed on federally subsidized HMOs, the law finally compromised by retaining the social goals but deleting the subsidies. The result was said to be an excessively detailed set of requirements that asked more of HMOs than unsubsidized premiums could bear, and that made a mockery of a fair market test by depriving the plans of the flexibility they needed to make their way in local markets. This view was widely shared within the HMO industry and among academic analysts of the program.[11] After the amendments of 1976 granted the HMO industry most of the changes it sought and removed much of the force of this argument, the critics rested their indictment on the momentum lost as a result of the unworkable law and the federal government's continuing discrimination against HMOs in its other programs.[12]

These arguments are deficient in four main respects. They greatly overestimate the damage the federal government has done to HMOs. They misconceive the nature of the conflict between the federal government and the HMO industry. They place far too much emphasis on federal actions amid the wide variety of forces working for and against HMOs. And they greatly overstate the potential importance of HMO-building as a federal policy strategy. This and the next chapter will defend these propositions in detail.

The argument that federal programs discriminate pervasively and consistently against HMOs is questionable. Comprehensive medical plans (including prepaid group practices and independent practice associations) have been offered to government employees since the federal employees health benefits plan began in 1960. The federal government put no major obstacles in the way of state contracts with HMOs in Medicaid. (In the aftermath of the MediCal scandals it restricted such contracts to federally qualified HMOs, a provision that is at once an obstacle and a protection.) In 1973 it passed a law that (whatever its other effects) gave HMOs recognition, small sums of capital, exemption from some inhibiting state laws, and improved access to employee markets. It then amended this law twice to make it palatable to the HMO industry. The Health Planning and Resource Development Act of 1974 declared that promotion of HMOs and similar systems was a "national goal." When HMOs protested that state and local regulators were snubbing or discouraging them, legislators worked long and hard to revise the law to end these practices. The hospital costs containment plan the Carter administration developed in 1977 would have exempted hospitals run or dominated by HMOs from its revenue

11. See Paul Starr, "The Undelivered Health System," Public Interest, no. 42 (Winter 1976), pp. 66–85; Alain C. Enthoven, "Prepaid Group Practice and National Health Policy," Proceedings of the 26th Annual Group Health Institute, June 1976 (Washington: Group Health Association of America, 1976), pp. 2–19. H. E. Frech III and Paul B. Ginsburg, Public Insurance in Private Medical Markets: Some Problems of National Health Insurance (Washington: American Enterprise Institute for Public Policy Research, 1978) even suspect, (p. 67) that the law of 1973 was "written by interests hostile to HMOs."

12. For the argument that there is a "strong and pervasive anti-HMO bias in the policies of the Federal government," see Alain Enthoven, "Memorandum for Secretary Califano; Subject: National Health Insurance (NHI)," Draft, September 22, 1977, p. 19, app. 18.

ceilings. In all these instances the federal government accepted or actively encouraged HMOs. That more has not come of the effort to encourage HMOs is best explained, as chapter 7 points out, by attitudes and interests at the state and local levels of government and in the private sector, not by federal discrimination.

The charge of federal discrimination receives strongest support from one program: Medicare. As chapter 7 explained, however, the debate throughout the 1970s on HMO participation in Medicare raised many complex questions of fact and value—the propriety of using Medicare funds (which include beneficiary contributions) for HMO development; the dangers of underservice for very high utilizers; the possibilities of windfall profits; the problem of monitoring care and relating it fairly to cost in a system of prospective capitation—on both sides of which much could be said.

The case against the HMO act of 1973 deserves more extended attention. If the law was indeed unworkable, an unwitting exercise in putting obstacles in the path of HMO development, then the hypothesis suggested at the end of the last chapter is mistaken twice over. First, HMOs should be viewed not (as that chapter suggested) as an implausible strategy beyond the ability of politics to realize but rather as a promising strategy that has not yet had (or did not have until 1977) a fair chance. Second, the pessimistic prognosis for HMO growth may be wrong. One might expect that as the ill effects of 1973–76 wear off, and as the amendments of 1976 and 1978 take effect, HMOs may arise and thrive in larger numbers. To address these questions it is necessary to look in some detail at the asserted unworkability of the 1973 law.

As the previous chapter explained, almost every detail of the 1973 law offended at least one of the many HMO-related special interests in some way. The building of the consensus group, however, forced these interests to distinguish annoying features of the law from unworkable ones, and the list of the unworkables steadily dwindled. Here it will suffice briefly to examine two features of the 1973 act that generated very intense opposition: certain contents of the basic benefit package and the open enrollment requirement. These requirements, the industry argued in effect, made much of the difference between a disastrous law and a workable one. If these provisions were retained, if HMOs were unfairly asked to meet requirements not binding on their Blue Cross and other competitors, the plans' costs would rise, triggering premium increases, diminishing their competitive strength, and threatening their financial survival. In 1976 Congress accepted these arguments and changed the law.

Congress's willingness to accept the industry's arguments left the impression in some quarters that the unworkability argument rested on hard evidence and demonstrated fact, which only political naïveté and stubbornness had obscured from view. This is far from clear. In this instance as in many others throughout the HMO debate, issues of principle and organizational character masqueraded as objective, technical, and economic questions.

It is and always was impossible to assess the effect of the disputed provisions of the 1973 law on HMOs in general. Although more stringent requirements are obviously more costly to meet than are weaker ones, nothing follows automatically from this truism about premiums, competition, and survival. Health maintenance organizations are complex economic systems; they offer certain services in diverse local markets to consumers with diverse characteristics and preferences. The effect of service and enrollment requirements varies with the nature of local markets themselves. Moreover, HMOs are systems of political economy; managerial approaches to organizing and offering services also make a difference, and these approaches differ too. Third, HMOs vary by organizational structure; independent practice associations (IPAs), prepaid group practices (PGPs), and mixed types of different ages and sizes react differently to given requirements. The many possible and actual differences in the values of these three variables make generalization hazardous.

It is of course possible to assemble data and manipulate them to yield overall estimates of average costs in HMOs. It is difficult to put much confidence in such figures, however. As a high-ranking industry spokesman who had used such data many times acknowledged in an interview, they are all "gossamer" and could be collected and manipulated to support virtually any a priori position on the "true" costs of federal requirements. (He then chuckled as he recalled how he had once given a staff associate the "bottom line" he sought—the average cost of developing a plan—and instructed him to devise the detailed charts in any way he pleased, so long as they yielded that figure.) Indeed the HMO industry's estimates of rate increases that would be required to meet the minimum benefit package of the act leave much room for difference of interpretation (see table 8-1). In two cases—the New Haven and Boston plans—the increases were tiny. In the others they were larger, but no one could say scientifically how many

Table 8-1. *Estimated Increases in Rates of Selected Plans Necessary to Meet the Basic Health Services Requirements of the Health Maintenance Organization Act of 1973*

Plan	Monthly rate for adult subscriber (dollars)			Increase in monthly rates (percent)
	Current benefits	Additional benefits	Total	
Community Health Care Center Plan, Inc., New Haven	20.85	0.37	21.22	1.8
Group Health Association, Inc., Washington, D.C.	18.89	1.25	20.14	6.6
Group Health Cooperative of Puget Sound, Seattle	17.89	1.04	18.84	5.8
Health Insurance Plan of Greater New York	16.69	1.02	17.71	6.1
Harvard Community Health Plan, Boston	20.17	0.05	20.22	0.2
Kaiser-Permanente Medical Care Program				
Colorado region	17.88	1.00	18.88	5.6
Southern California region	18.92	1.38	20.30	7.3

Source: Letter from Jeffery Cohelan, Executive Director, Group Health Association of America, Inc., to Director, Bureau of Community Health Services, June 5, 1974, app. A, in HEW files, HMO Comments folder C.

subscribers to, say, Kaiser's Southern California plan who found a monthly premium of $18.92 tolerable would object to an increase to $20.30 when the new and presumably attractive services were taken into account.

To be sure, a rate increase of 7.3 percent (the highest increase in the table) imposed organizational costs. The increase might make the plan somewhat less attractive to healthy, low-risk subscribers, a point much on the mind of Kaiser officials, ever mindful of the relationship between rate and risk, and ever eager to hold the line on premiums. It might also place the plan's premium beyond the budgets of some low-paid groups—the oft-invoked culinary workers, for example.[13] That these were matters for concern may be granted; that they threatened financial disaster for Kaiser or for other solid plans may be doubted.

There is no reason to expect that each extra cent of premium necessarily produces a corresponding increment of uncompetitiveness. Insofar as

13. *Health Maintenance Organization Amendments of 1975*, Hearings before the House Subcommittee on Health and the Environment of the House Interstate and Foreign Commerce Committee, 94 Cong. 1 sess (GPO, 1975), pp. 84, 94.

competition is a function of costs (in fact, other variables enter in too), it depends mainly on the price of HMO membership relative to the price of the competition. Where HMOs are more expensive than the competition, a key variable in gaining and keeping members is widely agreed to be the size of the monthly payroll deduction the subscriber must incur. Although HMO industry spokesmen sometimes leave the impression that any increase in payroll deductions threatens to trigger mass defections from their plans, there appears to be little hard evidence relating such increases to enrollment or nonenrollment decisions. An HEW survey in 1976 of sixty-six employer groups found that "there appears to be no correlation between HMO penetration and differentials in out-of-pocket contributions by the employee" until the employee's monthly contribution reached $15.[14] If this finding is to be believed, it is questionable that the premium increases in table 8-1, ranging from $0.05 to $1.38 per month, would very often make the difference between a competitive and an uncompetitive plan. The increases are small enough, the apparent slack in consumer calculations large enough, and the other variables influencing competition numerous enough to suggest that arguments attributing the plans' prospects for competition and survival to the requirements of the HMO act's package of minimum benefits should be approached skeptically.

Equally important, critics generally damned the law without taking account of the plans' ability to meet its requirements without resorting to increases in premiums. Large plans could to some extent spread and therefore dilute the cost of the requirements among their members, and small new plans aided by the program could offset these added costs during their growth period with federal funds made available by the law.[15] Growth triggered by dual choice and by the addition of the new services themselves are also pertinent factors. Estimates holding everything else—size, federal grants, dual choice, and the services themselves—constant may mislead because everything else pertinent to the effects of the requirements on competitive premiums was not constant.

The frequent argument that the foolish generosity of the law's requirements was the major obstacle to widespread formation of HMOs in areas that lacked them is also implausible. In parts of the country—rural areas, the South, and parts of the Southwest, for example—where employers'

14. U.S. Department of Health, Education and Welfare, Division of Health Maintenance Organizations, *Health Maintenance Organization Program Status Report, December, 1976,* DHEW Publication (HSA) 77-13022 (HEW, 1977), p. 43.

15. Kappa Systems, Inc., "The Issues of Risk and Insolvency in the Health Maintenance Organization Act of 1973" (n.d.), pp. 8, 14.

contributions to employee health plans tend to be modest, the premiums of any reasonably comprehensive HMO would require unacceptably large contributions from employees. Although the federal requirements added a small, probably insignificant, increment to this already unacceptable gap, critics have sometimes blamed the law for precluding what they fondly claimed would otherwise have been an explosion of HMO formings and joinings.

The areas where HMOs take root most readily are those—especially metropolitan areas in highly industrialized and progressive states—where employer contributions to employee health benefits tend to be generous.[16] These of course are the areas where the additional deductions from the employee's paycheck required by the act could be most easily absorbed. And consumers' suspicion and providers' opposition would probably have limited HMO activities in urban and rural areas alike, even if there had been no federal law and even if employer contributions had been larger.

By the industry's own admission, two of the three controversial basic benefits—outpatient mental health services and alcoholism services—were not unworkable. The mental health requirement was modest, calling for no more than twenty short-term, outpatient visits for "evaluation and crisis intervention."[17] Some states—Massachusetts and Connecticut, for example—already required health insurers to include mental health benefits in their plans, and such provisions were growing steadily more common in conventional insurance plans even when they were not required by state law. Costs per member per month were estimated to be low.[18] The HMO

16. Richard McNeil, Jr., and Robert E. Schlenker, "HMOs, Competition, and Government," *Milbank Memorial Fund Quarterly/Health and Society*, vol. 53 (Spring 1975), p. 200. It is noteworthy that in a May 1974 survey of the attitudes of HMO officials toward the 1973 law, only 12 percent of respondents labeled the minimum basic benefits required by the law as a "significant disadvantage"; 28 percent considered the benefits to be a "moderate" disadvantage, while fully 58 percent thought them to be no or only a slight disadvantage (ibid., p. 219).

17. Public Law 93-222, sec. 1302 (1)(D).

18. In the early 1970s the Health Insurance Plan of Greater New York (HIP) was providing much broader mental health benefits than the 1973 HMO law required for about $7.50 per person per year; see Raymond Fink, "Financing Outpatient Mental Health Care Through Psychiatric Insurance," *Mental Hygiene*, vol. 55 (April 1971), p. 148; Sidney S. Goldensohn, "A Pre-Paid Group-Practice Mental Health Service As Part of a Health Maintenance Organization," *American Journal of Orthopsychiatry*, vol. 42 (January 1972), p. 156. Harold R. Hunter and others, *Development of Alternatives for an Evaluation of the Cost and Effectiveness of Inclusion of Mental, Dental and Pharmaceutical Benefits in Health Maintenance or Related Organizations* (American Public Health Association [n.d.]), p. 6, found that the cost of providing mental health services for regular (as distinct from low-income) plan members came to only $10.80 per enrollee per year for HIP, $4.65 for the Group Health Cooperative of Puget Sound, and $5.64 for Kaiser's Fontana facility. Robert W. Gibson, "Can Mental Health Be Included in the Health Maintenance Organization?" *American Journal of Psychiatry*, vol. 128 (February 1972), p. 925, offers further evidence that "the cost of including mental health benefits . . . would not be prohibitive." Irving

industry's consensus group itself decided that trying to persuade the legislators to eliminate the requirement was not worth the fight it would provoke with the mental health lobby.

The alcoholism treatment requirement was also modest, especially after HEW rules excluded from it treatment for chronic alcoholism. The service was not thought to be very expensive. In any event, HMOs would be obliged to treat alcohol-related medical problems of their members, and these services, like mental health services, required no large new capital outlays. Alcoholism benefits were included on the consensus group's list of unworkable provisions mainly as a bargaining chip to concede at the opportune moment to the chairman of the Senate committee responsible for HMO legislation.

Thus the indictment of the basic benefit package rests on one single, solitary service: preventive dental care for children. At first glance this is peculiar, for in many ways this benefit resembles the others that proved to be tolerable after all. The costs of providing the service were apparently not large;[19] it was another benefit that was growing in popularity and it

---

D. Goldberg and others, "Effects of a Short-term Outpatient Psychiatric Therapy Benefit on the Utilization of Medical Services in a Prepaid Group Practice Medical Program," *Medical Care*, vol. 8 (September–October 1970), p. 428, "strengthens the hypothesis of reduced utilization of medical services, and more efficient utilization of appropriate services," as a result of mental health benefits in the Kaiser, HIP, and GHA programs—a source of economies almost entirely neglected in critics' estimates of the costs of the provision. Harvard Community Health Plan, *A Study of Integrated Comprehensive Mental Health Services in a Health Maintenance Organization*, HSMHA Contract HSM-42-72-201 (February 1973), p. 46, reported mental health benefit costs per member per month were only $0.87. These studies were all available throughout the HMO industry's assault on the bankrupting effects of the provision. A 1978 study is consistent with the earlier ones. An Arizona HMO that in 1974 installed mental health benefits far broader than those required by the 1973 law shows that costs per member per year never exceeded $9.72; Thomas E. Bittaker and Scott Idzorek, "The Evolution of Psychiatric Services in a Health Maintenance Organization," *American Journal of Psychiatry*, vol. 135 (March 1978), p. 341.

19. A meeting of the American Public Health Association in May 1973 concluded that "it is feasible to include dental services within Health Maintenance Organizations, but not at a comprehensive level for all services." "Dental Meeting," in Hunter and others, *Development of Alternatives, Final Report: Dental Component*, p. 3. The authors of the report argued that although there had been little study of the costs of including a preventive program within a prepaid structure, "the cost of prevention would . . . be very small on a per capita basis" (pp. 47–48). In 1974 an elaborate effort to estimate the cost of the federal dental requirement using data from the Harvard Community Health Plan found that providing dental care for children under the age of twelve would cost only $0.82 per member per year (that is, less than $0.07 per member per month); Jerold M. Frankle and Joseph Boffa, *Prepaid Dental Care: Technical Assistance Manual* (1974), p. 58. In an excellent review of the subject a specialist in prepaid dental care, Max H. Schoen, "Dental Care and the Health Maintenance Organization Concept," *Milbank Memorial Fund Quarterly/Health and Society*, vol. 53 (Spring 1975), p. 188, argued that "limiting dental coverage to the basic benefit mandated by the HMO act would reduce costs to pennies per family per month." He then went on to make the fundamental *organizational* points: "The performance of this service to the exclusion of other dental care is of doubtful value, would probably be used by few persons, and would antagonize everyone. Patients would expect more or get a false sense of security, local dentists would

had the potential of attracting healthy young families of low utilizers to HMOs.[20]

The logistics of the benefit, however, posed organizational problems quite different from those raised by the other two services—rather than an incremental expansion of services already offered in some form, it meant entering a new and unfamiliar medical speciality; rather than occasional crisis care for a comparatively small number of members, it mandated recurring services to a sizable number of members; rather than increasing the workload of existing personnel or adding a psychologist or psychiatrist here and a counselor there, it meant recruiting a new type of personnel.

The nature of the task in turn raised a host of complex organizational questions. How many dentists would be needed? Could they be employed efficiently and full time on preventive child care alone? Did it make more sense to rely on dental hygienists? Should the plan press boldly ahead and offer more than preventive services to children and adult members? What would this cost? Should it contract with dentists or dental groups outside the plan for the required services? (This meant a loss of control and responsibility for service quality and costs.) Should it provide the minimum service itself and refer problems whose treatment went beyond the requirement to dentists in the community? (This course too abridged the plan's responsibility and carried the additional disadvantage of presenting the subscriber with a fee for these extra services.) Were sizable capital outlays for dental chairs and drills and the like justified by the minimum requirement? And even if the plan's officials reached agreement on the correct answers to these questions, they did not all have a free hand to implement them. Officials of the two-million-member Kaiser plans in California, in particular, were constrained by state laws governing professional corporations (in this case, dental groups) that prevented them from organizing the service in what they took to be the most efficient manner. And once the officials finally had decided just how they would organize the service, they must fit it into their many and diverse contracts with employee groups,

---

criticize the services, and the HMO itself would have to face the outcry." Earlier, Max H. Schoen and Charles R. Jerge, "The Provision of Dental Care Under the Health Maintenance Organization Act of 1973: A Position Paper" (April 1974), p. 5, had sought to assure critics that the mandated benefit would not be as costly "as most people imagine," and noted that "the trend in third party fringe benefit plans is clearly toward increasing coverage to include . . . dentistry."

20. In 1974 about 10 percent of dental expenditures were paid by third parties; Frankel and Boffa, *Prepaid Dental Care*, p. 77. In four years the percentage had nearly doubled, to 19 percent; Robert M. Gibson, "National Health Expenditures, 1978," *Health Care Financing Review*, vol. 1 (Summer 1979), p. 9. "Dental Insurance," *Insurance Marketing* (September 1979), p. 46, noted that "group dental insurance is the fastest growing health benefit in the United States."

negotiate premium adjustments, and estimate the impact on enrollment and on facilities and workloads.

To understand the problems the plans perceived in the dental requirement is to grasp the essence of the unworkability argument. In the words of a Kaiser vice-president: "Our first question is always, how do we organize it? Then we ask, what do we charge?" As a physician administrator at Kaiser explained: "We operate by consensus. If it doesn't seem right to everyone, there must be something wrong with it." The possibility of entering a qualitatively new field would be explored carefully, from every major institutional viewpoint, perhaps over a long time. Consensus among leading administrators and physicians might or might not emerge. Such a decision would never be taken rapidly or casually, and it was inconceivable that outside pressure could trigger a rapid, large innovation. Faced with the prospect that dental services would have to be designed and installed suddenly and purely as a consequence of federal decree, Kaiser bridled. So did other prominent plans. The essential problem was that the requirement threatened significant organizational dislocation and that the plans could see no immediately satisfactory answer to their first and basic question: how is it to be organized? Considerations of organizational integrity led the giants of the industry to agree that the provision must be killed.

Raw financial calculations must be similarly set in their organizational context in order to understand the industry's bitter objections to the open enrollment requirement. Obviously the requirement would raise HMO costs to some extent because more high users cost more to serve than do fewer. But the workability of the provision turned on a different question— whether the admittedly higher costs would make the plans' premiums uncompetitive. Answering this question meant exploring several intermediate variables between requirement and outcome: 1) the number of open enrollees, 2) the amounts and types of care they used, 3) the costs per member per month they generated, 4) the effects of their costs on the plan's community rate and on premiums, and 5) the relationship of the plan's premium (thus affected) to that of the competition. Moreover, a complete answer would set these variables in the context of the plan's size and financial condition (and hence its ability to absorb risks), and would consider the impact on the plan of the dual choice provision (which would presumably increase enrollment and spread risks).

The general effects of open enrollment when these intervening variables were taken into account were unknown. Too few plans had experimented with open enrollment to yield data on these questions. Even if data had been abundant, however, they would not have influenced the plans' attitudes, for these attitudes were grounded on normative and organizational concerns as well as on economics. The plans, in effect, followed the argument through the first three variables and then stopped and firmly refused to go further. The requirement would mean more open enrollees than they would otherwise have, these members would use more care than would the average member recruited in the usual way, and this higher use would cost the plan more than it would have to bear in the absence of the requirement. Pressed to complete the inquiry by considering variables four and five—exactly what effect would all this have on premiums and on the plan's competitive status?—the plans turned a deaf ear. A requirement that raised their costs was intrinsically a bad management practice. It also generated discontent among physicians within the organization. Physicians in HMOs tend to be acutely conscious of time pressures—and, in some plans, of the sources of the savings that comprise their annual bonuses—and therefore of the need to allocate time among patients efficiently. An infusion of cases in need of extensive, recurrent attention would not be welcomed. Finally, HMOs thought it unfair that they should be subjected to a requirement that was not enforced on Blue Cross and commercial firms.

The actual workability of the open enrollment provision was unknown and, to the plans, largely immaterial. The Marshfield Clinic's findings that open enrollment left its competitive position undamaged had no impact whatever on the HMO industry. Marshfield was different, spokesmen argued. But even if it had been a fine facsimile of their own operations, no conceivable data were likely to have changed the minds of industry spokesmen, for the interpretation of even the most elementary datum lay in the eye—and values and organizational interests—of the beholder. What a former aide to Senator Kennedy saw as a "small" increase in Marshfield's membership costs, an indication that the provision was not inherently unworkable, a Kaiser executive saw as "a lot," proof of the folly of the requirement. The issue turned on conflicting management philosophies and notions of justice, not on "facts," economic or other.[21]

21. A physician-administrator at one Kaiser site explained: "Open enrollment makes planning tough. Facility planning is hard enough to keep timely now, with HSAs and all that. Open enrollment would just make it harder, and so it would make access harder for all." A Kaiser financial expert, asked about the basis of his plan's opposition to the provision in the HMO Act of 1973, made a similar point: "No, we don't know what open enrollment would have cost us. Our concern stemmed from the community rating principle: we'd want to know about the group's characteristics before offering to it. In a community rating system it's very important to update changes in demographics. In fact, an HMO might take an adverse

The major counterexample is the North Communities Health Plan (North Care) of Evanston, Illinois, which held an open enrollment period when it opened early in 1975 and then two more in 1976–77 and 1978–79.[22] About 14 percent of the plan's first 9,000 members were individual enrollees, and their rate of hospital use was more than twice that of group enrollees.[23] The first open enrollment period alone "forced the plan to increase its premium to all enrollees by 20%."[24]

The question of competitiveness, however, turns not on HMO members' use and premiums but on these figures relative to the use and premiums of the competition. Although the individual enrollees used many hospital days, the more than 85 percent of members enrolled through groups used few. Comparing HMO data for nine federally qualified HMOs over two calendar quarters with 1975 data for Blue Cross, an HEW study found that North Care had used only 485 days per 1,000 members, half of the 972 days per 1,000 used by the Blue Cross plan in its area. North Care stood near the middle of the list—fourth in hospital use of the nine HMOs examined. Its Blue Cross counterpart stood highest among the nine Blue Cross plans listed.[25] In the fourth quarter of 1976, North Care used 572.6 days per 1,000, but in the first quarter of 1977 the rate was again 485. This, a consultant noted, was "an acceptable level," given the high demands of the open enrollees. The plan's family premium, $96 per month, was judged to be too high by $8–$10 to be competitive, however.[26]

One reason why lower use did not produce lower premiums was that the individual enrollees' hospital days were unusually expensive. Even so, it is difficult to disentangle the effects of open enrollment from those of other problems afflicting North Care, a veritable Job among HMOs. Contemporaneously with its open enrollment exercise, the plan suffered from lack of management expertise, a poorly "connected" consumer-dominated board, weak budget and financial controls, inadequate marketing, a failure to take advantage of favorable Medicare reimbursement possibilities, high fee-for-service payments to outside specialists, a location

---

group to get the revenue, expecting the risks to get absorbed later. Open enrollment would be no big problem in the bigger regions, and not much of one elsewhere. We cared about growth we couldn't control."

22. Only the first was a "true" open enrollment. The latter two used a health statement to screen out the worst risks.

23. *Health Services Information*, August 29, 1977, p. 3.

24. Strumpf and others, "Health Maintenance Organizations," p. 49.

25. HEW, *Health Maintenance Organization Program Status Report*, p. 42.

26. Gettys Associates, "General Management Review Conducted for the Board of Trustees" (1977), pp. 53–54.

inaccessible to some potential members, and an unfavorable financial contract with the hospital that handled most of its inpatient care. Nor, apparently, did the plan do all it could to cushion the financial effects of open enrollment. For example, the new management brought in to save the foundering plan negotiated a more favorable contract with a local Blue Cross plan for the reinsurance of high-risk members, and a consultant studying the plan's problems noted that members of individually enrolled families were charged individual rates, not higher family rates.[27] Plainly, North Care's problems went deeper than a struggle against the effects of open enrollment alone. Open enrollment was a federal requirement, however, while the plan's other problems were of its own making, and critics found in it a convenient proof of the federal government's foolishness.

Open enrollment surely did nothing to bring the plan closer to success. In the context of North Care's endless problems it may well have been one "unquestioned mistake"[28] among others. In a stronger plan, however, it might have raised costs without doing major damage to competitiveness.

A reasonable inference from the limited data at hand is that the open enrollment requirement would have proved tolerable for some plans and disadvantageous to others. It was precisely to address this possibility that the 1973 law allowed an administrative waiver, of course. Nor did HEW put obstacles in the plans' path. A former official of the qualification office recalled that "all [that asked] got waivers. It was no real problem. They got waivers because we basically ignored it [the requirement]." Some plans were content with an informal exemption; others, however, fumed that HEW had not published "criteria." But even if it had issued highly detailed criteria, these plans would not have been satisfied, for criteria might be changed. In short, enraged at the injustice of it all and at the government's blithe indifference to managerial considerations, and determined not to let disposition of the case hang on the whim of HEW, the giants of the industry determined to kill the provision.

Throughout the debate on the 1973 law, issues of organizational integrity and fairness were continually couched in the rhetoric of financial survival and competition. The reason is not entirely clear. Perhaps spokes-

---

27. Mark Perlberg, "Shaky Start Overcome by Illinois HMO," *Hospitals*, vol. 53 (August 16, 1979), pp. 70–72.

28. Ernest Libman, "North Communities Health Plan," in Robert A. Zelten and Susan Bray, eds., *Health Maintenance Organizations—Presentations to the 1976 Training Program in HMO Management* (Leonard Davis Institute of Health Economics, Wharton School, University of Pennsylvania), p. 77.

men for the HMO industry understood that arguments about organizational character and fairness would be hard to communicate and would appear unconvincing, subjective, soft, narrow-minded, and self-serving, whereas arguments addressing financial survival and competition—the hard, quantitative bottom line—appeared by contrast to be clearcut, powerful, and objective. Perhaps industry executives, long accustomed to perceiving what is good for the plan as a seamless web of sound business management, organizational security, and fiscal prudence, unconsciously melded the themes or failed to separate them analytically in their own minds and therefore in their public presentations. Whatever the reason, the industry played its "unworkable law" theme to the hilt and eventually prevailed.

The central problem of the 1973 law was not, however, that it was unworkable but rather that it was unacceptable to the HMO industry, and especially to the very large plans. The distinction is important, for it points to two very different explanations of the problems of the HMO program and to two quite different prognoses. If the law was indeed unworkable and if this law was the main obstacle to HMO development, then the consensus amendments of 1976 should have eliminated the program's major problem and set it on the road to large achievements. But whatever their success in making the law acceptable to the industry, the amendments have not made and are unlikely to make the difference between a feeble HMO development effort and a thriving one, or the difference between an implausible strategy and a fruitful one. These differences have little to do with the workability of the HMO law, or with other maltreatment of HMOs by the federal government.

Politicians versus PGPs

The clash between prepaid group practice plans and lawmakers over the merits of HMO law is a vivid instance of a general pattern in the corporatist politics of a collectivist age: the standard operating procedures of politics increasingly collide with those of business as usual in the large formal organizations, public and private, that the lawmakers aim to influence. As the coalition-building tasks of politicians at work in the highly decentralized U.S. political setting clash with the maintenance and enhancement needs of large formal organizations implicated in the politicians' plans, misunderstanding and conflict arise and grow. The development of HMO policy was an acute and aggravated case of an increasingly commonplace occurrence.

To understand why the 1973 law was unacceptable and why it generated bitter outcries over its "unworkable" and "anti-HMO" features, one must understand something of the organizational history and character of the HMO industry, the influence of this history and character on the world view of the industry's spokesmen, and the ways in which these perceptions clashed with those of the politicians who produced the law. The industry consisted of three major elements: the purists in organized labor and in high positions in some of the consumer-minded plans, who were mainly concerned with the moral and professional superiority of their movement; the Ellwood eclectics, mainly policy analysts with little practical experience in prepaid group practice, who had abstracted from real-world plans a set of economic principles and called the construct a health maintenance organization; and the pragmatic executives in large business-minded plans (especially Kaiser), less pure than the purists but further removed still from the abstract eclecticism of the policy analysts. The former two elements were largely audience-oriented, the first concerned with spreading the gospel of the moral and professional superiority of PGPs, the second bent on demonstrating the economic superiority of HMOs, and the two had almost nothing in common. The third element was constituency-oriented,[29] concerned with running successful organizations and therefore with maintaining a harmonious balance among their multiple constituencies of members, physicians, administrators, and others.

The official voice of the HMO industry on matters of public policy was the GHAA, a trade association which may not have been, as one federal official put it, "Kaiser's Charlie McCarthy," but which spoke mainly for the constituency-oriented executives and, to a lesser degree, for the purists. In 1970, however, the effective voice of the industry on policy matters was that of Paul Ellwood, the eclectic outsider who, single-handedly and virtually without the involvement of the GHAA, persuaded his audience of HEW generalists that the federal government should promote HMOs vigorously. Left to themselves, the purists and executives would probably not have attempted to sell this proposition to the government; had they tried to do so they would surely not have sold the inclusive, flexible Ellwood approach. In practice, however, they found themselves confronted with a

29. The distinction between audience and constituency is taken from James Q. Wilson, "The Mayors Vs. the Cities," *The Public Interest*, no. 16 (Summer 1969), pp. 25–37.

fait accompli. They and their constituencies had been pulled willy-nilly into the political arena.

Most of the leading lights of the giant PGP sector of the industry had little use for the federal government and did not look forward to dealing with it. Old hands retained unpleasant memories of the 1940s and 1950s when in the course of trying to establish and market their plans they were (as one former Kaiser executive recalled) "literally kicked out of all the best places in town." These executives had received little but trouble from government. They had not forgotten the fights against obstacles to their groups' operations imposed by state legislatures at the behest of fee-for-service doctors, blatant discrimination against them when they sought a share of Hill-Burton hospital construction funds, the federal government's inattention to them when the Medicare law was drafted in 1965, and the repeated rebuffs they had endured at HEW when they sought administrative measures to ease their participation in the Medicare program. They had made their organizations successful by applying sound business principles to private capital and by offering medical care of good quality to voluntarily enrolled populations. They had endured and overcome the slanders and dirty tricks of fee-for-service competitors, who had lost no chance to promote misunderstanding and distrust of prepaid group practice among the public. A small band of fierce organizational loyalists joined in a "fellowship of the persecuted," their first principle was responsibility, meaning a self-contained, self-sufficient, self-financed system that pulled together all major facets of medical care delivery and financing in one organizational structure. Maintaining such a system is a constant balancing act (see chapter 3) requiring not only allegiance to economic tenets of rationality and efficiency but also unfailing sensitivity to the complex organizational ecology that allows physicians and administrators to work together in harmony. Insular, proud, unused to change imposed from outside the organization, and mindful of past hurts inflicted by an alliance of fee-for-service enemies and government, these leaders viewed the growing federal interest in HMOs with an uneasy sense of vindication and trepidation.

Having suffered at the hands of enemies, they had no intention of yielding to the dictates of new and possibly false and fickle friends in Washington. Having asked of government nothing more than to be let alone to practice their brand of medical care without legal obstacles and on equal terms with the competition, they asked no more of the federal government now. Having built self-contained organizations on a responsible synthesis of sound management, hard business sense, and good medicine, they had little patience with political dilettantes dabbling in their little island of the health care world. In the established plans the antigovernmental ethos of businessman and physician came together with redoubled force. Antipolitical, largely outside the realm of government-group bargaining, conscious of minority status, a self-perceived island of rationality in a sea of inefficiency, resolutely committed to their distinctive blend of sound business and sound medicine in which the taint of politics and government had no proper place, the leaders were most unlikely to grasp the newly lit torch of federal HMO policy and carry it stoically and gracefully over the hurdles of the political process.

While Ellwood sold HMOs to HEW and the department then sold the approach to ever higher levels of the administration, the PGP leaders looked on ambivalently. Many found a certain sour satisfaction in the belated discovery that their oft-despised modes of care were superior to the illogical fee-for-service system. On the other hand they feared the consequences of the way the discovery was taking place. Ellwood had retitled the plans "health maintenance organizations," thereby seeming to promise a magic organizational formula for making and keeping people well. The old hands knew perfectly well that most of what they did involved caring for the sick and that although PGPs might emphasize preventive services more than fee-for-service plans did, there was nothing about their groups per se that would enable doctors to keep people well. Moreover, the new proponents were going about the country talking as if HMOs could spring up virtually anywhere, as if management problems would somehow take care of themselves, and as if the good name and reputation of existing plans could be readily emulated by virtually any prepaid group system. These contentions disturbed those who knew first-hand the rigors of founding and building successful PGPs. At the same time, they did believe that good things followed from the organizational union of prepayment and group practice and were themselves curious about the adaptability of their model.

The Ellwood-HEW efforts of spring 1970 triggered an intense debate between purists and pragmatists, and within each camp as well, but the Nixon administration's policy initiative did not wait upon their consensus. The president's speech of February 1971 put HMO development, Ellwood-style, high on the federal policy agenda.

The Nixon initiative put the PGP insiders in an acutely painful dilemma. On the one hand, they could go along with the new enthusiasm for HMOs and thereby condone overgeneralization, overpromising, and misunderstanding that might come back to haunt them. On the other hand, they could painstakingly and responsibly point out the contingencies in the eclectic, theoretical proposal and insist on a full consideration of complexities. But their words would then surely be used against them by watchful fee-for-service critics as an admission that PGPs were not all they were said to be. And their warnings would probably be lost on even intelligent and well-meaning politicians, most of whom knew next to nothing about the founding and running of prepaid plans. They would be accused of being wet blankets by some and of working to thwart competition by others. On balance, there was only one feasible, albeit uncomfortable, course: endorse the strategy in principle but seek, carefully and gingerly, to introduce specifics and safeguards into the Nixon proposal in the legislature.

On one general point the plan leaders and the Democratic health leaders in Congress were immediately of one mind: the flexible, inclusive administration initiative was an invitation to trouble. The approach might well produce a large number of HMOs quickly, but they would almost certainly not be desirable and successful health care systems. The administration's approach would open the door to officials of neighborhood and rural health centers and other well-meaning people in search of federal funds who had little understanding of prepaid group practice or of how such a system differed from government-subsidized clinics. If these sponsors were given funds to set up HMOs, solo physicians and medical groups serving Medicaid populations in the larger cities might become nervous and then attempt to save or retain their patients by erecting jerry-built HMOs. Indeed, even as the national HMO debate began, the prepaid health plans that proved so troublesome were forming in large numbers under California's MediCal law.

Worse still, the administration's plan was an open door to charlatans and get-rich-quick artists. The monthly prepaid premiums of many thousand subscribers add up to a handsome sum of money, and the prospect of establishing a skeletal plan, quickly building a large enrollment, collecting the prepaid premiums, and then either prolonging the plan's life and profits by skimping on service or collapsing the plan and skipping town with the cash was bound to attract the unscrupulous. The argument that such inferior plans could not survive in the market over time was beside the point: some entrepreneurs were quite content to make a killing and then disappear.[30] And if profit-making groups, which the Nixon plan made

30. A notorious case in point was a concern known as National Prepaid Health Plans, "which was highly successful in obtaining union business but had difficulty in servicing and paying its claims"; two weeks after the California attorney general ordered it to cease operation until its finances were corrected,

eligible for some forms of federal aid, were excluded, entrepreneurs could still channel their plan's business to profit-making equipment, laboratory services, and other "independent" enterprises in which they had a financial interest.

The problem was that a law such as the administration proposed would make it difficult for HEW to say no to shady or incompetent operators. Within a short time the program would probably be beset by failures and scandals, and even if these were comparatively few, the skeletal plans and the well-established ones might be tarred with one brush. The severe damage this might do led the plan leaders and legislators alike to agree that an HMO law should contain safeguards and specifics.

Writing acceptable safeguards and specifics into law was bound to be difficult, however. The nature of the industry (which of course included Ellwood as well as the purists and the pragmatists) imposed four criteria on any acceptable HMO law. First, it must keep out the charlatans and the fly-by-nights. Second, it must honor the industry's ambivalence about IPAs, which some leaders lumped with the charlatans and strongly opposed aiding and others viewed as tolerable under certain circumstances. Third, the law must recognize that most plans developed with federal aid would differ from the prototypes in many ways (some by virtue of being IPAs, or containing some of their elements). And fourth, it must not interfere with the settled, time-tested practices of the established plans.

As the legislative process got under way, the PGP leaders soon saw that even if a law meeting these four criteria was logically possible (and it might not be), it would never be produced by the politicians then setting to work on it. Not only were the politicians hopeless amateurs in the PGP field, but in their role as politicians they also felt bound to honor norms and decisionmaking procedures that had little to do with the merits of the issues surrounding HMO growth and management.

Misunderstanding began with the most elementary points and proceeded through the most arcane. Even politicians who were sensibly skeptical of the amorphous Nixon approach had apparently accepted much of the rhetoric on HMOs and had drawn what the plan leaders thought to be erroneous conclusions from it. Some politicians, for example,

---

it filed for bankruptcy, "leaving debts of more than $2 million including $1.5 million of unpaid medical claims." For a synopsis of the investigations of the Permanent Subcommittee on Investigations of the Senate Government Operations Committee into this and other health-related schemes see "Senate Investigating Subcommittee Airs Insurance Deals with T-H (Taft-Hartley) Funds," *Employee Benefit Plan Review*, November 4, 1977, pp. 7–8. See also "Senate Subcommittee Throws Light on Labyrinthine Operations of 'Hauser Group,'" ibid., November 11, 1977, pp. 3–5.

having heard that HMOs realized "savings of from 10–40 percent over fee-for-service," pictured large fiscal dividends—free and unencumbered sums—that might be allocated whenever and however they chose in exchange for political quid pro quos. The plan officials attempted to explain that the concept of an HMO "saving" did not support this vision.

The politicians proved to be erratic and uneven pupils, however. To the PGP leaders' distress, the lawmakers approached the HMO program as another exercise in federal grant-in-aid politics—the federal government proffers money (grants, loans, and so on) to recipients (state and local government agencies, private entrepreneurs, and so forth); in exchange it expects institutional or behavioral change, frequently in the form of new services provided by the recipient to new beneficiaries.

In the HMO case the politicians were only too aware of the benefits they intended to shower on HMOs. They would give them money, of course, and legitimacy and recognition—the federal "good housekeeping seal of approval." They would also override state laws interfering with HMO development and would give the plans access to the nation's largest employee groups by means of a dual choice provision. As they weighed all this largesse into the balance with the famous HMO savings, many legislators thought it only reasonable that the plans accept in exchange some earmarking of federal aid (and of a part of their savings) for new services and beneficiaries.

The plans soon recognized that the source of their strength and pride— the responsible, comprehensive character of their organizations—was their greatest source of vulnerability in the political arena. To the politicians, the comprehensiveness of the HMO concept offered up an unusually long list of items that might be incorporated in the quid pro quo and about which legislators of different persuasions might disagree and compromise. There ensued the lengthy debates over benefit packages, premium setting, enrollment practices, staffing, and quality assurance recounted in chapter 5. To the lawmakers, each facet of the HMO construct was fair game for negotiation. To the plans, a fine Swiss watch was being dismantled and reassembled before their eyes by blind men with sticky fingers.

The political logic of the politicians' approach was understandable, but from a practical standpoint it had one major flaw. Although new and growing HMOs might benefit from federal aid, the established plans had no need of it. The only tangible asset offered them was the dual choice provision. Some of them might benefit from new markets that followed upon their qualification under dual choice or suffer from the competition of a plan that qualified before they did, but these effects would probably be marginal. In theory, there was nothing to prevent them from simply ignoring the whole process.

The typical interest-group participant in federal grant-in-aid politics has a strong incentive (money) to exhibit loyalty as a program is being designed and then raise its voice about unwieldy requirements after the program and the funds are safely in place. For the PGPs, by contrast, exit was a real possibility.[31] The politicians were, in essence, attempting to bring two very different constituencies—new HMOs and long-standing plans—under the purview of one law. It is not strange that the flesh-and-blood constituency of established plans sought above all to protect their organizational characters from the politicians' exercises in concept-formation.

Tempted though they often were to make their way to the exit, the PGPs concluded that they could not simply detach themselves from the politicians' efforts. The true costs of ignoring the program were not tangible and present but intangible and in the future, those that might attend abdication of the leadership of a PGP-inspired movement and alienation of important leaders in government who might return the disfavor in future legislation, especially national health insurance legislation. The plan leaders therefore felt compelled to endure the frustrations of HMO-building in Washington and to insist patiently and repeatedly that HMOs are complex organizations based on fragile accommodations among administrators, physicians, and members, and endowed with staff patterns, premium structures, and facilities with a fine and interdependent logic that could not be altered at legislative whim without grave consequences. They were bound to insist, in a word, that HMO policymaking could not be grant-in-aid politics as usual.

As the legislative process wore on and PGP leaders got a clear glimpse of what the congressional health leaders, especially Edward Kennedy, had in mind, their early attempts to add safeguards and specifics to the Nixon bill gave way to an effort to delete various requirements from the Senate and House bills. Although they were reasonably successful in the House subcommittee chaired by Paul Rogers, HMO legislation depended on many other actors in many other forums. The Rogers subcommittee would send its bill to the full House Commerce Committee and then to the House as a whole, and the Kennedy subcommittee—very different from its House

31. The terms are taken from Albert O. Hirschman, *Exit, Voice and Loyalty* (Harvard University Press, 1970).

counterpart—would also take account of its Senate environment. A conference committee would then take up the handiwork of both chambers and would also aim at an outcome at least minimally acceptable to the White House (to avoid a veto) and to interest groups other than GHAA alone. Although the plans sniffed at this approach to HMO-building—the 1973 law, one Kaiser official said, reminded him of the facetious definition of a camel, "an animal created by a committee"—the legislators could work in no other way. To the plans, a responsible HMO law was one that did not interfere with sound management and good medicine as practiced in their organizations. To the politicians, a responsible law was one assembled by careful coalition-building, with give and take and negotiation and compromise at all stages. Each side was responsible in its fashion; alas, these fashions clashed sharply.

To the PGP executives the HMO was a reality whose complexity was confirmed daily. To the politicians it could be no more than a concept. That concept—or, better, concepts—consisted of two lists of attributes, one list positively and the other negatively valued. In each of the major legislative forums (administration, House, and Senate) HMO-builders, acting on and within the tenets and constraints of their own political games, would pick and choose from the conceptual cornucopia those attributes they viewed as good and would proscribe those they judged bad. They would then argue with one another and trade off or modify items on the list until all those actors who had to be made reasonably happy with the outcome were so. The result was a legislative hybrid—an eclectic amalgamation of present and possible fragments of real and imagined plans drawn to accentuate positives and eliminate negatives. The three hybrids thus fashioned would finally be fused into one compromise hybrid—the federally qualified HMO—and new plans and old were expected to design themselves in conformity to it. The plans could accept neither this hybrid nor the approach that generated it: that they should disrupt their stable, well-managed, time-tested organizations to conform to the federal camel struck them as absurd. The politicians, however, were bound to follow these sloppy procedures and were very likely to produce something like the hybrid that emerged: the legislative process runs on coalition-building within multiple, decentralized settings and ends in a final burst of coalition-building among the settings.

The politicians' approach embodied the precepts of U.S. legislative politics as usual. First, no special interest can expect to get all of what it seeks. Second, federal aid should involve a quid pro quo, not a giveaway.

Organizations receiving aid should be expected to do more and better, although how much more and better is of course subject to disagreement and compromise. Third, the nature of the quid pro quo is established by interaction among separated actors in a decentralized setting; proposals cannot become programs until they have been made acceptable to House, Senate, and (as a rule) administration. Fourth, no political actor can expect to get all of what he seeks. Fifth, where there is a political will there is a policy way—if two principles clash, the politic course is not to abandon one but to devise statutory language ambiguous enough to accommodate both. If it is feared that an admirable principle may prove unworkable in practice, the proper course is to retain it in law but also to allow administrators to waive it in suitable cases.

Unfortunately, none of these precepts had anything to do with the realities of running an HMO. What to the politicians was mere politics as usual struck the plans as a political miscarriage—unwise, unjust, and (therefore) unworkable. To the plans the law was unworkable *because* it was unacceptable—because it obligated them to take steps inconsistent with their sense of fairness and definitions of sound management. Apparently believing that a law should be written with the same economy and efficiency with which their groups were managed, the industry executives grew increasingly bitter, despite their skillful and often successful efforts to modify the HMO bills. Wondering how it happened that the federal government, inspired by prepaid prototypes, ended up creating in law a model HMO whose features the prototypes could adopt only by damaging themselves, some leaders began to discern the sinister workings of a coalition of enemies and fools. The hand of the AMA was seen everywhere—in Kennedy's inflated expectations, in the Rogers subcommittee's preoccupation with a demonstration program, in the White House reconsiderations of the summer of 1972. In retrospect none of this is surprising. Indeed the remarkable thing is not that the industry found the HMO law objectionable, but that it found so little of it highly objectionable.

The clash of ethos between politicians and practitioners continued into the administrative process. The deep distrust that medical businessmen at the head of minority enterprises had for federal bureaucrats meant (as chapter 6 points out) that anything less than substantial abandonment by HEW of disliked provisions of the law failed to satisfy the industry. In essence the plans wanted unambiguous administrative assurances, spelled out in absolutely clear regulatory language, that they would enjoy the flexibility to interpret controversial provisions of the law as they saw fit.

Working with a detailed law and subject to the cross pressures of responsibility (to the law and its drafters) and of responsiveness (to the HMO
industry), HEW struck a balance as best it could. The plans, however, were
not about to entrust their fate to bureaucratic balancing, which not only
failed to give them the assurances they sought but also might become
imbalanced against them in the future. Despairing of administrative
assurances, the plans, working through the GHAA, set out to amass enough
data, marshall enough arguments, concert enough action within the
industry, and—in all these ways—bring enough discredit on the 1973 law
to generate a consensus among politicians that the law was indeed
unworkable, and in need of amendment.

Late in 1976 the industry prevailed. Almost three years of experience
with the HMO program had made it clear to the politicians that it could
not sustain the contempt of the industry giants and hope to succeed. The
largest plans were avoiding the program, refusing to seek qualification
until the law was amended. Moreover, these plans and the GHAA occupied
a crucial position between the federal government and would-be HMO
entrepreneurs. Although not all entrepreneurs were deterred by the giants'
critique, controversy over the unworkable law deterred some and created
a climate of anxiety and uncertainty that suited very poorly the development
of new small businesses. Unless the government managed to mobilize the
consent of the PGPs, in short, it could not energize the formation of new
plans on a large scale.[32]

By 1976 the politicians, with the exception of Kennedy, either accepted
the plans' critique of the law or declined to bother to contest it. Clearly the
plans cared very deeply about matters that to the politicians seemed minor,
and no one wanted the HMO effort rendered unworkable by such details.
When the consensus group demonstrated that all the major interests within
the industry had unanimously agreed on a concrete set of amendments, no
major political figure save Kennedy would fight to withhold what they
sought. That the unworkability of the law may have been in part a self-
fulfilling prophecy—that by dismissing and attacking the law as unworkable, the plans may have helped to make it so—was beside the point.

It is not and will never be known whether the 1973 law was workable.
As a theoretical matter, it is impossible rigorously to disentangle the effects
of the law from the host of other problems and challenges facing young

32. The term "mobilizing consent" is taken from Samuel H. Beer, "The British Legislature and the
Problem of Mobilizing Consent," in Elke Frank, ed., *Lawmakers in a Changing World* (Prentice-Hall,
1966).

HMOs. As a practical matter, the demonstration of the law's effects ended with the passage of amendments in 1976.[33] Be that as it may, in the industry's celebration in 1976 the central point was lost from view: the law was amended not because it was demonstrably unworkable but because it had proved unacceptable to Kaiser and other well-established plans, which argued as if what was unacceptable to them was necessarily disastrous to the HMO industry as a whole.

When the issue is seen as one of acceptability to the industry giants, not workability for the industry as a whole, it ceases to be surprising that the amendments have failed to make the difference between a large HMO industry and a small one, or between a highly successful HMO program and a halting one. However much observers may have confused workability with acceptability and the HMO law with the HMO strategy, the distinctions remain of the essence: making the law acceptable to the industry giants is one thing; making the strategy workable is quite another.

Strategy versus Structure

The clash between the ethos of politicians and of PGPs produced six years (1971–76) of skirmishing over whether or not HMOs would partake of politics as usual. Few HMO proponents hesitated to claim an exemption. The politicians' refusal to grant dispensation accounts for the familiar charge that federal policymakers wrongheadedly insisted on combining two sets of incompatible objectives in one program, that they tried to blend a modest, fair market test of HMOs' cost-containment powers with an ambitious, social-goals approach that made HMOs the entering wedge of national health insurance.

The distinction between workability and acceptability suggests that the conventional wisdom may be posing the wrong question. The right question may not be, "why were HMOs forced to endure the coincidence of incompatible goals that could only drag them down?" but rather, "why did HMOs prove so incapable of withstanding expectations and demands under which other programs bear up better?"

33. More accurately, the demonstration ended sometime between June 1975 (when James Hastings, with Rogers as cosponsor, introduced amendments to the 1973 law) and November 1975 (when the House overwhelmingly passed these amendments). At these points it was widely believed that the HMO industry had successfully made its case and that it would be only a matter of time until the Senate followed suit. Thus the demonstration (which could be said to have begun in January 1974) lasted for little more than one and one-half years.

The nostrum that policymakers should above all clarify their objectives and then move to eliminate inconsistencies from programs is advice—no doubt sound theoretically—that a decentralized political system cannot easily follow. Without strong and responsible parties or other means of pulling its structural fragments into a coherent, coordinated whole, a decentralized system must make policy by means of ad hoc coalition-building with the raw materials of diverse and separated political games. Because coalition-building may grind to a halt over logical conflicts about inconsistent goals, politicians tend to seek means of including all goals with an important following. Proposals important enough to be considered and acted on are therefore usually destined to be saddled with unrelated or incompatible goals as they are transformed into public programs.

Examples are abundant. The social security and Medicare programs are both contributory, social insurance programs and redistribution programs.[34] Federal housing programs are frequently designed to aid the disadvantaged, spur the housing industry, and stimulate the economy. The tax laws raise revenue, manage the economy, offer incentives selectively, and reward influential political groups. The statutes governing many of the independent regulatory commissions seek at once to promote competition and to restrain it.[35] The general revenue-sharing program was expected to allot aid both on the basis of need and in response to local effort.[36] The model cities program was designed to encourage both citizen participation and administrative coordination.[37] The professional standards review organizations are expected to save money and improve quality of care. The health systems agencies are asked to constrain proliferation of medical facilities and improve access to care.

Although the multiple and incompatible goals incorporated in these programs may seem to guarantee unworkability, the effects are highly varied. In the general revenue-sharing program the clash between principles of need and effort produced a standoff between the two—an allocation of aid roughly corresponding to the population of recipient jurisdictions. Although the housing programs have been repeatedly attacked for their

34. Martha Derthick, *Policymaking for Social Security* (Brookings Institution, 1979).

35. Alan Stone, *Economic Regulation and the Public Interest: The Federal Trade Commission in Theory and Practice* (Cornell University Press, 1977), especially chaps. 2, 3.

36. Samuel H. Beer, "The Adoption of General Revenue Sharing: A Case Study in Public Sector Politics," *Public Policy*, vol. 24 (Spring 1976), pp. 132–49.

37. See James Q. Wilson's comments in *Journal of the American Institute of Planners*, vol. 32 (November 1966), p. 373; Lawrence D. Brown and Bernard J. Frieden, "Rulemaking by Improvisation: Guidelines and Goals in the Model Cities Program," *Policy Sciences*, vol. 7 (December 1976), pp. 457–88.

generosity to various middlemen in the housing industry, they have also been of significant benefit to the poor. The regulatory agencies have wrestled with the proper means of assuring a healthy mix of restrictions on and encouragement for competition with results that vary among agencies and within agencies over time. The social security and Medicare programs, although not free of problems, have been by any reasonable standards successful in improving the incomes and medical care of the elderly. Despite their various imperfections, none of these programs has been rendered clearly unworkable by the mixing of disparate goals. This is fortunate indeed, because it is very unlikely that any of them would have come into existence had such mixing been precluded.

All of these programs have their unintended consequences, which policy analysts have exposed at great length and have often traced back, with a fine Cartesian eye, to the mixed and inconsistent goals assigned them. The U.S. welfare state is perhaps now sufficiently mature that the early blush of scandal and revelation surrounding the discovery that things do not work out exactly as envisioned—an inevitable misfortune in any important public or private undertaking—may be allowed to fade. A distinct and equally important problem, as Albert O. Hirschman points out, may be seen in those governmental efforts whose intended consequences somehow fail to materialize at all.[38] The HMO program is perhaps a textbook case of this problem.

The programs most vulnerable to goal conflicts are those that require a rapid, large-scale construction of new organizations with complex missions. Model cities agencies did have difficulty reconciling coordination with participation, for example, and HSAs have been puzzled by the relationship between containing costs and improving access. Yet even here these tensions are of secondary importance; the fundamental problem is not that they were saddled with incompatible goals but rather that they were poorly conceived and ill designed to accomplish anything at all. Had model cities agencies confronted no participation requirement, for instance, they still would probably have failed to induce much coordination among municipal agencies. Were HSAs relieved of their mandate to improve access, they would still be badly equipped to contain costs. A similar argument may be made for HMOs.

The combination of disparate and competing goals in one program is not a sure recipe for failure. Some goals coexist more easily than do others,

---

38. *The Passions and the Interests* (Princeton University Press, 1977), p. 131.

and some programs improvise ways of managing tensions more successfully than do others. Although it can do no harm to urge policymakers to clarify their goals, a more practical piece of advice is that they should try, on the basis of experience, to distinguish between policy strategies that are able to accommodate disparate goals and those more fragile strategies likely to be undone or greatly troubled by inconsistencies. In general it will be wise to avoid the latter, or, if there are compelling reasons to press ahead with them, not expect to achieve large results quickly.

Viewed in this perspective, the conventional wisdom that the problems of the HMO program arose from its incompatible goals takes for granted what most needs to be explained. The critique implies that in the particular case of HMOs the lawmakers should have suspended the rules of their political games and passed a bill that met the criteria of greatest interest to the industry. In a word, the HMO program should have been depoliticized.

Such an approach, implausible in any program, was even less plausible in the HMO case than in others. A comprehensive proposal like HMOs, combining in one package a thoroughgoing rearrangement of basic elements of health care delivery and financing, naturally worked as a lightning rod attracting a comprehensive range of disagreements, or, to shift images, as a prolonged Rorschach test into which policymakers read what they wished. The inescapably synthetic nature of the undertaking—the forgone conclusion that the federally qualified HMO would be a replica of no living entity, but instead an exercise in concept-formation, a hybrid—reinforced these tendencies. In such an exercise it was inevitable that one man's small detail would be another's essential provision—that to some dental care, for example, would be a side issue, to others a tremendous need, one of the "greatest needs in the country."[39] No one who considered the political "technology" of policymaking could have doubted that the HMO law would be highly detailed and the product of endless compromises—or that this political technology would clash sharply with the organizational technology of running a PGP.

The larger setting of the politics of health care policy in the early 1970s worked in the same direction. Health maintenance organizations could not have entered the federal agenda and remained untainted by the effects of divided government, the skirmishing over national health insurance, the strong currents of reformist thinking about the social obligations of

39. Senator Kennedy, *Physicians Training Facilities and Health Maintenance Organizations,* Hearing before the Subcommittee on Health of the Senate Labor and Public Welfare Committee, 92 Cong. 1 and 2 sess., 6 pts. (GPO, 1971–72), pt. 2, p. 600.

medicine, legislative-executive conflicts over the nomination of an assistant secretary for health, vetoes of bills supporting the HEW budget and the Hill-Burton program, and more. And the HMO industry itself was badly split and uncertain of its aims. Purists in the labor movement and in some established plans stood almost as far from the Ellwood eclectics as Kennedy did from Nixon. The HMO initiative could hardly have withstood all these vicissitudes and emerged as a model of businesslike efficiency and rationality. The important question about HMOs is not why they were so grievously politicized but rather why the HMO proposal proved too fragile to withstand the inescapably rough hands of politics as usual.

One important source of this fragility was, as noted above, the peculiar nature of the HMO industry itself. The HMO initiative was sold to the Nixon administration by Paul Ellwood, an outsider, while the authentic voices of the industry before the legislature were those of the GHAA, Kaiser, and a few other large plans. The large plans were uncommonly insulated from grant politics, having no need of the largesse the federal government proposed to confer on HMOs. Persnickety, detached, and secure in the knowledge that their views were correct, the plans were not loath to insist that the law meet their demands in all major respects or to denounce and avoid it when their demands were not met.

Even if the large plans had been deeply implicated in the program and eager to realize federal intentions, however, the HMO undertaking would have remained extremely fragile. The basic reason is that organization-building by means of public policy is especially complicated. Throughout the HMO debate there seems to have been little awareness that the government was considering a distinctive policy strategy, an approach with definite limitations and pitfalls that might be viewed and studied against analytic variables derived from earlier governmental experience.

Organization-building is not merely one task among others that government may happen to undertake. It is a highly complex endeavor that rests on an elongated and contingent chain of causes and effects. This may be illustrated by a crude typology of governmental modes of intervention. Government's simplest activities are those that involve a direct grant of money to people or institutions. Examples are social security payments to individuals and general revenue-sharing payments to state and localities; in both cases government defines eligibility and then sends those eligible a check. This may be called a second-order policy because it consists of only two terms: government and recipient.

Somewhat more complex are typical grant-in-aid efforts, in which government extends aid to an institution in order to induce it to alter its behavior (usually at the margin of its continuing procedures) for the benefit of some third party or group. Thus government may fund medical schools on the condition that they expand the ranks of general practitioners (presumably an advantage to society as a whole and a special advantage to the underserved); it may give local school departments funds with which to create new programs for the educationally disadvantaged; it may impose rules on an industry in the expectation that the industry will treat its customers differently than it would in the absence of the rules. This third-order relationship involves government, recipient, and beneficiary.

Third-order processes include federal "agency-building" efforts. In these cases the federal government gives money to state or local governments to establish a new public administrative entity to carry out new, but nonetheless fairly clear and straightforward, purposes usually involving delivery of social services or physical redevelopment. Examples include urban renewal and public housing agencies.

Agency-building may be contrasted with organization-building, a more complex, fourth-order strategy in which government builds an organization which enters a larger universe of organizations and by its presence produces benefits for the general population or for some subset of it. Whereas agency-building usually takes place under the auspices of state or local government, develops new administrative entities with direct account-ability to public officials, and addresses fairly well-understood purposes, organization-building generally creates institutions with tenuous, ambiguous, or no relations with state and local government; is often catalytic or speculative in purpose, aiming to trigger "systems change," not merely to deliver services or do physical redevelopment; and frequently sets its sights on ambitious goals supported by problematic clients and no clear technology.

Like most strategies, organization-building has the vices of its virtues. It is attractive to policymakers because it promotes innovation, coordination, competition, or whatever without displacement or regulation. No one is driven from the scene or forced by government to change his ways. The seemingly nonconflictual, indirect nature of the strategy largely explains its political appeal. But this indirection is purchased at a high price in fragility, for organization-building depends on a long chain of links, weakness at any point of which may undercut the whole effort.

The HMO proposal suffered all the innate fragility of a fourth-order, organization-building enterprise: unless government designed the organizations correctly, they could not be expected to enter and revitalize health care markets correctly and therefore would not have the correct effects on the incentives and behavior of physicians, consumers, and competitors. It was therefore most pertinent to inquire how these inherent weaknesses might be repaired. And to guide such an inquiry, there was abundant empirical evidence—for example, the Tennessee Valley Authority (TVA), regional organizations, the comprehensive health planning bodies (later transformed into the health systems agencies), neighborhood health centers, community action agencies, model cities agencies, and small businesses launched by the Small Business Administration. The HMO enthusiasts might have tried to consider their plans as a species of this genus in order to divine problems and opportunities in the organization-building strategy. Apparently none did.

The record of most of these ambitious programs shows high hopes, much effort, and little accomplishment. The one clear exception is TVA,[40] and this exception may prove the rule. Unlike the other examples of the strategy, the TVA "had sweeping powers and, as it turned out, a rich source of independent revenue." Indeed its very success was an ironic source of failure: it may be that TVA "failed (that is, was not repeated as an organizational form) because it was so powerful and effective in one place. It became clear that putting such a creature into the larger universe of organizations again and again would be very disruptive."[41] Beyond question, the record shows that it is extremely difficult to achieve ambitious policy goals rapidly by means of organization-building, that the strategy tends to be cumbersome and highly inefficient.

The legacy of these efforts suggests some analytic variables and predictions of the degree of difficulty organization-building efforts are likely to encounter. Specifically, organization-building is easier when the organization is itself governmental—a public organization run by public money—and more difficult if it is launched by government and then expected to sink or swim as a business selling products in private markets; easier if the new organizations are incremental extensions of activities already performed by and familiar to the government or the private sector, and more difficult if they are truly innovative and new; easier if the organizations to be built are one (the TVA) or few in number, and harder if they are to be

40. Philip Selznick, *TVA and the Grass Roots* (Harper and Row, Torchbook, 1966). Neighborhood health centers are arguably another exception; see Karen Davis and Cathy Schoen, *Health and the War on Poverty: A Ten-Year Appraisal* (Brookings Institution, 1978), chap. 6.

41. Martha Derthick, Brookings Institution, personal communication, February 29, 1980.

numerous and nationwide; easier if the federal government delegates substantial portions of the enterprise to subnational governments, and harder if it runs the process itself.

The HMO proposal combined these four variables in the least favorable possible way. It deliberately avoided creating publicly maintained or subsidized plans—the federal government would give them funds at the start, and the competitive rigors of the private market would then decide their fate. The enterprises were highly innovative, not incremental extensions of existing activities. The genius of Ellwood's proposal (and of the Congress's work), after all, was precisely that, transcending all existing models, it was a creative, synthetic, largely untried blend. The proposal envisioned large numbers of plans quickly—seventeen hundred in less than ten years, proclaimed HEW. And the program would be run by HEW, according to firm federal criteria, not delegated to the states and localities. There was every reason to believe that the policy approach adopted would make an inherently fragile fourth-order strategy more fragile still.

Furthermore, the strategy's requirements for success were in important ways at odds with the intricacies of U.S. political structures. The fourth-order logic of organization-building assumes that an unbroken chain of theoretical ifs and thens can be put in place intact in the real world, but this assumption is most unlikely to be met in a highly decentralized political system. As a practical matter, the four-term chain must extend across three levels of a federal system, among three separated branches of government (with further divisions within each branch) at each level, and beyond government itself to a powerful private sector. These forms of decentralization allow many independent actors and institutions to interfere with the orderly working-out of the program's theoretical presuppositions.

Ironically, a decentralized system is at once most likely to find the organization-building strategy attractive and least likely to be able to make it work. The HMO strategy was politically appealing precisely because instead of resorting to more government and more regulation it worked by means of private market processes at the local level. Unfortunately, no one seems to have dwelled on the possibility that making HMOs marketable at local levels might presuppose centralization in both the political and health care systems that would sully the appeals of the strategy itself.

The program's designers bumped into the refractory prerogatives of decentralized actors at every turn. The states are of central importance to HMOs, for in the United States, which lacks a national health insurance scheme, the states mainly regulate health insurance plans and insurers, and

HMOs, which offer health coverage as well as health services, come under their diverse and sometimes unfavorable laws. Delegating the HMO effort to them was out of the question.

The private sector too is of great importance. In the absence of national health insurance, most health benefit plans in the United States are either offered by employers directly to employees or determined by collective bargaining between union representatives and management. Contents of health plans vary from firm to firm. Health maintenance organizations can enter forcefully into the prevailing pattern only if employers offer them, union bargaining agents accept them, employers contribute enough to the HMO premium to make them financially attractive, and employees, taking account of financial and many other factors, choose to enroll in them. Unless the federal government could firmly influence these state and private forces toward a more favorable position on HMOs, the organization-building strategy could not hope to take off. But merely to list these decentralized prerogatives is to suggest the difficulty of changing them rapidly and significantly.

These private and subnational prerogatives stoked the fires of disagreement within the political games of the separated powers of the national government in two ways. First, they generated severe ideological disputes about the proper role of government. Second, they aroused a range of affected interests to pressure the lawmakers to protect their holdings. The result was the continuing displacement of ends and transformation of issues that extensive decentralization often produces.

Open enrollment and the scope of the benefit package to be written into the HMO law, for example, could not simply be treated as health care issues. Open enrollment and such additional benefits as dental care for children could be imposed fairly on the HMOs only if (so the industry argued) they were imposed on the competition too. But this equitable arrangement involved much more than a mere particular application of federal decisionmaking; it meant a radical shift of regulatory responsibility from the states to the federal government. What began as an issue of health care coverage was soon transformed into one of states' rights. Even those legislators who, like Kennedy, were sympathetic to a broader federal role, knew that such a shift was not worth seriously proposing; the insurance industry, organized medicine, and the states would not stand for it.

But if the states' regulatory authority over HMOs were left entirely untouched, state laws could thwart the federal government's HMO-building plans in many parts of the country. Hence the proposal that such laws be overridden in the federal HMO law. This proposal was enormously controversial, however, triggering lengthy debates within the administration, in the Rogers subcommittee, and in conference. When the law finally emerged, the American Medical Association and the states' righters (including the administration) had succeeded in limiting the provision to an exemption of only federally aided HMOs from some interfering state laws.

So too the extreme privatism and variety of employee health benefits left the definition of a marketable plan largely indeterminate. Any proposed benefit package or set of other requirements was immediately subject to endless debate sustained by data dismissable as unrepresentative. Kennedy's approach—design the HMOs right and then subsidize them to cover the market disadvantages that might be imposed by the design—was adamantly opposed by the AMA, which protested that private practitioners should not be asked to compete with federally subsidized HMOs, and by conservatives for whom the word subsidy was a red flag. But the need to design and aid the plans without subsidizing them produced endless debates over the proper permutations and combinations among grants, loans, and loan guarantees; public, private, and for-profit HMOs; stages of aid; and more. And the dual choice provision, which recognized that most health coverage is provided in the work place, failed initially to take account of the prerogatives of organized labor—an omission that proved very costly to the program in its formative years, for union rights were no less crucial to the resolution of health care issues than were states' rights and those of private practitioners.

The lawmakers' concern for states' rights and private prerogatives not only deflected attention from the substance of health care questions but also made it extremely difficult to write one HMO law that would apply well, let alone equally well, to the entire country. Decentralization was fundamentally at odds with the political logic of the quid pro quo, which led the federal government to ask federally qualified HMOs to do more and be better than the mainstream, in exchange for the advantages of start-up grants and loans, dual choice, and an override of obstructive state laws. The requirements posed an immediate threat to the organizational norms of existing groups, and the compensating advantages to them and to new plans alike were of uncertain dollar value and would vary greatly with individual markets and locales. Requirements met easily by some plans might prove onerous or disastrous to others. The industry therefore found it easy to brand the unacceptable provisions of the law as unworkable. If they could not prove that they were right, no one could prove them wrong either, and the fact was that no one could tell how often they or their critics would prove right until the law had been extensively tested in practice.

For the federal policymakers the task of designing plans that would prove marketable in the decentralized U.S. setting imposed extreme rigidity on customarily fluid political processes. Negotiating, trading, and compromising within committees and chambers and between chambers and branches grew precarious when experts warned that even one small slip— inclusion of so seemingly small a requirement as preventive dental care for children, for example—could render the whole package uncompetitive and all the politicians' work unworkable.

The politics of HMO-building were of course no less frustrating to the industry. In its eyes, the politicians were bent on making trade-offs in a most cavalier fashion between unreasonable requirements and unknown compensations. The results at once violated the established plans' notions of sound management and left the infants of the industry unclear as to what effects the law would have on any plan, let alone on all. Thus the apparent clash between incompatible goals concealed a deeper, more important clash between the strategic requirements of HMO-building and the structural features of U.S. politics. A federal law to launch marketable plans in decentralized medical and political settings required the politicians to forgo what they could not do without—negotiating flexibility—and the HMOs to accept what they as businessmen could least tolerate—extreme uncertainty.

In view of the difficulties of fitting one federal law to highly varied subnational and private circumstances, the logical course might seem to have been the all-inclusive, highly flexible Nixon bill. This approach, after all, would have allowed almost any self-proclaimed HMO to adapt as it saw fit to almost any local market. But apart from the question of merits, the decentralized politics of policymaking were inconsistent with this approach. Nixon's game was but one of three, in fact the least important. Democratic health leaders in Congress would not accept a law without specific conditions and safeguards to take account of the double-edged sword of prepayment incentives, to exclude charlatans from the program, and for other equally good reasons. Moreover, the HMO industry itself was sharply divided over the role of IPAs, for-profit plans, and other entities the Nixon bill would have included. In sum, when a strategy with the characteristics of the HMO proposal was entrusted to political structures and processes with the characteristics of the U.S. government, the outcome could hardly fail to be much like that of the 1973 law.

A more centralized political system would have developed well-defined party positions on HMOs, not three separate political games interweaving partisan and other themes separately in each of two legislative chambers and the executive. National health insurance would have reduced or eliminated the marketing uncertainties associated with a diversity of work-related plans. Instead of a dual choice provision, government would have made HMOs one official option to which the citizenry might entrust its health entitlements. Central regulation of health insurers would have reduced or eliminated the states' rights issue and the problem of state-erected barriers to HMOs. Although such a system might produce a more rational HMO program, it presupposes precisely the policies—national health insurance and central regulation—that most U.S. policymakers hoped HMOs would avoid or supplant. In other words, any system that could implement the HMO strategy properly would have no need to adopt it.[42]

The political decentralization that made the HMO proposal so attractive in the United States also made its eventual legislative embodiment unacceptable to some and uncertain and controversial for all—the worst possible climate in which to launch new, small, vulnerable medical care businesses. This outcome is no one's fault: the problems of devising—by means of the interplay of political games among separate powers responsive to subnational and private interests as well as to their own—one law acceptable alike to all major political designers and to all market competitors under highly heterogenous conditions are insuperable. The irony of the HMO episode is that the hopes of policymakers who would use a decentralized strategy—reorganization of local markets by means of organization-building—as a bulwark against greater centralization were decisively stymied by the decentralization of the political system itself.

The entry of a low-consensus proposal into a decentralized political system greatly magnified the intrinsic fragility of the organization-building strategy. This strategy is attractive when there is wide agreement among policymakers on general goals ("the need to fight medical cost inflation") but little agreement on operational goals. New federally designed organizations easily become omnibus vehicles onto which a wide range of specific

---

42. More centralized governments have not adopted such systems. "Small closed panels" such as the American HMOs are "rare abroad," writes William Glaser; "where they exist, they are difficult to reconcile with the clauses in the [national health insurance] statute that were written during the political compromises with the office practitioners, guaranteeing every doctor the right to see any patient under national health insurance." Nonetheless, Glaser believes that the experience of the French *mutualités* might teach the United States how to make HMOs work. *Health Insurance Bargaining: Foreign Lessons for Americans* (Gardner Press, 1978), pp. 244–45.

goals are loaded as the political process plays on—a development that makes a fourth-order undertaking more fragile. Whereas Congress left the statutory definition of the model cities agency vague in most respects, allowing the agency's organizational character to be defined largely by political battles in the cities, the definition of federally qualified HMOs was fought over in detail in three distinct political games and within the HMO industry itself from the very beginning of the legislative process down to the last compromise in the conference that finally produced the controversial law of 1973.

The troublesome values that the HMO law assigned to the key organization-building variables discussed above stemmed largely from the incongruity between central theory and decentralized fact. Because injecting federally subsidized competition into the largely private fee-for-service system was unacceptable to those enamored of a fair market test, the plans had to be marketable. Because no HMO prototype struck the central players in the political games and in the HMO industry as simultaneously feasible and desirable, the federal law had to be based on a hybrid that borrowed features from all existing models but bore a clear family resemblance to none. Because the federal strategy would work on the scale anticipated only if it affected many private and subnational actors largely beyond the federal government's direct control, the plans had to be numerous enough to enroll a substantial share of the population in a relatively short time. And because the states were generally uninterested in or hostile to HMOs, the program had to be federally run, not delegated. Alas, these preconditions of successful program design warred with the preconditions of successful organization-building.

In short, HMOs are an extreme case of a general policymaking approach that suffers from a strong probability that high hopes will after long and painstaking efforts end in disappointment. The fourth-order, organization-building strategy usually combines high fragility with low consensus; the specific properties of the HMO subtype combined especially high fragility with especially low consensus. A reasonable inference—and practical lesson—is that the HMO-building strategy was not a plausible candidate for federal policy and that if it were to be pursued, little should have been expected from it and little promised of it, at least in the short run.

In 1976, by means of skillful and unusual diplomacy, the GHAA's legislative counsel, James Doherty, supplied, at least temporarily, the consensus that had been lacking. The amendments that made the HMO law finally acceptable to the industry were expected to make it workable at last. They were powerless, however, to reduce the fragility of the strategy. Neither consensus nor political responsiveness could undo the many difficulties of achieving fourth-order results in the health care field by public means.

The small accomplishments of the federal HMO effort, protracted, amended, and reorganized as it has been, are not explained by the failings of the federal government. The conflict between the requisites of organization-building by the central government and the workings of decentralized political and medical care systems suggests that the explanation should be sought not in Washington but in realms largely beyond federal control and in many cases even beyond effective federal influence.

CHAPTER NINE

Policy Analysis and Disembodied Incentives: HMOs as Idea and as Strategy

That the laws of supply and demand can be stated at all in elementary economics depends on certain institutional conditions. It depends on the existence of money as a standard in which prices can be expressed and on the existence of markets, whether the old market-place or its modern equivalents. It is much more difficult to explain the institutional conditions themselves than to explain behavior once the institutions are given. Elementary economics was lucky in being able to take institutions pretty much for granted.

George Homans, *The Nature of Social Science*

THE CLASH that explains the limitations of the federal HMO-building effort is not that between the policymakers and the industry. It is rather a clash of quite a different character, one between the analytical model that supported the transformation of the HMO idea into an HMO strategy and the medical care institutions that the model attempted at once to describe and to change. The key to the success of HMO-building lay not in Washington, but in the larger society—in private and largely local settings where the interactions among consumers, technology, physicians, hospitals, and insurers that make up the U.S. health care system take place. This chapter will argue that the HMO strategy accomplished little because it took for granted a conceptual image of the workings of health care institutions that was seriously incomplete and in important respects misleading. Ultimately the program's shortcomings lie in the realm of ideas, in the largely economics-based policy analysis on which the HMO proposal rested.[1] Failing to concern itself properly with the institutional properties of the health care system, the HMO proposal mistook what was—and indeed still is—in theory a good idea for what would prove in practice to be a good federal policy strategy.

1. Some readers may suspect that as used here the terms "policy analysis" and "policy analysts" are euphemisms for "economics" and "economists." This is not the case. "True" economists—that is,

Incentives versus Institutions

Throughout the 1970s, federal policymakers dealing with health maintenance organizations (HMOs) cheerfully relied on two code words reiterated by policy analysts—"incentives" and "competition"—tied together conceptually by the catchphrase "market approach." For professional economists these terms denote processes with reasonably clear definitions and concomitants. To most of the policy analysts and policymakers engaged in HMO-building these terms had a host of vague and imprecise, but nevertheless ambitious and seductive connotations. A market approach built on incentives and competition promised the policymakers a way of avoiding regulation, governmentally imposed constraint, and displacement of established interests. Health maintenance organizations promised such all-American ends as pluralism, choice, efficiency, and reorganization achieved by all-American means. The correct manipulation of conceptual elements produced a strategy that would yield both cost-containment, attractive to all, but especially to conservatives, and a challenge to fee-for-service medicine, attractive to the innovation-and-reform-minded. Equally important, it appeared to ensure that rarity, the Pareto-optimal improvement: according to the literal theory of HMOs, the organizations would contain costs, improve access, and enhance quality of care, without trade-offs among these goals. A federal HMO program would leave no one worse off than before and, more attractive still, could be conducted inexpensively. Policymakers seldom encounter so compact and glowing a package of policy assets and it is no wonder that they rushed to embrace it. Even those who, like Edward Kennedy, perceived the dangers of double-edged swords in the HMO incentive system did not appear to doubt that sustained legislative tinkering to add specifics and safeguards to the administration's proposal would realize its potential.

---

professors of and Ph.D.s in economics—were strikingly absent from the ranks of the policy entrepreneurs who promoted and sold the HMO proposal in the early 1970s, and some—Herbert Klarman, for example—discussed the proposal in several balanced and skeptical essays. As the 1970s wore on, some prominent health economists could be counted as vocal supporters of a public HMO development effort, but many more remained cautious and decidedly nonentrepreneurial. In short, the focus of this chapter is not economists but principally "those, sometimes found in high government positions, who are not economists but who behave as they believe economists would, preferring to rely more on their understanding of economic laws that 'cannot be repealed' than to exercise judgments that are open to dispute." Rashi Fein, "Social and Economic Attitudes Shaping American Health Policy," *Milbank Memorial Fund Quarterly/Health and Society*, vol. 58 (Summer 1980), p. 370.

Health economists, of course, offer long lists of the ways in which the health care system deviates from the preconditions of perfect or normal market behavior,[2] and these problems have often deterred proponents of market approaches from applying their solutions to that system. The HMO, however, seemed to overcome these deviations. For example, it ceased to matter that physician suppliers define the degree and type of consumer demand or that consumers lack the information and interest to shop around for efficient suppliers if physicians, by electing to work for an HMO, and consumers, by choosing to subscribe to one, could be made to "precommit" themselves to efficiency.[3]

Under the spell of the analysts' code words, policymakers failed to anticipate how difficult it might prove to be to build HMOs by means of public policy. As the difficulties became clear in the course of trials and errors, critics—including some of the policy analysts who had originally sold the proposal in Washington—concluded that politicians had taken up an excellent idea and somehow managed to ravish it. It occurred neither to them nor to the abashed politicians that even if the policy process had gone smoothly, and even if an entirely acceptable law had been constructed, the fundamental problems of HMO-building would all have remained largely undiminished. This possibility did not occur because much of the policy analysis behind the HMO effort was deficient. Instead of clarifying practical questions of central importance to the policymakers, it obscured them. Instead of pushing forward major operational issues for deliberation, it prevented them from being recognized as problematic.

The proposition that all good things in medical care could be realized simultaneously and without serious costs and trade-offs by means of HMOs rested on two basic conceptual elements: the incentive-based self-regulating organization and, as a result of the proliferation of these organizations, a competition-based self-regulating system of health care. These two ingredients defined the literal theory of HMOs, a theory that could be no stronger than these two elements. Flaws in the foundation inevitably produced shakiness in the superstructure built upon them.

The analysts' line of reasoning gained force from its close coincidence with the two major reformist strains of that school of thought within the health community that has long argued for a "reorganization" or "restruc-

---

2. For example, Herbert E. Klarman, *The Economics of Health* (Columbia University Press, 1965), pp. 10–19.
3. Victor R. Fuchs, "Economics, Health and Post-Industrial Society," *Milbank Memorial Fund Quarterly/Health and Society*, vol. 57 (Spring 1979), p. 170.

turing" of the U.S. health care system not by means of government rules but rather by means of changes in financial incentives. One group of reformers calls for "industrialization" of the health care system. On this view it is socially and economically absurd that a specialized, high-technology field such as medicine should continue to be organized in small "cottage industry" units of solo practitioners integrated ad hoc with hospitals, payment mechanisms, medical centers, and other institutional "fragments" in need of coordination on behalf of care of the "whole person." The reformers find the logical solution in a rearrangement and coordination of the fragments in larger-unit organizations, which would make the scale of production conform to the technology of the industry. The HMO, an organization that combines in one setting doctors, clinics, hospitals, administrators, and consumers (or at any rate brings them together in one plan) and, under a central financial administration, assumes full responsibility for the comprehensive health care needs of members struck some as the ideal embodiment of this reorganization.[4]

A second group of reformers calls for the replacement of fee-for-service payment with thoroughgoing prepayment. The critique is obvious and straightforward: fee-for-service reimbursement gives physicians an incentive to supply excessive care to the consumer. By requiring doctors to provide care on a fixed budget set in advance and to share in the risk of exceeding that budget, the HMO would reverse this illogical incentive system. The organizations' need to compete for customers would assure not only that doctors will avoid giving too little care for economic reasons, but, on the contrary, that they will treat patients early, even keep them well, in order to hold down costs.

The synthesis in one organization of comprehensive delivery and prepaid financing yielded a rational, self-regulating entity which, when set down in the larger system, would by the competitive pressures of its efficiency force that system to change its ways; the result would be improved health care through the self-regulation of the market. This fusion of reformist thinking popular among many "progressive" health professionals since the reports of the Committee on the Costs of Medical Care in the 1930s and of arguments widespread among health economists generated the

4. Paul M. Ellwood and others, "Health Maintenance Strategy," *Medical Care*, vol. 9 (May–June 1971), p. 298. By contrast, in the housing field, "economies of scale do seem possible, but the view that the housing industry could achieve huge savings by becoming 'industrialized' is now recognized as naive." William G. Grigsby and others, *Re-Thinking Housing and Community Development Policy* (Department of City and Regional Planning, University of Pennsylvania, 1977), p. 15.

reasoning that the HMO proponents advanced and the politicians accepted.

The proponents were far too ready to accept the assurances of the model that economic processes would reconcile quality, access, and cost in the desirable ways predicted. The limitations of the literal theory were explored in part 1 of this book and need not be reviewed again here. But even if one granted the proponents their predictions, the difficulty remained that they generally took for granted the most problematic element of the exercise, the organization-building process itself—those coordinated contributions needed to put an HMO together in the first place. To recall Homans's words, quoted at the head of this chapter, economic theory may have considerable success at explaining "behavior once the institutions are given," but "it is much more difficult to explain the institutional conditions themselves."[5] Although economic theory may be, as Homans put it, "lucky in being able to take institutions pretty much for granted," those who resort to economic theory for policy analyses may enjoy no such luck. The HMO episode demonstrates a central irony and limitation of economics-based policy analysis in the health field, that an orientation that takes so little direct account of the institution-building process should generate so often and so enthusiastically recommendations that presuppose heroic institution-building efforts.

Under the spell of the model, policymakers failed carefully to consider the HMO as an organization, as a system of contributions. Instead they tended to view it as some unitary entity whose existence was contingent mainly on the right amounts and composition of federal aid. In the eyes of the administration, as many as seventeen hundred HMOs could be launched with small federal sums because, so long as requirements were kept few and flexible, private sponsors would rush in with private capital. To Kennedy and other liberals, an indefinitely large number of HMOs could be started if only the federal government put up enough billions of dollars. Debate then turned to the problem of finding middle ground between these unacceptable extremes—to the relative importance of grants versus loans, to the role subsidies should play, to what type of plan should be eligible for what type of aid. Between the abstractions of the policy analysts and the details of the lawmakers, basic middle-range questions—assuming the presence of federal funds, large or small, who would want to claim them? what would they do with them? what results could be expected?—were largely overlooked.

5. George Homans, *The Nature of Social Science* (Harbinger, 1967), pp. 49–50.

Unfortunately, the plausibility of the HMO concept as a policy strategy depended heavily on answers to these and other questions, discussed in chapter 2. Who would sponsor HMOs? Why would physicians go to work for them? Why would consumers subscribe to them? Why would hospitals cooperate with them? Even if one granted the simplistic notion that the incentives of the ideal-typical HMO would work as intended if these contributors contributed, what incentives did the proposal offer them to contribute and keep contributing in harmonious interaction over time?

This simple question had an equally simple answer: few. But except for some program specialists in the health bureaucracy, whose advice on the Ellwood plan the HEW generalists politely sought in 1970 and then promptly ignored, no one appears fully to have recognized the importance of these questions. They did not fit the analysts' model, which addressed the behavior, not the creation, of institutions. Nor did they enter the early deliberations of politicians more accustomed to thinking expansively about the formidable leverage of federal grants than about their limits. As events soon showed, however, neglect of these questions proved to be a severe deficiency in the HMO strategy. The model as strategy fell victim to a great gaping black hole, which, like the fabled black holes of science, sucked up the voluminous proposal and compressed it to perhaps a half-pint of plausibility.

A little familiarity with the evolution of the U.S. health care system, or for that matter a little detached rumination, might have shown not only that it was unlikely that key contributors would find themselves strongly induced to form and support HMOs but also that they faced strong disincentives to do so. Basic, bedrock trends in the health care system— not by-products of "faulty incentives," but deeply rooted elements of consumer psychology, professional culture, and organizational character—worked against the growth and development of such plans. The tendency in the United States to entrust the financing and delivery of care to separate hands makes it unlikely that sponsors (some of which, such as hospitals, dealt only with one of these functions, and others of which, such as industrial firms, dealt directly with neither) would attempt to integrate both functions in an HMO under their own auspices. The growth of fee-for-service group practices allows physicians to enjoy most of the advantages of prepaid practice while accepting few of its constraints. Steady expansion of third-party-payment insurance plans reduces the consumer's direct share of medical costs and thus the appeals of an HMO. The tendency to perform more medical functions of an increasingly complex and costly technological character in hospitals sets hospitals at odds with the decreases in inpatient use (and therefore in revenues) that an HMO's accustomed mode of operation entails. All four contributors thus have strong interests in keeping separated processes that the HMO internalizes. In theory, industrialization—pulling together into one organization processes previously performed by interaction among several—is a highly rational and responsible approach to reforming the system. In practice, incorporating matters handled between organizations into a single organizational framework may raise levels of interdependence and problems of coordination and control, and, therefore, conflict, to levels that potential participants will prefer to avoid.

The picture is not unrelievedly grim; contributors face some incentives to sponsor, work for, subscribe to, and cooperate with HMOs. But these incentives appear to be strong enough only to support occasional, relatively small-scale HMO development here and there as favorable coalitions form for largely local reasons. They will not support a nationwide effort to use HMOs as the cutting edge of a "system reorganization." That ambitious objective could not be realized by mere benign manipulation of incentives; it would require instead costly and authoritative governmental measures.

Had the federal government been willing to commit very large sums of money to launch—and subsidize over time—exemplary HMOs offering such high salaries, such broad services, and such attractive facilities (including their own hospitals) that they would have approximated the appeals of a prestigious university medical or private research center or clinic, HMOs and their enrollees might have become numerous. If it had coupled this development strategy with changes in tax laws and in benefit packages and payment procedures in government programs such as Medicare and Medicaid that would discriminate strongly in favor of HMOs, plans and members might have grown more numerous still. (It is also possible, however, other sources of resistance to HMOs would have remained strong, keeping growth small in spite of these federal measures.) But these approaches violated the political rationale that made HMOs attractive in the first place. These organizations were supposed to save federal money, not spend large sums of it. However much HMO proponents in Congress argued the wisdom of spending more in the present in order to realize larger savings in the future, the hard common sense of the conservatives made them skeptical of such futuristic promises. Moreover, this course spelled favoritism, and the point of the exercise for the conservatives was to provide a fair market test. At any rate, few policymakers besides Kennedy were willing to travel this expansive road.

Likewise, manipulation of the incentives at the central government's direct disposal—tilting tax provisions and Medicare payments in favor of HMOs, for instance—violated the understanding that HMOs were a nonregulatory, competitive, nonconflictual approach to reform. At a certain point— that point at which the HMO strategy appeared to be in danger of imposing high budgetary or political costs—the end ceased to justify the means for the politicians. Understandably, therefore, they embraced the analysts' assurances that the HMO strategy was neither costly nor conflictual but merely a procompetitive use of small sums of federal seed money that would trigger large systemwide reforms. Unfortunately, these constraints on input were inconsistent with the proposal's grandiose promises of output. The "moral"—simple, unsubtle, but pertinent—is that incentive-based syllogisms that derive desirable conclusions from a chain of highly problematic institution-building processes should not be taken for finished and plausible pieces of policy analysis.

The fundamental weakness of the HMO proposal was that it rested on an uncritical application of the concept of incentives. This concept is, of course, one of the most useful and widely used in the social sciences, and perhaps the most widely used in policy analysis, but it is not the all-purpose tool it is sometimes taken to be. That policy should "change the incentives" to bring behavior into line with what government seeks has the ring of unassailable insight, eternal truth, elegant simplicity. Not surprisingly, some policy analysts have apparently persuaded themselves that the merest flick of an incentive system can, like Sumner's mores, make anything right. The right incentives, it is confidently declared, will lead businesses back into central cities and urban enterprise zones (the "urbank" proposals); make companies produce and consumers buy much less gasoline (decontrol of gas prices); lead polluting firms to pollute "optimally" (pollution taxes, fees, and "rights"); make lower-class persons behave like solid, hard-working middle-class citizens (improved "objective opportunities"); and lead doctors, who would otherwise treat patients only when they have become ill, to suddenly start keeping them well (HMOs). Very likely, incentives are capable of doing some of these things in some degree and others very little or not at all. Unfortunately, very little is now known about what policy problems successfully lend themselves to what types of incentive-based solutions.

An incentive is simply a reward or penalty. It is of course an elementary and powerful psychosocial truth that people respond to rewards and penalties. This truth, however, cannot be imported wholesale and unrefined into policy analysis and translated directly into useful practical advice. Individuals face incentives; systems have properties. Although system properties are not wholly distinct from individual incentives they are not wholly reducible to them either. Incentives are embodied in sociopolitical and psychocultural contexts, embedded in institutions, in a word. In some cases this fact may be disregarded without harm; in others, reliance on disembodied incentives may render policy advice useless or worse. It is therefore highly apposite to seek principles that distinguish between these situations.

Of any proposal to manipulate incentives as a policy device, three questions should be asked at the outset. Who must be made subject to the incentives if the desired outcome is to occur? How do these actors define rewards and penalties—that is, how do their values bear on the incentives under discussion? How large must the inducements be to bring about the desired outcome? The first question is institutional; it requires a canvass of the major participants in the system that is to be changed. The latter two are psychological and cultural; they require an analysis of values and norms. Unless the answers to these questions are relatively straightforward and favorable, the postulated play of incentives is likely to be impeded, and the incentive approach may not work.

In the case of what the previous chapter termed second-order strategies, where it is reasonable analytically to picture the policy problem as one of bringing about the proper relations between government and individual, the three questions may have direct and actionable answers. For instance, James Q. Wilson has shown that in thinking about crime it can be useful to disengage from deep causal issues, look at the problem as one of the available measures government may take vis-à-vis criminals, and then ask what incentives (in this case, deterrents) government possesses. The "who" is the criminal, the "what" is the loss of freedom, and the "how great" involves deprivations of liberty of greater or lesser length.[6]

Most relationships government attempts to influence by means of policy are of more than second-order complexity, however. In education, for example, the findings of James Coleman and his associates on the correlates of educational achievement among elementary and secondary school students introduced into the generally accepted third-order relationship of government, school, and student, a fourth order—family background.[7] Coleman threw new light on the relationship between government policy

6. *Thinking About Crime* (Vintage Books, 1977). On the difference between policy analysis and causal analysis, see especially chap. 3.
7. James S. Coleman and others, *Equality of Educational Opportunity* (U.S. Government Printing Office, 1966).

and educational achievement precisely because he refused to eschew causal analysis in favor of policy analysis, insisting instead on searching for the influence of hidden "orders" behind accepted images.[8] To be sure the Coleman findings left the policy question far less actionable than it had seemed before. Had the researchers limited themselves to policy analysis in the narrow sense, however—to discussion of readily available "policy tools" for the "manipulation of objective conditions"[9]—they would have missed what now appears to be the heart of the matter.

Failure to appreciate and allow for the nature and complexity of health care institutions is the most important explanation for the disappointments of the HMO strategy. Preoccupied with the theoretical virtues of the HMO as an institution, and overlooking the complexities of bringing these institutions into being, the analysts suggested that government dangle seed money (an incentive) before the eyes of entrepreneurs. But the organization-building process was of fourth-order, not second-order, complexity: government must attract sponsors who must recruit and socialize providers (physicians and hospitals) and then attract and place under the (properly functioning) providers' care a sizable number of consumers. In the assessment of this strategy, the crucial questions of who, what, and how large were generally neglected. The dependence of the comprehensive, responsible HMO on four sets of actors—sponsors, doctors, subscribers, and hospitals; the complex interplay of economic, political, cultural, psychological, and organizational variables in forming the tastes of each group for what an HMO offered them; and the strong forces working against HMO-building and -joining could not realistically be left out of account. Had the analysts' model taken them into account, however, the results would have disrupted the advocates' agenda. The contingent and high-risk nature of the HMO strategy would have been exposed, goals and expectations would have been scaled down, a systemwide reorganization would have been neither promised nor predicted, the numbers game would have appeared foolish, and politicians might have lost interest.

Competition versus Complexity

Even if health maintenance organizations could be built effortlessly and in large numbers, it is unclear what policy impact they would have.

8. James S. Coleman, "The Evaluation of *Equality of Educational Opportunity*," in Frederick Mosteller and Daniel P. Moynihan, eds., *On Equality of Educational Opportunity* (Vintage Books, 1972), pp. 149–50.

9. Wilson, *Thinking About Crime*, pp. 159, 161.

Proponents generally took it for granted that the competitive presence of HMOs in the larger system would engender incentives that would realize the theoretical virtues claimed on behalf of competition. Unfortunately, the outcome the analysts confidently predicted lies mainly in the realm of deduction—which is to say, conjecture and speculation—unsupported by germane empirical evidence.

Although the analysts' theories relied on a second-order image to deduce the benefits that the presence of cost-conscious HMOs would bring about—the unitary HMO "versus" its fee-for-service competition—the process is in reality multiordered, highly complex, and only partially responsive to economic and competitive forces. To accomplish their postulated effects, HMOs must make their presence felt on five variables—consumers, technology, physicians, hospitals, and third-party payers,[10] each of which is subject to a complicated mix of competitive and noncompetitive, monetary and nonmonetary forces of varying strength. In the health field there is no single, personalized object—the benefit-cost balancing criminal to be deterred, for example—at whom the government may beam its incentives. Each of the five loosely linked elements is driven by a distinct set of forces and therefore will respond differently from the others to a governmental stimulus. To predict whether an input injected at the beginning of the complex chain of cause and effect may be expected to generate a desired output, or indeed any recognizable output at all, all five factors should be kept simultaneously in view. Insofar as they fail to set HMOs in their full institutional setting and thus fail to keep interdependence and interaction constantly in view, analysts will fail to get an accurate reading of the efficacy of an HMO's competitive incentives. Unfortunately, not enough is known about the values of these five variables to support confident policy analysis, much less the bold promises of the HMO advocates.

Put simply, health care expenditures reflect five forces: the nature and extent of consumer expectations, the nature and extent of medical technologies, the number and behavior of physicians, the number and organizational character of hospitals, and the structure and scope of third-party-payment mechanisms.[11] These variables interact with one another in local

10. Three of these—consumers, doctors, and hospitals—are also vital to HMO-building. It should be borne in mind that the discussion here concerns not the degree to which these actors are willing to contribute to an HMO but rather the degree to which they may be influenced by an HMO in the course of competition with it. In other words, this section discusses these actors not as internal contributors but instead as the HMO's external objects.

11. The line of argument developed in these sections follows Lawrence D. Brown, "The Scope and Limits of Equality as a Normative Guide to Federal Health Care Policy," *Public Policy*, vol. 26 (Fall 1978), pp. 503–04.

"delivery systems" and therefore must be taken into account in formulating policies at the federal level designed to change these systems. Over time, all five variables have assumed values that call for more and better medical care. Larger numbers of consumers (some of whom find care newly accessible as a result of federal programs) bring ever higher expectations to the system. The growth of medical knowledge and the diffusion of medical technologies generate an ever larger number of more costly procedures that become part of popular and professional definitions of good care. A growing number of doctors, facing the expanding expectations of consumers and widening technological opportunities, have a strong professional and economic interest in giving each patient the most and the best. Hospitals in search of organizational prestige and high-caliber medical staffs expand their beds, facilities, equipment, and services—and therewith their costs. The growth of third-party-payment plans, in which insurers tend to reimburse providers with a less than sharply critical eye, adds fuel to all these expansive, expensive developments.

The number of variables and the complexity of their interaction place great obstacles in the way of policy analyses, that is, recommendations for governmental action based on some combination of theory and research. Sound analyses should neglect none of the five variables, but the variables embody processes very different from one another and therefore disrupt lines of disciplinary specialization. The behavior of physicians should be viewed not only from the standpoint of economics but also from those of the sociology of professions and anthropology. The expectations and behavior of consumers require the insights of psychology, sociology, and economics. Understanding medical technology demands these disciplines and an admixture of natural science. The behavior of hospitals and insurance firms is probably best illuminated by organizational analysis. Taking variables out of context and examining them in the light of one discipline alone (say, economics) guarantees distortion. But examining the full range of variables in the light of several pertinent disciplines mainly exposes the complexity of it all, induces humility and restraint in the student, and leads to cautious and circumscribed policy analyses or to none at all. Those who understand the system most fully tend therefore to be least entrepreneurial in their recommendations and tend least to seize or attract the ear of policymakers.[12] Policy advocacy in the health field presupposes a capacity for terrible simplifications.

12. There are a number of excellent balanced works, highly pertinent to the policy debate, by Eliot Freidson, David Mechanic, and Herbert Klarman, and cited in the footnotes to chapter 4 of this study. It appears, however, that these works had and still have little or no influence on thinking within the HMO

Unfortunately, the simplifications of the analysts may lead to misunderstandings, for if complexity may be willed away in the analytic world, it keeps breaking into the real world. A policy analytic input in the health field must make its way through five "black boxes," each with different institutional properties that skew and distort the input as surely as a prism does a ray of light. The HMO strategy "works" insofar as it injects competitive pressures that break into and change the interinstitutional processes that uncritically favor more and better—and more costly—medical care. The problems, then, are to specify how and how far these processes are subject to competitive pressures and how and how likely HMOs are to exert such pressures. In sum, how might HMOs affect the "market" characteristics of the health care system?

Judging by the confidence with which HMO proponents and other advocates of competitive solutions to high medical costs advance their various proposals, one might conclude that the market properties of the medical care system are well understood. They are not. In the cases of consumer and physician behavior there does not exist even a well-developed vocabulary with which to name and describe processes, let alone a model that links processes to one another in patterns useful to policymakers. As a policy tool, however, competition presupposes consistent behavior and an ability to make refined predictions about it: it works if, and only if, it moves the major variables in desired directions. The literal theory of HMOs promises precisely this: HMOs, offering broader benefits at substantial savings over fee-for-service competitors, will put pressure on third-party payers, physicians, and hospitals to curb their own costs and thereby alter both their uncritical uses of technology and the efficiency of the care they offer consumers. But it is doubtful that any of the five variables is highly susceptible to competition in the senses in which the term has traditionally been used in economics and in which the literal HMO theory used it.

The proposal presupposes that the efficiencies of HMOs can be brought to bear directly on the financial calculations of the consumer, and that he will respond primarily to these financial considerations. But as employers' contributions to health plans have grown more generous, the individual's incentive to choose the efficient plan has declined. In 1977, employers contributed 100 percent of the health insurance premiums of their em-

---

industry and within the federal government about HMO policy. For a similar observation in a different field, see Daniel P. Moynihan, *Maximum Feasible Misunderstanding*, paperback ed. (Free Press, 1970), pp. 171–77.

ployees in 57 percent of cases.[13] Besides, an efficient HMO may entail a larger payroll deduction than the competition, and consumers may not value the additional coverage enough to be willing to pay it. Moreover, consumers do not choose health insurance on financial grounds alone. Matters of style and taste—for a particular physician, against "clinic medicine," for "freedom of choice" in general, or against the HMO's hospital in particular, for example—also affect the decision. Little is known about these elements of consumer choice.

Nor is it clear that competition among plans will alter medical norms so as to make the technological imperative less powerful. In the quest for a competitive edge, HMOs may substitute less for more technically intensive care, but here too noneconomic variables intervene. Unless the plan offers the most and the best, and gives physicians a reasonably free hand to practice good medicine as defined by their professional training and outlook, it will have difficulty attracting and retaining good physicians. Consumers will expect that membership in an HMO will not oblige them to forgo the advances of modern medicine. The risk of malpractice suits will continue to stimulate physicians to do "all they can."

Moreover, unless the HMO owns or controls its own hospital, it will bear the costs of acquiring and using technology along with the hospital's other clients. In the quest for organizational maintenance and enhancement hospitals will, unless constrained by public regulation, seek to be the first in town with the latest medical gadget. If they acquire it they are apt to try to use it, and to the degree that they succeed, HMOs relying on that hospital will share in the costs. Presumably, sustained HMO competition will have some impact on the diffusion and use of technology by doctors, hospitals, and insurers subject to it. How such competition works and how large its effects might be under different circumstances are unclear, however.[14]

If competition is to make itself felt, responses must come mainly from providers of medical care and coverage—doctors, hospitals, and insurers. These providers display odd mixes of competitive and noncompetitive processes about which much remains to be learned. In most places, health

13. Charles E. Phelps, "National Health Insurance by Regulation: Mandated Employee Benefits," in Mark V. Pauly, ed., *National Health Insurance: What Now, What Later, What Never?* (Washington: American Enterprise Institute for Public Policy Research, 1980), p. 62.

14. The predictive problem goes well beyond the effects of HMOs. As Louise B. Russell observes, "the general literature on the effect of market structure on technological diffusion has been unable to come to any accepted conclusions about the links between them." *Technology in Hospitals: Medical Advances and Their Diffusion* (Brookings Institution, 1979), p. 26.

insurance is a competitive business carried on between nonprofit Blue Cross and Blue Shield plans and profit-making commercial plans in the economic media of premiums, costs, and benefits offered. Hospital costs, on the other hand, are usually driven by competition of a very different type—among predominately nonprofit institutions that meet their needs for organizational maintenance and enhancement by competition not in the currency of price but of quality, or the technological and professional trappings of quality. The production functions of the quality- or image-competitive hospitals and the costs that ensue naturally complicate the economic logic of predicting the behavior of the price-competitive insurers called on to pay hospital bills.

Physician behavior responds to still other forces; the degree to which the term "competition" accurately captures them has been little studied and is little understood. Physicians are often said to "monopolize" the provision of medical care services, and from this it is often thought to follow that new competition would be a good and efficient thing. This assessment of the problem, however, rests on an uncritical use of language. Throughout the U.S. economy, Lester Thurow writes, "it is becoming . . . less and less clear what a monopoly means."[15] In the health care sector, "which in the main consists of a multitude of relatively small private service units,"[16] the meaning of the term has never been clear at all.

The perplexities of applying these traditional economic terms to physician behavior are easily illustrated. It is sometimes said that doctors exercise monopoly power by artificially restricting the supply of physicians in order to increase their own incomes. Yet they have apparently done a poor job of it, for Americans are not notably underdoctored and indeed are said to face a serious physician surplus. It is sometimes argued that physicians fear and resist concentrations—and therefore competition—of new doctors in lucrative specialties and locations. If so, they have again done a poor job of exerting monopoly power, for physicians have crowded into remunerative specialties and practice sites. Perhaps this type of competition is in the collective interests of physicians: more doctors means more referrals and consultations and therefore more fees. Why then do physicians oppose HMOs? Presumably because HMOs do not entail "competition among physicians" but rather competition between "a

15. Lester C. Thurow, *New York Times*, October 19, 1980.

16. Basil J. F. Mott, "The New Health Planning System," in Arthur Levin, ed., *Health Services: The Local Perspective*, Proceedings of the Academy of Political Science, no. 32 (New York: The Academy, 1977), p. 238.

multitude of relatively small service units" and a relatively large, organized service unit which "monopolizes" patients by withdrawing them from communitywide referral and consultation networks. Obviously many complications and qualifications might be introduced into all of these propositions. The point is simply that it would be odd indeed if the traditional notions of monopoly and competition proved useful in analyzing "firm" behavior in this highly peculiar industry.

The problem is not that physicians monopolize services in the traditional economic sense (indeed those who charge monopoly sometimes acknowledge in the next breath that medicine in the United States is a "cottage industry") but rather that they claim expertise over the proper application of medical care in general and over the amounts and types of care that particular consumers ought to demand and that physicians ought to supply. The problem, in Freidson's words, is "professional dominance."[17] Using the term "monopoly" enthrones lack of competition as the central cost problem by semantic fiat. If monopoly is the problem, then breaking the monopoly must be the corrective. Viewing the problem as one of the demand-defining capacities of professional suppliers places the question in a different conceptual and practical light.

Physician behavior is a complex tapestry of professional (including personal, cognitive, peer-related, and ethical) and financial considerations about which abstract economic reasoning conceals at least as much as it clarifies. This complexity presumably explains the remarkable disagreement among policy-oriented economists on the effects of increasing the supply of physicians. Some argue that such a step would be a disastrous invitation to increases in treatments and costs as physicians use their demand-defining powers to maintain "target incomes," those incomes they believe they have a right to achieve after years and money spent in acquiring expertise. Others contend that the competition created by an increased supply of physicians would drive charges down and thereby strike a blow for cost-containment. The disagreement cannot be resolved because the scope and results of competition in physicians' behavior have hardly begun to be explored.[18]

17. See Eliot Freidson, *Professional Dominance: The Social Structure of Medical Care* (Atherton, 1970).

18. The most impressive evidence, derived from research on treatment patterns in Vermont, supports the view that the number of medical procedures performed varies positively with the number of physicians in an area, even controlling for pertinent medical and demographic differences. John Wennberg and Alan Gittelsohn, "Small Area Variations in Health Care Delivery," *Science,* vol. 182 (December 14, 1973), pp. 1102–08.

Amazingly little careful empirical attention has been given to exploring what such terms as "markets," "competition," and "well-functioning market competition" mean or might mean in health care services and what their actual or possible meanings mean in turn for public policy. One analyst will cite the private character of the U.S. health care system, apparently taking it for granted that nonpublic and market-based are synonymous. A second will compile long lists of the ways in which health care services deviate from the assumptions that support classical market theory and take an agnostic or highly cautious position on policy solutions. A third, looking at the very same list of deviations, will offer heated assurances that policymakers can solve their problems only by strengthening or introducing competition, market forces, cost-consciousness, and the like. A fourth will declare firmly that markets and market forces do not and cannot work in a field with the peculiar properties of health care, while a fifth bitterly deplores the American tendency to treat health care as a commodity to be bought and sold.

It is far from clear what should be expected from increased competition in the health care field. Empirically, only two competitive effects stand forth clearly. In the largely non-price-competitive hospital sector, organizational competition has fueled an arms race for newer and better technology without much regard for community or regional needs. And in the reasonably price-competitive insurance sector, competition has made it difficult for poor risks—those with unfortunate actuarial attributes or a bad health history—to get coverage; that is, it has promoted skimming and creaming. Competition with experience-rated commercial insurance plans forced Blue Cross to abandon most of its community rating long ago, thereby creating problems that made the case for government intervention by means of Medicare and Medicaid. Neither competitive effect is socially desirable, yet no others may be clearly attributed to competition in the health care field.

Because they gave little attention to the complexities of estimating the degree to which health care institutions constitute markets and are susceptible to competition, HMO proponents largely ignored the difficulties and uncertainties attending their promise that the growth of such organizations would, by means of revitalized competition and reinvigorated markets, produce efficient and desirable outcomes. Indeed they ignored these difficulties almost as assiduously as they ignored those attending the building of HMOs.

Given the institutional context, one should be skeptical of theoretical assertions that the introduction of an HMO into the larger system will produce all manner of reforms and improvements. A realistic assessment of the prospects requires answers to two questions. To what extent and how do HMOs compete? To what extent and how do conventional plans respond to this competition? Answers do not come easily.

The same factors that make HMOs difficult to build by blueprint also make it difficult to explain in general terms what makes them competitive. Competitiveness turns on highly particular and local aspects of a plan's setting: location, the attitudes of employers and employees, the generosity of employers' contributions to the health coverage of their workers, and more. It also turns on highly particular strategic choices of management: staffing decisions, the appearance and design of facilities, utilization controls, marketing assessments and efforts, and more. The correct inter-action and balance among these many variables defines a plan that is *able* to compete. But the list of variables yields no general formula for competitiveness that applies equally to all plans. Some will be more competitive than others for reasons of time, place, and circumstance.

Obviously HMOs must in some sense compete; this truism means nothing more than that HMOs cannot be indifferent to the way that the price and contents of their product compare with those of other products. Fewer conclusions follow logically from this fact than is sometimes supposed, however. It takes at least two parties to create a competitive setting and if one or both of the potential competitors is substantially insulated from the ordeals of competition, competitive discipline relaxes for the other also. Ability, will, and need to compete are different matters. None follows directly from the others.

Competition may be expected to have its intended effects only if both competitors must absorb their own true costs over time and both can control their costs. Medical care markets frequently violate both assumptions, or at least the HMO's usual major competitor, Blue Cross, does. Blue Cross plans convert increased costs into higher premiums passed mainly along to employers and thence to the public at large in the consumer price index. Not all—indeed sometimes not any—of the increases are borne directly by the person whose coverage the premium purchases. Nor are these plans well suited to control costs. Although they may monitor and investigate claims for payment submitted by enrollees and providers, too much fastidiousness and too many disallowances generate conflict and may be worse for business than premium increases. These important areas of competitive insulation in Blue Cross operations define in turn the competitive challenge faced by HMOs.

If the HMO's competitors are themselves inflationary and lax, the HMO can loosen up too and still remain competitive. So long as the HMO offers broader benefits for not a great deal more money, it will be, everything else being equal, competitive, even if it does not maximize its savings, indeed even if it is almost as inefficient as the competition.

The literal theory of HMO competition assumes that HMOs will attempt to maximize savings—that is, exploit to the hilt the various efficiencies "inherent" in the HMO structure; but plans may often prefer, in Herbert Simon's term, to "satisfice."[19] If a plan is attempting to reach the break-even enrollment or to grow very rapidly, it does indeed face incentives to maximize, that is, to offer the broadest possible benefits for the smallest possible price. There are high organizational costs to maximizing, however, and a plan that is running in the black and growing as fast as its facilities and preferences dictate will count these costs carefully. Two such costs are of special importance: first, the strict utilization controls required to ensure that care is allocated tightly and in accord with least-cost principles may alienate doctors and set them in conflict with administrators. Second, excessive economies and efficiencies might give members the impression that HMO care is a bargain basement brand with norms different from those prevailing in the mainstream. Plans with very well socialized physicians and members may be able to maximize savings without incurring these costs, but, as chapter 3 illustrates, no economic laws ensure that these human elements will behave as they should. Moreover, even plans in urgent need of building enrollment in order to break even need not force costs and premiums to their lowest feasible levels in order to do so. They may instead mount an aggressive marketing campaign by expanding contacts with unions and employers, for example, or by stepping up their advertising. These qualifications to the maximizing model—that stable plans need not maximize, that to maximize carries high organizational costs, and that alternatives to it exist—should be considered in estimates of the strength and nature of competitive pressures exerted by HMOs. The notion that HMOs may be "satisficers" has received little analytical attention. To the degree that they do satisfice, however, injecting HMOs into the larger system is unlikely to have the direct and sizable results predicted by the maximizing model.

A reasonable assessment of the competitive impact of HMOs should, in short, take close account of the market positions and organizational characters of both HMOs and their competition. A priori, one might

19. *Administrative Behavior*, 2d ed. (Free Press, 1957), p. xxiv.

expect competition to be most vigorous between young HMOs in search of a break-even enrollment and well-disciplined, comparatively efficient Blue Cross operations, that is, those with the least slack. Conversely, one would expect competition to be least vigorous between stable HMOs content with their market shares and growth rates and poorly disciplined, comparatively lax Blue Cross plans. Even as hypotheses, however, these generalizations are suggestive at best: organizational idiosyncracies and management philosophies in both HMOs and Blue Cross plans are of major, perhaps central, importance, and these factors lie outside the scope of economic laws. One assumes, for example, that the Kaiser plans are tough competitors not mainly because they fear going under if they ran a somewhat less tight ship but primarily because of their long-standing, deeply ingrained allegiance to sound management.

It may be expected that the vigor of competition will depend too on the market share of the HMOs. It would be strange indeed if the Blue Cross plans of California did not feel strong competitive pressure from the two Kaiser plans in that state, which have been in business for more than thirty years and have each surpassed a membership of one million. It would also be strange if these strong competitive pressures automatically accompanied HMOs of whatever age and size around the country.

Although a 1977 study of the competitive effects of HMOs by the Federal Trade Commission (FTC) found evidence of competition between HMOs and Blue Cross in the western states, where Kaiser and some other plans are strong and long established, little evidence could be found in other areas of the country. Some of the areas studied are the sites of old and comparatively large HMOs: Washington, D.C., for example, houses the Group Health Association (GHA), a forty-year-old plan of roughly 110,000 members, and New York City is the home of the Health Insurance Plan of Greater New York (HIP), a thirty-year-old plan with about 800,000 members. The FTC study shows that the usual maximizing assumption that any HMO able to survive over time must "compete" is simplistic. Plans like GHA and HIP survive but apparently do not compete, at least not aggressively, indeed, judging by the FTC findings, not even noticeably.[20] On "satisficing" assumptions, this is perfectly natural behavior for settled plans which for reasons of facility size or managerial philosophy, or some other reason, either are not eager to expand or conclude that the likelihood of significant expansion is too small to justify the organizational costs

20. Federal Trade Commission, *Staff Report on the Health Maintenance Organization and Its Effects on Competition* (FTC, 1977), pp. 60–72, especially pp. 65, 71.

required to make savings as great, premiums as low, or benefits as broad as possible.

These considerations have led some HMO proponents to argue that the benefits of competition will be realized best and perhaps only in areas where HMOs compete vigorously with each other.[21] When this happens, it is urged, an HMO cannot use Blue Cross inefficiency as an excuse for laxity of its own; instead efficiency will breed further pressure for efficiency. Recent experience in Minneapolis, where seven HMOs compete with one another, has received a wide press but the results of this competition are unclear.[22] Harold Luft observed that despite a doubling of HMO enrollment in Minneapolis–St. Paul between 1975 and 1977, and HMO hospital use averaging 42 percent below the Blue Cross group average, overall hospital use in the area "stayed constant or increased slightly," whereas the HMO reductions should have produced an areawide decrease of fifteen days per thousand, even *apart* from a competitive effect. The result, Luft remarks, might be explained in many ways, but is "consistent with both the notions of no major competitive response and the selective enrollment of low utilizers in the HMOs."[23]

Competition among HMOs may be expected to have its intended effects only if several conditions are met. First, the entrepreneurs and managers of HMOs must be willing to compete with each other. Unfortunately, there is no good reason why they would be. Most HMO executives want to succeed, not test academic notions about competition, and they succeed by building strong, stable organizations, not by subjecting themselves to the risk of failing a fair market test. Administrators of HMOs, like most

21. As Leonard Woodcock, head of the United Auto Workers, put it: "The idea of a 'health maintenance strategy' to my mind was invalid unless you believed that competition among group practice prepayment plans in the same geographical area made sense." "Health Security, Prepaid Group Practice and HMOs," in *Proceedings of the 25th Annual Group Health Institute* (Washington: Group Health Association of America, 1975), p. 244.

22. Jon B. Christianson and Walter McClure, "Competition in the Delivery of Medical Care," *New England Journal of Medicine*, vol. 301 (October 11, 1979), pp. 812–18. As the authors remark on p. 818: "Since the development of a competitive market in the Twin Cities is obviously in its initial stages, the data are incomplete. Further study of these HMOs is needed to determine whether any reductions in the supply of community physicians or hospital beds are precipitated by enrollment growth, whether competitive health plans will enroll the poor and elderly if the opportunity and incentive are provided, whether hospitalization rates lower than those of traditional providers will persist over time and whether constructive competitive behavior will continue as the market share of the health plans grows. A careful comparison of the quality of the medical care delivered by traditional providers and health-care plans is also needed."

23. Harold S. Luft, "Health Maintenance Organizations, Competition, Cost Containment, and National Health Insurance," in Pauly, *National Health Insurance*, p. 303.

other executives, tend to be averse to risks to their organization's stability and thus to their own reputations and careers. Competition is a very salient risk.

For this reason, HMO founders and executives tend to analyze markets carefully before they plunge in and tend to be wary of fragmenting HMO markets of uncertain strength. If they do enter a market already populated by HMOs, they will often try to differentiate their product. One approach is to specialize by location. In Massachusetts, for example, the state insurance commissioner licensed the state's first open-panel HMO only after requiring that its application be rewritten to ensure that it and other HMOs would not "be like the Mafia, dividing the state into families."[24] Another strategy is to specialize by "taste," challenging an HMO not with another similarly structured HMO but with an independent practice association, for instance. In short, HMOs may deliberately choose not to challenge each other's markets, a possibility that poses obvious problems for the theory of competition. According to Walter McClure, "the worst realistic scenario occurs if the first few health care plans in an area become content with their market share after they have acquired 20–30,000 enrollees or so to assure stability. Then, relatively few consumers, unions, and employers understand or demand fair market choice."[25] This worst realistic prospect is also the most realistic. As an HMO administrator put it in an interview, "many HMOs would be happy to get 25,000 and just leave it right there. It's easier to manage."

Second, if HMOs are to compete with one another, employers must be willing to offer more than one HMO and perhaps also to promote them to their employees. To the degree that HMOs specialize by area, this may be difficult. Employers are reluctant to bear the administrative costs of offering plans remote from work or convenient to the homes of only a few of their workers. Even if the plans are well located, employers may be diffident. Some resist the costs and inconvenience of reprogramming health offerings in any way. Others will do so to meet the legal requirement that they offer a federally qualified HMO if and when one exists in their area but will not offer another HMO before or afterward. Even employers willing to offer multiple HMOs may decline to promote them; many consider it imprudent to meddle in employees' health care decisions. In all these respects,

24. *Boston Evening Globe*, September 19, 1978.
25. *Comprehensive and Regulatory Strategies for Medical Care* (Excelsior, Minn.: InterStudy, 1980), p. 142.

Minneapolis appears to be distinctive if not unique; there several major employers have taken a lead not only in offering but also in promoting several HMOs.[26]

Third, competitive HMOs presuppose that unions bargaining collectively for employees will welcome multiple HMOs and will leave the choice of particular plans to their individual members. Unions sometimes welcome an HMO option as a chip in bargaining with conventional plans (the threat of taking their business elsewhere may thus be made credible). Occasionally unions welcome a new HMO as a club to hold over an established HMO in which membership is heavily enrolled and dissatisfied. Usually, however, they prefer to commit their membership to and consolidate their influence with one plan, not fragment both among several.

Fourth, to be a durable policy solution, competition among HMOs must be in some sense self-stabilizing. One requirement of a sound competitive system is that strong competitors be induced to compete by the prospect of enjoying the fruits of superior performance, including the acquisition of a commanding market share by beating the competition. Another requirement is that competitors be prevented from achieving monopoly power. Balancing these requirements is no simple matter, as FTC and other antitrust experience shows. If aggressively competitive HMOs rout their competition, will the weak HMOs be allowed to fail? Or will they be bailed out, sacrificing efficiency for a competition justified in the name of efficiency?

The analytical point of these reflections is that competition in health care should be treated not simply as an economic process, but also as a product (or casualty) of the interests of actors in formal organizations, especially HMO sponsors and managers, employers, unions, and those government agencies that oversee and regulate competition. The practical point is that the conditions required to support vigorous competition among HMOs are not likely to be met soon in many places.

Even if HMOs (one or several) came out seeking a competitive knockout, so to speak, they might find that Blue Cross had neither the ability, need, nor will to respond. If competition is an infallible road to lower costs, it may be asked, why has the persistent price-based competition between Blue Cross and commercial insurers not led to lower costs over time? The usual answer is that third-party payers are irresponsible, lacking control over the behavior of the doctors whose treatment decisions they

26. John K. Iglehart, "HMOs Are Alive and Well in the Twin Cities Region," *National Journal*, July 22, 1978, pp. 1160–65.

largely ratify. Because third-party payers tolerate inefficient treatments, pay the bills, raise their premiums, and then market mainly to employers who pay much or most or all of these higher premiums and pass the costs along to the public, and because Blue Cross and its commercial competition are on an equal footing in this respect, neither has an incentive for efficiency. An HMO, by contrast, can control its providers and must absorb its own costs in responsible fashion and therefore does face incentives for efficiency. The presence of an HMO, then, will have effects on a third-party payer different from those of another third-party competitor.

This reasoning makes questionable assumptions about both the HMO's demand for competition and the ability of Blue Cross to supply it. As noted above, it is arguable that the same lack of internal discipline that HMO competition is expected to combat may establish a ceiling or norm of maximum acceptable inflation that the HMO may find it more comfortable to hover around or just below than drastically to undercut. On the supply side, it is surely not evident—and to an organization theorist not even plausible—that the presence of an HMO with, say, twenty thousand members will make a Blue Cross plan long accustomed to and content with permissiveness suddenly begin fighting with doctors, hospitals, and enrollees over appropriate treatment and unwarranted claims. It is quite likely that here too the fundamental dynamic is organizational, not simply financial; it is a question of the strength of leadership and the nature of management philosophy in the highly varied Blue Cross plans. Even if an HMO is highly efficient (that is, able to offer a wider set of benefits at a cost well below that of the competition), Blue Cross officials may find it less costly on the whole to lose some members (it would be remarkable if an HMO's penetration rate in many areas exceeded 20 percent, after all, and extraordinary if it grew large enough to threaten a Blue Cross plan's survival) than to battle doctors, hospitals, and enrollees in an effort to drive costs and premiums sharply downward. Nothing follows automatically from the injection of competition, at least not from competition of the type and on the scale that HMOs now generally offer. If HMOs were set down amid all sixty-nine Blue Cross plans, the result would probably be sixty-nine different competitive responses ranging from none at all to vigorous, with most falling somewhere in between, but closer to none.

Nor does the consternation created by the prospect or presence of a new HMO among fee-for-service physicians and insurers prove that the requisites of a stable and continuing competitive system have been met. A competitor who might find it rational to do all he could to preempt or meet competition (by setting up an independent practice association, by altering conventional benefit packages, or by stirring local opinion, for example) might then choose to ignore or retreat from competition if these efforts failed. Local energies set off by the prospect of competition are one thing; long-lived and deep-reaching changes produced by the coexistence of competitors over time are another.

The argument here is not that Blue Cross plans will not respond competitively to the presence of an HMO, but rather that they need not and may not do so. The hypothesis that responses are a function not of economic laws but rather of organizational politics and managerial policies specific to each plan suggests the corollary that the most efficient Blue Cross plans may offer the most competitive responses. One might expect the toughest competitors, those well-run Blue Cross plans whose executives pride themselves on achieving and maintaining a high penetration rate and on offering an attractive product, who "hate to lose one member" (in the words of an HMO official describing the attitudes of his plan's competition), and who are determined to run a tight ship, to be most willing to take on doctors and other claimants in the interest of sound management and HMOs in the interest of organizational maintenance.

If these hypotheses are sound, analysts should guard against spuriously attributing to competition behavior that derives mainly from managerial philosophy and organizational politics. In the U.S. health care system, plans everywhere compete to some degree. This competition takes no single form and has no determinate result, however, but rather many forms and results. Competitors may take one another carefully into account (as apparently happens in California) or they may largely ignore one another (as apparently happens in Washington, D.C., and in New York City). Some plans facing sharp competition appear to be efficient, others less so. Correlation should not be mistaken for causation; one should no more automatically attribute to the presence of an HMO the efficiencies of competitors than one should conclude that continued inefficiencies in conventional plans faced with HMO competition are caused by the presence of an HMO.

If competition is contingent on organizational politics, Blue Cross plans with similar market shares might react quite differently to the entry of an HMO into their service areas. This does seem to be the case. For example, the Blue Cross plans serving Rochester, New York; Providence, Rhode Island; and Cleveland, Ohio, all command a strong share of the local health insurance market. Yet whereas Blue Cross of northwestern New York helped to establish HMOs in Rochester, Rhode Island's Blue Cross plan has been mildly supportive but not greatly enthusiastic about HMOs in Providence, and the Blue Cross plan serving Cleveland was described by one former HMO executive as uncooperative and hostile to HMOs. In short, Blue Cross responses vary with the managerial outlooks of their executives; to these executives, as to everyone else, HMOs are Rorschach tests into which one reads what one will. Some executives have resisted them strongly, some have welcomed them in hopes that they would fail and vindicate the status quo, some have become involved in them as means of cornering a share of the potential HMO market for themselves, some have participated in HMO development in the interest of product diversification, some have entered the field to demonstrate to the government and to the public the flexibility and open-mindedness of the insurance industry, and others have become involved, or have declined to get involved, for still other reasons. No abstract model describing the ideal-typical HMO locked in competition with the ideal-typical third-party payer, to the greater efficiency of both, begins to fit the facts. Useful models wait not upon the elaboration and refinement of theoretical "laws" of competition but rather upon careful qualitative research into organizational behavior in health insurance plans.

Even if HMOs could be made to compete aggressively and Blue Cross plans could be made to respond with fear and trembling and efficiency, the likely effects are not clear, and some of them might not be desirable. For one thing, competition can lead to underservice and abuse, as it did in California where Governor Reagan unleashed very vigorous competition among prepaid health plans, and between those plans and fee-for-service physicians, for Medicaid recipients. Reagan "relied on the market place to develop competition, believing the good would drive the bad out. It just didn't work that way."[27] Although the California experience had several unusual properties, the facts remain that one major means of competing is to hold premiums down, that one major way to do this is to realize internal economies, that some ways to do this are to underserve and to ration or restrict access to care, and that these possibilities will never be entirely absent from the minds of physicians and executives whose main attachment to prepaid plans is money. Exclusively money-minded executives and the abuses they practice may be few. Even solid and decent plans may give rise to questions about the source and consequences of internal economies, however. For example, Harold Luft's finding that HMOs achieve savings by reducing hospital admissions for "nondiscretionary" as well as for

27. Elizabeth Owen, director of a prepaid health project in the California Health Department, quoted in *Group Health News*, vol. 21 (December 1980), p. 3.

"discretionary" procedures by no means convicts HMOs of underservice, but it does raise questions worthy of further research.[28]

Second, there are adaptive costs of competition. For example, Blue Cross may respond to HMOs by broadening its own benefits, thereby encouraging utilization. California again may offer an instructive example. The FTC study notes that Blue Cross of Northern California claims to have "the broadest outpatient benefits package of any Blue Cross plan," a development that the authors view as a "competitive step" to meet the appeals of the huge Northern California Kaiser plan.[29] But Luft points out that although California ranks forty-sixth among states in the share of its expenditures for hospital care, it nonetheless stood third in per capita health spending in 1969, the last year for which such data were available. The explanation may be that "as a result of the improved ambulatory care coverage by conventional insurers, California ranked second in the share of per-capita expenditures for physicians' services." He concludes that "by some standards the mix of medical services bought by Californians may be more efficient, but there is no evidence that even massive HMO enrollment has resulted in overall cost containment."[30]

Another adaptive cost is that hospitals "may raise rates to compensate for reduced utilization" brought on by the presence of an HMO.[31] Consider, for example, the case of Washington, D.C., a city with three HMOs in 1978—a forty-year-old giant of more than 100,000 members, a rapidly growing plan of about 43,000 members, and a smaller HMO of about 15,000. In that year the *Washington Post* reported that the average cost of a day of care in Washington hospitals was rising 50 percent faster than the national average of 18.5 percent. (In Maryland, which had a strong rate-setting commission, the article noted, the increase had been held to 8.2 percent.) The reason appeared to be low occupancy and the resulting "high unit costs, since many expenses remain the same even when some beds or wards are not being used."[32]

It is doubtful that the presence of the HMOs affected this situation much one way or another. Yet the workings of vigorous competition might be expected to reduce occupancy further. The interesting policy question is what happens then. Will hospitals voluntarily redefine their services and facilities by means of cutbacks, mergers, and closures? Will they cling to

28. "How Do Health-Maintenance Organizations Achieve Their 'Savings'?" *New England Journal of Medicine*, vol. 298 (June 15, 1978), p. 1341.

29. *Staff Report on the Health Maintenance Organization*, p. 77, n. 3.

30. "Health Maintenance Organizations, Competition," p. 304.

31. FTC, *Staff Report on the Health Maintenance Organization*, p. 117, n. 1.

32. *Washington Post*, December 30, 1978.

their underused facilities and continue to cover rising unit costs in their per diem charges? Will competition by itself brake this tendency and produce a more efficient hospital sector? Or will the assistance of public regulation—rate-setting, decertification, and the like—be required, and perhaps more urgently and on a larger scale? The fact is that no one knows what effect HMO competition will have on costs, or even if it will be downward or upward. Likewise no one knows whether competition will prove to be an alternative to regulation or an invitation to further and more stringent regulation.

Finally, even if competition did lead to savings, the nature of these savings should be scrutinized carefully. As chapter 4 points out, the notion that savings are somehow snatched away from the more than 9 percent of the gross national product now devoted to health care may be misleading. Savings meet this expectation if they are converted directly into lower or more slowly rising premiums, but they need not be. They may go to broaden benefits, into the plan's reserves, to launch new plans, to expand old ones by building new facilities and acquiring new equipment, into higher salaries for physicians or administrators, and elsewhere. Indeed savings will have to be devoted to some of these alternatives in order to keep the plan competitive. Even if competition works as predicted, most of the savings will be recycled into, not reclaimed from, the national health care budget.

Although HMOs may save the system *some* money, there is, on balance, no reason to expect that HMO-building will produce the dramatic and far-reaching competitive effects often claimed on its behalf. Hasty applications of the theoretical virtues of competition in properly functioning markets to the real world of rising costs in the poorly functioning and partial markets of the health care system have masqueraded too often as policy analysis and supplanted research giving proper attention to the institutional properties of the health policy field. As a result, the effects that might attend systemwide HMO-building, even granting the doubtful assumption that it could take place, remain almost entirely conjectural.

Policy Analysis versus Policymaking

Perhaps the least attractive aspect of the HMO program has been the diligent search for villains on whom blame for its small accomplishments might be fixed. The Nixon-Ford administrations, the federal bureaucracy, Congress (especially Edward Kennedy), the American Medical Association, and others have at various times been labeled the wreckers of a simple and good idea. The arguments developed here lend no support to this search. Neither individual political actors and institutions nor the political process as a whole deserve much blame for the program's many problems. The familiar view that HMO-building is a highly opportune policy strategy badly mistreated by the political process is mistaken. A more accurate view, it has been urged here, is that HMOs were a good idea but a poor policy strategy on behalf of which the federal government has done all it reasonably can do. The antinomies reviewed in this and the preceding chapter—a workable law versus an acceptable one, prepaid practice plans versus politicians, strategy versus structure, incentives versus institutions, and competition versus the complexities of the U.S. health care system— describe an unfortunate mating of politics and policy whose outcomes betray not the hands of villains and fools but the mostly good intentions of reasonable and sincere men.

The central question, then, is why the nature and extent of the misfit between the HMO strategy and the nature of U.S. health care politics were never properly perceived. The difference between academic social science and policy analysis, after all, is presumably that the latter *asks* whether the good ideas of the former are indeed suitable for translation into public policy. The urgings of policy analysts that they be given greater opportunity to ply their trade in the policy process rests on their supposedly refined ability to make such distinctions. The HMO episode is therefore ironic twice over: first, because HMO policymaking was one of the rare instances in which policy analysts were granted their claim to be heeded attentively, and second, because the advice they gave showed little awareness of the difference between good ideas and good strategies.

But why were the politicians so vulnerable and so easily exploited? Why did intelligent men of at least average common sense embrace so enthusiastically and uncritically so abstract and theoretical a policy proposal? The executive branch generalists and the congressmen require different answers.

Six attributes of the executive branch policymakers in the early Nixon years explain why the HMO concept-strategy appealed so strongly to them. These men were: generalists, very busy, badly in need of a bold new health care initiative, unfamiliar with the complexities of the health care field, distrustful of the bureaucracy, and far more certain of what they did not want than of what they did want. An innovative, easily grasped, nonregulatory, inexpensive proposal designed outside the bureaucracy met their immediate needs. Officials in their situation are easily attracted to what might be called "free standing" policy proposals—bright ideas seemingly governed by their own internal logic and uncontaminated by the need to mesh with other programs or with troubling social facts. Health maintenance organizations were perceived as independent variables which themselves depended on little but could be depended on, once put in place, to generate large ripple effects. The seemingly self-contained, free-standing character of the proposal, which was so harshly and repeatedly challenged as the HMO legislative effort wore on, was precisely what made the proposal appealing to top HEW generalists in 1970–71.

More surprising, at least at first glance, is that the ambiguities and implausibilities of the proposal were able to survive the elaborate processes of review and clearance in the executive branch as it evolved from an enthusiasm at high levels of the Department of Health, Education, and Welfare (HEW). The explanation is that the nature of decisionmaking in the executive branch is not well suited to press the types of questions that were neglected in the HMO initiative. Important decisions often are taken in three stages, each in a different institutional setting. First, a strategy session is convened. Busy men with immediate needs and little substantive expertise discuss broad questions, philosophies, and intuitions and toss about appealing ideas, general approaches, and policy concepts. Political generalists tend to grow impatient with such conversations and therefore tend to react with quick and strong affirmation of possibilities that appear to meet their needs. Those that do not are buried, at least temporarily, while the favored strategies are entrusted to staffers or to outside proponents to be worked up in greater detail. (The meeting at the DuPont Plaza Hotel on February 5, 1970, to hear Paul Ellwood's views on HMOs was a strategy session.)

Second, officials hold option sessions to discuss various ways of moving from a general strategy to a specific proposal. These meetings usually include generalists of various agencies and perspectives, including those of the Executive Office of the President and the White House staff. If a proposal has a strong constituency in one of the agencies, is not out of sorts with the administration's general program, and has no determined opponents, it will probably be kept alive. It is usually assumed that the rough edges that grate on the particular institutional interests and agendas of the participants will be smoothed through compromise, refinement, and consensus-building. If hard questions are pressed, the assumption is that proponents will devise answers, not that the proposal will be put on hold indefinitely. (The meetings between officials in HEW and reviewers in the Office of Management and Budget were option sessions that produced the ambiguous compromises on the meaning and scope of the HMO initiative in late 1970 and early 1971 in preparation for President Nixon's health message.)

Third, the proposal thus refined goes to a decision session. At these meetings a single item is but one of several; the agenda is typically long, and because some "action-forcing process" such as a presidential message often triggers the gathering, time is short. If a proposal has survived the earlier option sessions, retains strong supporters, and has been compromised appropriately, the parties to these developments will be reluctant to undo past efforts and agreements or to generate time-consuming arguments by pushing fundamental objections to someone else's project. Top decisionmakers—the president and his highest aides, for example—will generally know little about the substance of the issue in question and will probably care most about its politics and public relations, about its sex appeal and costliness, not about the accumulation of small details that define its feasibility. In sum, if there is nothing overtly wrong with a proposal that has survived to this point, it may well continue its onward march to the public agenda. (The major decision sessions in the HMO process were the hectic, down-to-the-wire meetings that preceded Nixon's speech of February 1971 proposing HMOs to the Congress and to the nation.)

The policy planning process is not designed to elicit questions about the probability that a proposal is fit and ready to be set down in the real world. In this process the crucial middle ground between concept and detail, between a good idea and a good strategy, may be eclipsed. To be sure, proposals that fail to attract key supporters, that are thought to be clearly not in accord with the program of the president, or that are feared to be beyond redemption by compromise may be squelched. Nonetheless, a well-supported, conceptually attractive, but highly implausible proposal may make its way from idea to presidential initiative, shuttled along by rapidly taken decisions in negotiating sessions among generalists. This, at any rate, is what happened in the HMO case.

The more generalist-dominated the planning process, the more vulnerable is an administration to this risk. The HMO initiative, a generalist romp in which high administration officials smugly and contemptuously excluded the health bureaucracy from their deliberations, illustrates the danger well. The signature of the piece, in a phrase used by more than one administration official recalling these events, was: "No one knew what they were doing." As a result the executive largely abdicated the responsibility assigned to it by the civics texts to conduct the hard work of data-gathering and detail-sifting, to subject proposals to the informed scrutiny of specialists, to construct a coherent and well-considered initiative, and (only then) to entrust it to the broad and general considerations of the layman legislature.[33]

In the HMO case, traditional executive and legislative roles were reversed. It was left to Congress to ask hard questions, gather facts, canvass alternatives, and draft legislation in detail. In many ways Congress acquitted itself admirably. But in many ways too, the nature of decision-making in the legislature was as unsuited as that in the executive to identify and explore that practical middle ground that constitutes the difference between a good idea and a good strategy.

It ran against the legislative grain to press "fundamental" questions about the HMO strategy. Like the administration generalists, the lawmakers could not be against an all-American effort to contain costs by means of competition, pluralism, and efficiency, without regulation, and at little cost. Nor was it in the legislators' nature to brood over the possibility that even a sustained congressional effort to smooth the proposal's rough edges might not successfully transform it from a good idea into a good strategy. To the analysts, the incentives could make anything right; to the lawmakers, consensus and the right amounts and types of federal aid could make anything right. Once the congressmen accepted the surface plausibility of the proposal, the main question immediately became one of legislative craftsmanship and shaping, that is, of how the various images of the federally qualified HMO entertained by members of subcommittees, committees, and full chambers could be disassembled and recombined in ways that would command the obligatory consensus at each stage.

Each involved legislator began with a position of general support for HMOs, and some idiosyncracies in his personal image of a desirable HMO. The legislative process then traded off among idiosyncracies. At each stage—subcommittee sessions and drafts, full committee sessions and drafts, floor debate and amendments, and finally the conference committee and still another new draft—major legislators staked out their positions, advanced and defended them, held out for them until it appeared that

---

33. For a succinct statement of this traditional view of executive responsibility, see Arthur Maass, "System Design and the Political Process: A General Statement," in Arthur Maass and others, *Design of Water Resource Systems* (Harvard University Press, 1962), pp. 578–84.

compromise was necessary, looked for attractive terms of trade, and then yielded in part. The law took shape in a flurry of trades. No legislator could be sure what he would take or give up or live with until he had seen concretely what he could or could not get. At each stage this process altered the nature of the HMO hybrid substantially. In this way, the legislators, like the administration generalists, moved from general endorsement to compromise and trade-offs among details, squeezing out the middle ground.

Even if the legislators had posed probing questions, however, the nature of the legislative process itself would have obscured the answers. Given the nature of legislative bargaining, it was not easy to discern, for example, the precise impact of the (constantly changing) HMO bills on the industry. The giant plans did not say bluntly that they would ridicule and snub a program unacceptable to them; that would have been poor political form indeed. Instead, they hoped that their persuasive and political skills would head off an unacceptable law; only when the work of the conference committee had been completed and bargaining had come finally to an end did they learn that they had not entirely succeeded. Likewise, not knowing exactly how strongly the plans felt about open enrollment and preventive dental care for children, Kennedy and his aides had no reason to suppose that when nudged a little by a federal government that would now confer numerous advantages on HMOs, they would fail to do what was morally right, albeit grudgingly. Even skeptics on the House subcommittee, who prevailed on many more items at issue than did Kennedy, had no reason to assume that compromise with the Senate on a handful of issues out of the dozens resolved would prevent the program from taking off.

Middle-ground issues were not altogether ignored. Some congressmen did voice doubts about the organization-building process, about the ease with which HMOs could be launched and could take root around the nation. Individual legislators, however, could do little about this problem. Changes in federal financing programs—in Medicare and Medicaid, or in a national program of health insurance—and in the rules on reimbursement accompanying them might affect HMO growth more than a development effort based on grants and loans, but these matters lay in the hands of the ways and means and finance committees. The best the legislators on the Rogers and Kennedy subcommittees could do was to acknowledge the problem, call the program a demonstration, and proceed (Rogers), or acknowledge the problem, hope that large sums of development aid would overcome it, and proceed (Kennedy). The same applied to questions about the effects of HMO competition, where the obstacle to an answer was not dependence on other committees, but rather, sheer lack of knowledge about what to expect. The legislators were not about to treat uncertainty as an "excuse for inaction." Some hedged their bets and proceeded (Rogers); others pressed ahead with ambitious designs and funding schemes (Kennedy). They then assembled to split the differences, as legislators do and must.

In short, the process by which the HMO proposal moved from the first administration strategy session in February 1970 through many stages to the conference report of December 1973 was politics as usual. The problem—itself not unusual—was that the HMO program that finally emerged bore very little relation either to what Ellwood had proposed or to what existing plans knew. Although Ellwood's HMOs and the well-established plans were very different from one another, the fragile presuppositions of both had been shattered by the politicians' endless compromises. The two camps therefore joined in excoriating the politicians for taking up penetrating policy analyses and proven prototypes and caricaturing both in an unworkable law. Unnerved by the depth of the industry's wrath, the politicians, who had not themselves doubted the ability of politics to realize the benefits of HMOs, came to agree. (Kennedy of course was the major exception.) Consensus in the industry was answered by consensus—and amendments—in the legislature in 1976 and 1978.

The disappointing results of the newly "workable" law have been understandably perplexing; after all, the possibility that fulfillment of the theoretical promise of HMOs lay beyond the powers of ordinary politics and policy to accomplish was not seriously entertained. The question, is this likely to take root in the real world on the scale and with the results desired? was not given sustained examination, but this too is perfectly understandable. "This" (the HMO program) was continually in process of being shaped and revised to move toward a consensual hybrid. The particular "this" of the moment might appear to be flawed and unworkable, but a revised version, even then in process of being hammered out, would be better. The "this" that finally constituted Public Law 93-222 was not unveiled and could not be fully contemplated until the hectic moment of its creation in the conference committee. By then it was too late for probing questions to do any good. Nor is it clear how, in a highly decentralized system, policy can be made otherwise.

The explanation of the slim accomplishments of the federal HMO effort lies in the poor fit between politics and policy. A political process as decentralized and multistaged as that in the United States and a policy proposal as fragile and multitermed as the HMO initiative could not be happily united. Efforts by the central government of a highly decentralized political system to launch marketable health plans on a large scale throughout the system are likely to be fraught with difficulty. Policy proposals and political structures cannot be mixed and matched indiscriminately, for not all proposals fit well with all structures. Although it would be absurd to argue that structure dictates strategy, it is but simple prudence to recognize that some, perhaps many, items on any list of theoretically promising strategies may suffer from a poor fit between politics and policy. Indeed it might be a useful analytic exercise to ask that policy analysts append to their proposals "political impact statements" gauging the obstacles the proposals are likely to meet as they make their way from theory to program, and the damage the literal theories that support them are likely to sustain in and from the process.

Because the U.S. political system is not likely to change its structural properties in the near future, there are grounds for uneasiness about the proliferation of incentive-based, highly fragile policy analyses, in health and in other fields. The misunderstandings and disappointments of the HMO program may be repeated more frequently in the future, for a host of ingenious adaptations of market principles to public ends has been proposed. As discontent with public regulation mounts, infatuation with these alternatives may grow too.

The HMO case suggests that these approaches may not only fail to offer a workable alternative to regulation but also may produce new angry charges that the federal government is incapable and blundering. It is, therefore, important to ensure that the choice between regulation (or whatever) and the analysts' alternatives receives sensible consideration and full and informed debate. How, then, can policymakers be helped to distinguish between policy problems that are susceptible to these analytical solutions—and for all one knows many policy areas may be—and problems, like those in the health field, that probably are not?

One basic protection is a fuller awareness of the costs and complications of the organization-building strategy. Some of the appeals of institution-building for competition (or coordination or whatever)—indirection, avoidance of displacement and direct constraint, reduction of conflict, and innovation, for example—look less seductive when the extent and sources of the gross inefficiency of the process are examined.

Organization-building is not the only or most prominent incentive-based formula for solving policy problems, however. In appraising others, five sources of debate and devil's advocacy are of special importance.

One important means of encouraging a balanced consideration of the claims of incentive-based analyses, which usually purport to offer the most efficient means of attaining politically given ends, is to concentrate attention on the ends themselves, on moral, not technocratic considerations. Treating Medicare, for example, as an essentially moral question about the proper grounds of a citizen's claim to a public entitlement, policymakers concluded that social justice called for a program entitling the elderly to federal funds to help pay their medical bills. The just scope, contents, and design of the entitlement preoccupied the policymakers and suppressed speculative concern about complex incentive mechanisms. Indeed, the program was imbalanced in this respect. One reason why the question of national health insurance is treated today not as an issue of simple social justice, but rather in the technocratic terms of cost-estimation and cost-containment, is that the incentives accompanying retrospective cost-based reimbursement were not given due regard when Medicare was enacted.[34]

In the debates over a negative income tax and a family assistance plan policymakers refused to create an entitlement. Technocratic considerations were abundant—the optimal design of benefit structures, cutoff points, taxes on income derived from work, and the like—but these were subordinated to, and explored within the context of, essentially moral questions—the legitimacy of a fully federal income support program, the justification of means tests, the rights of all the poor versus some of the poor (children, for example) to public support, the merits of in-kind versus general cash aid, the social value of work, and the like.[35] No welfare reform proposal has been adopted. Whether this decision is right or not is beside the present point, which is that by refusing to pretend that technocratic manipulation could yield answers to moral issues, the policymakers have kept means subordinated to ends.

In the HMO case, the moral protection was largely ineffectual. Everyone agreed on ends—that society should contain medical costs without sacrificing access to or quality of care if possible. And everyone agreed about

34. See Theodore R. Marmor, *The Politics of Medicare* (Aldine, 1973), pp. 71–72, 85–86.

35. See, for example, Vincent J. Burke and Vee Burke, *Nixon's Good Deed: Welfare Reform* (Columbia University Press, 1974); Daniel P. Moynihan, *The Politics of a Guaranteed Income* (Random House, 1973); Alice M. Rivlin, *Systematic Thinking for Social Action* (Brookings Institution, 1971), pp. 16–35; and Otto A. Davis and John E. Jackson, "Senate Defeat of the Family Assistance Plan," *Public Policy*, vol. 22 (Summer 1974), pp. 265–66.

means—that HMOs, somehow defined, might achieve this end. The problem, therefore, turned on the "somehow defined," on those clusters of technocratic and secondary moral considerations that summed up to major strategic choices. In this case, other spurs to middle-level debate were needed.

A second force for balanced consideration is constituency politics. For example, well-staffed, well-connected, articulate, and assertive environmental protection lobbies stand ready to disabuse policymakers of the notion that exchanging standards and regulations for pollution fees, taxes, or rights is a simple, all-embracing, and uncontestable strategy. This is consistent with traditional pluralist and incrementalist theory, which maintains that the best brake on extravagant governmental enthusiasms is the pulling and hauling of organized interests that expose the vulnerable parts of proposals they find threatening or distasteful.

In the HMO case, this pulling and hauling broke down. The proposal was a case of "public sector politics,"[36] agitated within government itself. Most groups agreed with the policymakers that HMOs were a motherhood concept cloaked in American virtues no one could confute. The only important exception was the American Medical Association, and in 1970–71 its opposition was not only suspect but rather easily dismissed. Health maintenance organizations obviously did threaten organized fee-for-service medicine, but only with that most legitimate of challenges, market competition. Moreover, the AMA itself embodied the very problem—excesses of fee-for-service medicine—that the HMO program was intended to correct. Finally, the AMA had been so transparently and indulgently self-serving in other recent legislative battles that its opposition could not then derail so appealing a proposal as HMOs. When the organization was taken seriously, for example, in the House and in the Nixon administration in late 1972, the main effect was to reduce the scope of the enterprise, not to evoke serious consideration of the prospects for the strategy itself.

General as well as special-interest constituencies may shed skeptical light on an attractive piece of policy analysis. For instance, diffuse constituency pressures might well turn the carefully targeted program envisioned in various urbank or urban-enterprise-zone proposals into a national development program handing out aid right and left with little consideration to hardship, and the government might end up subsidizing firms or localities for steps they would have taken anyway. Moreover, a

---

36. The term comes from Samuel H. Beer, "The Adoption of General Revenue Sharing: A Case Study in Public Sector Politics," *Public Policy*, vol. 24 (Spring 1976), pp. 127–28.

fourth protection, past experience—in this case with the urban renewal program—suggests that the incentive would probably not be attractive enough to accomplish its ends unless it were infeasibly large. Such considerations did not make much impression in the HMO case because, except for a few legislators with established plans in their districts or states, the program's areal constituency was as yet unborn. Nor did past experience bear pertinently on what was intended. Kaiser was a prototype, not a model, after all, and the federal HMO would be a highly synthetic hybrid— not *an* increment, but rather a crazy-quilt of increments.

A fifth protection for balanced consideration is to rely on subject-matter specialists in government—meaning, as a rule, career civil servants, or bureaucrats—to analyze, criticize, and refine general proposals. These officials may have the acquaintance with institutional realities and with nonobvious connections among actors and facts that generalists lack. Strong generalists will not use fear of bureaucratic disagreement as an excuse for ignoring specialists' advice. In the HMO case, Medicare and Medicaid specialists in HEW who examined the Ellwood HMO proposal asked highly insightful questions about organization-building and competition. The generalists, however, persuaded that the bureaucrats were self-serving and unimaginative, asked their questions as a matter of mere form and did not stay for an answer.

These five protections, together with awareness of the risks of organization-building strategies, should ensure a reasonably full and fair debate on the merits of incentive-based schemes. But eternal vigilance is in order, for these protections may be breaking down over time. First, the proposition that institution-building based on "correct" incentives is a major alternative to regulation has been endorsed by influential writers[37] and appears increasingly attractive to policymakers besieged by complaints about regulation. A major approach to national health insurance, for instance— the so-called consumer-choice plan—presupposes that carefully drawn incentives for consumers to choose "efficient" plans will result in large-scale organization-building (of HMOs and other organized delivery systems).[38]

Second, after a spate of moral-breakthrough legislation, relatively technical issues surrounding repair jobs on existing programs are becoming more prominent. Because repairs often threaten to constrain or rescind

37. For example, Charles L. Schultze, in the widely cited and discussed *The Public Use of Private Interest* (Brookings Institution, 1977), p. 13.

38. Alain C. Enthoven, *Health Plan* (Reading, Mass.: Addison-Wesley, 1980).

benefits or otherwise upset industries and consumers affected by programs, the search for nonregulatory measures will probably proceed with greater urgency, and with it the temptation to lift from the texts intricate and fragile incentive-based prescriptions.

Third, as public sector politics aimed at rationalizing the ill effects of previous government commitments grow more vigorous, the number of programs with inchoate constituencies may grow too. Thus the pulling and hauling of groups with a vested interest in exposing the practical obstacles in the face of theoretically appealing ideas may play a weaker role in future policymaking. And insofar as groups with vested interests— the AMA, for instance—may be part of the problem, their views may be taken more lightly.

Fourth, as government does more, and as unintended and unwanted consequences arise, it must experiment increasingly with rationalizing strategies which, in the nature of the case, have little or no track record or prior experience. Because government is in these cases flying blind, a lucid, free-standing scheme that ties up all important variables into one uncluttered whole takes on great value. The outcry against the heavy hand of regulation makes the delicate sleight-of-hand of the policy analyst the more enticing.

Fifth, as programs develop problems that bureaucrats create, aggravate, or fail to solve, and as the outcry over bureaucratic regulation builds, subject-matter specialists in the federal bureaucracy may command less legitimacy and may be increasingly excluded from the policymaking process. Meanwhile, policy analysts in consulting firms, universities, and think tanks, and graduates of university programs in public policy grow more numerous, and more confident that their modules, models, and modes can train legislators to write, and administrators to implement, public policy.[39] Generalists, disenchanted with bureaucratic specialists, increasingly turn to the analysts or import them into government.

For all of these reasons, the union of policy analysts and political generalists in support of good ideas that turn out to be fragile and implausible strategies when government sets about attempting the transformation may reappear, albeit in other guises. The HMO program may be an early warning signal of some importance.

39. This trend is particularly evident in the health care field, where the federal government has showered millions of dollars on universities promising to establish programs to teach senior health care officials not only the state of academic wisdom about health care policy but how to make and administer more rational public policy. That there exists very little academic literature to serve as a foundation for the latter purpose and that the faculty of some of these programs know very little about government has not moderated the universities' demand for and the government's supply of such awards.

Some would argue that the problem in the HMO case was not that politicians relied too heavily on policy analysis but rather that they failed to avail themselves of the right kind. Perhaps if the incentive-based analyses of the literal model had been supplemented by approaches to policy analysis developed by political scientists, the policymakers would have been able to evaluate the future of the HMO strategy more fully. This is doubtful.

Political science today offers two major approaches to policy analysis. One, the comparative approach, often illustrates the workings of political institutions and structures in its descriptions and explanations and then proceeds to ignore them in its recommendations. On this view, the most reliable means of assessing what to expect from a policy and of learning how to make one work is to observe closely what other nations have done with similar policies or at any rate in similar situations. This approach can be instructive, but it would not have been very helpful in the HMO case for the simple reason that HMO-like groups are extremely uncommon in other nations. But of course one major reason why HMOs are now all-but-unknown in European nations is that European governments have not tried to develop them. The reason for this in turn is that they pursue very different cost-containment strategies—negotiated fee schedules, in particular—in the very different context of national health insurance. It was precisely this context that the U.S. policymakers could not presuppose and precisely these strategies that they hoped to avoid by means of HMOs.

These policy differences reflect, in their turn, the very different political structures of the United States and Europe. No European nation combines in so high a degree as the United States the decentralization of separated powers, federalism, and privatism. This extreme decentralization is an important reason why centralized health care financing and controls are difficult to generate here, and also a major reason why, in the absence of central financing and controls, the United States opted to experiment with HMOs. That Europe has not tried to do so proves little one way or the other. Comparative perspectives are of great, indeed unique, value in understanding why HMOs were singled out for government encouragement in the United States; that is, they are invaluable for setting a nation's policies in political context. They are less useful, however, in offering practical advice on how to make policy strategies work.

Although a comparative perspective would not have taught American policymakers how to make the HMO strategy work, it might have given them valuable, middle-range insights into the workability of the strategy. In Europe, prepaid arrangements were once widespread. Health care was provided under the auspices of unions, churches, fraternal groups, and other voluntary associations that offered doctors fixed prepaid sums on behalf of their members.[40] These arrangements rarely survived the introduction of national health insurance, with entitlements to basic benefits and free choice of physician for most of the population.

One implication of this experience is that although much of the population will accept, indeed welcome, care provided by HMO-like arrangements in the absence of universal coverage, broad entitlements lead to a demand for freedom of choice of provider. Another is that the principle of freedom of practice—that any qualified physician can treat any entitled beneficiary—is also very important to doctors. In Germany, "from 1892 on, these issues, the physicians' access to sickness fund practice and the patients' freedom-of-choice, dominated discussion between sickness funds and the medical profession,"[41] and "freedom" steadily gained ground, as it has also in other European nations.

To be sure, the United States differs from Europe in that the privatism and diversity of American health insurance policies permit extensive competition among insurers. By offering more value for the subscriber's dollar HMOs might attract a sizable market share. Even so, comparative analysis suggests that it is unlikely that the U.S. population, increasingly well covered by third-party plans allowing free choice of provider and financed in ever larger degree by employer contributions, will forsake these freedoms for closed panel plans. Comparison also shows the implausibility of the view that doctors, many of them resistant to group practice of any sort, will move in large numbers to prepaid group practices, or that many of them will voluntarily forsake fee-for-service reimbursement for salaries or capitation.

The second major political science approach to policy analysis, the study of implementation and so-called bargaining games, is homegrown, native American, and recent. Setting out from the undebatable proposition that much rugged terrain lies between the declaration of a program's broad and worthy goals and the achievement of outcomes, this persuasion concentrates on the implementation process, which is said to be dominated by large formal organizations that take up programs delegated to them and then assimilate them to the standard operating procedures and bargaining games that are at the heart of political life within and between

40. William A. Glaser, *Paying the Doctor* (Johns Hopkins Press, 1970), pp. 9–11.
41. Jan Blanpain and others, *National Health Insurance and Health Resources: The European Experience* (Harvard University Press, 1978), p. 27.

organizations. Along the way, goals are easily displaced or subverted.[42] According to this view, more informed attention to the implementation process and to internal bureaucratic politics in particular is vital to improving the workings of public policy. In the HMO case, the bureaucratic politics approach would call attention to HEW and its standard operating procedures and bargaining games. But many of the department's problems with the program arose from the failure of the HMO mission to fit the department's standard operating procedures. The problems lay not in mindless assimilation to agency norms, but instead in the vagaries of improvisation to do justice to a new and unusual task, defined by a watchful and critical political environment.

Internal bureaucratic jealousies were indeed important; the extreme deviation of the qualification task from the usual grant-giving activities of the Public Health Service led to a division of labor between developers and qualifiers that proved unwieldy and inefficient. The best sensitizer to the bureaucratic politics that arose would not have been the recent lore of implementation, however, but rather the ancient public administration principle prescribing clear lines of authority and responsibility.[43]

Even if foresight into the bargaining games between the developers and qualifiers (a rather forced description of the sullen noncommunication and sniping between Seubold and McLeod) could have improved the HMO program's implementation, the basic issues remained the content of the law—a product of legislative, not bureaucratic, bargaining games—and the cross pressures that pulled HEW now toward responsibility to the law and to the lawmakers, and then toward responsiveness to its nervous clientele, the HMO industry. These problems could not have been resolved by analysis or reform of internal HEW processes because they were grounded in decisions and attitudes external to the agency. As an explanation of the HMO program's problems and outcomes, the bureaucratic politics of HEW are of distinctly secondary importance.

If the politicians had had deeper insight into the standard operating procedures of Kaiser and other giants of the industry, they might have designed a more acceptable law, but the nature of the legislative bargaining games made this prospect unlikely. Implementation is unquestionably a highly complex process, beset by the need for many clearances, their nature

42. Well-known works in this area include Graham Allison, *Essence of Decision* (Little, Brown, 1971), and Jeffrey L. Pressman and Aaron B. Wildavsky, *Implementation* (University of California Press, 1973).

43. Luther Gulick, "Notes on the Theory of Organization," in Luther Gulick and L. Urwick, eds., *Papers on the Science of Administration* (New York: Institute of Public Administration, 1937), p. 9.

often unforeseen, among organizations with agendas that conflict with those of the designers of public programs.[44] It is a mistake, however, to assume that policymakers appear to overlook this insight out of ignorance. If they refuse to accept organizational agendas as given, this may be because—as in the HMO case—they are determined to change them and believe that the manipulation of federal grants and other inducements gives them the leverage they need. The grant-in-aid system has, after all, long been expected to use federal funds as a quid pro quo for institutional change. The finding that institutions tend to be reluctant to change is not, therefore, a highly compelling or useful piece of practical wisdom.

The problem in the HMO case was not a general lack of enlightenment among policymakers on the nature of organizational conservatism, but rather a lack of highly specific insights into the individual interests and attitudes of particular organizations in particular locales. Such information cannot be taught by policy analysis; the analysts' generalities are too general to guide behavior and their case studies too specific and circumstantial. The enlightenment needed comes from an unteachable—and usually unavailable—combination of experience, sensitivity, and intuition.

Even if policymakers had had these qualities in high degree, however, they would not have been determinative; that is, they would not have definitively ruled out unacceptable decisions and prescribed acceptable ones. For example, even if Nixon had foreseen with complete clarity what Kennedy would do to the administration's HMO initiative, he might very well have acted no differently. He might have pressed ahead with his approach, acquitted his obligation to act like a leader, and then blamed Kennedy for any mishaps in the program. Nixon, like Kennedy, Rogers, and others, was playing his own political game, with an internal logic that could not simply be sacrificed in the face of disagreement.

Again, even if the established plans had firmly promised Kennedy that they would publicly deplore and shun any program containing elements unacceptable to them, Kennedy might very well have acted no differently. Politicians know that special interests are always self-serving and that a prudent bargainer always overstates his case in hopes of winning more of it than he would if he came on less strongly. Thus it was natural for Kennedy and his allies to assume that a little pushing on a naturally conservative system would lead to compliance, even if it were accompanied by grumbling. And of course the plans refrained from declaring that they

44. Pressman and Wildavsky, *Implementation*, chap. 5.

would in fact shun the program; they hoped to achieve their goals with persuasion, not threats. Up until the last minute, indeed until the work of the conference committee was perused, the plans hoped that the most offensive provisions would be bargained out of the law. As it happened, both sides proved wrong, but neither could have known that beforehand.

The nature of legislative bargaining precludes extreme precision in weighing the effects of decisions on implementation. Actors naturally stake out preferred positions, argue and hold out for what they want as long as they can, and then under the pressure of time compromise quickly in a burst of trades and trade-offs that produce an amalgamation that all are expected to tolerate. By its political nature, lawmaking is an art, not a science, and a highly impressionistic art at that. Policy analyses that counsel, in effect, that Kennedy and the other politicians should have known that, despite their inexhaustible willingness to bargain and compromise, a handful of provisions among dozens would render the law unacceptable to the plans and lead them to propagandize against it as unworkable ask too much and offer too little.

In sum, the implementation–bargaining-games school of analysis boils down to the proposition that policymakers would do well to anticipate all the unanticipated consequences they will wish they had anticipated when these consequences bring their projects to grief later on. This advice is both beside the point and incapable of useful application to the bargaining games that matter most—those carried on between the affected industries and lawmakers—in the HMO case. And although the bureaucratic politics approach is a useful corrective to the excessive formalism of administrative doctrine in the past, the HMO example shows how it may go too far, failing to recognize that what may appear to be endogenous bureaucratic politics may be an agency's improvised efforts to cope with conflicting pressures imposed from outside by political superiors and industry clients. In short, the implementation of the HMO law cannot be understood apart from everything else about the HMO law—its formulation, and its reception by the industry, in particular. Insofar as the implementation–bargaining-games approach to policy analysis remains an "approach" it is too narrow. When it is broadened it ceases to be an approach, becoming merely an invitation to look at any and every thing.

No form of policy analysis would have served policymakers well in the HMO case. What was needed were not arcane analytical techniques and academic insights, but a combination of common sense and qualitative understanding of the workings of health care institutions in the United

States. Common sense was suppressed by the combined force of the generalists' urgent need for a bold new presidential initiative—the omnipresent need to "do something" that passes for leadership in the United States—and the constraints imposed on them by the political infeasibility of more substantively plausible possibilities. Qualitative understanding of the workings of U.S. health care institutions was excluded because those in possession of it—some bureaucrats in HEW and a few social scientists, mainly sociologists—were either despised by the generalists or unable to offer appealing, free-standing proposals within the constraints of political feasibility.

Policy analysts can best contribute to the solution of practical problems in the health field by sketching out the research needed to elucidate them, by suggesting the full range of policy possibilities that such research might support, by illuminating the likely strengths and shortcomings of items on the list, and by insisting that even after extensive and well-conceived research some questions of fact will remain unanswered and all major policy questions will still turn on the interpretation of facts through value-laden perspectives and will therefore remain essentially political, not scientific or analytic, questions. High on the research agenda might be development of a sound vocabulary with which to portray the behavior of consumers and physicians; development of realistic models that address the actual workings of health care institutions, not merely the ways in which they deviate from the profit-making presuppositions of economic theory; careful attention to the complex interactions among institutions and the influence of these interactions on the transformation of policy inputs into outputs; clarification of the meanings and workings of markets, competition, and kindred processes in the health field; and development of multidisciplinary vocabularies (and perhaps, in time, even models) that set the economics of these processes in their professional, psychological, historical, organizational, and political contexts.

If this agenda were discharged, the result might be more informed and sensible policy discussion among the public, the media, professional elites, other attentive elites, and policymakers. In a political system designed to make policy through the interaction of public and private power centers working in and on three separated governmental branches at each of three levels of a federal system, this is all that analysts may legitimately hope to accomplish and more than they usually do achieve.

Even if research were extremely abundant and of very high quality, the results could not be readily translated into public policy. Just as academicians sometimes seem to think that a rational policy process is one that approximates their own intellectual processes of puzzling problems out, so too they are inclined to believe that the acquisition and transmission of knowledge cannot fail to have direct beneficial effects on policy. As a rule, however, those most knowledgeable about complex social systems are least willing to offer immediate solutions to practical problems. Freidson's close, careful study of peer review processes among physicians, for instance, suggests that the social controls on which the federal government's professional standards review organizations rely are probably flawed. A workable peer review system must grow out of the felt needs and deliberate decisions of physicians themselves.[45] Government can do little about this, however, and may have its reasons not to wait for so remote and perhaps utopian an event.

Again, research into the organizational character of hospitals shows that in some respects they are broadly similar—all exhibit the peculiar problems inherent in the ambiguous hierarchies that develop when administrators and medical professionals join in running a complex institution—and in other respects each is unique—combinations of such characteristics as service area, specialization, and sponsorship vary greatly. Neither insight is very useful to policymakers seeking means of containing hospital costs, for any governmental cost-containment strategy will upset relations between administrators and physicians within hospitals to some degree and will also interfere with many particular needs of particular hospitals. Stringent measures in service of federal aims and flexibility in service of the hospitals' daily administrative and financial lives are bound to be in tension. Under the circumstances, the great simplifier, the research broker or policy entrepreneur able to apply a little knowledge and make perplexed policymakers view his recommendation as a lucid and useful rather than a dangerous thing, may find easy entry. No less important than a reduction in the claims policy analysts offer on behalf of their craft, therefore, is a reduction in the expectations policymakers entertain of it.

It would be naïve to promise or expect much on behalf of these protections, however. Even if analysts had been properly humble and policymakers appropriately wary, it is unlikely that the HMO initiative would have been pursued much differently. This judgment follows from the elementary facts of political life in the early 1970s: health care costs were rising rapidly, the administration felt compelled to do something

45. Eliot Freidson, *Doctoring Together: A Study of Professional Social Control* (Elsevier, 1975), pp. 246–59.

about the problem, the fee-for-service system was increasingly in bad odor, but the nation was not ready, or at any rate not thought ready, to address these problems by means of regulatory controls. Had there been no literal model, no Ellwood, no HMOs, the policymakers might well have invented them all. The substantive merits and plausibility of the HMO strategy were subordinated to, and should be viewed in the context of, the political functions of the strategy. This public program was, after all, a political response to a rapidly changing mix of objective conditions and public perceptions. The HMO strategy should be evaluated not only for its substantive policy achievements, but also and more broadly for its larger political meaning. As a policy strategy designed to correct the faulty incentives of the fee-for-service system and thereby reorganize American medicine, HMOs have been of little importance. But as a political response that mediated between the old and the new in an unsettled period in the interplay between health care politics and policy in the United States, HMOs have been extremely significant.

CHAPTER TEN

HMOs and the Future of Federal Health Care Policy

Lately there has been an upsurge of self-praise about the fact that "the time has come" for prepaid group practice. Has it?

Certainly the time has come for prepaid group practice to lead American medicine. But we have to remember that medical delivery systems, as well as legislative programs, are never self-fulfilling. We live by old habits, preferring well worn paths even if they lead nowhere. . . .

America has a habit of killing off good programs by overselling and overstatement. This is no time for hurrahs. Prepaid group practice can easily be swallowed in a sea of rhetoric. Prepaid practice is not the millennium.

Health Insurance Plan of Greater New York, *Health Almanac,* July 1971

THE SOCIAL and public functions of a program that has accomplished little of substance may not be inferred from that outcome, for programs are not only instruments aimed at tangible results and immediate changes in behavior but also links in complex chains reconciling past and future political circumstances and policy choices. Looking at the tangible dimension of U.S. health care policy in 1972, Robert R. Alford concluded that "dynamics without change" was the rule.[1] As an appraisal of some programs—Medicare, for example—this description is simply wrong.[2] But even in the case of less accomplished programs—health maintenance organizations, for example—it may be wise to cast an eye in nonobvious places for evidence of contribution to change. It is unreasonable to expect "genuine change" to occur quickly and dramatically in so decentralized a system as that of the United States. Change here is gradual and mediated, and public programs are major agents of mediation. Although its tangible importance has been modest, the HMO program has figured importantly

1. "The Political Economy of Health Care: Dynamics Without Change," *Politics and Society,* vol. 2 (Winter 1972), pp. 127–64. See also Robert R. Alford, *Health Care Politics: Ideological and Interest Group Barriers to Reform* (University of Chicago Press, 1975).

2. See the critique of Alford by Milton I. Roemer, "An Empirical Misadventure," *Journal of Health Politics, Policy and Law,* vol. 1 (Spring 1976), pp. 117–22; and the discussion of Medicare and Medicaid in Karen Davis and Cathy Schoen, *Health and the War on Poverty: A Ten-Year Appraisal* (Brookings Institution, 1978), chaps. 3, 4.

in what John Dewey called "the mediation of social transitions."[3] This chapter will sketch briefly the character of these social transitions, the directions in which they appear to be moving, and the role HMOs may be expected to play in them relative to other policy strategies.

Four Strategies of Intervention

The U.S. federal government has intervened in the health care system by means of four general strategies, each one in large measure a response to the perceived problems of the preceding ones.[4] Before World War II, that government intervened very little in the health system, confining its activities mainly to financial support of traditional public health functions of state and local governments. Soon after the war ended, however, the government, largely by means of congressional leadership, adopted grant programs subsidizing biomedical research in government and in universities (through the National Institutes of Health) and supporting the planning and construction of new hospitals (under the Hill-Burton program). In the early 1960s these programs were supplemented by new federal aid to train medical manpower, especially physicians. This general approach, which may be called the "subsidy" strategy because it gave federal funds to providers (broadly defined) to augment their continuing activities, dominated federal health care policy until 1965.

In 1965 the government enacted the Medicare and Medicaid programs, which entitled certain consumers to federal funds to pay a portion of their medical bills. Having discovered that subsidies to providers to expand research, hospitals, and medical manpower would not automatically trickle down to the population and remove the barriers to care the elderly and poor faced, the government adopted a "financing" strategy.

In 1970, concerned about medical cost increases that were aggravated by governmental programs that increased both the supply of medical care resources and the demand for them, the federal government considered means of building new organizational types to move the system toward greater efficiency. The major result was the HMO program. (Neighborhood health centers of the Office of Economic Opportunity and the model

3. *Liberalism and Social Action* (Capricorn, 1963), p. 48.
4. This section draws heavily on Lawrence D. Brown, "Health Care Policy Strategies and Political Coalitions in the United States," in Charles R. Foster, ed., *Comparative Public Policy and Citizen Participation* (Pergamon, 1980), pp. 194–214.

cities programs were earlier reorganization efforts, while the national health service corps, designed to encourage physicians to practice in underserved areas, was roughly contemporaneous with the emergence of the HMO initiative.)

While it was still evolving, the reorganization strategy was supplemented by a fourth approach, regulation. In 1972 the government created a program of professional standards review organizations (PSROs) mainly to monitor the appropriateness of hospital admissions and lengths of stay for Medicare and Medicaid patients. In 1974 it transformed the comprehensive health planning agencies into somewhat stronger health systems agencies (HSAs) and imposed new planning and grant review requirements on the states and localities. In the same legislation the government required that each state adopt a certificate-of-need program that forbade hospitals and other institutions to make major expansions of their facilities and equipment without the express approval of state reviewers. The federal government also began supporting efforts to set hospitals' rates prospectively in some states.

Broadly speaking, then, the federal role has moved from laissez faire and nonintervention, broken only by small-scale support for established public health activities at the state and local levels, to a period of support for system expansion, first by means of programs to increase the supply of medical care services by subsidizing the activities of providers and then by means of programs increasing the demand for services by financing care for the disadvantaged, and thence to efforts to impose on the system public controls, by means of reorganization and regulation, in hopes of moderating the costs of health care. Viewed in this light, federal health care policy has generated both dynamics and change. It should be borne in mind that the federal government has intervened in the health care system in a major way for only about thirty years. The breakthrough to a significant federal role in financing care occurred only in 1965, and the effort to control costs did not begin in earnest until five years later. In sum, health care policy has compressed a significant amount of change into relatively few years. Admittedly, it has not adopted national health insurance or a national health service or otherwise driven out the private practice and financing of medicine—the only measures that some critics would accept as genuine change. The United States has, however, moved toward stronger measures of centralization and regulation in a typically American fashion, taking a series of small steps, each of which institutionalizes new public commitments, sows the seeds of the next change, and thereby contributes subtly to a policy mosaic that embraces major changes over time. The significance of individual programs cannot be grasped fully apart from this context, for individual programs are at once effects and causes in a larger evolutionary pattern.

Discussion of the shift from laissez faire to active government intervention by means of the subsidy and financing strategies lies outside the scope of this work, which has focused on the shift from system-expanding measures to measures of control by means of HMOs, the main embodiment of one strategy, reorganization. This chapter, like those before, will confine itself to the "controls" period of the 1970s. However, it will attempt to set HMOs in at least part of their larger context, showing how the HMO program has been a small but important vehicle of change, making a subtle break with the past, embodying a new public philosophy and consciousness, and mediating the transition to more forceful and perhaps more plausible strategies.

Decentralized Incentive-based Controls

Any political system contemplating controls on health care costs must reach decisions along two policy dimensions or axes. First, it must choose between controls that involve direct public prescriptions as to what the controlled may or may not do (regulation) and those that work by way of monetary rewards encouraging or discouraging (but not flatly forbidding or requiring) certain behavior (incentives). Second, it must allocate control efforts among levels of government—either to the central government (a centralized approach) or to subnational governments or administrative units (decentralized). The two dimensions together yield four policy cells:

	Incentives	Regulation
Decentralized control	I	II
Centralized control	III	IV

The HMO strategy is an example—indeed the only prominent example—of a decentralized incentive-based strategy. It aims to control costs by encouraging the development of cost-conscious, competitive organizations in localities across the nation. It is not surprising that the difficult road to control of health care in the United States began with this strategy. Contemplating both the need to do something about the increase in medical costs and the infeasibility of doing anything authoritative and central, federal policymakers seized on a seemingly painless, inexpensive, nondepriving, nonconflictual, and nonregulatory approach. Instead of expanding or reducing public benefits, HMOs would give consumers incentives to choose more efficient modes of care. Instead of regulating or displacing or directly challenging fee-for-service practitioners, HMOs would subject them to the bracing challenge of market competition. Instead of obliging government to choose among preferred modes in the delivery and financing of health care, HMOs would simply add a new mode to the mix, thus enhancing pluralism. These virtues—efficiency, competition, and choice— proved irresistible to policymakers of the early 1970s, and they embraced the HMO strategy warmly.

Comfortable both politically and ideologically with this strategy, federal policymakers elaborated and pressed for the first time a sharp and expansive critique of the prevailing fee-for-service, third-party-payment system. In a remarkable, even historic, message to Congress in 1971, Republican President Richard M. Nixon in no uncertain terms denounced the system's incentives as "illogical." In this way the literal model of HMOs performed well a central task of policy analysis: it challenged the entrenched consensus of professional, in this case medical, elites.[5] It not only provided a reasoned and far-reaching challenge to the prevailing system but also gave government officials the courage to issue the challenge in their own words and on their own behalf. The HMO proposal began the gradual painful process of acclimating the federal government to the chill waters of intervention in the organization of health care. It put physicians, third-party payers, hospitals, and others on notice that they must expect federal pressure for major changes in their accustomed modes of operation and that the federal government was determined to raise the price of continued nonchalance about the problems of the prevailing system. By offering policymakers both a comprehensive critique of the dominant system and examples of a better way, the HMO proposal gave them the confidence to be critical and forthright. In sum, the HMO initiative at once emboldened government, challenged the prevailing system, and advanced a public philosophy of change. These were no small accomplishments, and in them lies the major positive significance of the federal HMO effort.

Judged against the literal theory and the practice of at least some prepaid group prototypes, many facets of the prevailing system were open to

5. See Rudolph Klein, "The Rise and Decline of Policy Analysis: The Strange Case of Health Policymaking in Britain," *Policy Analysis*, vol. 2 (Summer 1976), pp. 467–72.

criticism. The theory and the prototypes were indeed "partisan efficiency advocates"[6] on which generalist policymakers found they could rely in articulating a sophisticated critique of the tendencies of the prevailing system toward overprovision, the irresponsibilities of third-party payers, the apparent overuse of inpatient care, the system's seeming inattention to prevention and to early outpatient care, the overspecialization of manpower and facilities, and more. These were of course complex medical questions and in the search for answers the expertise and legitimacy of the medical profession easily intimidated government generalists. Health maintenance organizations, however, were a valuable ally of the generalists and a standing reproach and challenge to the professional mainstream. To the arcane quibbles of the professionally dominant, the generalists now had a simple and powerful (albeit simplistic) reply: "But the experience of the HMO prototypes shows that. . . ."[7] In short, the HMO proposal gave high government officials a rationale for federal endorsement of a revisionist model of medical care that had been gaining adherents among academicians and other observers in the private sector for some time. By endorsing and articulating the new perspectives, they helped publicize and legitimatize them.[8]

Into the mainstream assumption that a person should be able to get a doctor when he wants one, revisionists introduced the qualification that access should be channeled along a hierarchy of increasing specialization. Care should begin with a general practitioner or even a paraprofessional;

6. The term is taken from Charles L. Schultze, *The Politics and Economics of Public Spending* (Brookings Institution, 1968), p. 96.

7. In 1976, Paul Starr surmised that "the primary function of HMO's in the long run . . . may turn out to be as a yardstick for social policy, indicating what kinds of advantages are possible from more systematic organization of medical care." "The Undelivered Health System," *The Public Interest,* no. 42 (Winter 1976), p. 85. Such effects were soon visible. For example, Hale Champion, under secretary of HEW in the Carter administration, acknowledged that the 9 percent limit the administration proposed in its hospital cost-containment bill to put on annual revenue increases for hospitals was derived from an analysis of the experience of prepaid group practices. *Congressional Record,* September 26, 1977, pp. 31013–14. And in an interview in 1977 a state health planning official described the yardstick effect in Rhode Island: "We're utilizing HMO experience to a large extent. They provide us with standards for hospital utilization, ambulatory visit rates, etc.—guidelines, in short. We face a paucity of decent empirical or normative standards with which to measure the system. HMO statistics are useful for evaluation. If the feds say four beds per 1,000 population is standard and Rhode Island has 3.9 beds, the fact that HMOs manage with 2.0 puts it in context. If patient days run at 1,100 per 1,000 population and the HMO rate is 450 per 1,000, where does need really lie? We'd be at a great loss without these HMO statistics. They're real-world empirical data on the actual needs of a defined population. We gather them up as fast as they can produce them."

8. The summary of the revisionist viewpoint follows Lawrence D. Brown, "The Scope and Limits of Equality as a Normative Guide to Federal Health Care Policy," *Public Policy,* vol. 26 (Fall 1978), pp. 524–27.

a specialist's time and the high costs required to buy it should be reserved for cases that cannot be treated adequately by generalist personnel. This principle is basic to the operations of most HMOs.

Against the assumption that cost is no object, revisionists argued that considerations of cost-effectiveness could and should be introduced into medical care without necessarily reducing quality. Again, HMOs were the clearest concrete embodiment of this assumption. The HMO must care for members within a fixed annual budget, and must therefore think long and hard about the relative efficacy and importance of various services and allocate scarce resources accordingly.

Against the view that nothing but the best care is good enough, revisionists challenged the automatic equation of technologically advanced care with high-quality care. Tests and procedures should not be automatically employed because they are at hand and because they might conceivably find something wrong even if there is no good reason to think that they will. If diagnostic tests can be done outside the hospital, they should be. If patients can be sent home from the hospital a day or two early, they should not be kept in simply because unsuspected complications could conceivably occur. If a tighter supply of hospital beds means delays for elective surgery, this may be an acceptable, indeed desirable, outcome. (More surgery means more risk of iatrogenic disease.) If generic brand drugs are available, they, and not a more expensive brand name, should be prescribed. Health maintenance organizations gave both theoretical and practical testimony in favor of these revisionist positions.

Finally, against the mainstream view that health and health care are outcomes and services directly dependent on the activities and skills of doctors and hospitals, revisionists argued that health depends importantly, perhaps mainly, on personal preventive practices—life-style; diet; smoking; exercise; stress; exposure to carcinogens in food, water, the work place, and elsewhere—that are essentially "preinstitutional," that is, have little or nothing to do with doctors or hospitals or with the medical care system itself. The revisionist corollary—that doctors should aim at prevention and health maintenance, at keeping people well rather than just treating them when they are sick—however implausible, strengthened forces working to demystify traditional views of medical treatment. It also suggested that medical care and its costs were but one among a range of worthwhile and expensive social endeavors. If the absolute equation of medical care with life and health was unwarranted, then the costs and provision of medical care were no longer untouchable and sacrosanct but instead became fair game for public debate and trade-offs with other desired goods and services. The notion that "health maintenance organizations" could be set up around the nation both expressed and increased interest in the preinstitutional sources of health and health care.

Although the greater share of the critique had little to do with HMOs per se, the HMO model presented a comprehensive, integrated, seemingly logical, and easily grasped package that connected revisionist maxims to incentive-based, seemingly actionable policy strategies. The HMO model, in sum, offered government a uniquely attractive instrument with which to broadcast challenges to established arrangements and thereby both to tap and to build constituencies for change in the larger society. Although the HMO strategy served government poorly, the HMO idea served it very well.

Health maintenance organizations have changed federal attitudes and have themselves been changed in turn. The social bases of HMO development have been transformed since the federal government's discovery and endorsement of HMOs. Labor, once the foremost organization sponsor of HMOs, is now (with some exceptions) indifferent or detached. Business retains much of its traditional indifference and detachment, but some firms have shown new interest in HMO development. Fee-for-service physicians, once adamant opponents of HMOs, increasingly sponsor independent practice associations (IPAs), and some fee-for-service groups have begun devoting a portion of their time to HMO practice. Hospitals show enhanced interest in HMO development as a means of exerting leadership, responding to changing conceptions of their roles (in particular, to the call for a greater emphasis on ambulatory care), and finding outlets for capital. The interest of insurance companies, which ebbed as fear over national health insurance passed, now flows again as concern over their place in contemplated regulatory or competitive cost-containment schemes rises. Corporations owning chains of for-profit hospitals have recognized the rich business possibilities in cornering a complete health market by coupling their hospitals with HMOs. As these trends proceed, the traditional philosophical and professional motivations of contributors to prepaid group practice (PGP) increasingly yield to economic motivations; the old hands may soon find their vocation unrecognizable. In short, the future holds both a further social transformation within the HMO movement and a subtle penetration of mainstream medical institutions by HMOs of this newer entrepreneurial type.

Although it is impossible to predict in detail where these trends will lead, it is probably safe to anticipate extensive ideological and financial turmoil in the HMO industry. With capital more available, but purposive commitment less tenacious, entry may be more rapid and failures more frequent. The growth of IPAs will generate attacks both from purists of the left, moral critics of fee-for-service medicine who believe that thorough-going prepaid group practice is alone desirable, and from purists on the right, ardent competitive types who view IPAs as means by which fee-for-service providers thwart "real" competition. Moreover, greater involvement in HMO-building by Blue Cross and other insurers will aggravate fears of an industry takeover and will trigger cries for relief, perhaps by means of antitrust policy. There will be concern that businesses interested in cost cutting and hospitals in search of teaching material and secure patient markets—sponsors marginally committed to the HMO as an economic entity, and little committed to the supposed professional and moral superiority of prepaid group practices—will compromise access and quality of care. For better or worse, federal involvement has transformed the PGP movement into an HMO industry.

Prognoses about HMO growth and recommendations about the proper federal role in it are best addressed in this context. As a result of the plans' new legitimacy and (far less important) federal financial aid offered by the HMO program itself, HMOs are likely to continue to grow in number and enrollment. This growth is likely to take two distinct forms, a pattern that will aggravate splits within the industry and perhaps even lead some purists to regret the government's discovery of HMOs.

The most important and rapid growth will be among IPAs. Indeed their number is growing at a faster rate than that of PGPs and hybrid types and will probably continue to do so.[9] This pattern, a product of the federal government's legitimatizing of HMOs, is also an ironic and belated fulfillment of the original Nixon-Ellwood plan. As the taboo on HMOs has gradually diminished, physician attitudes toward them, at least in some areas, have changed. In the past, physicians viewed IPAs mainly as a distasteful but necessary means of countering the immediate and dangerous

9. Between 1977 and 1978, independent practice associations grew by a rate of 5 percent, rising to 29 percent of all plans, with 9.5 percent of the national HMO membership, an InterStudy survey showed ("HMO Growth," cited in *Health Services Information*, October 30, 1978, p. 4). In November 1978, they accounted for 36 percent of all HMOs and had 14.4 percent of total HMO membership; U.S. Department of Health, Education, and Welfare, Office of Health Maintenance Organizations, *National HMO Census of Prepaid Plans, 1978* (HEW, 1978), p. 1. By the middle of 1980, 41 percent of the nation's 236 HMOs were IPAs, with 18.6 percent of all HMO members. U.S. Department of Health and Human Services, Office of Health Maintenance Organizations, *National HMO Census of Prepaid Plans, June 30, 1980,* DHHS Publication (PHS) 80-50159 (HHS, 1980), p. 5.

presence of an HMO. In most cases, therefore, one got two plans for the price of one[10]—an HMO and an IPA. Increasingly, however, physicians recognize that they need not await the risk of competition; they might, so to speak, launch a preemptive strike instead of relying on their second-strike capability. Perceiving the value of cornering the prepaid market for themselves and perhaps heading off HMO competition altogether, local medical societies and medical groups have begun to discuss with local industries or cost-minded chambers of commerce the possibility that physicians might set up a prepaid plan (IPA) whose enrollees might amount to, say, 10 percent of the physicians' total practices. As these plans grow more numerous, PGP purists are likely to grow disheartened. These insiders have long believed that so small a percentage of patients winds up as second-class citizens and have viewed competition with a genuine HMO as a necessary, albeit imperfect, protection. There are also serious questions about how much money IPAs may be expected to save.[11]

Independent practice associations will probably be the most volatile element in an increasingly unstable HMO industry. Determination to preempt competition from a "real" HMO may motivate local physicians to form and join an IPA, but it does not necessarily supply commitment to the sacrifices—in particular, acceptance of utilization controls, constraints on referrals, and fees for enrollees set below usual and customary levels—required to make such a plan succeed. If physician leadership (or follow-ership) is weak, discipline may not develop and the plan may fail. If physician leadership is strong and the preemptive strike succeeds (that is, if a projected HMO is deterred from opening in the community), discipline may fade and the plan may fail too. In some areas, then, the result may be no plan for the price of one, or a succession of unstable plans in a chaotic local market.

A less prominent source of growth will be full-scale prepaid group practices or hybrid HMOs established by large industries or insurance companies. Groups like the Winston-Salem Health Care plan founded by R. J. Reynolds Company; Detroit's Health Alliance Plan, which the Ford Motor Company, with the advice of Kaiser, helped to enlarge; and the HMO begun in Dallas under the joint auspices of Kaiser and the Prudential Insurance Company may gladden the hearts of the purists. It would be surprising, however, if they grew very numerous, for they must be either

10. HEW staffer, quoted in *Health Services Information,* March 5, 1979, p. 8.
11. Harold S. Luft, "How Do Health-Maintenance Organizations Achieve Their 'Savings'?" *New England Journal of Medicine,* vol. 298 (June 15, 1978), p. 1337.

very generously capitalized or must grow quite large in order to succeed financially.

Such plans are most likely to arise in the headquarters cities of large and progressive industries whose management has the civic stature, influence, and sense of a hometown stake that create both the willingness to get involved and the ability to win others' support for an HMO effort. Branch plants are less likely to sponsor such efforts; local executives, sensitive to their outsider status, are often reluctant to generate or involve themselves in local controversies. On balance, it is likely that large corporations, sometimes described as the sleeping giants among HMO sponsors, will continue to lie dormant, content to meet the growing expectation that they should "do something" about health costs by means far less intricate and demanding than developing an HMO.

Although the *number* of HMOs is likely to grow, the extent of *membership* growth is difficult to predict. Although the number of HMOs grew dramatically during the 1970s, perhaps fivefold or more, the portion of the U.S. population enrolled rose only from around 2 percent in 1973 to about 4 percent in 1980. Various factors should encourage a higher penetration rate over time. In particular, the growth of IPAs will reduce the dislocations attending HMO membership, especially the requirement that the member exchange his personal physician for a plan physician. Increased familiarity with the HMO approach should generate favorable publicity that will reduce suspicion of the unknown, and should diminish still further the stigma attached to HMO care. And premiums in conventional insurance plans continue to rise rapidly, which may make HMOs appear to be attractive bargains.

Equally important factors are likely to work against dramatic growth of HMO enrollment, however. First, the steady spread of third-party-payment insurance, which covers not only about 90 percent of hospital costs but more than 60 percent of physician costs too, allows conventional plans to challenge the HMOs' traditional bargain—much improved outpatient coverage in exchange for more money or less freedom of choice of physicians and facilities, or both. Second, the growth of major medical coverage and the decrease in individual contributions to premiums in work-related plans further reduce consumers' financial stakes in HMO economies. Third, no one can now be sure precisely how economical the current breed of young HMOs will prove to be. Many of these plans depend importantly on fee-for-service physicians outside their direct control, do not own or control their hospitals, may lack strong utilization controls and well-socialized physicians, may be underpricing their services, must repay millions of federal loan dollars, and are themselves vulnerable in many ways to the ravages of inflation. Some plans may be driven to charge uncompetitive premiums and may therefore grow slowly. Some may go bankrupt and others may succumb to scandal.

Fourth, in areas where Blue Cross and other competitors stabilize premiums by means of tighter management and utilization controls, HMO efficiencies and savings will give less of a competitive edge than they do in areas where a tightly run HMO confronts an undisciplined competitor. Federal jawboning and threats of direct controls may lead Blue Cross plans in some areas increasingly to emulate HMOs, by denying or reducing reimbursement for diagnostic inpatient procedures and for procedures of doubtful efficacy. If government pressure and stronger organizational leadership make Blue Cross a keener economic competitor, this fact, added to the freedom of choice that already works strongly in Blue Cross's favor, may diminish the appeals of HMO membership. Indeed it is possible that some "true" HMOs will be squeezed out between more efficient conventional plans and more available IPAs. Finally, even if all these variables develop in ways favorable to HMOs, there are psychological, cultural, or other unknown variables that may suppress HMO growth.

In the future, as in the past, HMO growth will probably be strongest in fast-growing regions that attract a mobile population without strong ties to personal physicians and mobile physicians without deep roots in local medical societies and other community networks. The major growth centers, therefore, are likely to be in the sun belt, probably its western states. Even in the sun belt, however, low employer contributions to employee health benefits in some communities may limit HMO growth.

Even if HMO membership should reach roughly 10 percent of the U.S. population in the 1980s, it will not transform or reorganize the fee-for-service system. The probable effects of such growth on quality, access, and costs remain largely conjectural. And although HMOs will probably continue to realize their famous inpatient economies, the effects of these economies on competition in the larger system are also unpredictable.

Health maintenance organizations remain a good idea—a powerful critique of, and alternative to, the conventional system—but an implausible federal policy strategy. Ten years of very limited accomplishment with the strategy will probably not diminish policymakers' interest in HMOs, however. The reason is easily found; in 1980 as in 1970, policymakers were in search of relatively painless ways to contain costs, ones that neither curtail benefits nor impose large measures of federal regulation. Indeed, the quest is likely to become more urgent in the 1980s as a result of the growth of an antiregulatory mood and repeated failure among politicians to agree on a national health insurance plan. Therefore, HMOs, a "market alternative" that offers broader benefits for each dollar, may be more intriguing than ever.

In 1980 as in 1970, there was little familiarity with HMOs among policymakers, and little of the deep conviction that historically sustained the PGP movement. Health maintenance organizations remain largely an abstraction, a construct, a distillation and synthesis of ideal, but disembodied, incentives. Given the continuing political stimuli to promote them, policymakers will probably keep reminding themselves that HMOs are a very good idea and from that will conclude that there should be more of them, with more people in them. That only about 4 percent of the population had joined one after ten years of promotional effort will be attributed not to the complex realities of institutional life and consumer taste but to "faulty incentives." From this it will seem to follow logically that the government should busy itself in manipulating everyone's incentives until sizable numbers are induced to join an HMO. These proposals will in turn run aground on institutional-psychological-cultural questions and the recurrent debates will probably prove only that the same old problem—how to get from here (theory) to there (lots of HMOs with many members)—is intractable, depending on many variables other than the logical merits of HMOs and their incentives, and having no nonauthoritative, cheap solution.

Because the federal HMO strategy will probably continue to suffer from the problem of disembodied incentives, of embracing a concept without an institutional base, it will probably continue to be afflicted by topheaviness. One may expect that the secretaries and under secretaries of the executive branch, the health leaders in the Congress, top AFL-CIO officials, some high corporate "statesmen," the Group Health Association of America, and policy analysts and academicians seeking to wield influence will assemble periodically in Washington to celebrate the wonders and glories of HMOs and blame some unrepresented actor for their slow progress. The problems, however, will continue to be out there—in the middle levels of organizations remote from Washington, among state officials, benefit purchasing agents in unions, health benefit plan administrators in companies, and consumers, doctors, hospital administrators, and insurance executives, to whom an HMO is not a state of mind but a concrete organizational project. As Arnold R. Weber remarked in another context, it is sometimes "easier to bring the president of U.S. Steel to bay than a business agent in New Jersey."[12] For these persons, the infrastructure on which successful implementation of the HMO strategy depends, there is no reason to believe that the institutional forces that limited the strategy in the 1970s will change significantly.

That the HMO strategy is never likely to realize fully, or even very largely, the promise of the HMO concept is no reason to refrain from strengthening the strategy insofar as possible. The account developed here yields several modest recommendations on how this might be done. Policymakers seeking to advance the HMO strategy should, above all, acknowledge its practical limitations and stop overselling it. The fragile HMO-building strategy has been asked to bear policy burdens vastly greater than it can support. Although a measure of overselling and overpromising was no doubt necessary and useful in order to concert the force of the HMO idea and critique, this force has now been felt, and ten years' experience with the HMO strategy shows the need to scale down expectations. This scaling-down should take several forms.

First, policy analysts and policymakers should stop offering HMOs as the vehicle of a comprehensive, systemwide reorganization of the incentives of the dominant system, a reorganization that will avoid the need for regulation. Health maintenance organizations are not likely to grow large enough in numbers and in membership to do away with the need for regulation and even if they did grow very large and populous, there is no good reason to assume that the competition their presence would trigger would make regulation unnecessary. These organizations will be at most one small and probably minor element in what will necessarily be a fragmented and multifaceted quest for cost-containment. The properties of the U.S. health care system—high consumer expectations, expanding technology, professional dominance, third-party payment, institutional specialization, and welfare-state entitlements—cannot be made to obey the theoretical laws of the marketplace and must of necessity be subjected to some measure of regulation. The view that regulation is merely a product of the failure of mindless and captured politicians to recognize the easy and better way offered by incentives and competition and conveniently embodied in HMOs upholds a venerable American tradition of promising

---

12. "The Continuing Courtship: Wage-Price Policy through Five Administrations," in Craufurd D. Goodwin ed., *Exhortation and Controls: The Search for a Wage-Price Policy, 1945–71* (Brookings Institution, 1975), p. 374.

facile solutions to complex problems. Schemes to make HMOs the linchpin between national health insurance and cost-containment place excessive burdens on the organization-building strategy.

Second, an end to overselling should mean an end to the numbers game that has plagued the strategy all along. The idea that the progress of the strategy can be measured by the numbers of HMOs launched and by the size of their enrollment has all along been naïve. That plans have not sprung up in every nook and cranny of the land after continued federal efforts to make the HMO law acceptable has led to unwarranted confusion and disappointment, reflecting an overestimation of the potential of the strategy and of the efficacy of political consensus and change. Because HMO-building is at best a precarious process, the HMO program should aim not at creating large numbers of plans quickly, but at discerning competent, knowledgeable founders in plausible locations and encouraging their plans to achieve excellence.

Third, HMOs should not be viewed as a solution to the needs of the rural underserved, the unemployed, the sick, the elderly, and the poor. Several forces work against HMOs in rural areas: dispersed populations, physician and hospital opposition, consumer resistance, and, perhaps most important, low employer contributions to employee benefit plans. Unfortunately, the promise of rural HMOs breathed new life into the long-standing view that the federal government could attract providers to rural areas by erecting a critical mass of modern facilities (medical school branches, for example) that would make the hinterland blossom with a rich medical-professional culture. Lately this approach is properly being abandoned in favor of more modest efforts such as encouragement of paraprofessionals and small, generalist-staffed clinics. This misconceived promise of rural HMO-building should not be permitted to derail this overdue adjustment.

Nor is it likely that HMOs will prove to be a solution to the needs of the poor and the elderly. Unless the government makes it well worth their while, HMOs will remain reluctant to enroll atypically high users, especially difficult cases, and those whose cultural patterns may alienate the stable, employed, middle-class bulk of their memberships. Nor is it likely that the poor, who tend to seek mainstream care at facilities in their own communities, or the elderly, who are often attached to personal physicians who have treated them for many years, will join HMOs in large numbers unless the inducements are very large, and perhaps not even then. Health maintenance organizations offer an improvement in pluralism and choice for those who already enjoy mainstream care, not a solution to the problems of many of the underserved.

Fourth, much would be gained if the federal government and other HMO proponents candidly acknowledged the limits of existing knowledge about the benefits of HMOs and stopped pretending that the plans offer a sure and generalizable means of reconciling lower cost, higher quality, and improved access to care in one harmonious package. Milton I. Roemer, a leading advocate of "zealous," "inspired" promotional leadership in HEW's Office of Health Maintenance Organizations, admitted in 1977 that the office knew almost nothing about the nature and quality of medical care delivery in the federally qualified HMOs it was charged with monitoring.[13] Access is a highly subjective and ambiguous variable. The term "savings," ubiquitous among HMO promoters, should be clarified. Those who use the term should explain precisely which of its many senses they do and do not intend to employ. In particular, HMO savings on inpatient days should be adjusted for age, sex, and other important variables, and it should be recognized that in many cases dollar savings from inpatient economies are not diverted from health care spending to other uses but are instead redistributed among health care purposes. Finally, it should be acknowledged that the asserted systemwide benefits of market competition in the health care field are largely speculative possibilities, not demonstrated fact.

Fifth, the federal government should give up its emphasis on promotion and on zealous, inspired leadership tirelessly selling the HMO concept. After ten years of federal endorsement, it may be safely assumed that most of those actors in a position to launch or support HMOs are now acquainted with the concept. If they decline to engage themselves in HMO-building or expansion, this may well be because they are prudent men with good and sufficient reasons and a realistic reading of their local and organizational circumstances. Conversely, if they undertake HMO-building, they will do so for reasons of their own, not because federal promoters suddenly made the scales fall from their eyes.

Sixth, federal policymakers ought to give hard thought to the continuing justification for a federal role in HMO development. Top officials in the HMO program have admitted that development depends mainly on the funds and commitment of business and labor; federal funds have never

13. "Moving Ahead with HMO Development," University of California, Los Angeles, August 1, 1977, pp. 9, 25–27.

been more than seed money.[14] This suggests that the federal government might extract itself from the organization-building enterprise altogether with little loss. Plans arise and take root when and where local conditions are favorable to them; federal promotion cannot make it otherwise. Independent practice associations impose low capital costs, probably well within the range of coalitions of local business and medical group sponsors to meet or borrow on their own. The PGP prototypes developed almost entirely without federal aid, and if the will to launch a large plan is strong in such companies as Ford, Reynolds, and DuPont, capital should not be a major problem.[15] Needless to say, many sponsors would prefer to substitute federal capital for their own if possible. That the opportunity for such substitutions makes the difference between development and inaction may be doubted, however.

The continuing case for a federal role in HMO development rests on intermediate cases, where sponsors less well endowed than business, labor, and the insurance industry seek to launch plans more ambitious than IPAs. There is much to be said for a modest amount of federal aid concentrated mainly on these sponsors. There is little or nothing to be said for a much enlarged federal appropriation for HMO development.

In general, the federal government should involve itself as little as possible in HMO promotion and development. The much-touted federal promotional effort of the Carter administration rested on a misunderstanding of the obstacles in the way of HMO development and of the powers of oratory to remove them. Federal seed money for HMO development is in most cases a secondary consideration in local decisions about whether or not to proceed with HMO-building. Nor is the federal bureaucracy an appropriate source of guidance for contemplated or new plans in early stages of development. These plans have two principal needs. First, sponsors need advice in moving from a general commitment to HMO-

14. According to Howard R. Veit, director of the Office of Health Maintenance Organizations in the Carter administration, the "primary potential sponsors for HMO growth around the country" are "the business and labor communities." The federal role, Veit argued, should be "catalytic," because "we want to throw the ball to the private sector and let them run with it." "New Office in HEW Undertakes Campaign to Promote HMO Concept," in Federation of American Hospitals, *Review*, June 1978, pp. 22, 24. See also John K. Iglehart, "HMOs—An Idea Whose Time Has Come?" *National Journal*, February 25, 1978, p. 311.

15. See *Health Services Information*, March 5, 1979, pp. 7–9, for a review of some private-sector initiatives in HMO-building. An executive director who had come to an HMO from the insurance industry put it this way in an interview in 1977: "The money isn't the issue. For instance, if you're Ford Motors and spend three billion dollars on health care, what's three million for an HMO? Or take our company's support for this HMO; it's a few millions in a $45 billion budget."

building to operational plans and strategies. Second, HMO executives need counsel on detecting early and imminent dangers and on how to move to meet them. Such aid is best offered by those with long experience in building and running HMOs; it should come from Kaiser and other prototypes, and from other industry insiders. Federal officials for the most part do not have sustained administrative experience in HMOs, and although they may command an overview of the pitfalls and prospects of HMOs around the country, they generally lack the grasp of local circumstances (physician sentiments and organization, employer and employee attitudes, locational nuances, and health insurance benefit levels) and of physician-administrator interaction (recruitment procedures, utilization controls, and staff-facility-enrollment ratios) that permits them to speak in a timely and helpful way to the particular needs of particular plans.

The federal HMO program should concentrate its attention not on promotion and development but on qualification and compliance. The dual choice provision of the HMO law, which requires that most employers of twenty-five or more workers who offer those workers a health benefits plan include the offer of a federally qualified HMO if one exists in their service area and wishes to be offered, awards federal approval; the terms and conditions of the award ought to be taken seriously. If employers are required to offer federally qualified HMOs, the federal government ought to see to it that the plans are reasonably well organized and staffed, that they meet their contractual promises and responsibilities, that they are fiscally sound and likely to remain solvent—that they meet the terms of the HMO law, in short. The meaning of that law is best interpreted by those who must enforce it. If promotion and development were scaled down, leaving the federal program to deal mainly with qualification and compliance, there would be less friction attending checks and balances and fewer conflicts of viewpoint among the promoters and developers and the qualifiers and monitors. The leadership of the HMO program should aim mainly at superintending a small, tightly organized, closely defined, carefully monitored program designed to identify, reward (with the stamp of qualification), and document excellence in HMOs, wherever and however many or few they may be.

These steps would help to realize the potential of the HMO strategy, mainly by honoring its limitations. At best the substantive accomplishments of the program are likely to remain modest, and its true significance will probably continue to lie in the mediation of social transitions. As a matter of political history, the HMO program will be seen as a first, highly important step in the federal government's critique of the prevailing system of American medicine and in its growing willingness to do battle with it. In the future too HMOs will remain a powerful partisan of efficiency, empirical proof that a fee-for-service, third-party-payment system need not be regarded as the one right way. In all of this, irony may compound irony: just as the major substantive accomplishment of the development effort over time may be a proliferation of IPAs (conforming to the early Nixon vision), the main transitional achievement of the enthusiasm for HMOs may be to make a case for governmental regulation designed to bring the prevailing system closer to the efficiencies of HMOs. Having given federal policymakers the will and confidence to criticize the prevailing system, the HMO example may eventually help give them the will and confidence to regulate it.

Decentralized Regulatory Controls

Even as the HMO initiative was being debated, enacted, and launched, the federal government was adopting regulatory efforts in the health care field—the professional standards review organizations (PSROs), the health system agencies, the federal certificate-of-need requirement, and support for efforts at prospective hospital rate-setting and budget review in various states. In the development of the political consensus behind these measures, it is very probable that the critiques contained in HMO theory and practice, broadcast and diffused in the debate over the HMO proposal, hastened processes that would have proceeded more slowly in their absence. In sum, the political debate about the rationale for and design of decentralized incentive-based approaches probably strengthened the movement for decentralized regulatory controls.

Decentralized regulation reflected ambivalence among the public and among policymakers. It was widely agreed that providers sometimes behave wastefully and that public authority should do something about this waste, but there was no consensus about exactly what should be done. Lacking a clear national agenda, believing that the extent and nature of waste varies from place to place, concerned that regional variations be respected, hopeful that lessons of general application might be learned from diverse efforts at cost-containment in diverse settings, and eager to diffuse and deflect from themselves the conflicts inherent in public regulation, federal policymakers approached regulation cautiously, deliberately designed weak programs with few powers and sanctions, and delegated these new programs to state and local bodies.

The decentralized regulatory programs concentrate most of their energies on hospitals. (Even PSROs—aimed at physicians' behavior—have generally confined themselves to reviewing decisions about admission to and length of stay in hospitals.) This is the most opportune target for programs with little power and an ambiguous role. It is easier (though not easy) to promulgate regulations for a delimited set of formal organizations than for the much more numerous corps of private physicians. It is easier to monitor compliance by the former than by the latter. It is also easier to apply sanctions in cases of noncompliance to hospitals than to physicians.

The hospital focus also reflects prevailing notions of the nature of the problem of medical cost increases. Hospital charges account for by far the largest portion of the nation's medical care bill and are by far the fastest rising element of that bill. If the hospitals' tendency to compete with one another for a lustrous medical staff, a prestigious board, esoteric services, and a reputation for innovation can be curbed; if existing beds are not misused and new beds are not built; if scanners and other costly equipment are not too widely diffused; if, in short, hospitals can be made to respond to imperatives other than those of organizational aggrandizement, then, it is often argued, this most worrisome component of costs may be brought under control.

Not everyone accepts this diagnosis, however. Canada and much of Europe, after all, have significantly more hospital beds per thousand persons than the United States and hospital stays tend to be longer there.[16] The fundamental problem, some analysts argue, is not the size and number of facilities, nor admission rates and lengths of stay, but rather what happens to patients once they are in the hospital. The major source of rising hospital costs is said to be the battery of diagnostic, therapeutic, and surgical procedures ordered by physicians once the patient has been

16. On numbers of beds see Marc Lalonde, *A New Perspective on the Health of Canadians: A Working Document* (Ottawa: Government of Canada, 1974), p. 27. Of lengths of stay, William A. Glaser writes: "Closed medical staffs in European hospitals usually try to keep a patient until his recovery is assured. American medicine has much shorter stays because the physician continues to see the patient in his office, instead of referring him back to the primary doctor." *Paying the Doctor Under National Health Insurance: Foreign Lessons for the U.S.*, 2d ed. (Bureau of Applied Social Research, Columbia University, 1976), p. IV-23. For helpful figures on hospital use and facilities in the United States, Sweden, and England see Odin W. Anderson, *Health Care: Can There Be Equity?* (Wiley, 1972), pp. 234–38; and Odin W. Anderson and James Warner Bjorkman, "Equity and Health Care: Sweden, Britain and the United States," in Arnold J. Heidenheimer and Nils Elvander, eds., *The Shaping of the Swedish Health System* (St. Martin's, 1980), pp. 230–31.

hospitalized. Because hospitals are essentially passive agents—because, as is often said, hospitals have not patients, but rather medical staffs who have patients—tightening controls on the hospital is misconceived. If doctors are inclined to admit patients at the slightest hint of trouble, leave them in for long periods while insurance pays the bill, hospitalize them for procedures that could have been done as well in an outpatient setting, bombard them with ancillary services and tests, and perform a high volume of surgery (including elective surgery and surgery of questionable need), there is little the hospital can do. To be sure, it profits directly from all this overuse, as does the physician. Correlation, however, should not be mistaken for causation. "The elimination of unnecessary surgery, hospital admissions, tests, prescriptions, and the like is the surest, swiftest way of stopping runaway inflation of health care costs," Victor R. Fuchs declares, and the proper target of the effort is the physician.[17] The best way to reach this target, some urge, is to change the physician's incentives. And the best way to accomplish this change is to promote HMOs.

If this line of reasoning is correct, the hospital-targeted, decentralized regulatory programs might be expected to accomplish little. As might also be expected, however, evaluations are inconclusive. Scholars have argued that these programs cost more to run than they save (PSROs), have encouraged hospitals to channel funds from constrained objects of investment such as new hospital beds into less constrained objects such as new equipment (certificate-of-need), are poorly equipped to contain costs (HSAs), and unintendedly generate perverse incentives for overuse (rate-setting).[18] Other scholars have replied that the early studies were conducted before the programs had sufficient time to take root; that data, methods, and measures were all badly flawed; that the potential for savings when programs are implemented sincerely and energetically was obscured by the aggregate data; and that later studies using better data and methods to examine more mature programs have indeed shown some impressive savings.[19]

17. *Who Shall Live? Health, Economics, and Social Choice* (Basic Books, 1974), p. 60.

18. For example, Congressional Budget Office, *The Effects of PSROs on Health Care Costs: Current Findings and Future Evaluations* (CBO, 1979), p. x; David S. Salkever and Thomas W. Bice, *Hospital Certificate-of-Need Controls: Impact on Investment, Costs, and Use* (Washington: American Enterprise Institute for Public Policy Research, 1979); Bruce C. Vladeck, "Interest-Group Representation and the HSAs: Health Planning and Political Theory," *American Journal of Public Health*, vol. 67 (January 1977), pp. 23–29; Katharine G. Bauer, "Hospital Rate Setting—This Way to Salvation?" *Milbank Memorial Fund Quarterly/Health and Society*, vol. 55 (Winter 1977), pp. 117–58; reprinted in Michael Zubcoff and others, eds., *Hospital Cost Containment* (New York: PRODIST, 1978), pp. 324–69.

19. Paul M. Gertman and others, "Utilization Review in the United States: Results from a 1976–1977 National Survey of Hospitals," *Medical Care*, supplement, vol. 17 (August 1979); Donald R. Cohodes,

However these arguments may be resolved, it may be that the major significance of the decentralized regulatory programs, like that of HMOs, lies not in short-term dollar savings, but rather in longer-range and intangible sociopolitical changes, in their contribution to the mediation of social transitions. Two such effects deserve special scrutiny. First, it may be argued that a basic step toward effective control of health care costs in the United States is the development of functional substitutes for the more structured bargaining arrangements employed by the Europeans. In Europe, regulations—notably fee schedules—are negotiated between sickness funds and providers who come together in national and perhaps provincial forums under the watchful eye of unions, political party leaders, government ministries, and others. The national health insurance statute gives the central government the authority to set down procedures for and constraints on bargaining and (as a rule) to keep the major interests at the table. In the United States, which lacks a national health insurance scheme and which allows governmental financing to take a back seat to private arrangements, the central government cannot rely on these structural controls. It may therefore be sensible to look for functional substitutes that conform to the decentralized American pattern.

The decentralized regulatory programs may play this role. Although these programs are "regulatory," perhaps their major achievement is to bring important groups into negotiations with one another. In the PSRO program a government-sponsored body bargains with physicians. In the HSAs many local interests debate the proper allocation of present and future resources and draw up areawide plans. Certificate-of-need processes engage virtually any community, organizational, or governmental interest with a stake in the expansion of hospitals. In the rate-setting programs, hospitals and other affected institutions negotiate with state officials over rates and reimbursement. In all of these programs providers are obliged to negotiate with governmental authorities and with each other over behavior that was formerly considered their individual private preserve, and in most of them an array of community interests joins the fray. In the HMO these bargaining processes—among administrators, providers, board, and so on—are intraorganizational and are therefore contingent on the rigors of

---

"Interstate Variation in Certificate of Need Programs—A Review and Prospectus," and Lawrence D. Brown, "Some Structural Issues in the Health Planning Program," in Institute of Medicine, *Health Planning in the United States: Health Policy Issues*, vol. 2 (Washington: National Academy Press, 1981), pp. 1–79; Brian Biles and others, "Hospital Cost Inflation Under State Rate-Setting Programs," *New England Journal of Medicine*, vol. 303 (September 18, 1980), pp. 664–68.

organization-building and maintenance. In the decentralized regulatory programs they are interorganizational and are therefore capable of development from the ever-present raw materials of local medical systems.[20] Even if these programs are indeed too weak to become accomplished constrainers and regulators, they too contribute to the mediation of social transitions.

Second, these programs may produce subtle but important changes in the balance of power within hospitals. When government programs constrain hospital decisionmaking, administrators may no longer behave as passive registers of the preferences of the medical staff. Countervailing public power may force administrators aggressively to mediate, bargain, and apply pressure within their institutions, perhaps for the first time. Doctors may be obliged to accept that a state rate-setting body will not incorporate a favorite project in the rates it allows for the coming year, or that a new facility or piece of equipment may be challenged or denied by a certificate-of-need authority. Hospitals' plans will be debated by many participants at HSA meetings, and their admission procedures will be monitored by PSROs. Perhaps in time this governmental pressure will change the nature of the hospital administrator's tasks, the character of administrative-medical staff relations, and thus the power of professional dominance. These changes in communitywide bargaining and in organizational patterns within hospitals will not find their ways into quantitative indicators of cost-containment this year or next, but, sustained over time, they may have important effects on the nature of medical politics and practice.

The possibility that the decentralized regulatory programs may produce these subtle, seemingly latent, long-term results casts a skeptical light on the view that the one best way to cost-containment is incentive-based solutions aimed at changing physicians' behavior. The familiar notion that everything that argues for the importance of physician behavior in health care services automatically argues for an incentive-based approach in preference to regulation rests on a rigid image of the relation between physicians and hospitals. One may grant the primacy of physician behavior—the importance of consumer deference to their demand-governing decisions, the expression of the technological imperative in physicians' conduct, the maxim that hospitals have doctors who have patients, the

---

20. This is not, of course, to say that they are easily developed. See Lawrence D. Brown, "Political Conditions of Regulatory Effectiveness: The Case of PSROs and HSAs," *Bulletin of the New York Academy of Medicine*, vol. 58 (January–February 1982), pp. 77–90.

roots of hospital aggrandizement in the need to attract and retain prominent medical staffs, and more. One may then go on to concede that cost-containment depends on altering physician behavior; entertain the theoretical arguments for incentive-based means of doing so, such as HMOs; explore the practical difficulties of putting such strategies in place; and finally despair of their working on a large scale. And one may still retain hope, or at any rate the hypothesis, that hospital-based regulatory approaches aimed at altering the environment and constraints within which physicians employ this costliest component of medical care may gradually bring about changes in physicians' attitudes and practices. These arguments generate the hypothesis that U.S. health care policy may find it "easier" to achieve cost-containment by altering physicians' *environments* than by altering physician *incentives*. A fair test of the hypothesis will require time and the application of evaluative methodologies far different from those that equate rigor with quantification.

Centralized Incentive-based Controls

In the 1970s, the federal government launched in earnest the search for acceptable health care cost controls, beginning with decentralized approaches, both incentive-based and regulatory. In the 1980s, there will be debate over more centralized measures toward which the efforts of the 1970s may prove to be transitional.

The debate over centralization grew intense in 1977 when the Carter administration proposed that Congress enact a health care cost-containment plan that would impose federal revenue and capital "ceilings" on hospitals.[21] Congress rejected the plan decisively in 1979. Meanwhile, pricked by the threat of this escalation of regulatory power, opponents of regulation scrambled with new urgency to devise or revise incentive-based alternatives.

These efforts repeatedly returned to HMOs, but as the 1970s closed, incentive theorists increasingly recognized the limits of a decentralized market-building strategy. An effective HMO strategy would at the very least require changes in financial incentives initiated by the central government; these changes might reinforce, but would remain essentially inde-

---

21. See William L. Dunn and Bonnie Lefkowitz, "The Hospital Cost Containment Act of 1977: An Analysis of the Administration's Proposal," in Zubcoff and others, *Hospital Cost Containment*, pp. 166–214.

pendent of, the HMO strategy. This rethinking of the requisites of an effective incentive-based strategy is one of the more important products of the HMO experience. In the 1970s, policy logic took the form: "If HMOs are launched (with modest federal start-up aid), then consequences x, y, and z will follow." Increasingly the logic takes the form: "If the federal government makes changes a, b, and c in programs and laws d, e, and f, then HMOs may catch on in greater numbers and then consequences x, y, and z, including the elimination of many obstacles to market competition, will follow." This belated acknowledgment that the HMO strategy is not free-standing and independent of painful change is an important step toward realism. What is realistic is not necessarily feasible or desirable, however.

The proposals to use federal law to encourage market approaches to cost-containment are complex, diverse, and difficult to summarize. (In part, this results from the tendency of authors of these measures to rush to the hopper with their "solutions," reflect afterward on the full complexity of what they have suggested, and then modify their proposals substantially.) Most, though not all, of these proposals build on three basic elements. First, they would require that all employers who offer health benefits to a work force above a certain size offer "multiple" choices, usually meaning two or three distinct plans. Second, so that employees have not only a choice but also an incentive to choose the inexpensive option, they would require that employers make equal contributions to the various offerings. Employees choosing more expensive options would pay for the extras out-of-pocket. Third, in order to sharpen the incentive to choose the inexpensive plan, the proposals would depart from present practice and treat employer contributions above a certain dollar limit to employee health insurance premiums as taxable employee income.[22] Some versions would give a tax rebate to employees choosing cheaper plans. These measures, it is argued, will guarantee that consumers have both a choice among plans and an incentive to choose the more efficient plans. The result would be price competition among plans.[23]

It will be difficult to translate these principles into legislation for four

22. For a balanced discussion of this and related proposals, see Congressional Budget Office, *Tax Subsidies for Medical Care: Current Policies and Possible Alternatives* (CBO, 1980).

23. See *Proposals to Stimulate Health Care Competition*, Hearings before the Subcommittee on Health of the Senate Finance Committee, 96 Cong. 2 sess. (U.S. Government Printing Office, 1980); Alain C. Enthoven, *Health Plan* (Addison-Wesley, 1980); Lawrence S. Seidman, "Income-Related Consumer Cost Sharing: A Strategy for the Health Sector," in Mark V. Pauly, ed., *National Health Insurance: What Now, What Later, What Never?* (Washington: American Enterprise Institute for Public Policy Research, 1980), pp. 307–28.

major reasons. First, the approach is not likely to be highly popular with the electorate. One may assume that most people view their insurance purchases as acts of prudence, not extravagance, that they regard their present direct share of health expenses as an adequate, or perhaps even excessive, check on frivolous use, and that they will not be pleased to see the tax code manipulated to manipulate their coverage decisions while other taxes rise and tax cuts are promised. Moreover, these proposals would disrupt established collective bargaining prerogatives and are strongly opposed by organized labor.

Second, the proposals raise many seemingly small questions that assume great significance when viewed through the eyes of major organizations affected by them. For example, what will be the minimum number of employees in firms made subject to the multiple choice requirement? How does the choice of one or another number affect administrative costs to employers and carriers, ability to experience rate, bargaining leverage, and more? What is to constitute a distinct offering? Can one carrier—for instance, Blue Cross—offer separate plans or must the plans be offered by separate carriers? Must one or more of the offerings be an HMO? Must one or all HMO offerings be federally qualified? Or state qualified? How is the precise dollar cap on employer contributions excluded from federal tax to be derived? Can a national cap work or must regional caps be installed to compensate for variations in costs?

Third, using the tax code for purposes of health cost-containment may prove to be highly frustrating to government and citizen alike. In Herbert Kaufman's words: "It does not take a vivid imagination to visualize the consequences of using taxation for purposes besides raising revenue. The multiplication of categories would itself necessitate a flood of instructions, which would be followed by more instructions as unanticipated ambiguities presented new problems." There would follow "requests for advisory opinions," "complaints about the length of time needed to get answers," appeals and court battles, and "a larger body of enforcement agents." According to Kaufman, "taxation has already become one of the major sources of what people think of as red tape. The more purposes it is made to serve, the worse it is likely to get."[24]

Finally, even assuming that agreement could be reached on all these "details," there is a fourth element contained in some market proposals, notably Alain Enthoven's consumer choice plan, but absent from others,

24. *Red Tape: Its Origins, Uses, and Abuses* (Brookings Institution, 1977), pp. 84–85.

that elicits strong controversy. This is the requirement that all of the multiple plans offered market a minimum, federally defined, benefit package and observe other federally imposed constraints on rate-setting and recruitment. The provision would protect HMOs and other comprehensive plans from the adverse selection likely to occur in a pure competitive setting. Under the market approach, offerings may be expected to run from very inexpensive indemnity-type plans with high deductibles and copayments, and many exclusions and limitations, to HMOs offering wide benefits and few deductibles, copayments, exclusions, or limitations, but charging a higher premium. Given a choice and financial incentives (a tax rebate and a loss of tax exclusion) tied to premium levels, families with good health histories and little expected need for care might choose the cheap indemnity plans while those expecting to use much care might opt for the HMO. Over time, indemnity costs would fall while HMO costs rose, eventually driving HMOs from the market. The only way to avoid this outcome is to define a minimum benefit package and require that all eligible plans offer it.[25]

This proposal has created dissension within the ranks of those who support market approaches and consumer choice in general. Proponents of cost sharing argue, in essence, that although HMOs have their uses and merits, there is no good reason to circumscribe the limits of free competition so sharply simply to protect them. The point of a market approach should be, in the words of Alfred Kahn, "to see the market free to offer consumers the widest range of choices they are willing to select."[26]

The prospect that cost sharing will be the main outcome of freer markets and wider choices has in turn evoked a long list of familiar objections. Cost sharing, opponents contend, deters relatively inexpensive preventive and outpatient care and may actually raise costs over time by increasing the need for hospitalization; indiscriminately deters beneficial medical procedures along with ones of little expected value; inequitably imposes higher costs on those with the greatest needs; asks people to make complex benefit-cost calculations in moments of anxiety and stress; and invites privately purchased supplementary insurance plans, filling gaps in the primary policies. However, the Enthoven approach—multiple offerings, equal contributions, and a tax cap combined with minimum benefit packages and other regulatory measures designed to make the world safe for HMOs and other comprehensive, organized systems—seems to some

25. Enthoven, *Health Plan*, pp. 78–82.
26. *Proposals*, Hearings, p. 192.

market-builders to put unacceptable limits on the free play of market competition.

Even if these various difficulties could be overcome, no one knows what effect a market approach would have if it were adopted. As Karen Davis explained, "there is little evidence to indicate that these efforts can provide substantial immediate relief from health care inflation or that competitive approaches can effect more than marginal changes in the health care system," for "we have little practical experience which shows how the majority of consumers would actually behave in such circumstances."[27]

Evidence from the federal employees health benefits plan (FEHBP), sometimes cited as a rough prototype of a consumer choice plan, suggests that responses may be small. The plan offers workers a choice among Blue Cross, commercial plans, and HMOs (where available), requires that the plans meet certain minimum requirements, and pays 60 percent of the average of premiums of a sample of major plans, but no more than 75 percent of the premium of any plan selected. The program has been offered since it began in 1960, and the number of HMOs offered jumped from 21 in that year to 84 in 1980. Yet the number of program beneficiaries enrolled in HMOs has grown slowly over time, from 5.8 percent in 1960 to 10 percent in 1980. Moreover, the Kaiser plans have all along accounted for more than 40 percent of this enrollment. There is no reason to assume that the general population will prove more Pavlovian in responding to such financial incentives than has the federal work force.

None of these incentive approaches is the answer their proponents sometimes take them to be. Indeed no one has the slightest idea how any of them would work if put into practice. Their principal contribution is that when scrutinized closely, they dispel the illusion that simple, painless, inoffensive federal strategies can be devised to improve the efficiency of the health care system by means of HMOs or otherwise. Modest sums of seed money and manipulation of financial incentives at the margin will not do. If the incentives are just incentives—that is, one or more benefit or cost added at the margin of freely taken decisions—they may well turn out to be too small to accomplish their purpose. To meet its objectives, the federal government must be prepared to manipulate the particulars of the tax code and of financing programs strongly and unequivocally toward HMOs or other exemplars of efficiency. That is, it must award windfalls or impose burdens large enough reliably to constrain decisions on a large scale. But

27. Ibid., p. 37.

then, of course, it will no longer be benignly manipulating incentives; it will instead be authoritatively withdrawing familiar benefits such as tax exclusions or first-dollar coverage, and thereby imposing costs and disincentives to continue accustomed and widely accepted behavior. To some, this approach to efficiency is preferable to regulation. Be this as it may, calling it an incentive approach strains language severely. To put the point in the plain Benthamite terms it deserves, both regulatory and market approaches work by means of governmental imposition of various types and degrees of pain. The policy choice lies, therefore, not between a libertarian, free-spirited, "incentive" approach honoring consumer choice and an oppressive, coercive, "regulatory" approach forcing narrow options down the throats of a resistant populace, but rather between types and degrees of publicly imposed pain. Efforts to achieve efficiency and cost control by means of incentives, markets, and competition would not be, if taken seriously, an inconspicuous exercise in constructing new consumer choices. They would instead demand extensive social engineering that would impose large changes on the structure of the American health care system. To "work," these efforts must penalize significantly the vast majority of the population, which has given no indication whatever that it wishes to be forced to be free to choose between extensive cost sharing that renders meaningless its accompanying freedom of choice of providers and comprehensive coverage in closed panel HMOs.

The habit of describing the so-called incentive approaches with the hallowed term "markets" confers an undeserved respectability on approaches that share little in common with markets as traditionally understood and obscures the enormous differences between new markets and old. Traditionally, a market approach has denoted social arrangements that facilitate the aggregation and channel the expression of decentralized, "atomized," individually taken preferences within broad and general public rules of conduct (contracts shall be upheld, fraud and violence are prohibited, and so forth). The so-called market approaches recommended to policymakers today as means of employing private interests in the service of public ends have a very different character. They invite the central government to design, with care and specificity, a set of top-down rewards and penalties that, when applied to "the system" from above, may be depended on to change millions of individual choices significantly in directions that government prefers and that the individuals affected hitherto dismissed. The object of the old markets was to express preferences; that of the new markets is to shape them. Old markets facilitated expression of a range of choices limited mainly by persons' willingness and ability to pay, with institutions held constant, so to speak. New markets construct a range of choices and then stack the decks by manipulating incentives toward what government defines as the right choice, with the explicit intention of producing institutional change. If the new approach were described accurately—as, for example, "centrally planned social engineering by the federal government involving the manipulation of material rewards and penalties to trigger major behavioral changes"— instead of in code words with ancient and honored libertarian connotations, the nature of the enterprise and of the policy options would be much clearer.[28]

Options would grow clearer still if market advocates curbed their tendency to misconstrue the nature of the regulatory alternative in the health care field. This alternative is not old-style regulation—decisionmaking by independent regulatory commissions in Washington on the pricing, routing, programming, and other requests of public utilities and of profit-making firms—but rather a new regulation carried on by decentralized, political, interdependent, and variously structured bodies working at the state and local levels to constrain the excesses of mainly nonprofit organizations.[29] A fair appraisal of the choice between market and regulatory approaches requires that both be examined in their true new forms. Analysis that contrasts the theoretical virtues of old markets with the known evils of old regulation errs twice over.

It is logically possible that a market approach to cost-containment without serious drawbacks could be devised. This logical possibility is unlikely to be realized in practice, however, because at bottom these approaches, however ingenious or theoretically elegant, rest on questionable assumptions about the nature of the demand for health insurance. The usual image portrays consumers whose principal concern is the dollar cost to them of their insurance, and whose overriding interest lies in achieving as much of a free ride as possible, that is, in acquiring for themselves as much coverage with as few limitations as possible at the lowest possible out-of-pocket costs, thereby removing financial deterrents

28. Some of the best contemporary examples of confused thinking on this point come from the environmental field, where environmentalists sometimes join in the general outcry over excessive governmental regulation and agree with some economists that a tax or fee system would prove less constraining and more libertarian—provided that the taxes and fees are set to be "unacceptably high" to polluters!

29. For differing perspectives on these questions, see Richard S. Gordon, ed., *Issues in Health Care Regulation* (McGraw-Hill, 1980).

to their consumption—and waste—of care. The problem, wherein consumers lose interest in restricting the amount of care they receive because third parties pay most of the bill, is called "moral hazard."[30]

This image of the demand for health insurance and of the effects of moral hazard on the consumption of care is open to question. For example, the cost the consumer bears is certainly not the only relevant aspect of his choice among health insurance plans. Matters of taste and style of care also enter in, especially when, as in the case of the choice between an HMO and a conventional competitor, choosing the health coverage offered by the HMO entails choosing its delivery system also. This has always been a major obstacle to HMO growth despite the tendency of HMOs to offer broad benefits and to impose lower out-of-pocket costs on consumers. The propensity to join HMOs cannot be predicted or manipulated by financial incentives alone.

Nor are present health insurance patterns adequately pictured as a product of thoroughgoing moral hazard, of free riders run riot. One might begin by distinguishing between two types of free rider problems. The first describes a situation in which some ride free at the expense of others because the former class has somehow exempted or insulated itself from the costs of goods or services generally ("collectively") enjoyed. Group A enjoys a benefit but pays little or nothing, allowing group B to bear all the costs of providing the benefit. One group rides free, and one is taken for a ride. The nature of the collective good itself prevents group A from being excluded from its provision even though the group declines to contribute to the costs of its production.

Although the problems arising from widespread third-party payment of health care costs are sometimes described in similar terms, the description is misleading. The two classes that constitute the classic collective good–free rider problem do not exist in the case of health care services and costs. For no one is health care a free collective good; everyone pays for it—in higher insurance premiums, higher taxes, higher out-of-pocket costs, higher prices, forgone wage increases, or in all of these and in other ways—and everyone knows it. And in one respect the problem is the reverse of the classic free rider problem: whereas classically, nonpayers cannot be excluded from collective benefits, in the health insurance case some payers are excluded from the collective good—unemployed or self-employed persons, for example, who bear health-related increases in taxes, prices,

30. Kenneth J. Arrow, "Uncertainty and the Welfare Economics of Medical Care," *American Economic Review*, vol. 53 (December 1963), pp. 961–62.

and otherwise, but who have declined to purchase, or have been denied, health coverage.

Most analysts of moral hazard, however, appear to have in mind a different version of the free rider problem. This problem is not that there exist two classes, exploiters and the exploited, but rather that under third-party payment each member of the single payer-consumer class lacks a personal financial incentive to restrain the amount of care he consumes, if and when he consumes care, because abstinence on his part would not be emulated by others and would therefore make an imperceptible dent in the total social cost of medical care. In this sense, it is said, each rides free at the expense of all. The rational solution, it is argued, is to devise arrangements to force more of the true costs of care directly onto consumers so that they will weigh possible costs of care against the likely benefit or value of care as measured by their own willingness to pay for it.

Critics have often pointed out that this approach overlooks important elements in the interplay between individual decisionmaking and the peculiar properties of medical care. Concrete evaluation of the benefits and costs of particular services carrying particular costs "at the point of service delivery" are largely irrelevant when the point is to achieve insurance against risk. Health care is not merely another valued product or consumer good. As Bruce C. Vladeck argues,

> the theoretical proposition that free goods tend to be overconsumed and that eliminating "moral hazard" will reduce consumption has considerable intuitive appeal, especially to those naturally sympathetic to economic models of human behavior. As applied to medical care, however, it is an insidious principle, imposing hardship on the healthy and sick alike, violating the very purposes of medical assistance programs, and perpetuating the linkage between access to care and ability to pay. If, as a society, we choose to treat health care as a merit good, then it is absurd to assume that its demand function resembles that for ice cream.[31]

A person insures against risk precisely because he does not want to be confronted with such questions of willingness to pay in the unhappy event of illness. He buys health insurance because he does not know what objective conditions (illnesses) may strike; because he does not know exactly how he will feel about the value of alternative treatments for various objective conditions of various degrees of severity; and because he does not feel capable of deciding, and does not want to be forced to decide, what the benefit-cost ratios are for various combinations of treatment and

31. "On 'Cutting the Cost of Medical Assistance,' " *Policy Analysis*, vol. 2 (Summer 1976), pp. 497–98.

illness. Anxiety levels are apt to be too high and the professional expertise of the patient too low to permit him to make rational decisions when an illness strikes.

The result is that all (or most) persons purchase generous insurance benefits so that all (or most) may ride free if something unfortunate happens. The favored political status of health spending lies here. In William A. Glaser's words, "most other spending programs are transfers to other persons, but health spending is viewed as a potential benefit to one's self when it is urgently needed."[32] To some critics this social behavior is the irrational, irresponsible log-rolling that defines moral hazard. From another point of view, however, it is a highly rational, or at any rate entirely understandable, form of collective risk-spreading and -sharing. To be sure, consumers ride free when they partake of the most and best care available because they do not bear a burdensome share of the costs. On the other hand, consumers buy the right to enjoy such care with awareness of the aggregate costs of their (collective) decisions—everyone knows that health care is expensive and that it is wrong to waste it—and in the expectation and hope that they will never be forced to exercise their right. Although there are no doubt some Scrooges fully convinced that third-party payment of health services leads consumers to seek care recklessly and for the sheer perverse fun of it, in this respect too, medical insurance departs from the usual free rider problem, where the consumers' incentive to consume varies positively and directly with the scope of third-party coverage. Thus in its second sense too the free rider diagnosis misses the mark. Analyses of health insurance that see in it only or mainly the perversities of heedlessness and waste-shifting set policy discussion off in misleading directions.

The usual analyses of health insurance today offer neither useful policy advice nor convincing explanations of prevailing patterns. These analyses either over- or under-explain present arrangements. If moral hazard is indeed the central dynamic and the universe of consumers is peopled with crafty, wasteful free riders, it is difficult to explain why this universe, acting in the political marketplace, did not bring about in its self-interest a cradle-to-grave program of national health insurance some time ago. This would be the logical outcome of the moral hazard–free rider diagnosis, but it is one the United States has resisted. Instead the nation relies on a mix of public and private arrangements that generally offer less than comprehensive benefits and less than first-dollar coverage for care, and that generally

32. "Health Politics—Lessons from Abroad," in Theodore J. Litman and Leonard S. Robins, eds., *Health Politics, Policy and the Public Interest* (Wiley, forthcoming), draft, p. 61.

incorporate some of the cost-sharing features of which the market theorists would like to see more.

There is no obvious explanation for this electoral self-restraint, but a reasonable hypothesis is that the electorate fears that the enactment of comprehensive national health insurance might lead many citizens to start acting as economic theory says they now act, and that it fears the collective costs of this. But if consumer-voters show this much cost-consciousness and self-restraint, why do they not show more? Why does the same willingness to avoid the temptations of national health insurance not generate a cost-containing, efficiency-favoring set of arrangements, including truly deterrent cost-sharing provisions? Reasonable hypotheses are that although the electorate wants something less than comprehensive services at very high costs, it wants very full coverage for the most intensive and costly services, notably inpatient and surgical services, and that although it does not demand full first-dollar coverage (at least not by way of public financing), it wants enough coverage to ensure that out-of-pocket costs do not become truly burdensome. The result of these preferences would be a middle ground between the two logical extremes to which the assumptions of the moral hazard theory lead. And it is this "illogical" middle ground that U.S. patterns of health care coverage occupy.

Several derivative hypotheses follow. First, consumers may make a distinction between consumer-initiated and physician-initiated treatments, and although they tend to be willing to bear a sizable share of the cost of the former (as a check on extravagance), they wish to bear few of the costs of the latter (as a check on anxiety and inexpertise). Second, this distinction may correspond very roughly to that between outpatient (consumer-initiated) and inpatient (physician-initiated) care. Consumers may prefer to see the two types of care treated differently in insurance arrangements. Although they may be willing to continue to bear some share of the cost of the former, they may strongly resist schemes that impose large costs of the latter on them. If so, schemes that merge the two types and entitle the consumer to government aid after he has incurred, from his own pocket, costs (for whichever purpose) established by a sliding, income-related scale may prove to be unpopular.

As for HMOs, consumers in general may prefer good coverage for inpatient procedures combined with some risk of incurring out-of-pocket costs for outpatient procedures to the comprehensive bargain offered by an HMO, especially when HMO care restricts the consumer to the staff and facilities of the plan itself. Finally, consumers are likely to resist strongly any scheme that obliges them to incur large out-of-pocket costs for either outpatient or inpatient care.

It is a mistake to assume that these patterns can only be explained by the absence of consumer choice, meaning the consumer's ability to buy coverage from sources more efficient than fee-for-service, third-party-payment plans like Blue Cross. In the United States, consumers exercise choice in many ways—notably, through their choice of health plans in the work place or in the market, through collective bargaining, and through the political process. An efficient system of cost-sharing provisions or incentives encouraging HMOs could be widely in place within a few months—if consumer-voters wanted it and were willing so to instruct insurance agents, employers, union representatives, and politicians. The same may be said of comprehensive national health insurance. The problem is not that consumers cannot make choices among alternative modes of care, but that they have chosen, for good and sufficient if little understood reasons of their own, alternatives of which some analysts disapprove, and have exercised those choices by means of nonmarket decision mechanisms that the analysts distrust.

It should be emphasized that the arguments advanced here are crude hypotheses, and that, unfortunately, very little is known about consumer attitudes and preferences on these matters. Policy analysts have become so entangled in the counterfactual logic of trying to devise ways in which consumers would convey what they might be willing to pay for health services if battered, creaky health care markets could be made to resemble the handsome creature in the text books that they have devoted little attention to studying—by means of interviews, surveys, and other empirical research techniques—what people do in fact want from a health insurance system and how they prefer to pay for it.

Centralized Regulatory Controls

It would be gratifying to end this study with a wide-ranging set of predictions and recommendations. Unfortunately, this is not possible, both because an examination of the HMO program is a poor foundation for these tasks, and, more important, because the primitive state of understanding of the dynamics of health care cost increases makes predictions little better than guesses, and recommendations little more than well-meant wishes. The sources of the health care cost problem are many and their relative contributions are difficult to assign.

A long list of causes of rising health care costs may be spun out. Causes include: consumers who are morally hazardous, overexpectant, too demanding, uninformed, excessively deferential, or irrational; doctors who are greedy, defensive, subservient to technological imperatives, and overspecialized; hospitals that are over-bedded, mindlessly acquisitive of technology, badly managed, or in the habit of cow-towing to doctors; third-party payers who are unconcerned, timid, or insulated from market forces; and more. These factors constitute what might be termed that "profligate provider" model of rising health costs.

A second model, however, points to such cost-increasing variables as longevity (larger numbers of persons live to be elderly and then incur costly illnesses in the course of their prolonged old age); greater demand by previously disadvantaged groups (for example, the poor served by Medicaid); legitimate technological breakthroughs; and overdue upgrading of work conditions, especially in hospitals (higher pay for nurses, larger staffs, and shorter hours). This might be called the "price of progress" model.

The two models point in different policy directions. The profligate provider model holds that the major problems are waste and inefficiency, even fraud and abuse, all captured under the general headings of "duplication," "unnecessary utilization," and "overutilization." It implies that utilization can and should be whittled down to the hard, justifiable core of "medically necessary and appropriate" care. The price of progress model does not (or at any rate need not) deny that waste and inefficiency contribute to rising costs. It emphasizes, however, that the progressive variables to which it points would nonetheless combine to drive costs up even in an efficient and waste-free system. On this latter view, then, cost-containment is not mainly a matter of finding new efficiencies to separate the chaff of overuse from the wheat of medically appropriate care; rather it evokes the disturbing prospect of somehow rationing medically appropriate procedures among truly needy beneficiaries, accepting that not all in need can have all of what they need. Recommendations and predictions follow in large part from one's choice of model.

The main perplexity for policy is that existing knowledge does not support a confident choice between the two models; indeed it does not even permit one to assign relative weights to the many and interdependent causal variables within each model. More research is surely desirable, and possibly such research will yield clear and actionable findings. Probably, however, such research will discover that both models explain some of the variance, that all the various factors within each help to explain each model's contribution, that the variables are annoyingly interactive and resistant to quantification and control, that much depends on the assumptions one makes and the methods one employs—in short, that policy "science" can recommend little more than that public policy might want to design a "comprehensive and multifaceted assault on multiple and interdependent causal variables," no doubt by means of "fundamental reform" and "system reorganization." In short, the quest for cost-containment cannot and need not wait upon research; it should proceed on politicians' common sense, shaped by the clash of conventional and unconventional wisdoms, and ultimately by a sense of what the populace wants, or at any rate will tolerate.

In practice, politicians may stumble their way along a continuum of six cost-containment strategies, listed below in order of increasing regulatory stringency. The choice of a strategic mix is in large part a game of political roulette, dependent on poorly understood trends, accidental forces, and chance. Where it stops, nobody knows.

Competition. It is possible that the federal government will try to contain costs by expanding its efforts to promote competition between traditional and "organized, efficient" health care systems. It may do so by continuing to support development of HMOs or by means of such centralized incentive-based strategies as cost sharing, changes in the federal tax treatment of health insurance premium payments, Enthoven's consumer choice health plan, or others. The limitations of this general approach have been discussed throughout this book and need not be reviewed again here.

The Status Quo. Possibly, the combined effects of decentralized regulatory programs, HMOs, federal jawboning, the voluntary efforts of providers to hold the line on cost increases, and other factors will bring medical cost increases down to approximately the rate of inflation of the economy as a whole. In this case the health care cost crisis may be declared over, or more likely, may be allowed to fade away through inattention as other crises replace it. If this happens, the nation may be content to make do with the present mélange of decentralized cost-containment strategies.

This prospect is not entirely farfetched, as table 10-1 shows. After a large jump in hospital expenditures in 1975, following the end of wage

Table 10-1. *Annual Rates of Increase of Hospital Expenditures,*
1975–80

Year	Increase in expenditures by community hospitals (percent)	Increase in adjusted expenses per inpatient day (percent)
1975	19.5	17.8
1976	15.4	13.4
1977	14.2	13.9
1978	12.6	11.7
1979	13.4	11.8
1980	16.4	12.8

Source: American Hospital Association, *Hospital Statistics, 1976 Edition*, pp. xiii, xv; *1977 Edition*, pp. xiii, xvi; *1978 Edition*, pp. x, xi; *1979 Edition*, pp. ix, x; *1980 Edition*, pp. xvi, xvii; *1981 Edition*, pp. xvi, xvii.

and price controls, annual increases slowed. The increase in community hospital expenditures between 1977 and 1978 was the lowest yearly jump since 1965, and the increase in adjusted expenditures per patient day was the lowest since 1974 and lower than occurred in all but three of the previous ten years.[33] The deceleration reflected the hospitals' self-imposed "voluntary effort" at restraint in hopes of avoiding enactment of the hospital cost-containment bill proposed by the Carter administration. But as the regulatory threat waned,[34] rates of increase turned up again, and the federal government is likely to feel pressure to contain costs more aggressively.

Incrementalism. The federal government may attempt to strengthen and expand such decentralized regulatory programs as the PSROs, HSAs, certificate-of-need reviews, and hospital rate-setting at the state level. These programs generally rest on the profligate provider model and aim to discourage waste by influencing the use of hospital care. Insofar as the model is mistaken, or hospitals the wrong target, or the programs too weak, this approach will prove disappointing.

Bargaining. A fourth possibility is that the United States will enact some form of comprehensive national health insurance and strong central regulatory and incentive-based controls to accompany it. These controls would mainly be reimbursement schedules negotiated between providers and payers, subject to governmentally defined rules of the game. This, of course, is the European approach.

33. American Hospital Association, *Hospital Statistics, 1979*, pp. ix–x.
34. On November 15, 1979, the House voted 234–166, with 99 Democrats among the "nays," to reject the bill. (Elizabeth Wehr, "House Rejects Hospital Cost Control Plan," *Congressional Quarterly Weekly Report*, November 17, 1979, p. 2575.)

Some contend that this approach alone will permit the United States to address rationally the problem of health care costs. In the largely private, partly public U.S. system most health insurance is privately purchased or negotiated. Lacking the leverage that accompanies national health insurance, the central government has been reluctant to impose central reimbursement controls. To be sure, it finances the care of some of the poor, the elderly, and others, under Medicaid, Medicare, and other programs, and it has attempted to regulate costs and use in these programs with some authority. However, tight federal controls in a largely private system might drive providers out of the public programs (as has indeed happened) or might lead them to render second-class care to public beneficiaries, and these dangers—along with the political power of organized recipients and their ideological allies—check the government's aggressiveness. The result is a frustrating Alphonse-Gaston routine. Lacking public control over the major sources of health care cost increases, government fears to enact the broader entitlements of national health insurance, lest such a program aggravate costs severely. But in the absence of national health insurance, government lacks the financial leverage to impose strong controls on costs. Hence the argument for enactment of a national health insurance plan coherently coordinated with a comprehensive set of public controls.

One problem with this recommendation is politics; in the negotiations and trading involved in passing a sizable national plan, controls might well be compromised into extreme weakness in order to win support and diffuse provider opposition. Unless controls are strong and strict, they will probably be unable to contain the cost increases accompanying enlarged entitlements. But even if the federal government enacted comprehensive health insurance and far-reaching controls to go with it, it is doubtful that the combination would check medical cost increases decisively. German, French, and other Continental politicians and health ministers describe health costs in their nations in terms very like those used in the United States: "insupportable," growing at an "alarming" rate, and threatening to "bankrupt" social services budgets. Their expenditure rates and levels bear them out.[35] The reason is presumably that in these nations tighter

35. West Germany, France, the Netherlands, and Sweden have "witnessed a substantial rise in the percentage of GNP spent on health and in per capita expenditure for health" in recent years, observe Jan Blanpain and others. Between 1968 and 1972 the share of GNP spent on health services in the Netherlands rose from 5.9 percent to 7.3 percent. In Sweden it rose from 6.4 percent to 7.0 percent in the single year between 1969 and 1970. *National Health Insurance and Health Resources: The European Experience* (Harvard University Press, 1978), p. 247. In West Germany, expenditures for all public health insurance plans between 1970 and 1975 increased by an annual average of more than 19 percent—"the central problem of national health-care policy." Klaus-Dirk Henke, "Health Care: Policy Alternatives and Research Directions," in Kenneth J. Arrow and others, eds., *Applied Research for Social Policy: The*

controls are counterbalanced and offset by broader entitlements, whereas in the United States, narrower entitlements are counterbalanced and offset by weaker controls. The roads to inflation are different but parallel, and although the United States could adopt the way of the Continent, it would probably reach the same costly outcome.

The one European nation that has successfully contained costs—Great Britain, which devoted 5.6 percent of its gross national product to health care in 1975[36]—has not only national health insurance, but a national health service—that is, genuine socialized medicine, not the superimposition of national health insurance on a fee-for-service system, as found on the Continent. It is most unlikely that the United States would adopt the British model.

Rationing. It is possible that the federal government will eventually lose faith in the profligate provider model and adopt the view that health care cost increases are mainly the result of desirable medical progress, but that progress imposes higher prices than American society can afford. Louise Russell, for example, argues that across-the-board assaults on sources of waste and inefficiency within the norm of more and better services for everyone are unlikely to make a major dent in the cost problem. "True" controls, she notes, will mean some type of rationing.[37] One approach is to allocate entitlements: government could set limits on how much of what type of care it will finance for whom. The premise is—and the result will be—that not everyone can have all of the medical care he "objectively" needs. It would be surprising if the federal government showed an interest in detailed rationing of this type.

A plausible alternative to rationing entitlements is to impose a "cap"— an aggregate limit on dollars, days of care, or some other measure, enforced for a given period of time—and then to allow rationing to take place in still decentralized but newly constrained interactions among providers, consumers, and payers. Caps may be legislated—for example, the Carter administration's losing effort to persuade Congress to enact an annual ceiling on allowable revenue increases for hospitals and on national

United States and the Federal Republic of Germany Compared (Cambridge, Mass.: Abt Books, 1979), pp. 144–45. In response, West Germany enacted in 1977 a health care cost containment act. See Deborah A. Stone, "Health Care Cost Containment in West Germany," *Journal of Health Politics, Policy and Law*, vol. 4 (Summer 1979), pp. 176–99.

36. Joseph G. Simanis and John R. Coleman, "Health Care Expenditures in Nine Industrialized Countries, 1960–76," *Social Security Bulletin*, vol. 43 (January 1980), p. 4.

37. Louise B. Russell, *Technology in Hospitals: Medical Advances and Their Diffusion* (Brookings Institution, 1979), especially pp. 153–55.

expenditures for hospital capital projects. They may be formulated admin-istratively, as when a state rate-setting agency establishes a formula limiting increases in hospital rates, revenues, or budgets for the coming year. They may be negotiated, as when, for example, hospitals and payers in a state agree voluntarily that hospital charges will rise no higher than, say, 10 percent in the next year. Caps take many forms, employ diverse units and measures, and come into being by different political routes. Their essence, however, is a ceiling on increases (in dollars, days, or whatever) within which providers agree or are obliged to remain either individually or collectively. Despite their obvious arbitrariness and insensitivity to the nuances of individual situations, caps have their appeals: they acknowledge that scarce resources require discipline beyond that achievable by cutting obvious elements of waste and inefficiency in the system; they put a brake on increased health care spending; and yet in imposing an aggregate constraint, they leave the particulars of such rationing as ensues to individual providers, consumers, and payers. If less firm measures fail to bring the rate of health cost increases within acceptable limits, the federal government will probably show growing interest in indirect rationing by means of caps.

Planning. If rationing and capping fail to bring medical costs within acceptable bounds, it is possible—though highly unlikely—that the federal government will consider altering the service mix, and especially the health facility mix, directly by means of a central plan. Until recently the United States has taken a laissez faire attitude toward the founding and growth of hospitals. Hospitals have been treated as local monuments, chips in political games played with energy and commitment by local medical societies, churches, women's groups, community service organizations, philanthro-pists, and others. Administrators' needs to maintain and enhance their institutions have frequently been at one with the interests of the medical staff. These interests have in turn been largely consonant with the political games of community notables. These community interests were reinforced by the federal Hill-Burton program, which put up funds for hospital planning, construction, and renovation. The result of this government deference, many analysts concluded in the 1960s and early 1970s, was hospital construction and expansion largely unrelated to regional need and a proliferation of institutions whose occupancy and utilization rates were too low to be efficient.

In the 1970s the federal government and some state governments began trying to contain or reverse these developments. Hill-Burton aid for new hospital construction was greatly curtailed. Health maintenance organizations (famous above all for inpatient economies), certificate-of-need laws (which place the burden of proof for large-scale hospital building, expansion, and acquisition on hospitals themselves), PSROs (which attempt to stop needless admissions and needlessly long stays), rate-setting efforts (which tie hospitals' allowable revenues and charges to publicly approved processes and purposes), and HSAs (which attempt to view the future of hospital plans and operations in the wider context of areawide needs and resources) all began working for change. The Carter hospital cost-containment proposal and what one high official in HEW described as "vicious jawboning" by that department also gave notice that hospitals should expect closer federal scrutiny and tighter controls.

The closeness of the scrutiny and the rigor of the controls will depend on the perceived urgency of the battle against increases in the cost of health care. If the United States becomes determined to do something about these costs, the federal government—or perhaps the states—may eventually take a detached, critical, central look at the distribution of hospital facilities. It may then try to devise, on the basis of demographic need, an appropriate hospital distribution by location and specialty and may begin taking steps to implement its findings. This might mean closing down inefficient, underused, or overspecialized hospitals in unsuitable locations. It might involve indirect but determined efforts to force financially marginal or shaky hospitals to close their doors. It might entail an effort to act on the implications of Roemer's law—that a main determinant of hospital bed use is bed availability, so that if beds are available, they will be used. The government might, in short, seek to act on the major lesson of HMO experience, that the surest route to economy and efficiency is to avoid using inpatient care for treatments that do not require it. The process and the result might resemble those recommended by A. L. Cochrane to British planners:

> The main change will be the movement of the center of gravity of medicine from the hospital to the community, associated with a rise in the importance of the GP in relation to the consultant, and the disappearance of the pathologist as the final medical arbiter. . . .
> The district general hospital will either become smaller or there will be fewer of them. The number of acute hospital beds will probably fall below two per thousand. . . . The hospitals will be very intensive. In most cases investigations will be completed before admission and no-one will be admitted unless there is a reasonable probability of effective therapy. Lengths of stay will be very much shorter, partly due to earlier discharge to community hospitals. Out-patient

departments will be transformed. There will be very few chronic out-patients as they will be increasingly under the care of their GPs. New out-patients will increasingly be seen in health centers. . . .

Another change in out-patient departments will be their increased use for cold surgery and investigations. Assessment by the hospital staff with continuous care by the GP in the community will become the general rule for mental abnormalities, geriatric, and chronic disease in general. Only those requiring very specialized care will be retained in the hospitals.

In the community there will be health centres, community hospitals, and other specialized units providing care near the patients' homes for all the various types of disability. In urban areas a health centre and community hospital will usually be located in the grounds of the district general hospital.[38]

If this strategy worked, the result would be a significant measure of rationing and queuing. Inpatient beds would be reserved for those in serious need of them; elective surgery would be deferred or conducted elsewhere. As Cochrane suggests, major new efforts would be needed to build outpatient centers, infirmaries for minor surgery, and generalist community institutions—in theory according to careful regional plans. Health maintenance organizations would have something to teach planners should this path ever be followed.

Of course the United States is no more likely to adopt such central planning than it is to cut entitlements drastically, to impose fee schedules on physicians, or to pressure much of the population to join HMOs. Such rationing would force many blue-collar workers out of jobs, would wreak havoc on the practice patterns of physicians and the expectations of consumers, and would require a degree of centralization—and a degree of immunity from the pressures of local doctors, unions, consumers, hospitals, politicians, health planning bodies, and other community interests—that is strongly at odds with the biases of the highly decentralized U.S. political structure.

The gradual but steady movement from decentralized incentive-based controls toward centralized regulatory controls results from and renews a continuing social debate over how to sort out the cost-increasing factors that are inseparable from such good things as greater equality in ability to pay for care, improved access, enhanced quality, and technological progress from those factors that lie in the realm of waste. No simple solution is in the cards; no tolerable strategy will end soaring medical costs. In this area, as in so many others, victory will mean losing ground more slowly in some

38. A. L. Cochrane, *Effectiveness and Efficiency: Random Reflections on Health Services* (London: Nuffield Provincial Hospitals Trust, 1972), pp. 83–84.

respects (cost increases) while gaining ground in others (improved access and quality). Making policy is inescapably and properly a political project, one undertaken in the unsettling foreknowledge that although there are endless social transitions to be mediated, there are no right answers to discover or learn.

Index